D0164367

The School in the United States

The School in the United States collects a wide range of essential primary documents of the history of education in the United States, from colonial America to present-day reform efforts. Expertly chosen by historian and education scholar James Fraser, these documents incorporate many different sources, from first-person accounts to textbook excerpts and presidential speeches. As Fraser demonstrates, the history of American education is also a history of national debates and decisions about schooling, and he places the prominent voices of these debates in conversation through carefully curated selections, including the work of famous thinkers like Thomas Jefferson and W. E. B. DuBois, as well as that of ordinary classroom teachers.

Organized by era, each chapter begins with a brief introduction intended to spark student interest, while a detailed bibliography suggests opportunities for further research. In addition, the fourth edition also offers an alternative structure that allows easy use of the book by topic as an alternative to chronology. Comprehensive enough to be used as a main text, but selective enough to be used alongside another, *The School in the United States* makes accessible key readings in the history of American education in a format that encourages students to make their own evaluations as they engage with major historical debates.

Updates to this fourth edition include:

- New documents throughout including additional teacher voices and a focus on technology.
- The last two chapters have been extensively revised to include material on school shootings, debates about charter schools, teacher strikes, and the purposes of public education in the United States.
- A number of older documents have been shortened to point students more clearly to the most important ideas of a document. Overall the fourth edition is shorter than previous editions.
- Online resources that include a full Instructor's Manual and sample syllabi.

James W. Fraser is Professor of History and Education at the Steinhardt School of Culture, Education, and Human Development at New York University, USA. He was the 2013–2014 President of the History of Education Society.

"This is my favorite book that I use with my students. It allows me a lot of creativity in planning the course curriculum and I like that students can learn from the primary sources without me having to search for all of the documents."

—*Josephine Tabet Sarvis, PhD, Dominican University*

"James Fraser provides an excellent comprehensive collection of primary sources that provide the student with an opportunity for reflecting, constructing meaning, and establishing relationships with the past through the ideas and experiences of those who lived it and helped form American education as we know it."

—*Sam F. Stack Jr., Professor, Social and Cultural Foundations,*
West Virginia University

"Fraser has most certainly achieved his goal of providing students 'with a way to immerse themselves in some of the major debates that have consumed educators over the decades.' His book enables students to become historians."

—*Christine A. Ogren, Associate Professor, Educational Policy and*
Leadership Studies, the University of Iowa

The School in the United States

A Documentary History

Fourth Edition

Edited by James W. Fraser

Routledge
Taylor & Francis Group

NEW YORK AND LONDON

Fourth edition published 2019
by Routledge
52 Vanderbilt Avenue, New York, NY 10017

and by Routledge
2 Park Square, Milton Park, Abingdon, Oxon, OX14 4RN

Routledge is an imprint of the Taylor & Francis Group, an informa business

First edition published by McGraw Hill 2000
Third edition published by Routledge 2014

Library of Congress Cataloging-in-Publication Data
Names: Fraser, James W., 1944- editor.
Title: The school in the United States : a documentary history / edited by
    James W. Fraser.
Description: Fourth edition. | New York : Routledge, 2019. | "Third edition
    published by Routledge 2014"—T.p. verso. | Includes bibliographical
    references and index.
Identifiers: LCCN 2018051648| ISBN 9781138478848 (hardback : alk. paper) |
Subjects: LCSH: Education—United States—History. | Schools—
    United States—History.
Classification: LCC LA205 .S34 2019 | DDC 370.973—dc23
LC record available at https://lccn.loc.gov/2018051648

ISBN: 978-1-138-47884-8 (hbk)
ISBN: 978-1-138-47887-9 (pbk)

Typeset in Minion
by Swales & Willis Ltd, Exeter, Devon, UK

Visit the eResource: www.routledge.com/9781138478879

Chronological Contents

Permissions Page   xiv
Preface to the Fourth Edition   xv

ORGANIZED CHRONOLOGICALLY

1   The School in Colonial America, 1620–1770   1

    Introduction   1

    Virginia Council [London], Instructions to Sir Thomas Gates, Knight,
       Governor of Virginia, 1636   3

    Virginia Statutes on the Education of Indian Children Held Hostage,
       from the *Virginia Statutes at Large,* 1656   4

    South Carolina Statute on Conversion of Slaves to Christianity;
       Digest of the Public Statute Law of South Carolina, 1711   4

    A Missionary Report from Mr. Taylor to the Society in North
       Carolina on the Baptism of Slaves, April 23, 1719   5

    Virginia's Cure, or an Advisive Narrative Concerning Virginia,
       London, 1662   6

    Sir William Berkeley, Governor of Virginia, Response to "Enquiries
       to the Governor of Virginia," from the Lords' Commissioners of
       Foreign Plantations, 1671   7

    Massachusetts' Old Deluder Satan Law, 1647   7

    Benjamin Franklin, *Autobiography* 1714–1718   8

    John Adams, Diary Entries, 1756   9

    The New England Primer, 1768   10

2   The American Revolution and Schools for the New Republic, 1770–1820   17

    Introduction   17

    Thomas Jefferson, A Bill for the More General Diffusion of Knowledge, 1779   20

    Thomas Jefferson, Notes on the State of Virginia, 1783   21

    Benjamin Rush, Thoughts Upon Female Education, 1787   23

    Noah Webster, On the Education of Youth in America, Boston, 1790   25

    Noah Webster, *The American Spelling Book,* 1783   30

    United States Congress, the Northwest Ordinance, July 13, 1787   32

    United States Congress, Civilization Fund Act, March 3, 1819   33

3   The Common School Movement, 1820–1860   34

    Introduction   34

    Horace Mann, *Tenth* and *Twelfth Annual Reports to the Massachusetts
       Board of Education,* 1846 and 1848   38

Catharine E. Beecher, *An Essay on the Education of Female Teachers for the United States*, 1835 43

The *Common School Journal*, Debate Over Plan to Abolish the Board of Education, 1840 45

Petition of the Catholics of New York for a Portion of the Common School Fund: To the Honorable Board of Aldermen of the City of New York, 1840 49

The Desegregation of the Boston Public Schools, 1846–1855 53

4 Schooling Moves West, 1835–1860 .... **60**

Introduction 60

Selections from *McGuffey's Sixth Eclectic Reader*, 1836 (With Many Subsequent Editions) 61

Calvin E. Stowe, Report on Elementary Public Instruction in Europe, 1837 66

Board of National Popular Education, Correspondence, 1849–1850 68

Mary Augusta Roper, Letters from Mill Point, Michigan, 1852–1854 71

The Speech of Red Jacket, the Seneca Chief, to a Missionary, circa 1805 73

5 Slavery, Reconstruction, and the Schools of the South, 1820–1937 .... **76**

Introduction 76

Frederick Douglass, *The Narrative of the Life of Frederick Douglass: An American Slave*, 1845 78

The New England Freedmen's Aid Society—Official Records, 1862–1872 83

The New England Freedmen's Aid Society—Correspondence, 1865–1874 85

Charlotte Forten, *The Journal of Charlotte Forten*, 1862 88

Booker T. Washington, *The Future of the American Negro*, 1899 93

W. E. B. DuBois, *The Souls of Black Folk*, 1903 97

Marcus Garvey, *Lessons from the School of African Philosophy: The New Way to Education*, 1937 101

6 The Emergence of the High School, 1821–1959 .... **104**

Introduction 104

National Education Association, *Report of the Committee on Secondary School Studies* (The Committee of Ten), 1893 109

G. Stanley Hall, *Adolescence*, 1904 116

John Dewey, "A Policy of Industrial Education," 1914 119

David Snedden, "Vocational Education," 1915 121

John Dewey, "Education vs. Trade-Training—Dr. Dewey's Reply," 1915 124

National Education Association, *Cardinal Principles of Secondary Education*, 1918 126

Thomas Edison Predicts Film Will Replace Teacher, Books, 1923 134

William Jennings Bryan, "Who Shall Control?", 1925 135

James Bryant Conant, *The American High School Today*, 1959 136

7 Growth and Diversity in Schools and Students, 1880–1960   **140**

Introduction   140

Third Plenary Council of Baltimore, 1884   142

Mary Antin, *The Promised Land*, 1912   145

Lewis Meriam, *The Problem of Indian Administration*, 1928   149

The Asian Experience in California, 1919–1920   155

Beatrice Griffith, *American Me*, 1948   163

Teaching Children of Puerto Rican Background in the New York
City Schools, 1954   169

8 The Progressive Era, 1890–1950   **175**

Introduction   175

James Jackson Storrow, *Son of New England*, 1932   177

Margaret Haley, *Why Teachers Should Organize*, 1904   181

Ella Flagg Young, *Isolation in the School*, 1901   185

Grace C. Strachan, *Equal Pay for Equal Work*, 1910   187

Cora Bigelow, "World Democracy and School Democracy," 1918   189

John Dewey, *The School and Society*, 1899   191

Lewis M. Terman, *National Intelligence Tests*, 1919   199

George Counts, *Dare the School Build a New Social Order?*, 1932   205

The Social Frontier, 1934   210

9 Schools in the Cold War Era, 1950–1970   **214**

Introduction   214

F. James Rutherford, Sputnik and Science Education,
Reflections on 1957   215

National Defense Education Act, 1958   220

The *Scott Foresman Readers*, 1955   221

H. G. Rickover, *Education for All Children: What We Can Learn
from England*, 1962   224

Herbert Kohl, *Thirty-Six Children*, 1967   227

John Holt, *How Children Fail*, 1964   235

10 Civil Rights, Integration, and School Reform, 1954–1980   **240**

Introduction   240

Federal District Court, *Mendez v. Westminster*, 1946   242

Septima Clark, *Ready from Within*, ca. 1950   245

Supreme Court of the United States, *Brown v. Board of Education
of Topeka, Kansas*, 1954   250

Kenneth B. Clark, "How Children Learn About Race," 1950   253

School Desegregation in the South: Little Rock, 1957   256

NAACP Boston Branch, Statement to the Boston School Committee,
June 11, 1963   260

School Desegregation in the North: Boston, 1965   264

Looking Back at an Era: Rucker C. Johnson, *The Dream Revisited—In
Search of Integration: Beyond Black and White*, 2014   271

11 Rights, Opportunities, and Limits in American Education, 1965–1980   **275**

Introduction   275

Supreme Court of the United States, *Engel v. Vitale*, 1962   278

The Elementary and Secondary Education Act and the Great Society, 1965   281

Supreme Court of the United States, *Tinker et al. v. Des Moines Independent Community School District*, 1969   285

Title IX, the Education Amendments of 1972   292

Supreme Court of the United States, *Lau et al. v. Nichols et al.*, 1974   292

Public Law 94-142, Education for All Handicapped Children Act, 1975   295

Dillon Platero, The Rough Rock Demonstration School, Navajo Nation, 1970   296

Supreme Court of the United States, *San Antonio Independent School District v. Rodriguez*, Argued October 12, 1972, Decided March 21, 1973   300

12 Reform Efforts of the 1980s and 1990s and the New Century, 1980–2005   **304**

Introduction   304

National Commission on Excellence in Education, *A Nation at Risk: The Imperative for Educational Reform*, 1983   306

Ann Bastian, Norm Fruchter, Marilyn Gittell, Colin Greer, and Kenneth Haskins, *Choosing Equality: The Case for Democratic Schooling*, 1985   310

David C. Berliner and Bruce J. Biddle, *The Manufactured Crisis*, 1995   313

Sonia Nieto, *Affirming Diversity: The Sociopolitical Context of Multicultural Education*, 1992   317

Arthur M. Schlesinger, Jr., *The Disuniting of America*, 1991   322

Seymour Papert, *The Children's Machine*, 1993   327

Neil Postman, *Technopoly*, 1993   329

United States Department of Education, Executive Summary of the No Child Left Behind Act, 2002   330

Different Schools of Thought Regarding the No Child Left Behind Act (NCLB), 2003–2004   334

13 Curriculum, Technology, and New Tensions, 2005–2018   **337**

Introduction   337

Common Core State Standards Initiative, FAQ, 2018   338

Joseph P. McDonald, James W. Fraser, and Susan B. Neuman, *Where Are the Common Core State Standards Headed? Oblivion, Probably*, 2016   344

Arthur Levine, "Digital Students, Industrial-Era Universities," 2010   348

Benjamin Harold, "Technology in Education: An Overview," *Education Week*, February 5, 2016   349

Emma Gonzalez, Address at Gun Control Rally, 2018   355

President Donald Trump, Governor Jay Inslee (D-Washington), and Governor Greg Abbott (R-Texas) on Guns in Schools, 2018   358

Secretary of Education Betsy DeVos, Remarks to Turning Point USA
    High School Leadership Summit, July 25, 2018   362
AFT Resolution, "Defeating the DeVos Agenda," 2018   365
Josh Eidelson and Sarah Jaffe, "Defending Public Education:
    An Interview with Karen Lewis of the Chicago Teachers Union,"
    Dissent, Summer 2013   366
Frederick M. Hess, "The Facts Behind the Teacher Strikes," *Forbes*,
    April 30, 2018   370
Randi Weingarten, "Hope in Darkness," 2018   372
Johann N. Neem, "Schools Have a Nobler Purpose Than Just Career
    Prep," 2018   376

Bibliography: For Further Reading   378
About the Author   385
Index   386

Thematic Contents

Permissions Page   xiv
Preface to the Fourth Edition   xv

ORGANIZED THEMATICALLY

**How Has the Job of Teaching Changed Over Time and How Have
Teachers Helped Change It?**

John Adams, Diary Entries, 1756   9
Catharine E. Beecher, *An Essay on the Education of Female Teachers
    for the United States*, 1835   43
Board of National Popular Education, Correspondence, 1849–1850   68
Charlotte Forten, *The Journal of Charlotte Forten*, 1862   88
Margaret Haley, *Why Teachers Should Organize*, 1904   181
Grace C. Strachan, *Equal Pay for Equal Work*, 1910   187
Herbert Kohl, *Thirty-Six Children*, 1967   227
John Holt, *How Children Fail*, 1964   235
United States Department of Education, Executive Summary of the
    No Child Left Behind Act, 2002   330

How Is Technology Changing Schools? For Better? For Worse?

Thomas Edison Predicts Film Will Replace Teacher, Books, 1923   134
Seymour Papert, *The Children's Machine*, 1993   327
Neil Postman, *Technopoly*, 1993   329
Arthur Levine, "Digital Students, Industrial-Era Universities," 2010   348
Benjamin Harold, "Technology in Education: An Overview,"
    Education Week, February 5, 2016   349

Who Pays for Schools? Who Decides What to Do with the Money?

Horace Mann, *Tenth* and *Twelfth Annual Reports to the Massachusetts
    Board of Education*, 1846 and 1848   38
Petition of the Catholics of New York for a Portion of the Common School
    Fund: To the Honorable Board of Aldermen of the City of New York, 1840   49
William Jennings Bryan, "Who Shall Control?", 1925   135
The Elementary and Secondary Education Act and the Great Society, 1965   281
Supreme Court of the United States, *San Antonio Independent School District
    v. Rodriguez*, Argued October 12, 1972, Decided March 21, 1973   300
Josh Eidelson and Sarah Jaffe, "Defending Public Education: An Interview
    with Karen Lewis of the Chicago Teachers Union," *Dissent*,
    Summer 2013   366

Are Schools Fair? What Should Fairness in Schooling Look Like?

Federal District Court, *Mendez v. Westminster*, 1946   242

Septima Clark, *Ready from Within*, ca. 1950   245

Supreme Court of the United States, *Brown v. Board of Education
of Topeka, Kansas*, 1954   250

Kenneth B. Clark, "How Children Learn About Race," 1950   253

School Desegregation in the South: Little Rock, 1957   256

NAACP Boston Branch, Statement to the Boston School Committee,
June 11, 1963   260

School Desegregation in the North: Boston, 1965   264

Looking Back at an Era: Rucker C. Johnson, *The Dream Revisited—In
Search of Integration: Beyond Black and White*, 2014   271

A Broadening Quest for Rights and Opportunities in American Education

Supreme Court of the United States, *Engel v. Vitale*, 1962   278

The Elementary and Secondary Education Act and the Great Society, 1965   281

Supreme Court of the United States, *Tinker et al. v. Des Moines
Independent Community School District*, 1969   285

Title IX, the Education Amendments of 1972   292

Supreme Court of the United States, *Lau et al. v. Nichols et al.*, 1974   292

Public Law 94-142, Education for All Handicapped Children Act, 1975   295

Dillon Platero, The Rough Rock Demonstration School, Navajo
Nation, 1970   296

**School Violence, School Choice, Teacher Unions, Liberal and Conservative
Views of Fairness**

Emma Gonzalez, Address at Gun Control Rally, 2018   355

President Donald Trump, Governor Jay Inslee (D-Washington), and
Governor Greg Abbott (R-Texas) on Guns in Schools, 2018   358

Secretary of Education Betsy DeVos, Remarks to Turning Point
USA High School Leadership Summit, July 25, 2018   362

AFT Resolution, "Defeating the DeVos Agenda," 2018   365

Frederick M. Hess, "The Facts Behind the Teacher Strikes," *Forbes*,
April 30, 2018   370

Randi Weingarten, "Hope in Darkness," 2018   372

**What Gets Taught? What Should Get Taught? Hidden and Overt
Curriculum?**

The New England Primer, 1768   10

Noah Webster, *The American Spelling Book*, 1783   30

Selections from *McGuffey's Sixth Eclectic Reader*, 1836 (With Many
Subsequent Editions)   61

The *Scott Foresman Readers*, 1955   221

Sonia Nieto, *Affirming Diversity: The Sociopolitical Context of
Multicultural Education*, 1992   317

Arthur M. Schlesinger, Jr., *The Disuniting of America*, 1991 322
Common Core State Standards Initiative, FAQ, 2018 338
Joseph P. McDonald, James W. Fraser, and Susan B. Neuman, *Where Are the Common Core State Standards Headed? Oblivion, Probably*, 2016 344

What Is the Purpose of Public Schools? How Has the Purpose Changed Over Time?

Thomas Jefferson, A Bill for the More General Diffusion of Knowledge, 1779 20
Benjamin Rush, Thoughts Upon Female Education, 1787 23
Noah Webster, On the Education of Youth in America, Boston, 1790 25
United States Congress, the Northwest Ordinance, July 13, 1787 32
United States Congress, Civilization Fund Act, March 3, 1819 33
Horace Mann, *Tenth* and *Twelfth Annual Reports to the Massachusetts Board of Education*, 1846 and 1848 38
Calvin E. Stowe, Report on Elementary Public Instruction in Europe, 1837 66
Booker T. Washington, *The Future of the American Negro*, 1899 93
W. E. B. DuBois, *The Souls of Black Folk*, 1903 97
Marcus Garvey, *Lessons from the School of African Philosophy: The New Way to Education*, 1937 101
John Dewey, "A Policy of Industrial Education," 1914 119
David Snedden, "Vocational Education," 1915 121
John Dewey, "Education vs. Trade-Training—Dr. Dewey's Reply," 1915 124
National Education Association, *Cardinal Principles of Secondary Education*, 1918 126
National Commission on Excellence in Education, *A Nation at Risk: The Imperative for Educational Reform*, 1983 306
Johann N. Neem, "Schools Have a Nobler Purpose Than Just Career Prep," 2018 376

Bibliography: For Further Reading 378
About the Author 385
Index 386

Permissions Page

Preface to the Fourth Edition

Few things are more gratifying to an author than to have multiple editions of one's work published. In the case of *The School in the United States*, the need for new editions confirms an assumption that led me to collect these documents in the first place. While I have taught the History of Education in the United States for three decades, I have often found myself frustrated with my inability to find just the right textbook for the course. There continue to be many wonderful books that have been published in the History of Education; many more than when I began my career. This is a vibrant field that includes careful studies of some of the major events and figures, critical reviews of the changing role of the school, and thoughtful new inquiries into the place of the school in different communities. In the last few years several excellent textbooks have also appeared.

But I wanted something that could stand on its own or be used in conjunction with other material. It was important to me to have something that engaged students in looking at primary documents—first-person accounts, reports, and textbooks published in the era under consideration so that students could make their own evaluations and engage with some of the major debates of the day. I suspected I was not alone in wanting this sort of collection of materials and the response of colleagues to the earlier editions of this book indicates that I was right. Too often an instructor in History of Education courses is reduced to supplementing secondary sources with online material, photocopies, and library and internet research assignments, all of which students may or may not explore. In the end, far too much time is wasted chasing documents instead of studying them. I wanted something that would make the material much more easily accessible.

My goal in this volume is to provide students—future teachers, emerging historians, and others who are interested in learning more about the history of education in the United States—a way to immerse themselves in some of the major debates that have consumed educators, teachers, students, administrators, and philosophers over the decades. It has been my experience that being deeply engaged in these very real debates makes history come alive far more than simply reading about the issues. It is one thing for a student to read about Horace Mann's role from the perspective of an historian, whether that historian is an admirer or critic of Mann. It is something quite different for a student to read Mann's own words and then the words of some of his sharpest contemporary critics, such as the Massachusetts Democrats who advocated abolishing his position, and draw their own conclusions. The latter approach leads students to a much deeper engagement with the issues and certainly results in more lively class sessions in my seminars. Students read one way if they are preparing for class discussions and examinations. They read far more deeply if they are preparing for a class debate in which they will be expected to defend or attack the author's position on the major issues of the day. I prefer the kind of energy that comes with the latter type of class activity.

In this fourth edition, I have inserted two different tables of contents. The first table follows the chronological organization of the book itself and of most history and History of Education courses. But I have added a second version of the contents, organized not chronologically but thematically. Having taught Introduction to Education or other foundation courses, I have found that this thematic approach works well in some cases and I wanted to offer teachers and students both. Of course, instructors will pick and choose which specific documents to assign with either approach.

I imagine this volume used in several different ways:

- As a primary text for a History of Education or Introduction to Education course in which this volume provides the framework around which various monographs and student-initiated research projects can be used.
- As a documentary supplement to one of the excellent textbooks in the field, especially Wayne Urban, Jennings Wagoner, and Milton Gaither, *American Education: A History*, 6th edition (Routledge, 2019).
- As a tool for structuring a class around some of the major debates in American education, debates that might be reenacted in the class and for which students would need to prepare first by reading the documents and then by further research around the issues (hence the organization of the second table of contents around key themes).

The School in the United States is designed as a textbook for History of Education and related courses, whether these are offered through education departments and other teacher education programs or through history departments. While courses of this sort cover some of the same material, those in education departments—whether called History of Education, Foundations of Education, or Introduction to Education—often have more of a professional focus, while those in history departments treat education as one of many topics appropriate for historical inquiry. This volume is specifically designed for use in both kinds of courses. Supplemented in different ways, it can serve different kinds of courses and both undergraduate and graduate students. Indeed, I have personally used it in multiple kinds of courses. The purpose of this book is to help students of American history and especially prospective teachers understand and gain a feel for the historical, philosophical, and cultural roots of public schooling in the United States.

Why These Documents?

The documents presented here are only a small part of a vast array of documents that could have been used. Any effort to develop a documentary history of any reasonable length will inevitably disappoint some. And this selection certainly represents my own judgments about what is most important to include. In this volume I have used six primary criteria in selecting documents:

- There are some authors that no reasonable history of education could exclude. These include Thomas Jefferson, Horace Mann, W. E. B. DuBois, Margaret Haley, and John Dewey. In these cases I have attempted to provide a representative sample that is both illustrative and engaging.

- I believe that the voices of teachers must also be heard in this sort of collection. Whether it is John Adams in 1756, Mary Augusta Roper from the 1850s, Cora Bigelow in 1918, or Herb Kohl's reflection on his first year in the classroom in the 1960s, teacher voices are an essential part of this history.
- Textbooks are also a major part of the history as generations of students have struggled with them. From the colonial *New England Primer* to the *McGuffey's Reader* to the Scott Foresman series, the stories used to teach generations of students to read also shed light on the important issues of the day.
- The history of education is also a history of national debates and decisions about schooling. Presidential speeches—from Thomas Jefferson to Donald Trump—Congressional actions, and Supreme Court decisions have shaped the world in which teachers teach and students learn.
- I have tried to include documents—sometimes less familiar documents—that shed light on unique moments in the history of schooling. The Virginia Council in London's 1636 "Instruction to the Governor of Virginia" helps us understand the education of the young, both European and Native American in that colony, while other documents bring to life the battle over desegregation in the Boston Public Schools—in the 1840s and again in the 1960s. Yet other documents tell of the experience of student experiences from Mary Antin's autobiography to Beatrice Griffith's study of Mexican American students in the 1940s.
- Finally for this fourth edition, I have attended to many issues of concern in the twenty-first century including school shootings, debates about charter schools, teacher strikes, etc.

I have also offered a brief introduction to each section of the book but my primary goal has been to let the documents speak for themselves. My introductions are designed to spark interest and understanding, not to substitute for further reading. To further students' research I have included a brief bibliographical list at the end of the book.

Acknowledgments

I owe a special debt to my students and colleagues over the years. For the last ten years I have been fortunate to teach courses in the History of American Education and Introduction to Education as part of an extraordinary program in this field at the Steinhardt School of Culture, Education and Development at New York University. I am especially grateful to my colleague Jonathan Zimmerman who has welcomed me to NYU and facilitated my role in this course. I am also grateful to other Steinhardt historians, Robby Cohen, Joan Malczewski, Diana Turk, and Harold Wechsler. I am in debt to Heather Lewis, Jeffrey Snyder, Noah Kippley-Ogman, and Stacie Brensilver Berman, and more recently to Lauren Lefty, Brittney Lewer, Amy Karwoski, Adrienne Nguyen, Daniel Olson, Briana Royster, and Troy Smith, all of whom as NYU doctoral students helped me with the History of Education course and my thinking about what should be included in it. I also owe a debt to other colleagues at Northeastern University, the Divinity School at Harvard University, Lesley University, Wheelock College, The University of Massachusetts at Boston, Boston University, and Wellesley College. I have been privileged to teach the History of Education in many different places and to work with many wonderful people who have allowed me to test and build my own approach to this material. To all of those students who assumed the roles of Horace Mann, Catharine Beecher, Bishop John Hughes, and many others in class debates, many thanks. My fellow historians, beginning with my mentor Lawrence A. Cremin, have shaped my thinking about every one of these documents. I owe a special debt to Christine Ogren whose prodding is responsible for the chapter on the emergence of the high school, as well as to others who have sent me comments and suggestions about this book, and to Heather Lewis and Bethany Rogers who have organized special sessions of the History of Education Society to discuss the best ways to teach a course like this.

In developing this fourth edition, I have benefited from the enthusiasm and support of my long-time editor at Routledge, Catherine Bernard, as well as her colleague Rachel Dugan and the careful copyediting of Sally Evans-Darby.

I am also grateful to my earlier editors at McGraw-Hill, Allison McNamara, Beth Kaufman, and especially Cara Labell, who did so much of the preliminary work on this volume. Without all of them, this manuscript might have stayed on the shelf for a very long time. Gina Sartori, my undergraduate research assistant at Northeastern University and now a teacher in New York City, provided invaluable research assistance and critical commentary. I am also grateful to the historians and archivists who made it possible to locate some of these documents. My former Northeastern department chair, William Fowler, who also served as President of the Massachusetts Historical Society for a time, along with the Society's superb reference librarian, Nicholas Graham, made my work much easier. My former colleague David Ment was most helpful in locating material in the archives of the New York City Public Schools. Jennifer Dawson and Jacqueline Ramos did an extraordinary amount of typing in a very short time.

Those who reviewed the different editions of this book, especially Malcolm B. Campbell, Bowling Green State University; John Georgeoff, Purdue University; Frank Guldbrandsen, the University of Minnesota; B. Edward McClellan, the University of Indiana; Edna Mitchell, Mills College; Colleen A. Moore, Central Michigan University; and Norman Rose, Sonoma State University, all shaped it in ways I hope they will recognize.

Finally, of course, my family and especially my wife Katherine provided essential patience and support in the original development of the manuscript and again in the recent revisions.

James W. Fraser
January 2019

The School in Colonial America, 1620–1770

- Introduction
- Virginia Council [London], Instructions to Sir Thomas Gates, Knight, Governor of Virginia, 1636
- Virginia Statutes on the Education of Indian Children Held Hostage, from the *Virginia Statutes at Large*, 1656
- South Carolina Statute on Conversion of Slaves to Christianity; *Digest of the Public Statute Law of South Carolina*, 1711
- A Missionary Report from Mr. Taylor to the Society in North Carolina on the Baptism of Slaves, April 23, 1719
- Virginia's Cure, or an Advisive Narrative Concerning Virginia, London, 1662
- Sir William Berkeley, Governor of Virginia, Response to "Enquiries to the Governor of Virginia," from the Lords' Commissioners of Foreign Plantations, 1671
- Massachusetts' Old Deluder Satan Law, 1647
- Benjamin Franklin, *Autobiography* 1714–1718
- John Adams, Diary Entries, 1756
- *The New England Primer*, 1768

Introduction

The culture of the lands that would become the United States after 1776 was created out of the interaction of European colonists—especially those coming from England, France, and Spain; people of African descent—especially those taken as slaves from the west coast of Africa and increasingly from the heart of the continent; and, of course, the native peoples who had resided in North America for hundreds of years before the first Europeans or Africans arrived. All of these cultures had ways to educate the young and induct them into the culture of the adult world in which they were expected to live. But schools as we know them were a European invention (though both Europe and Africa also had universities for more advanced learning prior to American contact), and in the American context it was the Europeans who built schools and who designed them to be part of an effort to ensure that everyone in the colonies—Europeans, Africans, and American Indians—was inducted into a common culture, though hardly a culture that treated all of the colony's inhabitants equally. And as the English came to dominate North America, it was the English version of schooling that came over time to be the dominant form of education for most people living in the colonies that eventually became the United States.

Schools existed in the North American colonies almost from the beginning of European settlement. English settlers created schools as part of their effort to build a little England in their new home. But in order to understand the schools of colonial America, it is important to understand how they differed from, as well as how they were similar to, modern schools. First, schools were a relatively small part of English education. Family, church, community, and apprenticeship all ranked far above formal schooling as means to gain a good and useful education. In addition, schools were introduced into the lands which would become the United States at a unique historic moment—a time when three cultures were meeting in ways unimaginable to the English people who had designed the institution.

One of the earliest issues the English faced had to do with the education of the new peoples they were encountering. The Virginia Company, based in London, instructed their governor to ensure that the American Indians were inducted into Christianity and English culture whether they wanted to be or not. It was not the last time schooling would be imposed by those in power on others who did not want it. Later documents indicate the same approach to Indian education continued years later. The colonial era also saw great debates about the appropriate education of African-American slaves. Initially, some European settlers feared that literacy, and especially conversion to Christianity, might make the slaves eligible for freedom. In time, however, the governing authorities decided differently. Slaves could be educated, and they could convert to Christianity and join the European churches, but they would remain slaves. In the colonial era, this legislation unleashed a significant effort to educate the slaves in the rudiments of Christianity and a somewhat less enthusiastic, but still real, effort to encourage literacy among the slaves. Only much later, as literate slaves rebelled in the nineteenth century, did the southern states outlaw literacy among their slaves.

Slave owners were also not the only ones frightened by literacy. Virginia Governor Berkeley's oft-quoted statement reflected the thinking of many: "I thank God, *there are no free schools* nor *printing*, and I hope we shall not have these [for a] hundred years." While not everyone agreed with Berkeley, he was far from alone. Puritan New England had the strongest commitment to schooling of any part of what was then British North America. The Puritans saw education as one essential element in the larger structure of society's educational configuration. In Boston, which was founded in 1630, family, church, and of course the community were there from the beginning, but schools were added within five years. In April 1635, Boston Latin School was created by public vote. As was recorded, "At a general meeting upon public notice agreed that our brother Philemon Pormort shall be intreated to become schoolmaster for the teaching and nurturing of children with us." Pormort apparently agreed, although within a few years he was in trouble with the authorities for supporting the "heretic" Anne Hutcheson and was forced into exile in New Hampshire. His successor, Daniel Maude, continued the school in his own home until 1645, when the first schoolhouse for the Latin School was built.

Just as the first schools were opening, legislators were creating laws to ensure their availability—at least to the English. For example:

- In 1642, the first education-related legislation passed the Massachusetts legislature. It required that the head of every household teach every child in that household—male and female, biological children, apprentices, or servants—"to read and understand the principles of religion and the capital laws of the country."

- In 1647, legislation also required the creation of schools. "It being one chief project of that old deluder Satan," began one of the most famous pieces of education-related legislation ever written, "to keep men from the knowledge of the Scriptures." The legislature therefore ordered towns to "appoint one within their town to teach all such children as shall resort to him to write and read."

It is important to note what these laws did not require as well as what they did. Neither law required children to attend school; instead, parents needed to ensure that their children would learn, and the community had to ensure that schools were available. Thus, schools did not have to be the vehicle of learning—and for many they weren't, especially for many girls, but also for some boys.

Benjamin Franklin's *Autobiography* provides an excellent description of how colonial schooling actually worked for European Americans. Franklin was born in Boston in 1714. About a decade later, his formal schooling began after he had already learned to read and write at home when, "I was put to the grammar school [Boston Latin School] at eight years of age." But he did not stay at the grammar school for long. Franklin and his father decided that a trade was better than college and that, therefore, there was no further value in the grammar school, so he dropped out and went to a "school for writing and arithmetic." This was exactly what Franklin and his father thought he needed and in time it helped him become one of the richest and most influential citizens of North America.

While Benjamin Franklin described his experience as a student, another of the nation's founders, John Adams, began his post-college career as a teacher in the Center School, in Worcester, Massachusetts. In his *Diary* from those early years of his career, Adams recounted the joys of teaching even though, like most colonial teachers, he left the job after just two years to pursue a more lucrative career.

The documents that follow in this chapter give some sense of the variety of schools as well as the variety of intended purposes for those schools. In the colonial era nothing that could be called a system of schooling existed but for all of the variety, schools most assuredly did exist.

VIRGINIA COUNCIL [LONDON], INSTRUCTIONS TO SIR THOMAS GATES, KNIGHT, GOVERNOR OF VIRGINIA, 1636

The London-based Virginia Council gave clear instructions to one of their early governors, Sir Thomas Gates, regarding his responsibility to educate the native peoples in the ways of English Christianity. Their instructions revealed overt hostility to the religions, cultures, and educational systems of the original inhabitants of the New World; their orders also demonstrated their conviction that Christianity and English civilization offered important opportunities to native children.

You shall, with all propenseness and diligence, endeavor the conversion of the natives to the knowledge and worship of the true God and their Redeemer, Christ Jesus, as the most pious and noble end of this plantation, which the better to effect you must procure from them some convenient number of their children to be brought up in your language and manners. And if you find it convenient, we think it reasonable you first remove . . . them from their . . . priests by a surprise of them all and detain them prisoners, for they are so wrapped up in the fog and misery of their iniquity, and so terrified with their continual tyranny, chained under with the bond of Death unto the Devil, that while [the priests] live among them to poison and infect . . . their minds, you shall never make any great progress into this glorious work, nor have any civil peace or concur with them . . .

Susan M. Kingsbury, ed., *Virginia County Records.* The Record of the Virginia Company of London: Court Book. From the Manuscript in the Library of Congress. 4 volumes. Washington, D.C.: Government Printing Office, 1906–1935, Vol. III, pp. 14–15.

From Robert H. Bremner, ed., *Children and Youth in America: A Documentary History, Volume I: 1600–1865,* Cambridge, MA: Harvard University Press, 1970, p. 75.

VIRGINIA STATUTES ON THE EDUCATION OF INDIAN CHILDREN HELD HOSTAGE, FROM THE *VIRGINIA STATUTES AT LARGE,* 1656

Twenty years after the London-based Council sent its instructions, the Virginia legislature began to outline its own plan for the education of Indian children held hostage among them. The purpose it outlined for their schooling influenced the purpose of schooling for many in future generations. The legislature specified that it was the responsibility of those in charge of these youth to "do their best to bring them up in Christianity, civility, and the knowledge of necessary trades."

If the Indians shall bring in any children as gauges of their good and quiet intentions to us and amity with us, then the parents of such children shall choose the persons to whom the care of such children shall be entrusted; and the country by us their representatives do engage that we will not use them as slaves, but do their best to bring them up in Christianity, civility, and the knowledge of necessary trades. And on the report of the commissioners of each respective county that those under whose tuition they are do really intend the bettering of the children in these particulars, then a salary shall be allowed to such men as shall deserve and require it.

Susan M. Kingsbury, ed., *Virginia County Records.* The Record of the Virginia Company of London: Court Book. From the Manuscript in the Library of Congress. 4 volumes. Washington, D.C.: Government Printing Office, 1906–1935, Vol. I, p. 396.

From Robert H. Bremner, ed., *Children and Youth in America: A Documentary History, Volume I: 1600–1865,* Cambridge, MA: Harvard University Press, 1970, p. 75.

SOUTH CAROLINA STATUTE ON CONVERSION OF SLAVES TO CHRISTIANITY, *DIGEST OF THE PUBLIC STATUTE LAW OF SOUTH CAROLINA,* 1711

Colonial legislatures with the approval of the British government stepped in to resolve the controversy over the education of slaves in religion and literacy. Slave owners were worried about losing their "property rights" if baptism or literacy might lead slaves to claim the right to be free. Soon after 1700 colonial legislatures, as this example from South Carolina illustrates, made it clear that neither baptism into the Christian religion nor acquiring literacy gave a slave any right to claim freedom. From then on, masters were free to educate their slaves, secure in the knowledge that they would still remain slaves no matter what level of education or piety they achieved.

Since charity and the Christian religion which we profess obliges us to wish well to the souls of all men, and that religion may not be made a pretence to alter any man's property and right, and that no persons may neglect to baptize their Negroes or slaves, or suffer them to be baptized for fear that thereby they should be manumitted and set free: Be it therefore enacted, that it shall be, and is hereby declared, lawful for any Negroe or Indian slave, or any other slave or slaves whatsoever, to receive and profess the Christian faith, and be thereunto baptized. But that notwithstanding such slave or slaves shall receive and profess the Christian religion, and be baptized, he or they shall not thereby be manumitted or set free, or his or their owner, master, or mistress lose his or their civil right, property, and authority over such slave or slaves, but that the slave or slaves, with respect to his or their servitude, shall remain and continue in the same state and condition that he or they was in before the making of this act.

J. Brevard, ed., *Digest of the Public Statute Law of South Carolina*, Charleston, SC, 1814, Vol. II, p. 229. From Robert H. Bremner, ed., *Children and Youth in America: A Documentary History, Volume I: 1600–1865*, Cambridge, MA: Harvard University Press, 1970, p. 97.

A MISSIONARY REPORT FROM MR. TAYLOR TO THE SOCIETY IN NORTH CAROLINA ON THE BAPTISM OF SLAVES, APRIL 23, 1719

Acts of colonial legislatures like South Carolina's did not satisfy everyone, as this letter from a missionary indicates. In Anglican North Carolina, Taylor was attempting to inculcate the slaves of one plantation in English Christianity by having them memorize selections from the Episcopal Book of Common Prayer. The plantation owner, however, feared that his slaves would be freed unless the British Parliament enacted a law specifically preventing it.

In this year I caused a pretty many of the children to learn our catechism, and catechized them in public. In this year I baptized one adult white young woman and thirty white children, and one adult Negro young woman, and one mustee [a person of European and Indian ancestry] young woman and three mustee young children, in all thirty-six. I hope I took a method with the Negro young man, and with the mustee young woman whom I baptized which will please the Society, which was this. I made them get our Church Catechism perfectly without book, and then I took some pains with them to make them understand it, and especially the baptismal covenant, and to persuade them, faithfully and constantly to perform the great things they were to promise at their baptism and ever after to perform to God. And then I caused them to say the catechism one Lord's Day, and the other Lord's Day before a large congregation without book, which they did both distinctly, and so perfectly that all that heard them admired their saying it so well. And with great satisfaction to myself I baptized these two persons . . .

I had for some time great hopes of being the minister that should convert and baptize the rest of Esquire Duckenfield's slaves, which I was very desirous and ambitious to be, and I would have begrudged no pains but would, most freely and with the greatest pleasure, have done all I could to promote and accomplish this so great, and so good work. And in order thereunto, I was preparing four more of them for baptism, and had taught one of those four [his] catechism very perfectly and the other three a good part of it, and now as I was about this good work, the enemies to the conversion and baptism of slaves industriously and very busily buzzed into the peoples' ears that all slaves that were baptized were to be set free. And this silly bugbear so greatly scared Esquire Duckenfield that he told me plainly I should baptize no more of his slaves till the Society had got a law made in England that no baptized slave should be set free because he is baptized, and sen[t] it here. And many more are of the same mind, and so this good work was knocked in the head, which is a great trouble to me because so many slaves are so very desirous to become Christians without any expectation of being set free when they are baptized. I fear this good work will not be revived and prosper here till such a law is enacted by the Parliament of Great Britain and this people are acquainted with it, for I perceive nothing else will satisfy them.

William L. Saunders, ed., *The Colonial Records of North Carolina (1662–1776)*. 10 volumes. Raleigh, NC: PM Hale, etc., 1886–1890, Vol. II (1886), pp. 331–333.

From Robert H. Bremner, ed., *Children and Youth in America: A Documentary History, Volume I: 1600–1865*, Cambridge, MA: Harvard University Press, 1970, p. 97.

VIRGINIA'S CURE, OR AN ADVISIVE NARRATIVE CONCERNING VIRGINIA, LONDON, 1662

As the next two documents show, caste, class, and race were not the only determinants in limiting the spread of schooling in the southern colonies. Because the territory was settled in plantations and farms scattered over large areas, formal schooling was logistically difficult. And the hierarchical attitudes of many, like Governor Berkeley, made schools an object of distrust. These two statements from Virginia show why an advocate for education like Thomas Jefferson would face an uphill battle in advocating for schools throughout the Commonwealth even a century later.

Their almost general want of schools for the education of their children is another consequence of their scattered planting, of most sad consideration, most of all bewailed of parents there; and therefore the arguments drawn from thence most likely to prevail with them cheerfully to embrace the remedy. This want of schools, as it renders a very numerous generation of Christians' children born in Virginia (who naturally are of beautiful and comely persons and generally of more ingenious spirits than these in England) unserviceable for any great employments either in Church or State; so likewise it obstructs the hopefullest way they have for the conversion of the heathen, which is, by winning the heathen . . . to bring in their children to be taught and instructed in our schools together with the children of the Christians.

I shall humbly . . . endeavor to contribute towards the compassing this remedy by propounding:

1. That your Lordship would be pleased to acquaint the King with the necessity of promoting the building [of] towns in each county of Virginia, upon the consideration of the forementioned sad consequences of their present manner of living there.
2. That your Lordship ... be pleased to move the pitiful and charitable heart of His Gracious Majesty (considering the poverty and needs of Virginia) for a collection to be made in all the churches of his three kingdoms ... for the promoting a work of so great charity to the souls of many thousands of his loyal subjects, their children, and the generations after them, and of numberless poor heathen; and that the ministers of each congregation be enjoined with more than ordinary care and pains to stir up the people to a free and liberal contribution towards it ...

Virginia's Cure, or An Advisive Narrative Concerning Virginia. London, 1662, pp. 5–6, 9–11.
From Robert H. Bremner, ed., *Children and Youth in America: A Documentary History, Volume I: 1600–1865*, Cambridge, MA: Harvard University Press, 1970, p. 90.

SIR WILLIAM BERKELEY, GOVERNOR OF VIRGINIA, RESPONSE TO "ENQUIRIES TO THE GOVERNOR OF VIRGINIA," FROM THE LORDS' COMMISSIONERS OF FOREIGN PLANTATIONS, 1671

Sir William Berkeley was the royal governor of Virginia from 1642 to 1676. In the more than thirty years that he ruled the colony he consolidated the authority of a small ruling elite and put down a rebellion against his authoritarian style organized by poor whites and African Americans, both slave and free. The governor's answer was blunt when authorities in London asked Berkeley, "What course is taken about instructing the people within your government in the Christian religion; and what provision is there made for the paying of your ministry?"

The same course that is taken in England out of towns; every man according to his ability instructing his children. We have forty-eight parishes, and our ministers are well paid, and by my consent should be better if *they would pray oftener and preach less*. But of all other commodities, so of this, *the worst are sent us*, and we had few that we could boast of, since the persecution in *Cromwell's* tyranny drove divers worthy men hither. But, I thank God, *there are no free schools* nor *printing*, and I hope we shall not have these hundred years; for *learning* has brought disobedience, and heresy, and sects into the world, and *printing* has divulged them, and libels against the best government. God keep us from both!

W. W. Herring, ed., *Statutes at Large of Virginia (1619–1782)*. 13 volumes. Richmond, VA: Samuel Pleasants, 1809–1823, Vol. II, p. 517.
From Robert H. Bremner, ed., *Children and Youth in America: A Documentary History, Volume I: 1600–1865*, Cambridge, MA: Harvard University Press, 1970, p. 90.

MASSACHUSETTS' OLD DELUDER SATAN LAW, 1647

Comparing this Massachusetts legislation of 1647 with contemporary educational laws, one might become wistful for the rhetoric of the past. In fact, however, the legislature was simply placing their commitment to education in the context of the Puritan faith, the official religion of the Massachusetts Bay colony. If the Puritan version of Protestant Christianity, which demanded that each believer read and study the Bible on their own, were to prevail, then literacy was absolutely essential. In 1642, the legislature passed their first significant school law, requiring that every head of household ensure the literacy of all children resident in that home. Five years later in this 1647 law, they added the requirement that every town offer a school as a means of supporting the householders in their quest to educate children. It is important to note, however, that the responsibility for literacy continued to rest on the family. The school was an adjunct, an option that might or might not be selected as the vehicle for accomplishing state-mandated skills.

It being one chief project of that old deluder Satan to keep men from the knowledge of the Scriptures, as in former times by keeping them in an unknown tongue, so in these latter times by persuading from the use of tongues, that so at least the true sense and meaning of the original might be clouded by false glosses of saint-seeming deceivers, that learning may not be buried in the grave of our fathers in the church and commonwealth, the Lord assisting our endeavors:

It is therefore ordered, that every township in this jurisdiction, after the Lord hath increased them to the number of fifty householders, shall then forthwith appoint one within their town to teach all such children as shall resort to him to write and read, whose wages shall be paid either by the parents or masters of such children, or by the inhabitants in general by way of supply, as the major part of those that order the prudentials of the town shall appoint. Provided, those that send their children be not oppressed by paying much more than they can have them taught for in other towns. And it is further ordered, that where any town shall increase to the number of 100 families or householders, they shall set up a grammar school, the master thereof being able to instruct youth so far as they may be fitted for the university. Provided, that if any town neglect the performance hereof above one year, that every such town shall pay five pounds to the next school till they shall perform this order.

Nathaniel Shurtleff, ed., *Records of the Governor and Company of Massachusetts Bay, 1628–1686.* 5 volumes. Boston, MA: W. White, 1853–1854, Vol. II, p. 203.
From Robert H. Bremner, ed., *Children and Youth in America: A Documentary History, Volume I: 1600–1865*, Cambridge, MA: Harvard University Press, 1970, p. 81.

Benjamin Franklin, *Autobiography* 1714–1718

Benjamin Franklin (1706–1790) wrote his famous Autobiography in four stages in his middle and late years. It was not fully published until 1868. The portion quoted here involves events that took place in 1714–1718. His report of his own childhood and education remains a classic description of the experience of many a white youth within the schools of the colonial era. Boston Latin School proudly claims Franklin as a graduate while, in fact, he dropped out of the "grammar school" after only a few months. But no one, least of all Franklin, thought that his departure was a problem. He moved on first to another school to learn the specific skills in mathematics and bookkeeping that it offered him and then to an apprenticeship that prepared him for his occupation as a printer. At the same time, his voracious out-of-school reading and keen observation of those around him prepared him intellectually for his role as one of the prime shapers of the new American nation.

My elder brothers were all put apprentices to different trades. I was put to the grammar school at eight years of age, my father intending to devote me as the tithe of his sons to the service of the church. My early readiness in learning to read (which must have been very early, as I do not remember when I could not read) and the opinion of all his friends that I should certainly make a good scholar, encouraged him in this purpose of his . . . I continued, however, at the grammar school rather less than a year, though in that time I had risen gradually from the middle of the class of that year to be at the head of the same class, and was removed into the next class, whence I was to be placed in the third at the end of the year. But my father, burdened with a numerous family, was unable without inconvenience to support the expense of a college education, considering, moreover, as he said to one of his friends in my presence, the little encouragement that line of life afforded to those educated for it. He gave up his first intentions, took me from the grammar school, and sent me to a school for writing and arithmetic kept by a then famous man, Mr. Geo. Brownell. He was a skillful master, and successful in his profession, employing the mildest and most encouraging methods. Under him I learned to write a good hand pretty soon, but I failed in the arithmetic and made no progress in it. At ten years old, I was taken home to help my father in his business, which was that of a tallow chandler and soap boiler—a business he was not bred to but had assumed on his arrival in New England, because he found his dyeing trade, being in little request, would not maintain his family. Accordingly, I was employed in cutting wick for the candles, filling the molds for cast candles, attending the shop, going of errands, etc . . .

From my infancy I was passionately fond of reading, and all the little money that came into my hands was laid out in the purchasing of books . . . There was among them Plutarch's *Lives,* in which I read abundantly, and I still think that time spent to great advantage. There was also a book of Defoe's called an *Essay on Projects* and another of Dr. Mather's called *Essays to do Good,* which perhaps gave me a turn of thinking that had an influence on some of the principal future events of my life.

This bookish inclination at length determined my father to make me a printer, though he had already one son (James) of that profession. In 1717 my brother, James, returned from England with a press and letters to set up his business in Boston. I liked it much better than that of my father, but still had a hankering for the sea. To prevent the apprehended effect of such an inclination, my father was impatient to have me bound to my brother. I stood out some time, but at last was persuaded and signed the indenture, when I was yet but twelve years old.

Benjamin Franklin, *The Works of Benjamin Franklin, with Notes and a Life of the Author by Jared Sparks*, London: Benjamin Franklin Stevens, 1882, pp. 9–16.

JOHN ADAMS, DIARY ENTRIES, 1756

When John Adams graduated from Harvard College in 1755, the town of Worcester, Massachusetts was looking for a new school master for its Central School. Reverend Thaddeus McCarty from Worcester was at the commencement ceremony and hired Adams that day. He began teaching in the fall. His diary, which he kept throughout his life, has more reflections on life in the town of Worcester than on his actual teaching, but in the spring of his first year, he wrote one entry which is included here. During Adams's second year of teaching he also studied law with James Putnam and once he completed his studies he left teaching behind forever.

MONDAY, March 15, 1756

I sometimes, in my sprightly moments, consider my self, in my great Chair at School, as some Dictator at the head of a commonwealth. In this little State I can discover all the great Genius's, all the surprizing actions and revolutions of the great World in miniature. I have severall renowned Generalls but 3 feet high, and several deep projecting Politicians in peticoats. I have others catching and dissecting Flies, accumulating remarkable pebbles, cockle shells &c., with as ardent Curiosity as any Virtuoso in the royal society. Some rattle and Thunder out A, B, C, with as much Fire and impetuosity, as Alexander fought, and very often sit down and cry as heartily, upon being out spelt, as Cesar did, when at Alexanders sepulchre he recollected that the Macedonian Hero had conquered the World before his Age. At one Table sits Mr. Insipid foppling and fluttering, spinning his whirligig, or playing with his fingers as gaily and wittily as any frenchified coxcomb brandishes his Cane or rattles his snuff box. At another sitts the polemical Divine, plodding and wrangling in his mind about Adam's fall in which we sinned all as his primmer has it. In short my little school like the great World, is made up of Kings, Politicians, Divines, L.D. [LL.D.'s?], Fops, Buffoons, Fidlers, Sychophants, Fools, Coxcombs, chimney sweepers, and every other Character drawn in History or seen in the World. Is it not then the highest Pleasure my Friend to preside in this little World, to bestow the proper applause upon virtuous and generous Actions, to blame and punish every vicious and contracted Trick, to wear out of the tender mind every thing that is mean and little, and fire the new born soul with a noble ardor and Emulation. The World affords no greater Pleasure. Let others waste the bloom of Life, at the Card or biliard Table, among rakes and fools, and when their minds are sufficiently fretted with losses, and inflamed by Wine, ramble through the Streets, assaulting innocent People, breaking Windows or debauching young Girls. I envy not their exalted happiness. I had rather sit in school and consider which of my pupils will turn out in his future Life, a Hero, and which a rake, which a phylosopher, and which a parasite, than change breasts with them, tho possest of 20 lac'd wast coats and 1000 a year.

SUNDAY, August 22, 1756

Yesterday I compleated a Contract with Mr. Putnam, to study Law under his Inspection for two years.

John Adams, *Diary*, Adams Electronic Archive, Massachusetts Historical Society.

THE NEW ENGLAND PRIMER, 1768

The New England Primer was the premier textbook for basic literacy in colonial New England. Children learned the alphabet and their catechism through it at the same time. Moving from "In Adam's Fall We Sinned All," through "Zaccheus He Did Climb the Tree, Our Lord to See," children were inducted into a holistic worldview. The primer continued in use for some time after the Revolution, although references to the English king were removed. One could date the beginnings of American civil religion to the replacement of an earlier Calvinist "Whales in the Sea God's Voice Obey" with "Washington Brave His Country Did Save."

The New England Primer. Boston, MA: Printed and sold by John Perkins, 1768. MHS Neg.#1313, #1314, #1315, #1316, #1319, and #1490. Reprinted courtesy of the Massachusetts Historical Society.

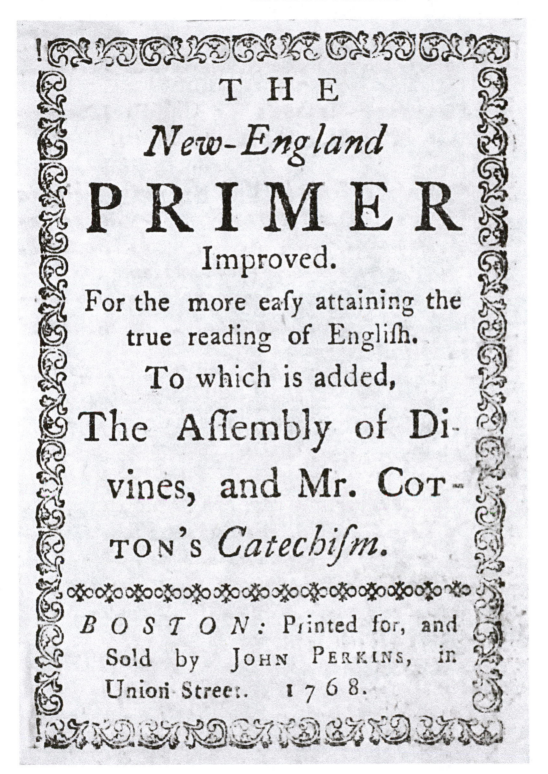

Figure 1.1 New England Primer. Title page. Boston, MA: Printed and sold by J. Perkins, 1768.

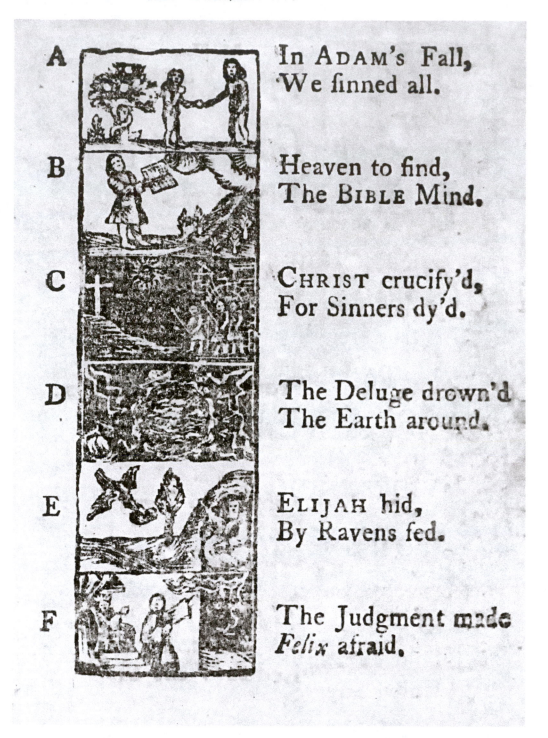

Figure 1.2 New England Primer. Illustrated Alphabet, letters A–F. Boston, MA: Printed and sold by J. Perkins, 1768.

G
As runs the Glass,
Our Life doth pass.

H
My Book and Heart
Must never part.

I
Job feels the Rod,
Yet blesses GOD.

K
Proud *Korah's* Troops
Was swallow'd up.

L
Lot fled to *Zoar*,
Saw fiery Shower
On *Sodom* pour.

M
Moses was he
Who *Israel's* Host
Led thro' the Sea.

Figure 1.3 New England Primer. Illustrated Alphabet, letters G–M. Boston, MA: Printed and sold by J. Perkins, 1768.

N — *Noah* did view
The old world & new.

O — Young *Obadias,*
David, Josias,
All were pious.

P — *Peter* deny'd
His Lord and cry'd.

Q — Queen *Esther* sues,
And saves the *Jews.*

R — Young pious *Ruth,*
Left all for Truth.

S — Young *Samuel* dear,
The Lord did fear.

Figure 1.4 New England Primer. Illustrated Alphabet, letters N–S. Boston, MA: Printed and sold by J. Perkins, 1768.

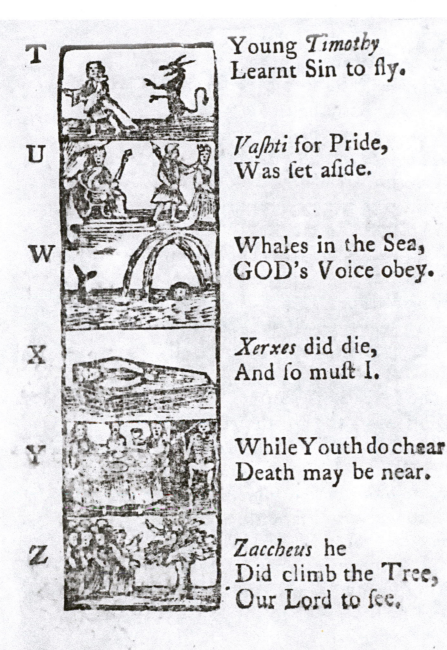

T   Young *Timothy*
Learnt Sin to fly.

U   *Vashti* for Pride,
Was set aside.

W   Whales in the Sea,
GOD's Voice obey.

X   *Xerxes* did die,
And so must I.

Y   While Youth do chear
Death may be near.

Z   *Zaccheus* he
Did climb the Tree,
Our Lord to see.

Figure 1.5 New England Primer. Illustrated Alphabet, letters T–Z. Boston, MA: Printed and sold by J. Perkins, 1768.

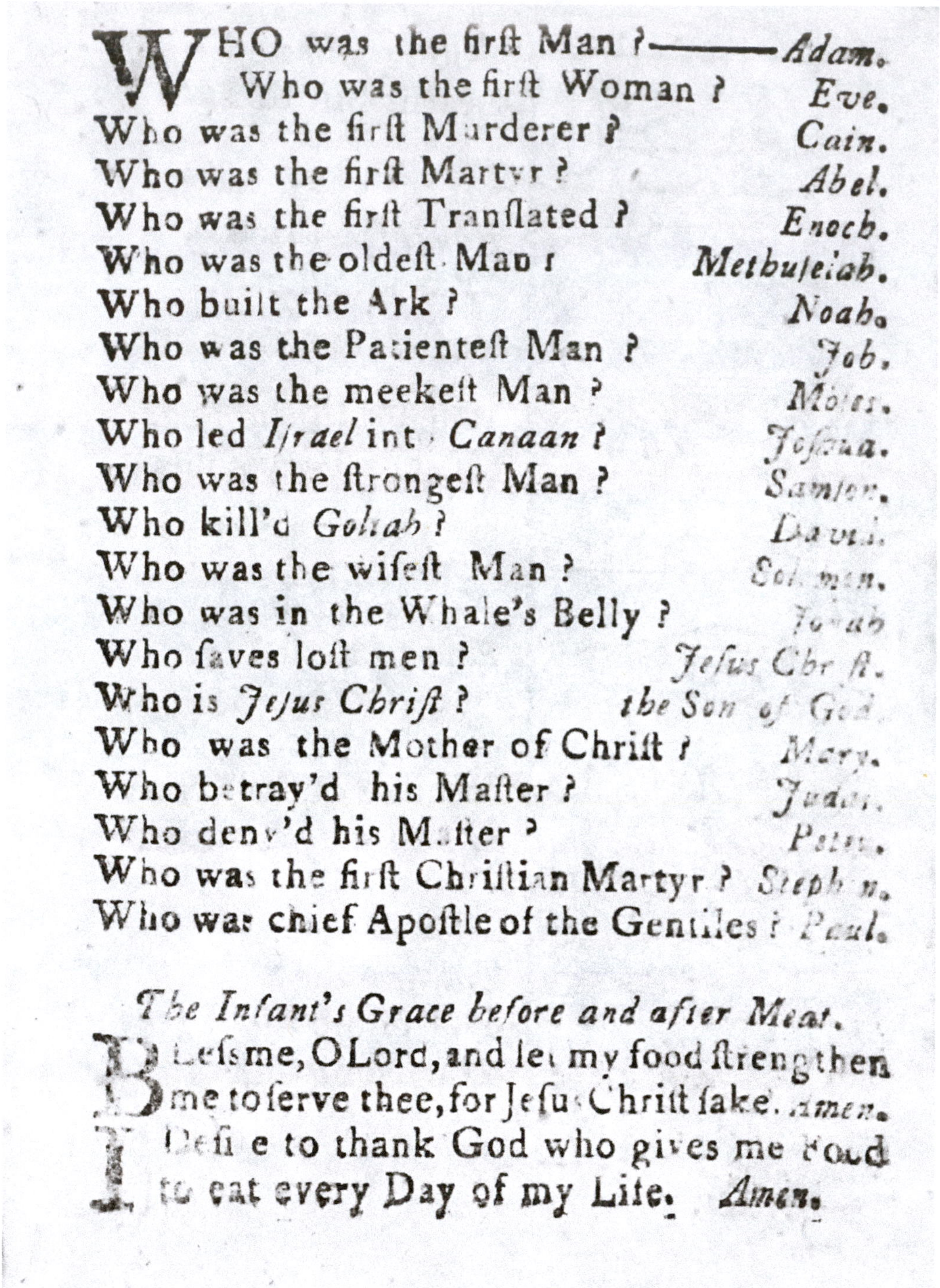

WHO was the first Man ? ——— *Adam.*
  Who was the first Woman ? *Eve.*
Who was the first Murderer ? *Cain.*
Who was the first Martyr ? *Abel.*
Who was the first Translated ? *Enoch.*
Who was the oldest Man ? *Methuselah.*
Who built the Ark ? *Noah.*
Who was the Patientest Man ? *Job.*
Who was the meekest Man ? *Moses.*
Who led *Israel* into *Canaan* ? *Joshua.*
Who was the strongest Man ? *Samson.*
Who kill'd *Goliah* ? *David.*
Who was the wisest Man ? *Solomon.*
Who was in the Whale's Belly ? *Jonah*
Who saves lost men ? *Jesus Christ.*
Who is *Jesus Christ* ? *the Son of God.*
Who was the Mother of Christ ? *Mary.*
Who betray'd his Master ? *Judas.*
Who deny'd his Master ? *Peter.*
Who was the first Christian Martyr ? *Stephen.*
Who was chief Apostle of the Gentiles ? *Paul.*

The Infant's Grace before and after Meat.

BLess me, O Lord, and let my food strengthen
me to serve thee, for Jesus Christ sake. *Amen.*

I Desire to thank God who gives me Food
to eat every Day of my Life. *Amen.*

Figure 1.6 New England Primer. "Who Was the First Man . . . Adam." Boston, MA: Printed and sold by J. Perkins, 1768.

2
The American Revolution and Schools for the New Republic, 1770–1820

- Introduction
- Thomas Jefferson, A Bill for the More General Diffusion of Knowledge, 1779
- Thomas Jefferson, Notes on the State of Virginia, 1783
- Benjamin Rush, Thoughts Upon Female Education, 1787
- Noah Webster, On the Education of Youth in America, Boston, 1790
- Noah Webster, *The American Spelling Book*, 1783
- United States Congress, the Northwest Ordinance, July 13, 1787
- United States Congress, Civilization Fund Act, March 3, 1819

Introduction

The colonial pattern of schooling was imported from England. After the American Revolution, citizens of the new nation needed to decide what to keep and what to discard from their English inheritance. Clearly, they intended to keep schools, but they also intended to change them. The *New England Primer's* editorial change, from "Whales in the Sea, God's Voice obey," to "Washington brave his country did save," was symbolic of the changes to come as a new generation sought to create a uniquely American and slightly more secular form of education for the young citizens of the new republic.

Thomas Jefferson was one of several leaders of the revolutionary generation who addressed issues of schooling. Although Jefferson was a prime voice for the development of schools for Virginia and throughout the new nation, his home state did not adopt his recommendations until long after his death. Nevertheless, Jefferson's 1779 "Bill for the More General Diffusion of Knowledge" and his subsequent 1783 "Notes on the State of Virginia" represent perhaps the best (and certainly the best known) statement of the demands a democratic revolution places on schooling. Jefferson argued for schooling for all citizens for two reasons. First, he argued that the best safeguard against tyranny is "to illuminate, as far as practicable, the minds of the people at large." He articulated the American faith in education as the only true safeguard of democracy as clearly as would ever be done. Of course, students of history recognize the irony that Jefferson's definition of "the people at large" was fairly limited. Jefferson seldom included women in his definition of citizens, and his own role as a slaveholder dramatically undermined all of his democratic rhetoric, including his call for universal schooling. And secondly, Jefferson saw quality education as a means of finding a few leaders of the future among the poor of the Commonwealth. If education could "rake from the rubbish" a few good leaders, the whole society would be better off. It was only long after Jefferson had died that a post-Civil War government in Virginia, with the voices of newly freed slaves included in the debate, adopted Jefferson's earlier proposals for pre-collegiate schooling. For all of his failings, however, Jefferson outlined a democratic political vision and system of education in his writings that later generations would embrace far more fervently than the author ever dreamed possible.

Less remembered but probably more effective in the educational politics of their own generation were two other philosophers of education, Benjamin Rush and Noah Webster. Rush shared Jefferson's opinion that a new form of education was needed in the new nation. In one area, however, Rush went far beyond Jefferson. In a series of lectures that were later published as "Thoughts Upon Female Education," in 1787, Rush outlined his version of republican virtues and education, including a specific, if somewhat limited—but radical for his day—vision of the educational needs of female citizens. His rationale for women's education fit perfectly with what was known as "Republican motherhood": the belief that women had to be educated—to have their minds cultivated—if they were to be fit partners for their husbands and fit mothers to raise their sons for active citizenship.

Noah Webster, best remembered for his dictionary, also played a key role in shaping American English. In his 1790 "On the Education of Youth in America," Webster outlined his democratic goals. In his three-volume *Grammatical Institute of the English Language*, Webster produced a spelling book, a grammar, and a reader, and in his later dictionary he put his ideas into practice, creating a new American language, consciously different from the English of the mother country. As important as Webster's dictionary was to subsequent generations—and it was very important—it was through Webster's "blue-backed speller" with its blue cover and its detailed instructions on how to read, speak, and spell in American English that many in the post-revolutionary generation of Americans learned to read and write.

While Jefferson, Rush, and Webster wrote about the kind of education the new nation needed, each of the newly freed thirteen colonies wrote a new constitution. Many of these earliest constitutions deemed a system of free public schooling essential to democracy. In Massachusetts, for example, John Adams drafted a new constitution in 1780 that included a state for the development of a school system to encourage a literate citizenry. Adams framed his rationale for schooling as follows:

Wisdom, and knowledge, as well as virtue, diffused generally among the body of the people, being necessary for the preservation of their rights and liberties . . . [schools should be established] to countenance and inculcate the principles of humanity and general benevolence, public and private charity, industry and frugality, honesty and punctuality in their dealings; sincerity, good-humour, and all social affections, and generous sentiments among the people.

Thus as the new state governments took shape, the school was emerging with a new role: It should not only support literacy, but encourage a quasi-religious morality among citizens.

The federal government also took an early lead in educational issues. While schooling was left to the states, the national government did play a role. Even before the Constitution was adopted, while still under the Articles of Confederation in 1787, Congress adopted the Northwest Ordinance, setting up a government for the new territories of the northwest (the present states of Michigan, Wisconsin, Ohio, Indiana, and Illinois). The ordinance included its famous edict that "Religion, morality, and knowledge being necessary to good government and the happiness of mankind, schools and the means of education shall forever be encouraged."

Congress and the presidents, from Washington on, also had to address the education of the Indian populations, with whom they were developing a series of treaties. Throughout the nation's history, the government's attitude toward Native Americans has been ambivalent, but the Civilization Fund Act of 1819 represents one of the earliest efforts to force Indians into the American system of society and government and the use of schools to accomplish the task. Almost without exception, at least until the era of the New Deal in the 1930s, federal policy assumed that schooling for Indians meant schooling that separated them from their cultures—and usually their lands—by making them adopt the culture and work ethic of European Americans. Respect for cultural diversity was not on the horizon.

Of course, the issues were more complex than these brief documents indicate. Jefferson understood all too well that women, Native Americans, and African Americans were excluded from the Republic his schools were designed to serve. Who would be included—in the schools and in definitions of democracy—would be debated for the next two hundred years. Attending

Figure 2.1 Thomas Jefferson. Courtesy of the Library of Congress, LC-USZ62-53985.

to the real diversity of the nation's citizens and to the institutionalization of the revolutionary era's dreams for schools would be left to later generations. In the field of schooling, the founders' primary contribution was their articulation of a vision of what they thought schooling should be. Institutionalizing this vision and answering questions of who would be included was left to future generations.

THOMAS JEFFERSON, A BILL FOR THE MORE GENERAL DIFFUSION OF KNOWLEDGE, 1779

In 1779, in the midst of the American Revolution, a young Thomas Jefferson proposed three interconnected bills to the Virginia legislature, one to make the College of William and Mary more democratic, one proposing a public library system, and the third to create a state-wide school system for his newly independent home state. None of the bills passed. Having failed to get the College of William and Mary to adopt his goals, Jefferson, long after he left the White House, launched the University of Virginia in 1819. But in Jefferson's lifetime, no progress was seen at the pre-college level. Indeed, none of the southern states had a meaningful system of public education in place until after the Civil War. But in his "Bill for the More General Diffusion of Knowledge," Jefferson outlined the system that he believed appropriate to the education of the youth of a new democracy.

Whereas it appeareth that however certain forms of government are better calculated than other to protect individuals in the free exercise of their natural rights, and are at the same time themselves better guarded against degeneracy, yet experience hath shewn, that even under the best forms, those entrusted with power have, in time, and by slow operations, perverted it into tyranny; and it is believed that the most effectual means of preventing this would be, to illuminate, as far as practicable, the minds of the people at large, and more especially to give them knowledge of those facts, which history exhibiteth, that, possessed thereby of the experience of other ages and countries, they may be enabled to know ambition under all its shapes, and prompt to exert their natural powers to defeat its purposes; And whereas it is generally true that people will be happiest whose laws are best, and are best administered, and that laws will be wisely formed, and honestly administered, in proportion as those who form and administer them are wise and honest; whence it becomes expedient for promoting the publick happiness that those persons, whom nature hath endowed with genius and virtue, should be rendered by liberal education worthy to receive, and able to guard the sacred deposit of the rights and liberties of their fellow citizens, and that they should be called to that charge without regard to wealth, birth or other accidental condition or circumstance; but the indigence of the greater number disabling them from so educating, at their own expence, those of their children whom nature hath fitly formed and disposed to become useful instruments for the public, it is better that such should be sought for and educated at the common expence of all, than that the happiness of all should be confided to the weak or wicked . . .

At every of these schools shall be taught reading, writing, and common arithmetick, and the books which shall be used therein for instructing the children to read shall be such as will at the same time make them acquainted with Graecian, Roman, English, and American history. At these schools all the free children, male and female, resident within the respective hundred, shall be intitled to receive tuition gratis, for the term of three years, and as much longer, at their private expence, as their parents, guardians or friends, shall think proper . . .

Paul Leicester Ford, ed., *The Writings of Thomas Jefferson*, Volume III, 1781–1784, New York: G.P. Putnam's Sons, 1894, pp. 242–243, 251–255.

THOMAS JEFFERSON, NOTES ON THE STATE OF VIRGINIA, 1783

Four years after the failure of his proposal for a general system of schooling, Jefferson wrote from Paris, where he was then serving as the ambassador of the rebellious Americans, describing the conditions of his home state and especially his continuing hopes for a revision of Virginia's system of public education once the revolutionary war was won. This piece provides a nice overview of Jefferson's goals but also interesting insight into Jefferson's views about what later generations would call child development and age-appropriate instruction. Unfortunately for Jefferson's goals, the post-revolutionary government still declined to act, but Jefferson's Notes make it clear just what he wanted.

Many of the laws which were in force during the monarchy being relative merely to that form of government, or inculcating principles inconsistent with republicanism, the first assembly which met after the establishment of the commonwealth, appointed a committee to revise the whole code, to reduce it into proper form and volume, and report it to the assembly. This work has been executed by three gentlemen, and reported; but probably will not be taken up till a restoration of peace shall leave to the legislature leisure to go through such a work.

. . .

Another object of the revisal is, to diffuse knowledge more generally through the mass of the people. This bill proposes to lay off every county into small districts of five or six miles square, called hundreds and in each of them to establish a school for teaching, reading, writing, and arithmetic. The tutor to be suported by the hundred, and every person in it entitled to send their children three years gratis, and as much longer as they please, paying for it. These schools to be under a visitor who is annually to chuse the boy of best genius in the school, of those whose parents are too poor to give them further education, and to send him forward to one of the grammar schools, of which twenty are proposed to be erected in different parts of the country, for teaching Greek, Latin, geography, and the higher branches of numerical arithmetic. Of the boys thus sent in any one year, trial is to be made at the grammar schools one or two years, and the best genius of the whole selected, and continued six years, and the residue dismissed. By this means twenty of the best geniuses will be raked from the rubbish annually, and be instructed, at the public expence, so far as the grammar schools go. At the end of six years instruction, one half are to be discontinued (from among whom the grammar schools will probably be supplied with future masters); and the other half, who are to be chosen for the superiority of their parts and disposition, are to be sent and continued three years in the study of such sciences as they shall chuse, at William and Mary college, the plan of which is proposed to be enlarged, as will be hereafter explained, and extended to all the useful sciences. The ultimate result of the whole scheme of education would be the teaching all the children of the State reading, writing, and common arithmetic; turning out ten annually, of superior genius, well taught in Greek, Latin, geography, and the higher branches of arithmetic; turning out ten others annually, of still superior parts, who, to those branches of learning, shall have added such of the sciences as their genius shall have led them to; the furnishing to the wealthier part of the people convenient schools at which their children may be educated at their own expence. The general objects of this law are to provide an education adapted to the years, to the capacity and the condition of every one, and directed to their freedom and happiness. Specific details were not proper for the law. These must be the business of the visitors entrusted with its execution. The first stage of this education being the schools of the hundreds, wherein the great mass of the people will receive their instruction, the principle foundations of future order will be laid here. Instead, therefore, of putting the Bible and Testament into the hands of the children at an age when their judgments are not sufficiently matured for religious inquires, their memories may here be stored with most useful facts from Grecian, Roman, European, and American history. The first elements of morality too may be instilled into their minds; such as; when further developed as their judgments advance in strength, may teach them how to work out their greatest happiness, by shewing them that it does not depend on the condition of life in which chance has placed them, but is always the result of a good conscience, good health, occupation, and freedom in all just pursuits.

Those whom either the wealth of their parents or the adoption of the state shall destine to higher degrees of learning, will go on to the grammar schools, which constitute the next stage, there to be instructed in the languages. The learning Greek and Latin, I am told, is going into disuse in Europe. I know not what their manners and occupations may call for: but it would be very ill-judged in us to follow their example in this instance. There is a certain period of life, say from eight to fifteen or sixteen years of age, when the mind like the body is not yet firm enough for laborious and close operations. If applied to such, it falls an early victim to premature exertion; exhibiting, indeed, at first, in these young and tender subjects, the flattering appearance of their being men while they are yet children, but ending in reducing them to be children when they should be men. The memory is then most susceptible and tenacious of impressions; and the learning of languages being chiefly a work of memory, it seems precisely fitted to the powers of this period, which is long enough too for acquiring the most useful languages, ancient and modern. I do not pretend that language is science. It is only an instrument for the attainment of science. But that time is not lost which is employed in providing tools for future operation: more especially as in this case the books put into the hands of the youth for this purpose may be such as will at the same time impress their minds with useful facts and good principles. If this period be suffered to pass in idleness, the mind becomes lethargic and impotent, as would the body it inhabits if unexercised during the same time. The sympathy between body and mind during their rise, progress and decline, is too strict and obvious to endanger our being misled while we reason from the one to the other. As soon as they are of sufficient age, it is supposed they will be sent on from the grammar schools to the university, which constitutes our third and last stage, there to study those sciences which may be adapted to their views. By that part of our plan which prescribes the selection of the youths of genius from among the classes of the poor, we hope to avail the state of those talents which nature has sown as liberally among the poor as the rich, but which perish without use, if not sought for and cultivated. But of all the views of this law none is more important, none more legitimate, than that of rendering the people the safe, as they are ultimate, guardians of their own liberty. For this purpose the reading in the first stage, where they will receive their whole education, is proposed, as has been said, to be chiefly historical. History, by apprising them of the past, will enable them to judge of the future; it will avail them of the experience of other times and other nations; it will qualify them as judges of the actions and designs of men; it will enable them to know ambition under every disguise it may assume; and knowing it, to defeat its views. In every government on earth is some trace of human weakness, some germ of corruption and degeneracy, which cunning will discover, and wickedness insensibly open, cultivate and improve. Every government degenerates when trusted to the rulers of the people alone. The people themselves therefore are its only safe depositories. And to render even them safe, their minds must be improved to a certain degree. This indeed is not all that is necessary, though it be essentially necessary. An amendment of our constitution must here come in aid of the public education. The influence over government must be shared among all the people. If every individual which composes their mass participates of the ultimate authority, the government will be safe; because the corrupting the whole mass will exceed any private resources of wealth; and public ones cannot be provided but by levies on the people. In this case every man would have to pay his own price. The government of Great Britain has been corrupted, because but one man in ten has a right to vote for members of parliament. The sellers of the government, therefore, get nine-tenths of their price clear. It has been thought that corruption is restrained by confining the right of suffrage to a few of the wealthier of the people: but it would be more effectually restrained by an extension of that right to such numbers as would bid defiance to the means of corruption.

Thomas Jefferson, *Notes on the State of Virginia*, London: John Stockdale, 1787, pp. 136–137, 143, 146–149.

BENJAMIN RUSH, THOUGHTS UPON FEMALE EDUCATION, 1787

In addition to his general thoughts on the education needed for a newly democratic nation, Benjamin Rush had quite specific designs for the education he thought women needed. This essay, which was originally a speech to the Board of Visitors of the young Ladies' Academy at Pennsylvania given in July 1787, of which Rush was one of the founders, outlines Rush's desire to create a distinctly American and democratic form of education that included the expectation that democratic women will have a level of independence and responsibility far greater than their predecessors. Not all women accepted the still limited role that Rush or proponents of Republican motherhood held for them. When Priscilla Mason graduated from the Young Ladies' Academy in 1794, she gave a graduation address in which she condemned limitations to women's education that "have denied us the means of knowledge, and then reproached us for the want of it." She continued, "The Church, the Bar, and the Senate are shut against us. Who shut them? Man, despotic man." An education that produced such a speaker may have been more than Rush envisioned when he proposed the school.

Gentlemen,

I have yielded with diffidence to the solicitations of the Principal of the Academy, in undertaking to express my regard for the prosperity of this seminary of learning by submitting to your candor a few thoughts upon female education.

The first remark that I shall make upon this subject is that female education should be accommodated to the state of society, manners, and government of the country in which it is conducted.

This remark leads me at once to add that the education of young ladies in this country should be conducted upon principles very different from what it is in Great Britain and in some respects different from what it was when we were a part of a monarchical empire.

There are several circumstances in the situation, employments, and duties of women in America which require a peculiar mode of education.

I. The early marriages of our women, by contracting the time allowed for education, renders it necessary to contract its plan and to confine it chiefly to the more useful branches of literature.

II. The state of property in America renders it necessary for the greatest part of our citizens to employ themselves in different occupations for the advancement of their fortunes. This cannot be done without the assistance of the female members of the community. They must be the stewards and guardians of their husbands' property. That education, therefore, will be most proper for our women which teaches them to discharge the duties of those offices with the most success and reputation.

III. From the numerous avocations to which a professional life exposes gentlemen in America from their families, a principal share of the instruction of children naturally devolves upon the women. It becomes us therefore to prepare them, by a suitable education, for the discharge of this most important duty of mothers.

IV. The equal share that every citizen has in the liberty and the possible share he may have in the government of our country make it necessary that our ladies should be qualified to a certain degree, by a peculiar and suitable education, to concur in instructing their sons in the principles of liberty and government.

V. In Great Britain the business of servants is a regular occupation, but in America this humble station is the usual retreat of unexpected indigence; hence the servants in this country possess less knowledge and subordination than are required from them; and hence our ladies are obliged to attend more to the private affairs of their families than ladies generally do of the same rank in Great Britain. "They are good servants," said an American lady of distinguished merit in a letter to a favorite daughter, "who will do well with good looking after." This circumstance should have great influence upon the nature and extent of female education in America.

The branches of literature most essential for a young lady in this country appear to be:

I. A knowledge of the English language . . .

II. Pleasure and interest conspire to make the writing of a fair and legible hand a necessary branch of female education . . .

III. Some knowledge of figures and bookkeeping is absolutely necessary to qualify a young lady for the duties which await her in this country . . .

IV. An acquaintance with geography and some instruction in chronology will enable a young lady to read history, biography, and travels, with advantage, and thereby qualify her not only for a general intercourse with the world but to be an agreeable companion for a sensible man . . .

V. Vocal music should never be neglected in the education of a young lady in this country . . .

VI. Dancing is by no means an improper branch of education for an American lady. It promotes health and renders the figure and motions of the body easy and agreeable . . .

VII. The attention of our young ladies should be directed as soon as they are prepared for it to the reading of history, travels, poetry, and moral essays . . .

VIII. It will be necessary to connect all these branches of education with regular instruction in the Christian religion . . .

IX. If the measures that have been recommended for inspiring our pupils with a sense of religious and moral obligation be adopted, the government of them will be easy and agreeable. I shall only remark under this head that *strictness* of discipline will always render *severity* unnecessary and that there will be the most instruction in that school where there is the most order . . .

The attempt to establish this new mode of education for young ladies was an experiment and the success of it hath answered our expectations. Too much praise cannot be given to our principal and his assistants, for the abilities and fidelity with which they have carried the plan into execution. The proficiency which the young ladies have discovered in reading, writing, spelling, arithmetic, grammar, geography, music, and their different catechisms since the last examination is a less equivocal mark of the merits of our teachers than anything I am able to express in their favor.

But the reputation of the academy must be suspended till the public are convinced by the future conduct and character of our pupils of the advantages of the institution. To you, therefore, YOUNG LADIES, an important problem is committed for solution; and that is, whether our present plan of education be a wise one and whether it be calculated to prepare you for the duties of social and domestic life. I know that the elevation of the female mind, by means of moral, physical, and religious truth, is considered by some men as unfriendly to the domestic character of a woman. But this is the prejudice of little minds and springs from the same spirit which opposes the general diffusion of knowledge among the citizens of our republics. If men believe that ignorance is favorable to the government of the female sex, they are certainly deceived, for a weak and ignorant woman will always be governed with the greatest difficulty.

Benjamin Rush, M. D., Thoughts upon Female Education, accommodated to the Present State of Society, Manners and Government, Boston, MA: John W. Folsom, 1791, pp. 3–14 from an original copy at the Massachusetts Historical Society.

NOAH WEBSTER, ON THE EDUCATION OF YOUTH IN AMERICA, BOSTON, 1790

While his name continues to be remembered through the omnipresent Webster's Dictionary, Noah Webster himself has been virtually forgotten. He was, in fact, the single most influential person in the early development of a uniquely American version of the English language. His dictionary as well as his speller, grammar, and reader were designed to clearly differentiate a democratic American English from the more flowery language of monarchical England. The fact that to this day people in the United States use a simpler form of spelling—"honor" rather than "honour," for example—is due to Webster's work. In addition to his schoolbooks, Webster was one of the most prolific authors of the revolutionary generation on the question of the appropriate kind of education for the new nation. In the following essay Webster outlined his beliefs. Following that essay is a brief selection from his American Spelling Book, known to generations because of its cover as the Blue-Backed Speller, in which Webster made his ideas concrete in a textbook with stories and lists of words to be learned with guides to good spelling and good pronunciation.

Education is a subject which has been exhausted by the ablest writers, both among the ancients and moderns. I am not vain enough to suppose I can suggest any new ideas upon so trite a theme as education in general; but perhaps the manner of conducting the youth in America may be capable of some improvement. Our constitutions of civil government are not yet firmly established; our national character is not yet formed; and it is an object of vast magnitude that systems of education should be adopted and pursued which may not only diffuse a knowledge of the sciences but may implant in the minds of the American youth the principles of virtue and of liberty and inspire them with just and liberal ideas of government and with an inviolable attachment to their own country. It now becomes every American to examine the modes of education in Europe, to see how far they are applicable in this country and whether it is not possible to make some valuable alterations, adapted to our local and political circumstances . . .

The first error that I would mention is a too general attention to the dead languages, with a neglect of our own.

This practice proceeds probably from the common use of the Greek and Roman tongues before the English was brought to perfection. There was a long period of time when these languages were almost the only repositories of science in Europe. Men who had a taste for learning were under a necessity of recurring to the sources, the Greek and Roman authors. These will ever be held in the highest estimation both for style and sentiment, but the most valuable of them have English translations, which, if they do not contain all the elegance, communicate all the ideas of the originals. The English language, perhaps, at this moment, is the repository of as much learning as one half the languages of Europe. In copiousness it exceeds all modern tongues, and though inferior to the Greek and French in softness and harmony, yet it exceeds the French in variety; it almost equals the Greek and Roman in energy and falls very little short of any language in the regularity of its construction . . .

But the principal defect in our plan of education in America is the want of good teachers in the academies and common schools. By good teachers I mean men of unblemished reputation and possessed of abilities competent to their stations. That a man should be master of what he undertakes to teach is a point that will not be disputed, and yet it is certain that abilities are often dispensed with, either through inattention or fear of expense.

To those who employ ignorant men to instruct their children, permit me to suggest one important idea: that it is better for youth to have no education than to have a bad one, for it is more difficult to eradicate habits than to impress new ideas. The tender shrub is easily bent to any figure, but the tree which has acquired its full growth resists all impressions.

Yet abilities are not the sole requisites. The instructors of youth ought, of all men, to be the most prudent, accomplished, agreeable, and respectable. What avail a man's parts, if, while he is the "wisest and brightest," he is the "meanest of man-kind?" The pernicious effects of bad example on the *minds* of youth will probably be acknowledged, but with a view to *improvement* it is indispensably necessary that the teachers should possess good breeding and agreeable manners. In order to give full effect to instructions, it is requisite that they should proceed from a man who is loved and respected. But a low-bred clown or morose tyrant can command neither love nor respect, and that pupil who has no motive for application to books but the fear of a rod will not make a scholar.

The rod is often necessary in school, especially after the children have been accustomed to disobedience and a licentious behavior at home. All government originates in families, and if neglected there, it will hardly exist in society, but the want of it must be supplied by the rod in school, the penal laws of the state, and the terrors of divine wrath from the pulpit. The government both of families and schools should be absolute. There should in families be no appeal from one parent to another, with the prospect of pardon for offenses. The one should always vindicate, at least apparently, the conduct of the other. In schools the matter should be absolute in command, for it is utterly impossible for any man to support order and discipline among children who are indulged with an appeal to their parents. A proper subordination in families would generally supersede the necessity of severity in schools, and a strict discipline in both is the best foundation of good order in political society.

The only practicable method to reform mankind is to begin with children, to banish, if possible, from their company every low-bred, drunken, immoral character. Virtue and vice will not grow together in a great degree, but they will grow where they are planted, and when one has taken root, it is not easily supplanted by the other. The great art of correcting mankind, therefore, consists in prepossessing the mind with good principles.

For this reason society requires that the education of youth should be watched with the most scrupulous attention. Education, in a great measure, forms the moral characters of men, and morals are the basis of government. Education should therefore be the first care of a legislature, not merely the institution of schools but the furnishing of them with the best men for teachers. A good system of education should be the first article in the code of political regulations, for it is much easier to introduce and establish an effectual system for preserving morals than to correct by penal statutes the ill effects of a bad system. I am so fully persuaded of this that I shall almost adore that great man who shall change our practice and opinions and make it respectable for the first and best men to superintend the education of youth.

Another defect in our schools, which, since the Revolution, is become inexcusable, is the want of proper books. The collections which are now used consist of essays that respect foreign and ancient nations. The minds of youth are perpetually led to the history of Greece and Rome or to Great Britain; boys are constantly repeating the declamations of Demosthenes and Cicero or debates upon some political question in the British Parliament. These are excellent specimens of good sense, polished style, and perfect oratory, but they are not interesting to children. They cannot be very useful, except to young gentlemen who want them as models of reasoning and eloquence in the pulpit or at the bar.

But every child in America should be acquainted with his own country. He should read books that furnish him with ideas that will be useful to him in life and practice. As soon as he opens his lips, he should rehearse the history of his own country; he should lisp the praise of liberty and of those illustrious heroes and statesmen who have wrought a revolution in her favor.

A selection of essays respecting the settlement and geography of America, the history of the late Revolution and of the most remarkable characters and events that distinguished it, and a compendium of the principles of the federal and provincial governments should be the principal schoolbook in the United States. These are interesting objects to every man; they call home the minds of youth and fix them upon the interests of their own country, and they assist in forming attachments to it, as well as in enlarging the understanding ...

In our American republics, where government is in the hands of the people, knowledge should be universally diffused by means of public schools. Of such consequence is it to society that the people who make laws should be well informed that I conceive no legislature can be justified in neglecting proper establishments for this purpose. When I speak of a diffusion of knowledge, I do not mean merely a knowledge of spelling books and the New Testament. An acquaintance with ethics and with the general principles of law, commerce, money, and government is necessary for the yeomanry of a republican state. This acquaintance they might obtain by means of books calculated for schools and read by the children during the winter months and by the circulation of public papers ...

In a system of education that should embrace every part of the community, the female sex claim no inconsiderable share of our attention.

The women in America (to their honor it is mentioned) are not generally above the care of educating their own children. Their own education should therefore enable them to implant in the tender mind such sentiments of virtue, propriety, and dignity as are suited to the freedom of our governments. Children should be treated as children, but as children that are in a future time to be men and women. By treating them as if they were always to remain children, we very often see their childishness adhere to them, even in middle life. The silly Language called *baby talk*, in which most persons are initiated in infancy, often breaks out in discourse at the age of forty and makes a man appear very ridiculous. In the same manner, vulgar, obscene, and illiberal ideas imbibed in a nursery or a kitchen often give a tincture to the conduct through life. In order to prevent every evil bias, the ladies, whose province it is to direct the inclinations of children on their first appearance and to choose their nurses, should be possessed, not only of amiable manners, but of just sentiments and enlarged understandings.

But the influence of women in forming the dispositions of youth is not the sole reason why their education should be particularly guarded; their influence in controlling the manners of a nation is another powerful reason. Women, once abandoned, may be instrumental in corrupting society, but such is the delicacy of the sex and such the restraints which custom imposes upon them that they are generally the last to be corrupted. There are innumerable instances of men who have been restrained from a vicious life and even of very abandoned men who have been reclaimed by their attachment to ladies of virtue. A fondness for the company and conversation of ladies of character may be considered as a young man's best security against the attractives of a dissipated life. A man who is attached to good company seldom frequents that which *is bad*. For this reason, society requires that females should be well educated and extend their influence as far as possible over the other sex ...

In all nations, a good education is that which renders the ladies correct in their manners, respectable in their families, and agreeable in society. That education is always *wrong* which raises a woman above the duties of her station.

In America, female education should have for its object what is *useful*. Young ladies should be taught to speak and write their own language with purity and elegance, an article in which they are often deficient. The French language is not necessary for ladies. In some cases it is convenient, but, in general, it may be considered as an article of luxury. As an accomplishment, it may be studied by those whose attention is not employed about more important concerns.

Some knowledge of arithmetic is necessary for every lady. Geography should never be neglected. *Belles-lettres* learning seems to correspond with the dispositions of most females. A taste for poetry and fine writing should be cultivated, for we expect the most delicate sentiments from the pens of that sex which is possessed of the finest feelings . . .

Before I quiet this subject, I beg leave to make some remarks on a practice which appears to be attended with important consequences; I mean that of sending boys to Europe for an education or sending to Europe for teachers. This was right before the Revolution, at least so far as national attachments were concerned, but the propriety of it ceased with our political relation to Great Britain.

In the first place, our honor as an independent nation is concerned in the establishment of literacy institutions adequate to all our own purposes, without sending our youth abroad or depending on other nations for books and instructors. It is very little to the reputation of America to have it said abroad that after the heroic achievements of the late war these independent people are obliged to send to Europe for men and books to teach their children A B C.

But in another point of view, a foreign education is directly opposite to our political interest and ought to be discountenanced, if not prohibited.

Every person of common observation will grant that most men prefer the manners and the government of that country where they are educated. Let ten American youths be sent, each to a different European kingdom, and live there from the age of twelve to twenty, and each will give the preference to the country where he has resided.

The period from twelve to twenty is the most important in life. The impressions made before that period are commonly effaced; those that are made during that period *always* remain for many years and *generally* through life . . .

A foreign education is the very source of this evil; it gives young gentlemen of fortune a relish for manners and amusements which are not suited to this country, which, however, when introduced by this class of people will always become fashionable.

But a corruption of manners is not the sole objection to a foreign education; an attachment to a *foreign* government, or rather a want of attachment to our *own, is* the natural effect of a residence abroad during the period of youth . . .

Americans, unshackle your minds and act like independent beings. You have been children long enough, subject to the control and subservient to the interest of a haughty parent. You have now an interest of your own to augment and defend: you have an empire to raise and support by your exertions and a national character to establish and extend by your wisdom and virtues. To effect these great objects, it is necessary to frame a liberal plan of policy and build it on a broad system of education. Before this system can be formed and embraced, the Americas must *believe* and *act* from the belief that it is dishonorable to waste life in mimicking the follies of other nations and basking in the sunshine of foreign glory.

Noah Webster, *A Collection of Essays and Fugitive Writings on Moral, Historical, Political and Literary Subjects*, Boston, MA: L. Thomas and E. T. Andrews, 1790, pp. 3–36, from an original copy at the Massachusetts Historical Society.

Noah Webster, *The American Spelling Book*, 1783

The design of this Grammatical institute is to furnish schools in this country with an easy, accurate, and comprehensive system of rules and lessons for teaching the English language.

To frame a complete system upon such an extensive plan, it was judged requisite to compile a small cheap volume for the use of beginners, containing words methodically arranged, sufficient to give the learner a just idea of spelling.

FABLE I. *Of the* BOY *that stole Apples.*

AN old man found a rude boy upon one of his trees stealing apples, and desired him to come down; but the young saucebox told him plainly he would not. Won't you, said the old man, then I will fetch you down; so he pulled up some tufts of grass and threw at him; but this only made the youngest laugh to think he should pretend to beat him out of the tree with grass only.

Well, well, said the old man, if neither grass nor words will do, I must try what virtue there is in stones: so the old man pelted him heartily with stones: which soon made the young cha hasten down from the tree and beg the old man's pardon.

MORAL

If good words and gentle means will not reclaim the wicked, they must be dealt with in a more severe manner.

Table XXVII.
In all words ending in *ow* unaccented, *w* is silent, and *o* has its first sound. Many of these words are corrupted in vulgar pronunciation; *follow* is called *foller*, &c. for which reason the words of this class are collected in the following table.

2

Bar-ro*w*	bel-lo*ws*	hal-low	win-no-*w*
bel-low	har-ro*w*	shad-o*w*	yel-low
bil-low	cal-low	shal-low	5
el-bo*w*	mal-lo*ws*	spar-row	bor-row
fel-o*w*	mar-ro*w*	tal-low	fol-low
fal-low	mead-o*w*	whit-low	mor-row
far-row	mel-low	wid-o*w*	sor-row
fur-row	min-now	wil-low	wal-low
gal-lo*ws*	nar-ro*w*	win-dow	swal-low

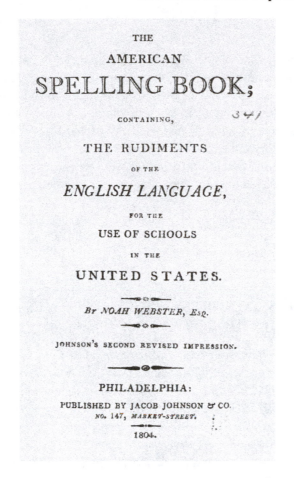

Figure 2.2 The American Spelling Book by Noah Webster. Courtesy of the Library of Congress, LC-USZ62-51905.

FABLE II. *The* COUNTRY MAID *and her* MILK-PAIL.

WHEN men suffer their imaginations to amuse them with the prospect of distant and uncertain improvement of their condition, they frequently suffer real losses by their inattention to those affairs in which they are immediately concerned.

A country maid was walking very deliberately with a pail of milk upon her head, when she fell into the following train of reflections; The money for which I shall sell this milk, will enable me to increase my flock of eggs to three hundred. These eggs allowing for what may prove addle, and what may be destroyed by vermin will produce at least two hundred and fifty chickens. The chickens will be fit to carry to market about Christmas, when poultry always bears a good price; so that by May-day I cannot fail of having money enough to purchase a new gown. Green—let me consider—yes, green become my complexion best, and green it shall be. In this dress I will go to the fair, where all the young fellows will strive to have me for a partner; but I shall perhaps refuse every one of them, and with an air of disdain toss from them. Transported with this triumphant thought, she could not forbear acting with her head what passed in her imagination, when down came the pail of milk, and with it all her imaginary happiness.

FABLE III. *The* FOX *and the* SWALLOW.

ARISTOTLE informs us that the following fable was spoken by Æsop to the Samians, on a debate upon changing their minister, who were accused of plundering the commonwealth.

A fox, swimming across a river, happened to be entangled in some weeds that grew near the bank, from which he was unable to extricate himself. As he lay thus exposed to whole swarms of flies who were galling him, and sucking his blood, a swallow observing his distress, kindly offered to drive them away. By no means, said the Fox, for if these should be chased away, who are already sufficiently gorged, another more hungry swarm would succeed, and I should be robbed of every remaining drop of blood in my veins.

Noah Webster, *The American Spelling Book: Containing the Rudiments of the English Language for the Use of Schools in the United States*, I. Thomas and E. T. Andrews. Boston, MA: Printed by T. W. White, for West & Richardson.

United States Congress, the Northwest Ordinance, July 13, 1787

Few pieces of legislation have been cited as often as the one from the Northwest Ordinance that stated, "schools and the means of education shall forever be encouraged." While most of the 1787 legislation dealt with setting up the five new states that would eventually be admitted as Ohio, Indiana, Illinois, Michigan, and Wisconsin, the clause on schooling constituted the new national government's first commitment to support schools, a topic not included in the Constitution or other early legislation. Nevertheless, from 1787 onward, Congress made it clear that new states were expected to provide at least a rudimentary education for their citizens. And the authorities in the new territories did take the admonishment seriously; public support for schools became part of the new state constitution in all five states.

It is hereby ordained and declared, by the authority aforesaid, That the following articles shall be considered as articles of compact between the original States, and the people and States in the said territory, and forever remain unaltered, unless by common consent, to wit: . . .

Religion, morality, and knowledge being necessary to good government and the happiness of mankind, schools and the means of education shall forever be encouraged. The utmost good faith shall always be observed towards the Indians; their lands and property shall never be taken from them without their consent; and in their property, rights, and liberty, they never shall be invaded or disturbed, unless in just and lawful wars authorized by Congress; but laws founded in justice and humanity shall from time to time be made, for preventing wrongs being done to them, and for preserving peace and friendship with them.

United States Congress, "An Ordinance for the Government of the Territory of the United States northwest of the river Ohio," July 13, 1787, in *Public Statues at Large of the United States of America*, edited by Richard Peters, Boston, MA: Little, Brown, and Company, 1856, Vol. I, pp. 52–53.

UNITED STATES CONGRESS, CIVILIZATION FUND ACT, MARCH 3, 1819

From its earliest years, the United States government struggled with the issue of how best to relate to the Indians. Early administrations viewed the various tribes as separate nations with whom the United States could wage war or conclude peace treaties. All too many inside and outside of the government preferred war and the taking of Indian lands. At the same time, others argued that the best course was to "civilize" the Indians, inducting them slowly into American culture—as defined by European Americans—and citizenship. While European missionaries had gone to the Indians from the earliest settlements in the sixteenth century, missionary efforts expanded in the national period. In 1810, some of the largest Protestant denominations expanded their Indian missions with government support. The Civilization Fund of 1819 formalized government support, allowing direct payments to "capable persons of good moral character" (that is, Protestant missionaries) who sought to bring European culture and religion to the various tribes.

An Act making provision for the civilization of the Indian tribes adjoining the frontier settlements:

Be it enacted by the Senate and House of Representatives of the United States of America, in Congress assembled, That for the purpose of providing against the further decline and final extinction of the Indian tribes, adjoining the frontier settlements of the United States, and for introducing among them the habits and arts of civilization, the President of the United States shall be, and he is hereby authorized, in every case where he shall judge improvement in the habits and condition of such Indians practicable, and that the means of instruction can be introduced with their own consent, to employ capable persons of good moral character, to instruct them in the mode of agriculture suited to their situation; and for teaching their children in reading, writing, and arithmetic, and performing such other duties as may be enjoined, according to such instructions and rules as the President may give and prescribe for the regulation of their conduct, in the discharge of their duties.

And be it further enacted, That the annual sum of ten thousand dollars be, and the same is hereby appropriated, for the purpose of carrying into effect the provisions of this act; and an account of the expenditure of the money, and proceedings in execution of the foregoing provisions, shall be laid annually before Congress.

Approved, March 3, 1819.

United States Congress, "An Act making provision for the civilization of the Indian tribes adjoining the frontier settlement," March 3, 1819, in *Public Statues at Large of the United States of America*, edited by Richard Peters, Boston, MA: Little, Brown, and Company, 1856, Vol. III, pp. 516–517.

3
The Common School Movement, 1820–1860

- Introduction

- Horace Mann, *Tenth* and *Twelfth Annual Reports to the Massachusetts Board of Education*, 1846 and 1848

- Catharine E. Beecher, *An Essay on the Education of Female Teachers for the United States*, 1835

- The *Common School Journal*, Debate Over Plan to Abolish the Board of Education, 1840

- Petition of the Catholics of New York for a Portion of the Common School Fund: To the Honorable Board of Aldermen of the City of New York, 1840

- The Desegregation of the Boston Public Schools, 1846–1855

Introduction

The pattern of public schooling we know today—tax-supported, free, essentially compulsory, and too often racially segregated—emerged in the United States during the four decades prior to the Civil War. As we have seen, schools existed from the early 1600s in the colonies that would become the United States. But the role schools played changed significantly after the American Revolution. While the colonial school had been an adjunct to family, apprenticeship, church, and community—offering on an elective basis those skills not learned at home, at church, or through apprenticeship—schools became the central institution of education during the early nineteenth century. And while Jefferson, Rush, and Webster argued in favor of schooling, it was the leaders of a succeeding generation—the school reformers of the 1820s–1850s—who actually implemented their ideas.

Horace Mann, who served as the first Secretary of the Massachusetts State Board of Education from 1837 to 1848, was perhaps the most articulate and certainly the most widely heard voice in the common school movement. Mann never tired of reminding audiences of the importance of the common school enterprise. As he wrote in his last (1848) Annual Report to the Board, "Without undervaluing any other human agency, it may be safely affirmed that the Common School, improved and energized, as it can easily be, may become the most effective and benignant of all the forces of civilization." Mann had two reasons for placing so much faith in the schools and in his efforts to consolidate school policy at the state level rather than leaving it to individual school districts. First, schools were becoming universal. The words "common school" did not mean a school for the "common people," but rather a school experience that Mann hoped would be common to all. In an era of increasing diversity, when no one religion could claim such loyalty, the church could no longer serve as a unifying force as it once had in Massachusetts. But the school, reaching all citizens, could replace the church as the carrier of culture and creator of social cohesion. Secondly, the school reached citizens when they were young, when they could be molded into good Americans—as Mann and his fellow school reformers defined the term. Adults would not be as easy to influence.

While Mann's was the most prominent voice in the common school movement, similar reformers, including Henry Barnard in Connecticut and Calvin Stowe and Samuel Lewis in Ohio, could be found in virtually every state of the Northeast and the Midwest (then simply called the West). All of the leaders who were involved in the creation of the Common Schools had a sense that they were participants in a heroic movement and treated each other in this way.

Two important anchors stabilized and strengthened the common school movement. One was an assumption, articulated by Mann in his *Twelfth Report*, that a generic Protestantism would serve the needs of the nation well. As historian Timothy L. Smith has written of the "common faith," which lay behind the emergence of the common school, "By the middle of the nineteenth century, leading citizens assumed that Americanism and Protestantism were synonyms and that education and Protestantism were allies." This was not the assumption of the more secular revolutionary generation, but with the major religious revivals of the early nineteenth century, and the significant growth of Catholic immigration, the nation's older leaders shifted their views toward a "vision of the future [which] was not the heavenly city of the eighteenth-century enlightenment but the New Jerusalem of the Christian millennium" (Timothy L. Smith (1967), "Protestant Schooling and American Nationality, 1800–1850," *Journal of American History*). For reformers like Mann, the common school would replace the church as the carrier of the culture. It would not reflect any one Protestant sect, but the very definition Mann gave to nonsectarianism: "Reading the Bible without note or comment" was a deeply Protestant approach to the scriptures.

The second equally important anchor of the common school movement was the replacement of the traditional male schoolmaster with the much lower-paid female schoolteacher. No one was more effective than Catharine Beecher in convincing school reformers that the key to their whole enterprise was the preparation and hiring of low-cost female teachers. Beecher was anxious to create a niche outside the home for single women like herself and was willing to accept second-class citizenship as the means to an education and professional career for women. Beecher was careful to include a moral dimension to her argument: she was among the advocates of the idea that women were more suited to teaching the young than men. As she said,

What is the most important and peculiar duty of the female sex? It is the physical, intellectual, and moral education of children. It is the care of the health, and the formation of the character, of the future citizen of this great nation.

Her 1835 *Essay on the Education of Female Teachers* is one of many such talks and pamphlets that she prepared in a lifetime devoted to transforming the teaching profession from an overwhelmingly male to an overwhelmingly female profession.

Not everyone was as enthusiastic in support of common schools as Mann, Beecher, and their allies. Historian Michael Katz has documented a series of failed school tax proposals that working-class voters rejected because they believed that the schools would primarily serve middle- and upper-class students, while the tax burden would fall on all citizens. (See Katz's *The Irony of Early School Reform: Educational Innovation in Mid-Nineteenth Century Massachusetts* (1968) and *Class, Bureaucracy, and Schools* (1971).) Many well-off voters also saw no reason why they should pay taxes to support the education of other people's children, especially because they were quite prepared to use their own funds to pay for the education of their own children. Yet others feared the increased power of the state as it came to control more and more spheres of public life and public consciousness. Opposition to the common school movement took many forms. In 1840, the Massachusetts legislature considered abolishing the State Board of Education and the office of Secretary that Mann held. In the end, the legislature did not do so, and Mann held office for another eight years. But the reasons for the legislature's actions, reported in the selections from the *Common School Journal* included in this chapter, cast an illuminating light on the political battles surrounding education reform in the 1840s. As they made clear in their report, Mann's opponents were not anti-education, but they were democratic localists who objected to what they saw as a state takeover of a local matter. Voices clamoring for community control of education have emerged in every era since Mann's time. They have supported different causes and expressed different concerns, but the question of who should hold authority and responsibility for the education and enculturation of the youth is as unresolved an issue today as it was in Mann's time.

One group more than any other had cause to worry about the common school movement— and worry they did. New York City's Catholic bishop at that time, John Hughes, took the lead in opposing the schools of the Public School Society, which, he rightly saw, were not non-sectarian but merely pan-Protestant. For him, the requirement that Catholic students attend such schools was a direct attack on his faith and on the religious freedom on which the nation prided itself.

Clearly Hughes and his allies meant to stop the movement toward a common Protestant culture and a common Protestant faith. They understood, far better than Mann or others, that in many ways the common school of the 1840s and 1850s was actually a state-supported Protestant parochial school. They certainly meant to have none of it. The "Petition of the Catholics of New York for a Portion of the Common School Fund," a petition signed by a number of Catholic laymen and included in this chapter, represents Hughes's arguments at their clearest.

In spite of their many protests, Catholics in New York and most of the rest of the country failed to get a portion of the funds for their own schools. Instead, they resigned themselves to what they called the "double taxation," paying taxes to support public schools they did not use and paying the church for religious schools that worked for them. The result was an alternative system of education—the Catholic parochial school system. But it is only possible to understand the Catholic system in the context of the Protestant flavor of the public schools.

The debates about schooling between 1820 and 1860 focused almost exclusively on the schooling of white children. It was not surprising the South was left out of the movement, for the issue of slavery divided the South's population far too deeply for anything that focused on commonality. But racism was not confined to the South. In the North, most African Americans were free, but they were still restricted in terms of attending school. While Mann himself was an abolitionist, one can search in vain for material on the education of his state's African American population within his education reports.

In the North, the racial segregation of schools was challenged in Massachusetts. In Boston, an independent African American school was founded soon after the turn of the century. In the early 1800s most of the city's small African American community seemed to prefer having a separate education for their children. By 1821, a subcommittee of the Boston School Committee was charged with looking after the "African School." And in 1834, the School Committee built the Abiel Smith School, with four teachers and 300 students, operating as a segregated school on Beacon Hill.

A later generation of African Americans and white abolitionist allies began a campaign for school integration in the 1840s. Led by William C. Nell (an African American) and William Lloyd Garrison (a European American abolitionist), this coalition petitioned the School Committee to end segregation in 1840, 1844, 1845, 1846, and 1849. In 1849, they took the issue to court in the *Roberts* case, which is included in the readings. The plaintiffs lost this case; on April 8, 1850, Massachusetts Chief Justice Lemuel Shaw ruled that "separate but

Figure 3.1 Horace Mann. Courtesy of the Library of Congress, LC-USZ62-60506.

equal" facilities were legally acceptable. Decades later, Judge Shaw's decision was cited by the U.S. Supreme Court in *Plessy v. Ferguson*, the 1896 decision allowing segregation throughout the nation. This ruling was finally overturned in *Brown v. Board of Education* in 1954. However, in the nineteenth century, the issue did not end in the courts but in the legislature. In April 1855, the Massachusetts legislature passed new laws saying that the public schools of the state must be racially integrated. The Smith School was closed and the Boston Public Schools fully integrated—at least for the time being. This chapter closes with the 1846 Petition to the School Committee for Integrated Schools, the School Committee's rejection of the petition, arguments from the *Roberts* case before the Massachusetts Supreme Judicial Court, and finally the legislature's 1855 action abolishing racial segregation in the public schools of the Commonwealth. It is important to realize how long the struggle for true educational equality has been going on.

HORACE MANN, *TENTH* AND *TWELFTH* ANNUAL *REPORTS TO THE MASSACHUSETTS BOARD OF EDUCATION*, 1846 AND 1848

Horace Mann's twelve annual reports, written between 1837 and 1848, were his most powerful and effective tool in building support for his notion of the kind of school the new nation needed. Many of the reports had a specific theme, but each pushed the need for the public to support a common school education, as defined by Mann and the state Board of Education, if democracy was to thrive. Mann elaborated this theme in detail in his Tenth Report *in 1846. As the short selection from that report, included here, demonstrates, Mann firmly believed in the transfer of private resources to the public good through taxation when necessary for a cause such as public education. The twelfth—and last—report, also included here, was Mann's opportunity to sum up. He had already resigned his position to take the congressional seat to which he had been elected. In this report, he affirmed the importance of the schools while stressing their fundamentally religious character. What looked like state-sponsored Protestantism to others was, to Mann, simply the affirmation of universal religious and ethical values.*

Tenth Annual Report (1846)

I believe in the existence of a great, immutable principle of natural law, or natural ethics,—a principle antecedent to all human institutions and incapable of being abrogated by any ordinances of man,—a principle of divine origin, clearly legible in the ways of Providence as those ways are manifested in the order of nature and in the history of the race,—which proves the *absolute right* of every human being that comes into the world to an education; and which, of course, proves the correlative duty of every government to see that the means of that education are provided for all.

In regard to the application of this principle of natural law,—that is, in regard to the extent of the education to be provided for all, at the public expense,—some differences of opinion may fairly exist, under different political organizations; but under a republican government, it seems clear that the minimum of this education can never be less than such as is sufficient to qualify each citizen for the civil and social duties he will be called to discharge;—such an education as teaches the individual the great laws of bodily health; as qualified for the fulfillment of parental duties; as is indispensable for the civil functions of a witness or a juror; as is necessary for the voter in municipal affairs; and finally, for the faithful and conscientious discharge of all those duties which devolve upon the inheritor of a portion of the sovereignty of this great republic.

The will of God, as conspicuously manifested in the order of nature, and in the relations which he has established among men, places the *right* of every child that is born into the world to such a degree of education as will enable him and, as far as possible, will predispose him, to perform all domestic, social, civil and moral duties, upon the same clear ground of natural law and equity, as it places a child's *right*, upon his first coming into the world to distend his lungs with a portion of the common air, or to open his eyes to the common light or to receive that shelter, protection and nourishment which are necessary to the continuance of his bodily existence. And so far is it from being wrong or a hardship, to demand of the possessors of property their respective shares for the prosecution of this divinely-ordained work, that they themselves are guilty of the most far-reaching injustice, who seek to resist or to evade the contribution. The complainers are the wrong-doers. The cry, "Stop thief," comes from the thief himself.

To any one who looks beyond the mere surface of things, it is obvious, that the primary and natural elements or ingredients of all property consist in the riches of the soil, in the treasures of the sea, in the light and warmth of the sun, in the fertilizing clouds and streams and dews, in the winds, and in the chemical and vegetative agencies of nature. In the majority of cases, all that we call property, all that makes up the valuation or inventory of a nation's capital, was prepared at the creation, and was laid up of old in the capacious store-house of nature. For every unit that a man earns by his own toil or skill, he receives hundreds and thousands, without cost and without recompense, from the All-bountiful Giver . . .

These few references show how vast a proportion of all the wealth which men presumptuously call their own, because they claim to have earned it, is poured into their lap, unasked and unthanked for, by the Being, so infinitely gracious in his physical, as well as in his moral bestowments.

But for whose subsistence and benefit, were these exhaustless treasuries of wealth created? Surely not for any one man, nor for any one generation; but for the subsistence and benefit of the whole race, from the beginning to the end of time . . .

The three following propositions, then, describe the broad and ever-during foundation on which the Common School system of Massachusetts reposes:

The successive generations of men, taken collectively, constitute one great Commonwealth.

The property of this Commonwealth is pledged for the education of all its youth, up to such a point as will save them from poverty and vice, and prepare them for the adequate performance of their social and civil duties.

The successive holders of this property are trustees; bound to the faithful execution of their trust, by the most sacred obligations; because embezzlement and pillage from children and descendants are as criminal as the same offences when perpetrated against contemporaries.

Twelfth Annual Report (1848)

Without undervaluing any other human agency, it may be safely affirmed that the Common School, improved and energized, as it can easily be, may become the most effective and benignant of all the forces of civilization. Two reasons sustain this position. In the first place, there is a universality in its operation, which can be affirmed of no other institution whatever.

If administered in the spirit of justice and conciliation, all the rising generation may be brought within the circle of its reformatory and elevating influences. And, in the second place, the materials upon which it operates are so pliant and ductile as to be susceptible of assuming a greater variety of forms than any other earthly work of the Creator. The inflexibility and ruggedness of the oak, when compared with the lithe sapling or the tender germ, are but feeble emblems to typify the docility of childhood, when contrasted with the obduracy and intractableness of man. It is these inherent advantages of the Common School, which, in our own State, have produced results so striking, from a system so imperfect, and an administration so feeble. In teaching the blind, and the deaf and dumb, in kindling the latent spark of intelligence that lurks in an idiot's mind, and in the more holy work of reforming abandoned and outcast children, education has proved what it can do, by glorious experiments. These wonders, it has done in its infancy, and with the lights of a limited experience; but, when its faculties shall be fully developed, when it shall be trained to wield its mighty energies for the protection of society against the giant vices which now invade and torment it;—against intemperance, avarice, war, slavery, bigotry, the woes of want and the wickedness of waste, then, there will not be a height to which these enemies of the race can escape, which it will not scale, nor a Titan among them all, whom it will not slay . . .

Moral Education

Moral Education is a primal necessity of social existence. The unrestrained passions of men are not only homicidal, but suicidal; and a community without a conscience would soon extinguish itself. Even with a natural conscience, how often has Evil triumphed over Good! From the beginning of time, Wrong has followed Right, as the shadow the substance . . . The race has existed long enough to try many experiments for the solution of this greatest problem ever submitted to its hands; and the race has experimented, without stint of time or circumscription of space, to mar or modify legitimate results. Mankind have tried despotisms, monarchies, and republican forms of government. They have tried the extremes of anarchy and of autocracy. They have tried Draconian codes of law; and, for the lightest offences, have extinguished the life of the offender. They have established theological standards, claiming for them the sanction of Divine authority, and the attributes of a perfect and infallible law; and then they have imprisoned, burnt, massacred, not individuals only, but whole communities at a time, for not bowing down to idols which ecclesiastical authority had set up. These and other great systems of measure have been adopted as barriers against error and guilt; they have been extended over empires, prolonged through centuries, and administered with terrible energy; and yet the great ocean of vice and crime overleaps every embankment, pours down upon our heads, saps the foundations under our feet, and sweeps away the securities of social order, of property, liberty, and life . . .

But to all doubters, disbelievers, or despairers in human progress, it may still be said, there is one experiment which has never yet been tried. It is an experiment which, even before its inception, offers the highest authority for its ultimate success. Its formula is intelligible to all; and it is as legible as though written in starry letters on an azure sky. It is expressed in these few and simple words:—*"Train up a child in the way he should go, and when he is old he will not depart from it."* This declaration is positive. If the conditions are complied with, it makes no provision for a failure. Though pertaining to morals, yet, if the terms of the direction are observed, there is no more reason to doubt the result, than there would be in an optical or a chemical experiment.

But this experiment has never yet been tried. Education has never yet been brought to bear with one hundredth part of its potential force, upon the natures of children, and, through them, upon the character of men, and of the race. In all the attempts to reform mankind which have hitherto been made, whether by changing the frame of government, by aggravating of softening the severity of the penal code, or by substituting a government-created, for a God-created, religion;—in all these attempts, the infantile and youthful mind, its amenability to influences, and the enduring and self-operating character of the influences it receives, have been almost wholly unrecognized. Here, then, is a new agency, whose powers are but just beginning to be understood, and whose mighty energies, hitherto, have been but feebly invoked; and yet, from our experience, limited and imperfect as it is, we do know that, far beyond any other earthly instrumentality, it is comprehensive and decisive . . .

Religious Education

On this subject, I propose to speak with freedom and plainness, and more at length than I should feel required to do, but for the peculiar circumstances in which I have been placed. It is a matter of notoriety, that the views of the Board of Education—and my own, perhaps still more than those of the Board—on the subject of religious instruction in our Public Schools, have been subjected to animadversion. Grave charges have been made against us, that our purpose was to exclude religion; and to exclude that, too, which is the common exponent of religion—the Bible—from the Common Schools of the State; or, at least, to derogate from its authority, and destroy its influence in them. Whatever prevalence a suspicion of the truth of these imputations may have heretofore had, I have reason to believe that further inquiry and examination have done much to disabuse the too credulous recipients of so groundless a charge. Still, amongst a people so commendably sensitive on the subject of religion, as are the people of Massachusetts, any suspicion of irreligious tendencies, will greatly prejudice any cause, and, so far as any cause may otherwise have the power of doing good, will greatly impair that power.

It is known, too, that our noble system of Free Schools for the whole people, is strenuously opposed;—by a few persons in our own State, and by no inconsiderable numbers in some of the other states of this Union;—and that a rival system of "Parochial" or "Sectarian Schools," is now urged upon the public by a numerous, a powerful, and a well-organized body of men. It has pleased the advocates of this rival system, in various public addresses, in reports, and through periodicals devoted to their cause, to denounce our system as irreligious and anti-Christian. They do not trouble themselves to describe what our system is, but adopt a more summary way to forestall public opinion against it, by using general epithets of reproach, and signals of alarm . . .

All the schemes ever devised by governments, to secure the prevalence and permanence of religion among the people, however variant in form they may have been, are substantially resolvable into two systems. One of these systems holds the regulation and control of the religious belief of the people to be one of the functions of government, like the command of the army or the navy, or the establishment of courts, or the collection of revenues. According to the other system, religious belief is a matter of individual and parental concern; and, while the government furnishes all practicable facilities for the independent formation of that belief, it exercises no authority to prescribe, or coercion to enforce it. The former is the system, which, with very few exceptions, has prevailed throughout Christendom, for fifteen hundred years. Our own government is the almost solitary example among the nations of the earth, where freedom of opinion, and the inviolability of conscience, have been even theoretically recognized by the law . . .

The elements of a political education are not bestowed upon any school child, for the purpose of making him vote with this or that political party, when he becomes of age; but for the purpose of enabling him to choose for himself, with which party he will vote. So the religious education which a child receives at school, is not imparted to him for the purpose of making him join this or that denomination, when he arrives at years of discretion, but for the purpose of enabling him to judge for himself, according to the dictates of his own reason and conscience, what his religious obligations are, and whither they lead. But if a man is taxed to support a school, where religious doctrines are inculcated which he believes to be false, and which he believes that God condemns; then he is excluded from the school by the Divine law, at the same time that he is compelled to support it by the human law. This is a double wrong. It is politically wrong, because, if such a man educates his children at all, he must educate them elsewhere, and thus pay two taxes, while some of his neighbors pay less than their due proportion of one; and it is religiously wrong, because he is constrained, by human power, to promote what he believes the Divine Power forbids . . .

[But] Surely, that system cannot be an irreligious, an anti-Christian, or an un-Christian one, whose first and cardinal principle it is, to recognize and protect the highest and dearest of all human interests and of all human rights . . .

Is it not, indeed, too plain, to require the formality of a syllogism, that if any man's creed is to be found in the Bible, and the Bible is in the schools, then that man's creed is in the schools? This seems even plainer than the proposition, that two and two make four; that is, we can conceive of a creature so low down in the scale of intelligence, that he could not see what sum would be produced by adding two and two together, who still could not fail to see, that, if a certain system, called Christianity, were contained in, and inseparable from, a certain book called the Bible, then wherever the Bible might go, there the system of Christianity must be . . .

Such, then, in a religious point of view, is the Massachusetts system of Common Schools. Reverently, it recognizes and affirms the sovereign rights of the Creator; sedulously and sacredly it guards the religious rights of the creature; while it seeks to remove all hindrances, and to supply all furtherances to a filial and paternal communion between man and his Maker. In a social and political sense, it is a *Free* school system. It knows no distinction of rich and poor, of bond and free, or between those who, in the imperfect light of this world, are seeking, through different avenues, to reach the gate of heaven. Without money and without price, it throws open its doors, and spreads the table of its bounty, for all the children of the State. Like the sun, it shines, not only upon the good; and, like the rain, its blessings descend, not only upon the just, but upon the unjust, that their injustice may depart from them, and be known no more.

Horace Mann, *Annual Reports on Education*, Boston, MA: Lee and Shepard, 1872, pp. 533–536, 544–550, 650–651, 701–706, 715–717, 731, 734–737, 753–754, from an original copy at the Massachusetts Historical Society.

CATHARINE E. BEECHER, *AN ESSAY ON THE EDUCATION OF FEMALE TEACHERS FOR THE UNITED STATES*, 1835

Catharine Beecher was a tireless advocate for expanding women's opportunities by educating them and allowing them to be teachers. She was convinced that women of backgrounds like her own were the ideal guardians of morality in a rapidly changing nation and she wanted to create new opportunities for women—again, middle-class white Protestant women like herself—that had not existed prior to her time. Along with her allies, Beecher succeeded in changing the teaching profession from being overwhelmingly male to overwhelmingly female. Future chapters tell the stories of women who went west to teach in the new settlements and later south to teach the newly freed slaves. Prior to Beecher's generation, most middle-class white women simply would not have worked outside the home. Beecher convinced these women, their families, and local and state governments that women's maternal natures and their willingness to work at lower salaries made them ideal candidates for this fast-growing profession. At the same time, she argued forcefully for women's education, made all the more necessary by their new role.

What is the most important and peculiar duties of the female sex? It is the physical, intellectual, and moral education of children. It is the care of the health, and the formation of the character, of the future citizen of this great nation.

Woman, whatever are her relations in life, is necessarily the guardian of the nursery, the companion of childhood, and the constant model of imitation. It is her hand that first stamps impressions on the immortal spirit, that must remain forever. And what demands such discretion, such energy, such patience, such tenderness, love, and wisdom, such perspicacity to discern, such versatility to modify, such efficiency to execute, such firmness to persevere, as the government and education of all the various characters and tempers that meet in the nursery and school-room? Woman also is the presiding genius who must regulate all those thousand minutiae of domestic business, that demand habits of industry, order, neatness, punctuality, and constant care. And it is for such varied duties that woman is to be trained. For this her warm sympathies, her lively imagination, her ready invention, her quick perceptions, all need to be cherished and improved; while at the same time those more foreign habits, of patient attention, calm judgment, steady efficiency, and habitual self-control, must be induced and sustained.

Is a weak, undisciplined, unregulated mind fitted to encounter the responsibility, weariness, and watching of the nursery; to bear the incessant care and perplexity of governing young children; to accommodate with kindness and patience to the peculiarities and frailties of a husband; to control the indolence, waywardness, and neglect of servants; and to regulate all the variety of domestic cares? The superficial accomplishments of former periods were of little avail to fit a woman for such arduous duties; and for this reason it is, that as society has advanced in all other improvements, the course of female education has been gradually changing, and some portion of that mental discipline, once exclusively reserved for the other sex, is beginning to exert its invigorating influence upon the female character. At the same time the taste of the age is altered; and, instead of the fainting, weeping, vapid, pretty plaything, once the model of female loveliness, those qualities of the head and heart that best qualify a woman for her duties, are demanded and admired.

None will deny the importance of having females properly fitted for their peculiar duties; and yet few are aware how much influence a teacher may exert in accomplishing this object. School is generally considered as a place where children are sent, not to form their habits, opinions, and character, but simply to learn from books. And yet, whatever may be the opinion of teachers and parents, children do, to a very great extent, form their character under influences bearing upon them at school. They are proverbially creatures of imitation, and accessible to powerful influences. Six hours every day are spent with teachers, whom they usually love and respect, and whose sentiments and opinions, in one way or another, they constantly discover. They are at the same time associated with companions of all varieties of temper, character, and habit. Is it possible that this can exist without involving constant and powerful influences, either good or bad? The simple fact that a teacher succeeds in making a child habitually accurate and thorough in all the lessons of school, may induce mental habits that will have a controlling influence through life. If the government of schools be so administered as to induce habits of cheerful and implicit obedience, if punctuality, neatness, and order in all school employment's are preserved for a course of years, it must have some influence in forming useful habits. On the contrary, if a child is tolerated in disobedience and neglect, if school duties are performed in a careless, irregular, and deficient manner, pernicious habits may be formed that will operate disastrously through life. It is true that mismanagement and indulgence at home may counteract all the good influences of school; and the faithful discharge of parental duty may counteract, to some extent, the bad influences of school: but this does not lessen the force of these considerations . . .

While Prussia, for years, has been pouring out her well-educated teachers from her forty-five seminaries, at the rate of one for every ten pupils; while France is organizing her Normal schools in all her departments for the education of her teachers; what is done in America, wealthy, intelligent, and free America, whose very existence is depending on the virtuous education of her children? In New England, we hear of one solitary institution for the preparation of teachers; and, in New York, eight are just starting into being; and this is all! Now, at this moment, we need at least thirty thousand teachers, and four thousand every year in addition, just to supply the increase of youthful population. And we must educate the nation, or be dashed in pieces, amid all the terrors of the wild fanaticism, infidel recklessness, and political strife, of an ungoverned, ignorant, and unprincipled populace. What patriot, what philanthropist, what Christian, does not see that all that is sacred and dear in home, and country, and liberty, and religion, call upon him to waken every energy, and put forth every effort?

Does the heart fail, and the courage sink, at the magnitude of the work, and the apparent destitution of means? We have the means—we have the power. There is wealth enough, and benevolence enough, and self-denying laborers enough. Nothing is wanting but a knowledge of our danger, our duty, and our means, and a willing mind in exerting our energies. Our difficulties and danger have been briefly noticed. It is the object of this essay to point out one important measure in the system of means that must be employed.

When we consider the claims of the learned professions, the excitement and profits of commerce, manufactures, agriculture, and the arts; when we consider the aversion of most men to the sedentary, confining, and toilsome duties of teaching and governing young children; when we consider the scanty pittance that is allowed to the majority of teachers; and that few men will enter a business that will not support a family, when there are multitudes of other employments that will afford competence, and lead to wealth; it is chimerical to hope that the supply of such immense deficiencies in our national education is to come chiefly from that sex. It is woman, fitted by disposition, and habits, and circumstances, for such duties, who, to a very wide extent, must aid in educating the childhood and youth of this nation; and therefore it is, that females must be trained and educated for this employment. And, most happily, it is true, that the education necessary to fit a woman to be a teacher, is exactly the one that best fits her for that domestic relation she is primarily designed to fill.

Catharine Beecher, *An Essay on the Education of Female Teachers*, New York: Van Nostrand & Dwight, 1835. From an original in the Lane Theological Seminary collection at the Library of McCormack Theological Seminary, Chicago.

The *Common School Journal*, Debate Over Plan to Abolish the Board of Education, 1840

Not everyone supported Horace Mann in his crusade to organize common schools. Some argued schools were a private family matter. Mann's strongest opponents in Massachusetts supported publicly financed and controlled schools, but they wanted the individual cities and towns of the Commonwealth to maintain local control. They distrusted Mann's advocacy for a state Board of Education, even if its authority was severely limited, and they predicted, correctly, that once a board was in place, its authority would only grow. The debate came to a head in 1840 when, during Mann's third year in office, the state legislature came very close to abolishing the state board and Mann's office as its secretary. The effort failed but the debate, reproduced here from Mann's Common School Journal, *is enlightening regarding the continuing battle over local versus state and federal control of education.*

An attempt may be made to identify the interest of Common Schools with the existence of the Board of Education; and any objections to that Board may, perhaps, be regarded by some, as a covert assault upon our long-established system of public instruction. But, since our system of public schools did not owe its origin to the Board of Education, but was in existence for two centuries before that Board was established, a proposal to dispense with its further services cannot be reasonably considered as indicating any feelings of hostility or of indifference towards our system of Common Schools. It is, indeed, the attachment of your Committee to that system, which has induced them to investigate, with care and attention the tendencies of the Board of Education. And, it is the conclusion to which they have arrived, that the operations of that Board are incompatible with those principles upon which our Common Schools have been founded and maintained, that leads them to make this Report.

The first question to be considered is, what is the power of the Board of Education? Upon this point, very great difference of opinion appear to prevail. By the terms of the Act, the Board seems to have only a power of recommending, but it is the opinion of many, that this power of recommendation, exercised by such a Board, must of necessity be soon converted into a power of regulation; and even if it were not, the vantage ground which such a board occupies, must obviously give it, for all practical purposes, an equivalent power.

One manifest means by which this power of recommending measures may become, and, in several instances, has already become, equivalent to a power of regulation, is to be found in the circumstance, that the Legislature will naturally lend a ready ear to the suggestions of the Board, and will be apt, without much examination, to clothe with a legal sanction such rules and regulations, as the Board may recommend. It would thus appear, that the Board has a tendency, and a strong tendency, to engross to itself the entire regulation of our Common Schools, and practically to convert the Legislature into a mere instrument for carrying its plans into execution. If, however, this result should be disclaimed, and the Legislature is left as independent as before, and with the same feeling of responsibility for all enactments on the subject of schools, the Board seems to be useless; for the Legislature will not lack suggestions from a variety of other quarters, equally well-adapted to furnish them. If then the Board has any actual power, it is a dangerous power, trenching directly upon the rights and duties of the Legislature; if it has no power, why continue its existence, at annual expense to the Commonwealth? . . .

Considering the degree of interest which pervades this community, on the subject of education, and the large number of intelligent persons whose lives are devoted to that profession, your Committee do not apprehend that any discoveries, which may be made in the art or science of teaching, will remain undisseminated, through want of zeal to spread information, or of disposition to acquire it. Your Committee can well imagine that in a different state of society, such as is to be found in the newly-settled States, where Common Schools are a novelty, and teachers are generally ill-qualified for their office, some artificial means, such as a Board of Education, might be useful, in stimulating a spirit of inquiry and in disseminating knowledge. But, among us, with so many accomplished teachers, a public Board, established for the benefit of the profession of teaching, seems as little needed as a public Board for the benefit of divinity, medicine, or the law. Undoubtedly, in all these professions, great improvements might be made; but it is better to leave them to private industry and free competition, than for the Legislature to put them under the superintendence of an official Board.

The true way to judge of the practical operations of the Board of Education is not merely to consult the statutes by which the Board is established, but also to examine its own reports. They will furnish an unquestionable means of discovering what are the objects, which the Board actually proposes for itself. A very cursory examination of these documents will suffice to show, that, so far from continuing our system of public instruction, upon the plan upon which it was founded, and according to which it has been so long and so successfully carried on, the aim of the Board appears to be, to remodel it altogether after the example of the French and Prussian systems.

These systems have a central Board, which supplies the ignorance and incapacity of the administrators of local affairs, and which models the schools of France and Prussia all upon one plan, as uniform and exact as the discipline of an army. On the other hand, our system of public instruction has proceeded upon the idea, that the local administrators of affairs, that is to say, the school committees of the several towns and districts, are qualified to superintend the schools, and might best be trusted with that superintendence. This different method of operating is not confined to public schools, but extends to every other department of life. In France or Prussia, the smallest bridge cannot be built, or any village road repaired, until a central Board has been consulted, a plan, which, in its practical operations, and notwithstanding the science of the central Board, and the skill of the engineers whom it has at command, is found not at all comparable with our system of local authority.

De Tocqueville, whose work upon America has been so much admired, dwells at great length and with great emphasis, upon the advantages which New England derives from its excellent system of local authority; while he points out the want of local public spirit in the countries of Europe, and the deficiency of interest in local affairs, as the greatest obstacle in the way of public improvements. This system of local authority is as beneficial to the schools, as to any thing else. It interests a vast number of people in their welfare, whose zeal and activity, if they find themselves likely to be overshadowed by the controlling power of a central Board, will be apt to grow faint. Improvements, which a teacher or school committee have themselves hit upon, will be likely to be pushed with much more spirit, than those which are suggested, or, as it were, commanded, by a foreign and distant power.

After all that has been said about the French and Prussian systems, they appear to your Committee to be much more admirable, as a means of political influence, and of strengthening the hands of the government, than as a mere means for the diffusion of knowledge. For the latter purpose, the system of public Common Schools, under the control of persons most interested in their flourishing condition, who pay taxes to support them, appears to your Committee much superior. The establishment of the Board of Education seems to be the commencement of a system of centralization and of monopoly of power in a few hands, contrary, in every respect, to the true spirit of our democratical institutions; and which, unless speedily checked, may lead to unlooked for and dangerous results.

As to the practical operation of this centralizing system, your Committee would observe, that some of the rules and regulation already devised by the Board of Education, and doubtless considered by it as of very useful tendency, have proved, when carried into execution in the schools, very embarrassing, and have engrossed much of the time and attention of the teachers, which might better have been bestowed upon the instruction of their pupils, than in making out minute and complicated registers of statistics. The Board passes new regulations respecting the returns to be made out by the school committees, and sends forth its blanks; the school committees are abruptly notified of them, without being informed of the reasons upon which they are founded. The rules and regulations become so numerous and complicated, as to be difficult of apprehension, as well as of execution. Indeed, a periodical commentary seems necessary, from the Secretary of the Board, in order to enable school committees to discharge their duties. Your committee are strongly of opinion, that nothing but a prevailing impression, well- or ill-founded, that a compliance with the rules and regulations of the Board is necessary to secure to towns their annual share of the school fund, has enabled those rules and regulations to be at all regarded. The multiplicity and complexity of laws, with respect to any subject, are matter of just complaint; and is especially the case with respect to Common Schools, the teachers of which have a great variety of arduous duties, which must, of necessity, be performed, and which ought not to be aggravated by any requirements, not essential to the welfare of the schools. A central Board, the members of which are not practical teachers, will be easily led to imagine, that minute statistical facts and other like information, may be obtained at much less expense of valuable time, than is actually needed for procuring them.

Your Committee have already stated, that the French and Prussian system of public schools appears to have been devised, more for the purpose of modifying the sentiments and opinions of the rising generation, according to a certain government standard, than as a mere means of diffusing elementary knowledge. Undoubtedly, Common Schools may be used as a potent means of engrafting in to the minds of children, political, religious and moral opinions; but, in a country like this where such diversity of sentiments exists, especially upon theological subjects and where morality is considered a part of religion, and is, to some extent, modified by sectarian views, the difficulty and danger of attempting to introduce these subjects into our school, according to one fixed and settled plan, to be devised by a central Board, must be obvious. The right to mould the political, moral, and religious, opinions of his children, is a right exclusively and jealously reserved by our laws to every parent; and for the government to attempt directly or indirectly, as to these matters, to stand in the parent's place, is an undertaking of very questionable policy. Such an attempt cannot fail to excite a feeling of jealousy, with respect to our public schools, the results of which could not but be disastrous . . .

Another project, imitated from France and Prussia, and set on foot under the superintendence of the Board of Education, is the establishment of Normal Schools. Your Committee approach this subject with some delicacy, inasmuch as one half the expense of the two Normal schools already established has been sustained by private munificence. If, however, no benefit, in proportion to the money spent, is derived from these schools, it is our duty, as legislators, in justice not only to the Commonwealth but to the private donor, to discontinue the project. Comparing the two Normal Schools already established with the academies and high school of the Commonwealth, they do not appear to your Committee to present any peculiar or distinguishing advantages.

Academies and high schools cost the Commonwealth nothing; and they are fully adequate, in the opinion of your Committee, to furnish a component supply of teachers. In years past, they have not only supplied our own schools with competent teachers, but have annually furnished hundreds to the West and the South. There is a high degree of competition existing between these academies, which is the best guaranty for excellence. It is insisted by the Board, however, that the art of teaching is a peculiar art, which is particularly and exclusively taught at Normal Schools; but it appears to your Committee, that every person, who has himself undergone a process of instruction, must acquire, by that very process, the art of instructing others. This certainly will be the case with every person of intelligence; if intelligence be wanting, no system of instruction can supply its place. An intelligent mechanic, who has learned his trade, is competent, by that very fact, to instruct others in it; and needs no Normal School to teach him the art of teaching his apprentices.

Considering that our district schools are kept, on an average for only three or four months in the year, it is obviously impossible, and perhaps it is not desirable, that the business of keeping these schools should become a distinct and separate profession, which the establishment of Normal Schools seems to anticipate . . .

In conclusion, the idea of the State controlling Education whether by establishing a central Board, by allowing that Board to sanction a particular Library, or by organizing Normal Schools, seems to your Committee a great departure from the uniform spirit of our institutions, a dangerous precedent, and an interference with a matter more properly belonging to those hands, to which our ancestors wisely intrusted it. It is greatly to be feared, that any attempt, to form all our schools and all our teachers upon one model, would destroy all competition, all emulation, and even the spirit of improvement itself. When a large number of teachers and school committees are all aiming at improvement, as is doubtless the case, to a great extent, in this Commonwealth, improvements seem much more likely to be found out and carried into practice, than when the chief right of experimenting is vested in a central Board.

With these views, your Committee have come to the conclusion, that the interest of our Common Schools would rest upon a safer and more solid foundation, if the Board of Education and the Normal Schools were abolished . . . For the Committee,

Allen W. Dodge

The *Common School Journal*, Boston, MA, August 1, 1840, Vol. II, No. 15, pp. 225–240. From an original copy of the journal, Gutman Library, Harvard Graduate School of Education.

PETITION OF THE CATHOLICS OF NEW YORK FOR A PORTION OF THE COMMON SCHOOL FUND: TO THE HONORABLE BOARD OF ALDERMEN OF THE CITY OF NEW YORK, 1840

The petition included here is a clear example of the views of one group of citizens who disagreed sharply with school reformers like Horace Mann. From the earliest days of the republic to the present, some have argued, as did Mann, that public funds and public control of schools should always be aligned. Others have argued that groups who held different views on essential matters of faith and culture should have the freedom to take their share of the public funds and educate children according to the dictates of their own consciences. One of the clearest examples of this conflict was in the great "school wars" in New York City in the 1840s. While the Public School Society wanted to consolidate its control over all of the schools, Roman Catholics, led by Bishop John Hughes, argued that such consolidation threatened the basic freedom of Catholic parents to educate their children in an atmosphere sympathetic to their Catholic faith. The debate about the appropriate use of public funds for different kinds of schools remains unresolved in the twenty-first century, but the New York crisis of 1840 provides one of its most dramatic moments. The petition from a number of Roman Catholic lay leaders gives eloquent testimony to their reasons for their perspective.

The Petition of the Catholics of New York, Respectfully represents:

That your Petitioners yield to no class in their performance of, and disposition to perform all the duties of citizens. They bear, and are willing to bear, their portion of every common burden; and feel themselves entitled to a participation in every common benefit.

This participation, they regret to say, has been denied them for years back, in reference to Common School Education in the city of New York, except on conditions with which their conscience, and, as they believe their duty to God, did not, and do not leave them at liberty to comply.

The rights of conscience, in this country, are held by the constitution and universal consent to be sacred and inviolate. No stronger evidence of this need be adduced than the fact, that one class of citizens are exempted from the duty or obligation of defending their country against an invading foe, out of delicacy and deference to the rights of conscience which forbids them to take up arms for any purpose.

Your Petitioners only claim the benefit of this principle in regard to the public education of their children. They regard the public education which the State has provided as a common benefit, in which they are most desirous and feel that they are entitled to participate; and therefore they pray your Honorable Body that they may be permitted to do so, without violating their conscience.

But your Petitioners do not ask that this prayer be granted without assigning their reasons for preferring it.

In ordinary cases men are not required to assign the motives of conscientious scruples in matters of this kind. But your petitioners are aware that a large, wealthy, and concentrated influence is directed against their claim by the Corporation called the Public School Society. And that this influence, acting on a public opinion already but too much predisposed to judge unfavorably of the claims of your petitioners, requires to be met by facts which justify them in thus appealing to your Honorable Body, and which may at the same time, convey a more correct impression to the public mind. Your petitioners adopt this course the more willingly, because the justice and impartiality which distinguish the decisions of public men, in this country, inspire them with the confidence that your Honorable Body will maintain, in their regard, the principle of the rights of conscience, if it can be done without violating the rights of others, and on no other condition is the claim solicited.

It is not deemed necessary to trouble your Honorable Body with a detail of the circumstances by which the monopoly of the public education of children in the city of New York, and of the funds provided for that purpose at the expense of the State, have passed into the hands of a private corporation, styled in its Act of Charter, "The Public School Society of the City of New York" . . . This Society, however, is composed of gentlemen of various sects, including even one or two Catholics. But they profess to exclude all sectarianism, from their schools. If they do not exclude sectarianism, they are avowedly no more entitled to the school funds than your petitioners or any other denomination of professing Christians. If they do, as they profess, exclude sectarianism, then your petitioners contend that they exclude Christianity and leave to the advantage of infidelity the tendencies which are given to the minds of youth by the influence of this feature and pretension of their system.

If they could accomplish what they profess, other denominations would join your petitioners in remonstrating against their schools. But they do not accomplish it. Your petitioners will show your Honorable Body that they do admit what Catholics call sectarianism, (although others may call it only religion) in a great variety of ways.

In their 22d report, as far back as the year 1827, they tell us, page 14, that they *"are aware of the importance of early RELIGIOUS INSTRUCTION,"* and that none but what is *"exclusively general and scriptural in its character should be introduced into the schools under their charge."* Here, then, is their own testimony that they did introduce and authorize "religious instruction" in their schools. And that they solved, with the utmost composure, the difficult question on which the sects disagree, by determining *what kind* of *"religious instruction"* is *"exclusively general and scriptural in its character."* Neither could they impart this "early religious instruction" themselves. They must have left it to their teachers and these, armed with official influence, could impress those "early religious instructions" on the susceptible minds of the children, with the authority of dictators.

The Public School Society in their report for the year 1832, page 10, describe the effect of these "early religious instruction," without, perhaps, intending to do so; but yet precisely as your petitioners have witnessed it, in such of their children as attended those schools. *"The age at which children are usually sent to school affords a much better opportunity to mold their minds to peculiar and exclusive forms of faith than any subsequent period of life."* In page 11, of the same report, they protest against the injustice of supporting "religion in any shape" by public money; as if the early religious instruction which they had themselves authorized in their schools five years before, was not "religion in some shape," and was not supported by public taxation. They tell us again in more guarded language, "The Trustees are deeply impressed with the importance of imbuing the youthful mind with religious impressions, and they have endeavored to attain this object, as far as the nature of the institution will admit." Report of 1837.

In their Annual Report they tell us, that "They would not be understood as regarding religious impressions in early youth as unimportant; on the contrary, they desire to do all which may with propriety be done, to give a right direction to the minds of the children intrusted to their care. Their schools are uniformly opened with reading of the Scriptures, and the class-books are such as recognize and enforce the great and generally acknowledged principles of Christianity." Page 7.

In their 34th Annual Report, for the year 1839, they pay a high compliment to a deceased teacher for "the moral and religious influence exerted by her over the three hundred girls daily attending her school," and tell us that "it could not but have had a lasting effect on many of their susceptible minds." Page 7. And yet in all these "early religious instruction, religious impressions, and religious influence," essentially anti-Catholic, your petitioners are to see nothing sectarian; but if in giving the education which the State requires, they were to bring the same influences to bear on the "susceptible minds" of their own children, in favor, and not against, their own religion, then this society contends that it would be sectarian!

Your petitioners regret that there is no means of ascertaining to what extent the teachers in the schools of this Society carried out the views of their principles on the importance of conveying "early religious instructions" to the "susceptible minds" of their children. But they believe it is in their power to prove, that in some instances, the Scriptures have been explained, as well as read to the pupils.

Even the reading of the Scriptures in those schools your petitioners cannot regard otherwise than as sectarian; because Protestants would certainly consider as such the introduction of the Catholic Scriptures, which are different from theirs, and the Catholics have the same ground of objection when the Protestant version is made use of. Your petitioners have to state further, as grounds of their conscientious objections to those schools, that many of the selections in their elementary reading lessons contain matter prejudicial to the Catholic name and character. The term Popery is repeatedly found in them. This term is known and employed as one of insult and contempt towards the Catholic religion, and it passes into the minds of children with the feeling of which it is the outward expression. Both the historical and religious portions of the reading lessons are selected from Protestant writers, whose prejudices against the Catholic religion render them unworthy of confidence in the mind of your petitioners, at least so far as their own children are concerned.

The Public School Society have heretofore denied that their books contained anything reasonably objectionable to Catholics. Proofs of the contrary could be multiplied, but it is unnecessary, as they have recently retracted their denial, and discovered, after fifteen years' enjoyment of their monopoly, that their books do contain objectionable passages. But they allege that they have proffered repeatedly to make such corrections as the Catholic Clergy might require. Your petitioners conceive that such a proposal could not be carried into effect by the Public School Society without giving just ground for exception to other denominations. Neither can they see with what consistency that Society can insist, as it has done, on the perpetuation of its monopoly, when the Trustees thus avow their incompetency to present unexceptionable books, without the aid of the Catholic, or any other Clergy. They allege, indeed, that with the best intentions they have been unable to ascertain the passages which might be offensive to Catholics. With their intentions, your petitioners cannot enter into any question. Nevertheless, they submit to your Honorable Body, that Society is eminently incompetent to the superintendent of public education, if they could not see that the following passage was unfit for the public schools, and especially unfit to be placed in the hands of Catholic children.

They will quote the passage as one instance, taken from Putnam's Sequel, page 266:

Huss, John, a zealous reformer from Popery, who lived in Bohemia, towards the close of the fourteenth, and beginning of the fifteenth centuries. He was bold and persevering; but at length, trusting himself to the deceitful Catholics he was by them brought to trial, condemned as a heretic, and burnt at the stake.

The Public School Society may be excused for not knowing the historical inaccuracies of this passage; but surely assistance of the Catholic Clergy could not have been necessary to an understanding of the word "deceitful," as applied to all who profess the religion of your petitioners.

For these reasons, and others of the same kind, your petitioners cannot, in conscience, and consistently with their sense of duty to God, and to their offspring, intrust the Public School Society with the office of giving "a right direction to the minds of their children" . . . This class (your petitioners speak only so far as relates to their own denomination), after a brief experience of the schools of the Public School Society, naturally and deservedly withdrew all confidence from it. Hence the establishment by your petitioners of schools for the education of the poor. The expense necessary for this, was a second taxation, required not by the laws of the land, but by the no less imperious demands of their conscience.

They were reduced to the alternative of seeing their children growing up in entire ignorance, or else taxing themselves anew for private schools, whilst the funds provided for education, and contributed in part by themselves, were given over to the Public School Society, and by them employed as has been stated above.

Your petitioners, therefore, pray that your Honorable Body will be pleased to designate, as among the schools entitled to participate in the Common School Fund, upon complying with the requirements of the law, and the ordinances of the corporation of the city or for such other relief as to your Honorable Body shall seem meet, St. Patrick's School, St. Peter's School, St. Mary's School, St. Joseph's School, St. James School, St. Nicholas School, Transfiguration Church School, and St. John's School.

And your petitioners further request, in the event of your Honorable Body's determining to hear your petitioners on the subject of their petition, that such time may be appointed as may be most agreeable to your Honorable Body and that a full session of your Honorable Board be convened for that purpose.

> And your petitioners, &c.
> Thomas O'Connor, Chairman
> Gregory Dillon, Andrew Carrigan, Peter Duffy, Vice chairmen
> B. O'Conner, James Kelly, J. M'Louglin, Secretaries
> Of a general meeting of the Catholics of the City of New York, convened in the school-
> room of St. James Church, Sept. 21, 1840

Lawrence Kehoe, ed., *Complete Works of the Most Rev. John Hughes, D. D., Archbishop of New York,* 2 volumes, New York: Lawrence Kehoe, 1865, Vol. I, pp. 102–107.

THE DESEGREGATION OF THE BOSTON PUBLIC SCHOOLS, 1846–1855

Given Boston's turbulent experience with school integration in the 1970s, few realize that the legal desegregation of the Boston Public Schools took place more than a century earlier, in 1855. The various documents included here—the 1846 petition by the African American community for desegregated schools, the School Committee's response, the records of the 1849 Sarah C. Roberts v. The City of Boston court case, and finally the legislature's act ending segregation in 1855—together tell of an early and important effort by the African American community to control its own fate.

Report to the Primary School Committee on the Petition of Sundry Colored Persons for the Abolition of the Schools for Colored Children (Boston, June 15, 1846)

The campaign for school integration in Boston began in earnest with this petition from African American parents asking for racial integration of all schools in 1846.

To the Primary School Committee of the City of Boston:

The undersigned colored citizens of Boston, parents and guardians of children now attending the exclusive Primary Schools for children in this City, respectfully represent;— that the establishment of exclusive schools for our children is a great injury to us, and deprives us of those equal privileges and advantages in the public school to which we are entitled as citizens. These separate schools cost more and do less for the children than other schools, since all experience teaches that where a small and despised class are shut out from the common benefit of any public institutions of learning and confined to separate schools, few or none interest themselves about the school—neglect ensues, abuses creep in, the standard of scholarship degenerates, and the teachers and the scholars are soon considered, and of course, become, an inferior class.

But to say nothing of any other reasons for this change, it is sufficient to say that the establishment of separate schools for our children is believed to be unlawful, and it is felt to be if not in intention, in fact, insulting. If, as seems to be admitted, you are violating our rights, we simply ask you to cease doing so.

We therefore earnestly request that such exclusive schools be abolished, and that our children be allowed to attend the Primary Schools established in the respective Districts in which we live.

[Signed]
George Putnam
And Eighty-five Others

Report of the Primary School Committee in Response to the Petition

After receiving the petition from George Putnam and others, the Boston Primary School Committee voted fifty-nine to sixteen to reject it and issued the following report explaining their defense of segregated schools for the city.

This report was adopted by the Committee by a vote of 59 to 16. A dissenting minority report, advocating integrated schools, was also presented.

What we claim is, That, under the law giving to the School Committee "the general charge and superintendence of all the public schools," and the power to "determine the number and qualifications of the scholars to be admitted into the school," the Committee have the right to distribute, assign, and classify, all children, belonging to the schools in the City according to their best judgment:

In applying these principles to the case of colored children, we maintain,

1. That their peculiar physical, mental, and moral structure, requires an educational treatment, different, in some respects, from that of white children. Teachers of schools in which they are intermingled, remark, that, in those parts of study and instruction in which progress depends on memory, or on the imitative faculties, chiefly, the colored children will often keep pace with the white children, but, when progress comes to depend chiefly on the faculties of invention, comparison, and reasoning, they quickly fall behind.
2. That the number of colored children, in Boston, is so great, that they can be advantageously placed in separate schools, where all needful stimulus, arising from numbers and competition, may be felt, without their being degraded or discouraged.
3. That they live so compactly, that in very few (if in any) cases, is it at all inconvenient to attend the special Schools provided for them.
4. That the facts, connected with the origin and history of these Schools, show, that, without them, the colored people would have remained ignorant and degraded, and very few would have been found in the Schools.

5. That if these special Schools were now abolished, the number of colored children in the Public Schools would be greatly diminished, while serious injury would also be done to the other Schools, and no benefit would result.
6. That the majority of the colored, and most of the white people, prefer the present system.

As, then, there is no statute, nor decision of the civil Courts, against classifying children in schools according to a distinction in races, color, or mental and physical peculiarities, the Committee believe that we have the right to classify on these principles; nor do they believe, that, by so doing, we defeat the intent, or violate the spirit, of the law, the Constitution, or the invaluable common-school system established by our fathers; nor in any way infringe the rights of the colored child, or degrade the colored people. These Schools were established for their special benefit: for the same reason we would have them vigorously sustained. No man, colored or white, who understands their real value to the colored people, would seek their destruction.

Sarah C. Roberts v. The City of Boston, 5 Mass. Reports (1849)

Following the Primary School Committee's rejection of the call for school integration, leaders of the African American community turned to the courts, bringing a suit in what became known as the Sarah Roberts case. The white attorney for the parents, Charles Sumner, was one of the nation's best-known lawyers, and made an extensive argument for school integration on the grounds of the equity clauses of the federal and Massachusetts constitutions.

(The facts of the case:)

The plaintiff is a colored child, of five years of age, a resident of Boston, and living with her father, since the month of March, 1847, in Andover street, in the sixth primary school district. In the month of April, 1847, she being of suitable age and qualifications (unless her color was a disqualification) applied to a member of the district primary school committee, having under his charge the primary school nearest to her place of residence, for a ticket of admission to that school, the number of scholars therein warranting her admission, and no special provision having been made for her, unless the establishment of the two schools for colored children exclusively is to be considered.

The member of the school committee, to whom the plaintiff applied, refused her application, on the ground of her being a colored person, and of the special provision made as aforesaid. The plaintiff thereupon applied to the primary school committee of the district, for admission to one of their schools, and was in like manner refused admission, on the ground of her color and the provision aforesaid. She thereupon petitioned the general primary school committee, for leave to enter one of the schools nearest her residence. That committee referred the subject to the committee of the district, with full powers, and the committee of the district thereupon again refused the plaintiff's application, on the sole ground of color and the special provision aforesaid, and the plaintiff has not since attended any school in Boston. Afterwards, on the 15th of February, 1848, the plaintiff went into the primary school nearest her residence, but without any ticket of admission or other leave granted, and was on that day ejected from the school by the teacher.

The school established in Belknap Street (a school for Negro children) is twenty-one hundred feet distant from the residence of the plaintiff, measuring through the streets, and in passing from the plaintiff's residence to the Belknap Street school, the direct route passes the ends of two streets in which there are five primary schools . . . The distance from the plaintiff's residence to the nearest primary school is nine hundred feet. The plaintiff might have attended the school in Belknap Street, at any time, and her father was informed, but he refused to have her attend there.

Argument of Charles Summer, Esq. Against the Constitutionality of Separate Colored Schools in the Case of *Sarah C. Roberts v. The City of Boston* (1849)

I. I begin with the principle, that, according to the spirit of American institutions, and especially of the Constitution of Massachusetts, *all men, with out distinction of color or race, are equal before the law.*

I might, perhaps, leave this proposition without one word of comment. The equality of men will not be directly denied on this occasion, and yet it has been so often assailed of late, that I trust I shall not seem to occupy your time superfluously in endeavoring to show what is understood by this term, when used in laws, or constitutions, or other political instruments.

The equality which was declared by our fathers in 1776, and which was made the fundamental law of Massachusetts in 1780, *was equality before the law.* Its object was to efface all political or civil distinctions, and to abolish all institutions founded upon birth. "All men are created equal," says the Declaration of Independence. "All men are *born* free and equal," says the Massachusetts Bill of Rights. These are not vain words. Within the sphere of their influence no person can be *created*, no person can be *born*, with civil or political privileges, not enjoyed equally by all his fellow-citizens, nor can any institution be established recognizing any, distinctions of birth. This is the Great Charter of every person who draws his vital breath upon this soil, whatever may be his condition, and whoever may be his parents. He may be poor, weak, humble, black—he may be of Caucasian, of Jewish, of Indian, or of Ethiopian race—he may be of French, of German, of English, of Irish extraction—but before the Constitution of Massachusetts, all these distinctions disappear. He is not poor, or weak or humble, or black—nor Caucasian, nor Jewish, nor Indian, nor Ethiopian—nor French, nor German, nor English, nor Irish; he is a MAN,—the equal of all his fellowmen. He is one of the children of the State, which, like an impartial parent, regards all its offspring with an equal care. To some it may justly allot higher duties, according to their higher capacities, but it welcomes all to its equal, hospitable board. The State, imitating the divine justice, is no respecter of persons.

II. I now pass to the second stage of this argument, and ask attention to this proposition. The legislature of Massachusetts, in entire harmony with the Constitution, has made no discrimination of color or race, in the establishment of Public Schools.

If such discrimination were made by the laws, they would be unconstitutional and void. But the legislature of Massachusetts has been too just and generous, too mindful of the Bill of

Rights, to establish any such privilege of *birth*. The language of the statutes is general, and applies equally to all children, of whatever color or race.

The provisions of the law regulating this subject are entitled, *Of the Public Schools* (Revised Statutes, chap. 23). It is to these that we must look in order to ascertain what constitutes a Public School. None can be legally such which are not established in conformity with the law. They may, in point of fact, be more or less public: yet, if they do not come within the terms of the law, they do not form a part of the beautiful system of our public schools—they are not public schools.

I conclude . . . that there is but one kind of public school established by the laws of Massachusetts. This is the general Public School, free to all the inhabitants. There is nothing in these laws establishing any exclusive or separate school for any particular class, whether rich or poor, whether Catholic or Protestant, whether white or black. In the eye of the law there is but *one class*, in which all interests, opinions, conditions and colors commingle in harmony—excluding none, comprehending all . . .

As the State receives strength from the unity and solidarity of its citizens, without distinction of class, so the school receives new strength from the unity and solidarity of all classes beneath its roof. In this way the poor, the humble, and the neglected, share not only the companionship of their presence, in drawing towards the school a more watchful superintendence. A degraded or neglected class, if left to themselves, will become more degraded or neglected. To him that hath shall be given; and the world, true to these words, turns from the poor and outcast to the rich and fortunate. It is the aim of our system of Public Schools, by the blending of all classes, to draw upon the whole school the attention which is too apt to be given only to the favored few, and thus secure to the poor their portion of the fruitful sunshine. But the colored children, placed apart by themselves, are deprived of this blessing.

Sarah C. Roberts v. The City of Boston, Decision of the Supreme Judicial Court

In spite of Sumner's eloquent plea, the Massachusetts Supreme Judicial Court sided with the school committee. In its decision, written by Chief Justice Lemuel Shaw, the court laid the legal groundwork for "separate but equal" schools.

The great principle, advanced by the learned and eloquent advocate of the plaintiff, is, that, by the constitution and laws of Massachusetts, all persons without distinction of age or sex, birth or color, origin or condition, are equal before the law. This, as a broad general principle, such as ought to appear in a declaration of rights, is perfectly sound; it is not only expressed in terms, but pervades and animates the whole spirit of our constitution of free government. But, when this great principle comes to be applied to the actual and various conditions of persons in society, it will not warrant the assertion, that men and women are legally clothed with the same civil and political powers, and that children and adults are legally to have the same functions and be subject to the same treatment; but only that the right, of all, as they are settled and regulated by law, are equally entitled to the paternal consideration and protection of the law, for their maintenance and security. What those rights are, to which individuals, in the infinite variety of circumstances by which they are surrounded in society, are entitled, must depend on laws adapted to their respective relations and conditions.

Conceding, therefore, in the fullest manner, that colored persons, the descendants of Africans, are entitled by law, in this commonwealth, to equal rights, constitutional and political, civil and social, the question then arises, whether the regulation in question, which provides separate schools for colored children, is a violation of any of these rights.

Legal rights must, after all, depend upon the provisions of law; certainly all those rights of individuals which can be asserted and maintained in any judicial, tribunal. The proper providence of a declaration of rights and constitution of government, after directing its form, regulating its organization and the distribution of its powers, is to declare great principles and fundamental truths, to influence and direct the judgment and conscience of legislators in making laws, rather than to limit and control them, by directing what precise laws they shall make. The provision, that it shall be the duty of legislatures and magistrates to cherish the interests of literature and the sciences, especially the university at Cambridge, public schools, and grammar schools, in the towns, is precisely of this character. Had the legislature failed to comply with this injunction, and neglected to provide public schools in the towns, or should they so far fail in their duty as to repeal all laws on the subject, and leave all education to depend on private means, strong and explicit as the direction of the constitution is, it would afford no remedy or redress to the thousands of the rising generation, who now depend on these schools to afford them a most valuable education, and an introduction to useful life.

In the absence of special legislation on this subject, the law has vested the power in the committee to regulate the system of distribution and classification; and when this power is reasonably exercised, without being abused or perverted by colorable pretenses, the decision of the committee must be deemed conclusive. The committee, apparently upon great deliberation, have come to the conclusion, that the good of both classes of schools will be best promoted, by maintaining the separate primary schools for colored and for white children, and we can perceive no ground to doubt, that this is the honest result of their experience and judgment.

It is urged, that this maintenance of separate schools tends to deepen and perpetuate the odious distinction of caste, founded in a deep-rooted prejudice in public opinion. This prejudice, if it exists, is not created by law, and probably cannot be changed by law. Whether this distinction and prejudice, existing in the opinion and feelings of the community, would not be as effectually fostered by compelling colored and white children to associate together in the same schools, may well be doubted; at all events, it is a fair and proper question for the committee to consider and decide upon, having in view the best interests of both classes of children placed under their superintendence, and we cannot say, that their decision upon it is not founded on just grounds of reason and experience, and in the results of a discriminating and honest judgment.

The increased distance, to which the plaintiff was obliged to go to school from her father's house, is not such, in our opinion, as to render the regulation in question unreasonable, still less illegal.

An Act in Amendment of An Act Concerning Public Schools, Chapter 256, Massachusetts Acts and Resolves, 1854–1855 (Boston, 1855)

While the Massachusetts Supreme Court ruling in the Roberts case allowed segregation to continue, the Massachusetts legislature ended the practice with the brief 1855 law that follows.

In determining the qualifications of scholars to be admitted into any public school or any district school in this Commonwealth, no distinction shall be made on account of the race, color, or religious opinions of the applicant or scholar.

Any child who, on account of his race, color, or religious opinions, shall be excluded from any public or district school in this Commonwealth, for admission to which he may be otherwise qualified, shall recover damages therefore in an action of tort, to be brought in the name of said child by his guardian or next friend, in any court of competent jurisdiction to try the same, against the city or town by which such school is supported.

"Report to the Primary School Committee, June 15, 1846, on the Petition of Sundry Colored Persons for the Abolition of the Schools for Colored Children," Boston, MA, 1846, pp. 2 and 28–30; "*Sarah C. Roberts v. The City of Boston*, 5 Mass. Reports," 1849, pp. 200–210; "Argument of Charles Sumner, Esq. Against the Constitutionality of Separate Colored Schools in the Case of *Sarah C. Roberts v. The City of Boston*," Boston, MA, 1849, pp. 4–30, selections; "An Act in Amendment of An Act Concerning Public Schools," Chapter 256, Massachusetts Acts and Resolves, 1854–1855, Boston, MA, 1855, pp. 674–675. From Robert H. Bremner, ed., *Children and Youth in America: A Documentary History, Volume I: 1600–1865*, Cambridge, MA: Harvard University Press, 1970, pp. 528–535.

Figure 3.2 Abiel Smith School, Museum of African American History, National Park Service, Joy Street, Boston. The Smith School was built in 1834 as a public school with the sole purpose of serving African American children in Boston's then segregated public school system.

4
Schooling Moves West, 1835–1860

- Introduction

- Selections from *McGuffey's Sixth Eclectic Reader*, 1836 (With Many Subsequent Editions)

- Calvin E. Stowe, Report on Elementary Public Instruction in Europe, 1837

- Board of National Popular Education, Correspondence, 1849–1850

- Mary Augusta Roper, Letters from Mill Point, Michigan, 1852–1854

- The Speech of Red Jacket, the Seneca Chief, to a Missionary, circa 1805

Introduction

During the early decades of the nineteenth century, after the U.S. Army defeated the Indian tribes, European Americans rapidly settled in the lands of western New York and Pennsylvania and soon moved west of the Alleghenies in the region known as the old Northwest, forming the new states of Ohio, Indiana, Illinois, Michigan, and Wisconsin. The center of gravity for the United States was shifting west. And with the North and South growing further apart in their irreconcilable differences over slavery, the West was seen as the hope of the future. But who would control the culture of the West? Not only was there competition between the cultures of the North and South, but new European immigrants were moving directly to the West. As German and Irish Catholics moved into the new areas, members of the nation's older Protestant elite worried about the character of the region and, therefore, of the nation. What better institution to "rescue" the West than the public school as envisioned by Horace Mann, Catharine Beecher, and their many eastern allies? If the New England model of schooling could be established in what was to be the Midwest, then perhaps New England culture—and cultural dominance—could also be established. Thus, by the 1830s, a major effort emerged to shape the culture of the West, with the public school at the center of the action.

In 1835, Lyman Beecher, one of the nation's best-known preachers (and Catharine's father), who had recently moved from Boston to Cincinnati, published *A Plea for the West*. Asking for Eastern funds to support institutions in the West, he wrote:

> The thing required for the civil and religious prosperity of the West, is universal education, and moral culture, by institutions commensurate to that result—the all-pervading influences of schools, and colleges, and seminaries, and pastors, and churches. When the West is well-supplied in this respect, though there may be great relative defects, there will be, as we believe, the stamina and vitality of a perpetual civil and religious prosperity.

Beecher and his allies, including his daughter Catharine and his son-in-law Calvin Stowe, were part of the nucleus of people who started public schools in Ohio. Other teams of ministers and educators helped found public schools in the other states of the Midwest. Even more than on the East Coast, schooling took off in the Midwest. The school was the ideal institution to help shape the culture of the new region.

By the late 1840s, Midwestern schools were well established, but they still lacked teachers. As a result, one of the nation's first major internal missionary campaigns was developed. The Board of National Popular Education, founded by Catharine Beecher, and other groups sponsored by various religious and charitable organizations, began raising funds and recruiting young women to go west as school teachers. As an earlier version of the Teacher Corps, the Board of National Popular Education offered young women adventure in a new place, a sense of purpose and meaningful effort, and a fresh start in life. Many responded. The official publications of the Board reported the successes of the adventure. Some of the teachers' private correspondence reported the hardships more vividly. Both are included in this chapter.

While midwestern schools initially relied on eastern funds and eastern teachers, it was for midwestern schools themselves that the most successful textbook ever known in the United States was published. A small Cincinnati publishing house offered William Holmes McGuffey $1,000 for a primer, a speller, and four Readers. The first Readers were published in 1836; McGuffey received his $1,000, and the publisher became a millionaire. Between 1836 and 1920, over 122,000,000 copies of the Readers were sold. *McGuffey's Reader* reflected American white middle-class Protestant morality as it existed circa 1836, and this and later editions continued to both shape and reflect American morality until well after 1900. As generations of school children learned to read from these stories, they also learned what it meant to be an American and a participant in a larger society that had clear expectations of its citizens.

Reading most of the material published before the Civil War, one might conclude that only Europeans and their descendants lived in the United States. That was far from the truth. All of the states of the upper Midwest were free states, and numbers of free Blacks lived there, often in less-than-easy circumstances. And while most of the previous Indian residents had been moved farther west, there continued to be Indian communities and conflicts in the region. Subsequent chapters include most of the material on Indian and African American educational experiences, but this chapter closes with an 1805 speech by Red Jacket, a Seneca leader in New York State, emphatically rejecting European culture, religion, and schooling. And in New York, small groups of Seneca and other tribes for the Iroquois confederation were able to maintain their tribal ways. Nevertheless, by the time of the Civil War, schools teaching American culture as defined in textbooks like McGuffey's were the norm throughout the North and no part of the country had such a clearly established and organized system of public schools, so much popular support for the institution, or such widespread participation as the Midwest.

SELECTIONS FROM *MCGUFFEY'S SIXTH ECLECTIC READER*, 1836 (WITH MANY SUBSEQUENT EDITIONS)

For generations of Americans, McGuffey's Readers were the textbook from which they learned the alphabet, grammar, spelling, pronunciation, and morality. In his foreword to a modern edition of the Readers, the historian Henry Steele Commager noted that "part of the greatness

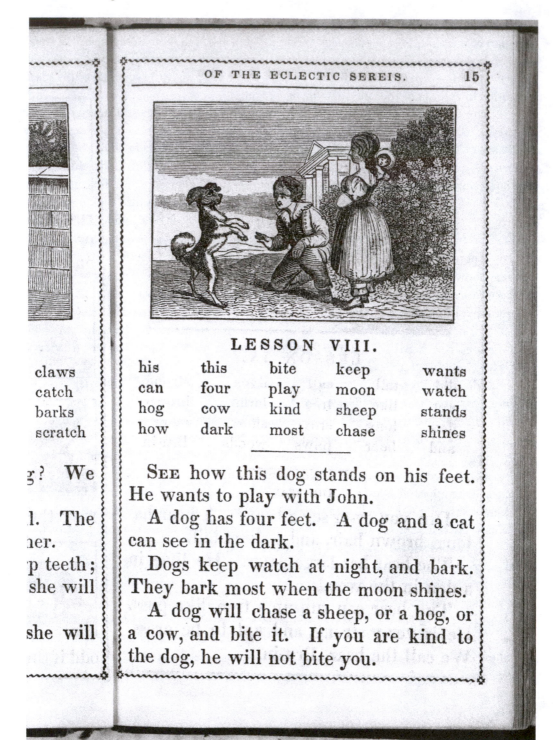

OF THE ECLECTIC SEREIS. 15

LESSON VIII.

his	this	bite	keep	wants
can	four	play	moon	watch
hog	cow	kind	sheep	stands
how	dark	most	chase	shines

SEE how this dog stands on his feet. He wants to play with John.

A dog has four feet. A dog and a cat can see in the dark.

Dogs keep watch at night, and bark. They bark most when the moon shines.

A dog will chase a sheep, or a hog, or a cow, and bite it. If you are kind to the dog, he will not bite you.

Figure 4.1 A page from a *McGuffey's Reader* showing good children with their dog is typical of the stories and morality of the Readers. Courtesy of the Library of Congress, LC-USZ62-51288.

of the McGuffey Readers was that they were there at the right time—they were there to be read by millions of children from all parts of the country." Just as the schools were growing, a textbook came along that fit the culture, the morality, and the patriotism of the institution and the times. The examples that follow are typical of McGuffey: an introduction that continues Noah Webster's stress on articulation, elocution, and reading in a single form of Americanized English (see Chapter 2), Patrick Henry's speech advocating the cause of the American Revolution before the Virginia Legislature, and the indomitable Lyman Beecher's sermon calling on the nation's increasingly diverse peoples to view the Puritan founders of Massachusetts as their true forebearers, no matter who their biological ancestors might be. While later editions of the Readers became somewhat less overtly religious, the patriotic themes, the celebration of the virtues of European Protestant ethics, and the focus on male leaders continued throughout. The readings that follow are from the 1879 edition.

Introduction [to the 1879 Edition]

Articulation is the utterance of the elementary sounds of a language, and of their combinations.

As words consist of one or more elementary sounds, the first object of the student should be to acquire the power of uttering those sounds with *distinctness, smoothness,* and *force.* This result can be secured only by careful practice, which must be persevered in until the learner has acquired a perfect control of his organs of speech . . .

Vocals are sounds which consist of pure tone only. They are the most prominent elements of all words, and it is proper that they should first receive attention. A vocal may be represented by one letter, as in the word *hat,* or by two or more letters, as in *heat, beauty.* A *diphthong* is a union of two vocals, commencing with one and ending with the other. It is usually represented by two letters, as in the words *oil, boy, out, now.*

Each of these can be uttered with great force, so as to give a distinct expression of its sound, although the voice be suddenly suspended, the moment the sound is produced. This is done by putting the lips, teeth, tongue, and palate in their proper position, and then expelling each sound from the throat in the same manner that the syllable "ah!" is uttered in endeavoring to deter a child from something it is about to do; thus, a'—a'—a'—.

Let the pupil be required to utter every one of the elements in the Table with all possible suddenness and percussive force, until he is able to do it with ease and accuracy. This must not be considered as accomplished until he can give each sound with entire clearness, and with all the suddenness of the "crack" of a rifle. Care must be taken that the *vocal alone* is heard: there must be no consonantal sound, and no vocal sound other than the one intended.

At first, the elementary sounds may be repeated by the class in concert; then separately . . .

Elocution and Reading

The business of training youth in elocution, must be commenced in childhood. The first school is the nursery. There, at least, may be formed a distinct articulation, which is the first requisite for good speaking. How rarely is it found in perfection among our orators.

Words, says one, referring to articulation, should "be delivered out from the lips, as beautiful coins, newly issued from the mint; deeply and accurately impressed, perfectly finished; neatly struck by the proper organs, distinct, in due succession, and of due weight." How rarely do we hear a speaker whose tongue, teeth, and lips, do their office so perfectly as to answer to this beautiful description! And the common faults in articulation, it should be remembered, take their rise from the very nursery . . .

Reading is, indeed, a most intellectual accomplishment. So is music, too, in its perfection. We do by no means undervalue this noble and most delightful art, to which Socrates applied himself even in his old age. But one recommendation of the art of reading is, that it requires a constant exercise of the mind. It involves, in its perfection, the whole art of criticism of language. A man may possess a fine genius without being a perfect reader; but he can not be a perfect reader without genius.

Speech Before the Virginia Convention

Patrick Henry, 1736–1799, was born in Hanover County, Virginia. He received instruction in Latin and mathematics from his father, but seemed to develop a greater fondness for hunting, fishing, and playing the fiddle than for study. Twice he was set up in business, and twice failed before he was twenty-four. He was then admitted to the bar after six weeks of study of the law. He got no business at first in his profession, but lived with his father-in-law. His wonderful powers of oratory first showed themselves in a celebrated case which he argued in Hanover Court-House, his own father being the presiding magistrate. He began very awkwardly, but soon rose to a surprising height of eloquence, won his case against great odds, and was carried off in triumph by the delighted spectators. His fame was now established; business flowed in, and he was soon elected to the Virginia Legislature, where, in 1765, he made his famous speech on his resolutions against the Stamp Act, of which the following selection is a portion. He was a delegate to the Congress of 1774, and during the Revolution he was, for several years, Governor of Virginia. In 1788, he earnestly opposed the adoption of the Federal Constitution. When he died, he left a large family and an ample fortune. In person, Mr. Henry was tall and rather awkward, with a face stern and grave. When he spoke on great occasions, his awkwardness forsook him, his face lit up, and his eyes flashed with a wonderful fire. In his life, he was good-humored, honest, and temperate. His patriotism was of the noblest type; and few men in those stormy times did better service for their country than he.

I have but one lamp by which my feet are guided; and that is the lamp of experience. I know of no way of judging the future but by the past; and, judging by the past, I wish to know what there has been in the conduct of the British ministry for the last ten years to justify those hopes with which gentlemen have been pleased to solace themselves and the house? Is it that insidious smile with which our petition has been lately received? Trust it not: it will prove a snare to your feet. Suffer not yourselves to be betrayed with a kiss. Ask yourselves, how this gracious reception of our petition comports with those warlike preparations which cover our waters and darken our land. Are fleets and armies necessary to a work of love and reconciliation? Have we shown ourselves so unwilling to be reconciled that force must be called in to win back our love? Let us not deceive ourselves. These are the implements of war and subjugation,—the last arguments to which kings resort.

I ask, gentlemen, what means this martial array, if its purpose be not to force us into submission? Can gentlemen assign any other possible motive for it? Has Great Britain any enemy in this quarter of the world, to call for all this accumulation of navies and armies? No, she has none. They are meant for us: they can be meant for no other. They are sent over to bind and rivet upon us those chains which the British ministry have been so long forging. And what have we to oppose to them? Shall we try argument? We have been trying that for the last ten years. Have we any thing new to offer upon the subject? Nothing. We have held the subject up in every light in which it was capable; but it has been all in vain. Shall we resort to entreaty and humble supplication? What terms shall we find which have not been already exhausted? Let us not, I beseech you, deceive ourselves longer. We have done everything that could be done, to avert the storm which is now coming on. We have petitioned; we have remonstrated; we have supplicated; we have prostrated ourselves at the foot of the throne, and implored its interposition to arrest the tyrannical hands of the ministry and parliament. Our petitions have been slighted; our remonstrances have produced additional violence and insult; our supplications disregarded; and we have been spurned with contempt from the foot of the throne.

In vain, after these things, may we indulge the fond hope of peace and reconciliation. There is no longer any room for hope. If we wish to be free; if we mean to preserve inviolate those inestimable privileges for which we have been so long contending; if we mean not basely to abandon the noble struggle in which we have been so long engaged, and which we have pledged ourselves never to abandon until the glorious object of our contest shall be obtained-we must fight! I repeat it, we must fight! An appeal to arms and the God of Hosts, is all that is left us . . .

It is vain to extenuate the matter. Gentlemen may cry peace, peace; but there is no peace. The war is actually begun. The next gale that sweeps from the north, will bring to our ears the clash of resounding arms! Our brethren are already in the field! Why stand we here idle? What is it that gentlemen wish? What would they have? Is life so dear, or peace so sweet, as to be purchased at the price of chains and slavery? Forbid it, Almighty God! I know not what course others may take; but as for me, give me liberty or give me death.

The Memory of Our Fathers

Lyman Beecher, 1775–1863, a famous Congregational minister of New England, was born in New Haven, graduated from Yale College in 1797, and studied theology with Dr. Timothy Dwight. His first settlement was at East Hampton, LI at a salary of three hundred dollars a year. He was pastor of the church in Litchfield, CT from 1810 till 1826, when he removed to Boston, and took charge of the Hanover Street Church. In the religious controversies of the time, Dr. Beecher was one of the most prominent characters. From 1832 to 1842, he was President of Lane Theological Seminary, in the suburbs of Cincinnati. He then returned to Boston, where he spent most of the closing years of his long and active life. He died in Brooklyn, NY. As a theologian, preacher, and advocate of education, temperance, and missions, Dr. Beecher occupied a very prominent place for nearly half a century. He left a large family of sons and two daughters, who are well known as among the most eminent preachers and authors in America.

We are called upon to cherish with high veneration and grateful recollections, the memory of our fathers. Both the ties of nature and the dictates of policy demand this. And surely no nation had ever less occasion to be ashamed of its ancestry, or more occasion for gratulation in that respect; for while most nations trace their origin to barbarians, the foundations of our nation were laid by civilized men, by Christians. Many of them were men of distinguished families, of powerful talents, of great learning and of pre-eminent wisdom, of decision of character, and of most inflexible integrity. And yet not unfrequently they have been treated as if they had no virtues; while their sins and follies have been sedulously immortalized in satirical anecdote.

The influence of such treatment of our fathers is too manifest. It creates and lets loose upon their institutions, the vandal spirit of innovation and overthrow; for after the memory of our fathers shall have been rendered contemptible, who will appreciate and sustain their institutions? "The memory of our fathers" should be the watchword of liberty throughout the land; for, imperfect as they were, the world before had not seen their like, nor will it so, we fear, behold their like again. Such models of moral excellence, such apostles of civil and religious liberty, such shades of the illustrious dead looking down upon their descendants with approbation or reproof, according as they follow or depart from the good way, constitute a censorship inferior only to the eye of God; and to ridicule them is national suicide.

The doctrines of our fathers have been represented as gloomy, superstitious, severe, irrational, and of a licentious tendency. But when other systems shall have produced a piety as devoted, a morality as pure, a patriotism as disinterested, and a state of society as happy, as have prevailed where their doctrines have been most prevalent, it may be in season to seek an answer to this objection.

The persecutions instituted by our fathers have been the occasion of ceaseless obloquy upon their fair fame. And truly, it was a fault of no ordinary magnitude, that sometimes they did persecute. But let him whose ancestors were not ten times more guilty, cast the first stone, and the ashes of our fathers will no more be disturbed. Theirs was the fault of the age, and it will be easy to show that no class of men had, at that time, approximated so nearly to just apprehensions of religious liberty; and that it is to them that the world is now indebted for the more just and definite views which now prevail.

The superstition and bigotry of our fathers are themes on which some of their descendants, themselves far enough from superstition, if not from bigotry, have delighted to dwell. But when we look abroad, and behold the condition of the world, compared with the condition of New England, we may justly exclaim, "Would to God that the ancestors of all the nations had been not only almost, but altogether such bigots as our fathers were."

McGuffey's Sixth Eclectic Reader, Cincinnati, OH: Van Antwerp, Bragg & Co., 1879, pp. 11–12, 57–59, 115–118, 128–129.

CALVIN E. STOWE, REPORT ON ELEMENTARY PUBLIC INSTRUCTION IN EUROPE, 1837

While Calvin Stowe never held public office—he was a professor of New Testament at Lane Theological Seminary in Cincinnati—he did have an influence in Ohio not unlike that of Horace Mann in Massachusetts. A tireless advocate for an expanded public school system in his adopted state, he also wanted a school that inculcated the young with his version of morality and knowledge. A year before Horace Mann made his trip to view the schools of Prussia, Stowe made a similar trip. His subsequent report to the Ohio legislature advocates adopting the Prussian model in Ohio.

Internal Arrangements of the Prussian Schools

I will now ask your attention to a few facts respecting the internal management of the schools in Prussia and some other parts of Germany, which were impressed on my mind by a personal inspection of those establishments.

One of the circumstances that interested me most was the excellent order and rigid economy with which all the Prussian institutions are conducted. Particularly in large boarding schools, where hundreds, and sometimes thousands of youths are collected together, the benefits of the system are strikingly manifest. Every boy is taught to wait upon himself— to keep his person, clothing, furniture, and books, in perfect order and neatness; and no extravagance in dress, and no waste of fuel or food, or property of any kind is permitted. Each student has his own single bed, which is generally a light mattress, laid upon a frame of slender bars of iron, because such bedsteads are not likely to be infested by insects, and each one makes his own bed and keeps it in order. In the house, there is a place for every thing and every thing must be in its place. In one closet are the shoe brushes and blacking, in another the lamps and oil, in another the fuel. At the doors are good mats and scrapers, and every thing of the kind necessary for neatness and comfort, and every student is taught, as carefully as he is taught any other lesson, to make a proper use of all these articles at the right time, and then to leave them in good order at their proper places. Every instance of neglect is sure to receive its appropriate reprimand, and if necessary, severe punishment . . .

At Weisenfels, near Lutzen where the great battle was fought in the Thirty Years' War, there is a collection of various schools, under the superintendent of Dr. Harnisch, in what was formerly a large convent. Among the rest there is one of those institutions peculiar to Prussia, in which the children of very destitute families are taken and educated at the public expense, to become teachers in poor villages where they can never expect to receive a large compensation; institutions of a class which we do not *need here*, because no villages in this country *need* be poor. Of course, though they have all the advantages of scientific advancement enjoyed in the most favored schools, frugality and self-denial form an important part of their education. Dr. Harnisch invited me to this part of the establishment to see these boys dine. When I came to the room, they were sitting at their writing tables, engaged in their studies as usual. At the ringing of the bell they arose. Some of the boys left the room, and the others removed the papers and books from the tables, and laid them away in their places. Some of the boys who had gone out, then re-entered with clean, coarse tablecloths in their hands, which they spread over their writing tables. These were followed by others with loaves of brown bread, and plates provided with cold meat and sausages, neatly cut in slices, and jars of water, which they arranged on the table. Of these materials, after a short religious service, they made a cheerful and hearty meal; then arose, cleared away their tables, swept their room, and after a suitable season of recreation, resumed their studies. They are taught to take care of themselves, independent of any help, and their only luxuries are the fruits and plants which they cultivate with their own hands, and which grow abundantly in the gardens of the institution . . .

Character of the System

The entirely practical character of the system is obvious throughout. It views every subject on the practical side, and in reference to its adaptedness to use. The dry technical abstract parts of science are not those first presented; but the system proceeds, in the only way which nature ever pointed out, from practice to theory, from parts to demonstrations. It has often been a complaint in respect to some systems of education, that the more a man studied, the less he knew of the actual business of life. Such a complaint cannot be made in reference to this system, for being intended to educate for the actual business of life, this object is never for a moment lost sight of.

Another striking feature of the system is its moral and religious character. Its morality is pure and elevated, its religion entirely removed from its narrowness of sectarian bigotry. What parent is there, loving his children and wishing to have them respected and happy, who would not desire that they should be educated under such a kind of moral and religious influence as has been described? Whether a believer in revelation or not, does he not know that without sound morals there can be no happiness, and that there is no morality like the morality of the New Testament? Does he not know that without religion, the human heart can never be at rest, and that there is no religion like the religion of the Bible? Every well-informed man knows, that, as a general fact, it is impossible to impress the obligations of morality with any efficiency on the heart of a child, or even on that of an adult, without an appeal to some mode which is sustained by the authority of God; and for what code will it be possible to claim this authority if not for the code of the Bible?

But perhaps some will be ready to say, the scheme is indeed an excellent one, provided only it were practicable; but the idea of introducing so extensive and complete a course of study into our common schools is entirely visionary and can never be realized. I answer, that it is not theory which I have been exhibiting, but a matter of fact, a copy of actual practice. The above system is no visionary scheme emanating from the closet of a recluse, but a sketch of the course of instruction now actually pursued by thousands of schoolmasters in the best district schools that have ever been organized. It can be done, for it has been done, it is now done, and it ought to be done. If it can be done in Europe, I believe it can be done in the United States: If it can be done in Prussia, I know it can be done in Ohio. The people have but to say the word and provide the means, and the thing is accomplished; for the word of the people here is even more powerful than the word of the King there; and the means of the people here are altogether more abundant for such an object than the means of the sovereign there. Shall this object, then, so desirable in itself, so entirely practicable, so easily within our reach, fail of accomplishment? For the honor and welfare of our State, for the safety of our whole nation, I trust it will not fail; but that we shall soon witness in this commonwealth the introduction of a system of common school instruction, fully adequate to all the wants of our population.

Calvin Stowe, "Report on Elementary Public Instruction in Europe, made to the Thirty-Sixth General Assembly of the State of Ohio, December 19, 1837 by C.E. Stowe," reprinted, Boston, MA: Dutton and Wentworth, State Printers, 1838, pp. 17–21, 51–54. Copy at Massachusetts Historical Society.

BOARD OF NATIONAL POPULAR EDUCATION, CORRESPONDENCE, 1849–1850

The success of school reformers in actually establishing schools and systems of schooling in the Midwest led to a desperate shortage of teachers. With so many schools in place there were not nearly enough teachers to go around. The logical step, some thought, was to recruit teachers from the East Coast. Eastern teachers were not only literate, they also shared the values of the midwestern school leaders. A number of organizations began sending teachers west. The largest was founded by Catharine Beecher and led by William Slade, former Governor of Vermont. Recruiting young women to teach in schools hundreds of miles from their homes was a radical departure from previous sex-role stereotypes which assumed that a woman needed to stay with her family of origin until marriage. Nevertheless, the effort to recruit young women to move to places where they were needed as teachers was the forerunner of similar efforts after the Civil War to send missionaries to the South to teach newly freed slaves and twentieth-century efforts to send young women—and occasionally men—abroad or into high-need urban and rural areas of the United States to teach. In many cases, young women found adventure and a sense of purpose for their lives as teachers. The National Board publicized extracts from letters of teachers. While these letters were carefully selected to portray the work in its most positive and romantic light—they were part of a continuing recruitment and fundraising campaign—they also give one a glimpse of the morality, dedication, and sense of adventure among these teachers. The letters also leave little doubt that it was a Protestant public school system that the National Board meant to establish.

St. Paul, Minnesota
Aug. 8, 1849

A new school house is about being prepared, so that Miss B. and myself will be kept from idleness. In performing my duty as a teacher and a Christian I have been supported far better than I had dared to hope—so true is it that God never forsakes his children. For encouragement to continue my labors, I have but to look at what this town was two years ago, and what it is at present. I rejoice that I have been thrown here at so early a period in the history of this Territory, and trust that, as one of the many now weaving the future web of society, my thread may be ever redolent with Christian love, and my efforts ever on the side of Christian Education. This is truly, an important field, and when the germ now budding shall have reached maturity, mighty will be the results. I believe Minnesota is yet to be a leader in the cause of Religion and Education.

Oct. 31 [1849]

My labors have been abundantly blessed during the past season. Not only the day school but the Sabbath school has doubled in interest. I have in my mind an idea of starting a "Youth's Total Abstinence Society," which I think would operate well. This is a young community, and it is impossible to tell what may be the result even of a day.

The Governor told me that we should be supplied with a room and furniture to make a school comfortable. Besides improvement in educational matters, there is a decided advancement in the cause of religion, and morality. Laws have been passed for the suppression of gambling and drinking . . . The different towns are filling up somewhat slowly, but the probability is, that, next spring, the emigration will be greater than ever.

This is a great country to make one grow. All the faculties are brought into action. I feel as if it was one of heaven's best blessings, that I was sent here, where there can be no shirking of labor—no release from responsibility, and no lack of room to work in. May God bless you and the cause in which you labor, and grant you full faith in the promise, that "in due season you shall reap if you faint not."

From Another Teacher in Minnesota
Nov. 12, 1849

I find no difficulty in managing the most turbulent spirits. But were there no Bible to teach me the secret of success in this department of my labors, I should be like the mariner without a compass. As it is, I am often allowed to look at the effect of the great principles of *right* and *wrong*, upon minds unused to the sweet, the subduing power of the gospel. Through the influence of the precept, "Be ye kind one to another, tender hearted, forgiving one another, even as God for Christ's sake hath forgiven you," the habits of some of my scholars are so far changed, that instead of raising the clenched fist at every little affront, they refer all their childish feuds to me. The satisfaction which they manifest with my decisions, is a rich reward for all my exertions and privations. I conduct my Sabbath school with so little parade that I presume the Priest does not know of its existence. I infer from this, from the circumstance that the Catholic children attend regularly. My prospects for continued and increasing usefulness are flattering. I am happy—very happy.

From a Teacher in Southern Indiana
Nov. 12, 1849

I very soon learned after coming here, that much prejudice existed against eastern teachers, and many unkind remarks were made; but, this feeling is fast passing away. Indeed, some of the very individuals have since apologized to me, and now treat me with much respect, while those who have children, have wished to send to my school, and are now waiting with much impatience for admission . . . All who are able, join with me each morning in reading from the Bible. These are seasons of deep interest—and the effect on the school is most salutary. Indeed I could not commence the duties of the day without it, with any hope that I should get through successfully. I often talk with them about the lesson, endeavoring to impress on their minds the necessity of having a new heart—of loving the Savior, and in general am listened to with much apparent interest . . . My pupils are constant in their attendance, and have an increasing interest in their studies. The community generally have a very high opinion of the teachers sent out by the Board, and the confidence in them, as far as I have had an opportunity to judge, is increasing. I am content and happy. I do not regret that I left home, although I often *feel* that I am *not at home*. Society is divided, which is to be expected, where it is composed of so many different elements. There are Swiss, French, Irish, and Dutch. I love the work; and if I can be useful shall continue to be happy. I feel grateful for the favors received at Hartford. My stay there was of much benefit—the preparatory course aiding me essentially in my work as a teacher.

"Second Annual Report of the General Agent of the Board of National Popular Education," Cleveland, OH: Steam Press of M.C. Younglove & Co., 1849, pp. 29–32.
"Third Annual Report of the General Agent of the Board of National Popular Education," Cleveland, OH: Steam Press of M.C. Younglove & Co., 1850, pp. 35–39.

Figure 4.2 Catharine Beecher not only advocated for women becoming school teachers but she opened the Hartford Female Seminary and helped found the Board of National Popular Education to prepare women and send them to schools in the Midwest and beyond.

MARY AUGUSTA ROPER, LETTERS FROM MILL POINT, MICHIGAN, 1852–1854

The Board of National Popular Education selected a certain kind of letter for publication while other matters are reflected in unpublished letters contained in the Board's files. Polly Welts Kaufman's Women Teachers on the Frontier *traces the lives of these women primarily through their correspondence. Kaufman's careful study gives the reader a sense of the adventure offered to a generation of women who escaped the social restrictions of their home towns, as well as their sense of dedication to the welfare of others. At the same time, the difficulty and the loneliness of the enterprise is clear. Moving far away from family and friends, without easy communications, living in a strange place, and dealing with illness made the experience precarious for many. Mary Augusta Roper of Templeton, Massachusetts was sent by the National Board to Mill Point, Michigan in the 1850s. Her letters to the women in Hartford, Connecticut who selected and trained her to be a teacher, written in 1852, illustrate the challenges many of these teachers faced.*

Mill Point, Ottawa County, Michigan
October 18 '52
Committee for Selecting Teachers, Hartford, C.T.

Ladies,

Since leaving Hartford last May, I have been actively engaged in the school of this place, which has been quite large, averaging 40 scholars. No time has been left unoccupied, to be filled up with unavailing regrets, that home and friends are so far away, and I had been unconscious that time had flown so rapidly until the arrival of Miss Bell at Grand Haven reminded me that another class had been collected and scattered over the broad west, and I had not written one word to you . . .

Mill Point is a village separated from Grand Haven entirely by water, containing about 400 inhabitants. A collection of foreigners mostly, who are employed in the steam mills which give the place its name. There are only four families in the place of intelligence. A few other families possess influence but are bad men. A few men in the place wished for a teacher from Governor Slade's class to supply the place of Miss E. Chandler (a lady sent out several years ago and who had taught in this place a year) who was going to leave on account of her health wishing a smaller school. The other party said "they had had a pious teacher long enough" and wished for a Universalist in principle. Mr. Smith was appointed school Director, and he, with the advice of two other of the officers, applied for a teacher, and I was sent here. At the same time a lady destitute of religious principle was hired to teach the children of the dissatisfied ones. No effort was left untried to injure my school. I fortunately succeeded in gaining the affection and confidence of my scholars, so that all avenues to that were closed up.

Completely foiled in their attempts to break up the school in this, they resorted to another expedient which has alike failed. They cautiously circulated suspicions of my good character, and growing bold, finally asserted with barefaced boldness the most indecent stories . . .

At the last school meeting a great effort was made to take from Mr. Smith the office of Director, had it been accomplished, I should not have continued the school, but the cause of right and virtue triumphed, they failed to elect an officer consequently, my employers are still at the head of affairs. They assure me of their unbounded confidence and respect and will not hear on any account of my leaving unless it is so unpleasant that I should *greatly* prefer a location elsewhere. I am firmly attached to my scholars, and I think I can say that they are to me. Attempts have been made repeatedly upon members of my school, to induce them to find fault with school, and leave it for the other, but never have they in but one instance succeeded, and that was the case of two Dutch [German] boys of passionate tempers, who combined in their character the worst traits I ever met in children, their absence was an advantage rather than a loss to the school.

I open my school with prayer and I never have seen any disposition to levity during devotions. We have a large Sabbath School, with only three teachers, we have hitherto felt the want of books, but a large library is on its way hither from my native place, a donation from the church of which I am a member.

We have had no regular preaching but are now making an effort to raise money for the support of a minister, and I think shall succeed. The same opposition has been made to that movement as to all others of such a nature, but it has succeeded beyond our expectations. I think that eventually the cause of religion will triumph but there is a great amount of irreligion, skepticism if not infidelity now.

Miss Bell arrived safely and has commenced her school under favorable circumstances, but she has to fill the place of one of the most successful teachers the state affords, viz. Miss

Mary White, her scholars were singularly attached to her, always speaking of her with all the tenderness of a mother.

Mill Point and Grand Haven are favored with the most beautiful natural scenery, the views from Lake Michigan's shores are very fine, sand hills of the purest white sand lying as steep as it is possible for sand to lie and in some instances covered with wild roses to the water's edge. Our sunsets on the Lake are magnificent in the extreme, and now in midsummer when the forests are robed in their varied hues the effect is fine.

Lake Michigan announces the approach of winter by his deep, wild roar and it is a beautiful scene to see his snow-crested breakers, dashing in fury and dying upon the shores.

I have heard from no member of the class of last spring, a wide correspondence of my own has prevented my writing to them and I have received no letters.

I shall ever retain the most grateful recollections of the kindness experienced at Hartford. I have found the facts learned by visiting schools there most important, enabling me to have a standard of school discipline in my own mind which if never reached, is a constant incentive to active exertion.

With an humble wish that your society may receive Heaven's blessing I will close.

Respectfully yours,

Mary Augusta Roper

Polly Welts Kaufman, *Women Teachers on the Frontier,* New Haven, CT: Yale University Press, 1984. Reprinted by permission of Yale University Press. From the Archives of the Board of National Popular Education, Connecticut State Historical Archives, cited in Polly Welts Kaufman, *Women Teachers on the Frontier,* New Haven, CT: Yale University Press, 1984, pp. 160–165. Reprinted by permission of Polly Kaufman.

THE SPEECH OF RED JACKET, THE SENECA CHIEF, TO A MISSIONARY, CIRCA 1805

The missionary preachers and school teachers who moved into the new European American settlements during the first half of the nineteenth century focused their energies almost exclusively on the development of white settlements. While of mixed opinions on slavery, the majority were probably moderate abolitionists; perhaps not concerned enough about slavery to do much about it, but opposed to its expansion. But the descendants of the earliest inhabitants of the lands had not entirely disappeared. While many had moved further west or into Canada, Indian tribes could be found throughout western New York, western Pennsylvania, and the new territories of the Midwest. When Protestant missionaries sought to educate Native Americans and convert them to Christianity, they met resistance by those who saw little reason to adopt the ways of those who had conquered them. Red Jacket or Sagoyewatha (1750–1830), a leader of the Seneca, one of the six nations of the Iroquois confederation, confronted a white missionary, Jacob Cram, in western New York in 1805. Red Jacket was clear in his rejection of white education and especially white religion.

Friend and Brother, it was the will of the Great Spirit that we should meet together this day. He orders all things, and he has given us a fine day for our council. He has taken his garment from before the sun, and caused it to shine with brightness on us. Our eyes are opened, that we see clearly: our ears are unstopped, that we have been able to hear distinctly the words that you have spoken; for all these favors we thank the Great Spirit, and him only.

Brother, this council fire was kindled by you; it was at your request that we came together at this time; we have listened with attention to what you have said; you requested us to speak our minds freely; this gives us great joy, for we now consider that we stand upright before you, and can speak what we think; all have heard your voice, and all speak to you as one man; our minds are agreed.

Brother, you say you want an answer to your talk before you leave this place. It is right you should have one, as you are a great distance from home, and we do not wish to detain you; but we will first look back a little and tell you what our fathers have told us, and what we have heard from the white people.

Brother, listen to what we say. There was a time when our forefathers owned this great land. Their seats extended from the rising to the setting sun. The Great Spirit had made it for the use of the Indians. He had created the buffalo, the deer, and other animals for food. He had made the bear and the beaver, and their skins served us for clothing. He had scattered them over the country, and taught us how to take them. He had caused the earth to produce corn for bread, all this he had done for his red children, because he loved them. If we had any disputes about hunting grounds, they were generally settled without the shedding of much blood; but an evil day came upon us; your forefathers crossed the great waters, and landed on this island. Their numbers were small; they found tribes, and not enemies; they told us they had fled from their own country for fear of wicked men, and come here to enjoy their religions. They asked for a small seat; we took pity on them, granted their request, and they sat down among us; we gave them corn and meat; they gave us poison in return.

The white people had now found our country, tidings were carried back, and more came among us, yet we did not fear them, we took them to be friends; they called us brothers; we believed them, and gave them a larger seat. At length their numbers had greatly increased; they wanted more land; they wanted our country. Our eyes were opened, and our minds became uneasy. Wars took place; Indians were hired to fight against Indians; and many of our people were destroyed. They also brought strong liquors among us; it was strong and powerful, and has slain thousands.

Brother, our seats were once large, and yours were very small; you have now become a great people, and we have scarcely a place left to spread our blankets; you have got our country, but are not satisfied; you want to force your religion upon us.

Brother, continue to listen. You say that you are sent to instruct us how to worship the *Great Spirit* agreeable to his mind, and if we do not take hold of the religion you white people teach, we shall be unhappy hereafter; you say that you are right, and we are lost; how do we know this to be true? We understand that your religion is written in a book; if it was intended for us as well as you, why has not the Great Spirit given it to us, and not only to us, but why did he not give to our forefathers the knowledge of that book, with the means of understanding it rightly? We only know what you tell us about it; how shall we know when to believe, being so often deceived by the white people?

Brother, you say there is but one way to worship and serve the Great Spirit; if there is but one religion, why do you white people differ so much about it? Why not all agree, as you can all read the book?

Brother, we do not understand these things; we are told that your religion was given to your forefathers, and has been handed down from father to son. We also have a religion which was given to our forefathers, and has been handed down to us, their children. We worship that way. *It teaches us to be thankful for all the favors we receive; to love each other, and to be united; we never quarrel about religion.*

Brother, the Great Spirit has made us all; but he has made a great difference between his white and red children; he has given us a different complexion, and different customs; to you he has given the arts; to these he has not opened our eyes; we know these things to be true. Since he has made so great a difference between us in other things, why may we not conclude that he has given us a different religion according to our understanding; the Great Spirit does right; he knows what is best for his children; we are satisfied.

Brother, we do not wish to destroy your religion, or take it from you; we only want to enjoy our own.

Brother, you say, that you have not come to get our land or our money, but to enlighten our minds. I will now tell you that I have been at your meetings, and saw you collecting money from the meeting. I cannot tell what this money was intended for, but suppose it was for your minister, and if we should conform to your way of thinking, perhaps you may want some from us.

Brother, we are told that you have been preaching to white people in this place; these people are our neighbors, we are acquainted with them; we will wait a little while and see what effect your preaching has upon them.

[The same document also reports a statement by Red Jacket on another occasion in which he alluded to the crucifixion of Christ]

Brother, if your white men murdered the son of the Great Spirit, we Indians had nothing to do with it, and it is none of our affair. If he had come among us we would not have killed him; we would have treated him well, you must make amends for that crime yourselves.

John McIntosh, *History of the North American Indians: Their Origin with a Faithful Description of their manners and customs, both civil and military, their religions, languages, dress, and ornaments*, New Haven, CT: H. Mansfield, 1859. Copy in the Harvard College Library, Cambridge, Massachusetts.

Slavery, Reconstruction, and the Schools of the South, 1820–1937

- Introduction

- Frederick Douglass, *The Narrative of the Life of Frederick Douglass: An American Slave*, 1845

- The New England Freedmen's Aid Society—Official Records, 1862–1872

- The New England Freedmen's Aid Society—Correspondence, 1865–1874

- Charlotte Forten, *The Journal of Charlotte Forten*, 1862

- Booker T. Washington, *The Future of the American Negro*, 1899

- W. E. B. DuBois, *The Souls of Black Folk*, 1903

- Marcus Garvey, *Lessons from the School of African Philosophy: The New Way to Education*, 1937

Introduction

In 1935, W. E. B. DuBois wrote in *Black Reconstruction in America* that "Public education for all at public expense was, in the South, a Negro idea" (pp. 168–169). He was several decades ahead of most other historians in correctly interpreting the history of school development in the states of the former Confederacy. While many historians described the experiences of northern philanthropists and northern missionary teachers in working with newly freed slaves during and after the Civil War, until recently few noted the essential role the recently freed African Americans themselves played in seeking literacy and in building a system of public schooling.

Northern missionaries who went south during and after the Civil War were greatly surprised to find that, in spite of southern laws and all of the efforts to stamp out literacy among slaves, there were many literate slaves. While they constituted a small minority of the total ex-slave population, these individuals had learned to read and write in spite of great danger during their years of slavery. Frederick Douglass was hardly a typical slave. He had run away from a plantation and gained his freedom in the North before the war and was among the great abolitionist and national leaders of the Civil War generation. Nevertheless, his autobiographical account of how he learned to read and write—despite severely repressive measures designed to keep him illiterate—exemplifies the experience of many others.

James D. Anderson's *The Education of Blacks in the South, 1860–1935* (Chapel Hill, NC: The University of North Carolina Press, 1988) provides a very important historical corrective to much of the history written prior to the 1980s. Anderson describes the educational scene at slavery's end:

Blacks emerged from slavery with a strong belief in the desirability of learning to read and write. This belief was expressed in the pride with which they talked of other ex-slaves who learned to read or write in slavery and in the esteem in which they held literate blacks. It was expressed in the intensity and the frequency of their anger at slavery for keeping them illiterate. "There is one sin that slavery committed against me," professed one ex-slave, "which I will never forgive. It robbed me of my education." The former slaves' fundamental belief in the value of literate culture was expressed most clearly in their efforts to secure schooling for themselves and their children. Virtually every account by historians or contemporary observers stresses the ex-slaves' demand for universal schooling. In 1879, Harriet Beecher Stowe said of the freedmen's campaign for education: "They rushed not to the grog-shop but to the schoolroom—they cried for the spelling-book as bread, and pleaded for teachers as a necessity of life." Journalist Charles Nordhoff reported that New Orleans's ex-slaves were "almost universally . . . anxious to send their children to school." Booker T. Washington, a part of this movement himself, described most vividly his people's struggle for education: "Few people who were not right in the midst of the scenes can form any exact idea of the intense desire which the people of my race showed for education. It was a whole race trying to go to school. Few were too young, and none too old, to make the attempt to learn." When supervising the first contrabands at Fortress Monroe in 1861, Edward L. Pierce "observed among them a widespread desire to learn to read."

The documents in this chapter reflect the power of this commitment to literacy. In particular, the New England Freedmen's Aid Society records shift in tone from offering help to passive blacks to respecting and cooperating with newly freed slaves.

It is important to read first-person accounts of what happened in the South in the immediate aftermath of the Civil War. The records of the New England Freedmen's Aid Society provide one such window into the educational effort that swept the South during the 1860s and 1870s. A first-person account of what it was like to teach former slaves in the South is contained in the journal of Charlotte Forten. Forten was among the first northern teachers to go south. She volunteered early in the Civil War to teach some of the first slaves to be freed by the Union Army. Her perspective is unique because she herself was an African American, a free black who had taught school in Massachusetts prior to the war, but many other women shared her experiences.

Reconstruction, and the literacy campaign that was part of it, was always under siege. As Reconstruction came to a painful end during the 1870s and 1880s, many northern allies turned to other matters after, leaving southern blacks at the mercy of the reconstituted segregationist governments. Nevertheless the public schools founded under Reconstruction continued, surviving as ill-funded, segregated institutions but still serving as centers of learning and community building for African Americans across the segregated South.

Under the difficult circumstances of the post-1876 South, Booker T. Washington emerged as a leading voice in the African American community. Washington urged other blacks to find ways to accommodate to the expectations of the white power structure to gain a degree of freedom and autonomy for black institutions, especially his own institute at Tuskegee, Alabama. Washington was by far the most widely recognized African American voice in the United States during the late nineteenth century. He was able to channel northern philanthropy into southern schools as long as the schools stayed focused on practical matters; or at least maintained the illusion of doing so. He—and his supporters—viewed his industrial education as a first step in the long, slow process of increasing the educational and economic opportunities available to southern blacks.

Some of Washington's African American contemporaries challenged his ideas, believing he was too much of an accommodationist and a gradualist. But by far his strongest challenge came from W. E. B. DuBois, destined to be one of the greatest African American leaders of the first half of the twentieth century. DuBois had no patience with Washington's industrial education. For him, the key for African Americans was to demand the full rights of citizens and to develop an intellectual elite, a "talented tenth" who could receive the best of what a classical education could offer, who could be philosophical and moral leaders in the campaign for freedom. Examples from the Washington–DuBois debates are reproduced here in this chapter. It is essential to understand these educational struggles within the African American community and also read them as illustrative of all debates about the meaning and purpose of education.

While historians rightly focus on the Washington–DuBois debate as providing an essential understanding of the tensions about education that existed within the African American community at the beginning of the twentieth century, such a focus omits a key person and school of thought. Marcus Garvey was born in Jamaica in 1887, studied in London, came to the United States in 1917, and soon thereafter launched the Universal Negro Improvement Association from a base in Harlem in New York City. In the 1920s the UNIA was by far the largest civil rights organization in the United States, claiming a membership of between 2 and 4 million people. Often remembered for gaudy uniforms and a call for African Americans to return to Africa, Garvey articulated a widely popular approach to education that differed dramatically from both Washington's and DuBois'. Where Washington called for vocational education and DuBois sought a Harvard-type education for a "talented tenth" within the black community, Garvey called on African Americans in the United States to make common cause with Africans and blacks around the world to create a new culture, literature, and approach to education that reflected their pride in who they were rather than any effort to seek access to the cultural or political worlds of white America. While the movement lasted little more than a decade, its heritage can be seen in separatist and black pride movements through the remainder of the twentieth century and beyond.

FREDERICK DOUGLASS, *THE NARRATIVE OF THE LIFE OF FREDERICK DOUGLASS: AN AMERICAN SLAVE*, 1845

The Narrative of the Life of Frederick Douglass: An American Slave *was published in 1845. It immediately brought national fame to Douglass, and it also provided an intimate portrait of what slavery was like. Douglass was born as a slave about 1817 on the eastern shore of Maryland. He escaped in 1838 and moved to New Bedford, Massachusetts. After the publication of his autobiography, he became a leader, along with William Lloyd Garrison, in the Massachusetts Anti-Slavery Society, a confidant—and sometimes opponent—of both John Brown and Abraham Lincoln, and probably the most respected leader of the African American community in the years immediately after the Civil War. In the account that follows, Douglass was a young slave, desperate—like many others—to gain the window of freedom that literacy would open on a larger world.*

Very soon after I went to live with Mr. And Mrs. Auld, she very kindly commenced to teach me the A, B, C. After I had learned this, she assisted me in learning to spell words of three or four letters. Just at this point of my progress, Mr. Auld found out what was going on, and at once forbade Mrs. Auld to instruct me further, telling her, among other things, that it was unlawful, as well as unsafe, to teach a slave to read. To use his own words, further, he said, "If you give a nigger an inch, he will take an ell. A nigger should know nothing but to obey his master—to do as he is told to do. Learning would *spoil* the best nigger in the world. Now," said he, "if you teach that nigger (speaking of myself) how to read, there would be no keeping him. It would forever unfit him to be a slave. He would at once become unmanageable, and of no value to his master. As to himself, it could do him no good, but a great deal of harm. It would make him discontented and unhappy." These words sank deep into my heart, stirred up sentiments within that lay slumbering, and called into existence an entirely new train of thought. It was a new and special revelation, explaining dark and mysterious things, with which my youthful understanding had struggled, but struggled in vain. I now understood what had been to me a most perplexing difficulty—to wit, the white man's power to enslave the black man. It was a grand achievement, and I prized it highly. From that moment, I understood the pathway from slavery to freedom. It was just what I wanted, and I got it at a time when I the least expected it. Whilst I was saddened by the thought of losing the aid of my kind mistress, I was gladdened by the invaluable instruction which, by the merest accident, I had gained from my master. Though conscious of the difficulty of learning without a teacher, I set out with high hope, and a fixed purpose, at whatever cost of trouble, to learn how to read. The very decided manner with which he spoke, and strove to impress his wife with the evil consequences of giving me instruction, served to convince me that he was deeply sensible of the truths he was uttering. It gave me the best assurance that I might rely with the utmost confidence on the results which, he said, would flow from teaching me to read. What he most dreaded, that I most desired. What he most loved, that I most hated. That which to him was a great evil, to be carefully shunned, was to me a great good, to be diligently sought; and the argument which he so warmly urged, against my learning to read, only served to inspire me with a desire and determination to learn. In learning to read, I owe almost as much to the bitter opposition of my master, as to the kindly aid of my mistress. I acknowledge the benefit of both . . .

I lived in Master Hugh's family about seven years. During this time, I succeeded in learning to read and write. In accomplishing this, I was compelled to resort to various stratagems. I had no regular teacher. My mistress, who had kindly commenced to instruct me, had, in compliance with the advice and direction of her husband, not only ceased to instruct, but had set her face against my being instructed by any one else. It is due, however, to my mistress to say of her, that she did not adopt this course of treatment immediately. She at first lacked the depravity indispensable to shutting me up in mental darkness. It was at least necessary for her to have some training in the exercise of irresponsible power, to make her equal to the task of treating me as though I were a brute.

My mistress was, as I have said, a kind and tender-hearted woman; and in the simplicity of her soul she commenced, when I first went to live with her, to treat me as she supposed one human being ought to treat another. In entering upon the duties of a slaveholder, she did not seem to perceive that I sustained to her the relation of a mere chattel, and that for her to treat me as a human being was not only wrong, but dangerously so. Slavery proved as injurious to her as it did to me. When I went there, she was a pious, warm, and tender-hearted woman. There was no sorrow or suffering for which she had not a tear. She had bread for the hungry, clothes for the naked, and comfort for every mourner that came within her reach. Slavery soon proved its ability to divest her of these heavenly qualities. Under its influence, the tender heart became stone, and the lamb-like disposition gave way to one of tiger-like fierceness. The first step in her downward course was in her ceasing to instruct me. She now commenced to practice her husband's precepts. She finally became even more violent in her opposition than her husband himself. She was not satisfied with simply doing as well as he had commanded; she seemed anxious to do better. Nothing seemed to make her more angry than to see me with a newspaper. She seemed to think that here lay the danger. I have had her rush at me with a face made all up of fury, and snatch from me a newspaper, in a manner that fully revealed her apprehension. She was an apt woman; and a little experience soon demonstrated, to her satisfaction, that education and slavery were incompatible with each other.

From this time I was most narrowly watched. If I was in a separate room any considerable length of time, I was sure to be suspected of having a book, and was at once called to give an account of myself. All this, however, was too late. The first step had been taken. Mistress, in teaching me the alphabet, had given me the *inch*, and no precaution could prevent me from taking the *ell*.

The plan which I adopted, and the one by which I was most successful, was that of making friends of all the little white boys whom I met in the street. As many of these as I could, I converted into teachers. With their kindly aid, obtained at different times and in different places, I finally succeeded in learning to read. When I was sent of errands, I always took my book with me, and by going one part of my errand quickly, I found time to get a lesson before my return. I used also to carry bread with me, enough of which was always in the house, and to which I was always welcome; for I was much better off in this regard than many of the poor white children in our neighborhood. This bread I used to bestow upon the hungry little urchins, who, in return, would give me that more valuable bread of knowledge. I am strongly tempted to give the names of two or three of those little boys, as a testimonial of the gratitude and affection I bear them; but prudence forbids;—not that it would injure me, but it might embarrass them; for it is almost an unpardonable offence to teach slaves to read in this Christian country. It is enough to say of the dear little fellows, that they lived on Philpot Street, very near Durgin and Bailey's shipyard. I used to talk this matter of slavery over with them. I would sometimes say to them, I wished I could be as free as they would be when they got to be men. "You will be free as soon as you are twenty-one, *but I am a slave for life!* Have not I as good a right to be free as you have?" These words used to trouble them; they would express for me the liveliest sympathy, and console me with the hope that something would occur by which I might be free.

I was now about twelve years old, and the thought of being *a slave for life* began to bear heavily upon my heart. Just about this time, I got hold of a book entitled, *The Columbian Orator*. Every opportunity I got, I used to read this book. Among much other interesting matter, I found in it a dialogue between a master and his slave. The slave was represented as having run away from his master three times. The dialogue represented the conversation which took place between them, when the slave was retaken the third time. In this dialogue, the whole argument in behalf of slavery was brought forward by the master, all of which was disposed of by the slave. The slave was made to say some very smart as well as impressive things in his reply to his master—things which had the desired though unexpected effect; for the conversation resulted in the voluntary emancipation of the slave on the part of the master.

In the same book, I met with one of Sheridan's mighty speeches on and in behalf of Catholic emancipation. These were choice documents to me. I read them over and over again with unabated interest. They gave tongue to interesting thoughts of my own soul, which had frequently flashed through my mind, and died away for want of utterance. The moral which I gained from the dialogue was the power of truth over the conscience of even a slaveholder. What I got from Sheridan was a bold denunciation of slavery, and a powerful vindication of human rights. The reading of these documents enabled me to utter my thoughts, and to meet the arguments brought forward to sustain slavery; but while they relieved me of one difficulty, they brought on another even more painful than the one of which I was relieved. The more I read, the more I was led to abhor and detest my enslavers. I could regard them in no other light than a band of successful robbers, who had left their homes, and gone to Africa, and stolen us from our homes, and in a strange land reduced us to slavery. I loathed them as being the meanest as well as the most wicked of men. As I read and contemplated the subject, behold! That very discontentment which Master Hugh had predicted would follow my learning to read had already come, to torment and sting my soul to unutterable anguish. As I writhed under it, I would at times feel that learning to read had been a curse rather than a blessing. It had given me a view of my wretched condition, without the remedy. It opened my eyes to the horrible pit, but to no ladder upon which to get out. In moments of agony, I envied my fellow-slaves for their stupidity. I have often wished myself a beast. I preferred the condition of the meanest reptile to my own. Any thing, no matter what, to get rid of thinking! It was this everlasting thinking of my condition that tormented me. There was no getting rid of it. It was pressed upon me by every object within sight or hearing, animate or inanimate. The silver trump of freedom had roused my soul to eternal wakefulness. Freedom now appeared, to disappear no more forever. It was heard in every sound, and seen in every thing. It was ever present to torment me with a sense of my wretched condition. I saw nothing without seeing it, I heard nothing without hearing it, and felt nothing without feeling it. It looked from every star, it smiled in every calm, breathed in every wind, and moved in every storm.

I often found myself regretting my own existence, and wishing myself dead; and but for the hope of being free, I have no doubt but that I should have killed myself, or done something for which I should have been killed. While in this state of mind, I was eager to hear any one speak of slavery. I was a ready listener. Every little while, I could hear something about the abolitionists. It was some time before I found what the word meant. It was always used in such connections as to make it an interesting word to me. If a slave ran away and succeeded in getting clear, or if a slave killed his master, set fire to a barn, or did any thing very wrong in the mind of a slaveholder, it was spoken of as the fruit of *abolition*. Hearing the word in this connection very often, I set about learning what it meant. The dictionary afforded me little or no help. I found it was "the act of abolishing;" but then I did not know what was to be abolished. Here I was perplexed. I did not dare to ask any one about its meaning, for I was satisfied that it was something they wanted me to know very little about. After a patient waiting, I got one of our city papers, containing an account of the number of petitions from the north, praying for the abolition of slavery in the District of Columbia, and of the slave trade between the States. From this time I understood the words *abolition* and *abolitionist*, and always drew near when that word was spoken, expecting to hear something of importance to myself and fellow-slaves. The light broke in upon me by degrees. I went one day down on the wharf of Mr. Waters; and seeing two Irishmen unloading a scow of stone, I went, unasked, and helped them. When he had finished, one of them came to me and asked me if I were a slave. I told him I was. He asked, "Are ye a slave for life?" I told him that I was. The good Irishman seemed to be deeply affected by the statement. He said to the other that it was a pity so fine a little fellow as myself should be a slave for life. He said it was a shame to hold me. They both advised me to run away to the north; that I should find friends there, and that I should be free. I pretended not to be interested in what they said, and treated them as if I did not understand them; for I feared they might be treacherous. White men have been known to encourage slaves to escape, and then, to get the reward, catch them and return them to their masters. I was afraid that these seemingly good men might use me so; but I nevertheless remembered their advice, and from that time I resolved to run away. I looked forward to a time at which it would be safe for me to escape. I was too young to think of doing so immediately; besides, I wished to learn how to write, as I might have occasion to write my own pass. I consoled myself with the hope that I should one day find a good chance. Meanwhile, I would learn to write.

The idea as to how I might learn to write was suggested to me by being in Durgin and Bailey's shipyard, and frequently seeing the ship carpenters, after hewing, and getting a piece of timber ready for use, write on the timber the name of that part of the ship for which it was intended. When a piece of timber was intended for the larboard side, it would be marked thus—"L." When a piece was for the starboard side, it would be marked thus—"S." A piece for the larboard side forward, would be marked thus—"L.F." When a piece was for starboard side forward, it would be marked thus—"S.F." For larboard aft, it would be marked thus—"L.A." For starboard aft, it would be marked thus—"S.A." I soon learned the names of these letters, and for what they were intended when placed upon a piece of timber in the shipyard. I immediately commenced copying them, and in a short time was able to make the four letters named. After that, when I met with any boy who I knew could write, I would tell him I could write as well as he. The next word would be, "I don't believe you. Let me see you try it." I would then make the letters which I had been so fortunate as to learn, and ask him to beat that. In this way I got a good many lessons in writing, which it is quite possible I should never have gotten in any other way. During this time, my copy-book was the board fence, brick wall, and pavement; my pen and ink was a lump of chalk. With these, I learned mainly how to write. I then commenced and continued copying the italics in Webster's *Spelling Book*, until I could make them all without looking on the book. By this time, my little Master Thomas had gone to school, and learned how to write, and had written over a number of copy-books.

These had been brought home, and shown to some of our near neighbors, and then laid aside. My mistress used to go to class meeting at the Wilk Street meeting-house every Monday afternoon, and leave me to take care of the house. When left thus, I used to spend the time in writing in the spaces left in Master Thomas's copy-book, copying what he had written. I continued to do this until I could write a hand very similar to that of Master Thomas. Thus, after a long, tedious effort for years, I finally succeeded in learning how to write.

Frederick Douglass, *Narrative of the Life and Times of Frederick Douglass, Written by Himself*, Boston, MA: Published at the Anti-Slavery Office, 1845, pp. 33–44.

THE NEW ENGLAND FREEDMEN'S AID SOCIETY— OFFICIAL RECORDS, 1862–1872

In the early years of the Civil War, the army called the freed slaves "contrabands" because they were still viewed as property forfeited by the rebelling southerners. Even before the Emancipation Proclamation changed the war to one for the abolition of slavery in 1863, large numbers of former slaves were finding freedom beyond Union Army lines and, once there, they asked for help in learning to read and write. Boston abolitionists responded quickly to the federal government's call to help educate the newly freed slaves. The three brief excerpts from the records of the New England Freedmen's Aid Society report the evolving view of both northern abolitionists and southern African Americans during and after the war. In the organizational meetings of the society in 1862, the newly freed are viewed as "unfortunate human beings," passive and helpless. By 1867, experience in the South had taught the societies that schooling could—and should—be a cooperative effort between northern philanthropic efforts and southern African American communities. And by the 1870s, the focus was in turning the schools over to the local communities and focusing instead on teacher education. This represents a dramatic change in the views of at least one small group of northern whites. Some of these whites went south initially thinking they would have to do everything for the former slaves, only to discover that they were welcome only if they respected ex-slaves enough to engage in cooperative efforts with them.

February 1, 1862

The undersigned were appointed a committee to bring to your notice a letter recently received in this city from E. S. Pierce, Esq., Agent of the U. S. Government for the "Contrabands," at Port Royal. In that letter, the writer urges the importance of immediately sending out teachers for the 8,000 unfortunate human beings now within the lines of our army in South Carolina.

February 7, 1862

I. The object of the Educational Commission shall be the industrial, social, intellectual, moral, and religious improvement of persons released from slavery in the course of the War for the Union . . .

II. The educational commission shall employ as its laborers, persons of undoubted loyalty to the Federal Government, who shall not permit their work to interfere with the proper discipline and regulating of the camps; and it will expect and gratefully welcome any facilities which the Government may be pleased to grant, such as passes for teachers, and supplies, and rations, and due protection for said teachers while engaged in their work.

New York City, Sept. 10, 1867

   I. *Resolved*, That the best interests of the freed people require the permanent establishment of free schools in the South: that, as in the Northern free-school system, the people should cooperate in their support; and, therefore, that no new schools should be established, except where co-operation can be secured.

  II. *Resolved*, That our teachers and agents in the South should organize the people into associations to raise means to aid in the establishment and support of their schools.

 III. *Resolved*, That, in the opinion of this meeting, all books should be sold at a price to be fixed by the Teachers' Committee; and that none should be given away except by special permission of the Committee . . .

Lyman Abbot, General Secretary
1872

The annual meeting of the N. E. Freedmen's Aid Society was held yesterday afternoon, in the Freeman Place Chapel, the vice-president, Mr. William Lloyd Garrison in the chair . . . From this report, it appeared that the number of teachers at the South had been greatly reduced, the attention being turned especially to the normal schools. These are under the most experienced teachers and their good results are already apparent, the graduates being the best teachers which can be procured for their peculiar work. In Maryland two teachers are retained, the expense being chiefly borne by the citizens of Baltimore. More than two hundred scholars are now in the school. A letter was read from one of the teachers giving an encouraging report of progress. The work in Richmond has ceased on account of the action of the local authorities in receiving colored pupils into their schools. In Virginia, there are two schools with five teachers and two hundred and thirty-seven scholars. In North Carolina there is one school kept by two teachers and educating seventy-seven scholars. In South Carolina, there are five schools, twenty-one teachers, and six hundred and sixty-five pupils. In Georgia, eleven schools, thirty-three teachers and twelve hundred scholars.

Minutes. February 1, 1862, February 7, 1862, and September 10, 1862. Volume of Minutes, 1862–1874. Ms. N-10 New England Freedmen's Society Records. Reprinted courtesy of the Massachusetts Historical Society.

Annual Meeting. 1872. Volume of Minutes, 1862–1874. Ms. N-10 New England Freedmen's Aid Society Records. Reprinted courtesy of the Massachusetts Historical Society.

THE NEW ENGLAND FREEDMEN'S AID SOCIETY—CORRESPONDENCE, 1865–1874

While the official records provide a glimpse into the thinking of the northern social leaders who supported the society, the society's correspondence with the teachers who went south provides a better look at the reality of daily life in the schools. As with the National Board in the 1850s, so in the 1860s and 1870s, young people from across the north—mostly women, but also some men—responded to the call to go south to aid in the instruction of the newly freed citizens. The letters that follow give a sense of what life was like, revealing the excitement and challenge of teaching but also the more personal concerns and stories of the teachers.

Winchester
Mar 14, 1865

Yours of the 9th is at hand. I hope those two good teachers from Boston will be sent out so as to be here the 1st of April. The school numbered ninety-one at present. Perhaps Miss Moore will leave in a day or two, but a short vacation will be no injury. Don't fail to send a supply of books. Many of them can purchase their books, if they can find them to purchase. There seems to be but one thing to render the success of the enterprise uncertain, viz: "the occupation of the town by our troops." From present appearances, I think there is little doubt that the town will be held. I will meet the teachers at the depot . . . four miles from this place at anytime, if I can be notified.

N. E. Brackett

Boston
Sept 29, 1869
Mr. Jillson,

Dear Sir,

We have had the pleasure of a visit from our friend, Mr. Tomlinson, and have arranged with him in regard to our work in South Carolina. We hope to keep up as many schools in the state as last year and shall employ the native teachers as far as possible. In order to do so, we must have the co-operation of the colored people themselves and Mr. Tomlinson agrees with us that they should pay one half of the teachers' salaries whenever they are able.

But we see no prospect of our being able to do anything in South Carolina beyond this year, except in keeping up the Shaw School at Charlestown. It seems to us that the time has already come when the people can and ought to support and manage the schools themselves and the legislating of last year shows a disposition to do so, although the desired result was not obtained.

We give you this timely notice that in your plans for the promotion of public education you may know on what help from us you can rely. We shall be very glad to give you any aid in our power and hope that this year's work will show a great progress in the schools.

Will you be kind enough to give us any information you think would be interesting to us in regard to your plans for the schools in South Carolina?

Yours very respectfully,

Edward D. Cheney

Columbus, Ga
January 8th, 1874

My Dear Mr. Cheney:

Enclosed please find Report from Dec. which I should have forwarded earlier, but during Christmas vacation both Marian Lucy and myself were on the sick list and I did not find the time to settle accounts.

Our school seems quite prosperous, though not quite as large as usual at this time of year, owing no doubt to the harsh times which press very heavily on this people . . .

We have rather more pupils, who come from the country, and who walk long distances, and a smaller number who board in the city, than we have had for the last three years, and this is quite conclusive evidence of poverty. During Aunt Lucy's illness she was visited by pupils of whom, I dare say, you have heard, and in the course of conversation one day she spoke of the gratitude which to him the colored people had always evinced, and also of their forgiving spirit instancing one case which it seems to me is worth preserving. A certain Rev. Mr. DeLawson, an Episcopal minister, was noted under the old regime for his cruel treatment of his slaves. I fancy he did not amount to much as a preacher, for he raised then—as now—vegetables for market and sent "Hannah" to town with them every morning. The stripping and whipping of Hannah were inevitable if she failed to sell the entire contents of her wagon. But Hannah was a favorite and she was thus spared the beating by the kindness of some of his patrons and they gave her small pieces of money for herself so that she had gotten together about $60.00 in small pieces of silver which she gave to the Rev. to keep for her. When "the freedom" came Hannah wanted to go by herself and meekly asked the preacher for his six penses, but he, evidently intending to do his small part toward the fulfillment of the Scripture "from him that hath not, shall be taken away even that which he hath," utterly refused to give her a cent.

She had no clothes, but she went away and now in her old age has managed to make a comfortable home for herself. The old mistress had been even harder with Hannah than the master (an almost universal experience) but last summer "old missus" was very sick with a lingering fever and with no one to do for her.

Hannah left her comfortable home, tended to her day and night, killed her own chickens to make broth for her, and took the entire care of her for two months without any prospect of wages. Could either you or I have done as much?

The old preacher brings vegetables to market himself now, but it seems to me his strawberries are always sour.

We are all "tolerably" well now. We have had a most delightful winter, though it was very cold at Christmas.

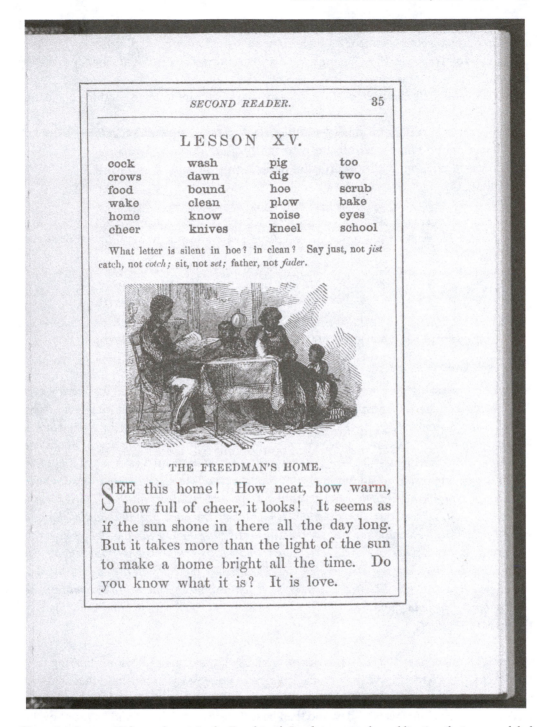

Figure 5.1 Lesson 15 from a lesson in the *Freedman's Reader*—a popular publication that was modeled on the McGuffey *Reader* but with far greater emphasis on African American history and on teaching basic morality and a strong work ethic to newly freed African Americans in search of literacy.

The children were quite disappointed at not having a Christmas tree and so was I, but I mean to get up an entertainment for them some time next month.

Did you receive a box of _____ some week or two since? They will, I am sure, prove very beautiful creatures if they live.

You spoke of a Library to be added to this one. Are you intending to send the books this year?

Mr. Harris is expecting to come to Columbus this month and then most likely there will be a change of one Trustee.

With love to the cousins, I am cordially yours

Caroline Alfred

N. E. Brackett. Letters to Edward D. Cheney, March 14, 1865 and September 29, 1869. Ms. N-10 New England Freedmen's Aid Society Records. Reprinted courtesy of the Massachusetts Historical Society.

N. E. Brackett. Letter to Caroline Alfred, January 8, 1874. Ms. N-10 New England Freedmen's Aid Society Records. Reprinted courtesy of the Massachusetts Historical Society.

CHARLOTTE FORTEN, *THE JOURNAL OF CHARLOTTE FORTEN*, 1862

European Americans were not the only ones to go south to teach the newly freed slaves. The Journal of Charlotte Forten provides the story of a free African American who joined other northern women to go to the schools of the South. Forten was born as a free black in Philadelphia in 1837. She later moved to Salem, Massachusetts, where she taught in the Epes Grammar School in the late 1850s. As the readings below indicate, with the coming of the war, she was anxious to go south to teach in the schools of the recently freed slaves. One of the earliest experiments of the federal government in opening schools for the ex-slaves was in Port Royal, South Carolina, where the military had taken over control of the coastal islands as part of the effort to blockade southern ports. The portions of the journal that follow cover the weeks after her initial decision, her travels south, and her first impressions of the schools. The danger she describes was not exaggerated. She was literally teaching on the edge of the Civil War battle lines. In such a context the mix of her commitment to the cause of abolition, her descriptions of teaching, and her wonderful notes about flowers, climate, and daily life is all the more intriguing.

Wednesday, September 3 [1862]. Have been anxious and disappointed at not hearing from Dr. P[eck]. But a letter from Mrs. J. to-day tells me that she has seen him, and that he is very sanguine about my going. Dr. [Seth] R.[ogers] and others to whom he spoke about it, wish it. The Com.[mission] meets to-day, and then he will write immediately and let me know the final decision. Last week I heard from home that there was no doubt of my being able to go from the Phil[adelphia] Com[mittee]. Mr. [J. Miller] McK.[im] had spoken to them about it. So if I cannot go from Boston I am sure of going from P[hiladelphia] but w'ld rather go under Boston auspices . . .

Monday, September 8. No further news from B.[oston]. I am determined to go tomorrow and see for my-self what the trouble is. Have paid a last visit to the W.[ater] C.[ure]. Am so grieved that I shall not see Dr. [Seth] R.[ogers]. He has gone to N.[ehant]. S.[allie] walked here to see me. We sat on the doorstep in the lovely moonlight, and talked for hours. We talked of self-sacrifice. What a girl S.[allie] is! Full of originality and genius—strange and wayward to the last degree. What will become of her? What will her life be? I ask myself often. She interests me deeply.

Wednesday, October 21. To-day rec'd a note from Mr. McK.[im] asking me if I c'ld possibly be ready to sail for Port Royal, perhaps tomorrow. I was astonished, stupefied, and, at first thought it impossible, but on seeing Mr. McK.[im] I found there was a excellent opportunity for me to go. An old Quaker gentleman is going there to keep store, accompanied by his daughter, and he is willing to take charge of me. It will probably be the only opportunity that I shall have of going this winter, so at any cost I will go. And so now to work. In greatest haste.

At Sea. October 27, Monday. Let me see. Where am I? What do I want to write? I am in a state of utter bewilderment. It was on Wed. I reed the note. On Thursday I said "good bye" to the friends that are so dear, and the city that is so hateful, and went to N.Y. Spent the night with Mrs. [Peter] W.[illiams]. The next morn did not hurry myself, having heard that the Steamer "United States" w'ld not sail till twelve. Mrs. W[illiams] and I went to "Lovejoy's" to meet the Hunns' and found there a card from Mr. H.[unn] bidding me hasten to the steamer, as it was advertised to sail at nine. It was then between ten and eleven. After hurrying down and wearying ourselves, found when I got on board that it was not to sail till twelve. But I did not go ashore again. It was too bad, for I had not time to get several things that I wanted much, among them *Les Miserables*, which my dear brother H.[enry] had kindly given me the money for. He had not had time to get it in Phila[delphia].

Enjoyed the sail down the harbor perfectly. The shipping is a noble sight. Had no symptoms of sea-sickness until eve. when being seated at the table inexpressibly singular sensation caused me to make a hasty retreat to the aft-deck, where by keeping perfectly still sitting on a coil of ropes spent a very comfortable eve. and had a pleasant conversation with one of the passengers. Did not get out of sight of land until after dark, I regretted that.

Early this morn. Mr. [John] H.[unn] came to our door to tell us that we were in sight of the blockading fleet in Charlestown harbor. Of course, we sprang to the window eagerly; and saw the masts of the ships looking like a grove of trees in the distance. We were not near enough to see the city. It was hard to realize that we were even so near the barbarous place.

Later. We are again in sight of land. Have passed Edisto and several other islands, and can now see Hilton Head. Shall reach it about one. 'Tis nearly eleven now. The S.[outh] C.[arolina] shore is flat and low—along line of trees. It does not look very inviting. We are told that oranges will be ripe when we get to Beaufort, and that in every way this is just the loveliest season to be there, which is very encouraging.

We approach Hilton Head. Our ship has been boarded by Health Officer and Provost Marshal. We shall soon reach the landing. All is hurry and confusion on board. I must lay thee aside, friend journal, and use my eyes for seeing all there is to be seen. When we reach our place of destination I will give to thee, oh faithful friend, the result of my observations. So *au revoir*.

Tuesday night. 'T'was a strange sight as our boat approached the landing at Hilton Head. On the wharf was a motley assemblage—soldiers, officers, and "contrabands" of every hue and size. They were mostly black, however, and certainly the most dismal specimens I ever saw. H.[ilton] H.[ead] looks like a very desolate place; just a long, low sandy point running out into the sea with no visible dwellings upon it but the soldiers' white-roofed tents.

Thence, after an hour's delay, during which we signed a paper, which was virtually taking the oath of allegiance, we left the "United States," most rocking of rockety propellers—and took a steamboat for Beaufort. On board the boat was General [Rufus] Saxton, to whom we were introduced. I like his face exceedingly. And his manners were very courteous and affable. He looks like a thoroughly *good* man.—From H.[ilton] H.[ead] to B.[eaufort] the same low line of sandy shore bordered by trees; almost the only object of interest to me were the remains of an old Huguenot Fort, built many, many years ago . . .

Went into the Commissary's Office to wait for the boat which was to take us to St. Helena's Island which is about six miles from B.[eaufort]. 'Tis here that Miss [Laura] Towne has her school, in which I am to teach, and that Mr. Hunn will have his store. While waiting in the office we saw several military gentleman [sic], *not* very creditable specimens, I sh'ld say. The little Commissary himself, Capt. T., is a perfect little popinjay, and he and a Colonel somebody who didn't look any too sensible, talked in a very smart manner, evidently for our especial benefit. The word *nigger* was plentifully used, whereupon I set them down at once as *not* gentleman [sic]. Then they talked a great deal about rebel attacks and yellow fever, and other alarming things, with significant nods and looks at each other. We saw through them at once, and were not at all alarmed by any of their representations. But if they are a fair example of army officers, I sh'ld pray to see as little of them as possible.

To my great joy I found that we were able to be rowed by a crew of negro boatmen. Young Mr. F.[rench]—whom I like—accompanied us, while Mr. H.[unn] went with a flat to get our baggage. The row was delightful. It was just at sunset—a grand Southern sunset; and the gorgeous clouds of crimson and gold were reflected in the waters below, which were smooth and calm as a mirror. Then, as we glided along, the rich sonorous tones of the boatmen broke upon the evening stillness. Their singing impressed me much. It was so sweet and strange and solemn. "Roll, Jordan, Roll" was grand, and another

Jesus make de blind to see
Jesus make de deaf to hear
Jesus make de cripple walk
Walk in, dear Jesus,
And the refrain,
No man can hender me.

It was very, very impressive. I want to hear these men sing [John Greenleaf] Whittier's "Song of the Negro Boatmen." I am going to see if it can't be brought about in some way.

It was nearly dark when we reached St. Helena's, where we found Miss T.[owne]'s carriage awaiting us, and then we three and our driver, had a long drive along the lonely roads in the dark night. How easy it sh'ld have been for a band of guerillas had any chanced that way to seize and hang us. But we found nothing of the kind. We were in a jubilant state of mind and sang "John Brown" with a will as we drove through the pines and palmettos. Arrived at the Superintendent's house[;] we were kindly greeted by him and the ladies and shown into a lofty *ceilinged* parlor where a cheerful wood fire glowed in the grate, and we soon began to feel quite at home in the very heart of Rebeldom; only that I do not at all realize yet that we are in S.[outh] C.[arolina]. It is all a strange wild dream, from which I am constantly expecting to awake. But I can write no more now. I am tired, and still feel the motion of the ship in my poor head. Good night, dear A!

Wednesday, October 29. A lovely day, but rather cool, I sh'ld think, for the "sunny South." The ship still reals [sic] in my head, and everything is most unreal, yet I went to drive . . . We drove to Oaklands, our future home. It is very pleasantly situated, but the house is in rather a dilapidated condition, as are most of the houses here, and the yard and garden have a neglected look, when it is cleaned up, and the house made habitable; I think it will be quite a pleasant place. There are some lovely roses growing there and quantities of ivy creeping along the ground, even under the house, in wild luxuriance—the negroes on the place are very kind and polite. I think I shall get on amicably with them.

After walking about and talking with them, and plucking some roses and ivy to send home, we left Oaklands and drove to the school. It is kept by Miss [Ellen] Murray and Miss Towne in the little Baptist Church, which is beautifully situated in a grove of live oaks. Never saw anything more beautiful than these trees. It is strange that we do not hear of them at the North. They are the first objects that attract one's attention here. They are large, noble trees with small, glossy green leaves. Their beauty consists in the long bearded moss with which every branch is heavily draped. This moss is singularly beautiful, and gives a solemn, almost funereal, aspect to the trees.

We went into the school, and heard the children read and spell. The teachers tell us that they have made great improvement in a very short time, and I noticed with pleasure how bright, how eager to learn many of them seem. The singing delighted me most. They sang beautifully in their rich, sweet, clear tones, and with that peculiar swaying motion which I had noticed before in the older people, and which seems to make their singing all the more effective. Besides several other tunes they sang "Marching Along" with much spirit, and then one of their own hymns, "Down in the Lonesome Valley," which is sweetly solemn and most beautiful. Dear children! Born in slavery, but free at last? May God preserve you all the blessings of freedom, and may you be in every possible way fitted to enjoy them. My heart goes out to you. I shall be glad to do all that I can to help you.

As we drove homeward I noticed that the trees are just beginning to turn; some beautiful scarlet berries were growing along the roadside, and everywhere the beautiful live oak with its moss drapery. The palmettos disappoint me much. Most of them have a very jagged appearance, and are yet stiff and ungraceful. The country is very level—as flat as that in eastern Penn[sylvania]. There are plenty of woods, but I think they have not the grandeur of our Northern woods. The cotton fields disappoint me too. They have a very straggling look, and the pods are small, not at all the great snowballs that I had imagined. Altogether the country w'ld be rather desolate looking were it not for my beautiful and evergreen oaks.

Friday, October 31. Miss T[owne] went to B.[eaufort] to-day, and I taught for her. I enjoyed it much. The children are well-behaved and eager to learn. It will be a happiness to teach here. I like Miss [Ellen] Murray so much. She is of English parentage, born in the

Provinces. She is one of the most whole-souled, warm-hearted women I ever met. I felt drawn to her from the first (before I knew she was English) and of course I like her none the less for that. Miss Towne also is a delightful person. "A Charming lady" Gen. Saxton calls her, and my heart echoes the words. She is housekeeper, physician, everything, here. The most indispensable person on the place, and the people are devoted to her. And indeed she is quite a remarkable young lady. She is one of the earliest comers, and has done much good in teaching and superintending the negroes. She is quite young; not more than twenty-two or three, I sh'ld think, and is superintendent of two plantations. I like her energy and decision of character. Her appearance, too, is very interesting. Mr. [Richard] S.[oule], the superintendent, is a very kind, agreeable person. I like him.

Wednesday, November 5. Had my first regular teaching experience, and to you and you only friend beloved, will acknowledge that it was *not* a very pleasant one. Part of my scholars are very tiny—babies, I call them—and it is hard to keep them quiet and interested while I am hearing the larger ones. They are too young even for the alphabet, it seems to me. I think I must write home and ask somebody to send me picture-books and toys to amuse them with. I fancied Miss T.[owne] looked annoyed when, at one time, the little ones were usually restless. Perhaps it was only my fancy. Dear Miss M.[urray] was kind and considerate as usual. She is very lovable. Well, I *must* not be discouraged. Perhaps things will go on better to-morrow. I am sure I enjoyed the walk to school. Through those lovely woods, just brightening to scarlet now. Met the ladies about halfway, and they gave me a drive to the church . . .

Monday, November 10. We taught—or rather, commenced teaching—the children "John Brown," which they entered into eagerly. I felt the full to the significance of *that* song being sung here in S.[outh] C.[arolina] by little negro children, by those whom he—the glorious old man—died to save. Miss [Laura] T.[owne] told them about him. A poor mulatto man is in one of our people's houses, a man from the North, who assisted Mr. [Samuel D.] Phillips (a nephew of Wendell P.[hillips]) when he was here, in teaching school; he seems to be quite an intelligent man. He is suffering from fever. I shall be glad to take as good care of him as I can. It is so sad to be ill, helpless, and poor, and so far away from home. This eve, though, I felt wretchedly, had a long exercise in irregular French verbs. The work of reviewing did me good. Forgot bodily ills—even so great an ill as a bad cold in the head for a while.

Thursday, November 13. Was there ever a lovelier road than that through part of my way to school lies? . . . Talked to the children a little while to-day about the noble Toussaint. They listened very attentively. It is well that they sh'ld know what one of their own color c'ld do for his race. I long to inspire them with courage and ambition (of a noble sort), and high purposes. It is noticeable how very few mulattoes there are here. Indeed in our school, with one or two exceptions, the children are all black. A little mulatto child strayed into the school house yesterday—a pretty little thing with large beautiful black eyes and lovely long lashes. But so dirty! I longed to seize and thoroughly cleanse her. The mother is a good-looking woman, but quite black. "Thereby," I doubt not, "hangs a tale." This eve. Harry, one of the men on the place, came in for a lesson. He is most eager to learn, and is really a scholar to be proud of. He learns rapidly. I gave him his first lesson in writing to-night, and his progress was wonderful. He held his pen almost perfectly right the first time. He will very soon learn to write, I think. I must inquire who w'ld like to take lessons at night. Whenever I am well enough it will be a real pleasure to teach them . . .

Monday, November 17. Had a dreadfully wearying day in school, of which the less said the better. Afterward drove the ladies to "The Corner," a collection of negro houses, whither Miss T[owne] went on a doctoring expedition. The people there are very pleasant. Saw a little baby, just borne today—and another—old Venus' great grandchild for whom I made the little pink frock. These people are very grateful. The least kindness that you do them they insist on repaying in some way. We have had a quantity of eggs and potatoes brought us despite our remonstrances. Today one of the women gave me some Tanias. Tania is a queer-looking root. After it is boiled it looks a little like potato, but is much larger. I don't like the taste.

Thursday, November 27. Thanksgiving Day. This, according to Gen. [Rufus] Saxton's noble Proclamation, was observed as a day of "Thanksgiving and praise." It has been a lovely day—cool, delicious air, golden, gladdening sunlight, deep blue light, with soft white clouds floating over it . . . This morning a large number—Superintendents, teachers, and freed people, assembled in the little Baptist church. It was a sight that I shall not soon forget—that crowd of eager, happy black faces from which the shadow of slavery had forever passed. "Forever free!" "Forever free!" Those magical words were all the time singing themselves in my soul, and never before have I felt so truly grateful to God.

Brenda Stevenson, ed., *The Journals of Charlotte Forten Grimke*, New York: Oxford University Press, 1988, pp. 380–407.

BOOKER T. WASHINGTON, *THE FUTURE OF THE AMERICAN NEGRO*, 1899

Other documents by Washington were more famous, but none stated his view on the proper education of southern African Americans better than his book, The Future of the American Negro, *published in 1899. In this selection, Washington makes his argument that education for basic economic development (industrial education) must precede education for "high culture."*

It seems to me that, as a general thing, the temptation in the past in educational and missionary work has been to do for the new people that which was done a thousand years ago, or that which is being done for a people a thousand miles away, without making a careful study of the needs and conditions of the people whom it is designed to help. The temptation is to run all people through a certain educational mould, regardless of the condition of the subject or the end to be accomplished. This has been the case too often in the South in the past, I am sure. Men have tried to use, with these simple people just freed from slavery and with no past, no inherited traditions of learning, the same methods of education which they have used in New England, with all its inherited traditions and desires. The Negro is behind the white man because he has not had the same chance, and not from any inherent difference in his nature and desires. What the race accomplishes in these first fifty years of freedom will at the end of these years, in a large measure, constitute its past. It is, indeed, a responsibility that rests upon this nation—the foundation laying for a people of its past, present, and future at one and the same time.

One of the weakest points in connection with the present development of the race is that so many get the idea that the mere filling of the head with a knowledge of mathematics, the sciences, and literature, means success in life. Let it be understood, in every corner of the South, among the Negro youth at least, that knowledge will benefit little except as it is harnessed, except as its power is pointed in a direction that will bear upon the present needs and conditions of the race. There is in the heads of the Negro youth of the South enough general and floating knowledge of chemistry, of botany, of zoology, of geology, of mechanics, of electricity, of mathematics, to reconstruct and develop a large part of the agricultural, mechanical, and domestic life of the race. But how much of it is brought to a focus along lines of practical work? In cities of the South like Atlanta, how many colored mechanical engineers are there? Or how many machinists? How many civil engineers? How many architects? How many house decorators? In the whole State of Georgia, where 80 percent of the colored people depend upon agriculture, how many men are there who are well-grounded in the principles and practices of scientific farming? Or dairy work? Or fruit culture? Or floriculture?

For example, not very long ago I had a conversation with a young colored man who is a graduate of one of the prominent universities of this country. The father of this man is comparatively ignorant, but by hard work and the exercise of common sense, he has become the owner of two thousand acres of land. He owns more than a score of horses, cows, and mules and swine in large numbers, and is considered a prosperous farmer. In college, the son of this farmer has studied chemistry, botany, zoology, surveying, and political economy. In my conversation I asked this young man how many acres his father cultivated in cotton and how many in corn? With a far-off gaze up into the heavens he answered he did not know. When I asked him the classification of the soils on his father's farm, he did not know. He did not know how many horses or cows his father owned nor of what breeds they were, and seemed surprised that he should be asked such questions. It never seemed to have entered his mind that on his father's farm was the place to make his chemistry, his mathematics, and his literature penetrate and reflect itself in every acre of land, every bushel of corn, every cow, and every pig.

Let me give other examples of this mistaken sort of education. When a mere boy, I saw a young colored man, who had spent several years in school, sitting in a common cabin in the South, studying a French grammar. I noted the poverty, the untidiness, the want of system and thrift, that existed about the cabin, notwithstanding his knowledge of French and other academic studies.

Again, not long ago I saw a colored minister preparing his Sunday sermon just as the New England minister prepares his sermon. But this colored minister was in a broken-down, leaky, rented log cabin, with weeds in the yard, surrounded by evidences of poverty, filth, and want of thrift. This minister had spent some time in school studying theology. How much better it would have been to have had this minister taught the dignity of labor, taught the theoretical and practical farming in connection with his theology, so that he could have added to his meager salary, and set an example for his people in the matter of living in a decent house, and having a knowledge of correct farming! In a word, this minister should have been taught that his condition, and that of his people, was not that of a New England community; and he should have been trained as to meet the actual needs and conditions of the colored people in this community, so that a foundation might be laid that would, in the future, make a community like New England communities.

Since the Civil War, no one object has been more misunderstood than that of the object and value of industrial education for the Negro. To begin with, it must be borne in mind that the condition that existed in the South immediately after the war, and that now exists, is a peculiar one, without a parallel in history. This being true, it seems to me that the wise and honest thing to do is to make a study of the actual condition and environment of the Negro, and do that which is best for him, regardless of whether the same thing has been done for another race in exactly the same way. There are those among the white race and those among the black race who assert, with a good deal of earnestness, that there is no difference between the white man and the black man in this country. This sounds very pleasant and tickles the fancy; but, when the test of hard, cold logic is applied to it, it must be acknowledged that there is a difference—not an inherent one, not a racial one, but a difference growing out of unequal opportunities in the past.

If I may be permitted to criticize the educational work that has been done in the South, I would say that the weak point has been in the failure to recognize this difference. Negro education, immediately after the war in most cases, was begun too nearly at the point where New England education had ended. Let me illustrate. One of the saddest sights I ever saw was the placing of a three-hundred-dollar rosewood piano in a country school in the South that was located in the midst of the "Black Belt." Am I arguing against the teaching of instrumental music to the Negroes in that community? Not at all; only I should have deferred those music lessons about twenty-five years. There are numbers of such pianos in thousands of New England homes. But behind the piano in the New England home there are one hundred years of toil, sacrifice, and economy; there is the small manufacturing industry, started several years ago by hand power, now grown into a great business; there is ownership in land, a comfortable home, free from debt, and a bank account. In this "Black Belt" community where this piano went, four-fifths of the people owned no land, many lived in rented one-room cabins, many were in debt for food supplies, many mortgaged their crops for the food on which to live, and not one had a bank account. In this case, how much wiser it would have been to have taught the girls in this community sewing, intelligent and economical cooking, housekeeping, something of dairying and horticulture? The boys should have been taught something of farming in connection with their common-school education, instead of awakening in them a desire for a musical instrument which resulted in their parents going into debt for a third-rate piano or organ before a home was purchased. Industrial lessons would have awakened, in this community, a desire for homes, and would have given the people the ability to free themselves from industrial slavery to the extent that most of them would have soon purchased homes. After the home and the necessaries of life were supplied could come the piano. One piano lesson in a home of one's own is worth twenty in a rented log cabin.

All that I have just written, and the various examples illustrating it, show the present helpless condition of my people in the South—how fearfully they lack the primary training for good living and good citizenship, how much they stand in the need of a solid foundation on which to build their future success. I believe, as I have many times said in various addresses in the North and in the South, that the main reason for the existence of this curious state of affairs is the lack of practical training in the ways of life.

There is, too, a great lack of money with which to carry on the educational work in the South. I was in a country in a Southern State not long ago where there are some thirty thousand colored people and about seven thousand whites. In this country, not a single public school for Negroes had been open that year longer than three months, not a single colored teacher had been paid more than $15 per month for his teaching. Not one of these schools was taught in a building that was worthy of the name of schoolhouse. In this country, the State or public authorities do not own a single dollar's worth of school property—not a school-house, a blackboard, or a piece of crayon. Each colored child had spent on him that year for his education about fifty cents, while each child in New York or Massachusetts had had spent on him that year for education not far from $20. And yet each citizen of this country is expected to share the burdens and privileges of our democratic form of government just as intelligently and conscientiously as the citizens of New York or Boston. A vote in this country means as much to the nation as a vote in the city of Boston. Crime in this country is as truly an arrow aimed at the heart of the government as a crime committed in the streets of Boston.

A single school-house built this year in a town near Boston to shelter about three hundred pupils cost more for building alone than is spent yearly for the education, including buildings, apparatus, teachers, for the whole colored school population of Alabama. The Commissioner of Education for the State of Georgia not long ago reported to the State legislature that in that State there were two hundred thousand children that had entered no school the year past and one hundred thousand more who were at school but a few days,

Figure 5.2 Booker T. Washington. Courtesy of the Library of Congress, LC-USZ62-120526.

making practically three hundred thousand children between six and eighteen years of age that are growing up in ignorance in one Southern State alone. The same report stated that outside of the cities and towns, while the average number of school-houses in a country was sixty, all of these sixty school-houses were worth in lump less than $2,000, and the report further added that many of the schoolhouses in Georgia were not fit for horse stables. I am glad to say, however, that vast improvement over this condition is being made in Georgia under the inspired leadership of State Commissioner Glenn, and in Alabama under the no less zealous leadership of Commissioner Abercrombie.

These illustrations, so far as they concern the Gulf States, are not exceptional cases; nor are they overdrawn.

Until there is industrial independence, it is hardly possible to have good living and a pure ballot in the country districts. In these States, it is safe to say that not more than one black man in twenty owns the land he cultivates. Where so large a proportion of a people are dependent, live in other people's houses, eat other people's food, and wear clothes they have not paid for, it is pretty hard to expect them to live fairly and vote honestly.

Booker T. Washington, *The Future of the American Negro*, Boston, MA: Small, Maynard & Company, 1899, pp. 16–41.

W. E. B. DuBois, *The Souls of Black Folk*, 1903

At the end of the nineteenth century, Booker T. Washington had become the acknowledged voice of the African American community in the South and generally in the nation. However, with the new century, a young Harvard graduate rose to challenge Washington. Believing that Washington's vision was too narrow and ultimately sold the African American community short, DuBois argued, first in The Souls of Black Folk *and then in a long line of subsequent publications, that the African American community needed a larger vision and a wider dream if liberation was to be found. The previous reading from Washington, combined with the two selections from* The Souls of Black Folk *that follow, frame the DuBois–Washington debate.*

Of Mr. Booker T. Washington and Others

Easily the most striking thing in the history of the American Negro since 1876 is the ascendancy of Mr. Booker T. Washington. It began at the time when war memories and ideals were rapidly passing; a day of astonishing commercial development was dawning; a sense of doubt and hesitation overtook the freedmen's sons—then it was that his leading began. Mr. Washington came, with a single definite programme, at the psychological moment when the nation was a little ashamed of having bestowed so much sentiment on Negroes, and was concentrating its energies on Dollars. His programme of industrial education, conciliation of the South, and submission and silence as to civil and political rights, was not wholly original; the Free Negroes from 1830 up to wartime had striven to build industrial schools, and the American Missionary Association had from the first taught various trades; and Price and others had sought a way of honorable alliance with the best of Southerners. But Mr. Washington first indissolubly linked these things; he put enthusiasm, unlimited energy,

Figure 5.3 W. E. B. Dubois. Courtesy of the Library of Congress, LC-DIG-ggbain-07435.

and perfect faith into this programme, and changed it from a by-path into a veritable Way of Life. And the tale of the methods by which he did this is a fascinating study of human life.

It startled the nation to hear a Negro advocating such a programme after many decades of bitter complaint; it startled and won the applause of the South, it interested and won the admiration of the North; and after a confused murmur of protest, it silenced, if it did not convert, the Negroes themselves.

To gain the sympathy and cooperation of the various elements comprising the white South was Mr. Washington's first task; and this, at the time Tuskegee was founded, seemed, for a black man, well-nigh impossible. And yet ten years later it was done in the word spoken at Atlanta: "In all things purely social we can be as separate as the five fingers, and yet one as the hand in all things essential to mutual progress." This "Atlanta Compromise" is by all odds the most notable thing in Mr. Washington's career. The South interpreted it in different ways: the radicals received it as a complete surrender of the demand for civil and political equality; the conservatives, as a generously conceived working basis for mutual understanding. So both approved it, and today its author is certainly the most distinguished Southerner since Jefferson Davis, and the one with the largest personal following.

Next to this achievement comes Mr. Washington's work in gaining place and consideration in the North. Others less shrewd and tactful had formerly essayed to sit on these two stools and had fallen between them; but as Mr. Washington knew the heart of the South from birth and training, so by singular insight he intuitively grasped the spirit of the age which was dominating the North. And so thoroughly did he learn the speech and thought of triumphant commercialism, and the ideals of material prosperity, that the picture of a lone black boy poring over a French grammar amid the weeds and dirt of a neglected home soon seemed to him the acme of absurdities. One wonders what Socrates and St. Francis of Assisi would say to this.

And yet this very singleness of vision and thorough oneness with his age is a mark of the successful man. It is as though Nature must needs make men narrow in order to give them force. So Mr. Washington's cult order has gained unquestioning followers, his work has wonderfully prospered, his friends are legion, and his enemies are confounded. To-day he stands as the one recognized spokesman of his ten million fellows, and one of the most notable figures in a nation of seventy millions. One hesitates, therefore, to criticize a life which, beginning with so little, has done so much. And yet the time is come when one may speak in all sincerity and utter courtesy of the mistakes and shortcomings of Mr. Washington's career, as well as of his triumphs, without being thought captious or envious, and without forgetting that it is easier to do ill than well in the world.

The criticism that has hitherto met Mr. Washington has not always been of this broad character. In the South especially, has he had to walk warily to avoid the harshest judgements—and naturally so, for he is dealing with the one subject of deepest sensitiveness to that section. Twice—once when at the Chicago celebration of the Spanish-American War he alluded to the color-prejudice that is "eating away the vitals of the South," and once [when] he dined with President Roosevelt—has the resulting Southern criticism been violent enough to threaten seriously his popularity. In the North the feeling has several times forced itself into words, that Mr. Washington's counsels of submission overlooked certain elements of true manhood, and that his educational programme was unnecessarily narrow. Usually, however, such criticism has not found open expression, although too, the spiritual sons of the Abolitionists have not been prepared to acknowledge that the schools founded before Tuskegee, by men of broad ideals and self-sacrificing spirit, were wholly failures or worthy of ridicule. While, then, criticism has not failed to follow Mr. Washington, yet the prevailing public opinion of the land has been but too willing to deliver the solution of a wearisome problem into his own hands, and say, "If that is all you and your race ask, take it."

Among his own people, however, Mr. Washington has encountered the strongest and most lasting opposition, amounting at times to bitterness, and even to-day continuing strong and insistent even though largely silenced in outward expression by the public opinion of the nation. Some of this opposition is, of course, mere envy; the disappointment of displaced demagogues and the spite of narrow minds. But aside from this, there is among educated and thoughtful colored men in all parts of the land a feeling of deep regret, sorrow, and apprehension at the wide currency and ascendancy which some of Mr. Washington's theories have gained. These same men admire his sincerity of purpose, and are willing to forgive much to honest endeavor, which is doing something worth the doing. They cooperate with Mr. Washington as far as they conscientiously can; and, indeed, it is no ordinary tribute to this man's tact and power that, steering as he must between so many diverse interests and opinions, he so largely retains the respect of all . . .

Booker T. Washington arose as essentially the leader not of one race but of two—a compromiser between the South, the North, and the Negro. Naturally the Negroes resented, at first bitterly, signs of compromise which surrendered their civil and political rights, even though this was to be exchanged for larger chances of economic development. The rich and dominating North, however, was not only weary of the race problem, but was investing largely in Southern enterprises, and welcomed any method of peaceful cooperation. Thus, by national opinion, the Negroes began to recognize Mr. Washington's leadership; and the voice of criticism was hushed.

Mr. Washington represents in Negro thought the old attitude of adjustment and submission; but adjustment at such a peculiar time as to make his programme unique. This is an age of unusual economic development, and Mr. Washington's programme naturally takes an economic cast, becoming a gospel of Work and Money to such an extent as apparently almost completely to overshadow the higher aims of life. Moreover, this is an age when the more advanced races are coming closer in contact with the less developed races, and the race-feeling is therefore intensified; and Mr. Washington's programme practically accepts the alleged inferiority of the Negro races. Again, in our own land, the reaction from the sentiment of war time has given impetus to race-prejudice against Negros, and Mr. Washington withdraws many of the high demands of Negros as men and American citizens. In other periods of intensified prejudice all the Negro's tendency to self-assertion has been called forth; at this period a policy of submission is advocated. In the history of nearly all other races and peoples, the doctrine preached at such crises has been that manly self-respect is worth more than lands and houses, and that a people who voluntarily surrender such respect, or cease striving for it, are not worth civilizing.

In answer to this, it has been claimed that the Negro can survive only through submission. Mr. Washington distinctly asks that black people give up, at least for the present, three things—

First, political power,
Second, insistence on civil rights,
Third, higher education of Negro youth—

and concentrate all their energies on industrial education, the accumulation of wealth, and the conciliation of the South. This policy has been courageously and insistently advocated for over fifteen years, and has been triumphant for perhaps ten years. As a result of this tender of the palm-branch, what has been the return? In these years there have occurred:

1. The disfranchisement of the Negro.
2. The legal creation of a distinct status of civil inferiority for the Negro.
3. The steady withdrawal of aid from institutions for the higher training of the Negro.

These movements are not, to be sure, direct results of Mr. Washington's teachings; but his propaganda has, without a shadow of a doubt, helped their speedier accomplishment. The question then comes: Is it possible, and probable, that nine millions of men can make effective progress in economic lines if they are deprived of political rights, made a servile caste, and allowed only the most meagre chance for developing their exceptional men? If history and reason give any distinct answer to these questions, it is an emphatic *No* . . .

The black men of America have a duty to perform, a duty stern and delicate—a forward movement to oppose a part of the work of their greatest leader. So far as Mr. Washington preaches Thrift, Patience, and Industrial Training for the masses, we must hold up his hands and strive with him, rejoicing in his honors and glorying in the strength of this Joshua called of God and of man to lead the headless host. But so far as Mr. Washington apologizes for injustice, North or South, does not rightly value the privilege and duty of voting, belittles the emasculating effects of caste distinctions, and opposes the higher training and ambition of our brighter minds—so far as he, the South, or the Nation, does this—we must unceasingly and firmly oppose them. By every civilized and peaceful method we must strive for the rights which the world accords to men, clinging unwaveringly to those great words which the sons of the Fathers would fain forget: "We hold these truths to be self-evident: That all men are created equal; that they are endowed by their Creator with certain unalienable rights; that among these are life, liberty, and the pursuit of happiness."

W. E. B. DuBois, *The Souls of Black Folk*, Chicago, IL: A. C. McClurg & Co., 1903, pp. 41–59.

MARCUS GARVEY, *LESSONS FROM THE SCHOOL OF AFRICAN PHILOSOPHY: THE NEW WAY TO EDUCATION*, 1937

Marcus Garvey opened the School of African Philosophy in Toronto, Canada in 1937 a decade after his 1927 deportation from the United States. But the lessons that he outlined in the late 1930s reflect the same approach to education that he advocated in the United States in the 1920s. While he saw himself as continuing some of Booker T. Washington's approach to education, and like Washington he fought bitterly with DuBois, his educational philosophy was significantly at odds with both. While he does not mention DuBois by name, there is little doubt who he means when he writes in this selection about the mis-education of "leading Negro intellectuals." As this document makes clear, Garvey wanted people of African descent around the world to develop their own institutions and their own culture and not to seek access to or be dependent on institutions or a culture that had both oppressed and ridiculed them for generations.

Aims and Objects of the U.N.I.A.—To Establish Universities, Colleges, Academies And Schools For the Racial Education And Culture of The People.

This means that we are not to become satisfied with the educational system of the white man which has been devised by him for his own purpose, and to lead others to obedience to his system.

The Negro must have an educational system of his own, based upon the history and tradition of his race. The text books, therefore, must be different to the white man's text books. The white man's books laud himself and outrages the Negro. In such textbooks the Negro should substitute all that is bad affecting himself for that which is good relating to him.

The Negro, therefore, should not be satisfied with a college or university education from white schools, but should add to his schooling by going to his own schools and universities where possible or reading such text books that have been adopted by his schools and colleges, which must all glorify the Negro, for the white man's system glorified the white man . . .

The present system of education is calculated to subject the majority and elevate the minority. The system was devised and has been promulgated by agents of the minority. This system was carefully thought out by those who desire to control others for their benefit, and the disadvantage of others to the extent that the others would not immediately rise into happiness and enjoyment of life simultaneously and equally with them. It was never originally intended to make all the people equal at the same time, and more so was it not intended to elevate the darker races to the immediate standard of the white races from whom the minority sprung to establish the system of education. All text books and general literature therefore were coloured to suit the particular interest of those who established the system of education, and the group they represent as against the interest of others whom they did not want to immediately elevate to their standard.

There is always a limited process in the education of other races by the race that originates the system of education. As for instance, if a Negro attends a university with other students of the race that postulates or projects the educational system, whilst the Negro would have the privilege of the class room for general instruction to learn commonly, he may not have the privilege of his fellow students of the other race who may be admitted to certain club fraternities within the University from which he would be debarred. Such fraternities generally enjoy the privilege of special instructions and special discussions which convey a wider range of enlightenment on the subjects taught than would be possible to the Negro. Hence when he graduates even from the same text books his technical knowledge is not as wide as that of others who have had fuller explanation in the technical interpretation of the particular text books and at the same time is only trained to reflect the system that props the intentions of the creators of the system, so that at his best he is making use of his education as a slave of a system that was not intended for him but to which he renders service.

It is necessary, therefore, that the Negro be additionally educated or re-educated after he has imbibed the system of the present education. The best way to do this is to educate him racially in the home, in the meeting hall or in his own club where he will be put under the closest scrutiny and analysis of what appears to be education, as coming from other people, because their system of education may not completely fit into the Negro's ideas of his own preservation.

By not being able to do this in the past, educated Negros have not been able to assume proper leadership of their race, because their education was of the nature as to cause them to support the present system which is of no advantage to the Negro, except as a servant, serf and slave, for which purpose really the system was devised to a certain extent. This explains the behavior of leading Negro intellectuals who are not able to dissect the educational system of others and use only that portion that would be helpful to the Negro race, and add to it for a complete curriculum that would be satisfactory as a complete education for the race. Do not swallow wholly the educational system of any other group except you have perfectly analysed it and found it practical and useful to your group. There is still room for the Negro educational system free from the prejudices that a present educational system upholds against him. Never fail to impress upon the Negro that he is never thoroughly educated until he has imbibed racial education.

It is by education that we become prepared for our duties and responsibilities in life. If one is badly educated he must naturally fail in the proper assumption and practice of his duties and responsibilities because the Negro has been badly educated. He has universally failed to measure up to his duties and responsibilities as a man and as a race. His education has been subversive. He must now make his education practical and real, hence he must re-arrange everything that affects him in his education to be of assistance to him in reaching out to his responsibilities and duties.

As you shouldn't expect another man to give you the clothing that you need to cover your own body so you should not expect another race to give you the education to challenge their rights to monopoly and mastery to take for yourself that which they also want for themselves. If you are going to distrust the other man in his honesty because you know him to be dishonest, then you must maintain the attitude in every respect, for if he is dishonest in one, he may be dishonest in all. If he will rob you your wages he will also rob you your education that would enable you to know that he is robbing you of your wages. Trust only yourself and those you know, and those who look like you and are related to you ought to be known first before you know others.

Marcus Garvey, "Lessons from the School of African Philosophy" (1937), pp. 181–352 in Robert A. Hill, ed., Marcus Garvey: *Life and Lessons: A Centennial Companion to the Marcus Garvey and Universal Negro Improvement Association Papers*, Berkeley, CA: University of California Press, pp. 209, 263–265.

6

The Emergence of the High School, 1821–1959

- Introduction

- National Education Association, *Report of the Committee on Secondary School Studies* (The Committee of Ten), 1893

- G. Stanley Hall, *Adolescence*, 1904

- John Dewey, "A Policy of Industrial Education," 1914

- David Snedden, "Vocational Education," 1915

- John Dewey, "Education vs. Trade-Training—Dr. Dewey's Reply," 1915

- National Education Association, *Cardinal Principles of Secondary Education*, 1918

- Thomas Edison Predicts Film Will Replace Teacher, Books, 1923

- William Jennings Bryan, "Who Shall Control?", 1925

- James Bryant Conant, *The American High School Today*, 1959

Introduction

The opening of Boston's English Classical High School in 1821 is usually noted as the date when the American high school was born. The reality is that the new high school was created to give Boston boys an alternative to the much older Boston Latin School that had been founded in 1635, which, in time, also became a high school. As the historian William Reese has noted, the English Classical High School was really an English-focused school designed for those who wanted a more practical education than the classical, college-preparatory curriculum offered at the venerable Latin School.

Nevertheless, in the decades after the 1820s more and more high schools were opened not only in Massachusetts—which had twenty-six high schools by 1840—but across the nation. Philadelphia opened Central High School to boys in 1838, followed in 1848 by its Girls High School. In Cleveland, Ohio, Central High School opened in 1846, followed a year later by a similar school in Cincinnati. Chicago High School opened in 1856. At the same time many older public schools, such as the already two-hundred-year-old Boston Latin School, and many long-established private academies transformed themselves into public high schools. To use a single date may be misleading, but in the 1820s and 1830s the public high school was emerging in several major cities as a new kind of school. Only much later did high schools spread to small towns and rural areas, but by the 1920s, nearly every town of any size saw the creation of a high school as a civic responsibility and a key to its respectability.

Figure 6.1 High School, Palmyra, Wisconsin. Courtesy of the Wisconsin Historical Society, Image ID 43450.

While a few cities, especially on the east coast of the United States, followed the Boston and Philadelphia models and opened single-sex schools, in most parts of the United States the model of Chicago, where the high school was coeducational from the beginning, was the norm. There were too few high school students to justify opening separate boys and girls schools. On the other hand, not only in the Deep South, but in many parts of the country, where a high school education was even offered for African Americans (which was far from universal), it was usually offered in separate, segregated, and nearly always second-rate schools.

High schools offered a curriculum that was significantly more advanced than the common schools—what we now think of as elementary schools—that had spread across the nation earlier in the century. Whatever one's future, for those who were lucky enough to attend, high school was a place to strengthen skill in reasoning and do more advanced study in English and mathematics. In most cases the nineteenth-century high schools offered college-preparatory courses, but also so-called English courses leading directly to the world of work in business, and often "normal courses" leading to a career in teaching. (Before long the high school normal course was the prime route to a career as an elementary teacher through the rest of the nineteenth century.) In most schools, the college-prep, English, and normal programs were found under the same roof, mixing students of both genders and many ultimate goals in one institutional setting.

For a twenty-first-century student for whom high schools are a permanent fixture, it is also important to remember that for much of their history only a tiny proportion of the nation's population attended high school. In 1892, as the Committee of Ten was debating its recommendations about the high school curriculum, less than 4 percent of eligible young people graduated from high school. By 1900 that number had risen to 6.3 percent, hardly an impressive amount. Indeed, part of what fueled the intensity of the debate between John Dewey and David Snedden that is included in this chapter is their mutual worry about the fact that as they wrote in 1914–1915, less than one-fifth of the nation's eligible young people graduated from high school. Though they represented quite different approaches to what should be done, both Dewey and Snedden were motivated by a desire to increase the number of young people completing some form of secondary education.

By the 1920s, as high school spread rapidly to many places which had not seen them before, high schools functioned as a source of civic pride. New high schools were often built at the very center of town in an imposing building meant to tell the world—or at least the part of the world that noticed—that the town was now a center of educational excellence.

At the same time, the widespread distribution of high schools brought controversy. In the 1910s and again in the 1920s, the nation's leading inventor, Thomas Edison, predicted that instruction would be much better and student interest stronger if motion pictures (which he had invented) replaced books and teachers as the means of instruction.

With the growth of schools, more and more people also became concerned with what was being taught in these schools and in many parts of the country. Biology texts and teachers teaching evolution became an especially heated topic. Some states banned the topic, including Tennessee where the famous Scopes Trial ignited a national debate about the teaching of evolution. This was not only about academic freedom and the scientific expertise of the teacher but, as William Jennings Bryan—who opposed such teaching—argued, a debate about who, in the end, decided the school curriculum.

It was only after World War I that high school graduation rates began to grow and only after World War II that the majority of the nation's youth received a high school diploma. The growth in the percentage of seventeen-year-olds who were high school graduates during these years was impressive. According to the United States Department of Commerce, the numbers are dramatic:

1920	16.3%
1930	28.8%
1940	49.0%
1950	57.4%
1960	63.4%
1970	75.6%

And while the percentage of adolescents who graduated from high school more or less stabilized at around three out of four between 1970 and 2000, it rose slightly to over 80 percent in the first decades of the twenty-first century. In addition, more and more young people are taking advantage of alternative programs, GED programs, and other routes to the equivalent of a diploma so that today a much higher percentage of those in their mid-twenties hold a high school diploma or its equivalent. High school today has become close to universal. Indeed much of the current concern about high school drop-out rates is fueled by the expectation that virtually everyone should attend and graduate from high school. Those who do not—and they are still many—are virtually guaranteed to be marginalized in the economy and the society for the rest of their lives.

But what does a high school diploma mean? And how did these schools come to have their place in the configuration of American educational institutions? A number of historians including Edward A. Krug, David F. Labaree, William J. Reese, Jurgen Herbst, as well as David L. Angus and Jeffrey E. Mirel have offered compelling portraits of the historical development of high schools in the nineteenth and twentieth centuries. Perhaps most useful for understanding the documents in this chapter is Herbert M. Kliebard's *The Struggle for the American Curriculum, 1893–1958*. Kliebard traces the major battles about what should be taught in high school from the end of the nineteenth century to the mid-twentieth century and describes most of the players who wrote the documents in this chapter.

In the 1890s, with some 6 or 7 percent of young people attending high school, and 3.5 percent graduating—less than half of whom went on to college—there began to be a growing tension around both the high school curriculum and the expectations that colleges were coming to have for high school graduates. In 1892 the National Education Association appointed a Committee on Secondary School Studies which came to be known as the Committee of Ten. The committee was initially appointed to deal with a very specific problem: Different colleges had widely differing admission requirements and high school leaders were finding it more and more difficult to offer a curriculum that prepared graduates to gain admission to institutions of higher education that had such widely differing requirements. Why couldn't the colleges agree on some basic requirements that would allow high schools to regularize their curricular offerings? The NEA appointed a committee to solve the problem and asked the president of Harvard, Charles W. Eliot, to chair it.

Eliot was happy to take on the assignment. But he also determined to use the committee to do more than bring uniformity to college entrance requirements. For Eliot this was an opportunity to argue for what he believed was a good education at every level and to critique what he saw as a growing tendency to sort and track students within high school according to assumptions about their future vocations. In the report that his committee issued, Eliot and his colleagues argued that there should be one basic high school curriculum for everyone—for those intending to go on to college and for those for whom high school—even only a year or two of high school—was the end of their formal education. He acknowledged that some students might stay with the curriculum longer than others, and might even take somewhat different courses while in school, but he insisted that all students studying the same subject study it in the same way and with the same degree of rigor. He feared that anything less would create grave divisions in society.

The Report of the Committee of Ten received much praise but also significant criticism for being impractical at a time when rapid industrialism was creating new divisions in the work lives of different Americans. Perhaps the sharpest critic of the report was G. Stanley Hall, then the president of Clark University in Worcester, Massachusetts, and one of the leaders in the new field of psychology. For Hall new developments in psychology meant that school leaders could—indeed, must—make distinctions between those fit for college and the "great army of incapables, shading down to those who should be in schools for the dullards or subnormal children." In Hall's opinion, to pretend that schools should offer the same education to all when some were meant for college and others were capable of much less, and to do so when science allowed the sorting of students to be done with new precision, was simply irresponsible. When Hall published what would be his magnum opus, *Adolescence,* in 1904, it included two volumes on all aspects of adolescents' psychological development but it also included a direct and very sharp critique of the report of the Committee of Ten that is included in this chapter.

The arguments between Eliot and Hall about the nature of the high school curriculum were hardly the end of the story. In 1914 when President Woodrow Wilson appointed a commission to study the future of vocational education, the debate was opened once again, if in slightly different form. The report that Wilson's commission issued called for federal funding of education for specific trades and industrial tasks. For John Dewey, this report represented a serious threat to democratic education. While Dewey had long advocated linking education more closely to the "real world," and using aspects of the trades and farming to help all children understand their studies in mathematics, history, English, and other fields in richer detail, he was opposed to using public schools for any kind of job training program. Making the school experience meaningful to students was at the heart of progressive education as Dewey saw it, but using schools, and public money, to slot students into specific trades was the height of anti-progressivism in his mind.

For David Snedden, Commissioner of Education in Massachusetts and a nationally recognized advocate of vocational education, Dewey's critique was "discouraging" to say the least. Snedden, following on Hall's earlier approach, believed that public schools needed to help students prepare for specific jobs depending on their ability and financial status. Indeed for Snedden it was irresponsible for schools to provide a general education, even a very good one, while leaving students on their own when it came to finding a career. What Dewey saw as the imposition of the needs of industrialists for trained workers on unsuspecting students, Snedden saw as the heart of a sane national policy in education.

The debate between these two educators, which took place in the pages of *The New Republic* in 1914 and 1915, represents a set of readings that offer insight into arguments that were taking place in the era of World War I but which have been echoed ever since. At the time, Snedden clearly won on the policy front. The Smith-Hughes Act that passed Congress and was signed by President Wilson in 1917 created a steady stream of federal funding—the first federal funding for education—that has continued to support vocational education programs in high schools to the present day.

As World War I was drawing to a close, the National Education Association issued another report on high schools, "The Cardinal Principles of Secondary Education." The Cardinal Principles were very different from the principles that had guided Eliot's committee twenty-five years earlier. The 1918 document called for a highly differentiated high school curriculum offering different students very different subjects and ways to study at a time when the high school population was growing in numbers. The "comprehensive high school" envisioned in this report was comprehensive in that all students gathered in the same place; but they gathered for very different programs. The unity envisioned in this report was not Eliot's unity in the study of traditional academic disciplines, but in the cultivation of a common understanding of family life, civic participation, and ethical character among all students. Compared to the work of the Committee of Ten, The Cardinal Principles envisions a radically different kind of high school, though both reports claimed that their version was the best kind of program for serving democratic ideals.

While many educators argued about the nature of high schools—what they should teach, how they should be organized, who they might serve—communities across the nation built high schools at a rapid pace and more and more students attended them. What had begun as an educational opportunity for residents of a few of the nation's largest urban areas became in the twentieth century an omnipresent part of the nation's educational landscape. No town was too small and few rural areas were too isolated to offer high school opportunities for their young people. And starting with the Great Depression, when jobs for young people were extremely scarce, and expanding rapidly with the baby boom generation after World War II, the vast majority of the nation's young people attended high school and most graduated by the time they were eighteen. The unique had become the national norm.

Not only did high schools become universal across America, but the institutional form of secondary education in the United States became surprisingly uniform. The coeducational comprehensive high schools offered courses for the college bound, for the "general population," and trade-specific vocational education for those who saw in their high school a key to a specific career in the trades. (Teacher preparation had long since moved from high schools to colleges and universities.) In the late 1950s when the Carnegie Corporation of New York asked James Bryant Conant to study the American high school, he found an amazing level of uniformity across the land; a uniformity all the more surprising because administrative control of high schools was not centralized at the federal or even the state level but in thousands of school boards and districts which had, to a surprising degree given their independence, adopted the same institutional model. A selection from Conant's 1959 *The American High School* in which he described the comprehensive high school of the mid-twentieth century rounds out the documents for this chapter and describes the post-World War II high school as it was seen through the eyes of this former college president.

NATIONAL EDUCATION ASSOCIATION, *REPORT OF THE COMMITTEE ON SECONDARY SCHOOL STUDIES* (THE COMMITTEE OF TEN), 1893

In his introduction to the Report of the Committee of Ten—created by the National Education Association and named for the number of its members—William T. Harris, then the United

States Commissioner of Education, wrote, "It has been agreed on all hands that the most defective part of the education in this country is that of secondary schools." Harris saw the Committee of Ten's work as important because, he said, it led educators "to a better understanding of what the pupil should study to gain the most from his work in school." Probably the most noted contribution of the report is its absolute insistence that "every subject which is taught at all in a secondary school should be taught in the same way and to the same extent to every pupil so long as he pursues it, no matter what the probable destination of the pupil may be, or at what point his education is to cease." No tracking or advanced or remedial courses would be allowed in a high school that followed the committee's recommendations. At the same time, as this selection from the report illustrates, the committee was well aware that their clause "as long as he pursues it" was significant. At the time they wrote, the majority of high school students stayed for at most two years and so they wanted to be sure that the first two years provided a broad general education for as many citizens as possible. In spite of the emphasis on uniformity, the authors of the report also sought student choice. In the committee's ideal high school not every student should take exactly the same subjects. But they were nevertheless clear. Whatever subjects a student did take should be taught in the same way and on the same schedule to all students taking them. Finally, the committee recommended major improvements in the preparation of teachers so that both elementary and secondary students could be taught by those who understood their subjects more fully. The Committee of Ten, led by Harvard's Charles W. Eliot, also appointed nine sub-committees of ten members each on different secondary school subjects. Thus one hundred educators, divided more or less equally between college faculty and high school principals and teachers—but all white men—participated in the deliberations that led to this report.

The Committee of Ten appointed at the meeting of the National Educational Association at Saratoga on the 9th of July, 1892, have the honor to present the following report:— . . .

Anyone who reads these nine reports consecutively will be struck with the fact that all these bodies of experts desire to have the elements of their several subjects taught earlier than they are now; and that the Conferences on all the subjects except the languages desire to have given in the elementary schools what may be called perspective views, or broad surveys, of their respective subjects—expecting that in later-years of the school course parts of these same subjects will be taken up with more amplitude and detail. The Conferences on Latin, Greek, and the Modern Languages agree in desiring to have the study of foreign languages begin at a much earlier age than now,—the Latin Conference suggesting by a reference to the European usage that Latin be begun from three to five years earlier than it commonly is now. The Conference on Mathematics wish to have given in elementary schools not only a general survey of arithmetic, but also the elements of algebra, and concrete geometry in connection with drawing. The Conference on Physics, Chemistry, and Astronomy urge that nature studies should constitute an important part of the elementary school course from the very beginning. The Conference on Natural History [Biology] wish the elements of botany and zoology to be taught in the primary schools. The Conference on History wish the systematic study of history to begin as early as the tenth year of age, and the first two years of study to be devoted to mythology and to biography for the illustration of general history as well as of American history. Finally, the Conference on Geography recommended that the earlier course treat broadly of the earth, its environment and inhabitants, extending freely into fields which in later years of study are recognized as belonging to separate sciences . . .

On one very important question of general policy which affects profoundly the preparation of all school programmes, the Committee of Ten and all the Conferences are absolutely unanimous. Among the questions suggested for discussion in each Conference were the following:—

1. Should the subject be treated differently for pupils who are going to college, for those who are going to a scientific school, and for those who, presumably, are going to neither?
2. At what age should this differentiation begin, if any be recommended?

The [1st] question is answered unanimously in the negative by the Conferences, and the [2nd] therefore needs no answer. The Committee of Ten unanimously agree with the Conferences. Ninety-eight teachers, intimately concerned either with the actual work of American secondary schools, or with the results of that work as they appear in students who come to college, unanimously declare that every subject which is taught at all in a secondary school should be taught in the same way, and to the same extent to every pupil so long as he pursues it, no matter what the probable destination of the pupil may be, or at what point his education may cease. Thus, for all pupils who study Latin, or history, or algebra, for example, the allotment of time and the method of instruction in a given school should be the same year by year. Not that all the pupils should pursue every subject for the same number of years; but so long as they do pursue it, they should all be treated alike. It has been a very general custom in American high schools and academies to make up separate courses of study for pupils of supposed different destinations, the proportions of the several studies in the different courses being various. The principle laid down by the Conferences will, if logically carried out, make a great simplification in secondary school programmes. It will lead to each subject's being treated by the school in the same way by the year for all pupils, and this, whether the individual pupil be required to choose between courses which run through several years, or be allowed some choice among subjects year by year . . .

At this point it is well to call attention to the list of subjects which the Conferences deal with as proper for secondary schools. They are: 1. languages—Latin, Greek, English, German, and French, (and locally Spanish); 2. mathematics—algebra, geometry, and trigonometry; 3. general history, and the intensive study of special epochs; 4. natural history—including descriptive astronomy, meteorology, botany, zoology, physiology, geology, and ethnology, most of which subjects may be conveniently grouped under the title of physical geography; and 5. physics and chemistry. The Committee of Ten assent to this list, both for what it includes and for what it excludes, with some practical qualifications to be mentioned below.

Table [6.1] exhibits the total amount of instruction (estimated by the number of weekly periods, assigned to each subject) to be given in a secondary school during each year of a four years' course, on the supposition that the recommendations of the Conferences are all carried out.

Table 6.1 The total amount of instruction to be given in a secondary school during each year of a four-year course

1st Secondary School Year	2nd Secondary School Year
Latin . . . . 5 p.	Latin . . . . 5 p.
English Literature, 3 p. . . . . 5 p.	Greek. . . . . 5 p.
" Composition 2 p.	English Literature, 3 p. . . . . 5 p.
German or French . . . . 4 p.	" Composition 2 p.
Algebra . . . . 5 p.	German. . . . . 4 p.
History . . . . 3 p.	French. . . . . 4 p.
<div align="right">22 p.</div>	Algebra* 2½ p. . . . . 5 p.
	Geometry, 2 ½ p.
	Astronomy (12 weeks) . . . . 5 p.
	Botany or Zoology . . . . 5 p.
	History . . . . 3 p.
	<div align="right">37 ½ p.</div>
	* Option of book-keeping and commercial arithmetic.
3rd Secondary School Year	4th Secondary School Year
Latin . . . . 5 p.	Latin . . . . 5 p.
Greek. . . . . 4 p.	Greek. . . . . 4 p.
English Literature, 3 p. . . . . 5 p.	English Literature, 3 p. . . . . 5 p.
" Composition 1 p.	" Composition 1 p.
Rhetoric 1 p.	Rhetoric 1 p.
German. . . . . 4 p.	German. . . . . 4 p.
French. . . . . 4 p.	French. . . . . 4 p.
Algebra* . . . . 2 ½ p.	Trigonometry, 2 p. ½ yr. . . . . 2 p.
Geometry . . . . 2 ½ p.	Higher Algebra, 2 p. ½ yr.
Chemistry. . . . . 5 p.	Physics . . . . 5 p.
History . . . . 3 p.	Anatomy, Physiology, and
<div align="right">35 p.</div>	Hygiene, ½ yr. . . . . 5 p.
* Option of book-keeping and commercial arithmetic.	History . . . . 3 p.
	Geol. or Physiography, 3 p.1/2 yr.
	Meteorology, 3 p.½ yr. . . . . 3 p.
	<div align="right">37 ½ p.</div>

Abbreviations: p. = a recitation period of 40–45 minutes.

Every one of these years, except the first, contains much more instruction than any one pupil can follow; but looking at the bearing of the table on the important question of educational expenditures, it is encouraging to observe that there are already many secondary schools in this country in which quite as many subjects are taught as are mentioned in this table, and in which there are more weekly periods of instruction provided for separate classes than are found in any year of the table. In some urban high schools which provide from five to nine different courses of three to five years each, and in some endowed secondary schools which maintain two or three separate courses called Classical, Latin-scientific, and English, or designated by similar titles, the total number of weekly periods of unrepeated instruction given to distinct classes is even now larger than the largest total of weekly periods found in Table [6.1]. The annual expenditure in such schools is sufficient to provide all the instruction called for by Table [6.1]. The suggestions of the Conferences presuppose that all the pupils of like intelligence and maturity in any subject study it in the same way and to the same extent, so long as they study it at all,—this being a point on which all the Conferences insist strongly. No provision is made, therefore, for teaching Latin, or algebra, or history to one portion of a class four times a week, and to another portion of the same class only thrice or twice a week. Such provisions are very common in American schools; but the recommendations of the Conferences, if put into effect, would do away with all expenditures of this sort . . .

With slight modifications, they would prepare pupils for admission to appropriate courses in any American college or university on the existing requirements; and they would also meet the new college requirements which are suggested below.

In preparing these programmes, the Committee were perfectly aware that it is impossible to make a satisfactory secondary school programme, limited to a period of four years, and founded on the present elementary school subjects and methods. In the opinion of the Committee, several subjects now reserved for high schools,—such as algebra, geometry, natural science, and foreign languages,—should be begun earlier than now, and therefore within the schools classified as elementary; or, as an alternative, the secondary school period should be made to begin two years earlier than at present, leaving six years instead of eight for the elementary school period. Under the present organization, elementary subjects and elementary methods are, in the judgment of the Committee, kept in use too long. They believed that this bifurcation [choices of some courses] should occur as late as possible, since the choice . . . often determines for life the youth's career. Moreover, they believed that it is possible to make this important decision for a boy on good grounds, only when he has had opportunity to exhibit his quality and discover his tastes by making excursions into all the principal fields of knowledge. The youth who has never studied any but his native language cannot know his own capacity for linguistic acquisition; and the youth who has never made a chemical or physical experiment cannot know whether or not he has a taste for exact science. The wisest teacher, or the most observant parent, can hardly predict with confidence a boy's gift for a subject which he has never touched. In these considerations the Committee found strong reasons for postponing bifurcation, and making the subjects of the first two years as truly representative as possible. Secondly, inasmuch as many boys and girls who begin the secondary school course do not stay in school more than two years, the Committee thought it important to select the studies of the first two years in such a way that linguistic, historical, mathematical, and scientific subjects should all be properly represented. Natural history being represented by physical geography, the Committee wished physics to represent the inorganic sciences of precision. The first two years of any one of the four programmes presented above will, in the judgment of the Committee, be highly profitable by themselves to children who can go no farther.

In the construction of the sample programmes the Committee adopted twenty as the maximum number of weekly periods, but with two qualifications, namely, that at least five of the twenty periods should be given to unprepared work, and that laboratory subjects should have double periods whenever that prolongation should be possible.

The omission of music, drawing, and elocution from the programmes offered by the Committee was not intended to imply that these subjects ought to receive no systematic attention. It was merely thought best to leave it to local school authorities to determine, without suggestions from the Committee, how these subjects should be introduced into the programmes in addition to the subjects reported on by the Conferences ...

One of the subjects which the Committee of Ten were directed to consider was requirements for admission to college; and particularly they were expected to report on uniform requirements for admission to colleges, as well as on a uniform secondary school programme. Almost all the Conferences have something to say about the best mode of testing the attainments of candidates at college admission examinations; and some of them, notably the Conferences on History and Geography, make very explicit declarations concerning the nature of college examinations. The improvements desired in the mode of testing the attainments of pupils who have pursued in the secondary schools the various subjects which enter into the course will be found clearly described under each subject in the several Conference reports; but there is a general principle concerning the relation of the secondary schools to colleges which the Committee of Ten, inspired and guided by the Conferences, feels it their duty to set forth with all possible distinctness.

The secondary schools of the United States, taken as a whole, do not exist for the purpose of preparing boys and girls for colleges. Only an insignificant percentage of the graduates of these schools go on to colleges or scientific schools. Their main function is to prepare for the duties of life that a small proportion of all the children in the country—a proportion small in number, but very important to the welfare of the nation—who show themselves able to profit by an education prolonged to the eighteenth year, and whose parents are able to support them while they remain so long at school. There are, to be sure, a few private or endowed secondary schools in the country, which make it their principal object to prepare students for the colleges and universities; but the number of these schools is relatively small. A secondary school programme intended for national use must therefore be made for those children whose education is not to be pursued beyond the secondary school. The preparation of a few pupils for college or scientific school should in the ordinary secondary school be the incidental, and not the principal object. At the same time, it is obviously desirable that the colleges and scientific schools should be accessible to all boys or girls who have completed creditably the secondary school course. Their parents often do not decide for them, four years before the college age, that they shall go to college, and they themselves may not, perhaps, feel the desire to continue their education until near the end of their school course. In order that any successful graduate of a good secondary school should be free to present himself at the gates of the college or scientific school of his choice, it is necessary that the colleges and scientific schools of the country should accept for admission to appropriate courses of their instruction the attainments of any youth who has passed creditably through a good secondary school course, no matter to what group of subjects he may have mainly devoted himself in the secondary school. As secondary school courses are now too often arranged, this is not a reasonable request to prefer to the colleges and scientific schools; because the pupils may now go through a secondary school course of a very feeble and scrappy nature—studying a little of many subjects and not much of any one, getting, perhaps, a little information in a variety of fields, but nothing which can be called a thorough training. Now the recommendations of the nine Conferences, if well carried out, might fairly be held to make all the main subjects taught in the secondary schools of equal rank for the purposes of admission to college or scientific school. They would all be taught consecutively and thoroughly, and would all be carried on in the same spirit; they would all be used for training the powers of observation, memory, expression, and reasoning; and they would all be good to that end, although differing among themselves in quality and substance . . . Every youth who entered college would have spent four years in studying a few subjects thoroughly; and, on the theory that all subjects are to be considered equivalent in educational rank for the purposes of admission to college, it would make no difference which subjects he had chosen from the programme—he would have had four years of strong and effective mental training . . .

Every reader of this report and of the reports of the nine Conferences will be satisfied that to carry out the improvements proposed more highly trained teachers will be needed than are now ordinarily to be found for the service of the elementary and secondary schools. The Committee of Ten desire to point out some of the means of procuring these better trained teachers. For the further instruction of teachers in actual service, three agencies already in existence may be much better utilized than they now are. The Summer Schools which many universities now maintain might be resorted to by much larger numbers of teachers, particularly if some aid, such as the payment of tuition fees and traveling expenses, should be given to teachers who are willing to devote half of their vacations to study, by the cities and towns which these teachers serve. Secondly, in all the towns and cities in which colleges and universities are planted, these colleges or universities may usefully give stated courses of instruction in the main subjects used in the elementary and secondary schools to teachers employed in those towns and cities. This is a reasonable service which the colleges and universities may render to their own communities. Thirdly, a superintendent who has himself become familiar with the best mode of teaching any one of the subjects which enter into the school course can always be a very useful instructor for the whole body of teachers under his charge. A real master of any one subject will always have many suggestions to make to teachers of other subjects. The same is true of the principal of a high school, or other leading teacher in a town or city. In every considerable city school system the best teacher in each department of instruction should be enabled to give part of his time to helping the other teachers by inspecting and criticizing their work, and showing them, both by precept and example, how to do it better.

In regard to preparing young men and women for the business of teaching, the country has a right to expect much more than it has yet obtained from the colleges and normal schools. The common expectation of attainment for pupils of the normal schools has been altogether too low the country over. The normal schools, as a class, themselves need better apparatus, libraries, programmes, and teachers. As to the colleges, it is quite as much an enlargement of sympathies as an improvement or apparatus or of teaching that they need. They ought to take more interest than they have heretofore done, not only in the secondary, but in the elementary schools; and they ought to take pains to fit men well for the duties of a school superintendent. They already train a considerable number of the best principals of high schools and academies; but this is not sufficient. They should take an active interest, through their presidents, professors, and other teachers, in improving the schools in their respective localities, and in contributing to the thorough discussion of all questions affecting the welfare of both the elementary and the secondary schools.

National Education Association, Report of the Committee on Secondary School Studies, Washington, DC: U.S. Government Printing Office, 1893, pp. 14–17, 36–39, 44–54.

G. Stanley Hall, *Adolescence*, 1904

G. Stanley Hall is often referred to as the "father of American psychology" and remembered for bringing Sigmund Freud on his only trip to America. Among other things, Hall played a major role in enshrining "adolescence" as a distinct developmental period for those in transition from childhood to adulthood and his two-volume study of that title was considered definitive for decades. While exploring what he called the "psychology, anthropology, sociology, sex, crime, religion, and education" of adolescents, Hall also took time to explore the current state and future needs of adolescent education. In the process he challenged virtually every aspect of the Report of the Committee of Ten. While some of Hall's language seems terribly disparaging of students, his call for differentiated instruction, for building on students' enthusiasms, and for avoiding the dominance of the college curriculum in the life of high schools foreshadows many of the concerns of the progressive educators and their successors in future generations.

The last decade has witnessed a remarkable new movement on the part of colleges to influence high schools, which began with the Report of the Committee of Ten, printed in 1893. We have also had Reports of the Committee of Seven, Nine, Twelve, Fourteen, Fifteen, besides that of the National Education Association in 1890 on entrance requirements which invoked the aid of the American Historical and Philological Associations. In general these influences have worked from above downward, the dominating influence and the initiative in most cases coming from colleges or universities. That this movement did good for a time no one can deny. It has made many junctures between secondary and higher education; greatly increased the interest of faculties in high schools; given the former fruitful pedagogic themes for their own discussions; brought about a more friendly feeling and better mutual acquaintance; given slow colleges a wholesome stimulus; made school courses richer, given them better logical sequence; detected many weak points; closed many gaps; defined standards of what education means; brought great advantages from uniformity and cooperation, and no doubt, on the whole, has improved the conditions of college entrance examinations and aided in continuity.

One interesting result is the standardizing of high school knowledge, as hardware and even agricultural products, foodstuffs and machines are standardized by sizes, weight, and other measures—six weeks, twelve chapters, four or six hundred pages, forty weeks, eighteen courses, seventy experiments, four hours a week, three and four years of preparatory study, with 3,200 periods, fifteen credits, age eighteen, average mark seventy, so many Latin and Greek words to learn a month, so many minutes of recitation, home work, courses, text-books and examination tests all reduced to arithmetical or quantified dimensions. Knowledge is no longer bullion from the mine, but is minted with a hall-mark of at least some numerical committee. Everything must count and so much, for herein lies its educational value. There is no more wild, free, vigorous growth of the forest, but everything is in pots or rows like a rococo garden. Intellectual pabulum has lost all gamey flavor and is stall-fed or canned. These bales or blocks of condensed and enriched knowledge, which are used to calibrate the youthful mind or test its lifting or carrying power, seem to it stale; the stints become monotonous, mechanical, factory work to the pupil but to the teacher they acquire an excessive value, as if the world of knowledge had been canonized and certain things set apart as more sacred than other fields of knowledge. Some institutions allow more options between the blocks and assert greater freedom because they offer more patterns and more sizes of essentially the same material. Such scientific goods as can be metered, inspected, and examined by mass methods, tabulated and schematized, always soon seem shopworn to youth who want somewhere room for individuality, if not for distinction, and resist curricularization and, as the French call it, the canalization of knowledge. The pupil is in the age of spontaneous variation which at no period of life is so great. He does not want a standardized, overpeptonized mental diet. It palls on his appetite. He suffers from mental *ennui* and dyspepsia, and this is why so many and an increasing number refuse some of the best prepared courses . . . As we saw above, truancy is often due to a restlessness which, all unconscious of the cause, is really where the home dietary lacks nutritiousness. To enforce a curriculum without interest suggests the dream of a great Leipzig psychologist who predicted that sometime foods could be prepared so like chyme as to be inserted into the veins through a stop-cock, dispensing with the digestive function of the alimentary canal, and thus the time of eating would be saved and energy set free for a new upward march of culture greater even than that caused by cooking and the control of fire which the legend of Prometheus marks. It is now often painful to set limits to science, and results as surprising as all these may emerge in the future, but they will be different and by yet undiscovered methods. Once beneficent, college entrance requirements, as now enforced in some parts of our country and in some respects, are almost an unmitigated curse to high schools, exploiting them against their normal interests and the purpose of the people who support them, and thus perverting their natural development, enforcing artifacts of both method and matter, and sacrificing the interests of the vast majority who will never *go* to college.

This invasion and subjection has been rendered plausible even to its victims by three extraordinary fallacies. *(a)* The Committee of Ten "unanimously declare that every subject which is taught at all in a secondary school should be taught in the same way and to the same extent to every pupil so long as he pursues it, no matter what the probable destination of the pupil may be or at what point his education is to cease." This is a masterpiece of college policy. But in the first place this principle does not apply to the great army of incapables, shading down to those who should be in schools for dullards or subnormal children, for whose mental development heredity decrees a slow pace and early arrest, and for whom by general consent both studies and methods must be different. To refuse this concession to the wide range of individual differences is a specious delusion, which in a democracy may be perfectly honest. Difficulties must be omitted, the interest of the hour more appealed to, illustrations multiplied, and different beginnings, means, and goals early sought. Nor does this principle, of course, apply to geniuses. The school is not constructed for such. They go by leaps and find their own way. We must consider, then, only pupils that lie between these extremes. Again, this is unknown in other lands, where it would bring the direst confusion. European systems seem constructed on the converse principle that subjects should be approached in as many different ways as there are ultimate goals, while choices between academic and other careers are made before the teens, and methods and matter in the same topics diverge increasingly up the grades . . . With all this precious development the principle of the Committee of Ten would make havoc, lacking as it does all proper conception of the magnitude of each science and its vast variety of approaches. In topics like astronomy and physics, even the question where to begin the mathematical side, how much stress to lay upon it, or whether to omit it entirely, like Tyndall, is largely a problem of destination.

(b) Closely associated with this is the principle that "all subjects are of equal educational value if taught equally well." This, too, has been reiterated until with some it has almost become a dogma . . . The history of education is rich in warnings, but I can recall no fallacy that so completely evicts content and enthrones form. If true, the greatest educational battles from the Greeks to the present time have been fought for naught, and seas of pedagogic ink will have been spilled in vain.

(c) Another related surd that has acquired wide vogue and wrought only mischief is that fitting for college is essentially the same as fitting for life. Indeed, life, it is said, is preparing for an examination. The lawyer crams for his cases; the doctor for his critical trials; the business man for crises. Life itself is an examination. Therefore, that state of man where he is fitting for college is really the best school for life. This involves the colossal assumption that the college has so adjusted itself to the demands of the world as it now is . . . Here the counter assertion is that to fit for present entrance examinations involves an at least temporary unfitting for life. It is too sedentary, clerical, bookish, and noetic, and above all, arbitrary and by an alien master who offers at best only a limited range of choices, all of which may fail to appeal to the best powers of youth. Life is not coaching nor cramming, and very few of its tests consist in getting up subjects and writing them, while too many examinations stunt and clog, and if too prolonged, make real life seem tenuous and afar because it lacks the vital element of decision and application . . .

These three so-called principles thus turn out to be only clever recruiting precepts, special pleas of able advocates holding briefs for the college rather than the judicial decisions of educational statesmanship. The strategists of this policy urge that social classes are favored by European schools, and that it is an American idea of unique value that every boy should as long as possible feel that he is on the high road to the bachelor's degree and will reach it, if he does not stop, just as we teach that he may become president, but they ignore the fact that there are as great differences in natural ability as those artificially created in any aristocracy, and that the very life of a republic depends on bringing these out, in learning how to detect betimes, and give the very best training to, those fittest for leadership . . . It is an infinitely greater problem to fit for life than to fit for college, and requires far more thought and a larger accumulation of experiences. It was natural, therefore, that college interests, which are so simple and easy, should be the first on the ground and should come to power. The evils of this dominance are now so great and manifest that they must be transient.

G. Stanley Hall, *Adolescence: Its Psychology and Its Relations to Physiology, Anthropology, Sociology, Sex, Crime, Religion and Education*, two volumes, New York: D. Appleton, 1904, Vol. II, pp. 508–515.

JOHN DEWEY, "A POLICY OF INDUSTRIAL EDUCATION," 1914

By 1914, John Dewey was probably the best-known educator in the United States. In this article in the first volume of The New Republic, *Dewey outlined his concerns about the way education policy was developing in the United States in the second decade of the twentieth century, specifically the recommendations of a federal Commission on National Aid to Vocational Education; recommendations that would eventually lead to the Smith-Hughes Act of 1917. Dewey was deeply concerned with the direction of vocational education policy—a direction that he feared would be toward tax-supported training for specific jobs rather than the more progressive use of the world of work to make schooling interesting and engaging—"vital," he said— to all students, whatever their vocational futures. For Dewey, who was a major critic of the industrial system but a powerful advocate for making education more closely connected to the "real world," the choice was clear even if the nation was tending in the opposite direction.*

The habitual American attitude towards public education is, to say the least, paradoxical. Belief in publicly supported education is the most vital article of the average citizen's creed. Money devoted to educational purposes makes the largest item in the budget, and payment of taxes for school purposes is accompanied with the least amount of grumbling. The man who ridicules his legislature, who is suspicious of his judiciary and openly flouts his police system, is enthusiastic about public education. But the connection of the public with its schools ends for the most part with their support. There is next to no provision for public control, and that little is generally felt to be a nuisance when it extends to activities beyond the financial support of the schools under its nominal charge. The direction of educational policy is no part of statesmanship; the divorce of school from politics—which presumably means matters of public policy—is thought to represent the ideal state of things. Educators have reciprocated by taking an astonishingly slight interest in the public functions attached to their own work. Social settlements, amateur philanthropists and voluntary associations, rather than professional educators, have agitated the questions of child labor and juvenile crime, of adequate recreative facilities and the wider use of the school plant, and even of preparation for making a livelihood . . .

The reasons thus far advanced for making industrial training an organic part of public school education are an undigested medley. The need for a substitute for the disappearing apprenticeship system, the demand of employers for more skilled workers, the importance of special training if the United States is to hold its own in international competitive commerce, figure side by side with the educational need of making instruction more "vital" to pupils.

The oft-cited experience of Germany as to the importance of industrial education must be weighed in connection with the purpose which has dominated her efforts. This has been frankly nationalistic. The available statistics indicate that the effect of industrial education upon wages has been almost negligible, skilled workers receiving but little more than unskilled. But the effect of industrial education upon the worker's individual wage or happiness was not the animating motive. Germans claim with justice that their systematized and persistent applications of intelligence to military affairs, public education, civic administration, and trade and commerce, have a common root and a converging aim. The wellbeing of the state as a moral entity is supreme. The promotion of commerce against international competitors is one of the chief means of fostering the state. Industrial training is a means to this means, and one made peculiarly necessary by Germany's natural disadvantages.

One does not need to grudge admiration for the skill and success with which this policy has been pursued. But as a policy it is extraordinarily irrelevant to American conditions. We have neither the historic background nor the practical outlook which make it significant. There is grave danger that holding up as a model the educational methods by which Germany has made its policy effective will serve as a cloak, conscious or unconscious, for measures calculated to promote the interests of the employing class. It is the privilege of large employers of labor to supplement public schooling by classes which they themselves support in order to give the special knowledge and skill required in their operations. There are many interesting and successful attempts of this kind. It is natural that employers should be desirous of shifting the burden of this preparation to the public tax-levy. There is every reason why the community should not permit them to do so. Class against class, there is no reason why the community should be more interested in the laboring class than the employing class, save the important reason that the former constitutes a larger part of itself. But every ground of public policy protests against any use of the public school system which takes for granted the perpetuity of the existing industrial regime, and whose inevitable effect is to perpetuate it, with all its antagonisms of employer and employed, producer and consumer.

In the lack of enlightened public opinion as to the place of industrial training in the public schools in a would-be democracy, even the enumeration of commonplaces may be of some help; unfortunately they are not as yet current commonplaces. In the first place, its aim must be first of all to keep youth under educative influences for a longer time. Were it not for historic causes which explain the fact, it would be a disgrace that the larger portion of the school population leaves school at the end of the fifth or sixth grade. Irrespective of its causes, the continuance of this situation is a menace. Meagre as are the efforts already put forth in adapting industry to educational ends, it is demonstrated in Chicago, Gary and Cincinnati, that such adaptation is the first need for holding pupils in school and making their instruction significant to them. In these places the aim has not been to turn schools into preliminary factories supported at public expense, but to borrow from shops the resources and motives which make teaching more effective and wider in reach.

In the second place, the aim must be efficiency of industrial intelligence, rather than technical trade efficiency. Schemes for industrial education thus far propounded ignore with astonishing unanimity many of the chief features of the present situation. The main problem is not that of providing skilled workers in the superior crafts. Taken by itself, this is a comparatively simple problem. But it cannot be taken by itself, for the reason that these crafts are the ones already best organized and most jealous of efforts to recruit their numbers beyond the market demand, and for the reason also that automatic machinery is constantly invading the province of specially trained skill of hand and eye. Wherever automatic machines develop, high specialization of work follows. In the larger cities even the building trades now represent a grouping of a very larger number of separate occupations, demanding for the most part simple skill in managing machines. The automobile is a complicated machine, nevertheless ninety-five percent of the labor of manufacture in the cheaper cars is unskilled. Such facts are typical. The rapid change by means of new inventions of the forms of machine industry is another controlling consideration. The mobility of the laboring populations in passing from one mode of machine work to another is important. Such facts cry aloud against any trade-training which is more than an incidental part of a more general plan of industrial education. They speak for the necessity of an education whose chief purpose is to develop initiative and personal resources of intelligence. The same forces which have broken down the apprenticeship system render futile a scholastic imitation of it.

In a word, the problem in this country is primarily an educational one and not a business and technical one as in Germany. It is nothing less than the problem of the reorganization of the public school to meet the changed conditions due to the industrial revolution. In view of this consideration, the absence of all educators from the Commission on National Aid to Vocational Education has a peculiar significance. Professional educators are not free from blame, because of their indisposition to face the question of educational reorganization. But to leave educators out of the discussion of an educational problem is a curious proceeding. They will have to take a larger share in the execution of any plan which may be adopted. If they cannot be trusted to have a responsible share in the making of the plan, the chances of their successful execution of it are indeed slight. The situation also adds peculiar significance to the fact that the Commissioner of Education is made by the bill an executive clerk of various departments of the Government which have direct concern with certain forms of industry but none with education. It is not an immediately important question whether there be a minister of education in the Cabinet. It is a fundamentally important question whether or not a Federal policy with respect to industrial education be initiated which relegates the educational interest to the background.

The New Republic, December 19, 1914, pp. 11–12.

DAVID SNEDDEN, "VOCATIONAL EDUCATION," 1915

David Snedden, Commissioner of Education in Massachusetts, was also a nationally recognized educator in 1915. Snedden considered himself a progressive educator and admired Dewey. But Dewey's New Republic *critique struck a nerve with Snedden. Only a few months after it appeared, he answered it in the same journal. Just at the moment when advocates of vocational education saw federal support as a real possibility, here was Dewey acting as a critic. Unlike Dewey, Snedden valued a program of vocational education that was designed to prepare a young person for a specific job. The more advanced professions—lawyers, physicians, architects, etc.—had long had such specific preparation. Why not, Snedden asked, future workers in factories and farms? And why shouldn't the specific industries, rather than educators, have control of such educational programs? For Snedden and many like him, the need for the United States to develop a strong program of vocational education was critical and they did not mean to have anyone, even someone they admired as much as John Dewey, stand in their way.*

Sir: Some of us school men, who have profound respect for the insight of Dr. Dewey where the underlying principles of social organization and of education are under discussion, are somewhat bewildered on reading the contributions which he has recently made to *The New Republic*. Those of us who have been seeking to promote the development of sound vocational education in schools have become accustomed to the opposition of our academic brethren, who, perhaps unconsciously still reflect the very ancient and very enduring lack of sympathy, and even the antipathy, of educated men towards common callings, "menial" pursuits and "dirty trades." We have even reconciled ourselves to the endless misrepresentations of numerous reactionaries and of the beneficiaries of vested educational interests and traditions. But to find Dr. Dewey apparently giving aid and comfort to the opponents of a broader, richer and more effective program of education, and apparently misapprehending the motives of many of those who advocate the extension of vocational education in schools designed for that purpose, is discouraging.

To many of us the question of the so-called dual or unit control are not fundamental at all. The fundamental questions are, first, as to what constitutes sound pedagogic theories as to the aims and methods suited to vocational education in schools, and secondly, the most effective organization and administration of the means designed to realize them. There are fewer mysterious and uncertain features in vocational education, whether carried on by schools or by other agencies, when such education is rightly interpreted and defined, than in the fields of the so-called general or liberal education. Vocational education—not as carried on in schools, of course—is the oldest as well as even yet the most widely distributed form of education of all, since all grown men and women have always had vocations for which, with some measure of purposiveness, they have been trained in the home, the field, the workshop, the commercial establishment or on shipboard. Vocational education is, irreducibly and without unnecessary mystification, education for the pursuit of an occupation. In all stages of social development men have always sought, with more or less conscious method, to train their youth efficiently to follow a vocation—to hunt, fight, fish, farm, work metals, weave, bake, trade, transport, teach, heal, lead in worship or to govern. Vocational education is not all of education—never was that fact more clearly recognized than to-day; but vocational education at the right time and of the right kind is supremely important—and of that fact we have recently been in danger of losing sight. Hence questions as to what constitutes right vocational education, when and by whom it shall be given, and how it shall be effectively correlated with other forms of education, are just now of the greatest importance.

It has long been recognized that vocational education for many of the leading callings could no longer be successfully carried on by the historic methods of apprenticeship. Hence have appeared in succession vocational schools for the training of lawyers, theologians, military leaders, physicians, pharmacists, dentists, teachers, engineers, navigators, accountants, architects, telegraphers, stenographers and many others. Vocational schools for delinquents and for children without homes were organized many years ago by philanthropists. More recently the state itself has entered this field. In many of our cities far-sighted men have been active in establishing vocational trade schools as a means of extending educational opportunities.

Now, many of us have been forced, and often reluctantly, to the conclusion that if we are to have vocational education for the rank and file of our youth as well as for the favored classes, we shall be obliged to provide special vocational schools for this purpose, because the historic agencies of apprenticeship training have in most cases become less rather than more effective as means of sound vocational education. A few industries are indeed still so organized as to be able to give good vocational education, and it may be that as a result of movements now taking place others will readjust themselves so that in them workers can be assured of progressive development of their capacities.

But in general, modern economic conditions are such as to impair rather than enhance the capacity of employers to give satisfactory vocational training. The mobility of labor has enormously increased in the western world, and more particularly in America. Competition among the various units of a given industry has, with rare exceptions, become keener, and the success of a given employer is often dependent upon his ability to attract immigrant labor or to lure skilled workmen away from his competitors. American manufacturers have long been accustomed to await a supply of foremen and competent workmen from European countries. Western railroads by paying higher wages attract firemen, engineers and mechanics away from Eastern roads. The city employer tempts county-trained hands.

There are some indications that a wise cooperation among employers, now beginning to be manifested in certain fields, will soon remedy this condition of affairs. Already the printers of America have joined forces to establish vocational schools for their apprentices. Railroads are stealing workmen from each other far less than formerly, and some of them now systematically train their own workmen. A few large manufacturers have established successful schools for machinists. But is it not yet clear just how far this movement can be carried, in view of the competitive conditions still persisting in such fields as the building trades, the manufacturing of textiles, the food-packing industries and numerous smaller lines of manufacture. It is hardly to be expected that government can effectively force all employers to cooperate in the important function of training workers.

The function of the state in this as in other fields of education is clear. The state should consider the good of the individual and the needs of society, and where private agencies cannot accomplish a desired end the collective action of the state must be enlisted for this purpose. This is fundamentally the reason why the various commonwealths of the United States now, in greater or less degree, assist such special forms of vocational education as engineering, agriculture and even law and medicine. Massachusetts, usually conservative as regards state support of higher schools, nevertheless maintains a free agricultural college, makes large contributions towards engineering education, and supports three schools designed for the training of leaders in the textile industries . . .

When and under what conditions a youth should be permitted to enter a vocational school is debatable. In Massachusetts the law carefully provides that a youth shall be eligible to enter a vocational school only at the time when he is equally eligible to leave the regular public schools and to become a factory or farm hand. The administrative theory under which Massachusetts vocational schools are being conducted assumes that the youth ready to embark on wage-earning who instead turns aside for a period in a vocational school, should be able to concentrate his efforts largely in learning the occupation selected. It is not desirable to blend so-called liberal and vocational education at this period, it being always within the possibilities of the youth to continue in the regular or general elementary or high school if he so elects.

It is sometimes asserted that vocational education given by schools under state support is beneficial chiefly to employers. It is incredible that men acquainted with the economic conditions of our time, the competition of employers for labor and the mobility of labor itself, should take this view. In every occupation in the country there is constant competition for superior ability, as is manifested in the varying wage rates usually found. The only sound point of view is to regard vocational education as being primarily of significance to the boys and girls concerned, and ultimately, of course, to society as a whole. If vocational education does not result in greater productive capacity, and if greater productive capacity does not result in a larger share to the laborer, then, indeed, are the times very much out of joint.

If vocational education is to be successfully established in those states where academic tradition strongly persists, it may prove absolutely essential that some form of separate control should, at least temporarily, be inaugurated with a view to obtaining the best results. School men, however well-intentioned, are apt to be impractical and to fail to appreciate actual conditions.

Some successful beginnings of vocational education of the kind discussed in this paper have been made in Massachusetts. The present stage of development would not have been reached if it had not been for the activities of the Commission on Industrial Education during the years 1906 to 1910. The ultimate merger of this body with the Board of Education may have represented what should happen in every state after particular forms of development have arrived at some degree of maturity.

The New Republic, May 15, 1915, pp. 40–42.

John Dewey, "Education vs. Trade-Training— Dr. Dewey's Reply," 1915

The editors of The New Republic *invited Dewey to respond to Snedden's critique of his article and Dewey's reply was published side by side with Snedden's piece in May 1915. Responding to criticism forced Dewey to sharpen his own rhetoric. In this piece his distrust of any form of education that predetermines the vocational future for a young person still in their teens is clear. But more than that, Dewey distrusted an education designed to slot future workers into current industrial positions when the purpose of democratic education, he said, should be the "development of such intelligent initiative, ingenuity and executive capacity as shall make workers, as far as may be, the master of their own industrial fate." For Dewey such mastery included leading in the transformation of the nation's industrial order rather than accepting it as it existed. Although Dewey may have had the last word in* The New Republic, *Snedden's approach dominated the future of vocational education in the United States. Nevertheless, the debate has continued to raise its head many times in the century since the two educators first carried it on just prior to World War I.*

Sir: I have written unclearly indeed when Dr. Snedden interprets me as giving, even in appearance "aid and comfort to the opponents of a broader, richer and more effective program of education," or else Dr. Snedden has himself fallen a victim to the ambiguity of the word vocational. I would go farther than he is apparently willing to go in holding that education should be vocational, but in the name of a genuinely vocational education I object to the identification of vocation with such trades as can be learned before the age of say, eighteen or twenty; and to the identification of education with acquisition of specialized skill in the management of machines at the expense of an industrial intelligence based on science and a knowledge of social problems and conditions. I object to regarding as vocational education any training which does not have as its supreme regard the development of such intelligent initiative, ingenuity and executive capacity as shall make workers, as far as may be, the masters of their own industrial fate. I have my doubts about theological predestination, but at all events that dogma assigned predestinating power to an omniscient being; and I am utterly opposed to giving the power of social predestination, by means of narrow trade-training, to any group of fallible men no matter how well-intentioned they may be. Dr. Snedden has been fortunate if he has not met those who are not so well-intentioned, and if he is so situated that he believes that "the interests" are a myth of muckrakers and that none of "the interests" have any designs upon the control of educational machinery.

Dr. Snedden's criticisms of my articles seem to me couched in such general terms as not to touch their specific contentions. I argued that a separation of trade education and general education of youth has the inevitable tendency to make both kinds of training narrower, less significant and less effective than the schooling in which the material of traditional education is reorganized to utilize the industrial subject matter—active, scientific and social—of the present-day environment. Dr. Snedden would come nearer to meeting my points if he would indicate how such a separation is going to make education "broader, richer and more effective." If he will undertake this task there will be something specific to discuss. In order that the discussion may be really definite, I suggest that he tell the readers of *The New Republic* what he thinks of the Gary system, and whether he thinks this system would have been possible in any of its significant features except by a mutual interpretation of the factors of general education and of industry. And as his article may be interpreted as an apology for the Cooley bill in Illinois, I should like to ask him whether he is familiar with the educational reorganization going on in Chicago, and whether he thinks that it would be helped or hindered if the Chicago schools came under a dual administration, with one agency looking after a traditional bookish education and another after a specific training for mechanical trades. I should like to know, too, how such educational cleavage is to be avoided unless each type of school extends its work to duplicate that of the other type.

Apart from light on such specific questions, I am regretfully forced to the conclusion that the difference between us is not so much narrowly educational as it is profoundly political and social. The kind of vocational education in which I am interested is not one which will "adapt" workers to the existing industrial regime; I am not sufficiently in love with the regime for that. It seems to me that the business of all who would not be educational time-servers is to resist every move in this direction, and to strive for a kind of vocational education which will first alter the existing industrial system, and ultimately transform it.

I can readily understand how a practical administrator becomes impatient with the slowness of social processes and becomes eager for a short cut to desired results. He has a claim upon the sympathy of those who do not have to face the immediate problems. But as long as there are so many debatable questions as Dr. Snedden admits there are, and as long as conditions are as mobile as he indicates, it is surely well that those outside the immediate administrative field insist that particular moves having short-run issues in view be checked up by consideration of issues more fundamental although remoter.

The New Republic, May 15, 1915, pp. 42–43.

NATIONAL EDUCATION ASSOCIATION, *CARDINAL PRINCIPLES OF SECONDARY EDUCATION*, 1918

Where the Committee of Ten, led by Charles Eliot, had recommended that all high school students study basically the same subjects and do so in the same way, a very different National Education Association Committee, chaired by Clarence D. Kingsley, a former high school teacher from Brooklyn, New York who was then serving as David Snedden's assistant Commissioner of Education for high schools in Massachusetts, recommended a highly differentiated high school curriculum in their 1918 report on the Cardinal Principles of Secondary Education. This latter report, reflecting the findings of researchers in the new fields of psychology and testing as well as the move toward social efficiency in the curriculum, recommended a comprehensive high school in which different students would be taught different subjects in different ways. The goal here, unlike the earlier report, was a secondary curriculum that would help prepare students for the widely different roles in life that the report's authors were certain they were destined to find.

I. The Need for Reorganization

Secondary education should be determined by the needs of the society to be served, the character of the individuals to be educated, and the knowledge of educational theory and practice available. These factors are by no means static. Society is always in process of development; the character of the secondary-school population undergoes modification; and the sciences on which educational theory and practice depend constantly furnish new information. Secondary education, however, like any other established agency of society, is conservative and tends to resist modification. Failure to make adjustments when the need arises leads to the necessity for extensive reorganization at irregular intervals. The evidence is strong that such a comprehensive reorganization of secondary education is imperative at the present time.

1. *Changes in society.*—Within the past few decades changes have taken place in American life profoundly affecting the activities of the individual. As a citizen, he must to a greater extent and in a more direct way cope with problems of community life, State and National Governments, and international relationships. As a worker, he must adjust himself to a more complex economic order. As a relatively independent personality, he has more leisure. The problems arising from these three dominant phases of life are closely interrelated and call for a degree of intelligence and efficiency on the part of every citizen that can not be secured through elementary education alone, or even through secondary education unless the scope of that education is broadened.

   The responsibility of the secondary school is still further increased because many social agencies other than the school afford less stimulus for education than heretofore. In many vocations there have come such significant changes as the substitution of the factory system for the domestic system of industry; the use of machinery in place of manual labor; the high specialization of processes with a corresponding subdivision of labor; and the breakdown of the apprentice system. In connection with home and family life have frequently come lessened responsibility on the part of the children; the withdrawal of the father and sometimes the mother from home occupations to the factory or store; and increased urbanization, resulting in less unified family life. Similarly, many important changes have taken place in community life, in the church, in the State, and in other institutions. These changes in American life call for extensive modifications in secondary education.

2. *Changes in the secondary-school population.*—In the past 25 years there have been marked changes in the secondary-school population of the United States. The number of pupils has increased, according to Federal returns, from one for every 210 of the total population in 1889–90, to one for every 121 in 1899–1900, to one for every 89 in 1909–10, and to one for every 73 of the estimated total population in 1914–15. The character of the secondary-school population has been modified by the entrance of large numbers of pupils of widely varying capacities, aptitudes, social heredity, and destinies in life. Further, the broadening of the scope of secondary education has brought to the school many pupils who do not complete the full course but leave at various stages of advancement. The needs of these pupils can not be neglected, nor can we expect in the near future that all pupils will be able to complete the secondary school as fulltime students.

At present only about one-third of the pupils who enter the first year of the elementary school reach the four-year high school, and only about one in nine is graduated. Of those who enter the seventh school year, only one-half to two-thirds reach the first year of the four-year high school. Of those who enter the four-year high school about one-third leave before the beginning of the second year, about one-half are gone before the beginning of the third year, and fewer than one-third are graduated. These facts can no longer be safely ignored.

3. *Changes in educational theory.*—The sciences on which educational theory depends have within recent years made significant contributions. In particular, educational psychology emphasizes the following factors:

(a) *Individual differences in capacities and aptitudes among secondary-school pupils.*—Already recognized to some extent, this factor merits fuller attention.

(b) *The reexamination and reinterpretation of subject values and the teaching methods with reference to "general discipline."*—While the final verdict of modern psychology has not as yet been rendered, it is clear that former conceptions of "general values" must be thoroughly revised.

(c) *Importance of applying knowledge.*—Subject values and teaching methods must be tested in terms of the laws of learning and the application of knowledge to the activities of life, rather than primarily in terms of the demands of any subject as a logically organized science.

(d) *Continuity in the development of children.*—It has long been held that psychological changes at certain stages are so pronounced as to overshadow the continuity of development. On this basis secondary education has been sharply separated from elementary education. Modern psychology, however, goes to show that the development of the individual is in most respects a continuous process and that, therefore, any sudden or abrupt break between the elementary and the secondary school or between any two successive stages of education is undesirable.

The foregoing changes in society, in the character of the secondary school population, and in educational theory, together with many other considerations, call for extensive modifications of secondary education. Such modifications have already begun in part. The present need is for the formulation of a comprehensive program of reorganization, and its adoption, with suitable adjustments, in all the secondary schools of the Nation. Hence it is appropriate for a representative body like the National Education Association to outline such a program. This is the task entrusted by that association to the Commission on the Reorganization of Secondary Education.

II. The Goal of Education in a Democracy

Education in the United States should be guided by a clear conception of the meaning of democracy. It is the ideal of democracy that the individual and society may find fulfillment each in the other. Democracy sanctions neither the exploitation of the individual by society, nor the disregard of the interests of society by the individual. More explicitly—

The purpose of democracy is so to organize society that each member may develop his personality primarily through activities designed for the well-being of his fellow members and of society as a whole.

This ideal demands that human activities be placed upon a high level of efficiency; that to this efficiency be added an appreciation of the significance of these activities and loyalty to the best ideals involved; and that the individual choose that vocation and those forms of social service in which his personality may develop and become most effective. For the achievement of these ends democracy must place chief reliance upon education.

Consequently, education in a democracy, both within and without the school, should develop in each individual the knowledge, interests, ideals, habits, and powers whereby he will find his place and use that place to shape both himself and society toward ever nobler ends.

III. The Main Objectives of Education

In order to determine the main objectives that should guide education in a democracy, it is necessary to analyze the activities of the individual. Normally he is a member of a family, of a vocational group, and of various civic groups, and by virtue of these relationships he is called upon to engage in activities that enrich the family life, to render important vocational services to his fellows, and to promote the common welfare. It follows, therefore, that worthy home membership, vocation, and citizenship demand attention as three of the leading objectives.

Aside from the immediate discharge of these specific duties, every individual should have a margin of time for the cultivation of personal and social interests. This leisure, if worthily used, will recreate his powers and enlarge and enrich life, thereby making him better able to meet his responsibilities. The unworthy use of leisure impairs health, disrupts home life, lessens vocational efficiency, and destroys civic-mindedness. The tendency in industrial life, aided by legislation, is to decrease the working hours of large groups of people. While shortened hours tend to lessen the harmful reactions that arise from prolonged strain, they increase, if possible, the importance of preparation for leisure. In view of these considerations, education for the worthy use of leisure is of increasing importance as an objective.

To discharge the duties of life and to benefit from leisure, one must have good health. The health of the individual is essential also to the vitality of the race and to the defense of the Nation. Health education is, therefore, fundamental.

There are various processes, such as reading, writing, arithmetical computations, and oral and written expression, that are needed as tools in the affairs of life. Consequently, command of these fundamental processes, while not an end in itself, is nevertheless an indispensable objective.

And, finally, the realization of the objectives already named is dependent upon ethical character, that is, upon conduct founded upon right principles, clearly perceived and loyally adhered to. Good citizenship, vocational excellence, and the worthy use of leisure go hand in hand with ethical character; they are at once the fruits of sterling character and the channels through which such character is developed and made manifest. On the one hand, character is meaningless apart from the will to discharge the duties of life, and, on the other hand, there is no guaranty that these duties will be rightly discharged unless principles are substituted for impulses, however well-intentioned such impulses may be. Consequently, ethical character is at once involved in all the other objectives and at the same time requires specific consideration in any program of national education.

This commission, therefore, regards the following as the main objectives of education: 1. Health. 2. Command of fundamental processes. 3. Worthy home membership. 4. Vocation. 5. Citizenship. 6. Worthy use of leisure. 7. Ethical character.

The naming of the above objectives is not intended to imply that the process of education can be divided into separated fields. This can not be, since the pupil is indivisible. Nor is the analysis all-inclusive. Nevertheless, we believe that distinguishing and naming these objectives will aid in directing efforts; and we hold that they should constitute the principal aims in education.

IV. The Role of Secondary Education in Achieving these Objectives

The objectives outlined above apply to education as a whole—elementary, secondary, and higher. It is the purpose of this section to consider specifically the role of secondary education in achieving each of these objectives.

For reasons stated in Section X, this commission favors such reorganization that secondary education may be defined as applying to all pupils of approximately 12 to 18 years of age.

1. *Health*
2. *Command of fundamental processes*

3. *Worthy home membership.* This objective applies to both boys and girls. In the education of every high-school girl, the household arts should have a prominent place because of their importance to the girl herself and to others whose welfare will be directly in her keeping . . . In the education of boys, some opportunity should be found to give them a basis for the intelligent appreciation of the value of the well-appointed home and of the labor and skill required to maintain such a home, to the end that they may cooperate more effectively.
4. *Vocation*
5. *Civic education* should develop in the individual those qualities whereby he will act well his part as a member of neighborhood, town or city, State, and Nation, and give him a basis for understanding international problems.
6. *Worthy use of leisure*
7. *Ethical character*

VII. Education as a Process of Growth

Education must be conceived as a process of growth. Only when so conceived and so conducted can it become a preparation for life. In so far as this principle has been ignored, formalism and sterility have resulted.

For example, civic education too often has begun with topics remote from the pupil's experience and interest. Reacting against this formalism, some would have pupils study only those activities in which they can engage while young. This extreme, however, is neither necessary nor desirable. Pupils should be led to respond to present duties and, at the same time, their interest should be aroused in problems of adult life. With this interest as a basis, they should be helped to acquire the habits, insight, and ideals that will enable them to meet the duties and responsibilities of later life. Similarly in home-making education, to neglect present duties and responsibilities toward the family of which the pupil is now a member, is to court moral insincerity and jeopardize future right conduct. With present duties as a point of departure, home-making education should arouse an interest in future home-making activities and with that interest as a basis give the training necessary . . .

X. Division of Education into Elementary and Secondary

Individual differences in pupils and the varied needs of society alike demand that education be so varied as to touch the leading aspects of occupational, civic, and leisure life. To this end curriculums must be organized at appropriate stages and the work of pupils progressively differentiated.

To accomplish this differentiation most wisely the pupil should be assisted ordinarily at about 12 or 13 years of age to begin a preliminary survey of the activities of adult life and of his own aptitudes in connection therewith, so that he may choose, at least tentatively, some field of human endeavor for special consideration. Following the period of preliminary survey and provisional choice, he should acquire a more intimate knowledge of the field chosen, including therewith an appreciation of its social significance. Those whose schooling ends here should attain some mastery of the technique involved. The field chosen will be for some as sharply defined as a specific trade; for others, it will be but the preliminary choice of a wider domain within which a narrower choice will later be made.

These considerations, reinforced by others, imply, in the judgment of this commission, a redivision of the period devoted to elementary and secondary education. The eight years heretofore given to elementary education have not, as a rule, been effectively utilized. The last two of these years in particular have not been well adapted to the needs of the adolescent. Many pupils lose interest and either drop out of school altogether or form habits of dawdling, to the serious injury of subsequent work. We believe that much of the difficulty will be removed by a new type of secondary education beginning at about 12 or 13. Furthermore, the period of four years now allotted to the high school is too short a time in which to accomplish the work above outlined.

We, therefore, recommend a reorganization of the school system whereby the first six years shall be devoted to elementary education designed to meet the needs of pupils of approximately 6 to 12 years of age; and the second six years to secondary education designed to meet the needs of pupils of approximately 12 to 18 years of age . . .

XV. The Specializing and Unifying Functions of Secondary Education

1. *Their significance.*—The ideal of a democracy, as set forth in Section II of this report, involves on the one hand specialization whereby individuals and groups of individuals may become effective in the various vocations and other fields of human endeavor, and on the other hand unification whereby the members of that democracy may obtain those common ideas, common ideals, and common modes of thought, feeling, and action that make for cooperation, social cohesion, and social solidarity.

   Without effective specialization on the part of groups of individuals there can be no progress. Without unification in a democracy there can be no worthy community life and no concerted action for necessary social ends. Increasing specialization emphasizes the need for unification, without which a democracy is a prey to enemies at home and abroad.

2. *The specializing function.*—Secondary education in the past has met the needs of only a few groups. The growing recognition that progress in our American democracy depends in no small measure upon adequate provision for specialization in many fields is the chief cause leading to the present reorganization of secondary education. Only through attention to the needs of various groups of individuals as shown by aptitudes, abilities, and aspirations can the secondary school secure from each pupil his best efforts. The school must capitalize the dominant interest that each boy and girl has at the time and direct that interest as wisely as possible. This is the surest method by which hard and effective work may be obtained from each pupil.

   Specialization demands the following provisions in secondary education:

   (a) *A wide range of subjects.*—In order to test and develop the many important capacities and interests found in pupils of secondary-school age, the school should provide as wide a range of subjects as it can offer effectively.

   (b) *Exploration and guidance.*—Especially in the junior high school the pupil should have a variety of experience and contacts in order that he may explore his own capacities and aptitudes. Through a system of educational supervision or guidance he should be helped to determine his education and his vocation. These decisions should not be imposed upon him by others.

(c) *Adaptation of content and methods.*—The content and teaching methods of every study should be adapted to the capacities, interests, and needs of the pupils concerned. In certain studies these factors may differ widely for various groups of pupils, e.g., chemistry should emphasize different phases in agricultural, commercial, industrial, and household-arts curriculums.

(d) *Flexibility of organization and administration.*—Flexibility should be secured by "election" of studies or curriculum, promotion by subjects from the beginning of the junior high school, possible transfer from curriculum to curriculum, provision for maximum and minimum assignments for pupils of greater and less ability, and, under certain conditions, for the rapid or slow progress of such pupils.

(e) *Differentiated curriculums.*—The work of the senior high school should be organized into differentiated curriculums. The range of such curriculums should be as wide as the school can offer effectively. The basis of differentiation should be; in the broad sense of the term, vocational, thus justifying the names commonly given, such as agricultural, business, clerical, industrial, fine-arts, and household-arts curriculums. Provision should be made also for those having distinctively academic interests and needs. The conclusion that the work of the senior high school should be organized on the basis of curriculums does not imply that every study should be different in the various curriculums. Nor does it imply that every study should be determined by the dominant element of that curriculum. Indeed any such practice would ignore other objectives of education just as important as that of vocational efficiency.

3. *The unifying function.*—In some countries a common heredity, a strongly centralized government, and an established religion contribute to social solidarity. In America racial stocks are widely diversified, various forms of social heredity come into conflict, differing religious beliefs do not always make for unification, and the members of different vocations often fail to recognize the interests that they have in common with others. The school is the one agency that may be controlled definitely and consciously by our democracy for the purpose of unifying its people. In this process the secondary school must play an important part because the elementary school with its immature pupils can not alone develop the common knowledge, common ideals, and common interests essential to American democracy. Furthermore, children of immigrant parents attend the secondary school in large and increasing numbers; secondary education comes at a stage in the development of boys and girls when social interests develop rapidly; and from the secondary school the majority of pupils pass directly into participation in the activities of our society . . .

4. *Specialization and unification as supplementary functions.*—With increasing specialization in any society comes a corresponding necessity for increased attention to unification. So in the secondary school, increased attention to specialization calls for more purposeful plans for unification. When there was but little differentiation in the work within the secondary school, and the pupils in attendance were less diversified as

to their heredity and interests, social unification in the full sense of the term could not take place.

The supplementary character of these functions has direct bearing upon the subjects to be taken by secondary-school pupils. To this end the secondary school should provide the following groups of studies:

(a) *Constants*, to be taken by all or nearly all pupils. These should be determined mainly by the objectives of health, command of fundamental processes, worthy home-membership, citizenship, and ethical character.

(b) *Curriculum variables*, peculiar to a curriculum or to a group of related curriculums. These should be determined for the most part by vocational needs, including, as they frequently do, preparation for advanced study in special fields.

(c) *Free electives*, to be taken by pupils in accordance with individual aptitudes or special interests, generally of a nonvocational nature. These are significant, especially in preparation for the worthy use of leisure.

The constants should contribute definitely to unification, the curriculum variables to specialization, and the free electives to either or both of these functions . . .

XVI. The Comprehensive High School as The Standard Secondary School

The comprehensive (sometimes called composite, or cosmopolitan) high school, embracing all curriculums in one unified organization, should remain the standard type of secondary school in the United States.

Junior high schools must be of the comprehensive type, whatever policy be adopted for the senior high schools, since one of the primary purposes of the junior high school is to assist the pupil through a wide variety of contacts and experiences to obtain a basis for intelligent choice of his educational and vocational career. In the judgment of the commission senior high schools and four-year high schools of the older organizations should, as a rule, be of the comprehensive type . . .

XX. Conclusion

In concluding this report on the cardinal principles of secondary education the commission would call attention to its 17 other reports in which the principles herein set forth are applied to the various aspects of secondary education. The reports now available are listed on the last page of this bulletin, and others are nearly ready for publication. One report will consider in detail the application of these principles to the organization and administration of secondary schools. Thirteen reports deal with the aims, methods, and content of the various subjects of study and curriculums in the light of these principles. Three others discuss vocational guidance, physical education, and the moral values that should be derived from secondary school organization and instruction.

It is becoming increasingly apparent that the problems of secondary education merit much more serious attention than they have received heretofore. The study of the best methods for adapting secondary education to the needs of modern democratic life is but begun. The physical, intellectual, emotional, and ethical characteristics of young people are still but vaguely comprehended. Such knowledge of social needs and educational theory and practice as is already available has been seriously studied by comparatively few administrators and teachers. Progress will depend very largely upon adequate professional training of teachers both before and after entering upon service. Plans must be adopted for pooling the results of successful experimentation on the part of individual teachers. To make the reorganization effective, competent supervision and constructive leadership must be provided in the various fields of secondary education.

It is the firm belief of this commission that secondary education in the United States must aim at nothing less than complete and worthy living for all youth, and that therefore the objectives described herein must find place in the education of every boy and girl.

Finally, in the process of translating into daily practice the cardinal principles herein set forth, the secondary school teachers of the United States must themselves strive to explore the inner meaning of the great democratic movement now struggling for supremacy. The doctrine that each individual has a right to the opportunity to develop the best that is in him is reinforced by the belief in the potential, and perchance unique, worth of the individual. The task of education, as of life, is therefore to call forth that potential worth.

While seeking to evoke the distinctive excellencies of individuals and groups of individuals, the secondary school must be equally zealous to develop those common ideas, common ideals, and common modes of thought, feeling, and action, whereby America, through a rich, unified, common life, may render her truest service to a world seeking for democracy among men and nations.

National Education Association, *The Cardinal Principles of Secondary Education*, Department of the Interior, Bureau of Education, Bulletin No. 35, Washington, DC: Government Printing Office, 1918, pp. 7–18, 21–24, 31–32.

THOMAS EDISON PREDICTS FILM WILL REPLACE TEACHER, BOOKS, 1923

The rapid growth of schooling in the early twentieth century led to many predictions about the future, especially for high schools that demanded more specialized expertise by teachers and more effort at maintaining student interest. Thomas A. Edison, perhaps the most famous inventor in U.S. history, invented many things besides the electric light bulb including modern motion pictures. In 1913, Frederick James Smith, a newspaper reporter for the New York Dramatic Mirror, asked Edison, "What is your estimation of the future educational value of pictures?" Edison replied, "Books will soon be obsolete in the public schools. Scholars will be instructed through the eye. It is possible to teach every branch of human knowledge with the motion picture. Our school system will be completely changed inside of ten years." Ten years later, though his prediction had not yet come true, Edison repeated it in testimony to the U.S. Federal Trade Commission, though he allowed a longer time span for it to come to fruition.

(By The Associated Press.) New York, May 15, 1923. —The children of today's school children will get their education at school in which the movie screen will supplant the blackboard and the motion picture film will take the place of textbooks, Thomas A. Edison predicted today at the investigation by the federal trade commission of charges that the Famous-Players-Laskey corporation and six allied organizations constituted a motion picture, trust. The famous inventor whose recent questionnaires have led him to say harsh things about present educational methods in the United States was called for the purpose of developing the importance of the film industry and its possibilities for the future. He disclosed for the first time experiments with school children which he said had convinced him that 85 per cent of all knowledge is received through the eye and that motion pictures are 100 per cent efficient for its dissemination. "I have made a good many experiments in the line of teaching children by other methods than books," Mr. Edison told the commission. "I made an experiment with a lot of pictures to teach children chemistry. I got twelve children and asked them to write down what they had learned, from the pictures. I was amazed that such a complicated subject as chemistry was readily grasped by them to a large extent through pictures. The parts of the pictures they did not understand I did over and over again until they finally understood the entire picture. I think motion pictures have just started and it is my opinion that in 20 years children will be taught through pictures and not through textbooks," he said.

Monterey, Virginia *Recorder*, May 18, 1923, downloaded from the Virginia Chronicle/Library of Virginia (virginiachronicle.com), August 25, 2018.

William Jennings Bryan, "Who Shall Control?", 1925

William Jennings Bryan was nominated three times for president of the United States, but he is probably best known today for the last act of his career. In 1925 he volunteered to serve as a counsel for the prosecution at the famous Scopes Trial in Dayton, Tennessee, in which John T. Scopes was accused—and ultimately convicted—of teaching evolution in the town's high school although it was then against state law to do so. Bryan believed passionately that teaching evolution contributed to the arrogance of the rich (who claimed to be the most fit in society) and also undermined respect for religion. He also believed, perhaps even more strongly, that in a democratic society, the elected representatives had the right to control the curriculum of public schools and prohibit any topic they wished. In 1925, a week after the conclusion of the trial, he wrote the following article defending the Tennessee legislature's right to ban evolution.

The first question to be decided is: Who shall control our public schools? . . . Four sources of control have been suggested. The first is the people, speaking through their legislatures. That would seem to be the natural source of control. The people are sovereigns and governments derive their just powers from the consent of the governed . . . If not the legislatures, then who shall control? Boards of Education? It is the legislature that authorizes the election of boards . . . All authority goes back at last to the people; they are the final source of authority.

[But] Some have suggested that the scientists should decide what shall be taught . . . If the number [of scientists in the U.S.] is put at eleven thousand, it makes about one scientist for every ten thousand people—a pretty little oligarchy to put in control of the education of all the children . . .

The fourth source suggested is the teacher. Some say, let the teacher be supreme and teach anything that seems best to him . . . Professor Scopes, the defendant in the Tennessee case, has a right to think as he pleases—the law does not attempt to regulate his thinking. Professor Scopes was not arrested for doing anything as an individual. He was arrested for violating a law as a representative of the state and as an employee in a school . . . as an employee, he is compelled to act under the direction of his employers and has no right to defy instructions and still claim his salary.

William Jennings Bryan, "Who Shall Control?" (June 1925) in William Jennings Bryan and Mary Baird Bryan, *The Memoirs of William Jennings Bryan*, Philadelphia, PA: United Publishers of America, 1925, pp. 526–528; reprinted pp. 189–191.

JAMES BRYANT CONANT, *THE AMERICAN HIGH SCHOOL TODAY*, 1959

James Bryant Conant was one of the nation's most prestigious educators in 1957 when he accepted an invitation from John W. Gardner, President of the Carnegie Corporation of New York, to write a report on the state of American high schools. Conant had just stepped down as U.S. Ambassador to Germany, having been the president of Harvard University from 1933 to 1953. In the late 1950s more and more Americans were worried about the state of their high schools, and that worry only grew with the launch of Sputnik, the world's first space satellite by the Soviet Union in 1957. The year that Conant began his work was also the year in which the impact of the Supreme Court's Brown decision, ordering an end to legally segregated high schools, reached a crisis in Little Rock, Arkansas (see Chapter 10). Having such a leading educator tell the nation that the comprehensive high school, while in need of reform, was basically solid and here to stay was reassuring to many. Conant's report does not deal with the fact that many high schools in the nation were segregated by race in 1959. And he wrote before most educators were attending to the issues of socioeconomic and gender divisions in the schools (see Chapter 11). Nevertheless, Conant's report provides a glimpse into the way many—but not all—Americans viewed secondary education in the mid-twentieth century: a time when the comprehensive high school—first described in the Cardinal Principles report of 1918—was the national norm, when suburbanization was having an impact never seen before, and when the demands on schools, while significant, were limited in comparison to those that would emerge in subsequent decades.

As a consequence of the changes in universities and colleges in the nineteenth century and the alteration of the employment situation since World War I, the American public high school has become an institution which has no counterpart in any other country. With few exceptions, for the most part in large eastern cities, the public high school is expected to provide education for *all* the youth living in a town, city, or district. Such a high school has become known as a "comprehensive" high school in contrast to the "specialized" high schools which provide vocational education or which admit on a selective basis and offer only an academic curriculum. The local factors which have determined, and still determine, some of the features of a comprehensive high school are discussed later in this report, as are the pros and cons of the selective academic high school and the specialized vocational school.

Thousands of comprehensive high schools of considerable size exist throughout the United States. Though generalization about American public education is highly dangerous (and I shall avoid it as far as possible in this report), I believe it is accurate to state that a high school accommodating all the youth of a community is typical of American public education. I think it safe to say that the comprehensive high school is characteristic of our society and further that it has come into being because of our economic history and our devotion to the ideals of equality of opportunity and equality of status.

It is hardly necessary to say that a European finds the educational tasks facing the teachers and administrators of a comprehensive high school almost beyond his comprehension. (But this is the case also with some Americans whose children have not attended such a school.) Almost as incomprehensible as the American college and the American high school is the characteristic arrangements in the United States for managing our tax-supported schools. When one tells a foreign visitor that we have tens of thousands of local school boards with vast powers over the elementary schools and the high schools, he is apt to say, "This is not a system but a chaos." To which I always reply, "But it works; most of us like it; and it appears to be as permanent a feature of our society as most of our political institutions." And then, in hope of giving him some glimpse of the reasons why such an arrangement has developed and why, in spite of its obvious drawbacks, it has so many friends, one falls back again on history . . .

I have already defined the comprehensive high school as a high school whose programs correspond the educational needs of *all* the youth of the community. In those cities in which there are specialized high schools, particularly vocational schools, it may well happen that some of the boys and girls who reside in the district served by a comprehensive high school attend the specialized schools, and to this degree the breadth of the program in the comprehensive high school is limited. Likewise, in those states in which separate vocational schools have been developed and supported, the comprehensive high school will not have among its programs the vocational offerings supported by federal funds. One can therefore speak of the "degree of comprehensiveness" of a high school.

As will be pointed out more than once in the course of this report, there are high schools whose comprehensiveness is limited not by the existence of a specialized high school, but by lack of interest in the community in certain types of programs which develop special skills immediately useful upon graduation. High schools whose comprehensiveness is thus limited by the nature of the community are to be found particularly in suburban areas and in high-income residential sections of large cities. In these schools one finds that the vast majority of boys and girls desire to enter a four-year college or university, largely because of the collegiate ambitions of parents. In such schools, one will find that courses in stenography, auto mechanics, mechanical drawing, or the building trades are either not offered or are elected by very few students . . .

As I indicated in Section I of this report, the comprehensive high school is an American development of this century. It has no equivalent, so far as I am aware, in any European country. If the high school is of sufficient size and located in a community where parental pressure for preparing for college is not overriding, those boys and girls who desire to pursue education beyond the high school level will be in a minority. The question arises whether, being in a minority, such students can obtain an adequate education. Stating it another way, one can raise the question whether, under one roof and under the same management, it is possible for a school to fulfill satisfactorily three functions: Can a school at one and the same time provide a good general education for *all* the pupils as future citizens of a democracy, provide elective programs for the majority to develop useful skills, and educate adequately those with a talent for handling advanced academic subjects—particularly foreign languages and advanced mathematics? The answer to this question would seem to be of considerable importance for the future of American education. If the answer were clearly in the negative, then a radical change in the structure of American public secondary education would be in order. If the students in a given geographic area who have the ability to profit from the study of foreign languages and advanced mathematics on the high school level cannot obtain an adequate education in a comprehensive high school, then one can argue that separate high schools for these students should be maintained, as is now the case in some of the large eastern cities. On the other hand, if the answer is in the affirmative, then no radical change in the basic pattern of American education would seem to be required.

The problem of protecting the interest, so to speak, of a minority in an institution arises not only in connection with the pupils who are scholastically able, but also in many schools in connection with the education of those boys who desire to make progress in learning a skilled trade during the high school years. A generation and more ago, in certain states those who were urging the expansion of vocational education with the aid of federal funds decided that it was impossible to do justice to the needs of boys desiring a vocational education within the framework of a general high school. In these states the administrators of the vocational funds insisted on setting up separate vocational schools or, at least, were lukewarm in their enthusiasm for vocational programs in the comprehensive high school. Knowing of this situation, I was curious to discover not only whether in a comprehensive high school the interests of the minority who are academically able were well protected, but also whether it was possible for such a school to provide a satisfactory program for developing certain vocational skills through shopwork if the state permitted the use of federal funds in the comprehensive high school . . .

To repeat, the three main objectives of a comprehensive high school are: *first*, to provide a general education for all the future citizens; *second*, to provide good elective programs for those who wish to use their acquired skills immediately on graduation; *third*, to provide satisfactory programs for those whose vocations will depend on their subsequent education in a college or university . . .

Conclusion

I can sum up my conclusions in a few sentences. The number of small high schools must be drastically reduced through district reorganization. Aside from this important change, I believe no radical alteration in the basic pattern of American education is necessary in order to improve our public high schools. If all the high schools were functioning as well as some I have visited, the education of all American youth would be satisfactory, except for the study of foreign languages and the guidance of the more able girls. Most of the schools which I found unsatisfactory in one or more respects could become satisfactory by relatively minor changes, though I have no doubt that there are schools even of sufficient size where major improvements in organization and instruction would be in order. If the fifty-five schools I have visited, all of which have a good reputation, are at all representative of American public high schools, I think one general criticism would be in order: The academically talented student, as a rule, is not being sufficiently challenged, does not work hard enough, and his program of academic subjects is not of sufficient range. The able boys too often specialize in mathematics and science to the exclusion of foreign languages and to the neglect of English and social studies. The able girls, on the other hand, too often avoid mathematics and science as well as the foreign languages. As I have indicated in the preceding paragraph, a correction of this situation in many instances will depend upon an altered attitude of the community quite as much as upon action by a school board or school administration.

James Bryant Conant, *The American High School Today: A First Report to Interested Citizens*, New York: McGraw-Hill, 1959, pp. 7–8, 12–17, 40.

Growth and Diversity in Schools and Students, 1880–1960

- Introduction
- Third Plenary Council of Baltimore, 1884
- Mary Antin, *The Promised Land*, 1912
- Lewis Meriam, *The Problem of Indian Administration*, 1928

- The Asian Experience in California, 1919–1920
- Beatrice Griffith, *American Me*, 1948
- Teaching Children of Puerto Rican Background in the New York City Schools, 1954

Introduction

Students in the United States have always been a diverse lot. How the schools have handled this diversity has changed dramatically over the years, however. Before the nation was founded, the thirteen colonies all had immigrants from many different European countries mingling with Africans and their descendants, both slave and free, as well as with Indians who predated both on these shores. Spanish-speaking residents of Puerto Rico and much of the American southwest did not immigrate to the United States; they simply happened to be in lands conquered by the growing nation, though many more people immigrated from Mexico to the U.S. in the twentieth century. Asian immigrants began coming to the United States in the middle of the nineteenth century. All of these groups had to engage with schools in one way or another.

Schools as they existed in the United States were often alien places to many from other countries and cultures. Some immigrants embraced them enthusiastically (see Mary Antin story) while many others experienced marginalization and disrespect. The result, far too often, has been a definition of schooling as an institution for the dominant classes. At times non-Europeans were simply excluded from schools. At times they were welcomed, but only on the dominant culture's terms. At yet other times, schools were segregated by race and ethnicity. Including and respecting a diverse population within schools remains a major issue in schooling at the beginning of the twenty-first century.

While the last chapter focused on the African American experience, this chapter looks at the ways in which schools related to a wide range of immigrant groups—nineteenth-century Roman Catholics, turn-of-the-century Jewish immigrants from eastern Europe, Asian immigrants on the West Coast, Mexican Americans in California, and Puerto Rican migrants to the New York City Public Schools in the 1950s. The individual documents are illustrative;

no one should assume that all Catholics followed the directives of their bishops to attend parochial schools; and certainly not all Jewish immigrants had as positive an experience with American schools as Mary Antin. Taken as a whole, however, the readings give a flavor of the responses of people from different cultures to U.S. schools.

By the time the Third Plenary Council of the nation's Roman Catholic bishops met in Baltimore in 1884, the Catholic leadership had given up on any meaningful chance to gain public support for their separate schools. For all the energy put into the campaign by New York's Bishop John Hughes and others, Catholics remained a minority in the nation, and the majority was not about to lend financial support to their schools. The bishops decided that the alternative was to withdraw from the public schools and develop an alternative school system that reflected Catholic faith and values in spite of the cost. Mary Antin's embrace of public schools represents the opposite end of the spectrum. For Antin, as for many immigrants, the public schools represented an opportunity to become an American. Her autobiography, *The Promised Land*, has been critiqued for casting a romantic haze around the immigrant experience. Nevertheless, it remains a powerful first-person account. Many of the hundreds of thousands of young people who flocked to these shores between 1880 and 1920 shared her enthusiasm for the schools.

The Native American experience with education has always been unique. More than any other group, Native Americans were truly a conquered people who had no say in their decision to become part of the United States. The U.S. government developed a wide range of programs to acculturate Indians to European American ways. At their worst, these programs were designed to "kill the Indian but save the human." Other educators and missionaries were more respectful of Indian culture. But few Europeans were successful in developing a truly respectful engagement with American Indians. By the 1920s, the failure of U.S. educational practices in regard to Native Americans was clear. As a result, the U.S. Department of the Interior commissioned a survey, subsequently known as the Meriam report for its author, Lewis Meriam, which offered a devastating critique of previous efforts at Indian education. It took an additional three decades before some of the issues raised in the Meriam report were fully addressed, but the report did represent a turning point in Indian education. In addition, the report offers the twenty-first-century student a good picture of the nature of Indian education as it existed in the late nineteenth and early twentieth centuries.

The petition of the Japanese Association of America to President Woodrow Wilson in 1919 describes the experience of many Asian immigrants between 1880 and World War I, while the two documents that follow reflect the lack of understanding and the fears of California's white leaders that resulted in further marginalization of Asians in the 1920s. The Latino experience with schooling has long been problematic. In the middle of the nineteenth century, the United States conquered northern Mexico, adding California, Arizona, New Mexico, and Texas to the union. Many Mexican citizens suddenly became American citizens, but the change in political citizenship did not change their cultural or linguistic traditions. Schools often treated these new citizens as distinctly second-class citizens. The passing of a century did not fully ameliorate these issues. The reports describing the difficulties of Mexican American students—children of long-time California residents or of recent immigrants—in the Los Angeles public schools from the 1940s provide a picture of what school life was like for many children on the West Coast. In the 1950s, large

Figure 7.1 "Steamer Glass" in Hancock School, Boston. Courtesy of the Library of Congress, LC-DIG-nclc-04529.

numbers of Puerto Rican students who were by birth in Puerto Rico American citizens began immigrating to New York City. The circular included here was issued by the New York Board of Education and offers a glimpse of how Puerto Rican students were welcomed into the city's schools.

No one set of documents can cover all the groups of people who have interacted with American schools, or the many different perspectives of individuals within each group. Nevertheless, the documents in this chapter should give the reader some sense of the incredibly diverse experiences of many children over many years in public schools in the United States.

THIRD PLENARY COUNCIL OF BALTIMORE, 1884

The first Roman Catholic bishop in the United States was appointed shortly after the Revolution. Bishop John Carroll was based in Baltimore, and he and a small number of priests ministered to a small Catholic population clustered in the middle colonies. By 1850, Catholicism had become the nation's largest single denomination, with parishes, priests, and bishops spread throughout the land. The bishops held three national meetings, or ecumenical councils, in Baltimore in 1866, 1874, and 1884 to develop goals and policies that would guide American Catholics in the future. Each of these meetings addressed the issue of the proper education for a Catholic school child. At the third and final of these councils, the bishops issued a decree that was quite unmistakable in its direction. In spite of the difficulties and financial constraints, the bishops insisted "that near every church a parish school, where one does not yet exist, is to be built and maintained" and "that all Catholic parents should be bound to send their children to the parish school." The direction was set, and the Catholic parochial school system was fully launched.

Few, if any, will deny that a sound civilization must depend upon sound popular education. But education, in order to be sound and to produce beneficial results, must develop what is best in man, and make him not only clever but good. A one-sided education will develop a one-sided life; and such a life will surely topple over, and so will every social system that is built up of such lives. True civilization requires that not only the physical and intellectual, but also the moral and religious, well-being of the people should be promoted, and at least with equal care. Take away religion from a people, and morality would soon follow; morality gone, even their physical condition will ere long degenerate into corruption which breeds decrepitude, while their intellectual attainments would only serve as a light to guide them to deeper depths of vice and ruin. This has been so often demonstrated in the history of the past, and is, in fact so self-evident, that one is amazed to find any difference of opinion about it. A civilization without religion, would be a civilization of "the struggle for existence, and the survival of the fittest," in which cunning and strength would become the substitutes for principle, virtue, conscience and duty. As a matter of fact, there never has been a civilization worthy of the name without religion; and from the facts of history the laws of human nature can easily be inferred.

Hence, education, in order to foster civilization, must foster religion. Now the three great educational agencies are the home, the Church, and the school. These mould men and shape society. Therefore, each of them, to do its part well, must foster religion. But many, unfortunately, while avowing that religion should be the light and the atmosphere of the home and of the Church, are content to see it excluded from the school, and even advocate as the best school system [that] which necessarily excludes religion.

Few surely will deny that childhood and youth are the periods of life when the character ought especially to be subjected to religious influences. Nor can we ignore the palpable fact that the school is an important factor in the forming of childhood and youth, so important that its influence often outweighs that of home and Church. It cannot, therefore, be desirable or advantageous that religion should be excluded from the school. On the contrary, it ought there to be one of the chief agencies for molding the young life to all that is true and virtuous, and holy. To shut religion out of the school, and keep it for home and the Church, is logically, to train up a generation that will consider religion good for home and the Church, but not for the practical business of real life. But a more false and pernicious notion could not be imagined. Religion, in order to elevate a people, should inspire their whole life and rule their relations with one another. A life is not dwarfed, but ennobled by being lived in the presence of God.

Therefore the school, which principally gives the knowledge fitting for practical life, ought to be preeminently under the holy influence of religion. From the shelter of home and school, the youth must soon go out into the busy way of trade or traffic or professional practice.

In all these, the principles of religion should animate and direct him. But he cannot expect to learn these principles in the workshop or the office or the counting room. Therefore, let him be well and thoroughly imbued with them by the joint influences of home and school, before he is launched out on the dangerous sea of life.

All denominations of Christians are now awaking to this great truth, which the Catholic Church has never ceased to maintain. Reason and experience are forcing them to recognize that the only practical way to secure a Christian people, is to give the youth a Christian education. The avowed enemies of Christianity in some European countries are banishing religion from the schools, in order gradually to eliminate it from among the people. In this they are logical, and we may well profit by the lesson. Hence the cry for Christian education is going up from all religious bodies throughout the land. And this is no narrowness and "sectarianism" on their part; it is an honest and logical endeavor to preserve Christian truth and morality among the people by fostering religion in the young. Nor is it any antagonism to the State; on the contrary, it is an honest endeavor to give to the State better citizens, by making them better Christians. The friends of Christian education do not condemn the State for not imparting religious instruction in the public schools as they are now organized; because they well know it does not lie within the province of the State to teach religion. They simply follow their conscience by sending their children to denominational schools, where religion can have its rightful place and influence.

Two objects therefore, dear brethren, we have in view, to multiply our schools, and to perfect them. We must multiply them, till every Catholic child in the land shall have within its reach the means of education. There is still much to do ere this be attained. There are still thousands of Catholic children in the United States deprived of the benefit of a Catholic school. Pastors and parents should not rest till this defect be remedied. No parish is complete till it has schools adequate to the need of its children, and the pastor and people of such a parish should feel that they have not accomplished their entire duty until the want is supplied.

But then, we must also perfect our schools. We repudiate the idea that the Catholic school need be in any respect inferior to any other school whatsoever. And if hitherto, in some places, our people have acted on the principle that it is better to have an imperfect Catholic school than to have none, let them now push their praiseworthy ambition still further, and not relax their efforts till their schools be elevated to the highest educational excellence. And we implore parents not to hasten to take their children from school, but to give them all the time and all the advantages that they have the capacity to profit by, so that, in after life, their children may "rise up and call them blessed."

We need hardly remind you, beloved brethren, that while home life would not, as a rule, be sufficient to supply the absence of good or counteract the evil of dangerous influences in the school, it is equally true, that all that the Christian school could accomplish would be inadequate without the cooperation of the Christian home. Christian schools sow the seed, but Christian homes must first prepare the soil, and afterwards foster the seed and bring it to maturity.

Decrees of the Council—Title IV

After full consideration of these matters, we conclude and decree:

1. That near every church a parish school, where one does not yet exist, is to be built and maintained *in perpetuum* within two years of the promulgation of this council, unless the bishop should decide that because of serious difficulties a delay may be granted.

2. That all Catholic parents should be bound to send their children to the parish school, unless it is evident that a sufficient training in religion is given either in their own homes, or in other Catholic schools; or when because of sufficient reason, approved by the bishop, with all due precautions and safeguards, it is licit to send them to other schools. What constitutes a Catholic school is left to the decision of the bishop.

Acta et Decreta Concili Plenaryi Baltimorensis Terti, Baltimorae: Typis Joannis Murphy et sociorumn, MDCCCLXXXVI (English text, pp. lxxxvii–lxxxvi).

MARY ANTIN, *THE PROMISED LAND*, 1912

The years between 1880 and 1920 saw massive immigration from southern and eastern Europe to the United States. As a result, the diversity of students and the sheer number of children attending school were radically different after the arrival of these immigrants. While Mary Antin's autobiography, The Promised Land, *is a very personal story of her own encounter with the public schools as a young Russian Jewish girl freshly arrived in Boston, it certainly is one example of what the immigrant experience was like for young students.*

The apex of my civic pride and personal contentment was reached on the bright September morning when I entered the public school. That day I must always remember, even if I live to be so old that I cannot tell my name. To most people, their first day at school is a memorable occasion. In my case, the importance of the day was a hundred times magnified, on account of the years I had waited, the road I had come, and the conscious ambitions I had entertained.

I am wearily aware that I am speaking in extreme figures, in superlatives. I wish I knew some other way to render the mental life of the immigrant child of reasoning age. I may have been ever so much an exception in acuteness of observation, powers of comparison, and abnormal self-consciousness; none the less were my thoughts and conduct typical of the attitude of the intelligent immigrant child toward American institutions. And what the child thinks and feels is a reflection of the hopes, desires, and purposes of the parents who brought him overseas, no matter how precocious and independent the child may be. Your immigrant inspectors will tell you what poverty the foreigner bring in his baggage, what want in his pockets. Let the overgrown boy of twelve, reverently drawing his letters in the baby class, testify to the noble dreams and high ideal that may be hidden beneath the greasy caftan of the immigrant. Speaking for the Jews, at least, I know I am safe in inviting such an investigation.

Father himself conducted us to school. He would not have delegated that mission to the President of the United States. He had awaited the day with impatience equal to mine, and the visions he saw as he hurried us over the sun-flecked pavements transcended all my dreams. Almost his first act on landing on American soil, three years before, had been his application for naturalization. He had taken the remaining steps in the process with eager promptness, and at the earliest moment allowed by the law, he became a citizen of the United States. It is true that he left home in search of bread for his hungry family, but he went blessing the necessity that drove him to America. The boasted freedom of the New World meant to him far more than the right to reside, travel, and work wherever he pleased; it meant the freedom to speak his thoughts, to throw off the shackles of superstition, to test his own fate, unhindered by political or religious tyranny. He was only a young man when he landed—thirty-two; and most of his life had been held in leading-strings. He was hungry for his untasted manhood . . .

If education, culture, the higher life were shining things to be worshipped from afar, he still had a means left whereby he could draw one step nearer to them. He could send his children to school, to learn all those things that he knew by fame to be desirable. The common school, at least, perhaps high school; for one or two, perhaps even college! His children should be students, should fill his house with books and intellectual company; and thus he would walk by proxy in the Elysian Fields of liberal learning. As for the children themselves, he knew no surer way of their advancement and happiness.

So it was with a heart full of longing and hope that my father led us to school on that first day. He took long strides in his eagerness, the rest of us running and hopping to keep up.

At last the four of us stood around the teacher's desk; and my father, in his impossible English, gave us over in her charge, with some broken word of his hopes for us that his swelling heart could no longer contain. I venture to say that Miss Nixon was struck by something uncommon in the group we made, something outside of Semitic features and the abashed manner of the alien. My little sister was as pretty as a doll, with her clear pink-and-white face, short golden curls, and eyes like blue violets when you caught them looking up. My brother might have been a girl, too, with his cherubic contours of face, rich red color, glossy black hair, and fine eyebrows. Whatever secret fears were in his heart, remembering his former teachers, who had taught with the rod, he stood up straight and uncringing before the American teacher, his cap respectfully doffed. Next to him stood a starved-looking girl with eyes ready to pop out, and short dark curls that would not have made much of a wig for a Jewish bride.

All three children carried themselves rather better than the common run of "green" pupils that were brought to Miss Nixon. But the figure that challenged attention to the group was the tall, straight father, with his earnest face and fine forehead, nervous hands eloquent in gesture, and a voice full of feeling. This foreigner, who brought his children to school as if it were an act of consecration, who regarded the teacher of the primer class with reverence, who spoke of visions, like a man inspired, in a common schoolroom, was not like other aliens, who brought their children in dull obedience to the law; was not like the native fathers, who brought their unmanageable boys, glad to be relieved of their care. I think Miss Nixon guessed what my father's best English could not convey. I think she divined that by the simple act of delivering our school certificates to her he took possession of America.

Initiation

It is not worthwhile to refer to voluminous school statistics to see just how many "green" pupils entered school last September, not knowing the days of the week in English, who next February will be declaiming patriotic verses in honor of George Washington and Abraham Lincoln, with a foreign accent, indeed, but with plenty of enthusiasm. It is enough to know that this hundred-fold miracle is common to the schools in every part of the United States where immigrants are received. And if I was one of Chelsea's hundred in 1894, it was only to be expected, since I was one of the older of the "green" children, and had had a start in my irregular schooling in Russia, and was carried along by a tremendous desire to learn, and had my family to cheer me on.

I was not a bit too large for my little chair and desk in the baby class, but my mind, of course, was too mature by six or seven years for the work. So as soon as I could understand what the teacher said in class, I was advanced to the second grade. This was within a week after Miss Nixon took me in hand. But I do not mean to give my dear teacher all the credit for my rapid progress, nor even half the credit. I shall divide it with her on behalf of my race and family. I was Jew enough to have an aptitude for language in general, and to bend my mind earnestly to the task; I was Antin enough to read each lesson with my heart, which gave me an inkling of what was coming next, and so carried me along by leaps and bounds. As for the teacher, she could best explain what theory she followed in teaching us foreigners to read. I can only describe the method, which was so simple that I wish holiness could be taught in the same way.

There were about half a dozen of us beginners in English, in age from six to fifteen. Miss Nixon made a special class of us, and aided us so skillfully and earnestly in our endeavors to "see-a-cat," and "hear-a-dog-bark," and "look-at-the-hen," that we turned over page after page of ravishing history, eager to find out how the common world looked, smelled, and tasted in the strange speech. The teacher knew just when to let us help each other out with a word in our own tongue—it happened that we were all Jews—and so, working all together, we actually covered more ground in a lesson than the native classes, composed entirely of little tots.

But we stuck—stuck fast—at the definite article; and sometimes the lesson resolved itself into a species of lingual gymnastics, in which we all looked as if we meant to bite our tongues off. Miss Nixon was pretty, and she must have looked well with her white teeth showing in the act; but at the time I was too solemnly occupied to admire her looks. I did take great pleasure in her smile of approval, whenever I pronounced well; and her patience and perseverance in struggling with us over that thick little word are becoming to her even now, after fifteen years. It is not her fault if any of us to-day give a buzzing sound to the dreadful English *th*.

I shall never have a better opportunity to make public declaration of my love for the English language. I am glad that American history runs, chapter for chapter, the way it does; for thus America came to be the country I love so dearly. I am glad, most of all, that Americans began by being Englishmen, for thus did I come to inherit this beautiful language in which I think. It seems to me that in any other language happiness is not so sweet, logic is not so clear. I am not sure that I could believe in my neighbors as I do if I thought about them in un-English words. I could almost say that my conviction of immortality is bound up with the English of its promise. And as I am attached to my prejudices, I must love the English language!

Whenever the teachers did anything special to help me over my private difficulties, my gratitude went out to them, silently. It meant so much to me that they halted the lesson to give me a lift, that I needs must love them for it. Dear Miss Carrol of the second grade, would be amazed to hear what small things I remember, all because I was so impressed at the time with her readiness and sweetness in taking notice of my difficulties.

Says Miss Carrol, looking straight at me:

"If Johnnie has three marbles, and Charlie has twice as many, how many marbles has Charlie?"

I raise my hand for permission to speak. "Teacher, I don't know vhat is tvice?"

Teacher beckons me to her, and whispers to me the meaning of the strange word, and I am able to write the sum correctly. It's all in the day's work with her; with me, it is a special act of kindness and efficiency.

She whom I found in the next grade became so dear a friend that I can hardly name her with the rest, though I mention none of them lightly. Her approval was always dear to me, first because she was "Teacher," and afterwards, as long as she lived, because she was my Miss Dillingham. Great was my grief, therefore, when, shortly after my admission to her class, I incurred discipline, the first, and next to the last, time in my school career.

The class was repeating in chorus the Lord's Prayer, heads bowed on desks. I was doing my best to keep up by the sound; my mind could not go beyond the word "hallowed," for which I had not found the meaning. In the middle of this prayer, a Jewish boy across the aisle trod on my foot to get my attention. "You must not say that," he admonished in a solemn whisper; "It's Christian." I whispered back that it wasn't, and went on to the "Amen." I did not know but what he was right, but the name of Christ was not in the prayer, and I was bound to do everything that the class did. If I had any Jewish scruples, they were lagging away behind my interest in school affairs. How American this was: two pupils side by side in the schoolroom, each holding to his own opinion, but both submitting to the common law; for the boy at least bowed his head as the teacher ordered.

But all Miss Dillingham knew of it was that two of her pupils whispered during morning prayer, and she must discipline them. So I was degraded from the honor row to the lowest row, and it was many a day before I forgave that young missionary; it was not enough for my vengeance that he suffered punishment with me. Teacher, of course, heard us both defend ourselves, but there was a time and a place for religious arguments, and she meant to help us remember that point.

I remember to this day what a struggle we had over the word "water," Miss Dillingham and I. It seemed as if I could not give the sound of w: I said "eater" every time. Patiently my teacher worked with me, inventing mouth exercises for me, to get my stubborn lips to produce that w; and when at last I could say "village" and "water" in rapid alteration, without misplacing the two initials, that memorable word was sweet on my lips. For we had conquered, and Teacher was pleased.

Getting a language in this way, word by word, has a charm that may be set against the disadvantages. It is like gathering a posy blossom by blossom. Bring the bouquet into your chamber, and these nasturtiums stand for the whole flaming carnival of them tumbling over the fence out there; these yellow pansies recall the velvet crescent of color glowing under the bay window; this spray of honeysuckle smells like the wind-tossed masses of it on the porch, ripe and bee-laden; the whole garden in a glass tumbler. So it was with one who gathers words, loving them. Particular words remain associated with important occasions in the learner's mind. I could thus write a history of my English vocabulary that should be at the same time an account of my comings and goings, my mistakes and my triumphs, during the years of my initiation.

If I was eager and diligent, my teachers did not sleep. As fast as my knowledge of English allowed, they advanced me from grade to grade, without reference to the usual schedule of promotions. My father was right, when he often said, in discussing my prospects, that ability would be promptly recognized in the public schools. Rapid as was my progress, on account of the advantages with which I started, some of the other "green" pupils were not far behind me; within a grade or two, by the end of the year. My brother, whose childhood had been one hideous nightmare, what with the stupid *rebbe* [rabbi], the cruel whip, and the general repression of life in the pale, surprised my father by the progress he made under intelligent, sympathetic guidance. Indeed, he soon had a reputation in the school that the American boys envied; and all through the school course he more than held his own with pupils his own age. So much for the right and wrong way of doing things.

Mary Antin, *The Promised Land*, Boston, MA: Houghton Mifflin, 1912, pp. 198–215.

LEWIS MERIAM, *THE PROBLEM OF INDIAN ADMINISTRATION*, 1928

Beginning in the seventeenth century, educators and missionaries sought to bring European-style schooling to American Indians. After 1875, many within the federal government advocated a shift in policy, removing Indians from their familiar surroundings to boarding schools far from tribe, family, and friends so that the process of acculturating them into a European American lifestyle and learning system would be more effective. In 1928, after a half-century of boarding schools and three centuries of other forms of schooling, Lewis Meriam, a well-known policy expert, was asked by the Secretary of the U.S. Department of the Interior to examine the education of Indians, and especially the role of the federal government in that effort. His report is devastating, but also very informative. The "Meriam Report," as it came to be known, represented a turning point of sorts and the beginning of a thorough reorganization of federal priorities in Indian education based on a new level of respect for tribal culture.

The work of the government directed toward the education and advancement of the Indian himself, as distinguished from the control and conservation of his property, is largely ineffective. The chief explanation of the deficiency in this work lies in the fact that the government has not appropriated enough funds to permit the Indian Service to employ an adequate personnel properly qualified for the task before it.

Absence of Well-Considered, Broad Education Program

The outstanding evidence of the lack of an adequate, well-trained personnel is the absence of any well-considered, broad educational program for the Service as a whole. Here the word *education* is used in its widest sense and includes not only school training of adults to aid them in adjusting themselves to the dominant social and economic life which confronts them, but it also embraces education in economic production and in living standards necessary for the maintenance of health and decency.

Figure 7.2 U.S. School for Indians at Pine Ridge, South Dakota. Courtesy of the Library of Congress, LC-DIG-ppmsc-02511.

Formal Education of Indian Children

For several years, the general policy of the Indian Service has been directed away from the boarding school for Indian children and toward the public schools and Indian day schools. More Indian children are now in public schools maintained by the state or local governments than in special Indian schools maintained by the nation. It is, however, still the fact that the boarding school, either reservation or nonreservation, is the dominant characteristic of the school system maintained by the national government for its Indian wards.

The survey staff finds itself obliged to say frankly and unequivocally that the provisions for the care of the Indian children in boarding schools are grossly inadequate.

The outstanding deficiency is in the diet furnished the Indian children, many of whom are below normal health. The diet is deficient in quantity, quality, and variety. The effort has been made to feed the children on a per capita of eleven cents a day, plus what can be produced on the school farm, including the dairy. At a few, very few, schools, the farm and the dairy are sufficiently productive to be a highly important factor in raising the standard of the diet, but even at the best schools these sources do not fully meet the requirements for the health and development of the children. At the worst schools, the situation is serious in the extreme. The major diseases of the Indians are tuberculosis and trachoma. Tuberculosis unquestionably can be best combated by a preventive, curative diet and proper living conditions, and a considerable amount of evidence suggests that the same may prove true of trachoma. The great protective foods are milk and fruit and vegetables, particularly fresh green vegetables. The diet of the Indian children in boarding schools is generally notably lacking in these preventive foods. Although the Indian Service has established a quart of milk a day per pupil as the standard, it has been able to achieve this standard in very few schools. At the special school for children suffering from trachoma, now in question at Fort Defiance, Arizona, milk is not part of the normal diet. The little produced is mainly consumed in the hospital, where children acutely ill are sent. It may be seriously questioned whether the Indian Service could do very much better than it does without more adequate appropriations.

Next to dietary deficiencies comes overcrowding in dormitories. The boarding schools are crowded materially beyond their capacities. A device frequently resorted to in an effort to increase dormitory capacity without great expense is the addition of large sleeping porches. They are in themselves reasonably satisfactory, but they shut off light and air from the inside rooms, which are still filled with beds beyond their capacity. The toilet facilities have in many cases not been increased proportionately to the increase in pupils, and they are fairly frequently not properly maintained or conveniently located. The supply of soap and towels has been inadequate.

The medical service rendered the boarding school children is not up to a reasonable standard. Physical examinations are often superficial and enough provision is not made for the correction of remediable defects.

The boarding schools are frankly supported in part by the labor of the students. Those above the fourth grade ordinarily work for half a day and go to school for half a day. A distinction in theory is drawn between industrial work undertaken primarily for the education of the child and production work done primarily for the support of the institution. However, teachers of industrial work undertaken ostensibly for education say that much of it is, as a matter of fact, production work for the maintenance of the school. The question may very properly be raised as to whether much of the work of Indian children in boarding schools would not be prohibited in many states by the child labor laws, notably the work in the machine laundries. At several schools, the laundry equipment is antiquated and not properly safe-guarded. To operate on a half-work, half-study plan makes the day very long, and the child has almost no free time and little opportunity for recreation. Not enough consideration has been given to the question of whether the health of the Indian children warrants the nation in supporting the Indian boarding schools in part through the labor of these children.

The medical attention given Indian children in the day schools maintained by the government is also below a reasonable standard.

In securing teachers for the government schools, and in recruiting other employees for the boarding schools, the Indian service is handicapped by low salaries and must accordingly adopt low standards for entrance. Although some of the nonreservation schools purport to be high schools, the qualifications of their teaching force do not entitle them to free and unrestricted recognition as accredited high schools. At best, they have been able to secure limited recognition from local universities. The teaching, taken as a whole, is not up to the standards set by reasonably progressive white communities.

Some years ago, in an effort to raise standards, the Indian Service adopted a uniform curriculum for all Indian schools. Modem experience has demonstrated that the effective device for raising standards is not curriculum control, but the establishment of high minimum qualifications for the teaching staff. The uniform curriculum works badly because it does not permit of relating teaching to the needs of the particular Indian children being taught. It requires the same work for Indian children who are the first generation to attend school and who do not speak English as it does for those who are of the third generation of school children, who have long been in contact with the whites, and speak English in the home.

The discipline in the boarding schools is restrictive rather than developmental. Routine institutionalism is almost the invariable characteristic of the Indian boarding school.

Although the problem of the returned Indian student has been much discussed, and it is recognized that in many instances the child returns to his home poorly adjusted to conditions that confront him, the Indian Service has lacked the funds to attempt to aid the children when they leave school either to find employment away from the reservation or to return to their homes and work out their salvation there. Having done almost no work of this kind, it has not subjected its schools to the test of having to show how far they have actually fitted the Indian children for life. Such a test would undoubtedly have resulted in a radical revision of the industrial training offered in the schools. Several of the industries taught may be called vanishing trades, and others are taught in such a way that the Indian students cannot apply what they have learned in their own homes, and they are not far enough advanced to follow their trades in a white community in competition with white workers without a period of apprenticeship. No adequate arrangements have been made to secure for them the opportunity of apprenticeship.

School System

The first and foremost need in Indian education is a change in point of view. Whatever may have been the official governmental attitude, education for the Indian in the past has proceeded largely on the theory that it is necessary to remove the Indian child as far as possible from his home environment; whereas the modern point of view in education and social work lays stress on upbringing in the natural setting of home and family life. The Indian educational enterprise is peculiarly in need of the kind of approach that recognizes this principle; that is less concerned with a conventional school system and more with the understanding of human beings.

The methods must be adopted to individual abilities, interests, and needs. Indian tribes and individual Indians within the tribes vary so greatly that a standard content and method of education, no matter how carefully they might be prepared, would be worse than futile.

Routinization must be eliminated. The whole machinery of routinized boarding school and agency life works against that development of initiative and independence which should be the chief concern of Indian education in and out of school. The routinization characteristic of the boarding schools, with everything scheduled, no time left to be used at the child's own initiative, every moment determined by a signal or an order, leads just the other way.

For the effort to bring Indian children schools up to standard by prescribing from Washington a uniform course of study for all Indian schools and by sending out from Washington uniform examination questions must be substituted the only method of fixing standards that has been found effective in other school systems, namely, that of establishing reasonably high minimum standards for entrance into positions in the Indian school system. Only thus can the Service get first-class teachers and supervisors who are competent to adapt the educational system to the needs of the pupils they are to teach, with due consideration of the economic and social conditions of the Indians in their jurisdiction and of the nature and abilities of the individual child.

The curriculum must not be uniform and standardized. The text books must not be prescribed. The teacher must be free to gather material from the life of the Indians about her, so that the little children may proceed from the known to the unknown and not be plunged at once into a world where all is unknown and unfamiliar. The little desert Indian in an early grade who is required to read in English from a standard school teacher about the ship that sails the sea has no mental background to understand what it is all about and the task of the teacher is rendered almost impossible. The material, particularly the early material, must come from local Indian life, or at least be within the scope of the child's experience.

To get teachers and school supervisors who are competent to fit the school to the needs of the children, the Indian Service must raise its entrance requirements and increase its salary scale . . . The Indian schools, as a matter of fact, require better teachers than do the city school systems for white children. The teacher in the Indian schools has the harder task and cannot secure so much assistance from supervisory officers.

The objection to the heavy assignments of purely productive labor must not be construed as a recommendation against industrial education. On the contrary, it is specifically recommended that the industrial education be materially improved. The industrial teachers must be free to plan the industrial teaching from the educational standpoint, largely unhampered by the demands for production to support the schools or the Service. The work must be an educational enterprise, not a production enterprise. The persons selected for industrial teachers must be chosen because of their capacity to teach and not because of their capacity to do the work themselves with the aid of the pupils as helpers. The industries taught must be selected not because they supply the needs of the institution, but because they train the pupil for work which he may get at home on the reservation or in some white community to which there is some possibility of his going.

The industrial training must be subjected to the tests of practical use. The Indian Service must attempt to place the Indians who leave the school and help them to become established in productive enterprise either on the reservation or in white communities. It must be prepared to enter into cooperative arrangements with employers so that boys and girls shall have opportunity to gain experience in commercial employment while still having some official connection with the school. In this way, the school can place its emphasis on helping the pupil acquire the necessary fundamental skills and then getting him a job which there is a local demand. The schools cannot train for all occupations, but they can aid the boy or girl in acquiring those types of skills that are common to many occupations. The Service should make a survey of the economic opportunities for its pupils and plan its industrial training to meet these ends.

In the discussion of health, it has been recommended that the over-crowding of boarding schools be corrected through the maximum possible elimination of young children from these schools. From the educational standpoint, the young child does not belong in a boarding school. For normal, healthy development, he needs his family, and his family needs him.

Young children, at least up to the sixth grade, should normally be provided for either in Indian Service day schools or in public schools. Not until they have reached adolescence and finished the local schools should they normally be sent to a boarding school.

Because of the nature of the Indian country, the boarding school will for many years to come be essential to provide secondary education of a type adapted to the needs of Indian youth. It can stress provision for their special needs in a way that the typical high school designed for white children already adjusted to the prevailing economic and social system could not do. It must emphasize training in health, in family, and community life, in productive efficiency, and in the management and use of property and income to a degree probably unnecessary in general public schools.

Although the boarding school must be distinctive in the emphasis on the special needs of the Indians, it should not be so distinctive that it will not dovetail into the general educational system of the country. The promising Indian boy or girl who has attended an Indian boarding school and who desires to go on with his education should not encounter any educational barrier because of the limitations of the Indian boarding schools. The faculties and their courses of study should be such that they can meet the standards set for accredited high schools. It may prove necessary for the Indian youth who wishes to go on to higher institutions to spend a little longer time in the boarding school than he would have spent in an accredited high school, but the way should exist and should be plainly marked.

The Indian Service should encourage promising Indian youths to continue their education beyond the boarding schools and to fit themselves for professional, scientific, and technical callings. Not only should the educational facilities of the boarding schools provide definitely for fitting them for college entrance, but the Service should aid them in meeting the costs.

The present policy of placing Indian children in public schools near their homes instead of in boarding schools or even in Indian Service day schools is, on the whole, to be commended. It is a movement in the direction of the normal transition, it results, as a rule, in good race contacts, and the Indians like it. The fact must be recognized, however, that often Indian children and Indian families need more service than is ordinarily rendered by public schools, as has been elaborated in the discussion of boarding schools. The Indian Service must, therefore, supplement the public school work by giving special attention to health, industrial, and social training, and the relationship between home and school. The transition must not be pushed too fast. The public schools must be really ready to receive the Indians, and for some years the government must exercise some supervision to see that the Indian children are really getting the advantage offered by the public school system. The policy of having a federal employee perform the duties of attendance officer is sound, but more emphasis should be placed on work with families in this connection, in an effort not so much to force attendance as to remove the causes of nonattendance.

The Indian day schools should be increased in number and improved in quality and should carry children at least through the sixth grade. The Hopi day schools are perhaps the most encouraging feature of the Indian school system. More can perhaps be done in providing transportation to day schools. Where Indians come in to camp near the day schools, special activities should be undertaken for them. In general, the day schools should be made community centers for reaching adult Indians in the vicinity as well as children, and they should be tied into the whole program adopted for the jurisdiction.

Lewis Meriam et al., *The Problem of Indian Administration*, Baltimore, MD: Johns Hopkins University Press, 1928, pp. 8–14, 32–37.

THE ASIAN EXPERIENCE IN CALIFORNIA, 1919–1920

The state of California has long been the main point of entry for Asians coming to the United States. While the first Chinese immigrants to California were welcomed, the situation quickly changed. Within a few years, immigrants from China and later Japan and Korea were met with exclusion and segregation. Efforts at Chinese exclusion date from the middle of the nineteenth century. The Chinese Exclusion Act of 1882 made such exclusion a matter of federal law. After the 1906 San Francisco earthquake the city segregated Chinese and Japanese students from white students in the city's schools, leading to major tensions between the United States and Japan. President Theodore Roosevelt mediated the so-called Gentlemen's Agreement by which San Francisco integrated its schools and Japan drastically limited future immigration to the U.S. In 1919, as President Woodrow Wilson was in California advocating for support of the League of Nations, Japanese residents of the state submitted a petition to him reviewing some of their historical harassment, asserting the rights of Japanese Americans to be recognized as full citizens in the state and students in the schools of California. Wilson and his immediate successors did not respond and, in fact, California reinstituted school segregation. The 1920 report, titled "California and the Oriental: Japanese, Chinese, and Hindus," is interesting for the three perspectives offered. The opening letter from the Governor of California to the Secretary of State clearly rejects Japanese immigration. The study conducted under the Governor's auspices is slightly less hostile but hardly welcoming, voicing as it does a fear of the failure of Japanese immigrants to assimilate and a statement of belief that assimilation is not possible. These documents serve as a reminder that school segregation was not only a black–white issue, but also, in the West, an Asian–white issue. They also help one understand the racism that lay behind the creation of internment camps for Japanese citizens during World War II.

Memorial Presented to the President While at San Francisco on September 18, 1919 from The Japanese Association of America, No. 444 Bush Street, San Francisco, California
Honorable Woodrow Wilson

President of the United States of America,
San Francisco, California

Mr. President: The Japanese Association of America, on behalf of resident Japanese in the State of California, extends greetings to you and begs to add its voice of welcome to that of the great state which you now honor by your presence. It sincerely hopes that the noble task in which you are now engaged may be fully realized, and that world peace and happiness may be the ultimate rewards of the labors for humanity to which your great efforts are devoted.

The Japanese people of this state, trusting implicitly in the lofty spirit of justice and fair dealing which have characterized your every public act and expression, take advantage of your presence in California to lay before you a few facts and figures bearing upon their relations to the community in which they reside, and they venture to ask for them your respectful and disinterested consideration.

The cry against our people may be historically traced as far back as 1887, when there were no more than 400 Japanese in the entire state. The so-called Japanese question did not, however, assume an acute character until 1906, when the school question arose. Unfortunately that question was settled by the politicians and not determined upon its true merits. At any rate, ever since that date, the Japanese "question" has become an issue of a most complicated nature-political, economic, racial, diplomatic—always resulting in the suffering of the Japanese residents. A few of the more familiar cases might be mentioned. The "Gentlemen's Agreement," under the workings of which America prohibits Japanese immigration, has been so strictly administered by the Japanese government that there has been no immigration from Japan. The alien land law of this state, enacted in 1913, prohibits Japanese ownership of land and limits the terms of lease to three years.

This limitation strikes at the very foundations of farming so far as the Japanese are concerned, and the limitation is substantially interfering with all Japanese agricultural enterprises. Not satisfied with these annoying measures, innumerable anti-Japanese bills were introduced at the last session of the State Legislature. One of those proposed to deprive the Japanese of the right to lease land while another proposed to segregate Japanese children in the public schools.

These facts, not to mention others, have tended to strain the historic friendly relations between the United States and Japan. We regret the situation. However, the Japanese residents, on the whole, have so far entertained the faith that the American Government would eventually protect them and render them justice and peace. A great deal of anxiety has, in the meantime, been experienced by them. This is but natural, and this unrest has been reflected across the ocean. Some of us who feel that we are better acquainted with the situation, have taken the position that our best course must come from education and we have been doing our utmost in what we characterize as an "Americanization campaign." We point out to our fellow-countrymen the better elements in American civilization, urging them to strive for their own improvement and better fit themselves for American life, hoping thereby to be relieved of the anxiety created and reinforced by the constant agitation against them. Our Americanization campaign will prove fruitless unless backed by true sympathy on the part of Americans. We regret to say that even to these efforts on our part there has been given but little response or sympathy.

May we not then appeal to you, Mr. President, and ask your powerful aid in so adjusting our condition on this coast that we may engage in legitimate pursuits and live in peace?

A brief statement may here be made concerning the anti-Japanese agitation in California. Before taking up the alleged reasons upon which the agitation is based, we may be allowed to quote one of the best general statements on the subject, which was prepared by Professor PJ Treat of Stanford University, an acknowledged authority on Oriental history. He says:

"It was in 1905 that the first suspicion of friction appeared. And in the next nine years a series of incidents occasioned some ill feeling, but it must be remembered that the friction was always between popular groups; the official relations were always cordial.

"The occasions for controversy were found in both the United States and in the far East. In the United States it arose from the agitation for the exclusion of the Japanese immigrants.

This movement began in California about 1905. It had a small basis in fact, for there were relatively few Japanese in this country, but if their number continued to increase as rapidly as it had since 1900, a real social and economic problem would be soon presented. Instead of meeting this problem through diplomatic channels, the agitators, remembering the Chinese exclusion movement of an earlier generation, commenced direct action. This took the form of the so-called 'schoolboy incident' in San Francisco. Using the excuse that school facilities were lacking after the great fire in 1906, the school board ordered all Oriental students to attend a designated school. The Japanese, recognizing the motive which prompted this action, justly resented it. And it was the more ungracious because at the time of the earthquake and fire the Japanese Red Cross had contributed to the relief of San Francisco more money than all other foreign countries combined. They had eagerly seized this opportunity of showing their appreciation of all that the United States had done for Japan in the past. The action of a local school board soon became a national and an international question. With the legal aspects we are not concerned here. The matter was settled, between the federal government and San Francisco, by a compromise. The Japanese students were admitted to all the schools as of old, and President Roosevelt promised to take up the question of immigration with Japan.

"When the matter was presented in proper form, the Japanese at once met our requests. Practically all thoughtful Japanese realized the dangers involved in a mass immigration of people from a land with low standards of living to one where they were high. The understanding took the form of the 'Gentlemen's Agreement,' under which Japan promised not to give passports to laborers desiring to emigrate to the United States, and our Government, in turn, agreed not to subject the Japanese to the humiliation of an exclusion act. Since this agreement went into effect in 1907, it has met every need. No one has found ground for questioning the scrupulous good faith of the Japanese foreign office in the issue of passports. In fact, the admission of Japanese under the passport system has worked out with fewer abuses than the admission of Chinese under the exclusion laws which we administer ourselves.

"Unfortunately, this good understanding did not quiet the agitation on the Pacific Coast. In the California Legislature in 1909, 1911, and 1913, a number of measures were proposed which would have caused discrimination against the Japanese residents of the state. These were reported to the Japanese press, and even though not passed, they kept alive the resentment. Japanese who accepted our views regarding immigration did not hesitate to assert that such Japanese as were admitted to our country should enjoy rights and privileges equal to those of any alien. A crisis was reached when, in 1913, a bill was proposed at Sacramento which would deny to Japanese the right to acquire land or to lease it for more than three years. The purpose of this bill was to prevent the accumulation of agricultural land by the industrious and thrifty Japanese farmers. But the danger was largely imaginary because, due to the 'Gentlemen's Agreement,' very few Japanese could enter the country, and in 1913, less than 13,000 acres were actually owned by them. In spite of the efforts of the national administration, the bill was passed in a modified form, which made it apply only to aliens ineligible for citizenship. This class included, specifically, the Chinese, and, by interpretation, all aliens who were not 'free white persons' or persons of African nativity or descent." . . .

Finally we beg to state a few facts concerning the more important of our positive efforts to uplift the Japanese residents. These may be classified under four headings: An organized movement for Americanization, the protection of Japanese immigrants, religious work, and schools for immigrants and their children.

The origin of our more or less organized movement for Americanization can be traced back to 1900. We first directed our effort to what we called social education and economic development. We tried to impart to our fellow countrymen elementary facts of American civilization so that they could better fit themselves for American life. We tried to teach them that assimilation was the first step for their success. Then we tried to convince them that by contributing to the national interests of America they could attain their own economic development.

In 1918, when the American government laid down the general plan of the "Americanization campaign," we made it the foundation of our work. In fact, we joined the movement. The Japanese associations of San Francisco, Los Angeles, Portland, and Seattle assumed the responsibility of directing the campaign in the coast states, Nevada, Utah, and Colorado.

The San Francisco Association employs a man educated in America to canvass the northern half of the state. His function was to organize, in conjunction with the local associations, work for the campaign. Meetings were held at which men and women familiar with America addressed the Japanese. These addresses are for the purpose of acquainting the local Japanese with America. The topics discussed are such as American history, spirit, politics, economics, industry, religion, education, society, customs and manners, hygiene, care of children, cooking, housekeeping, etc. Besides lectures, pamphlets on these subjects have been prepared, and these are freely distributed. We have asked the Japanese schools, churches, YMCA, YWCA clubs and other associations, newspapers and magazines to help us in our campaign, and they are enthusiastically responding. The Japanese Agricultural Association is also doing most effective work. We are also making a special effort to facilitate learning of the English language. We are helping to organize classes for women and children newly arrived and securing proper teachers for them. We are also helping them to select textbooks so that they can learn the language, and, at the same time, become familiar with America. Such is the nature and scope of our Americanization campaign.

To protect new arrivals, mostly women and children, we are cooperating with every institution connected with immigration at the time of their arrival, and after their landing in America. We distribute at ports of departure pamphlets on what they should know on the voyage and in America. We send one of our secretaries to the immigration station every time a ship arrives to facilitate the needs of newcomers. We do what we can for the unfortunate immigrants, acting as go-between [for] such and the Federal Bureau of Immigration. We make special efforts to protect wives whose husbands, for various reasons, fail to meet them at the station. We do our best to see that Japanese immigrants are accorded proper treatment from immigration officials. Our relations with these officials have been very cordial, and we are grateful.

The earlier Japanese immigrants were mostly students, and for many years students formed the bulk of Japanese immigrants. They began to come to America about forty years ago. The Christian missionaries saw a chance to do proselyting work among the young Japanese. First they taught them English and helped them to secure jobs. As the number of Japanese increased, missions were established. These conducted religious meetings, and schools and provided rooming facilities. The various denominations together now maintain fifty-nine missions in America and Canada. These are doubtless helping the Japanese in many ways. But Professor Millis says: "These missions are for Japanese alone, and a recognition of a difference between them and other races [is] a condition which lessens their value as an assimilative force." This inductment is, we are inclined to think, worthy of serious consideration by all who are interested in religious instruction as well as in the real Christianization of the Japanese. A stigma is attached to "mission" Christianity in the mind of many Japanese Christians, and they prefer to attend American churches, and they do. The mission work, if properly instituted, will no doubt have a far-reaching influence in Americanizing Japanese immigrants.

Aside from the schools for instructing Japanese in English, there are seventy-five so-called "supplementary" schools for teaching children the Japanese language. These are attended by the Japanese pupils after the public schools close for the day. They are primarily for the study of the Japanese language and are not intended to perpetuate the traditions and moral concepts of Japan. Of course, these are criticized by hostile Americans. But says Professor Millis, "They are supplementary schools, and at the worst, there is much less in them to be adversely criticized than in the parochial schools attended by many children of the South and European immigrants. No real problem is yet evident connected with Japanese children on American soil." These are some of the more obvious facts concerning the status of Japanese residents in California.

In conclusion, Mr. President, the undersigned, in their unofficial capacity as representatives of their countrymen, have thought this a fitting opportunity for directing your attention to the status of our people on this coast. We approach you in no spirit of complaint. If we have grievances, we recognize that such grievances are inseparable from the conditions which now exist and that they must be borne with patience. It is our firm belief, however, that fuller knowledge and better understanding on the part of the American people of our aims and aspirations as residents of the great State of California will tend to disabuse some prejudices and make our condition happier. We would convince the people of California that our presence and our activities are not a menace to the commonwealth, but that its dearest interests are our own. We are happy to be able to count with confidence upon your love of justice and we ask your powerful help in so shaping public thought and opinion that every obstacle to harmony may be removed. It is the earnest desire of the Japanese people in this state to dwell in peace and good will with their American neighbors, and they desire to so direct their energies that the best interests of the state and communities in which they live may be subserved.

If it is our good fortune to impress you with the sincerity of these, our purpose and aims, we shall feel that your visit to the West has been most fortunate and we shall remain gratified and grateful.

We have the honor to remain, Sir,
Most respectfully yours,
The Japanese Association of America

Letter from the Governor of California to the U.S. Secretary of State, 1920

Sacramento, June 19, 1920
State of California, Governor's Office

Hon. Bainbridge Colby
Secretary of State, Washington, D.C.
Sir:

I have the honor to transmit herewith the official report prepared and filed with me by the State Board of Control of California on the subject of Oriental immigration, population, and land ownership.

The subject is one of such transcendent importance to the people of California, and is so potential with future difficulties between the United States of America and the Oriental countries, that I deem it my duty in forwarding the report to outline in brief the history of the development of the Japanese problem in California, together with the legislation already enacted and that now pending. In doing so I trust I may be able clearly to lay before you the necessity of action by our Federal Government in the attainment of a permanent solution of this matter.

While the report deals with the problem as an entire Asiatic one, the present acute situation is occasioned specifically by the increase in population and land ownership of the Japanese. Forty years ago the California race problem was essentially a Chinese problem. At that time our Japanese population was negligible. The Chinese immigrants, however, were arriving in such numbers that the people of the entire Pacific slope became alarmed at a threatened inundation of our white civilization by this Oriental influx.

Popular feeling developed to such a pitch that many unfortunate incidents occurred of grave wrong done to individual Chinese as the result of mob and other illegal violence. Our country became awakened at the growing danger, and Congress passed the Chinese Exclusion Act, providing for the exclusion of all Chinese laborers and the registration of all Chinese at the time lawfully within the country. The statute was sufficiently comprehensive effectively to exclude further Chinese immigration and to make difficult, if not impossible, the evasion of the spirit of the act. As a result of this enactment, there has been a substantial reduction in the Chinese population of California.

Let me repeat that in submitting this report and transmitting this letter with its recommendations, the people of California only desire to retain the commonwealth of California for its own people; they recognize the impossibility of that peace-producing assimilability which comes only when races are so closely akin that intermarriage within a generation or two obliterates original lines. The thought of such a relationship is impossible to the people of California, just as the thought of intermarriage of whites and blacks would be impossible to the minds of the leaders of both races in the southern states; just as the intermarriage of any immigrant African would not be considered by the people of the Eastern States.

California is making this appeal primarily, of course, for herself, but in doing so she feels that the problem is hers solely because of her geographical position on the Pacific slope. She stands as one of the gateways for Oriental immigration to this country. Her people are the first affected, and unless the race ideals and standards are preserved here at the national gateway, the conditions that will follow must soon affect the rest of the continent.

I trust that I have clearly presented the California point of view, and that in any correspondence or negotiations with Japan which may ensue as the result of the accompanying report, or any action which the people of the State of California may take thereon, you will understand that it is based entirely on the principle of race self-preservation and the ethnological impossibility of successfully assimilating this constantly increasing flow of Oriental blood.

I have the honor to remain,
Yours very respectfully,
Wm. D. Stephens
Governor of California

State Report—"California and the Oriental: Japanese, Chinese, and Hindus"

Schools

Orientals attend the American public schools. In fact, until 1921, in some of the districts, the Japanese constituted the major part of the attendance, whites and Japanese attending the same schools together. The legislature of 1921, however, provided for separate schools for Orientals as follows: "The governing body of the school district shall have power . . . to establish separate schools for Indian children and for children of Chinese, Japanese, or Mongolian parentage. When such separate schools are established, Indian children or children of Chinese, Japanese, or Mongolian parentage must not be admitted into any other school."

Japanese Language Schools

The Japanese, besides attending the American public schools, thereby acquiring the English language and a knowledge of American customs, in many districts, also attend private Japanese schools conducted in the Japanese language in which are taught the language, laws, customs, history, and religion of Japan. How many there are at present of these Japanese language schools was not ascertained definitely. In a report submitted October 17, 1921, to the Superintendent of Public Instruction by the secretary of the Japanese Association of America, there was listed forty "Japanese Language Institutes" in northern and central California and fourteen in southern California. However, in a memorial address, prepared by the Japanese Association of America (in California), to the President of the United States, on the occasion of his visit to California in 1919, the Japanese Association stated that there were in California seventy-five such Japanese language schools, which they designate as "supplementary" schools.

While the Japanese schools are said by the Japanese to be primarily for the study of the Japanese language, and not intended to perpetuate the traditions and moral concepts of Japan, nevertheless, when an attempt was made in the Territorial Legislature of Hawaii to require teachers in these Japanese language schools to qualify for a certificate to teach, by passing an examination in the English language, American history, and American civics, the measure introduced in the legislature for this purpose was strongly opposed by Japanese educators and editors on the ground that it would force Japanese schools in that territory to close. This opposition defeated the bill . . .

On June 3, 1921, Governor William D. Stephens signed Assembly Bill Number 836, which added section one thousand five hundred thirty-four to the Political Code. This section, based on the Hawaiian law for the regulation of foreign language schools, provides that:

1. No person shall conduct or teach in a private school, conducted in the language of a foreign nation, without first obtaining a permit to do so from the superintendent of public instruction.
2. Each applicant shall be examined as to his knowledge of American history and institutions and his ability to read, write and speak the English language. The latter provision, however, is to be liberally construed up to the first of July, 1923.
3. Before issuing a permit, the superintendent of public instruction shall require the applicant to file an affidavit pledging himself to abide by the requirements of the law, the regulations of the superintendent of public instruction, and to so direct the minds of the pupils as will tend to make them good and loyal American citizens.
4. No such private school shall be conducted in the morning before school hours, during the hours the public schools are in session, nor for a longer period each day than one hour, nor more than six hours per week, nor more than thirty-eight weeks per year. Pupils over the age of seventeen, who are not required to attend the public schools, are exempt from these provisions.
5. The superintendent of public instruction shall have full supervision of courses of study and the textbooks used.
6. Each school shall be open to the inspection of the superintendent of public instruction, who shall have power to revoke the permit granted and discontinue the school if it has not complied with the law . . .

Examinations have been held at Sacramento, Stockton, San Francisco, and Los Angeles. Each applicant was permitted to answer in English or his native language. While many of the applicants have shown an excellent understanding of the subject matter, the greater number have most definitely exposed the result of being crammed for the examinations. Although the standard set was that of an eighth grade pupil, many were unable to pass satisfactory examinations.

Japanese Home Influence Nullifies American School Teachings

It seems apparent that the teachings of the American public schools do not offset the Japanese home influence, for, after years of residence in California, the Japanese still continue to congregate in racial groups, speak the Japanese language among themselves, and adhere to the customs of the mother country. There is little evidence of their assimilation. Dr. Sidney L. Gulick, author of numerous books and articles on the Japanese question, lecturer in the Imperial University of Japan, and who is by no means unfriendly to the Japanese, has expressed this very aptly in his book, *The American-Japanese Problem*, in which, addressing himself to the subject as it relates to the teaching of Japanese children in the schools of Hawaii, he writes as follows:

"It is not to be assumed that the education they (Japanese children) receive in the public schools, which they leave at fourteen or fifteen years of age, is adequate to prepare them for citizenship during the six or seven years after they get out from under the influence of their American teachers. Most of the boys will be isolated from English-speaking Americans; they will be associated chiefly with men of their own race, imbibing, therefore, the Oriental ideas as they approach manhood. The mere fact, accordingly, of American birth, public school education, and the requisite age should not be regarded as adequate qualification for the suffrage; for it is to be remembered that during the entire period of schooling, not only have they been in Oriental homes, but the Japanese at heart have been diligently drilled in Japanese schools by Japanese teachers, many of whom have little acquaintance and no sympathy with American institutions or a Christian civilization.

"If, as Asiatics, they maintain their traditional conceptions of God, nature, and men, of male and female, of husband and wife, of parent and child, of ruler and ruled, of the state and the individual, the permanent maintenance in Hawaii of American democracy, American homes, and American liberty is impossible."

Concerning the Japanese language schools in California, the Japanese Association of America, in the memorial to the President, above-mentioned, has the following to say:

"Aside from the schools for instructing Japanese in English there are seventy-five so-called 'supplementary' schools for teaching children the Japanese language. These are attended by the Japanese pupils after the public schools close for the day. These are primarily for the study of the Japanese language and are not intended to perpetuate the traditions and moral concepts of Japan. Of course, these are criticised by hostile Americans. But says Professor Millis, 'They are supplementary schools, and at the worst, there is much less in them to be adversely criticised than in the parochial schools attended by so many children of the South and European immigrants. No real problem is yet evident connected with Japanese children on American soil.'"

"California and the Oriental: Japanese, Chinese, and Hindus, Report of State Board of Control of California to Gov. Wm. D. Stephens, June 19, 1920, revised to January 1, 1922," Sacramento, CA: California State Printing Office, 1922, pp. 213–215, 221–233. Copy in the Harvard College Library, Cambridge, Massachusetts.

BEATRICE GRIFFITH, *AMERICAN ME*, 1948

At the conclusion of World War II, Beatrice Griffith set out to capture the experience of young Latino Californians in coming to terms with the culture of their rapidly growing state. She interviewed young people, studied their schools, and reported the results in American Me *in 1948. Her report on the experience of Mexican Americans in the Los Angeles area is filled with warmth, humor, and powerful judgments about the workings of racism in the United States just as the World War was ending and the Cold War with the Soviet Union beginning. She began this report with a letter written by one of the students she was observing to President Roosevelt describing the good life. This is followed by Griffith's own analysis of the state of Mexican American schooling in the places she studied.*

I sat down on the fireplug. "Come on. Let's write a letter to Roosevelt like if he were still alive, and tell him what we want for a school."

Dear President Roosevelt,

The next time one of those dames asks what will make our school better, we're going to tell them what we're telling you. But you'll probably get this letter before they ask us. So here goes!

We want to know out of that school the things you are supposed to know in life. How to fill out papers for work. How to put money in the bank. To know about the world we're living in. Not to know nothing about nothing. To know about the stars and moon, about shorthand and penmanship and power machines, so we can sew for our kids when we have them. And how to give them understanding.

We want lots of clubs for all of us, not only honor clubs where you have wings like angels. To know what we're reading about, how to talk with people when they say, "Did you see this and that about Europe and Russia?" And how to say back, "Oh yes. I know. And did you know this and that, about some current events?" And if we could have one period to study health about ourselves, how our organs are made, and what to do if we get sick, that would be good.

And we would like, President Roosevelt, a course in beauty—combing hair, how to fix your make-up, what style and all that. Not this professional grooming course they give us, that means cutting paper dolls out of newspapers.

In grammar school we studied about things that were so fine, all about life in other countries, like you knew about. You know, all that one-world business. We live in one world too—the Mexican world. But we want to go places and do things everywhere. To get out of these little grapes-of-wrath houses we live in.

But mostly, President Roosevelt, we want to know about the living of life real real good.
Your friends,
The One-World Kids

The Schools

It is in the schools that children of Mexican ancestry learn of America: American life, American history, her great men, her cities, and government. Here they make their dreams—and often lose them. The school records of these youngsters are affected by the same factors that influence any other underprivileged children—poverty, bad housing, undernourishment, and ill health. Added to these are the bilingualism and segregation which make even worse the hard lot of underprivileged childhood.

To children required to live in segregated areas, the insecurity and sense of inferiority that comes early in childhood is intensified by school segregation. Throughout the Southwest, many Mexican-American children see the big school bus going through the streets of their town picking up the "Americans," one by one, to take them blocks away to the big school, with its auditorium, cafeteria, and play equipment. The "Mexican" youngsters often walk down the long road to the small school where "specially trained" teachers teach them about that almost unknown world that is America.

The segregated "Mexican schools" usually lack the play facilities, cafeteria, and auditorium of the big school, and there are also differences in teaching personnel. It is not uncommon for the teachers to be sent to the "Mexican" school as a matter of administrative discipline.

Again, they may be transferred to the school because of difficulty with children and parents. One administrator described such a situation accurately when he said, "There isn't a teacher in *that* school who could be kept in the Anglo school. The parents wouldn't stand for it. Mexicans don't care."

The two most common excuses justifying segregation of Mexican-American children are: "They don't speak good English," and "They're dirty." The truth is that where Mexican parents are given a chance, their youngsters come to school as clean, and some times cleaner than, the other children. Their clothes may be poorer, but parental pride keeps the blackened washtubs boiling in the backyard. As for not speaking good English—they speak good or bad English according to the opportunity given them to hear it.

Stereotyped thinking of prejudiced teachers often results in false generalizations about Spanish-speaking children. One school reported "severe problems" regarding the cleanliness, tardiness, and truancy among the Mexican-Americans who comprised 2 percent of the school's population. After some investigation it was found that "only three Mexican-American families were dirty. The rate of uncleanliness was actually greater among the Anglo-American families in the school. The same conclusion had to be drawn in terms of tardiness and truancy."

Another frequent complaint is: "They are so clannish . . . Mexican children always hang around together—they don't mix." The facts are that Mexican-American youngsters, particularly the younger ones, mix as well as any group if given encouragement. They are, however, sensitive and proud, and if they are made to feel a group apart, it is natural for them to cling together rather than push themselves where they are not welcome.

The pattern of segregation is occasionally lost to the casual observer. Teachers may say, "Why, we don't have segregation here—you see the children together there in the yard." Actually, after recess, the Mexican-American children may attend separate classes in the basement, or other rooms set aside for them, with "special teachers." Then, too, the children may attend classes together, yet graduate on different nights, as happened in one school in Los Angeles County.

It should not be inferred that most California schools are segregated, for such is not the case. The percentage throughout other Southwest states is considerably higher as a rule. Increasingly the schools in California are yielding to community pressure and abandoning the segregated school systems. Saticoy schools in Ventura County, El Monte, Chino, and all districts in Riverside County are among the schools that are no longer segregated. In several instances, the fair-minded and democratic school principals have led the fight to abandon segregation.

In 1945, parents of over five thousand Mexican-American children in Santa Ana, California, hired David Marcus, Los Angeles attorney, and proceeded to sue the Orange County Board of Education in an attempt to secure unsegregated schools for their sons and daughters. On March 22, 1946, Judge Paul J. McCormack handed down a permanent injunction against further segregation. He found such a policy "arbitrary and discriminatory and in violation of their constitutional rights and illegal and void." When the Orange County Board of Education appealed the case to the Ninth Circuit Court of Appeals in San Francisco, Justices Stevens and Denman handed down two court opinions which were scathing denunciations of this Board of Education. They then directed the Los Angeles Federal

Grand Jury to review the facts for the purpose of returning an indictment against the Board. [See *Mendez v. Westminster* in Chapter 10.]

One of the most damaging results of segregating Mexican-American children is that their bilingual handicap is intensified. They speak Spanish in the home and with their playmates, and when they do not play with Anglo-American children at school, they grow up thinking in Spanish, and acting with "Mexican" reactions to American situations. Contrary to the opinion of some teachers and parents, the Spanish-speaking child does not learn English more quickly in a school where there are only Mexican-American children. The English vocabulary with which a great many Spanish-speaking children enter school is negligible. It is safe to say that at the end of the first school year the vocabulary of these children consists of those words that the teacher has stressed, and those heard most often among their "American" playmates. The importance of unsegregated kindergartens for equipping the little Mexican-American youngsters with a minimum English vocabulary with which to enter school cannot be minimized.

The fallacy of the belief that segregated schools teach English better than unsegregated is well-demonstrated by the noticeable accent with which English is spoken by thousands of children who were born and raised in America, but educated in "Mexican" schools.

Another stereotyped belief held by some teachers is the conviction that Mexican-American children are inferior mentally. One elementary school teacher who attended a teachers' summer workshop in Los Angeles on "the Education of Mexican and Spanish-Speaking Pupils," showed how deeply ingrown this belief can be: "I've had a very entertaining experience but as far as I am concerned, they are still dirty, stupid, and dumb."

Too often a teacher's interest in her pupils is determined by the intelligence quotients registered in the class. Where this is so, the bilingual child starts out with a definite handicap, which is seldom eliminated in later school years.

Let's take an example, a Spanish-speaking child from a poor home and large family. Juanito's father and mother are immigrants from Mexico who speak little English. They are migratory workers in the seasonal crops, and return to the city when the harvesting season is over. Juanito works with them. During his nine years of living, he has missed a couple of months or more of schooling each year since he enrolled in the first grade. He is undernourished, nervous, and restless. He understands little of the English spoken around him when he enters school. He hears only Spanish in his crowded home and from the loud radio constantly playing Mexican songs. His father, tired and weary from his long work, may drink little or much to ease his own frustrations—to quench the thirst of the hot Mexican food.

Juanito comes to school, washed up or not, after a breakfast of beans and flour tortillas. When he is given his Binet test, there is a confusion in his mind as to what the words mean, what the teacher means, what the whole business means. He may "get through," but he may also have such an emotional or lingual block that he fails to get an I.Q. above 70. Does this mean that Juanito is innately a dull child? Can his teacher honestly say his "inborn capacity has been adequately measured?"

These youngsters, confronted with intelligence tests in schools, are under a real disadvantage. George I. Sanchez, professor of Latin-American Education at the University of Texas, says that, "There are no adequate group tests that do justice to the Mexican-American child." Nevertheless, the Mexican-American child is constantly being compared with his

"American" classmates by most of his teachers, and usually to his detriment. Too many teachers fail to realize that "there is no Nordic corner on brains." They disregard the personal, social, and cultural differences of their pupils. They forget that Binet himself warned that the tests could be safely used only if the various individuals have the same or approximately the same environmental opportunities.

The fact of the matter is, these children follow the same biological curve as any other group. Doctor Elizabeth Woods, psychologist for the Los Angeles City Schools, says, "Some are super, some slow, but in general their average is like that of any other children."

H. A. Overstreet puts it another way. "Tests of intelligence are as often as not tests of what communities do to the minds of their people. We know that I.Q.s can be improved by better surroundings. A generally low test score, therefore, in any part of the country and among large numbers of its inhabitants, may merely reveal that in that region society is an enemy of its people."

Probably the most important factor of all, however, in the school life of the Spanish-speaking child is the attitude of the teachers. One school administrator said, "If I find a teacher who can reach a Spanish-speaking child, I find that she influences that child's whole life very often. If she gets into his being and the child takes her understanding into his own complex little life, the influence is incalculable later on . . ." It takes most of these children about ten minutes in a class to determine a teacher's attitude. From then on, the behavior pattern is predetermined for many.

Unfortunately, however, the sympathetic and understanding teacher is not the usual one by any means. Besides these there are the teachers who are sentimental and those who are indifferent and prejudiced—and the latter group predominates.

In speaking of the sentimental attitude, Dr. Ethel P. Andrus, nationally known educator, said, "Some teachers wrap the Mexican child up in a Zarape. He's delightful, cute, picturesque, and dramatic—but that is not making him an American. He is a person apart. If America is to survive, these children must be part of us . . . *not apart from us.* The Zarape attitude is the sentimental approach that some of the best teachers are guilty of practicing."

It is the sentimental teachers who place an emphasis on handicrafts in place of academic work, saying, "You can't force these children into the Anglo-Saxon mold or pattern of schooling. They are different—they are elemental in their conception of things. They have different temperaments. The best program for them is one of intensive handicrafts in informal classrooms."

Such attitudes, and the common belief that they are good only in art, are malicious. Inasmuch as the Mexican-American children are not expected to measure up with other children academically, the teachers need not bother. Just praise them in the lower grades, celebrate Cinco de Mayo, brush them up in the jarabe tapatio . . . make pets out of the cutest ones . . . and pass them on to the next grade. "We just let them slide through if they don't measure up." In the higher grade levels, they are advised to take woodwork, machine and print shop, gardening, art, sewing, or cosmetology . . . "That's the best thing for them. Why give them big ideas—they're a simple people."

They're not so simple. Children are shrewd, and Mexican-American youngsters are particularly sensitive. The sentimentalists don't fool all of the children they teach, as the remark of one junior high girl shows. "You know, that teacher used to hate me until I played 'Dream of Love' and 'Bésame Mucho' on the piano. 'Oh, I didn't know you played such beautiful music,' she said . . . and a lot of stuff like that. She gave me the soft line . . . 'You Mexican girls are so artistic,' she'd say, just so I'd play more. But I knew she hated me, so I wouldn't wear that old Mexican costume and dance for her."

It is questionable whether sentimental principals and teachers basically like these children. Their sentimentality is a cover-up, a conscience soother, a failure to admit the equality of the Mexican group. "If America is to be strong, they must be a part of us," accepting the responsibilities of citizenship as do any other Americans. Furthermore, the sentimental teacher does not Americanize the children . . . she Mexicanizes them.

This is not intended as a criticism of those comparatively few teachers who show respect for these children as Americans by wanting to strengthen their pride in the Old Country's culture. That, too, is needed. It is good if directed properly, if the teacher keeps in mind the fact that the Mexican-Americans are, after all, Americans, and it is our culture they will live by, be judged by; it is our way of life they know so little about, and are so eager to learn.

The most common attitude is that of indifference. The principal of a school in San Fernando Valley, which has a large Mexican population, voiced the indifferent attitude neatly enough when she said, "If you teach them attitudes and responses and how to be good citizens, how to wash and iron and scrub and bake, that's all you need to do. Why teach them to read and write and spell? Why worry about it . . . they'll only pick beets anyway."

This attitude usually accompanies the happy belief that "they don't want to be any better. No matter what you teach them, they'll only marry, have lots of kids, and let the dishes stay dirty as they do now."

Instead of accepting these children as a challenge to their initiative, such teachers usually request to be placed in other schools where they do not have to observe "those dirty and stupid Mexican kids." If placement in other schools out of the Mexican neighborhoods were always effected, and these teachers replaced by sympathetic ones, it would be a beneficial arrangement all the way around. Unfortunately this is not always possible, and so some just sweat it out, with the children bearing the brunt of prejudice.

Others of the indifferent group prefer to stay in the "Mexican schools" because less is demanded of them as teachers and community leaders. They can slide along from year to year, half doing a vital job, complaining about their hard lot to everyone who will listen.

Against the many examples of indifference and prejudice, ignorance and sentimentality, the sincere work of capable, patient, and sincere teachers and principals stands out bright as sunlight. It is from their successful classes that Mexican-American children carry away the kind of dreams of achievement and plans that go to make America a great nation.

The hope and encouragement such teachers give are the best insurance agents against the Mexican-American child leaving school for factory and field work, even when economic pressures are great. One successful principal was told, "You seem to get a better class of Mexican pupils in your school than we do. They look so much more intelligent and brighter than ours." She replied, "Well, we insist that they be intelligent . . . We demand that they make the effort to come up to a standard . . . so we get work that is a standard."

Sometimes the teachers succeed just because of the high standards they demand of the children. Or they may get results if, combined with high expectations, they have a close relationship with the children and their Mexican parents. In schools where a real effort is made to minimize the wide cultural gulf, discipline is not the problem it is in other areas where poverty, racial antagonisms, and lack of home supervision foster rebellious and resentful youngsters.

An example of "accepting each child as he is" is shown in the attitude of one elementary teacher toward pupils who slept in their clothes. "There are too many kids sleeping together in small overcrowded homes, sleeping both ways with five in a bed. I figure my job is to teach them and not to smell them. Children can't sleep cold, that's all."

There is one school located in the heart of a congested Mexican-Negro district where the relationship between the teachers and parents is exceptionally good. In the Americanization classes and parties, the teachers and mothers share the benefits of "intercultural relations" on a practical basis by exchanging cooking recipes and folk dances. The PTA attendance is large (contrary to the usual Mexican PTA attendance), and the health education and immunization programs are successful.

Beatrice Griffith, *American Me*, Boston, MA: Houghton Mifflin Company, 1948, pp. 144–169.

TEACHING CHILDREN OF PUERTO RICAN BACKGROUND IN THE NEW YORK CITY SCHOOLS, 1954

While the schools of Los Angeles were coming to terms with the educational needs of the children of its longest-term residents—the citizens of its Mexican American community—the New York City Public Schools were experiencing a new wave of immigrants. New York had long been the entry point for European immigrants, and the city's schools often served as the first point of contact with the new culture. The schools had helped assimilate generations of Irish, Italian, Russian, and many other European immigrant children. After World War II, Puerto Ricans—American citizens since the U.S. War with Spain in 1898—also began moving to New York in large numbers. The public school administration responded with a major undertaking known as "The Puerto Rican Study," a multipronged effort conducted in the early 1950s to review the curriculum and the means of instruction so as to engage these new students. The study, and the 1954 brochure for teachers, "Teaching Children of Puerto Rican Background," part of which is included here, provide an interesting glimpse of the attitudes of the school administrators. At one moment wise and respectful, in the next filled with low expectations, the study reflects all of the ambiguity with which generations of newcomers have, in fact, been greeted.

There are in the New York City Schools today a large number of children of Puerto Rican background. Many of them have difficulties communicating in English. They come from a background different from that of our continental American way of living and learning. They present a situation similar, in some respects, to that of previous waves of newcomers to our city. The adjustment of the New York City schools to these latest arrivals again offers our staff a challenging opportunity.

These Spanish-speaking children have become a part of the student body of New York City. They are being helped to take their places and participate effectively in our city life, each child to the full extent of his individual potentialities. They are learning English as a second language and are adjusting to our ways of living on the continent and in the City of New York in particular . . .

Local schools and the districts have been studying for some time the problem of organizing classes for children of Puerto Rican background. Many clues to effective plans of organization have been investigated. The superiority of any one plan has not been established, however. Practices that are successful in one situation do not always seem to meet the needs of other situations. *Pending further study, therefore, the following pages are offered as descriptions of practices found successful in many instances, and not as prescriptions to be followed by all schools.* They describe procedures used in the reception of pupils, in the organization of classes, in the assignment of pupils to both orientation and regular classes, and in providing for adequate guidance until proper adjustment has been made. In the main these suggestions are tentative, based on practices which thus far have seemed successful.

Reception of New Arrivals

A. *Advance Preparation.* Schools situated in areas where large numbers of Puerto Rican families live have found it helpful to prepare all directions and routine notices in Spanish and to post them along with the English signs in corridors and rooms where they will be most useful. Reading the instructions in their own language enables parents to help in the routines to be followed.

It is good practice also to have prepared in advance a welcome booklet in Spanish, which is distributed during registration. Information given should answer questions about the school and its educational goals and practices. The welcome booklet can be a constant source of reference for the parents during the time the student remains in the school.

B. *During Registration.* Since many of the newcomers from Puerto Rico arrive at the school with little ability to make themselves understood, the assistance of a Spanish-speaking person, familiar with Puerto Rican backgrounds, is invaluable during registration. Ideally, this person is a member of the supervisory or teaching staff; however, parent or student translators can receive the newcomer with a friendly greeting in Spanish and thus do much to establish the initial rapport. Some elementary schools arrange to have bilingual parents on duty at regular times during the week; other schools on various levels make use of the older students organized as a bilingual group within the service squad or the General Organization.

In addition to greeting the children and parents upon their arrival, the bilingual group assists the schools in the following ways:

1. to convey to the newcomers that certain documents, such as birth certificate, previous school record, and evidence of vaccination are expected.
2. to answer questions that arise after parents and pupils have had an opportunity to read the welcome booklets distributed by the school.
3. to assure parents of the schools' readiness to cooperate in all matters involving the well-being of their children.

4. to explain to parents the value of Parents' Associations and urge participation in such organizations.
5. to give information about the club and extracurricular programs of secondary schools.
6. to answer questions (if any) about special orientation classes.
7. to reassure students that someone who speaks their language will be available to help translate for them.
8. to inform parents of requirements of school attendance, and of notification to the school when the family moves . . .

Assignment to Regular Classes

Assignment to Regular Classes After the Orientation Period. Experience has shown that many children will be able to profit from the work in the regular class after approximately six months. Children above the age of nine who have had no previous school experience may need a longer time in the orientation class. The administrator is guided by the following considerations in making the reassignment to a regular class.

A. *Teacher Judgment.* This should include results of observation of the pupil in all aspects of school living. His readiness to take his place in a regular class with students of his own age group should be a deciding factor. With a very young child, this might mean ability to express himself orally and to understand spoken English and ability to adjust to class routine. With an older child, this might mean ability to use reading as a tool for further learning and ability to participate in committee work.
B. *Judgment of Other School Personnel.* Anyone who comes in contact with the pupil— the principal, special teachers assigned to the program, the guidance counselor, other members of the teaching staff—may be asked to evaluate the readiness of the pupil to be transferred to a regular class. Simple forms have been worked out for this purpose by various schools.
C. *More Formal Evaluative Procedures.* The results of all examinations the teacher has given to ascertain degree of mastery of subject matter should be taken into account. These tests may have been simple questions and answers, dictation of previously prepared material, the reading of an experience chart, or the answers to questions based on a reading selection. The ability of the child to communicate orally should be the fundamental consideration. Formal standardized tests in English or Spanish have not proved useful thus far . . .

Curriculum and Procedures

The schools are adapting their curriculum and teaching procedures in various ways to meet the special needs of the Puerto Rican child. The immediate concern is the orientation of the pupils to the school, the home, and community environment. A few of the major responsibilities of the school in which there are Puerto Rican children are:

1. To plan for those experiences in social and community living which will lead to effective participation in our everyday New York City life.

2. To encourage the use of the English language for the communication of needs, wants, ideas, and desires.
3. To guide physical, intellectual, emotional, and social growth toward satisfactory personal and social adjustment.
4. To inculcate ideals of responsibility leading to active and effective citizenship.

To achieve these ideals, the school must stress:

a. Oral and written communication in English
b. Everyday living in a big city
c. Citizenship and our American heritage
d. Health and nutrition
e. Personal and community hygiene
f. Safety
g. Guidance—personal, educational, and vocational

This manual is a guide, especially for teachers who have had only limited experience in teaching children whose native language is not English. It will be helpful to them and to more experienced teachers in selecting and organizing units, in varying procedures, and in obtaining and using materials. Since it is undesirable to follow a predetermined program, and since the variables in each school and in each group make it impossible to do so, teachers will adapt the suggestions and procedures given here. After teachers have had some experience, they will select and develop units with their own groups, based on the experiences and needs of the individuals concerned.

A curriculum devised for the education of Puerto Rican children should:

1. *Allow for flexibility.*
   Everyday experiences and needs as they arise should form the basis for units of learning. The needs will vary from one school age to another.
2. *Make use of the background experiences of the child.*
   His life in Puerto Rico, his trip to the United States, his previous educational training, and his ability to use Spanish should be the starting point for new learnings.
3. *Provide for direct experiences.*
   Tours of the school and trips in the community as well as activities in the classroom are important for language readiness.
4. *Plan for different levels of language ability.*
   Even where attempts are made to group children homogeneously, it is usually necessary to provide experiences and activities on different levels. For example, there may be in the same class children who read Spanish well, and those who have difficulty in reading Spanish; those with some knowledge of English and those with little previous contact with English; those who learn rapidly and those who learn slowly.
5. *Use varied approaches to obtain the desired objectives.*
   In addition to providing for direct experiences, wide use should be made of media such as selected audio-visual aids.

6. *Stress language growth in all activities.*

    All play and work experiences should be made to yield new vocabulary, idioms, and sentence patterns and encourage spontaneous conversation.

7. *Make provision for repetition of newly acquired vocabulary, idioms, and sentence patterns in a variety of situations.*

    New learnings should be reinforced by practice in activities involving all curriculum areas.

8. *Emphasize growth in oral expression.*

    Speaking and aural comprehension are of primary importance. Reading and writing may be deferred for pupils unable to communicate orally. With older pupils, reading and writing are sometimes used to reinforce the learning of language patterns.

9. *Be paced to meet the individual needs of each child.*

    A feeling of security and progress stemming from mastery of each step must accompany all learning.

10. *Provide for full participation of the pupils in all school-wide activities where language competency is not of paramount importance.*

    Opportunities for immediate active participation in health education and shop programs, assemblies, activities of the students' General Organization, service squads, and monitorial service should be given.

11. *Take cognizance of the cultural and linguistic contributions that the Puerto Rican children can make.*

    Emotional needs such as the desire for status, belonging, and achievement may be satisfied by having pupils serve as interpreters or student helpers. They may also explain the Puerto Rican background to the class or school . . .

Developing Communication Skills

For most of our Puerto Rican children, the school has a major responsibility to develop the essential communication skills in oral and written English. The program for the teaching of English as a second language may consist of many facets. Some of these are: building a rich background of experience, teaching language patterns through a planned sequence, using Spanish to develop comprehension, and others. Some schools may emphasize one of these, while another school may reject it almost completely. Moreover, combinations of various elements of the program may vary from school to school. No clear experimental evidence of the most effective type of program is available as yet. The procedures described below are therefore to be considered *tentative* and *suggestive*.

In general, communication skills are built around meaningful concepts gained through a rich background of experience. Thus, the school and the teacher can promote growth in language competence by providing an environment so rich that children want to inquire and talk about it. In this way, the children are given direct contact with the materials on which the new language is based. For children who speak little or no English, comprehension may be developed through such media as pictures, objects, models, dramatization, and pantomime. Much practice is needed to fix associations with the new words and sentence patterns developed through the use of the materials.

The materials should be attractively arranged so as to invite initiative and stimulate conversation. The classroom environment should be such as to encourage children to use the English language . . .

The Teacher Should Not:

1. Speak loudly or at an exaggerated rate (either too quickly or too slowly). The children should become accustomed to a normal tone, and a normal rate in which the small words take their proper unstressed place, as, for example, "the book on the desk" is not to be said, "thee book on thee desk."
2. Speak in isolated words.
3. Imitate the sounds and intonation of the child.
4. Adapt her speech pattern to that of the child. Expressions such as, "You go library," should not be reinforced by being repeated by the teacher.
5. Underestimate the ability of the pupil to utter a complete sentence with proper prompting by her.
6. Become discouraged because constant repetition is necessary.
7. Assume that there is an automatic transfer of learning from a sound in one word to the same sound in a new word. By giving some time to the sounds mentioned in this report, and by pointing out that the same sound occurs in other words, phrases, and sentences, transfer of learning may be expected.
8. Expect mastery of contractions, such as, "won't," "can't," "don't," "couldn't," "wouldn't," etc., to come easily without special training.
9. Confuse the children by requiring the use of several sentence patterns at one time.
10. Forget her own experience in learning a second language, perhaps in high school or college; and that learning *her* first language actually covered a period of several years.

Board of Education of the City of New York, "Teaching Children of Puerto Rican Background in New York City Schools: Suggested Plans and Procedures," June 28, 1954, pp. 1–2, 6, 9–10, 13, 25–26.

The Progressive Era, 1890–1950

- Introduction
- James Jackson Storrow, *Son of New England*, 1932
- Margaret Haley, *Why Teachers Should Organize*, 1904
- Ella Flagg Young, *Isolation in the School*, 1901
- Grace C. Strachan, *Equal Pay for Equal Work*, 1910
- Cora Bigelow, "World Democracy and School Democracy," 1918
- John Dewey, *The School and Society*, 1899
- Lewis M. Terman, *National Intelligence Tests*, 1919
- George Counts, *Dare the School Build a New Social Order?*, 1932
- *The Social Frontier*, 1934

Introduction

Perhaps no reform movement in American education lasted so long or had so much influence as progressive education. Often associated with the work of John Dewey, progressive education dominated the educational landscape for a decade before the twentieth century began and for much of the first half of the century. Well into the 1950s, and sometimes into the twenty-first century, education-related debates have focused on the virtues and vices of progressive education. Progressive education had as many definitions as it had proponents—or, later, critics. Lawrence A. Cremin's *The Transformation of the School: Progressivism in American Education, 1876–1957* (New York: Alfred A. Knopf, 1961) has long been viewed as the definitive history of progressive education. For Cremin, progressive education could not be understood apart from the larger progressive movement which swept the country in the early twentieth century, electing first Teddy Roosevelt and later Woodrow Wilson as progressive presidents. For Cremin, the key to understanding the movement was clear:

> The word *progressive* provides the clue to what it really was: the educational phase of American Progressivism writ large. In effect, progressive education began as progressivism in education: a many-sided effort to use the schools to improve the lives of individuals.
>
> (p. viii)

In my own examination of progressivism, I have come to the surprising (to me, at least) conclusion that progressive education actually meant so many things; that it was an educational reform effort with so many facets that it is a virtually meaningless term. Like the words *school reform* in the twenty-first century, *progressive education* came to be a catchphrase for whatever any particular speaker thought should be done in education for the first several decades of the century. Only by clustering progressives into subgroups can we make any sense of the era. I propose at least five separate strands of school reform, all of which called themselves "progressive." They are:

- administrative progressives, who sought consolidated management
- militant teachers, who sought a greater role for themselves
- child-centered curriculum reformers
- advocates of testing and measurement
- political reformers who wanted teachers to help build a better society.

Selected readings from advocates of each of these strands are included in this chapter.

One can imagine the debates that must have taken place between administrative progressives like the financier James Jackson Storrow in Boston or Columbia University president Nicholas Murray Butler in New York, and their counterparts across the country, and the teacher leaders in their cities. Both called themselves progressives. But the administrative leaders believed that progressivism meant centralized authority in a board of "the brightest and best" citizens working closely with a professional administrator. The fact that the "brightest and best" were usually men from old-line English stock, and those they viewed as their opponents were more often Irish-Catholics or from other immigrant groups and included the overwhelmingly female teachers, was, to the administrative progressives, incidental. Militant teachers viewed the boards that people like Storrow and Butler led, with their hand-picked professional superintendents, as distant spectators who did not understand the realities that teachers faced. For the teachers, the key was to shift power away from centralized bureaucracies into the hands of individual teachers. In addition to the ethnic issues that divided these two groups, the vast majority of the board members and superintendents were male, and most of the teachers were female. This created gender differences of great significance.

The curriculum reformers tended to be closer to the teachers than to the administrative progressives. However, for them the child—and not the teacher or the administration—was the central focus of school reform. The advocates of a child-centered curriculum believed passionately that traditional schools were boring and that only by eliciting the full and active participation of every child in the learning process would real education take place. They opposed regimentation in every form and advocated the creation of a small-scale democracy in every classroom to promote active learning and help develop future adults who would be active participants in a larger democratic society.

The educational testing advocates saw themselves as scientists who were above the squabbles of the other groups. For them, the key to successful education was the scientific measurement of the innate ability each child possessed. Once that was measured—through the Stanford-Binet, IQ, or other intelligence tests—the school curriculum could be shaped to support that child. The notion that education might change children or society was foreign to the test advocates.

As the Great Depression of the 1930s replaced the prosperity of the teens and twenties, those who believed that progressive education meant using the school to build a larger progressive society became more and more militant and came to believe that educators needed to provide leadership for changes in the larger American society. George Counts became quite critical of a focus only on the individual child when it was all of society that needed to change. He and John Dewey called on teachers to be leaders in building the new society and replacing the corrupt and defeated capitalism of early twentieth-century America. To lump all of these extraordinarily diverse actors under a single banner of progressivism is to misunderstand both their similarities and their differences. But to fail to attend to the lasting impact all of these groups had is equally to miss some of the most interesting developments in the history of American education.

James Jackson Storrow, *Son of New England*, 1932

Every major city in the United States seemed to have groups of business and university leaders who advocated school reform in the early years of the twentieth century. These administrative progressives—as they have been called—took over local school boards and hired a new breed of educational leader, the professionally trained school superintendent, to be the chief executive officer of each school system. Administrative progressives believed schools could benefit from a dose of business sense. They said their goal was to "take the schools out of politics," but generally that meant they wanted political power in their own hands. The premier leader of the administrative progressive movement in Boston was James Jackson Storrow. An investment banker and urban reformer, Storrow had helped design a new pattern for the Charles River that flowed through Boston and he later helped design a new charter for Boston that strengthened the role of the mayor in city government, and then ran for mayor in a heated campaign in 1909. He was defeated and later turned from urban reform to take the lead in uniting a number of smaller automobile companies into General Motors. Along the way, he was involved in a significant effort to improve the Boston Public Schools, a portion of which—from his authorized biography—appears here. The story begins with Storrow's election to Boston's highly politicized twenty-four-member School Committee in 1901. As reported, Storrow—like his fellow administrative progressives in other cities—quickly moved to reduce the committee to a five-member group of elite citizens who would then turn management over to a carefully chosen professional administrator.

At the beginning of his term [in 1901], Storrow, who was not in the habit of letting grass grow under his feet, expected to make himself speedily familiar with the character and the working of this branch of the city government of which he was to be a part; but it proved a very difficult thing to do. Indeed, so clumsy and antiquated was the organization of the School Committee, and so much was it affected by the political atmosphere of the municipal administration, with its undercover methods, that even at the end of his three-year term he felt that he had learned little and, except for one innovation of his own, had accomplished even less. What the experience taught him, however, was really more important than what he expected to learn, for he became convinced that it was not possible to achieve anything constructive so long as the Committee continued to be constituted as it was.

Storrow's first term of service may be summarized in his own account of the conditions which he found existing in the School Committee. To preface it with the stage setting: The furniture and its arrangement in the School Committee room of the building on Mason Street were expressive of the character of the body. The plan was that of a legislative chamber: a desk on a high platform for the presiding officer; facing him, a semicircle of twenty-three desks for the members of the Committee. The secretary had a table in front of the rostrum; at the rear was a space reserved for the public and the reporters. Procedure always conformed exactly to that of a legislative body: Nothing was ever said in a conversational tone; every word was spoken as part of a speech.

As the multitudinous details of the School Committee's business could not possibly be attended to in full session, small committees were needed, and enough of them to provide at least one chairmanship for each of the twenty-four members. As Storrow describes the working of the system:

> Each subcommittee is forever creating upon its own motion, business for itself. It is always hacking at or placing patches upon our school system. The other members of the board have no notice of its sessions; they do not know what scheme the chairman may be hatching; and when it is hatched out, it needs only two of his fellow members to put it through. Even the superintendent, the actual executive head of the school system, and who ought to be held directly responsible for the efficiency of the schools, is for the most part not consulted. In fact, if the superintendent were obliged to be present at these continual meetings of these subcommittees, besides the meetings of the full Board, he would have a sorry time of it. For one thing, it would be a physical impossibility . . .
>
> But it is here the business of the School Board is carried on; here the plans are matured; here the appointments of teachers are passed or held up; here the new textbooks are settled upon and the school supplies bought, the janitors appointed and the budget for the year laid out . . .

From Storrow's account, it is easy to see that many members of the Committee were concerned chiefly in representing the local constituency which had elected them, in getting jobs for teachers and janitors in the schools of their districts, and in obtaining whatever else was desirable and profitable for Charlestown, South Boston, or Dorchester, as the case may be. Since the "master" of each school was beholden to the district committee for his appointment, it was with his members that he was wont to consult, rather than with the superintendent . . . Meanwhile, as has been stated, Storrow found himself impotent in any other direction; then, in the second year of his term, the majority maintained by Public School Association representatives was reduced, and in the third year, the group formed a helpless minority. Several incidents, more or less scandalous, showed the deterioration of the Committee, and its low estate became a matter of general comment.

Once Storrow was convinced that the reform of the School Committee as an organization was essential and that no one else was likely to make any move, he decided to undertake it himself. As his term of service drew to a close in 1904, he did not stand for reelection, but instead made plans for an appeal to the Legislature. In order to find out what was the best type of school board, he applied to professor Paul Hanus of the Division of Education at Harvard ("I have a wild Utopian idea of possibly trying to remodel the School Committee," he wrote), and thus obtained the assistance of Henry W. Holmes, now Dean of the Graduate School of Education, who made a careful study of the different methods of school administration in American cities and gave Storrow a report with recommendations, of which the essential point was a School Committee of five, its members appointed by the mayor. Indeed, this provision constituted practically alone the bill which Storrow finally decided to lay before the Legislature:

> We spent six months in drawing up a bill of a new school organization [he wrote afterwards], with many modern improvements, such as a longer term for the superintendent, etc., etc., but before we went up to the Legislature we pitched out all the modem improvements and came down to the transferring of the authority of the old Board to the new, feeling that if we got the new men on the new Board we would get any reasonable request granted by the Legislature, and in fact this was just what happened.

Next, he handled the campaign as he had handled that for the Charles River Basin. He formed no committee or association; he took all the responsibility, supplied the driving energy, and employed helpers to obtain signatures to his petition, to attend to publicity, and otherwise to get support for his project. At the hearing on his bill before the Committee on Cities he had important assistance from two ex-mayors of Boston—Josiah Quincy and Nathan Mathews— but the chief speaker was himself. Asked afterwards by someone who would emulate him to describe "his method of insuring favorable action by the Legislature," he replied simply, "I should be very glad indeed to tell you how you could accomplish what you desire, but I must confess that I do not know of any method of insuring favorable action by the Legislature upon such a proposition—or upon any other. The only method I know of is to expend all the energy and good sense one possesses in presenting the merits of one's case to the committee having it under consideration and to the members of the Legislature. They must be induced to take an interest in the matter, and convinced that the change is one the public interest requires."

Though, as was to be expected, Storrow's measure was opposed by the beneficiaries of the old system, their opposition proved so extravagant that it carried little weight with the Legislature. The objection of the Public School Association and of an organization known as the Independent Women Voters that appointment of five members of the Committee by the mayor would deprive women of their only opportunity to exercise the suffrage had more weight; their suggestion that the Committee be chosen by ballot was accepted by Storrow. With this change, the measure became law.

"Presenting the merits of one's case" to the voters of Boston in a municipal campaign was, however, a vastly different matter from talking informingly and persuasively to legislators individually and in groups; it was an undertaking with the methods of which Storrow was entirely unfamiliar and for which he was in many ways unsuited. Furthermore, as it happened, the elements of the campaign this year were so strangely mixed as to baffle even the seasoned politicians. At the outset, the Democratic control had been snatched from "smiling Jim Donovan," the city boss, by John F. Fitzgerald, "the young Napoleon of the North End." Besides these two factions in the party camp, there was a third, led by a woman, which, resenting the demolition of the old School Committee, went into action with a blind rage of vindictiveness. On the other side, the reformers were by no means in agreement as to methods, and Storrow, a newcomer, was felt by the seasoned campaigners of the P.S.A. to be imperiling its success by his independent acts. Some of his ideas he put into effect with a rapidity that astonished and alarmed them; but when they reasoned with him they were equally astonished at the way in which he listened to their argument and with no pride of opinion abandoned his own project.

After a good deal of negotiating, which on the Democratic side finally brought out the police, the School Committee slates were made up: one was as bad as possible; the other, composed of men of high character (G. E. Brock, D. A. Ellis, T. J. Kenny, W. S. Kenney, J. J. Storrow) was expected to appeal to all voters who wished to take the school system out of politics, and in that department of the city government, at least, to establish and maintain high standards of administration. Thanks to the endorsements that these five men received both from the two political parties and from the nonpartisan associations, thanks to vigorous campaigning in which the reform elements at last came together, thanks finally to the scandals in which some of their opponents were involved and which at this time became a matter of general knowledge, public opinion was roused to the point of voting to clean house. In fact, although on election day, the first Monday in December, Fitzgerald, the Democratic candidate for mayor, was successful, the greater triumph went to the Public School Association, which elected its entire ticket.

When this new Committee met on January 1, 1906, and as its first act elected Storrow chairman, it faced a strange situation. Only ten days before, the Superintendent of Schools had died suddenly, his death having been brought on, as most people believed, by a vituperative attack made on him at one of the last sessions of the old Committee by its most discredited member. The new Board therefore had as a pressing duty the selection of his successor. The most promising man for the position, Stratton D. Brooks, for some years past one of the assistant superintendents, or supervisors, as they were called, had just been elected Superintendent of Schools of Cleveland, and had gone thither to take up his new duties. Before his departure, however, Storrow had talked with him and obtained from him a comprehensive plan for reorganizing the school system. After the Committee had ransacked the nation, they returned to Brooks and persuaded the City of Cleveland to release him. Before the first of March, Storrow had taken the program of reform from its pigeonhole and given it to Brooks to put into execution.

In the hands of the new Board and its Superintendent lay the fate of 99,000 pupils and 3,300 employees, and the disposition of funds amounting annually to $3,673,800. From the beginning, the new School Committee was agreed that it could not possibly perform its work unless it limited itself to functions proper to a body of final authority. Accordingly, it lodged executive duties in the Superintendent, under whom were six Assistant Superintendents, a business agent, and a schoolhouse custodian. In the course of his reorganizing and reforming, Brooks had many a sharp contest, with much clamor from the public, especially on behalf of recalcitrant teachers. The old order was not of a kind to melt under the genial influence of a warm sun. Blows had to be given and received, and Brooks was every inch a fighter. When protests against his masterful ways poured in on the School Committee, they were listened to respectfully, but they did not impair its support of its executive officer. When a man received responsibility with which Storrow was connected he knew what he could count on . . .

To give a picture of Storrow's School Committee at work: The five men usually assembled on Mondays at half-past four, in the large room formerly consecrated to oratory. ("When I found how the new School Committee was made up," one of the Assistant Superintendents told an appreciative audience, "and saw that there was not an orator among them, I said, 'Thank God, the schools are safe.'") At this session, they held hearings for any citizen or group who had complaints or proposals to make. Some of the questions that Storrow put to these visitors, like his investigation of the fire drill, were not calculated to make them "quite so proud of themselves as they had been;" other questions were asked on purpose to see whether they would stand to their guns. Disconcerted, perhaps, at first, the visitor realized before he left the room that he had been paid the compliment of a genuine interview with a man, not in the least antagonistic, who wanted "real results." These hearings were followed by discussion amongst the members of the Committee, in which the measures to be voted on at the formal session in the evening were put into final shape. While they talked, the menu of the Adams House was passed about and each man gave his order for dinner. During dinner the talk continued, and presently it was time for the stated meeting.

At this session, the public was admitted, though usually, in the absence of speechmaking, it preferred not to come, and the audience consisted of two or three reporters. Motions were passed with a mere formality of discussion—all moot points had been settled beforehand—and at the end of half or three-quarters of an hour, the meeting adjourned. Then began the real business of the evening. In the Superintendent's office, with coats off, in relaxed positions, the atmosphere growing thicker and thicker from cigar smoke, these five men ran the gamut of Brooks's problems with him. The conversation was discursive—the school system, it seemed, opened the door to every subject known to the mind of man; it was not gay, not intense; but always it was absorbingly human. And it was as human beings that they dealt with what was before them. Storrow here was not the businessman absenting himself hurriedly from the world of high finance to perform a hard duty. He was merely a citizen—a simple citizen—threshing out with his municipal neighbors matters of common interest, coming to the work with zest and receiving from it refreshment. Like the talk of a group of familiars at a country store, their session was long, leisurely, and late, and it was frequently well after midnight when they broke up and went home to their waiting wives.

Henry Greenleaf Pearson, *Son of New England: James Jackson Storrow, 1864–1926*, Boston, MA: Thomas Todd Company, 1932, pp. 43–53.

MARGARET HALEY, *WHY TEACHERS SHOULD ORGANIZE*, 1904

When Margaret Haley spoke to the National Education Association in 1904 on the need for teachers to organize, she was already the best-known teacher advocate in the United States. Founder and leader of the Chicago Teachers Federation, Haley was a powerful and effective voice for the rights of teachers. In 1904, the NEA was dominated by the male elite of education. To this less-than-friendly audience, Haley asserted that teachers needed:

- *Increased salaries*
- *Job security and pensions*
- *An end to overwork in overcrowded schoolrooms*
- *Recognition of teachers as educators instead of "factoryized education."*

For Haley and her counterparts, change had to come quickly, so that teachers could be profes-
sionals who felt proud of themselves and of their service to the nation's children. Haley believed
an organized body of teachers—a union—was the key to change.

The responsibility for changing existing conditions so as to make it possible for the public schools to do its work rests with the people, the whole people. Any attempt on the part of the public to evade or shift this responsibility must result in weakening the public sense of civic responsibility and the capacity for civic duty, besides further isolating the public school from the people, to the detriment of both.

The sense of responsibility for the duties of citizenship in a democracy is necessarily weak in a people so lately freed from monarchical rule as are the American people, and who still retain in their educational, economic, and political systems so much of their monarchical inheritance, with growing tendencies for retaining and developing the essential weaknesses of that inheritance instead of overcoming them . . .

Practical experience in meeting the responsibilities of citizenship directly, not in evad-ing or shifting them, is the prime need of the American people. However clever or cleverly disguised the schemes for relieving the public of these responsibilities by vicarious perfor-mance of them, or however appropriate those schemes in a monarchy, they have no place in a government of the people, by the people, for the people, and such schemes must result in defeating their object; for to the extent that they obtain, they destroy in a people the capacity for self-government . . .

The methods as well as the objects of teachers' organizations must be in harmony with the fundamental object of the public school in a democracy, to preserve and develop the demo-cratic ideal. It is not enough that this ideal be realized in the administration of the schools, and the methods of teaching; in all its relations to the public, the public school must conform to this ideal.

Nowhere in the United States today does the public school, as a branch of the public service, receive from the public either the moral or financial support needed to enable it properly to perform its important function in the social organism. The conditions which are militating most strongly against efficient teaching, and which existing organizations of the kind under discussion here are directing their energies toward changing, briefly stated, are the following:

1. Greatly increased cost of living, together with constant demands for higher standards of scholarship and professional attainments and culture, to be met with practically station-ary and wholly inadequate teachers' salaries.
2. Insecurity of tenure of office and lack of provision for old age.
3. Overwork in overcrowded schoolrooms, exhausting both in mind and body.
4. And, lastly, lack of recognition of the teacher as an educator in the school system, due to the increased tendency toward "factoryizing education," making the teacher an automa-ton, a mere factory hand, whose duty it is to carry out mechanically and unquestioningly the ideas and orders of those clothed with the authority of position, and who may or may not know the needs of the children or how to minister to them.

The individuality of the teacher and her power of initiative are thus destroyed, and the result is courses of study, regulations and equipment which the teachers have had no voice in selecting, which often have no relation to the children's needs, and which prove a hindrance instead of a help in teaching.

Dr. John Dewey, of the University of Chicago, in the *Elementary School Teacher* for December 1903, says:

> As to the teacher: If there is a single public-school system in the United States where there is official and constitutional provision made for the submitting questions of methods of discipline and teaching, and the questions of the curriculum, text-books, etc., to the discussion of those actually engaged in the work of teaching, that fact has escaped my notice. Indeed, the opposite situation is so common that it seems, as a rule, to be absolutely taken for granted as the normal and final condition of affairs. The number of persons to whom any other course has occurred as desirable, or even possible—to say nothing of necessary—is apparently very limited. But until the public-school system is organized in such a way that every teacher has some regular and representative way in which he or she can register judgment upon matters of educational importance, with the assurance that this judgment will somehow affect the school system, the assertion that the present system is not, from the internal standpoint, democratic seems to be justified. Either we come here upon some fixed and inherent limitation of the democratic principle, or else we find in this fact an obvious discrepancy between the conduct of the school and the conduct of social life—a discrepancy so great as to demand immediate and persistent effort at reform . . .

It is necessary that the public understand the effect which teaching under these conditions is having upon the education of the children.

A word, before closing, on the relations of the public school teachers and the public schools to the labor unions. As the professional organization furnishes the motive and ideal which shall determine the character and methods of the organized effort of teachers to secure better conditions for teaching, so is it the province of the educational agencies in a democracy to furnish the motive and ideal which shall determine the character and methods of the organization of its members for self-protection.

There is no possible conflict between the good of society and the good of its members, of which the industrial workers are the vast majority. The organization of these workers for the mutual aid has shortened the hours of labor, raised and equalized the wages of men and women, and taken the children from the factories and workshops. These humanitarian achievements of the labor unions—and many others which space forbids enumerating—in raising the standard of living of the poorest and weakest members of society, are a service to society which for its own welfare it must recognize. More than this, by intelligent comprehension of the limitations of the labor unions and the causes of these limitations, by just, judicious, and helpful criticism and cooperation, society must aid them to feel the inspiration of higher ideals, and to find the better means to realize these ideals.

If there is one institution on which the responsibility to perform this service rests most heavily, it is the public school. If there is one body of public servants of whom the public has a right to expect the mental and moral equipment to face the labor question, and other issues vitally affecting the welfare of society and urgently pressing for a rational and scientific solution, it is the public school teachers, whose special contribution to society is their own power to think, the moral courage to follow their convictions, and the training of citizens to think and to express thought in free and intelligent action.

The narrow conception of education which makes the mechanics of reading, and arithmetic, and other subjects, the end and aim of schools, instead of a means to an end—which mistakes the accidental and incidental for the essential—produces the unthinking, mechanical mind in a teacher and pupil, and prevents the public schools as an institution, and the public school teachers as a body, from becoming conscious of their relation to society and its problems, and from meeting their responsibilities. On the other hand, that teaching which is most scientific and rational gives the highest degree of power to think and to select the most intelligent means of expressing thought in every field of activity. The ideals and methods of the labor unions are in a measure a test of the efficiency of the schools and other educational agencies.

How shall the public school and the industrial workers, in their struggle to secure the rights of humanity through a more just and equitable distribution of the products of their labor, meet their mutual responsibility to each other and to society?

Whether the work of coordinating these two great educational agencies, manual and mental labor, with each other and with the social organism, shall be accomplished through the affiliation of the organizations of brain and manual workers is a mere matter of detail and method to be decided by the exigencies in each case. The essential thing is that the public school teachers recognize the fact that their struggle to maintain the efficiency of the schools through better conditions for themselves is a part of the same great struggle which the manual workers—often misunderstood and unaided—have been making for humanity through their efforts to secure living conditions for themselves and their children; and that lack of the unfavorable conditions of both is a common cause.

Two ideals are struggling for supremacy in American life today: one, the industrial ideal, dominating through the supremacy of commercialism, which subordinates the worker to the products and the machine; the other, the ideal of democracy, the ideal of the educators, which places humanity above all machines, and demands that all activity shall be the expression of life. If this ideal of the educators cannot be carried over into the industrial field, then the ideal of industrialism will be carried over into the school. Those two ideals can no more continue to exist in American life than our nation could have continued half-slave and half-free. If the school cannot bring joy to the work of the world, the joy must go out of its own life, and work in the school, as in the factory, will become drudgery.

Viewed in this light, the duty and responsibility of the educators in the solution of the industrial question is one which must thrill and fascinate while it awes, for the very depth of the significance of life is shut up in this question. But the first requisite is to put aside all prejudice, all preconceived notions, all misinformation and half-information, and to take to this question what the educators have long recognized must be taken to scientific investigation in other fields. There may have been justification for failure to do this in the past, but we cannot face the responsibility of continued failure and maintain our title as thinkers and educators. When men organize and go out to kill, they go surrounded by pomp, display, and pageantry, under the inspiration of music and with the admiration of the throng. Not so the army of industrial toilers who have been fighting humanity's battles, unhonored and unsung.

It will be well indeed if the teachers have the courage of their convictions and face all that the labor unions have faced with the same courage and perseverance.

Today, teachers of America, we stand at the parting of the ways: Democracy is not on trial, but America is.

Margaret A. Haley, "Why Teachers Should Organize," *National Educational Association, Addresses and Proceedings*, St. Louis, MO, 1904, pp. 145–152.

ELLA FLAGG YOUNG, *ISOLATION IN THE SCHOOL*, 1901

While Margaret Haley of Chicago was the nation's best-known organizer of militant teachers, her close ally, Ella Flagg Young, was the most significant theoretical voice of the teacher movement of the progressive era. A colleague of John Dewey at the University of Chicago and later the Superintendent of the Chicago Public Schools, Young spoke for the belief that a democratic society required a democratic system of education in which the teacher was a respected citizen and not a passive cog in a machine run from above—especially one run from above by "administrative progressives" like Storrow and his counterparts in cities across the country. The selection here gives some flavor of Young's philosophy.

Two objections will be urged against the implication that all should be active, not only in realizing, but in setting, the aim of the school. (1) The school cannot have so many different aims as there are teachers connected with it. If active participation in originating and cooperating means diversity, then this objection is well grounded. (2) Teachers are satisfied with the present method. The relations are pleasant in the system. No one feels downtrodden. Consideration must be shown; teachers are too busy to have the duty of assisting in planning the course of study added to their labors . . .

The school cannot take up the question of the development of training for citizenship in a democracy while the teachers are still segregated in two classes, as are the citizens in an aristocracy.

No more un-American or dangerous solution of the difficulties involved in maintaining a high degree of efficiency in the teaching corps of a large school system can be attempted than that which is effected by what is termed "close supervision." Frequent visitations to the schools in the district, or ward, bring the minutiae of each schoolroom into the foreground, and develop a feeling of responsibility for matters of petty detail which are of a purely personal nature; and hence it follows that a ranking officer may be so near to the daily work as to have an exaggerated, or mistaken, conception of the obligations of a superintendent in determining the method in regard to even the non-essentials in the conduct of the school. In a short time the teachers must cease to occupy the position of initiators in the individual work of instruction and discipline, and must fall into a class of assistants, whose duty consists in carrying out instructions of a higher class which originates method for all. The reaction from close supervision with one set of dominant ideas to close supervision with another set has been the basis of procedure in every large system, with little recognition of the fundamental difficulty in the theory. In colleges and universities the benumbing theory of close supervision of the members of the faculties is unknown; and yet it is generally held as an inspiring, natural one for elementary schools. There must come a recognition of the law of life in those schools. The rights and obligations that inhere in members in different parts of the system

Figure 8.1 Ella Flagg Young. Courtesy of the Library of Congress, LC-DIG-ggbain-16585.

must be subjected to careful analysis, and then the teaching corps must be unfettered in its activity in striving to realize those things which will evolve themselves in a free play of thought in the individual and the community.

To secure this freedom of thought, there must be, within the various parts of the school, organizations for the consideration of questions of legislation. Such organizations have been effected in some universities and in a few schools systems, but in the latter they lack some essential features for securing freedom of thought; and yet they are deemed satisfactory; so little does the teaching corps know about origination of thought on questions concerning education. Without doubt, councils for discussion and recommendation may be organized, and seem to have an eminently successful life, and yet come far short of their potentialities. The voice of authority of position not only must not dominate, but must not be heard in the councils. There should be organized, throughout every system, school councils whose membership in the aggregate should include every teacher and principal. The membership of each school council should be small enough to make the discussions deliberative, not sensational. The necessity for such an organization that shall insure a free play of thought and its expression, rather than courage in opposing and declaiming, because restive under restraint, cannot be made too emphatic ... The deliberations would have familiarized all with the essentials involved, and those sharp breaks in theory and practice which have been made in the past would no longer be possible. Education would be a continuous process, based on theory; not mere experimentation, based on personal preferences ...

In America today more than leeway in individual opinion is needed; more than the recognition of the individual and his development. From the entrance upon the first year in the kindergarten till the close of the student life, if the school functions as an intrinsic part of this democracy, the child, the youth, and the teacher will each be an organic factor in an organization where rights and duties will be inseparable; where the free movement of thought will develop great personalities.

Ella Flagg Young, *Isolation in the School*, Chicago, IL: University of Chicago Press, 1901, pp. 24, 88–92, 106–111.

GRACE C. STRACHAN, *EQUAL PAY FOR EQUAL WORK*, 1910

While Margaret Haley and the Chicago teachers focused on a wide range of issues affecting teachers, Grace Strachan and the other leaders of New York City's Interborough Association of Women Teachers had a single focus: the unequal salaries paid to women teachers. Not only did women regularly occupy the lower rungs of the profession—they were the classroom teachers, while men were the superintendents—but even at the level of classroom teacher, most cities and towns had two different salary scales, one for women and one for men. From early in the nineteenth century onward, women had been recruited to the teaching profession because they were seen as more maternal than men, but also because school boards could hire them more cheaply. By 1900 women teachers had had enough of the lower salaries. Although it took some time, the campaign for equal pay was generally successful, and one of the legacies of the progressive era was a gradual end to the two-level pay scale. Schools tended to promote men to the higher-paying ranks much faster than women but at least at the same level, women won the right to equal salaries.

Salary—A periodical allowance made as compensation to a person for his official or professional services or for his regular work.—*Funk and Wagnalls.*

Notice the words, *a person.* Here is no differentiation between male persons and female persons.

Yet the City of New York pays a "male" person for certain "professional services" $900, while paying a "female" person only $600 for the same "professional services." Stranger still, it pays for certain experience for a "male" person $105, while paying a "female" person only $40 for the identical experience. These are but samples of the "glaring inequalities" in the teachers' salary schedules.

Why is the male in the teaching profession differentiated from the male in every other calling, when his salary is concerned?

Why does the city differentiate the woman it hires to teach its children from the woman it hires to take stenographic notes, use a typewriter, follow up truants, inspect a tenement, or issue a license?

Why are not the appointees from the eligible lists established by the Department of Education, entitled to the same privileges and rights as appointees from the Civil Service lists from other City and State Departments?

Some ask, "Shall the single woman, in teaching, be given the married woman's wage?" I do not know what they mean, I say, "Why not the single woman in teaching just as much as the single woman in washing, in farming, in dressmaking, in nursing, in telephoning?"

Again, some ask, is there such a thing as "equal work" by two people?

Technically, no. No two people do exactly the same work in the same way. This is true of all professional and official work. Compare Mayor Gaynor's work with Mayor McClellan's. Will anyone say their work as mayor is "Equal Work"? And yet the pay is the same: Do all policemen do "Equal Work"? Yet they receive equal pay. So with firemen, school physicians, tenement house inspectors. The taxpayers, no doubt, believe that, judged by his work, Mayor Gaynor is worth a far higher salary than many of his predecessors. But a great corporation like the City of New York cannot attempt to pay each of its employees according to the work of that particular street cleaner or fireman or stenographer, and so must be content with classifying its positions, and fixing a salary for each. So should it do for its teachers. That is all we ask.

The Family-to-Support Argument:

It is rather a sad commentary on our profession that its men members are the only men who object to women members of the same profession getting the same pay for the same work. Who ever heard of a man lawyer fighting a woman lawyer in this way? A man doctor arguing that another doctor should give her services for less pay simply because she happened to be a woman? And leaving the professions, what attitude do we find the men who form our "Labor Unions" taking on this question? They form a solid phalanx on the side of "Equal Pay." The most powerful of all unions in many respects—"Big Six"—has a by-law making it a misdemeanor to pay a woman less than a man working the same form. All Labor Unions fight "two prices on a job."

Is it not sad to see men, American men, shoving aside, trampling down, and snatching the life preservers from their sisters? I say life preservers seriously and mean it literally. For to the woman obliged to support herself, is not her wage-earning ability truly a life preserver? How can any man expect one whom she is legally privileged to assist, take from a woman any part of the wages she has earned and remain worthy even in his own eyes? The excuses he makes to himself and to hers in the attempt to justify his act, tends to belittle him more and more . . .

I am firmly convicted that while teaching is a natural vocation for most women, it is rarely the true vocation of a man. And that those who enter the vocation without the love for it which overshadows even the pocket returns, invariably deteriorate. Their lives are spent largely among those whom they consider their subordinates—in a position or in a salary, if not in intellect—the children and the woman teachers. They grow to have an inordinate opinion of themselves. No matter how ridiculous or absurd or unfair may be the attitudes they take and the things they say, there is no one to say, "Nonsense!" as would one of his peers in the outer world . . . Recently, in one of our schools, a male assistant to the principal resigned. The vacancy thus caused was filled by a woman. This woman is doing the same work as the man did, but with greater satisfaction to the principal. *But* she is being paid $800 a year less than the man was . . .

Under a system of equal pay, where services should be paid for irrespective of sex, some men to-day remain single because of relative economic independence, which they desire to maintain. These men are, however, relatively few. Women are as instinctive and as normal as men are, and independence, which they feared to lose, would prevent very few from marrying when they should make marriages which were attractive to them. Independence of women would improve marriage, since fewer women would marry because of necessity. By the same means, divorce would be decreased, and human happiness would have a boom.

Grace C. Strachan, *Equal Pay for Equal Work*, New York: B.F. Buck, 1910, pp. 117–122.

CORA BIGELOW, "WORLD DEMOCRACY AND SCHOOL DEMOCRACY," 1918

Cora Bigelow was the leader of the elementary school teachers' organization in Boston, a group she was able to turn briefly into one of the first teacher unions in the nation in 1919. She wrote the following article for their monthly newsletter in December 1918, a month after World War I ended. Bigelow's brief piece reflects the views of those classroom teachers who embraced the progressive vision of a reformed school, led by teachers, as part of a larger reformed society. Although Bigelow has kind words for school administrators, she—and many others like her across the country—often stood in opposition to the administrative progressives in Boston when they tried to centralize authority. For Bigelow, progressive education meant teacher power: adequate compensation for teachers and a central role for teachers in the development of the school's curriculum and goals.

World democracy and school democracy should go hand in hand. The world has reached a crisis where national autocracy must disappear. Business and commercial autocracy also must go. Autocracy, wherever it occurs in school affairs, must follow the trend of the times and give place to democracy.

Democracy has developed rapidly in the professional life of American schools, to the great advantage of the schools. It is not unusual for school superintendents and other professional officials to seek conferences regularly with teachers in the endeavor to work out school problems. There is no loss of dignity on the part of these higher officials and not the faintest assumption of arrogance on the part of teachers who meet in such conferences. It is but the earnest, natural, and democratic "getting together" of those mutually interested in the progress of education.

So long as the conferences deal solely with academic subjects, they are looked upon favorably by school committees in general, who themselves represent the financial end of school planning. But the moment conferences take up the subject of school business, however closely connected with school efficiency, they are called mercenary and self-seeking and are at once in great disfavor, if not in disgrace. School teaching is the one occupation where reasonable regard for one's own financial welfare is seemingly not a virtue.

Many school committees appear to expect professional progress to go on in the mind and soul of the teachers without equal regard for their bodily welfare. Professional heights, though fully recognized by the professional school officials, do not enable the teachers to meet their financial requirements of the times. Is it mercenary and selfish for teachers to show an interest in being able to meet their just debts?

School committees and teachers alike represent the average intelligence of the community, the former are temporarily representing the public, while the latter are permanently employed by the public. Any teacher who resigns may be elected to the school committee and fill the office admirably, but not one in many of the members of school committees (who has not previously been a teacher) can become an acceptable teacher. This being true, why are school committees in our cities and towns apparently fearful of advising with teachers in school planning?

The world has reached a time when there must be true cooperation in every walk of life, not operating from one party and cooperating from the other. Cooperation is mutual effort of equal earnestness. American teachers are ready to fulfill their part of the contract, and will accept at once any disposition on the part of school authorities to consummate such a mutual effort.

Figure 8.2 John Dewey. Chicago Daily News negatives collection, Chicago Historical Society, DN-0087487.

The professional officials connected with most American schools long since successfully adopted the democratic plan of mutual effort to develop the schools. There will never be peace and contentment in school systems until school committees become as democratic as the professional school officials, until school autocracy is exchanged for school democracy, and until school committees apply the deep, broad democratic principles to their temporary power, which are not being worked on in the great world issues, as the good which can come out of the present world war against autocracy.

The teachers are ready and the professional school officials have already become democratic. When will the other factor in American school affairs join hands with these two in honest endeavor to put the American schools on the broad basis of American democracy?

Then, and not until then, will the present cause of discord diminish. Democracy stands for mutual benefits derived from earnest mutual effort, regularly sustained.

Cora Bigelow, "World Democracy and School Democracy," Boston, MA: Boston Teachers Newsletter, December, 1918, pp. 10–11.

JOHN DEWEY, *THE SCHOOL AND SOCIETY*, 1899

The curriculum reformers—the advocates of the child-centered school—regarded the work of John Dewey as their theoretical base. The range of reformers, some predating Dewey and others building consciously on his work, included some of the best-known names in progressive education—Francis W. Parker, Randolph S. Bourne, Carleton Washburne, Agnes DeLima, and William K. Kilpatrick. These child-centered advocates developed their own progressive schools or their own differing brands of the child-centered curriculum. Still, to gain a flavor of the movement, it is best to start with Dewey's own work, such as the selection included here from The School and Society. *Dewey was often called "the father of progressive education" by both friends and detractors. He saw himself as primarily a philosopher. During his long life from 1859 to 1952, he started the Laboratory School at the University of Chicago in 1896, testing many of the progressive theories, and wrote a steady stream of commentaries on education, culminating in* Democracy and Education *in 1916.*

We are apt to look at the school from an individualistic standpoint, as something between teacher and pupil, or between teacher and parent. That which interests us most is naturally the progress made by the individual child of our acquaintance, his normal physical development, his advance in ability to read, write, and figure, his growth in the knowledge of geography and history, improvement in manners, habits of promptness, order, and industry—it is from such standards as these that we judge the work of the school. And rightly so. Yet the range of the outlook needs to be enlarged. What the best and wisest parent wants for his own child, that must the community want for all of its children. Any other ideal for our schools is narrow and unlovely; acted upon, it destroys our democracy. All that society has accomplished for itself is put, through the agency of the school, at the disposal of its future members. All its better thoughts of itself it hopes to realize through the new possibilities thus opened to its future self. Here individualism and socialism are at one. Only by being true to the full growth of all the individuals who make it up, can society by any chance be true to itself. And in the self-direction thus given, nothing counts as much as the school, for, as Horace Mann said, "Where anything is growing, one former is worth a thousand reformers."

Whenever we have in mind the discussion of a new movement in education, it is especially necessary to take the broader, or social, view. Otherwise, changes in the school institution and tradition will be looked at as the arbitrary inventions of particular teachers, at the worst transitory fads, and at the best merely improvements in certain details—and this is the plane upon which it is too customary to consider school changes. It is as rational to conceive of the locomotive or the telegraph as personal devices. The modification going on in the method and curriculum of education is as much a product of the changed social situation, and as much an effort to meet the needs of the new society that is forming, as are changes in modes of industry and commerce.

It is to this, then, that I especially ask your attention: the effort to conceive what roughly may be termed the "New Education" in the light of larger changes in society. Can we connect this "New Education" with the general march of events? If we can, it will lose its isolated character; it will cease to be an affair which proceeds only from the over-ingenious minds of pedagogues dealing with particular pupils. It will appear as part and parcel of the whole social evolution, and, in its more general features at least, as inevitable. Let us then ask after the main aspects of the social movement; and afterward turn to the school to find what witness it gives of effort to put itself in line. And since it is quite impossible to cover the whole ground, I shall for the most part confine myself in this chapter to one typical thing in the modern school movement—that which passes under the name of manual training—hoping, if the relation of that to changed social conditions appears, we shall be ready to concede the point as well regarding other educational innovations.

I make no apology for not dwelling at length upon the social changes in question. Those I shall mention are writ so large that he who runs may read. The change that comes first to mind, the one that overshadows and even controls all others, is the industrial one—the application of science resulting in the great inventions that have utilized the forces of nature on a vast and inexpensive scale. The growth of a worldwide market as the object of production, of vast manufacturing centers to supply this market, of cheap and rapid means of communication and distribution between all its parts. Even as to its feebler beginnings, this change is not much more than a century old; in many of its most important aspects, it falls within the short span of those now living. One can hardly believe there has been a revolution in all history so rapid, so extensive, so complete. Through it the face of the earth is made over, even as to its physical forms; political boundaries are wiped out and moved about, as if they were indeed only lines on a paper map; population is hurriedly gathered into cities from the ends of the earth; habits of living are altered with startling abruptness and thoroughness; the search for the truths of nature is infinitely stimulated and facilitated, and their application to life made not only practicable, but commercially necessary. Even our moral and religious ideas and interests, the most conservative because the deepest-lying things in our nature, are profoundly affected. That this revolution should not affect education in some other than a formal and superficial fashion is inconceivable.

Back of the factory system lies the household and neighborhood system. Those of us who are here today need go back only one, two, or at most three generations, to find a time when the household was practically the center in which were carried on, or about which were clustered, all the typical forms of industrial occupation. The clothing worn for the most part made in the house; the members of the household were usually familiar also with the shearing of the sheep, the carding and spinning of the wool, and the plying of the loom. Instead of pressing a button and flooding the house with electric light, the whole process of getting illumination was followed in its toilsome length from the killing of the animal and the trying of fat to the making of wicks and dipping of candles. The supply of flour, of lumber, of foods, of building materials, of household furniture, even of metal ware, of nails, hinges, hammers, etc., was produced in the immediate neighborhood, in shops which were constantly open to inspection and often centers of neighborhood congregation. The entire industrial process stood revealed, from the production on the farm of the raw materials till the finished article was actually put to use. Not only this, but practically every member of the household had his own share in the work. The children, as they gained in strength and capacity, were gradually initiated into the mysteries of the several processes. It was a matter of immediate and personal concern, even to the point of actual participation.

We cannot overlook the factors of discipline and of character-building involved in this kind of life: training in habits of order and of industry, and in the idea of responsibility, of obligation to do something, to produce something, in the world. There was always something which really needed to be done, and a real necessity that each member of the household should do his own part faithfully and in cooperation with others. Personalities which became effective in action were bred and tested in the medium of action. Again, we cannot overlook the importance for educational purposes of the close and intimate acquaintance got with nature at first hand, with real things and materials, with the actual processes of their manipulation, and the knowledge of their social necessities and uses. In all this there was continual training of observation, of ingenuity, constructive imagination, of logical thought, and of the sense of reality acquired through first-hand contact with actualities. The educative forces of the domestic spinning and weaving, of the sawmill, the gristmill, the cooper shop, and the blacksmith forge, were continuously operative.

No number of object-lessons, got up as object-lessons for the sake of giving information, can afford even the shadow of a substitute for acquaintance with the plants and animals of the farm and garden acquired through actual living among them and caring for them. No training of sense-organs in school, introduced for the sake of training, can begin to compete with the alertness and fullness of sense-life that comes through daily intimacy and interest in familiar occupations. Verbal memory can be trained in committing tasks, a certain discipline of the reasoning powers can be acquired through lessons in science and mathematics; but, after all, this is somewhat remote and shadowy compared with the training of attention and of judgment that is acquired in having to do things with a real motive behind and a real outcome ahead. At present, concentration of industry and division of labor have practically eliminated household and neighborhood occupations—at least for educational purposes. But it is useless to bemoan the departure of the good old days of children's modesty, reverence, and implicit obedience, if we expect merely by bemoaning and by exhortation to bring them back. It is radical conditions which have changed, and only an equally radical change in education suffices. We must recognize our compensations—the increase in toleration, in breadth of social judgment, the larger acquaintance with human nature, the sharpened alertness in reading signs of character and interpreting social situations, greater accuracy of adaptation to differing personalities, contact with greater commercial activities. These considerations mean so much to the city-bred child of today. Yet there is a real problem: how shall we retain these advantages, and yet introduce into the school something representing the other side of life—occupations which exact personal responsibilities and which train the child in relation to the physical realities of life?

When we turn to the school, we find that one of the most striking tendencies at present is toward the introduction of so-called manual training, shopwork, and the household arts—sewing and cooking.

This has not been done "on purpose," with a full consciousness that the school must now supply that factor of training formerly taken care of in the home, but rather by instinct, by experimenting and finding that such work takes a vital hold of pupils and gives them something which was not to be got in any other way. Consciousness of its real import is still so weak that the work is often done in a half-hearted, confused, and unrelated way. The reasons assigned to justify it are painfully inadequate or sometimes even positively wrong.

If we were to cross-examine even those who are most favorably disposed to the introduction of this work into our school system, we should, I imagine, generally find the main reasons to be that such work engages the full spontaneous interest and attention of the children. It keeps them alert and active, instead of passive and receptive; it makes them more useful, more capable, and hence more inclined to be helpful at home; it prepares them to some extent for the practical duties of later life—the girls to be more efficient house managers, if not actually cooks and seamstresses; the boys (were our educational system only adequately rounded out into trade schools) for their future vocations. I do not underestimate the worth of these reasons. Of those indicated by the changed attitude of the children, I shall indeed have something to say in the next chapter, when speaking directly of the relationship of the school to the child. But this point of view is, upon the whole, unnecessarily narrow. We must conceive of work in wood and metal, of weaving, sewing, and cooking, as methods of living and learning, not as distinct studies.

We must conceive of them in their social significance, as types of the processes by which society keeps itself going, as agencies for bringing home to the child some of the primal necessities of community life, and as ways in which these needs have been met by the growing insight and ingenuity of man; in short, as instrumentalities through which the school itself shall be made a genuine form of active community life, instead of a place set apart in which to learn lessons.

A society is a number of people held together because they are working along common lines, in a common spirit, and with reference to common aims. The common needs and aims demand a growing interchange of thought and growing unity of sympathetic feeling. The radical reason that the present school cannot organize itself as a natural social unit is because just this element of common and productive activity is absent. Upon the playground, in game and sport, social organization takes place spontaneously and inevitably. There is something to do, some activity to be carried on, requiring natural divisions of labor, selection of leaders and followers, mutual cooperation and emulation. In the schoolroom, the motive and the cement of social organization are alike wanting. Upon the ethical side, the tragic weakness of the present school is that it endeavors to prepare future members of the social order in a medium in which the conditions of the social spirit are eminently wanting.

The difference that appears when occupations are made the articulating centers of school life is not easy to describe in words; it is a difference in motive, of spirit and atmosphere. As one enters a busy kitchen in which a group of children are actively engaged in the preparation of food, the psychological difference, the change from more or less passive and inert recipiency and restraint to one of buoyant, outgoing energy, is so obvious as fairly to strike one in the face. Indeed, to those whose image of the school is rigidly set, the change is sure to give a shock. But the change in the social attitude is equally marked. The mere absorbing of facts and truths is so exclusively individual an affair that it tends very naturally to pass into selfishness. There is no obvious social motive for the acquirement of mere learning, there is no clear social gain in success thereat. Indeed, almost the only measure for success is a competitive one, in the bad sense of that term—a comparison of results in the recitation or in the examination to see which child has succeeded in getting ahead of others in storing up, in accumulating, the maximum of information. So thoroughly is this the prevailing atmosphere that for one child to help another in his task has become a school crime. Where the school work consists in simply learning lessons, mutual assistance, instead of being the most natural form of cooperation and association, becomes a clandestine effort to relieve one's neighbor of his proper duties. Where active work is going on, all this is changed. Helping others, instead of being a form of charity which impoverishes the recipient, is simply an aid in setting free the powers and furthering the impulse of the one helped. A spirit of free communication, of interchange of ideas, suggestions, results, both successes and failures of previous experiences, become the dominating note of the recitation. So far as emulation enters in, it is in the comparison of individuals, not with regard to the quantity of information personally absorbed, but with reference to the quality of work done—the genuine community standard of value. In an informal but all the more pervasive way, the school life organizes itself on a social basis.

Within this organization is found the principle of school discipline or order. Of course, order is simply a thing which is relative to an end. If you have the end in view of forty or fifty children learning certain set lessons, to be recited to a teacher, your discipline must be devoted to securing that result. But if the end in view is the development of a spirit of social cooperation and community life, discipline must grow out of and be relative to such an aim. There is little of one sort of order where things are in process of construction; there is a certain disorder in any busy workshop; there is not silence; persons are not engaged in maintaining certain fixed physical postures; their arms are not folded; they are not holding their books thus and so. They are doing a variety of things, and there is the confusion, the bustle, that results from activity. But out of the occupation, out of doing things that are to produce results, and out of doing these in a social and cooperative way, there is born a discipline of its own kind and type. Our whole conception of school discipline changes when we get this point of view. In critical moments, we all realize that the only discipline that stands by us, the only training that becomes intuition, is that got through life itself. That we learn from experience, and from books or the sayings of others *only* as they are related to experience, and not mere phrases. But the school has been so set apart, so isolated from the ordinary conditions and motives of life, that the place where children are sent for discipline is the one place in the world where it is most difficult to get experience—the mother of all discipline worth the name. It is only when a narrow and fixed image of traditional school discipline dominates that one is in any danger of overlooking that deeper and infinitely wider discipline that comes from having a part to do in constructive work, in contributing to a result which, social in spirit, is nonetheless obvious and tangible in form—and hence in a form with reference to which responsibility may be exacted and accurate judgment passed.

The great thing to keep in mind, then, regarding the introduction into the school of various forms of active occupation, is that through them the entire spirit of the school is renewed. It has a chance to affiliate itself with life, to become the child's habitat, where he learns through directed living, instead of being only a place to learn lessons having an abstract and remote reference to some possible living to be done in the future. It gets a chance to be a miniature community, an embryonic society. This is the fundamental fact, and from this arise continuous and orderly streams of instruction. Under the industrial regime described, the child, after all, shared in the work, not for the sake of the sharing, but for the sake of the product. The educational results secured were real, yet incidental and dependent. But in the school, the typical occupations followed are freed from all economic stress. The aim is not the economic value of the products, but the development of social power and insight. It is this liberation from narrow utilities, this openness to the possibilities of the human spirit, that makes these practical activities in the school allies of art and centers of science and history . . .

There is nothing which strikes more oddly upon the average intelligent visitor than to see boys as well as girls of ten, twelve, and thirteen years of age engaged in sewing and weaving. If we look at this from the standpoint of preparation of the boys for sewing on buttons and making patches, we get a narrow and utilitarian conception—a basis that hardly justifies giving prominence to this sort of work in the school. But if we look at it from another side, we find that this work gives the point of departure from which the child can trace and follow the progress of mankind in history, getting an insight also into the materials used and the mechanical principles involved. In connection with these occupations, the historic development of man is recapitulated. For example, the children are first given the raw material—the flax, the cotton plant, the wool as it comes from the back of the sheep (if we could take them to the place where the sheep are sheared, so much the better). Then a study is made of these materials from the standpoint of their adaptation to the uses to which they may be put. For instance, a comparison of the cotton fiber with wool fiber is made. I did not know, until the children told me, that the reason for the late development of the cotton industry as compared with the woolen is that the cotton fiber is so very difficult to free by hand from the seeds. The children in one group worked thirty minutes freeing cotton fibers from the boll and seeds, and succeeded in getting out less than one ounce. They could easily believe that one person could gain only one pound a day by hand, and could understand why their ancestors wore woolen instead of cotton clothing. Among other things discovered as affecting their relative utilities was the shortness of the cotton fiber as compared with that of wool, the former averaging, say, one-third of an inch in length, while the latter run to three inches in length; also that the fibers of cotton are smooth and do not cling together, while the wool has a certain roughness which makes the fibers stick, thus assisting the spinning. The children worked this out for themselves with the actual material, aided by questions and suggestions from the teacher.

They then followed the processes necessary for working the fibers up into cloth. They reinvented the first frame for carding the wool—a couple of boards with sharp pins in them for scratching it out. They redevised the simplest process for spinning the wool—a pierced stone or some other weight through which the wool is passed, and which as it is twirled draws out the fiber; next the top, which was spun on the floor, while the children kept the wool in their hands until it was gradually drawn out and wound upon it. Then the children are introduced to the invention next in historic order, working it out experimentally, thus seeing its necessity, and tracing its effects, not only upon that particular industry, but upon modes of social life—in this way passing in review the entire process up to the present complete loom, and all that goes with the application of science in the use of our present available powers. I need not speak of the science involved in this—the study of the fibers, of geographical features, the conditions under which raw materials are grown, the great centers of manufacture and distribution, the physics involved in the machinery of production; nor, again, of the historical side—the influence which these inventions have had upon humanity. You can concentrate the history of all mankind into the evolution of the flax, cotton, and wool fibers into clothing. I do not mean that this is the only, or the best, center. But it is true that certain very real and important avenues to the consideration of the history of the race are thus opened—that the mind is introduced to much more fundamental and controlling influences than appear in the political and chronological records that usually pass for history.

Now, what is true of this one instance of fibers used in fabrics (and, of course, I have only spoken of one or two elementary phases of that) is true in its measure of every material used in every occupation, and of the processes employed. The occupation supplies the child with a genuine motive; it gives him experience at first hand; it brings him into contact with realities. It does all this, but in addition it is liberalized throughout by translation into its historic and social values and scientific equivalencies. With the growth of the child's mind in power and knowledge it ceases to be a pleasant occupation merely and becomes more and more a medium, an instrument, an organ of understanding—and is thereby transformed . . .

But all this means a necessary change in the attitude of the school, one of which we are as yet far from realizing the full force. Our school methods, and to a very considerable extent our curriculum, are inherited from the period when learning and command of certain symbols, affording as they did the only access to learning, were all-important. The ideals of this period are still largely in control, even where the outward methods and studies have been changed. We sometimes hear the introduction of manual training, art, and science into the elementary, and even the secondary, schools deprecated on the ground that they tend toward the production of specialists—that they detract from our present scheme of generous, liberal culture. The point of this objection would be ludicrous if it were not often so effective as to make it tragic. It is our present education which is highly specialized, one-sided, and narrow. It is an education dominated almost entirely by the mediaeval conception of learning. It is something which appeals for the most part simply to the intellectual aspect of our natures, our desire to learn, to accumulate information, and to get control of the symbols of learning; not to our impulses and tendencies to make, to do, to create, to produce, whether in the form of utility or of art. The very fact that manual training, art, and science are objected to as technical, as tending toward mere specialism, is of itself as good testimony as could be offered to the specialized aim which controls current education. Unless education had been virtually identified with the exclusively intellectual pursuits, with learning as such, all these materials and methods would be welcome, would be greeted with the utmost hospitality.

While training for the profession of learning is regarded as the type of culture, or a liberal education, the training of a mechanic, a musician, a lawyer, a doctor, a farmer, a merchant, or a railroad manager is regarded as purely technical and professional. The result is that which we see about us everywhere—the division into "cultured" people and "workers," the separation of theory and practice. Hardly 1 percent of the entire school population ever attains to what we call higher education; only 5 percent to the grade of our high school; while much more than half leave on or before the completion of the fifth year of the elementary grade. The simple facts of the case are that in the great majority of human beings, the distinctively intellectual interest is not dominant. They have the so-called practical impulse and disposition. In many of those in whom by nature intellectual interest is strong, social conditions prevent its adequate realization. Consequently, by far the larger number of pupils leave school as soon as they have acquired the rudiments of learning, as soon as they have enough of the symbols of reading, writing, and calculating to be of practical use to them in getting a living. While our educational leaders are talking of culture, the development of personality, etc., as the end and aim of education, the great majority of those who pass under the tuition of the school regard it only as a narrowly practical tool with which to get bread and butter enough to eke out a restricted life. If we were to conceive our educational end and aim in a less exclusive way, if we were to introduce into educational processes the activities which appeal to those whose dominant interest is to do and to make, we should find the hold of the school upon its members to be more vital, more prolonged, containing more of culture.

But why should I make this labored presentation? The obvious fact is that our social life has undergone a thorough and radical change. If our education is to have any meaning for life, it must pass through an equally complete transformation. This transformation is not something to appear suddenly, to be executed in a day by conscious purpose. It is already in progress. Those modifications of our school system which often appear (even to those most actively concerned with them, to say nothing of their spectators) to be mere changes of detail, mere improvement within the school mechanism, are in reality signs and evidences of evolution. The introduction of active occupations, of nature-study, of elementary science, of art, of history; the relegation of the merely symbolic and formal to a secondary position; the change in the moral school atmosphere, in the relation of pupils and teachers—of discipline; the introduction of more active, expressive, and self-directing factors—all these are not mere accidents, they are necessities of the larger social evolution. It remains but to organize all these factors, to appreciate them in the fullness of meaning, and to put the ideas and ideals involved into complete, uncompromising possession of our school system. To do this means to make each one of our schools an embryonic community life, active with types of occupations that reflect the life of the larger society and are permeated throughout with the spirit of art, history, and science. When the school introduces and trains each child of society into membership within such a little community, saturating him with the spirit of service, and providing him with the instruments of effective self-direction, we shall have the deepest and best guaranty of a larger society which is worthy, lovely, and harmonious.

John Dewey, *The School and Society*, Chicago, IL: University of Chicago Press, 1899, pp. 6–29.

Lewis M. Terman, *National Intelligence Tests*, 1919

If there is any part of the progressive heritage that continues to impact contemporary students, it is the belief, strongly held by one faction of progressive educators, that educational testing is the key to understanding students and improving their education. Edward L. Thorndike voiced his confidence in educational measurement when he wrote in 1918 that, "Whatever exists at all exists in some amount. To know it thoroughly involves knowing its quality as well as its quantity." From this confidence in scientific measurement came the IQ test, the SAT, and all the rest of the range of educational testing that has impacted the lives of virtually every American student for the last century. The voice most consistently calling for testing was Lewis M. Terman, a long-time member of the faculty at Stanford University, member of the Commission that developed tests for the U.S. Army during World War I, and popularizer of the Stanford-Binet intelligence tests. In this selection, from his 1919 book, The Intelligence of School Children, *he wrote of his faith in a plea to schoolteachers to adopt his perspective.*

The Binet tests, a method of assaying intelligence. In order to find out how much gold is contained in a given vein of quartz, it is not necessary to uncover all the ore and extract and weigh every particle of the precious metal. It is sufficient merely to ascertain by borings the linear extent of the lode and to take a small amount of the ore to the laboratory of an assayer, who will make a test and render a verdict of so many ounces of gold per ton of ore.

A half-century ago, Francis Galton predicted that it would sometime be possible to obtain a general knowledge of the intellectual capacities of a man by sinking shafts, as it were, at a few critical points. Already Galton's dream is in process of realization, for in the last decade, mental testing has become one of the most fruitful branches of psychological science. The credit for pointing the way belongs largely to the French psychologist, Alfred Binet, who, after more than fifteen years of patient research, gave to the world in 1908 the system of mental tests now known as the Binet-Simon Intelligence Scale. In various revised forms, the method has come into general use in public schools, institutions for defectives, prisons, reform schools, and juvenile courts in the United States and in Europe. Our debt to Binet is very great, for he succeeded in bringing psychology down from the clouds and making it useful to men.

The Binet scale is made up of an extended series of tests in the nature of problems, success in which demands the exercise of the intellectual processes. As left by Binet, the scale consisted of fifty-four tests, ranging in difficulty from tests which are passed by the average child of three years, to tests which are difficult enough for the average adult. The Standard Revision has increased the number of tests to ninety and has extended the scale far enough to measure the intelligence of superior adults.

The ninety tests in the revised scale constitute an extremely variegated series. This is necessary, since their purpose is to measure the subject's *general intelligence*, not his special ability in a particular line. They include tests of memory, language comprehension, size of vocabulary, orientation in time and space, eye-hand coordinations, knowledge about familiar things, judgment, ability to find likenesses and differences between common objects, arithmetical reasoning, resourcefulness and ingenuity in difficult practical situations, ability to detect absurdities, apperception, the speed and richness of association of ideas, the power to combine the dissected parts of a form board or a group of ideas into a unitary whole, the capacity to generalize from particulars, the ability to deduce a rule from connected facts, etc. Thus the tests give a kind of composite picture of the subject's general mental ability, and since standards of comparison have been established for each of the individual tests by trying it out on hundreds of unselected normal children of all ages, it is possible to express the total result of an examination in terms of "mental age" norms.

Why a mental test is significant. Are we justified in attributing real diagnostic significance to the little intellectual "stunts" called for by an intelligence scale? Some of these may even appear trivial. What does it signify, for example, whether a given ten-year-old subject names forty words or a hundred words in three minutes? Whether he puts together the parts of a form board in thirty seconds or in two minutes? Whether he defines thirty words or sixty words of a hundred-word list? Whether his definitions of words are stated in terms of "use" or in terms "superior to use"? Whether a series of five digits or only a series of three digits can be repeated backwards after a single auditory presentation? Whether there are three, two, one, or no successes in the attempt to draw a diamond-shaped figure from copy?

The secret lies in the standardization of the tests upon normal children of different ages. Without such a standardization, the tests would mean nothing. Standardization is coming to play the same role in psychology that it has long played in the various branches of applied science. The architect or bridge engineer plans his structure with constant reference to foot-pounds of strain which various materials will withstand. The physician analyzes a drop of blood and, by comparison of corpuscle count and haemoglobin with the norms for health and disease, is able to render an important diagnosis. The psychologist working with mental tests may be compared with the palaeontologist who finds in a gravel bed of some prehistoric age a skull cap, a fragment of a jaw, and a broken humerus. Although the layman might not even recognize the human origin of such remnants, the palaeontologist is able to tell us that the bones are those of a middle-aged male, that the species to which he belonged had not yet learned to stand erect, that he probably did not know the use of fire (worn teeth indicate that he subsisted on uncooked foods), that his intelligence was inferior (cranial contents only two thirds that of modern man), and that he had probably evolved but limited power of speech (diminutive points of attachment for the speech muscles). A little technical acquaintance with the standards of shape, size, and structure of human bones has transformed the meaningless fragments into a "missing link"—*Homo neanderthalensis.*

Perhaps no two things could be more alike to casual inspection than the balls of two thumbs; yet one who has been taught to read fingerprints can ordinarily find from forty to seventy separate and individually sufficient points of identification. Just as many a man has been hanged on the evidence of his fingerprints, so many an individual might safely be committed to an institution for the feebleminded on the evidence of ten or a dozen intelligence tests which have been standardized according to age norms.

The meaning of mental age. Both the individual tests of the Binet scale and the scale as a whole have been standardized on the basis of age norms. The tests themselves are located in age groups in such a way as to bring it about that the *average* child of eight years will earn by the scale a "mental age" of eight years, the *average* twelve-year-old a "mental age" of twelve years, etc. Such an arrangement was arrived at empirically by trying out a series of tests upon hundreds of normal children of different ages. The Stanford Revision, for example, was based on tests of 1,700 children and 400 adults.

To illustrate the use of the scale, let us suppose we are testing a child of eight years. If our subject passes successfully as far as the average child of eight years, we say that his mental age is eight years, or in this case, normal. If he goes as far as the average ten-year-old, we say that he has a mental age of ten years. If he earns no more credit than the average six-year-old, his mental age is six years. Binet merely took a standard of comparison which everyone uses (namely, the standard of age) and made it definite by finding out what intellectual performances representative children of different ages are capable of.

It is necessary that the reader should at the outset arrive at a correct understanding of what the term *mental age is* and is not intended to signify. Two misconceptions are to be avoided:

1. That each "mental age" is a separate and qualitatively distinct level of mental attainment, contrasting markedly with both the mental age which precedes it and that which follows it. Such a use of the term is not in harmony with the facts. Mental development is consecutive and gradual. There is probably no mental power, capacity, or function which has a Minerva birth. The "faculty" in question develops first in rudimentary form, then grows gradually stronger and more definite until, by imperceptible stages, it reaches a state of maturity.

2. Another misunderstanding comes from the assumption that those who use the term believe a given mental age is a stage of development which all normal individuals pass through at the corresponding actual age. Such a belief would imply that the age of ten years, for example, all children who do not belong to some special type (defective, genius, etc.) should be found at the ten-year mental age, eight-year children at the eight-year mental age, etc. It is one of the main purposes of this book to show how widely children of a given age differ in mental age, and how greatly children of adjacent ages overlap each other in mental age.

The real meaning of the term is perfectly straightforward and unambiguous. By a given mental age, we mean *that degree of general mental ability which is possessed by the average child of corresponding chronological age.*

Mental age as a basis for school grading. The significance of mental age for the teacher lies in the fact that it can be used as a basis for grading the pupils so as to secure class groups of homogeneous ability. As will be shown in succeeding chapters, the pupils of given grades, or even the pupils of one grade in a single classroom, are far from equal in general intelligence or in ability to master the school work. Generally speaking, not far from a fourth of the pupils in any given grade have a mental level too low to make satisfactory work in that grade possible, while another fourth have reached a mental level which would enable them to succeed in a higher grade.

The intelligent quotient. The mental age merely indicates the level of development which a child has reached at a given time. Considered apart from chronological age it does not tell us whether a child is bright, dull, or average. Of three children all testing at the mental age of eight years, one might very well be exceptionally superior, one average, and one feeble-minded. Such would be the case if their chronological ages were six, eight, and twelve years.

In addition to an index of absolute mental level, we need an index of relative brightness. Such is the intelligence quotient (IQ), which is the ratio of mental age to chronological age. The six-year-old of eight-year mental age has an IQ of 8/6 or 133; the twelve-year-old with a mental age of eight years, an IQ of 8/12, or 67. In computing the IQ of an adult subject, years of chronological age in excess of sixteen are disregarded, as the development of native intelligence seems practically to cease not far from this age.

An idea of how greatly school children differ in brightness is shown by the analysis of the IQs of one-thousand representative children in which it was found that:

The lowest 1% go to 70 or below, the highest 1% reach 130 or above
The lowest 2% go to 73 or below, the highest 2% reach 128 or above
The lowest 3% go to 76 or below, the highest 3% reach 125 or above
The lowest 5% go to 78 or below, the highest 5% reach 122 or above
The lowest 10% go to 85 or below, the highest 10% reach 116 or above
The lowest 15% go to 88 or below, the highest 15% reach 113 or above
The lowest 20% go to 91 or below, the highest 20% reach 110 or above
The lowest 25% go to 92 or below, the highest 25% reach 108 or above
The lowest 33% go to 95 or below, the highest 33% reach 106 or above

The intelligent quotient as a basis for prediction. Just as mental age indicates the school grade in which a child normally belongs at a given time, so the IQ is the basis for prediction in regard to the child's later mental development. The possibility of such prediction comes from the fact that the IQ has been found in the large majority of cases to remain fairly constant, at least for the ages between three or four and fourteen or fifteen. For illustration, we will take the case of a four-year-old child who is found to have a mental age of five years, and whose IQ is therefore 125. The probability is that child will continue to have a mental age not far from 25 percent above his chronological age, with consequences which may be expressed as follows:

It would, of course, be absurd to expect the IQ to maintain itself at an absolutely constant figure. Fluctuations occur for at least three reasons: (1) There may be in exceptional cases a certain amount of irregularity in the actual rate of mental development. (2) The results of a test may be influenced to some extent by the conditions under which it is given, the state of the child's health, his attitude toward the test, fatigue, and other temporary or accidental factors. Retests after a brief interval indicate that errors from this source are ordinarily not large. (3) There is inevitably a certain amount of error in every IQ rating, due to imperfections in

Table 8.1

Chronological Age	Probable Mental Age	Probable School Ability
4 years	5 years	Upper kindergarten
6 years	7½ years	Second school grade
8 years	10 years	High fourth grade
10 years	12½ years	Low seventh grade
12 years	15 years	First year high school

the scale used. If the scale has been so standardized that it yields mental ages which are too low, the IQ found will be too low; if the scale errs in the direction of being too generous, the resulting IQ will be too high. A scale may err in one direction at one level and in the opposite direction at another level. It was the most serious fault of the original Binet scale that in the lower range of tests it yielded mental ages which were too high, and in the upper range mental ages which were too low. The effect of such errors is greatly to exaggerate the amount of fluctuation to which mental growth is subject. It was the main purpose of the Standard Revision to reduce these constant errors. Chapter XI shows in detail the degree of constancy which may be expressed for the IQ when the Standard Revision is used. While the law of constancy is subject to minor revisions, few things are more certain than the essential untruth of the widespread belief that mental development knows no regularity, and that the dullard of to-day becomes the genius of tomorrow. The fact is that, apart from minor fluctuations due to temporary factors, and apart from occasional instances of arrest or deterioration due to acquired nervous disease, the feeble-minded remain feeble-minded, the dull remain dull, the average remain average, and the superior remain superior. There is nothing in one's equipment, with the exception of character, which rivals the IQ in importance.

Effects of environment on the IQ. The question is always raised whether, in estimating a child's intelligence on the basis of the IQ it is not necessary to make allowance for the influence of social environment. For example, it is often argued that the child cannot know his age if he has never heard it, cannot read and report the memory passages if he has never attended school, cannot count from 20 to 1 if he has never been taught to count from 1 to 20, cannot name the days of the week or the months of the year unless he has heard others name them, and that therefore the IQ can have little significance except possibly as an index of the subject's social and educational environment.

It is, of course, true that an individual who for his entire life had been entirely deprived of human environment (assuming such a thing to be possible) could not pass a satisfactory Binet test, however normal his original endowment may have been. To use an extreme illustration, a child of ten years who had been reared in a cage, whose wants had been supplied while he was asleep, or by means of ingenious mechanical contrivances, who had never seen a human being, could hardly be expected to make a brilliant showing in defining words in the vocabulary test, detecting absurdities, repeating sentences, reading the Binet passage, answering comprehension questions, or naming sixty words. We may go further and assume that such a subject would be as little successful with the three-year as with the ten-year test.

Needless to say, the Binet scale was not intended for subjects of the type we have just described. Its use in a given case takes for granted that the ordinary and all but inevitable social contacts have been made, that the subject is not deaf or blind, and that he has had reasonable opportunity to learn the language in which the tests are given. Children who have attended school for any considerable time meet all of these requirements, whatever the social status of the home.

As a matter of fact, limited acquaintance with the language employed in the examination does not put the subject at great disadvantage in many of the tests. In some it does, and in testing subjects who are under this handicap the vocabulary test and a few others may very well be omitted. Following are two illustrations which show that the validity of the scale does not hinge entirely upon the subject's knowledge of English:

1. Kohs tested a Belgian refugee child of nine years who had been in America but two years. Although this child's acquaintance with the English language was very limited, the IQ earned on the Stanford-Binet scale was 99. The child was also doing schoolwork of average quality in the fourth grade.
2. Dickson tested a Japanese boy, aged five years, two months, who had never attended school and who had had little opportunity to learn English; yet this boy earned a mental age of seven years and an IQ of 133.

That lack of schooling does not prevent a subject from earning an average or superior score in the test is shown by the cases of S. S. and Gypsy Mary.

S. S. was tested at the age of seven years. He had never been to school, and although his home advantages were excellent, he had had no formal instruction and had never learned to read. The parents believed, perhaps rightly, that the important needs of childhood, apart from simple moral instruction, are food, fresh air, and freedom to play. Nevertheless, S. earned a mental age of ten years, eight months, and an IQ of 153.

In 1916, a gypsy girl of sixteen years was given the Stanford Binet test in a clinic in Oakland, California. This girl had been stolen by the gypsies when she was about four years old, had lived with them continuously until a few days before the test was made, and had never attended a school. The IQ found was approximately 100.

It is not denied that the cultural status of the home (even apart from heredity) may affect the result of the test to some extent, although the influence has never been accurately determined. If it were considerable, we should find a marked rise of IQ in the case of children who had been removed from an inferior to a satisfactory home environment. Our data on this point are not extensive, but of a dozen or more children of this kind whom we have retested, not one showed improvement. Two such children, Walter and Frank, have been under observation for several years. Until the ages of five and seven years they lived in an exceptionally poor home. The mother was dull, the father illiterate and a drunkard. Both of the parents died within a year, and the boys were adopted by a woman of decidedly more than average ability who treated them as her own sons. At the time of adoption, one tested at 73, the other at 82. Four years later, the IQ's were 70 and 77. It is a general rule that children of borderline intelligence improve little if at all in IQ as they get older, notwithstanding their increased school experience and the extra attention they receive in special classes.

That the environment of the home affects the result of the test but little is further shown by the fact that occasionally in a very inferior home, all of the children except one test low, as would be expected, while that one tests exceptionally high. In one such family (Portuguese) there are three children who test between 76 and 88, while a brother of these tests at 130. The latter is making a very superior record in high school, which he entered at the age of thirteen years. The others have not been able to complete the eighth grade. All have had the same home environment and the same educational opportunities.

Scales for group testing. To test each year the intelligence of all the children by the Binet method would involve a larger task than the school is likely to undertake. There is accordingly a wide field for tests which can be applied to an entire group, or class, at once. The various scales have been devised for this purpose. The group scales are given as written tests and can be applied to an entire class of fifty or more pupils in about an hour. To score the records requires about ten minutes for each pupil, or a total of about five or six hours for a class of average size. This can be done evenings or at odd times. Most group scales have the advantage of requiring little special psychological training either for giving the tests or scoring them. An unfortunate limitation of such scales is that they are not satisfactory in the lower grades, where the need for testing is greatest. As measures of intelligence they are probably somewhat less accurate than scales for individual testing, but their obvious advantages make them deserving of wide use with pupils of the upper grades and high school.

However, no group scale will ever do away with the necessity of individual testing. Rather it makes the need for individual testing more obvious. All the pupils in the fourth grade and beyond should be given a test by the group method every year, and those whose scores are either very high or very low in the group examination should be given a Binet test. As will be shown later, it is highly desirable that every pupil be given a mental test within the first half-year of his school life.

Lewis M. Terman, *The Intelligence of School Children*, Boston, MA: Houghton Mifflin Company, 1919, pp. 1–21.

GEORGE COUNTS, *DARE THE SCHOOL BUILD A NEW SOCIAL ORDER?*, 1932

One of the most powerful voices of dissent in the 1930s emerged from the heart of progressive education itself. In the midst of the Great Depression, George S. Counts found himself increasingly frustrated with child-centered progressives who, he thought, were drowning out the voices of all of the rest. "Like a baby shaking a rattle, we seem to be utterly content with action, provided it is sufficiently vigorous and noisy," he said. "The weakness of Progressive Education thus lies in the fact that it has elaborated no theory of social welfare, unless it be that of anarchy or extreme individualism." In a series of speeches to teacher union gatherings, Counts electrified his audience with his call for a very different progressivism in which teachers would take the lead in building a more democratic and egalitarian society for all. Counts' speeches were published as Dare the School Build a New Social Order?; *Chapter 2 of the book appears here.*

1. There is the fallacy that man is born free. As a matter of fact, he is born helpless. He achieves freedom, as a race and as an individual, through the medium of culture. The most crucial of all circumstances conditioning human life is birth into a particular culture. By birth one becomes a Chinese, an Englishman, a Hottentot, a Sioux Indian, a Turk, or a 100 percent American. Such a range of possibilities may appear too shocking to contemplate, but it is the price that one must pay in order to be born. Nevertheless, even if a given soul should happen by chance to choose a Hottentot for a mother, it should thank its lucky star that it was born into the Hottentot culture rather than entirely free. By being nurtured on a body of culture, however backward and limited it may be comparatively, the individual is at once imposed upon and liberated. The child is terribly imposed upon by being compelled through the accidents of birth to learn one language rather than another, but without some language, man would never become man. Any language, even the most poverty-stricken, is infinitely better than none at all.

In the life cycle of the individual, many choices must of necessity be made, and the most fundamental and decisive of these choices will always be made by the group. This is so obvious that it should require no elaboration. Yet this very obvious fact with its implications, is commonly disregarded by those who are fearful of molding the child.

One of the most important elements of any culture is a tradition of achievement along a particular line—a tradition which the group imposes upon the young and through which the powers of the young are focused, disciplined, and developed. One people will have a fine hunting tradition, another a maritime tradition, another a musical tradition, another a military tradition, another a scientific tradition, another a baseball tradition, another a business tradition, and another even a tradition of moral and religious prophecy. A particular society of the modern type has a vast number of different traditions, all of which may be bound together and integrated more or less by some broad and inclusive tradition. One might argue that the imposing of these traditions upon children involves a severe restriction upon their freedom. My thesis is that such imposition, provided the tradition is vital and suited to the times, releases the energies of the young, sets up standards of excellence, and makes possible really great achievement. The individual who fails to come under the influence of such a tradition may enjoy a certain kind of freedom, but it is scarcely a kind of freedom that anyone would covet for either himself or his children. It is the freedom of mediocrity, incompetence, and aimlessness.

2. There is the fallacy that the child is good by nature. The evidence from anthropology, as well as from common observation, shows that on entering the world the individual is neither good nor bad; he is merely a bundle of potentialities which may be developed in manifold directions. Guidance is, therefore, not to be found in child nature, but rather in the culture of the group and the purposes of living. There can be no good individual apart from some conception of the character of the *good* society; and the good society is not something that is given by nature: it must be fashioned by the hand and brain of man. This process of building a good society is to a very large degree an educational process. The nature of the child must of course be taken into account in the organization of any educational program, but it cannot furnish the materials and the guiding principles of that program. Squirm and wriggle as we may, we must admit that the bringing of materials and guiding principles from the outside involves the molding of the child.

3. There is the fallacy that the child lives in a separate world of his own. The advocates of freedom often speak of the adult as an alien influence in the life of the child. For an adult to intrude himself or his values into the domain of boys and girls is made to take on the appearance of an invasion by a foreign power. Such a dualism is almost wholly artificial. Whatever may be the view of the adult, the child knows but one society; and that is a society including persons of all ages. This does not mean that conflicts of interest may not occur, or that on occasion adults may not abuse and exploit children. It does mean that in a proper kind of society, the relationship is one of mutual benefit and regard in which the young repay in trust and emulation the protection and guidance provided by their elders. The child's conception of his position in society is well-expressed in the words of Plenty-coups, the famous Crow chieftain, who spoke thus of his boyhood: "We followed the buffalo herds over the beautiful plains, fighting a battle one day and sending out a war-party against the enemy the next. My heart was afire. I wished so to help

my people, to distinguish myself, so that I might wear an eagle's feather in my hair. How I worked to make my arms strong as a grizzly's, and how I practiced with my bow! A boy never wished to be a man more than I." Here is an emphatic and unequivocal answer to those who would raise a barrier between youth and age. Place the child in a world of his own and you take from him the most powerful incentives to growth and achievement. Perhaps one of the greatest tragedies of contemporary society lies in the fact that the child is becoming increasingly isolated from the serious activities of adults. Some would say that such isolation is an inevitable corollary of the growing complexity of the social order. In my opinion, it is rather the product of a society that is moved by no great commanding ideals and is consequently victimized by the most terrible form of human madness—the struggle for private gain. As primitive peoples wisely protect their children from the dangers of actual warfare, so we guard ours from the acerbities of economic strife. Until school and society are bound together by common purposes, the program of education will lack both meaning and vitality.

4. There is the fallacy that education is some pure and mystical essence that remains unchanged from everlasting to everlasting. According to this view, genuine education must be completely divorced from politics, live apart from the play of social forces, and pursue ends peculiar to itself. It thus becomes a method existing independently of the cultural milieu and equally beneficent at all times and in all places. This is one of the most dangerous of fallacies and is responsible for many sins committed in different countries by American educators traveling abroad. They have carried the same brand of education to backward and advanced races, to peoples living under relatively static conditions and to peoples passing through periods of rapid and fundamental transition. They have called it Education with a capital *E*, whereas in fact it has been American education with a capital *A* and a small *e*. Any defensible educational program must be adjusted to a particular time and place, and the degree and nature of the imposition must vary with the societal situation. Under ordinary conditions, the process of living suffices in itself to hold society together, but when the forces of disintegration become sufficiently powerful, it may well be that a fairly large measure of deliberate control is desirable and even essential to social survival.

5. There is the fallacy that school should be impartial in its emphases, that no bias should be given instruction. We have already observed how the individual is inevitably molded by the culture into which he is born. In the case of the school, a similar process operates and presumably is subject to a degree of conscious direction. My thesis is that complete impartiality is utterly impossible, that the school must shape attitudes, develop tastes, and even impose ideas. It is obvious that the whole of creation cannot be brought into the school. This means that some selection must be made of teachers, curricula, architecture, methods of teaching. And in the making of the selection, the dice must always be weighted in favor of this or that. Here is a fundamental truth that cannot be brushed aside as irrelevant or unimportant; it constitutes the very essence of the matter under discussion. Nor can the reality be concealed beneath agreeable phrases. Professor Dewey states in his *Democracy and Education* that the school should provide a *purified* environment for the child. With this view I would certainly agree; probably no person reared in our society would favor the study of pornography in the schools. I am sure, however,

that this means stacking the cards in favor of the particular system of value which we may happen to possess. It is one of the truisms of the anthropologist that there are no maxims of purity on which all people would agree. Other vigorous opponents of imposition unblushingly advocate the "cultivation of democratic sentiments" in children or the promotion of child growth in the direction of "a better and richer life." The first represents definite acquiescence in imposition; the second, if it does not mean the same thing, means nothing. I believe firmly that democratic sentiments should be cultivated and that a better and richer life should be the outcome of education, but in neither case would I place responsibility on either God or the order of nature. I would merely contend that as educators we must make many choices involving the development of attitudes in boys and girls and that we should not be afraid to acknowledge the faith that is in us or mayhap the forces that compel us.

6. There is the fallacy that the great object of education is to produce the college professor, that is, the individual who adopts an agnostic attitude towards every important social issue, who can balance the pros against the cons with the skill of a juggler, who sees all sides of every question and never commits himself to any, who delays action until all the facts are in, who knows that all the facts will never come in, who consequently holds his judgment in a state of indefinite suspension, and who before the approach of middle age sees his powers of action atrophy and his social sympathies decay. With Peer Gynt he can exclaim:

> Ay, think of it—wish it done—will it to boot,—
> But do it—! No, that's past my understanding!

This type of mind also talks about waiting until the solutions of social problems are found, when as a matter of fact there are no solutions in any definite and final sense. For any complex social problem worthy of the name there are probably tens and even scores, if not hundreds, of "solutions," depending upon the premises from which one works. The meeting of a social situation involves the making of decisions and the working out of adjustments. Also it involves the selection and rejection of values. If we wait for a solution to appear like the bursting of the sun through the clouds or the resolving of the elements in an algebraic equation, we shall wait in vain. Although college professors, if not too numerous, perform a valuable social function, society requires great numbers of persons who, while capable of gathering and digesting facts, are at the same time able to think in terms of life, make decisions, and act. From such persons will come our real social leaders.

7. There is the closely related fallacy that education is primarily intellectualistic in its processes and goals. Quite as important is that ideal factor in culture which gives meaning, direction, and significance to life. I refer to the element of faith or purpose which lifts man out of himself and above the level of his more narrow personal interests. Here, in my judgment, is one of the great lacks in our schools and in our intellectual class today. We are able to contemplate the universe and find that all is vanity. Nothing really stirs us, unless it be that the bath water is cold, the toast burnt, or the elevator not running; or that perchance we miss the first section of a revolving door. Possibly this is the fundamental reason why we are so fearful of molding the child. We are moved by no

great faiths; we are touched by no great passions. We can view a world rushing rapidly towards collapse with no more concern than the outcome of a horse race; we can see injustice, crime, and misery in their most terrible forms all about us and, if we are not directly affected, register the emotions of a scientist studying white rats in a laboratory. And in the name of freedom, objectivity, and the open mind, we would transmit this general attitude of futility to our children. In my opinion, this is a confession of complete moral and spiritual bankruptcy. We cannot, by talk about the interests of children and the sacredness of personality, evade the responsibility of bringing to the younger generation a vision which will call forth their active loyalties and challenge them to creative and arduous labors. A generation without such a vision is destined, like ours, to a life of absorption in self, inferiority complexes, and frustration. The genuinely free man is not the person who spends the day contemplating his own navel, but rather the one who loses himself in a great cause or glorious adventure.

8. There is the fallacy that the school is an all-powerful educational agency. Every professional group tends to exaggerate its own importance in the scheme of things. To this general rule the teachers offer no exception. The leaders of Progressive Education in particular seem to have an over-weening faith in the power of the school. On the one hand, they speak continually about reconstructing society through education; and on the other, they apparently live in a state of perpetual fear lest the school impose some one point of view upon all children and mold them all to a single pattern. A moment's reflection is sufficient to show that life in the modern world is far too complex to permit this: The school is but one formative agency among many, and certainly not the strongest at that. Our major concern consequently should be, not to keep the school from influencing the child in a positive direction, but rather to make certain that every progressive school will use whatever power it may possess in opposing and checking the forces of social conservatism and reaction. We know full well that, if the school should endeavor vigorously and consistently to win its pupils to the support of a given social program, unless it were supported by other agencies, it could act only as a mild counterpoise to restrain and challenge the might of less enlightened and more selfish purposes.

9. There is the fallacy that ignorance rather than knowledge is the way of wisdom. Many who would agree that imposition of some kind is inevitable seem to feel that there is something essentially profane in any effort to understand, plan, and control the process. They will admit that the child is molded by his environment, and then presumably contend that in the fashioning of this environment we should close our eyes to the consequences of our acts, or at least should not endeavor to control our acts in the light of definite knowledge of their consequences. To do the latter would involve an effort to influence deliberately the growth of the child in a particular direction—to cause him to form this habit rather than that, to develop one taste rather than another, to be sensitive to a given ideal rather than its rival. But this would be a violation of the "rights of the child," and therefore evil. Apparently his rights can be protected only if our influence upon him is thoroughly concealed under a heavy veil of ignorance. If the school can do no better than this, it has no reason for existence. If it is to be merely an arena for the blind play of psychological forces, it might better close its doors. Here is the doctrine of *laissez faire*, driven from the field of social and political theory, seeking refuge in the

domain of pedagogy. Progressive Education wishes to build a new world but refuses to be held accountable for the kind of world it builds. In my judgment, the school should know what it is doing, in so far as this is humanly possible, and accept full responsibility for its acts.

10. Finally, there is the fallacy that in a dynamic society like ours the major responsibility of education is to prepare the individual to adjust himself to social change. The argument in support of this view is fairly cogent. The world is changing with great rapidity; the rate of change is being accelerated constantly; the future is full of uncertainty. Consequently, the individual who is to live and thrive in this world must possess an agile mind, be bound by no deep loyalties, hold all conclusions and values tentatively, and be ready on a moment's notice to make even fundamental shifts in outlook and philosophy. Like a lumberjack riding a raft of logs through the rapids, he must be able with lightning speed to jump from one insecure foundation to another, if he is not to be overwhelmed by the onward surge of the cultural stream. In a word, he must be as willing to adopt new ideas and values as to install the most up-to-the-minute labor-saving devices in his dwelling or to introduce the latest inventions in his factory. Under such a conception of life and society, education can only bow down before the gods of chance and reflect the drift of the social order. This conception is essentially anarchic in character, exalts the irrational above the rational forces of society, makes of security an individual rather than a social goal, drives every one of us into an insane competition with his neighbors, and assumes that man is incapable of controlling in the common interest the creatures of his brain. Here we have imposition with a vengeance, but not the imposition of the teacher or the school. Nor is it the imposition of the chaos and cruelty and ugliness produced by the brutish struggle for existence and advantage. Far more terrifying than any indoctrination in which the school might indulge is the prospect of our becoming completely victimized and molded by the mechanics of industrialism. The control of the machine requires a society which is dominated less by the ideal of individual advancement and more by certain far-reaching purposes and plans for social construction. In such a society, instead of the nimble mind responsive to every eddy in the social current, a firmer and more steadfast mentality would be preferable.

George S. Counts, *Dare the School Build a New Social Order?*, New York: The John Day Company, 1932, pp. 13–27.

THE SOCIAL FRONTIER, 1934

In October 1934, in the midst of the Great Depression, the most politically minded of the progressive educators launched a new journal, The Social Frontier. *Under George Counts' leadership,* The Social Frontier *included such other progressives as William H. Kilpatrick, Harold Rugg, Harrison Elliott, and the venerable John Dewey among its directors. The journal's editors were clear in their goals, calling on teachers and progressive educators to engage in active political agitation for a more socially democratic school and to play a role in the reconstruction of American society. An editorial from the first issue of the journal gives a good sense of the urgency with which these educators faced the issues raised by the Great Depression.*

A subsequent article by John Dewey represents his own call to teachers to enlist in the crusade for social reconstruction.

Orientation—The Editors

The Social Frontier assumes that the age of individualism in economy is closing and that an age marked by close integration of social life and by collective planning and control is opening. For weal or woe, it accepts as irrevocable this deliverance of the historical process. It intends to go forward to meet the new age and to proceed as rationally as possible to the realization of all possibilities for the enrichment and refinement of human life. It will nurse no fantasies of returning to the simple household and neighborhood economy of the time of Thomas Jefferson; it will seek no escape from the responsibilities of today, either by longing for a past now gone beyond recovery or by imagining a future bearing the features of Utopia. It proposes to take seriously the affirmation of the Declaration of Independence that "all men are created equal" and are entitled to "life, liberty, and the pursuit of happiness." Also it proposes, in the light of this great humanist principle applied to the collective realities of industrial civilization, to pass every important educational event, institution, theory, and program under critical review. Finally, it will devote its pages positively to the development of the thought of all who are interested in making education discharge its full responsibility in the present age of social transition. Its editorial staff and board of directors hope that it will help fight the great educational battles—practical and theoretical—which are already looming above the horizon. And they trust that it will engage in the battles of the twentieth and not of the eighteenth century.

The Social Frontier acknowledges allegiance to no narrow conception of education. While recognizing the school as society's central educational agency, it refuses to *limit* itself to a consideration of the work of this institution. On the contrary, it includes within its field of interest all of those formative influences and agencies which serve to induct the individual— whether old or young—into the life and culture of the group. It regards education as an aspect of a culture in process of evolution. It therefore has no desire to promote a restricted and technical professionalism. Rather does it address itself to the task of considering the broad role of education in advancing the welfare and interests of the great masses of the people who do the work of society—those who labor on farms and ships and in the mines, shops, and factories of the world.

Can Education Share in Social Reconstruction?—John Dewey

That upon the whole schools have been educating for something called the *status quo* can hardly be doubted by observing persons. The fallacy in this attempt should be equally evident. There is no *status quo*—except in the literal sense in which Andy explained the phrase to Amos: a name for the "mess we are in." It is not difficult, however, to define that which is called the *status quo*; the difficulty is that the movement of actual events has little connection with the name by which it is called.

For the alleged *status quo* is summed up in the phrase "rugged individualism." The assumption is—or was—that we are living in a free economic society in which every individual has an equal chance to exercise his initiative and his other abilities, and that the legal and political order is designed and calculated to further this equal liberty on the part of all individuals. No grosser myth ever received general currency. Economic freedom has been either nonexistent or precarious for large masses of the population. Because of its absence and its tenuousness for the majority, political and cultural freedom has been sapped; the legally constituted order has supported the idea of a *bead possidentes*.

There is no need here to review the historic change from a simple agrarian order, in which the idea of equal opportunity contained a large measure of truth, to a complex industrial order with highly concentrated economic and political control. The point is that the earlier idea and theory persisted after it had lost all relevance to actual facts, and was then used to justify and strengthen the very situation that had undermined it in practice. What, then, is the real *status quo*? Is it the condition of free individuality postulated by the ruling theoretical philosophy, or is it the increasing encroachment of the power of a privileged minority, a power exercised over the liberties of the masses without corresponding responsibility?

It would not be difficult to make out a case for a positive and sweeping answer in favor of the latter alternative. Let me quote, as far as schools are concerned, from Roger Baldwin. "On the whole, it may be said without question that the public schools have been handed over to the keeping of the militant defenders of the *status quo*—the Daughters of the American Revolution, the American Legion, the Fundamentalists, the Ku Klux Klan, and the War Department. Look at rites and flag saluting by law in most states; compulsory reading of the Protestant Bible in eighteen states, contrary to the provision for the separation of church and state; compulsory teaching of the Constitution by prescribed routine; making a crime of the teaching of evolution in three states; special oaths of loyalty not required of other public servants in ten states; loyalty oaths required of students as a condition of graduation in many cities; history textbooks revised under pressure to conform to prejudice; restriction or ban on teachers' unions affiliated with the labor movement; laws protecting tenure beaten or emasculated; compulsory military training in both high schools and colleges, with inevitable pressure on students and teachers by the military mind." To these forms of outward and overt pressure may be added—as indeed Mr. Baldwin does add—more powerful, because more subtle and unformulated, pressures that act constantly upon teachers and students.

It might seem, then, that, judged by the present situation, limitation upon the efforts of teachers to promote a new social order—in which the ideal of freedom and equality of individuals will be a fact and not a fiction—tremendously outweighs the element of possibility in their doing so. Such is not the case, however, great as are the immediate odds against effort to realize the possibility. The reason is that the actual *status quo* is in a state of flux; there is no *status quo*, if by that term it means something stable and constant. The last forty years have seen in every industrialized society all over the world a steady movement in the direction of social control of economic forces. Pressure for this control of capital—or, if you please, for its "regimentation"—is exercised mostly through political agencies and voluntary organizations. Laissez faire has been dying of strangulation. Mr. Hoover, who gave currency to the phrase "rugged individualism" while President, acted repeatedly and often on a fairly large scale for governmental intervention and regulation of economic forces. The list of interferences with genuine educational freedom that has been cited is itself a sign of an effort, and often a conscious one, to stem a tide that is running in the opposite direction—that is, toward a collectivism that is hostile to the idea of unrestricted action on the part of those individuals who are possessed of economic and political power because of control [of the nation's resources] and the possibility of educational effort for establishing a new social order is fairly evident. Teachers and administrators often say they must "conform to conditions" rather than do what they would personally prefer to do. The proposition might be sound if conditions were fixed or even reasonably stable. But they are not . . .

In spite of the lethargy and timidity of all too many teachers, I believe there are enough teachers who will respond to the great task of making schools active and militant participants in creation of a new social order, provided they are shown not merely the general end in view but also the means of its accomplishment . . . Laying the bases, intellectual and moral, for a new social order is a sufficiently novel and inspiring ideal to arouse a new spirit in the teaching profession and to give direction to a radically changed effort. Those who hold such an ideal are false to what they profess in words when they line up with reactionaries in ridicule of those who would make the profession a reality. That task may well be left to educational fascists.

The Social Frontier: A Journal of Educational Criticism and Reconstruction, October 1934, Vol. I, No. 1, pp. 3–5, 11–12.

Schools in the Cold War Era, 1950–1970

- Introduction
- F. James Rutherford, Sputnik and Science Education, Reflections on 1957
- National Defense Education Act, 1958
- The *Scott Foresman Readers*, 1955

- H. G. Rickover, *Education for All Children: What We Can Learn from England*, 1962
- Herbert Kohl, *Thirty-Six Children*, 1967
- John Holt, *How Children Fail*, 1964

Introduction

By the 1950s, the progressive education movement that had dominated educational reform since 1890 was in a state of rapid decline. As Lawrence Cremin saw it, "By the 1950s, the enthusiasm, the vitality, and the drive were gone; all that remained were the slogans" (1961, p. 181). The loss of drive came on many fronts. The administrative progressives' effort to reform schools through top-down dictates had been frustrated because so many of the top positions had been captured by people with little vision. In too many cases bureaucrats replaced reformers. As for the militant teachers, from Margaret Haley to Ella Flagg Young to George Counts, the anticommunism of the Cold War ended whatever opportunities they had once had to tie teacher union organizing to the quest for a socialist and democratic society. A new generation of teacher union organizers that emerged in the 1950s carefully separated the movement from any controversial social changes and focused instead on bread-and-butter issues such as salary and working conditions. This move speeded their drive to organize, but separated them from efforts to improve the society in which children lived. Finally, as Counts had warned, the child-centered advocates fell victim to their own class limitations—since so many child-centered schools ended up serving mostly well-to-do students—and to societal concerns about what it took to prepare educationally successful youth.

At the same time, all of these movements came face to face with the major concern of the era: the Cold War and the launching of the Soviet satellite Sputnik in 1957. The fact that the Soviet Union was able to launch a satellite, before the United States, was a psychic shock unimaginable today. But that this event would awaken school reform efforts should be unsurprising in a nation that often turns to its schools to solve significant social problems. In the case of Sputnik, the result was a resurgence of interest in the capacity of schools to train scientists and engineers who could surpass the Russians—in space and in the more mundane matters of the Cold War. Suddenly, John Dewey and the progressive educators—diverse as they had been—were seen as the enemy, soft and mushy-headed sentimentalists who had let the nation's schools fall dangerously behind the rigorous and tough-minded schools of the Russian enemy. F. James Rutherford's reflections on the impact of Sputnik in education frame many of the educational reforms and debates of the 1950s and 1960s.

One immediate result of the Sputnik crisis was the passage of the National Defense Education Act by Congress in 1958. The title of the Act indicates both the urgency and the focus of federal education policy in the 1950s. The NDEA, as it was known, provided a major boost to efforts within the National Science Foundation to support school curricula as well as scientific research. The result was a significant expansion of the laboratory materials available to teachers as well as improvements in the quality of science textbooks. NDEA scholarships also supported a generation of college students who might otherwise have had difficulty financing higher education.

For school critics such as Navy Admiral Hyman Rickover, more needed to be done. For him the solution was clear—wipe away the vestiges of progressivism and replace them with a tough, basic education that would produce the leaders the nation needed. Rickover's *Education and Freedom*, a republication of his testimony before Congress, was both a direct attack on progressive education and a call for America to return to a more traditional curriculum taught in more traditional ways. Rickover and his allies were not, however, debating with progressive educators. They were simply putting the last nails into the coffin of a movement which—except in its educational testing phase, which had conveniently forgotten its progressive roots—had run its course.

Not everyone responded to the 1950s as Admiral Rickover and his educational colleagues did. A new generation of educational critics also emerged during this decade. Although they differed significantly among themselves, these critics did hark back to the concerns of the earlier child-centered educators. Herb Kohl, at the beginning of his long and distinguished career as an education reformer, was appalled at the antichild atmosphere he found in the New York City public schools when he first entered the classroom. He called for an education that began by exploring the wonderful curiosity of children and for the creation of classrooms and school systems founded on respect for each child. John Holt began with many similar observations. But where Kohl focused on changing schools, Holt gave up on them. His *How Children Fail* and subsequent books and lectures provided some of the philosophical foundation for both alternative schools and a growing home-school movement, but also describe the frustrations of classroom rigidity in ways that reflect Kohl and, indeed, many twenty-first-century teachers.

F. James Rutherford, Sputnik and Science Education, Reflections on 1957

Few events had so much impact on American society and American education as the launch by the Soviet Union of the first space satellite, Sputnik, in 1957 in the midst of the Cold War. While the Eisenhower administration then in office was not surprised or alarmed by Sputnik—they had enough intelligence information to know that in military matters the U.S. was far ahead of the Soviets—the American public was deeply disturbed. And for many citizens, as well as members of Congress, the problem was not a military one but an issue with American education, which a new generation of reformers said had grown flabby and was not producing the scientists and engineers that the country needed. As F. James Rutherford, who was a professor at Harvard and New York University, assistant director of the National Science Foundation, and then executive director of the education division of the American Association for the Advancement of Science, notes in his reflections on the fortieth anniversary of Sputnik's launch, American education was never the same again.

In this century, no two pieces of news so shocked America's world view of itself as the devastating attack on Pearl Harbor on December 7, 1942 and, a mere 15 years later, the successful launching of the Soviet space craft on October 5, 1957. Each provoked an enormous national response, the one leading ultimately to the Allied victory in World War II and the other to U.S. dominance in space. In each instance, the recovery from humiliation to vindication was surprisingly short, although, as we know, the political, economic, and technological ramifications of WWII and the space race, still being played out, have profoundly changed life in this country and much of the world.

Nationwide reform efforts in education followed both of these trials by fire. But there are some important differences between them that are worth bearing in mind as we look at the science education reform efforts following in Sputnik's wake. Where the post-war/pre-sputnik educational concerns were largely demographic—first the colleges trying to accommodate returning veterans, the likes of which had not been seen before, then quickly the schools doing the same for the young baby boomers. In contrast, the post-Sputnik concerns were curricular, focusing on what was being taught and how, rather than who was being taught. Another difference between the two eras was the assignment of blame. The military and the politicians received the blame for Pearl Harbor, not educators; in the Sputnik instance, the finger of blame quickly and sternly pointed at the schools. The third difference has to do with the public perception of the outcomes of the two reform movements: the first is almost unanimously regarded as a great success, a milestone in the history of American education not unlike that of the Morrill Act in the last century, while the second is widely regarded as having failed. I think that perception is only half right.

My remarks will focus on the Sputnik-associated science education reform efforts of the late 1950s and the 1960s, and argue that in fact they have left us a legacy of great value should we choose to draw on it in the current science education reform effort. (Parenthetically, the current effort was, like its predecessor, catalyzed by external matters—in this case the ascendancy of Japan in world trade—and quickly led to the perception that somehow our faltering industrial performance was in large measure the fault of the schools.) First I will propose a context for judging what happened, and then list what are, I believe, some of the major successes of the Sputnik reform effort.

Context

There is little to be gained by trying to arrive at global judgments on such matters as the overall success or failure of the Sputnik-era reforms. Education is simply too complex an enterprise for that—decisions in our disaggregated non-system are made by too many different persons in too many different places on too many different things at too many different times. Moreover, we lack the necessary conditions for deciding the matter on that scale: clear criteria for what constitutes success and failure and a reliable way for collecting valid evidence. (One can perhaps forgive the cynic for (spuriously) claiming that since the fact of the Soviets entering space before us was taken as evidence of the failure of the schools, our beating them to the moon can be taken (equally spuriously) as evidence of the success of the reforms.) What we *can* do is look at what happened with an eye to what seems to have contributed significantly to our ability to improve science and mathematics education in the schools.

Another important circumstance to keep in mind is that these spurts of reform activity, no matter what their motivation, are but part of a larger-scale movement reaching back at least to the first decade of this century—one might say, in science education, from John Dewey to James Conant and Vannevar Bush to today's White House and Congress. It is not as though everything remained placid in education between our bouts of reform, or that the schools were ever altogether free of criticism. Indeed, those of us teaching in the public schools before Sputnik remember well that Arthur Bestor's *Educational Wastelands*, Albert Lynn's *Quackery in the Public Schools*, and Rudolf Flesch's *Why Johnny Can't Read* were best sellers. Efforts to change education fluctuate in intensity but rarely disappear altogether for any length of time, although widespread public attention may only surface in response to a proclaimed crisis. It is interesting to note in that regard that both the Illinois Mathematics Project, the funding of the Physical Science Study Committee, and NSF-supported teacher institutes all were underway before Sputnik.

Dissatisfaction with schools not only waxes and wanes, it is sometimes general and sometimes local, and it is often domain specific (reading and mathematics head the list, of course). It seems to take a crisis—not some general move to "get ahead of the curve"—to mobilize nationwide action. But while the crisis occupies stage center, behind the scenes a set of persistent issues has been the focus of the reform struggles in this century. These issues came into play in the case of Sputnik and science education:

- Should progressive, child-centered education or basic, discipline-centered education have precedence in the schools?
- Should priority be given to building the nation's scientific capability or to creating nationwide science literacy?
- Who should decide what students are supposed to learn: the school community (teachers, school administrators and trustees, parents) or university scholars (scientists, mathematicians, and engineers, in our case)?
- What should the balance be between the stability that comes with maintaining traditional content and practices and the discombobulation that comes with the introduction of major changes? . . .

Successes

So how did it all turn out? As I claimed at the outset, I believe that there were many important advances made in the Sputnik years—if one takes increasing our capacity for reform in science education to be the measure, not the elimination of all the deficiencies of the schools.

Indeed, many of the greatest shortcomings in today's schools were there before and after Sputnik and are likely to be around for a long time to come, at today's reform pace. Here then is my (partial) list of Sputnik's positive contributions to science education.

1. We learned that under the right circumstances, some of the country's most prestigious scientists could be drawn into the fray, and that their presence alone helped to legitimize science education reform and elevate its status in the eyes of the public (or at least of legislators and the news media). And it turned out that the involvement of those leaders was more than symbolic, for they brought fresh ideas and new leadership energy to the challenge. Bentley Glass, Gerald Zacharias, and Glenn Seaborg come quickly to mind, but dozens of others could be named, including some, such as Gerald Holton, who are still engaged in science education reform.

2. The many course development projects founded in the Sputnik years revealed that teachers and scientists working together are able to accomplish far more than either alone. To be sure, at the start most scientists knew little of consequence about the realities of precollege education, and few educators had a firm grasp of the content and practice of science. But both learned—the scientists shedding their frequently condescending attitude toward teachers, and the latter their needless deference to scientists. More importantly, there emerged practical knowledge on how to go about curriculum development that is still drawn on in such places as the Lawrence Hall of Science, BSCS, and the Educational Development Corporation. This includes knowing how to frame curriculum design undertakings, assemble teams, create coordinated sets of course materials, conduct field testing all along the way, and more. Should we decide at some point to launch another large-scale course-design effort, we could quickly get underway and not have to repeat the entire learning curve.

3. One of the unintended but enormously valuable outcomes of the curriculum projects of the period was the formation of a relatively large pool of individuals—some from higher education, some from the schools—who became experts in science education R & D and leaders in the field generally. When the projects were phased out, many of the new specialists returned to their former roles, and the development of comparable successors came nearly to a halt.

4. There now exists a national treasury of exemplary science learning resources created by the NSF course development projects—the grand alphabet of PSSC, HPP, BSCS (in three colors, no less), Chem Study, ESCP, SAPA, and many more, including, yes, the infamous MACOS. Almost every one of these produced ideas, techniques, and activities that have already found their way into diverse instructional materials or could be adopted with benefit all around. I cannot list such active and dormant contributions for all the projects, but it would take little prodding for me to provide examples from Harvard Project Physics, and I have no doubt that others could do the same for those they know well.

5. Great stimulus was given to the inclusion of science in elementary school education and to having it be activity oriented. Prior to Sputnik little science was taught in the lower grades and what there was was bookish. While the textbook still predominates, we now know that young students respond well to doing science and know pretty well on how to teach science in those early years (whether we actually do so or not). Our experience

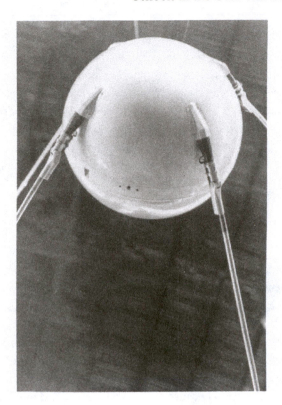

Figure 9.1 When the Soviet Union launched the world's first satellite, Sputnik, on October 4, 1957, Americans blamed the schools for allowing the Soviets to produce the scientists and engineers that allowed it to happen.

of the period showed, I believe, that when the elementary schools were provided with science specialists (as many were during the heyday of the National Defense Education Act) science instruction tended to be more investigative than when each teacher was held responsible for all science teaching without expert help.

6.   We found out that large numbers of teachers will respond enthusiastically and seriously to opportunities to improve their subject-matter knowledge and teaching skills and to upgrade their teaching circumstances. The summer and academic-year institutes—there were NSF institutes in all but five states by the summer before Sputnik, and the number mushroomed after that before tailing off by the early 1970s. Similarly, teachers and school administrators eagerly learned to write proposals to receive funding for laboratory facilities and equipment from the Office of Education's NDEA program. Of course this is not true for all teachers, maybe not even for a majority, but it was certainly true for enough to oversubscribe the opportunities and enough to change what science was like in a large number of classrooms.

F. James Rutherford, American Association for the Advancement of Science, Sputnik and Science Education, from a Forum sponsored by the Center for Science, Mathematics, Engineering Education of the National Academy of Sciences, October 4, 1997. Downloaded from www.nas.edu/sputnik/rhther1.htm, July 26, 2013.

National Defense Education Act, 1958

The NDEA was a significant development in a campaign that had begun more than half a century earlier to provide federal aid to the states to support schools. Ironically, while the NDEA represented a significant expansion in federal aid to education, it was couched in terms that diverted attention from the actual result. The Act was a direct response to the launch of the Sputnik satellite by the Soviet Union. The goal was very American—to use the schools to address the problem—by providing better curriculum materials, better teachers, and better financing for future scientists and engineers. At the same time, the framers of the Act went to great lengths to assure all concerned that federal aid did not mean federal control of the schools, but only federal assistance.

General Provisions

The Congress hereby finds and declares that the security of the Nation requires the fullest development of the mental resources and technical skills of its young men and women. The present emergency demands that additional and more adequate educational opportunities be made available. The defense of this Nation depends upon the mastery of modern techniques developed from complex scientific principles. It depends as well upon the discovery and development of new principles, new techniques, and new knowledge.

We must increase our efforts to identify and educate more of the talent of our Nation. This requires programs that will give assurance that no student of ability will be denied an opportunity for higher education because of financial need; [and that] will correct as rapidly as possible the existing imbalances in our educational programs which have led to an insufficient proportion of our population educated in science, mathematics, and foreign languages, and trained in technology.

The Congress reaffirms the principle and declares that the States and local communities have and must retain control over and primary responsibility for public education. The national interest requires, however, that the Federal Government give assistance to education for programs, which are important to our defense.

To meet the present educational emergency requires additional effort at all levels of government. It is therefore the purpose of this Act to provide substantial assistance in various forms to individuals, and to States and their subdivisions, in order to insure trained manpower of sufficient quality and quantity to meet the national defense needs of the United States.

Federal Control of Education Prohibited

Nothing contained in this Act shall be construed to authorize any department, agency, officer, or employee of the United States to exercise any direction, supervision, or control over the curriculum, program of instruction, administration, or personnel of any educational institution or school system . . .

Financial Assistance for Strengthened Science, Mathematics, and Modern Language Instruction

There are hereby authorized to be appropriated $70,000,000 for the fiscal year ending June 30, 1959, and for each of three succeeding fiscal years, for (1) making payments to State educational agencies under this title for the acquisition of equipment (suitable for use in providing education in science, mathematics, or modern foreign language) and for minor remodeling described in paragraph (1) of Section 303(a), and (2) making loans authorized in Section 305. There are also authorized to be appropriated $5,000,000 for the fiscal year ending June 30, 1959, and for each of the three succeeding fiscal years, for making payments to State educational agencies under this title to carry out the programs described in paragraph (5) of section 303(a) . . .

Science Information Service

The National Science Foundation shall establish a Science Information Service. The Foundation, through such Service, shall (1) provide, or arrange for the provision of, indexing, abstracting, translating, and other services leading to a more effective dissemination of scientific information, and (2) undertake programs to develop new or improved methods, including mechanized systems, for making scientific information available.

Laws of the 85th Congress, 2nd Session, 1958, P.L. 85–864, pp. 1896–1897, 1903–1904, 1919–1919.

THE *SCOTT FORESMAN READERS*, 1955

From the time of the New England Primer *in the 1700s and the* McGuffey's Readers *that began publication in the 1830s, textbook publishing has been a big business. The textbooks that emerged in the United States after World War II were no exception. No company was more successful in marketing its products than Scott Foresman and Company. Their readers, which began with the famous stories of Dick and Jane and their dog Spot—and which a generation of Americans used to learn to read—continued through the elementary grades. Like all textbooks, the* Scott Foresman Readers *reflected their times. They marked a turn away from progressivism to a more traditional pedagogy. In response to the Cold War, they were also filled with patriotic stories. Indeed, looking back from the perspective of half a century, one is struck in reading these stories with how similar they are to the* McGuffey's Readers *of a century before, linking literacy with learning to be a patriotic American citizen. The two examples that follow illustrate the tone and content of these readers.*

"How a Song Named a Flag," pages 184–194 from *The New Basic Readers: More Times and Places*, Grade Four, 1955

In the year 1814, a large new flag waved over the fort guarding the city of Baltimore.

"It's a grand flag," said Mary Pickersgill, who had made it. "It's a strong flag, too," Mary boasted. "Those broad stripes will never tear apart. I fastened them thread by thread, to hold together forever, like our United States."

Caroline Pickersgill regarded the flag with shining eyes and echoed her mother's words. "Yes, it's a grand flag," she said. Her own skillful sewing had helped make the brilliant banner in the Pickersgill flag shop.

The huge flag was about thirty-three feet long and twenty-seven feet wide. This was the largest flag that Mary Pickersgill had ever made. It could be seen from both land and sea.

In the streets of Baltimore, the citizens looked up thankfully at the huge flag waving over the fort. "As long as it waves, we'll be safe," they thought.

One day a small ship was sailing past the fort. On it was a young man who forgot all else as he admired the bright banner. How magnificent it looked against the sky! At the sight, Francis Scott Key bared his head. "A star-spangled banner!" he said to himself. Then he added a wish, "Long may it wave."

The United States was again at war with England. The nearby city of Washington had been attacked and some Americans had been captured.

Among these prisoners was an old doctor whom everyone loved. He was being held on an enemy ship. Naturally many Americans were anxious for Dr. Beans's safety. Francis Scott Key was sailing to rescue the prisoner. Key's ship carried a flag of truce to protect it from being fired upon by the enemy ships. But first he must find the ship on which Dr. Beans was held.

At last the English warships were found. The officer in charge of them permitted Dr. Beans to go aboard the truce ship at once. But the truce ship was forced to stay with the English fleet, which was preparing for a surprise attack on the fort that guarded Baltimore. Dr. Beans, Francis Scott Key, and another American aboard the truce ship spent a dreary week of anxious waiting.

Finally the English fleet sailed to attack, and the United States truce ship was taken along.

The truce ship was held back of the warships. The three Americans on deck took turns watching the battle through a powerful spyglass.

When the warships first started to bomb the fort, no guns answered from the shore. The three loyal watchers groaned. Then the enemy fleet moved up closer. Immediately, the guns of the fort roared violently.

The warships moved back, badly damaged. Francis Scott Key felt encouraged. All day long he stood on the ship's deck. His eyes were glued to the Stars and Stripes, still waving over the fort.

Before midnight the enemy renewed their attack. Again, the Americans on the deck of the distant truce ship watched the firing. By the light of the bursting bombs they saw their star-spangled flag clearly.

Just before dawn, the bombing ceased, and Francis Scott Key waited anxiously to see the fort. At daybreak he cried in triumph, "It's there! The flag is still there!"

In the meantime, under cover of darkness, the enemy fleet had sailed away. Now the truce ship was free to return to Baltimore. On the way, Key was busy writing something on a piece of paper.

"Listen!" he cried, showing the paper to his companions. He sang the words on it to an old, familiar tune. His friends joined in and sang, too.

'Tis the star-spangled banner.
Oh, long may it wave
O'er the land of the free
And the home of the brave.

People all over the country began singing Francis Scott Key's song. People still sing it. It is called "The Star-Spangled Banner."

"A Boy and His Book," pages 189–194, *The New Basic Readers: More Items and Places*, Grade Four, 1955

Pigeon Creek was a lonely place when the pioneers began to settle in Indiana. But as young Abraham Lincoln tramped across a field, he was thinking how much he loved his new home in the Indiana wilderness.

The Lincoln cabin was roughly built. At night from his bed in the loft, the lad could see the sky through the cracks between the logs. Great white stars shone down on him. Sometimes the yellow moon lighted his room like a bright candle. Sometimes, on warm summer nights, cooling raindrops fell gently over his face. In winter, feathery flakes of snow fell on his pillow.

Today the sturdy youth was hurrying home with good news. A school was starting nine miles from Pigeon Creek. Abe meant to go and get some book learning.

Early the next morning, Abe and his older sister, Sally, got ready for the long walk to school. Nancy, their mother, saw that they were neat and clean. Then she sent them off with a loving pat.

"Now go and learn all you can," she told them. And away they went. They were both dressed in clothing made entirely by their mother. She had even made Abe's coonskin cap. His boots were made from bearskin.

After a few days of school, Sally tired of the daily eighteen-mile walk. She did not go any more. But young Abraham considered no distance too great if only he could learn to spell and write and to read books.

About a month later, the school closed so that the pupils could help with the spring planting. Abe was much disappointed. He knew, however, that the pioneer farmers of Indiana needed all the help they could get to plow their fields and to raise and harvest their crops.

Abe was big and sturdy for a boy of his age. He tried his best to do a man's work. But as he worked, he never stopped thinking about books. He never stopped wishing that he knew what they contained.

The next year, a strange illness brought sorrow to the community at Pigeon Creek. The illness was so terrible that many people died. Abe's mother was one of them.

For a long time after her death, the boy did not go to school. He spent all his time helping Sally with the housework or hunting and fishing.

Then one day Mr. Lincoln brought home a new wife with three children of her own.

The new wife was a good mother to Abe and Sally. She knew how much Abe wanted book learning and sent him back to school. But in the Indiana wilderness, school was open for just a few weeks during the winter season. And Abe was often absent while he helped his father chop wood or pull fodder.

In those few weeks of school, the boy learned reading, writing, spelling, and some arithmetic. He liked reading best of all. But books were scarce in Pigeon Creek.

The Lincoln family owned only two books—a Bible and an arithmetic. The Bible was hard to read, and Abe often stumbled over the words. The arithmetic was easier. He studied it from cover to cover.

Abe borrowed every book anyone would lend him. He read each one until he knew it almost by heart.

One cold day he tramped five miles over rough fields to help a farmer pull cornstalks for fodder. When he came in to dinner at noon, he saw a book on a table. "Could I borrow it?" he asked.

Abe's eyes sparkled with pleasure when he left with the book tucked under his arm. At home he swallowed his supper quickly. Then he stretched out flat on the floor with his borrowed book. He read until midnight by the light of the crackling fire.

When Abe went up to his bed in the loft, he tucked the book between two logs of the wall. At dawn, when he reached for it, his fingers touched something wet and cold. The book was soaked with snow that had blown in through the cracks. Now it was ruined! The only honest thing he could do was to go and tell the owner. The boy did not hesitate. He set out without waiting for breakfast or combing his hair.

Abe told the farmer his sad story. "Oh, please, sir," he said anxiously, "I'll pull fodder or do anything you say to make up for your spoiled book."

"Well," drawled the farmer, "I reckon two days' work will pay for it. Pull fodder for two days and keep the book."

So Abe toiled for two days. He did not mind that his back ached and his hands were stiff with cold. The precious book was his! It was a story about George Washington.

Years afterwards, Abraham Lincoln often told about the Washington book. "It helped me become president of the United States," he always said.

The New Basic Readers: More Times and Places, Grade Four, Chicago, IL: Scott Foresman & Company, 1955, pp. 184–194.

H. G. RICKOVER, *EDUCATION FOR ALL CHILDREN: WHAT WE CAN LEARN FROM ENGLAND*, 1962

Navy Admiral Hyman Rickover gained national fame as the "father of the nuclear submarine." A crusty, tough-talking career Navy officer, Rickover had assembled a team of scientists, engineers, and Navy officers that had produced a nuclear-fueled submarine well ahead of schedule. In the 1960s, based on this experience, Rickover—although he continued on active duty as leader of the nuclear fleet—also turned his attention to the nation's schools. In a series of speeches and publications, he became a fierce critic of progressive pedagogy, blaming John Dewey and his fellow progressives for all that was wrong with education and demanding a return to the tough-minded, curriculum-centered pedagogy of an earlier time for the nation's youth. Note Rickover's direct critique of Dewey's The School and Society *which can be found in the previous chapter. While other critics of progressivism, such as Mortimer J. Adler, offered more nuanced views, Rickover, in part because of his plain-spokenness and in part because of his Navy hero aura, became the best-known advocate for a return to the basics.*

You can inform yourself about *anything* in two ways; by *personal* experience and by *studying* the experience of others. Personal experience is necessarily limited by the kind of life you lead and the kind of work you do. But study of the experience of others is limited only by the time you can find to study, to read, to correspond, or to talk with experts. Now, anybody can read books. They are available in public libraries and if your own library hasn't got what you want they will even order it for you—free of charge. When he was a young man, Lincoln remarked: "The things I want to know are in books; my best friend is the man who'll get me a book I ain't read."

Figure 9.2 Rear Admiral Hyman G. Rickover often testified before Congress not only in his area of expertise—nuclear submarines—but also regarding his critique of American education. Courtesy of the Library of Congress, LC-U9-1178–2-7 [P&P].

We are fortunate that we all have so many friends in our local library.

What you get out of books depends, of course, on how well you choose your authors, how reliable they are. I myself get most of my knowledge of education from official sources: from expressions by education authorities as to what objectives they believe the schools should pursue; writings of educators, which give one a good clue to how well or how badly they are educated, and how informed they are on their subject; also school curricula, examination questions and answers, the value given by outsiders to particular school diplomas and higher degrees, and so on. I am fortunate to be in contact by correspondence with eminent scholars and educators here and abroad who are kind enough to give me the benefit of their own wide practical experience and of a reasoned judgment in educational matters that ultimately rests upon their high intelligence and broad general and professional education.

The Value of Outsiders' Judgment

All this, I know, has no value whatsoever in the eyes of educational officialdom. Like most bureaucracies, this huge organization would like to escape lay criticism and tries to do so by constantly using the stereotyped argument that only "professionals" or "inside" critics can judge the performance of other professionals and anyway, nobody can judge the schools unless he has personally inspected every school in the country, sat in every classroom of every school, and listened to every child in every classroom of every school.

Now these are splendid gimmicks if all that the educators want is to save themselves the trouble to answer criticism of the schools. The most effective critics have almost always been outsiders—individuals working on their own, individuals who have no access to public funds that finance junkets of educators around the world. These days, they rarely obtain a foundation grant.

Dewey versus "Book Learning"

But I wonder sometimes whether this is merely a gimmick or whether the educators really mean it. I would feel much better if I thought it was only a gimmick, but what I am afraid of is that they actually believe what they say. This is what worries me so much, because if they do believe it, then they are denying the validity of our entire educational system, because all education is based on what humanity has learned throughout history. If you can only learn from what is going on *today*, then obviously we should do away with our educational system and just have our children make field trips to the firehouse and city hall.

It seems to me that the educators are in their own adult lives following the precepts Dewey used for *elementary school children* in his Chicago Laboratory School. He felt that children learned more by practical experience than out of books. Hence, his dogma that children should be "learning by doing." For instance, he had ten- and eleven-year-olds spend endless hours *reinventing* such things as how to make cotton, flax, and wool cloth, how to card wool, and so on. "You can concentrate the history of all mankind into the evolution of flax, cotton, and wool fibers into clothing," said Dewey. But would this not give you an utterly material-istic, worm's eye view of history and of man? And can modern children afford to devote so much time to learning the primitive origins of a manufacturing process that is unlikely to be important in their lives unless they all become managers of textile mills? At that, a manager could grasp the principle of primitive looms in half an hour from a book.

Ordinarily, mistrust of "book learning" is to be found only among uneducated people who do not themselves read books and whose schooling has not carried them from concrete things to abstract concepts. And so, quite naturally, they feel that to *know*, a person should have personally seen, heard, and touched the things he talks about; and before he can *criti-cize* anything; he must prove he can do the things he criticizes better himself.

Many people believe that unless a critic can demonstrate a better way, his criticism isn't "constructive." Doesn't the person who reports a fire perform a valuable service, even though the fire department puts it out? You sometimes hear people remark disparagingly of an art or literary critic—to take just one example—that they'd like to see this critic paint a better picture or write a better book. This way of thinking confuses *ability to judge art* with *artistic talent*, but the two are different. If it were not so, no layman could discriminate between good and bad art, or for that matter between a good and a bad doctor, lawyer, or teacher. The "pro-fessionals" would then have it all their own way. Many an administrator uses this stratagem of requiring his subordinates never to criticize unless it is "constructive," the administrator himself, of course, being the one who decides what is and what is not "constructive" criticism.

Judging Schools by Their Graduates

For myself, besides study and reading, correspondence and discussion, I have learned much about education through experience gained on my job with novel engineering development projects. Also, my many years in Washington have given me a unique opportunity to observe how greatly the United States is handicapped because we simply do not have enough people with the educational qualifications essential to keep us progressing satisfactorily. The lack is both in general or liberal education, and in the specialized education needed by professionals and technicians.

As a practical man, I am not much interested in the mystique or esoterics of education which fascinate so many of our professional educators. I freely admit I judge schools by their products. Literally thousands of these products pass through my hands and those of my leading scientists and engineers when we interview young people who apply for positions as designers and builders of nuclear reactors or as officers and men to operate our nuclear ships. I find the percentage so qualified to be deplorably small. Those selected we must send to special schools set up and run by our own naval reactors group. These schools do not teach reactor technology alone; they also have to teach many basic subjects which abroad have already been taught in the regular schools. My "school system" of six schools enrolls about 2,500 students at different levels from high school to graduate university. So I can claim some personal experience with educating young Americans.

H. G. Rickover, USN, *Education for All Children: What We Can Learn from England*, Hearings Before the Committee on Appropriations, House of Representatives, Eighty-Seventh Congress, Second Session, Washington, DC: U.S. Government Printing Office, 1962, pp. 3–5.

HERBERT KOHL, *THIRTY-SIX CHILDREN*, 1967

For all of the national debates about school reform, the day-to-day reality of many schools has remained much the same through the generations. Herb Kohl, who has become one of the nation's most respected commentators on the educational scene, began his career as a young graduate of Columbia University's Teachers College working in a school in Harlem. As Kohl reports, the school was only a few blocks from his home and his college, but miles away in terms of culture and the experiences of students and teachers. Kohl's first book, Thirty-Six Children, *became a bestseller, much respected for the harsh but clear light it shone on the reality of schools in urban America in the 1960s. His account of his first days on the job remains a classic description of what many experience upon entering the teaching profession.*

My alarm clock rang at seven-thirty, but I was up and dressed at seven. It was only a fifteen-minute bus ride from my apartment on 90th Street and Madison Avenue to the School on 119th Street and Madison.

There had been an orientation session the day before. I remembered the principal's words. "In times like these, this is the most exciting place to be, in the midst of ferment and creative activity. Never has teaching offered such opportunities . . . we are together here in a difficult situation. They are not the easiest children, yet the rewards are so great—a smile, a loving concern, what an inspiration, a felicitous experience."

I remembered my barren classroom, no books, a battered piano, broken windows and desks, falling plaster, and an oppressive darkness.

I was handed a roll book with thirty-six names and thirty-six cumulative record cards, years of judgments already passed upon the children, their official personalities. I read through the names, twenty girls and sixteen boys, the 6–1 class, though I was supposed to be teaching the fifth grade and had planned for it all summer. Then I locked the record cards away in the closet. The children would tell me who they were. Each child, each new school year, is potentially many things, only one of which the cumulative record card documents. It is amazing how "emotional" problems can disappear, how the dullest child can be transformed into the keenest, and the brightest into the most ordinary, when the prefabricated judgments of other teachers are forgotten.

The children entered at nine and filled up the seats. They were silent and stared at me. It was a shock to see thirty-six black faces before me. No preparation helped. It is one thing to be liberal and talk, another to face something and learn that you're afraid.

The children sat quietly, expectant. *Everything must go well; we must like each other.*

Hands went up as I called the roll. Anxious faces, hostile, indifferent, weary of the ritual, confident of its outcome.

The smartest class in the sixth grade, yet no books.

"Write about yourselves, tell me who you are." (I hadn't said who I was, too nervous.)

Slowly they set to work, the first directions followed—and if they had refused? Then arithmetic, the children working silently, a sullen, impenetrable front. *To talk to them, to open them up this first day.*

"What would you like to learn this year? My name is Mr. Kohl."

Silence. The children looked up at me with expressionless faces, thirty-six of them crowded at thirty-five broken desks. *This is the smartest class?*

Explain: They're old enough to choose, enough time to learn what they'd like as well as what they have to.

Silence, a restless movement rippled through the class. *They don't understand? There must be something that interests them, that they care to know more about.*

A hand shot up in the corner of the room.

"I want to learn more about volcanoes. What are volcanoes?"

The class seemed interested. I sketched a volcano on the blackboard, made a few comments, and promised to return.

"Anything else? Anyone else interested in something?"

Silence, then the same hand.

"Why do volcanoes form?"

And during the answer:

"Why don't we have a volcano here?"

A contest. The class savored it, I accepted. Question, response, question. I walked toward my inquisitor, studying his mischievous eyes, possessed and possessing smile. I moved to congratulate him, my hand went happily toward his shoulder. I dared because I was afraid.

His hands shot up to protect his dark face, eyes contracted in fear, body coiled, ready to bolt for the door and out, down the stairs into the streets.

"But why should I hit you?"

They're afraid, too!

Hands relaxed, he looked torn and puzzled. I changed the subject quickly and moved on to social studies—How We Became Modern America.

"Who remembers what America was like in 1800?"

A few children laughed; the rest barely looked at me.

"Can anyone tell me what was going on about 1800? Remember, you studied it last year. Why don't we start specifically? What do you think you'd see if you walked down Madison Avenue in those days?"

A lovely hand, almost too thin to be seen, tentatively rose.

"Cars?"

"Do you think there were cars in 1800? Remember that was over a hundred and fifty years ago. Think of what you learned last year and try again. Do you think there were cars then?"

"Yes . . . no . . . I don't know."

She withdrew, and the class became restless as my anger rose. At last another hand.

"Grass and trees?"

The class broke up as I tried to contain my frustration.

"I don't know what you're laughing about—it's the right answer. In those days, Harlem was farmland, with fields and trees and a few houses. There weren't any roads or houses like the ones outside, or streetlights or electricity. There probably wasn't even a Madison Avenue."

The class was outraged. It was inconceivable to them there was a time their Harlem didn't exist.

"Stop this noise and let's think. Do you believe that Harlem was here a thousand years ago?"

A pause, several uncertain "noes."

"It's possible that the land was green, then. Why couldn't Harlem also have been green a hundred and fifty or two hundred years ago?"

No response. The weight of Harlem and my whiteness and strangeness hung up in the air as I droned on, lost in my righteous monologue. The uproar turned into sullen silence. A slow, nervous drumming began at several desks; the atmosphere closed as intelligent faces lost their animation. Yet I didn't understand my mistake, the children's rejection of me and my ideas. Nothing worked, I tried to joke, command, play—the children remained joyless until the bell, then quietly left for lunch.

There was an hour to summon energy and prepare for the afternoon, yet it seemed futile. What good are plans, clever new methods and materials, when the children didn't— wouldn't—care or listen? Perhaps the best solution was to prepare for hostility and silence, become the cynical teacher, untaught by his pupils, ungluing himself, yet protected.

At one o'clock, my tentative cynicism assumed, I found myself once again unprepared for the children who returned and noisily and boisterously avoided me. Running, playing, lighting— they were alive as they tore about the room. I was relieved, yet how to establish order? I fell back on teacherly words.

"You've had enough time to run around. Everybody please go to your seats. We have work to begin."

No response. The boy who had been so scared during the morning was flying across the back of the room pursued by a demonic-looking child wearing black glasses. Girls stood gossiping in little groups, a tall boy fantasized before four admiring listeners, while a few children wandered in and out of the room. I still knew no one's name. "Sit down, we've got to work. At three o'clock you can talk all you want to." . . .

"Mr. Kohl, can we please talk to each other about the summer? We won't play around. Please, it's only the first day."

"I'll tell you what, you can talk, but on the condition that everyone, I mean *every single person in the room*, keeps quiet for one whole minute."

Teacher still had to show he was strong. To prove what? The children succeeded in remaining silent on the third attempt; they proved they could listen. Triumphant, I tried more.

"Now let's try for thirty seconds to think of one color."

"You said we could talk!"

"My head hurts, I don't want to think anymore."

"It's not fair!"

It wasn't. A solid mass of resistance coagulated, frustrating my need to command. The children would not be moved.

"You're right, I'm sorry. Take ten minutes to talk and then we'll get back to work." For ten minutes the children talked quietly; there was time to prepare for the last half-hour. I looked over my lesson plans: Reading, 9 to 10; Social Studies, 10 to 10:45, etc., etc. How absurd academic time was in the face of the real day. *Where to look?*

"You like it here, Mr. Kohl?"

I looked up into a lovely, sad face.

"What do you mean?"

"I mean do you like it here, Mr. Kohl, what are you teaching us for?"

What?

"Well, I . . . not now. Maybe you can see me at three and we can talk. The class has to get back to work. All right, everybody back to your seats, get ready to work." She had her answer and sat down and waited with the rest of the class. They were satisfied with the bargain. Only it was I who failed then; exhausted, demoralized, I only wanted three o'clock to arrive.

"It's almost three o'clock and we don't have much time left." I dragged the words out, listening only for the bell.

"This is only the first day, and of course we haven't got much done. I expect more from you during the year . . ."

The class sensed the maneuver and fell nervous again.

"Take out your notebooks and open to a clean page. Each day except Friday you'll get homework."

My words weighed heavy and false; it wasn't my voice but some common tyrant or moralizer, a tired old man speaking.

"There are many things I'm not strict about, but homework is the one thing I insist upon. In my class *everybody always* does homework. I will check your work every morning. Now copy the assignment I'm putting on the blackboard, and then when you're finished, please line up in the back of the room."

What assignment? What lie now? I turned to the blackboard, groping for something to draw the children closer to me, for something to let them know I cared. *I did care!*

"Draw a picture of your home, the room you live in. Put in all the furniture, the TV, the windows, and doors. You don't have to do it in any special way but keep in mind that the main purpose of the picture should be to show someone what your house looks like."

The children laughed, pointed, then a hand rose, a hand I couldn't attach to a body or face. They all looked alike. I felt sad, lonely.

"Do you have to show your house?"

Two boys snickered. *Are there children ashamed to describe their homes?—have I misunderstood again?* The voice in me answered again.

"Yes."

"I mean . . . what if you can't draw, can you let someone help you?"

"Yes, if you can explain the drawing yourself."

"What if your brother can't draw?"

"Then write a description of your apartment. Remember, *everybody always* does homework in my classes."

The class copied the assignment and lined up, first collecting everything they'd brought with them. The room was as empty as it was at eight o'clock. Tired, weary of discipline, authority, school itself, I rushed the class down the stairs and into the street in some acknowledged state of disorder.

The bedlam on 119th Street, the stooped and fatigued teachers smiling at each other and pretending *they* had had no trouble with their kids, relieved my isolation. I smiled, too, assumed the comfortable pose of casual success, and looked down into a mischievous face, the possessed eyes of the child who had thought I would hit him, Alvin, who kindly and thoughtfully said: "Mr. Kohl, how come you let us out so early today? We just had lunch . . ."

Crushed, I walked dumbly away, managed to reach the bus stop and make my way home. As my weariness dissolved, I only remembered of that first day Alvin and the little girl who asked if I liked being "there."

The books arrived the next morning before class. There were twenty-five arithmetic books from one publisher and twelve from another, but in the entire school there was no complete set of sixth-grade arithmetic books. A few minutes spent checking the first day's arithmetic assignment showed me that it wouldn't have mattered if a full set had existed, since half the class had barely mastered multiplication, and only one child, Grace, who had turned in a perfect paper, was actually ready for sixth-grade arithmetic. It was as though, encouraged to believe that the children couldn't do arithmetic judging from the school's poor results in teaching it, the administration decided not to waste any money on arithmetic books, thereby creating a vicious circle that made it even more impossible for the children to learn.

The situation was almost as dismal in reading—the top of the sixth grade had more than half of its members reading on fourth-grade level and only five or six children actually able to read through a sixth-grade book. There were two full sets of sixth-grade readers available, however, and after the arithmetic situation I was grateful for anything. Yet accepting these readers put me in an awkward position. The books were flat and uninteresting. They only presented what was pleasant in life, and even then limited the pleasant to what was publicly accepted as such. The people in the stories were all middle-class, and their simplicity, goodness, and self-confidence were unreal. I couldn't believe in this foolish ideal and knew that anyone who had ever bothered to observe human life couldn't believe it. Yet I had to teach it, and through it make reading important and necessary. Remembering the children, their anxiety and hostility, the alternate indifference, suspicion, and curiosity they approached me with, knowing how essential it is to be honest with children, I felt betrayed by the books into hypocrisy. No hypocrite can win the respect of children, and without respect one cannot teach.

One of the readers was a companion to the social studies unit on the growth of the United States and was full of stories about family fun in a Model T Ford, the first wireless radio in town, and the joys of wealth and progress. The closest the book touched upon human emotion or the real life of children was in a story in which children accepted a new invention before their parents did, even though the adults laughed at the children. Naturally, everything turned out happily.

The other reader was a miscellany of adventure stories (no human violence or antagonists allowed, just treasure hunts, animal battles, close escapes), healthy poems (no love except for mother, father, and nature), and a few harmless myths (no Oedipus, Elects, or Prometheus). I also managed to get twenty dictionaries in such bad condition that the probability of finding any word still intact was close to zero.

The social studies texts (I could choose from four or five) praised industrial America in terms that ranged from the enthusiastic to the exorbitant. Yet the growth of modern industrial society is fascinating, and it was certainly possible to supplement the text with some truth. I decided to work with what was given me and attempt to teach the sixth-grade curriculum as written in the New York City syllabus, ignoring as long as possible the contradictions inherent in such a task.

The class confronted me, surrounded by my motley library, at nine that second morning and groaned.

"Those phoney books?"

"We read them already, Mr. Kohl."

"It's a cheap, dirty, bean school."

My resolve weakened, and I responded out of despair.

"Let me put it straight to you. These are the only books here. I have no more choice than you do, and I don't like it any better. Let's get through them and maybe by then I'll figure out how to get better ones."

The class understood and accepted the terms. As soon as the books were distributed, the first oral reading lesson began. Some children volunteered eagerly, but most of the class tried not to be seen. The children who read called out the words, but the story was lost. I made the lesson as easy as possible by helping children who stumbled, encouraging irrelevant discussion, and not letting any child humiliate himself. It was bad enough that more than half the class had to be forced to use books they couldn't read. The lesson ended, and a light-skinned boy raised his hand.

"Mr. Kohl, remember that ten minutes you gave us yesterday? Couldn't we talk again now? We're tired after all this reading."

I wasn't sure how to take Robert's request. My initial feeling was that he was taking advantage of me and trying to waste time. I felt, along with the official dogma, that no moment in school should be wasted—it must all be preplanned and structured. Yet why shouldn't it be "wasted"? Hadn't most of the class wasted years in school, not merely moments?

I remembered my own oppressive school days in New York City, moving from one subject to another without a break, or at most, with a kind teacher letting us stand and stretch in unison; I remember reading moving into social studies into arithmetic. How hateful it seemed then. Is it a waste to pause, talk, or think between subjects? As a teacher I, too, needed a break.

"You're right, Robert, I'm tired too. Everybody can take ten minutes to do what you want, and then we'll move on to social studies."

The class looked fearful and amazed—freedom in school, do what you want? For a few minutes they sat quietly and then slowly began to talk. Two children walked to the piano and asked me if they could try. I said of course, and three more children joined them. It seemed so easy; the children relaxed. I watched closely and suspiciously, realizing that the tightness with time that exists in the elementary school has nothing to do with the quantity that must be learned or the children's needs. It represents the teacher's fear of loss of control and is nothing but a weapon used to weaken the solidarity and opposition of the children that too many teachers unconsciously dread.

After the ten minutes, I tried to bring the children back to work. They resisted, tested my determination. I am convinced that a failure of will at that moment would have been disastrous. It was necessary to compel the children to return to work, not due to my "authority" or "control" but because they were expected to honor the bargain. They listened, and at that moment I learned something of the toughness, consistency, and ability to demand and give respect that enables children to listen to adults without feeling abused or brutalized and, therefore, becoming defiant . . .

I am convinced that the teacher must be an observer of his class as well as a member of it. He must look at the children, discover how they relate to each other and the room around them. There must be enough free time and activity for the teacher to discover the children's human preferences. Observing children at play and mischief is an invaluable source of knowledge about them—about leaders and groups, fear, courage, warmth, isolation. Teachers consider the children's gym or free play time their free time too, and usually turn their backs on the children when they have most to learn from them.

I went through a year of teacher training at Teachers College, Columbia, received a degree, and heard no mention of how to observe children, nor even a suggestion that it was of value. Without learning to observe children and thereby knowing something of the people one is living with five hours a day, the teacher resorts to routine and structure for protection. The class is assigned seats, the time is planned down to the minute, subject follows subject—all to the exclusion of human variation and invention.

I witnessed the same ignorance of the children in a private school I once visited, only it was disguised by a progressive egalitarian philosophy. The teachers and students were on a first-name basis; together, they chose the curriculum and decided upon the schedule. Yet many of the teachers knew no more of their classes than the most rigid public-school teachers. They knew only of their pupils and their mutual relationships in contexts where the teacher was a factor. It was clear to me, watching the children when the teacher left the room, that the children's preferences "for the teachers" were not the same as their human preferences (which most likely changed every week). That is not an academic point, for observation can open the teacher to his pupils' changing needs, and can often allow him to understand and utilize internal dynamic adjustments that the children make in relation to each other, rather than impose authority from without.

After the first few days of the year, my students are free to move wherever they want in the room, my role being arbiter when someone wants to move into a seat whose occupant does not want to vacate or when health demands special consideration. I have never bothered to count the number of continual, self-selected seat changes in my classes, yet can say that they never disrupted the fundamental fabric of the class. Rather, they provided internal adjustments and compensations that avoided many possible disruptions. Children fear chaos and animosity. Often they find ways of adjusting to difficult and sensitive situations (when free to) before their teachers are aware they exist.

Only fourteen of the thirty-six children brought in homework that second afternoon, and twelve of them were girls. One of the boys, I noticed, was the quiet artist. Here was a critical moment that plunged me back into the role of participant and destroyed my objective calm. What was the best reaction to the children's lack of response, especially after I'd been so pompous and adamant about homework the first day? How many of the twenty-two missing homeworks were the result of defiance (perhaps merited), of inability, of shame at what the result might reveal? Was there a simple formula: *Good = do homework* and another *Bad = not do homework*? Or would these formulas themselves negate the honesty and sincerity that could lead the children to find a meaningful life in school? At that moment in the classroom, I had no criteria by which to decide and no time to think out my response. It would have been most just to react in thirty-six different ways to the thirty-six different children, but there was no way for me to be most just at that moment. I had to react intuitively and immediately, as anyone in a classroom must. There is never time to plot every tactic. A child's responses are unpredictable, those of groups of children even more so, unless through being brutalized and bullied they are made predictable. When a teacher claims he knows exactly what will happen in his class, exactly how the children will behave and function, he is either lying or brutal.

That means that the teacher must make mistakes. Intuitive, immediate responses can be right and magical, can express understanding that the teacher doesn't know he has, and lead to reorganizations of the teacher's relationship with his class. But they can also be peevish and petty, or merely stupid and cruel. Consistency of the teacher's response is frequently desirable, and the word *consistency* is a favorite of professors at teacher training institutions. Consistency can sometimes prevent discovery and honesty. More, consistency of response is a function of the consistency of a human personality, and that is, at best, an unachievable ideal.

I've said many stupid, unkind things in my classroom, hit children in anger, and insulted them maliciously when they threatened me too much. On the other hand, I've also said some deeply affecting things, moved children to tears by unexpected kindnesses, and made them happy with praise that flowed unashamedly. I've wanted to be consistent and have become more consistent. That seems the most that is possible, a slow movement toward consistency tempered by honesty. The teacher has to live with his own mistakes, as his pupils have to suffer them. Therefore, the teacher must learn to perceive them as mistakes and find direct or indirect ways to acknowledge his awareness of them and of his fallibility to his pupils.

The ideal of the teacher as a flawless moral exemplar is a devilish trap for the teacher as well as a burden for the child. I once had a pupil, Narciso, who was overburdened by the perfection of adults, and especially of teachers. His father demanded he believe in this perfection as he demanded Narciso believe in and acquiesce to absolute authority. It was impossible to approach the boy for his fear and deference. I had terrified him. He wouldn't work or disobey. He existed frozen in silence. One day he happened to pass by a bar where some other teachers and I were sitting having beers. He was crushed; *teachers don't do that*. He believed so much in what his father and some teachers wanted him to believe that his world collapsed. He stayed away from school for a while, then returned. He smiled, and I returned the smile. After a while he was at ease in class and could be himself; delightful, and defiant, sometimes brilliant, often lazy, an individual reacting in his unique way to what happened in the classroom.

It is only in the world of Dick and Jane, Tom and Sally, that the *always* right and righteous people exist. In a way, most textbooks, and certainly the ones I had to use in the sixth grade, protect the pure image of the teacher by showing the child that somewhere in the ideal world that inspires books all people are as "good" as the teacher is supposed to be! It is not insignificant that it is teachers and not students who select school readers, nor that, according to a friend of mine who edits school texts, the books were written for the teachers and not for children for this very reason.

Herbert Kohl, *Thirty-Six Children*, New York: The New American Library, Inc., 1967.

JOHN HOLT, *HOW CHILDREN FAIL*, 1964

While Herb Kohl and John Holt describe much the same feelings about many mid-century school classrooms, Kohl's response to the difficulty he experienced in his first days as a teacher was to devote his life to improving schools; others have reacted with less optimism. John Holt's How Children Fail, *another educational classic from the early 1960s, was the first of a series of books from an author who eventually came to believe that schools, public or private, could not be reformed. Holt believed that other efforts, including home schooling, were more likely to produce real success in the lives of children. Whether or not one accepts all of Holt's later thinking, his description of why children fail, or why schools fail children, is a valid reminder of what needs to change in American education.*

School tends to be a dishonest as well as a nervous place. We adults are not often honest with children, least of all in school. We tell them, not what we think, but what we feel they ought to think; or what other people feel or tell us they ought to think. Pressure groups find it easy to weed out of our classrooms, texts, and libraries whatever facts, truths, and ideas they happen to find unpleasant or inconvenient. And we are not even as truthful with children as we could safely be, as the parents, politicians, and pressure groups would let us be. Even in the most noncontroversial areas, our teaching, the books, and the textbooks we give children present a dishonest and distorted picture of the world.

The fact is that we do not feel an obligation to be truthful to children. We are like the managers and manipulators of news in Washington, Moscow, London, Peking, and Paris, and all the other capitals of the world. We think it our right and our duty, not to tell the truth, but to say whatever will best serve our cause—in this case, the cause of making children grow up into the kind of people we want them to be, thinking whatever we want them to think. We have only to convince ourselves (and we are very easily convinced) that a lie will be "better" for the children than the truth, and we will lie. We don't always need even that excuse; we often lie only for our own convenience.

Worse yet, we are not honest about ourselves, our own fears, limitations, weaknesses, prejudices, motives. We present ourselves to children as if we were gods, all-knowing, all-powerful, always rational, always just, always right. This is worse than any lie we could tell about ourselves. I have more than once shocked teachers by telling them that when kids ask me a question to which I don't know the answer, I say, "I haven't the faintest idea"; or that when I make a mistake, as I often do, I say, "I goofed again"; or that when I am trying to do something I am no good at, like paint in water colors or play a clarinet or bugle, I do it in front of them so they can see me struggling with it, and can realize that not all adults are good at everything. If a child asks me to do something that I don't want to do, I tell him that I won't do it because I don't want to do it, instead of giving him a list of "good" reasons sounding as if they had come down from the Supreme Court. Interestingly enough, this rather open way of dealing with children works quite well. If you tell a child that you won't do something because you don't want to, he is very likely to accept that as a fact which he cannot change; if you ask him to stop doing something because it drives you crazy, there is a very good chance that, without further talk, he will stop, because he knows what that is like.

We are, above all, dishonest about our feelings, and it is this sense of dishonesty of feeling that makes the atmosphere of so many schools so unpleasant. The people who write books that teachers have to read say over and over again that a teacher must love all the children in a class, all of them equally. If by this they mean that a teacher must do the best he can for every child in a class, that he has an equal responsibility for every child's welfare, an equal concern for his problems, they are right. But when they talk of love, they don't mean this; they mean feelings, affection, the kind of pleasure and joy that one person can get from the existence and company of another. And this is not something that can be measured out in little spoonfuls, everyone getting the same amount . . .

As we are not honest with them, so we won't let children be honest with us. To begin with, we require them to take part in the fiction that school is a wonderful place and that they love every minute of it. They learn early that not to like school or the teacher is *verboten*, not to be said, not even to be thought. I have known a child, otherwise healthy, happy, and wholly delightful, who at the age of five was being made sick with worry by the fact that she did not like her kindergarten teacher. Robert Heinemann worked for a number of years with remedial students whom ordinary schools were hopelessly unable to deal with. He found that what choked up and froze the minds of these children was, above all else, the fact that they could not express, they could hardly even acknowledge, the fear, shame, rage, and hatred that school and their teachers had aroused in them. In a situation in which they were able and felt free to express these feelings to themselves and others, they were able once again to begin learning. Why can't we say to children what I used to say to fifth graders who got sore at me, "The law says you have to go to school; it doesn't say you have to like it, and it doesn't say you have to like me, either." This might make school more bearable for many children . . .

Behind much of what we do in school lie some ideas, that could be expressed roughly as follows: (1) Of the vast body of human knowledge, there are certain bits and pieces that can be called essential, that everyone should know; (2) the extent to which a person can be considered educated, qualified to live intelligently in today's world and be a useful member of society, depends on the amount of this essential knowledge that he carries about with him; (3) it is the duty of schools, therefore, to get as much of this essential knowledge as possible into the minds of children. Thus we find ourselves trying to poke certain facts, recipes, and ideas down the gullets of every child in school, whether the morsel interests him or not, even if it frightens him or sickens him, and even if there are other things that he is much more interested in learning.

These ideas are absurd and harmful nonsense. We will not begin to have true education or real learning in our schools until we sweep this nonsense out of the way. Schools should be a place where children learn what they most want to know, instead of what we think they ought to know. The child who wants to know something remembers it and uses it once he has it; the child who learns something to please or appease someone else forgets it when the need for pleasing or the danger of not appeasing is past. This is why children quickly forget all but a small part of what they learn in school. It is of no use or interest to them; they do not want, or expect, or even intend to remember it. The only difference between bad and good students in this respect is that the bad students forget right away, while the good students are careful to wait until after the exam. If for no other reason, we could well afford to throw out most of what we teach in school because the children throw out almost all of it anyway.

The notion of a curriculum, an essential body of knowledge, would be absurd even if children remembered everything we "taught" them. We don't and can't agree on what knowledge is essential. The man who has trained himself in some special field of knowledge or competence thinks, naturally, that his specialty should be in the curriculum. The classical scholars want Greek and Latin taught; the historians shout for more history; the mathematicians urge more math and the scientists more science; the modern language experts want all children taught French, or Spanish, or Russian; and so on. Everyone wants to get his specialty into the act, knowing that as the demand for his special knowledge rises, so will the price that he can charge for it. Who wins this struggle and who loses depends not on the real needs of children or even of society, but on who is most skillful in public relations, who has the best educational lobbyists, who best can capitalize on events that have nothing to do with education, like the appearance of Sputnik in the night skies.

The idea of the curriculum would not be valid even if we could agree what ought to be in it. For knowledge itself changes. Much of what a child learns in school will be found, or thought, before many years, to be untrue. I studied physics at school from a fairly up-to-date text that proclaimed that the fundamental law of physics was the law of conservation of matter—matter is not created or destroyed. I had to scratch that out before I left school . . .

How can we say, in any case, that one piece of knowledge is more important than another, or indeed, what we really say, that some knowledge is essential and the rest, as far as school is concerned, worthless? . . .

It is not subject matter that makes some learning more valuable than others, but the spirit in which the work is done. If a child is doing the kind of learning that most children do in school, when they learn at all—swallowing words, to spit back at the teacher on demand—he is wasting his time, or rather, we are wasting it for him. This learning will not be permanent, or relevant, or useful. But a child who is learning naturally, following his curiosity where it leads him, adding to his mental model of reality whatever he needs and can find a place for, and rejecting without fear or guilt what he does not need, is growing—in knowledge, in the love of learning, and in the ability to learn. He is on his way to becoming the kind of person we need in our society, and that our "best" schools and colleges are not turning out, the kind of person who, in Whitney Griswold's words, seeks and finds meaning, truth, and enjoyment in everything he does. All his life he will go on learning. Every experience will make his mental model of reality more complete and more true to life, and thus make him more able to deal realistically, imaginatively, and constructively with whatever new experience life throws his way.

We cannot have real learning in school if we think it is our duty and our right to tell children what they must learn. We cannot know, at any moment, what particular bit of knowledge or understanding a child needs most, will most strengthen and best fit his model of reality. Only he can do this. He may not do it very well, but he can do it a hundred times better than we can. The most we can do is try to help, by letting him know roughly what is available and where he can look for it. Choosing what he wants to learn and what he does not is something he must do for himself.

There is one more reason, and the most important one, why we must reject the idea of school and classrooms as places where, most of the time, children are doing what some adult tells them to do. The reason is that there is no way to coerce children without making them afraid, or more afraid. We must not try to fool ourselves into thinking that that is not so. The would-be progressives, who until recently had great influence over most American public school education, did not recognize this—and still do not. They thought, or at least talked and wrote as if they thought, that there were good ways and bad ways to coerce children (the bad ones mean, harsh, cruel, the good ones gentle, persuasive, subtle, kindly), and that if they avoided the bad and stuck to the good they would do no harm. This was one of their greatest mistakes, and the main reason why the revolution they hoped to accomplish never took hold.

The idea of painless, nonthreatening coercion is an illusion. Fear is the inseparable companion of coercion, and its inescapable consequence. If you think it your duty to make children do what you want, whether they will or not, then it follows inexorably that you must make them afraid of what will happen to them if they don't do what you want. You can do this in the old-fashioned way, openly and avowedly, with the threat of harsh words, infringement of liberty, or physical punishment. Or you can do it in the modern way, subtly, smoothly, quietly, by withholding the acceptance and approval which you and others have trained the children to depend on; or by making them feel that some retribution awaits them in the future, too vague to imagine but too implacable to escape. You can, as many skilled teachers do, learn to tap with a word, a gesture, a look, even a smile, the great reservoir of fear, shame, and guilt that today's children carry around inside them. Or you can simply let your own fears, about what will happen to you if the children don't do what you want, reach out and infect them. Thus the children will feel more and more that life is full of dangers from which only the goodwill of adults like you can protect them, and that this goodwill is perishable and must be earned anew each day.

The alternative—I can see no other—is to have schools and classrooms in which each child in his own way can satisfy his curiosity, develop his abilities and talents, pursue his interests, and from the adults and older children around him get a glimpse of the great variety and richness of life. In short, the school should be a great smorgasbord of intellectual, artistic, creative, and athletic activities, from which each child could take whatever he wanted, and as much as he wanted, or as little. When Anna was in the sixth grade, the year after she was in my class, I mentioned this idea to her. After describing very sketchily how a school might be run, and what the children might do, I said, "Tell me, what do you think of it? Do you think it would work? Do you think the kids would learn anything?" She said, with utmost conviction, "Oh, yes, it would be wonderful!" She was silent for a minute or two, perhaps remembering her own generally unhappy schooling. Then she said thoughtfully, "You know, kids really like to learn; we just don't like being pushed around."

No, they don't; and we should be grateful for that. So let's stop pushing them around, and give them a chance.

John Holt, *How Children Fail*, New York: Putnam, 1964. Copyright © 1995. Reprinted by permission of Perseus Books Publisher, a member of Perseus Books, L.L.C.

10

Civil Rights, Integration, and School Reform, 1954–1980

- Introduction

- Federal District Court, *Mendez v. Westminster*, 1946

- Septima Clark, *Ready from Within*, ca. 1950

- Supreme Court of the United States, *Brown v. Board of Education of Topeka, Kansas*, 1954

- Kenneth B. Clark, "How Children Learn About Race," 1950

- School Desegregation in the South: Little Rock, 1957

- NAACP Boston Branch, Statement to the Boston School Committee, June 11, 1963

- School Desegregation in the North: Boston, 1965

- Looking Back at an Era: Rucker C. Johnson, *The Dream Revisited— In Search of Integration: Beyond Black and White*, 2014

Introduction

Contrary to more simplistic versions of history, the civil rights movement did not burst on the American scene with the Supreme Court's 1954 *Brown v. Board of Education* decision. That decision represented the culmination of years of activity by civil rights organizations.

While the heart of the civil rights movement—in education and beyond—was the black freedom struggle, African Americans were not alone in the effort for integrated schooling. As we saw in Chapter 7, Asian Americans in California were fighting for educational rights as early as the teens and twenties of the twentieth century. From Texas to California, Latinx Americans, especially Mexican Americans, also worked to end racial segregation and in the 1930s and 1940s had considerable success in California. African Americans and white allies understood that separate but equal schooling never meant equal. The Legal Defense Fund of the National Association for the Advancement of Colored People—the NAACP—led by lawyers such as Thurgood Marshall and his predecessor Charles Houston began a slow and systematic process of challenging widespread inequality and separation in schools in all parts of the U.S. in the 1930s. At the same time, a grassroots civil rights movement of African American parents, teachers, and various allies began to raise the issue of school segregation across the country. Septima Clark, one of the great leaders of the civil rights movement of the 1950s, reports her own experiences of teaching and being fired in the segregated South prior to the *Brown* decision. I have included the story of how she was fired as a public school teacher when she joined the NAACP in Charleston, South Carolina in the 1950s from her biography, *Ready from Within*. Clark went on to prepare a generation of teachers for Freedom Schools across the South from her base at the Highlander Center in Tennessee.

While it is important to view it in context, it is true that few Supreme Court decisions have had the impact of the 1954 *Brown v. Board of Education* decision, which declared racial segregation in public schools to be unconstitutional. Prior to *Brown* a decade of Court decisions, focusing primarily on higher education, were brought by the NAACP Legal Defense Fund. Yet *Brown* itself was only the beginning of a continuing struggle to end segregation and discrimination in education. A significant test came in the crisis at Little Rock (Arkansas) Central High School in 1957. When the governor of Arkansas, Orval Faubus, warned that blood would run in the streets if Central High School were integrated, President Eisenhower sent federal troops to enforce the Supreme Court's desegregation order. Nevertheless, the real heroes of Little Rock were the children who integrated the school. It was not an easy process. Daisy Bates, one participant in the Little Rock struggle, remembers what things were like in Arkansas in the 1950s. Many similar crises would follow in the succeeding decades.

It is important to read the school desegregation literature in this chapter and elsewhere in light of earlier works, however. While an end to *legal* segregation in schools (*de jure* segregation) was gained through the *Brown* decision, the reality of segregated, and unequal, schooling (*de facto* segregation) continues to the present.

It is also important to note the degree to which the American civil rights movement turned to the schools to provide the solution for many larger issues of social inequity. This was a deeply American point of focus. As with other issues noted throughout this volume, leaders of the civil rights movement of the 1950s believed that if the schools could treat children as equals—if segregation could end and a quality education could be provided for every child—then some large strides would have been made toward creating a larger society of freedom and justice for all.

In 1971, the United States Supreme Court ruled that the schools of Charlotte and surrounding Mecklenburg County in North Carolina could not continue a *de facto* pattern of segregation. The Court ordered that the school districts end segregation by busing students across district lines, triggering a new era for school desegregation. For the first decade and a half after the Court's *Brown* decision, desegregation efforts focused on the South. After 1970, the focus of desegregation shifted to the urban North. During the 1970s, few cities received more attention in its struggle with school desegregation than Boston. Long seen as the bastion of Northern liberalism, few noted the fact that only a handful of the graduates of the Boston public schools ever attended the city's famous universities and that the schools, like the city's ethnic neighborhoods, were highly segregated and too many students in the Boston public schools received a very poor-quality education.

Boston's African American community was not passive in the face of this situation. In 1963, the Education Committee of the Boston Branch of the NAACP, chaired by Ruth Batson, petitioned the School Committee for change. This was but the first of many petitions and pleas to improve the quality and end the segregation of the Boston schools.

In 1967, Jonathan Kozol, recently fired after a short-lived career as a teacher in the virtually all African American Gibson School, published *Death at an Early Age* (Boston, MA: Houghton Mifflin Company, 1967). This powerfully written book described Kozol's experience with the Boston public schools in the early 1960s and the school system's role, as the cover said, in the "destruction of the hearts and minds of Negro Children in the Boston Public Schools." While Kozol was teaching, and later writing his book, a coalition of local leaders (led by future state representative and candidate for mayor, Mel King—an African American—and a sitting member of the School Committee, Arthur Gartland—a European American) began grassroots efforts to elect a new School Committee. In the 1965 elections for School Committee, the new coalition was soundly defeated by a second emerging coalition; this one was led by Louise Day Hicks and others who took racist positions to defend the status quo. During the following decade, leaders in the African American community and their white allies used a variety of tactics to try to change the racist and antichild public schools. Only as a last resort did they turn to the federal courts, filing what would become the *Morgan v. Hennigan* case in 1972.

In the twenty-first century, researchers revised the long-simmering issue of school integration. Indeed the topic received new attention as more scholars and educators saw that since the 1980s schools had actually become more segregated, and even schools that were integrated in the whole student body were often segregated in individual classrooms, especially for classes offering the most advanced subjects, as Rucker Johnson discussed in the closing document of this chapter.

FEDERAL DISTRICT COURT, *MENDEZ V. WESTMINSTER*, 1946

At the conclusion of World War II, many school districts in California still operated racially segregated schools for Mexican American and Asian American students in spite of a limited court ruling against such practices in the 1931 case of Lemon Grove v. Alvarez. *In 1945 Felicitas and Gonzalo Mendez, along with four other Mexican American families, brought a suit in federal district court against school districts in Orange County in southern California for maintaining "schools for Mexicans" and barring their children from the regular public schools, claiming that such school segregation violated the California and United States Constitutions. The school district claimed that all school segregation was based on the language of the students but some of those involved, including the Mendez children, were clearly fluent in English. Nevertheless, the district fought the suit, claiming that the federal government had no role in education. A year after the suit was filed the federal district judge ruled in favor of the Mendez suit, finding that the district's claims about language instruction were merely a cover for segregation based on last names that identified the students as Mexican American, and in 1947 the federal appeals court upheld the ruling while the California legislature also amended the state's Education Code to prohibit all school segregation based on race or ethnicity. The 1946 federal district court ruling reflects some of the legal thinking of the 1940s but it is also clear in rejecting the school district's claims. The decision was hardly the end of schooling arrangements that undermined educational opportunities for students of color in California or the nation, but it was an important step. On the fiftieth anniversary of the appeals court ruling, the city of Santa Ana, California opened the Gonzalo and Felicitas Mendez School in that city to honor the desegregation effort.*

The complaint, grounded upon the Fourteenth Amendment to the Constitution of the United States and Subdivision 14 of Section 24 of the Judicial Code, Title 28, Section 41, subdivision 14, U.S.C.A., alleges a concerted policy and design of class discrimination against "persons of Mexican or Latin descent or extraction" of elementary school age by the defendant school agencies in the conduct and operation of public schools of said districts, resulting in the denial of the equal protection of the laws to such class of persons among which are the petitioning school children. Specifically, plaintiffs allege:

"That for several years last past respondents have and do now in furtherance and in execution of their common plan, design and purpose within their respective Systems and Districts, have by their regulation, custom and usage and in execution thereof adopted and declared: That all children or persons of Mexican or Latin descent or extraction, though Citizens of the United States of America, shall be, have been and are now excluded from attending, using, enjoying and receiving the benefits of the education, health and recreation facilities of certain schools within their respective Districts and Systems but that said children are now and have been segregated and required to and must attend and use certain schools in said Districts and Systems reserved for and attended solely and exclusively by children and persons of Mexican and Latin descent, while such other schools are maintained, attended and used exclusively by and for persons and children purportedly known as White or Anglo-Saxon children.

"That in execution of said rules and regulations, each, every and all the foregoing children are compelled and required to and must attend and use the schools in said respective Districts reserved for and attended solely and exclusively by children of Mexican and Latin descent and are forbidden, barred and excluded from attending any other school in said District or System solely for the reason that said children or child are of Mexican or Latin descent." ...

In the Westminster Garden Grove and El Modeno school districts the respective boards of trustees had taken official action, declaring that there be no segregation of pupils on a racial basis but that non-English-speaking children (which group, excepting as to a small number of pupils, was made up entirely of children of Mexican ancestry or descent), be required to attend schools designated by the boards separate and apart from English-speaking pupils; that such group should attend such schools until they had acquired some proficiency in the English language.

The petitioners contend that such official action evinces a covert attempt by the school authorities in such school districts to produce an arbitrary discrimination against school children of Mexican extraction or descent and that such illegal result has been established in such school districts respectively ...

The ultimate question for decision may be thus stated: Does such official action of defendant district school agencies and the usages and practices pursued by the respective school authorities as shown by the evidence operate to deny or deprive the so called non-English-speaking school children of Mexican ancestry or descent within such school districts of the equal protection of the laws? ...

The common segregation attitudes and practices of the school authorities in the defendant school districts in Orange County pertain solely to children of Mexican ancestry and parentage. They are singled out as a class for segregation. Not only is such method of public school administration contrary to the general requirements of the school laws of the State, but we think it indicates an official school policy that is antagonistic in principle to Sections 16004 and 16005 of the Education Code of the State.

Obviously, the children referred to in these laws are those of Mexican ancestry. And it is noteworthy that the educational advantages of their commingling with other pupils is regarded as being so important to the school system of the State that it is provided for even regardless of the citizenship of the parents. We perceive in the laws relating to the public educational system in the State of California a clear purpose to avoid and forbid distinctions among pupils based upon race or ancestry except in specific situations not pertinent to this action. Distinctions of that kind have recently been declared by the highest judicial authority of the United States "by their very nature odious to a free people whose institutions are founded upon the doctrine of equality." They are said to be "utterly inconsistent with American traditions and ideals." Kiyoshi Hirabayashi v. United States, 320 U.S. 81, 63 S.Ct. 1375, 1385, 87 L.Ed. 1774.

Our conclusions in this action, however, do not rest solely upon what we conceive to be the utter irreconcilability of the segregation practices in the defendant school districts with the public educational system authorized and sanctioned by the laws of the State of California. We think such practices clearly and unmistakably disregard rights secured by the supreme law of the land. Cumming v. Board of Education of Richmond County, supra. 6. and 7. "The equal protection of the laws" pertaining to the public school system in California is not provided by furnishing in separate schools the same technical facilities, text books and courses of instruction to children of Mexican ancestry that are available to the other public school children regardless of their ancestry. A paramount requisite in the American system of public education is social equality. It must be open to all children by unified school association regardless of lineage.

We think that under the record before us the only tenable ground upon which segregation practices in the defendant school districts can be defended lies in the English language deficiencies of some of the children of Mexican ancestry as they enter elementary public school life as beginners. But even such situations do not justify the general and continuous segregation in separate schools of the children of Mexican ancestry from the rest of the elementary school population as has been shown to be the practice in the defendant school districts—in all of them to the sixth grade, and in two of them through the eighth grade.

The evidence clearly shows that Spanish-speaking children are retarded in learning English by lack of exposure to its use because of segregation, and that commingling of the entire student body instills and develops a common cultural attitude among the school children which is imperative for the perpetuation of American institutions and ideals. It is also established by the record that the methods of segregation prevalent in the defendant school districts foster antagonisms in the children and suggest inferiority among them where none exists. One of the flagrant examples of the discriminatory results of segregation in two of the schools involved in this case is shown by the record. In the district under consideration there are two schools, the Lincoln and the Roosevelt, located approximately 120 yards apart on the same school grounds, hours of opening and closing, as well as recess periods, are not uniform. No credible language test is given to the children of Mexican ancestry upon entering the first grade in Lincoln School. This school has an enrollment of 249 so-called

Spanish-speaking pupils, and no so-called English-speaking pupils; while the Roosevelt (the other) school, has 83 so-called English-speaking pupils and 25 so-called Spanish-speaking pupils. Standardized tests as to mental ability are given to the respective classes in the two schools and the same curricula are pursued in both schools and, of course, in the English language as required by State law. Section 8251, Education Code . . .

There are other discriminatory customs, shown by the evidence, existing in the defendant school districts as to pupils of Mexican descent and extraction, but we deem it unnecessary to discuss them in this memorandum. We conclude by holding that the allegations of the complaint (petition) have been established sufficiently to justify injunctive relief against all defendants, restraining further discriminatory practices against the pupils of Mexican descent in the public schools of defendant school districts . . . Findings of fact, conclusions of law, and decree of injunction are accordingly ordered pursuant to Rule 52, F.R.C.P.

From: *Mendez et al. v. Westminster School District of Orange County et al.*, Civil Action No. 4292. 64 F. Supp. 544 District court, S. D. California, Central Division, February 18, 1946.

SEPTIMA CLARK, *READY FROM WITHIN*, CA. 1950

Septima Clark is one of the great heroes of the civil rights movement. The story of her life in the South, including her firing as a teacher in a segregated school because of her membership in the NAACP, and her subsequent career as a full-time civil rights educator, provide a powerful example of the issues southern African American educators faced in the years before the Brown decision. Clark was an exceptional human being, and her story therefore cannot be considered typical. But the struggles she endured and the choices she made in the years leading up to the Brown decision and during the subsequent flowering of the civil rights movement are representative of the experiences of many African American activists, especially in the field of education.

I want to start my story with the end of World War II because that is when the civil rights movement really got going, both for me personally and for people all over the South. After World War II, the men were coming home from fighting in Europe and Africa, and they weren't going to take segregation any more.

In 1947, I got a job in Charleston teaching seventh grade at the newest school in the system, the Henry P. Archer School. But soon my assignment was changed, and I was put in charge of a group of problem pupils in grades four through seven. Each period these children would come to me from their homerooms, and we did what was actually remedial reading. It was challenging work, and we made considerable progress . . .

In 1952, there was a childhood education meeting in Washington, D.C., and a worker from the black Y in Charleston, a Mrs. Anna Kelly, went to that meeting. There were some things that she wanted to discuss with both blacks and whites, and she couldn't discuss them down here because we couldn't have a black and white meeting together. Teachers couldn't meet together, and neither could community people. They had to meet separately.

At that meeting, Mrs. Kelly asked where in the South blacks and whites could meet together and talk over the problems that they talked about in that workshop. People told her that there was only one place—at the Highlander Folk School near Chattanooga.

Figure 10.1 Septima Clark. Courtesy of the Wisconsin Historical Society, Image ID 52578.

Mrs. Kelly decided to go there in the summer of '53, and she asked me would I sit on the desk of the YWCA while she was away. When she came back, she said, "Oh, that's a wonderful place. You don't even have to spend a nickel. You go up there, and they feed you, and they sleep you, and they ride you, and so everything is wonderful." I decided I should go to a place like that, so the next summer I went up, and I found what she said was true. I even found that blacks and whites were sleeping in the same room—that surprised me.

That's when I met Myles Horton and his wife Zilphia. Myles used to open the workshops by asking the people what they wanted to know, and he would close it with, "What you going to do back home?"

Zilphia played an accordion, and she would always lead the singing. She was a very good singer, and she had the songs of the people of the mountains, of the low country, of the labor unions, and whatever group. When she died, we really missed her.

Myles and Zilphia came to Charleston when we were having a testimonial for Judge Waring. Judge Waring had become the most hated fellow below Broad Street in Charleston; the white people learned to dislike him greatly. They said they disliked him because he married a Yankee woman. To marry a Yankee in their face was terrible. He also was hated because he had opened the Democratic primary to black people. For that, the black people of Charleston gave him a testimonial. That night we had large numbers of people at a school we were able to get. Afterwards Zilphia stayed at my house, and Mrs. Waring stayed at one of the other black women's houses.

I kept up my contacts with Myles and Zilphia and the Highlander Folk School. While I was at Highlander for the first time, the Supreme Court decided that segregation shall be no more. We were really happy over that, and I felt wonderful. But I didn't yet have the feeling that this thing was really a part of me.

I went to Highlander twice the first summer in '54, and the following summer I used my car to transport three groups of six persons each to Highlander workshops. At the end of that summer, we held a workshop to develop leadership, which I was directing. That was when I met Rosa Parks.

At that time Mrs. Parks lived in Montgomery, Alabama. Her husband was a barber, and he used to shave and cut hair for all of the high-class whites. Rosa was working with the youth group of the National Association for the Advancement of Colored People, or the N, double A, C, P, for short.

Rosa got to Highlander because she knew Virginia Durr, a great friend of Myles Horton, the director of the Highlander. Rosa and Virginia got to know each other by Rosa being a seamstress and Virginia's husband being the only lawyer in Montgomery who would take the legal cases brought by the NAACP. Working with the NAACP, Rosa was under fire. Virginia stayed under fire because she was a white woman who dared to take sides with blacks.

First Virginia Durr wrote a letter and asked that we send money for Rosa to come up to Highlander, which we did. Then Virginia took Rosa to Atlanta and saw her on a bus to Highlander.

We had a large group of people at that workshop. It was a two-week workshop on the United Nations. We knew that Rosa had been working with the youth group in Montgomery, so at the meeting I asked Rosa to tell how she was able to get the Freedom Train to come to Montgomery and get this youth group to go through the Freedom Train. She wouldn't talk at all at first.

People at the workshop knew only a little bit about the Freedom Train. It was being sent by the government around the country from Washington, D.C. as a lesson in democracy. It carried an exhibit of the original U.S. Constitution and the Declaration of Independence. Anyone could go inside for free, but segregation was not permitted.

One night up there in the bedroom (there were about six beds in one dormitory) everyone started singing and dancing, white kids and all, and they said, "Rosa, how in the world did you deal with that Freedom Train?"

Then she said, "It wasn't an easy task. We took our children down when the Freedom Train came, and the white and black children had to go in together. They wouldn't let them go in otherwise, and that was a real victory for us." But she said, "After that, I began getting obscene phone calls from people because I was president of the youth group. That's why Mrs. Durr wanted me to come up here and see what I could do with this same youth group when I went back home."

The next day in the workshop I say, "Rosa, tell these people how you got that Freedom Train to come to Montgomery." She hated to tell it. She thought that certainly somebody would go back and tell the white people. A teacher from Montgomery came at the same time, and she said she couldn't let them know she was coming to Highlander, because if these white people knew then she would have lost her job, too.

Anyway, Rosa got up and told that group about it. We had somebody there from the United Nations, and they said to her, "If anything happens, you get in touch with me, and I'll be sure to see that you have your rights."

After the workshop, Rosa was afraid to go from Highlander to Atlanta. Myles sent me with her. She was afraid that somebody had already spoken, and she didn't know what was going to happen. I went with her to Atlanta and saw her in a bus going down to Montgomery. She felt much better then.

I guess she kept thinking about the things at the workshop. At the end of the workshops we always say, "What do you plan to do back home?" Rosa answered that question by saying that Montgomery was the cradle of the Confederacy, that nothing would happen there because blacks wouldn't stick together. But she promised to work with those kids, and to tell them that they had the right to belong to the NAACP, that they had the right to do things like going through the Freedom Train. She decided that she was going to keep right on working with them.

Three months after Rosa got back to Montgomery, on December 1, 1955, she refused to get up from her seat on the bus. When I heard the news, I said, "Rosa? Rosa?" She was so shy when she came to Highlander, but she got enough courage to do that.

Rosa hadn't planned at Highlander that she was going to refuse to get up out of her seat. That evidently came to her that day after she got done at work. But many people at the Highlander workshop told about the discrimination on the buses. I guess practically every family around Montgomery had had trouble with people getting on buses. They'd had a hard time. They had a number of cases where bus drivers had beaten 15-year-olds who sat up to the front or refused to get up from their seat and give it to whites coming in. That was the kind of thing they had, and they had taken it long enough.

Now I had that all the time here in Charleston. I was living down on Henrietta Street. I caught the bus going to my school about a mile up. The Navy Yard men would be going to work at the same time. I would sit in that section that's designed for blacks. But if a white man came up, and the white section is all filled in, I'd have to stand up and give him my seat and stand up the rest of the way. I'd just get up and give him my seat. I knew I had to do it or be arrested. I'd sit in the back but when that front got crowded they'd come to the back and you had to get up and give them your seat. That's what they call justice. I had to do that for a long time until Rosa refused, and then that changed.

I don't know why it was, but it seems like that did not make me angry. I always felt that there would be a time when I could work on things. I never felt that getting angry would do you any good other than hurt your own digestion—keep you from eating, which I liked to do . . .

By the time that Rosa Parks refused to get up and give her seat to a white man, I had gotten into some trouble of my own back in Charleston. I began to realize that I might be dismissed from my position as an elementary teacher because I belonged to that same organization Rosa Parks did—the National Association for the Advancement of Colored People, the NAACP.

. . . I became very fond of the NAACP, and from that time on I worked with it.

There weren't too many black people who considered the NAACP worthwhile. They were still afraid, you know, so it was a very small group at first. But after many years of work by its lawyers, the United States Supreme Court ruled, in 1954, that racial segregation in public schools was unconstitutional. After that decision, the school authorities in South Carolina passed out questionnaires to every teacher requiring us to list all the organizations we belonged to. I refused to overlook my membership in the NAACP, as some of the teachers did. I listed it.

The next year the South Carolina legislature passed a law that said that no city or state employee could belong to the NAACP. You see, our legislature was joining others across the Deep South in a systematic campaign to wipe out the NAACP.

Our supervisor of Negro teachers was horribly concerned about it. She knew that she was going to lose her job because she was a member, and she did not want to give it up. She just got terribly ill in her mind. She became senile soon, and she died not too long after that, before they took her job away.

It wasn't too long before I got my letter of dismissal. The Board of Education wrote me that it would not be renewing my contract to teach remedial reading at the Henry Archer School. My goodness, somehow or other it really didn't bother me.

But it bothered my family. My sister said that when people called her she felt like she had something in her stomach, just like butterflies, working around. She was teaching then. I said, "You just let me answer the phone and tell the people I'm a member and I've been dismissed. I don't mind at all."

My mother had died by the time I was dismissed, but I know she would have said, "I told you so." She never joined the NAACP, nor my sister Edith. My brother Peter hasn't either. They weren't fighters. They didn't feel as if they could fight for freedom or for justice. They just didn't have that kind of feeling.

One hundred and sixty-nine teachers came from Washington and Baltimore to get our jobs, and there weren't but forty-two of us dismissed. Those teachers came down here because they had to have one year experience before they could teach in Baltimore or Washington. They came thinking they could get those jobs.

But they didn't get them. Other people already here got those jobs. Most of those forty-two teachers who were fired went to New York and Boston and other places in the North. A few of them came back and were able to get jobs teaching.

I never did try. I felt that they never would let me have one anyway because they considered me a Communist because I worked with the Highlander Folk School. I had been to Highlander two years before I was dismissed here. I know they felt that I was really a Communist then, I was too much of a head woman, a controversial leader, and I couldn't get any job here.

I feel the big failure in my life was trying to work with the black teachers to get them to realize, when that law was passed in South Carolina, that it was an unjust law. But there were such a few jobs that they didn't see how they could work against the law.

I had the feeling that if all of them would say, "We are members of the NAACP," that the legislature would not have said, "All of you will lose your jobs," because that would mean thousands of children out on the streets at one time.

But I couldn't get them to see that. I signed my name to seven-hundred twenty-six letters to black teachers, asking them to tell the state of South Carolina that it was unjust to rule that no city or state employee could belong to the NAACP. If whites could belong to the Ku Klux Klan, then surely blacks could belong to the NAACP.

I don't know why I felt that the black teachers would stand up for their rights. But they wouldn't. Most of them were afraid and became hostile. Only twenty-six of them answered my letter, and I wrote them that we should go and talk with the superintendent. Eleven decided that they would go talk to the superintendent, but when it was time to go, there were only five of us. The superintendent did everything he could before he would see us. He was writing out some plans on a board. Finally he talked, and the only thing he did was to let us know that we were living far ahead of our time. That's what he said.

I considered that one of the failures of my life because I think that I tried to push them into something that they weren't ready for. From that day on I say, "I'm going to have to get the people trained. We're going to have to show them the dangers or the pitfalls that they are in, before they will accept." And it took many years.

You always have to get the people with you. You can't just force them into things. That taught me a good lesson, because when I went into Mississippi and Alabama, I stayed behind the scene and tried to get the people in the town to push forward, and then I would come forth with ideas. But I wouldn't do it at first because I knew it was detrimental. That was a weakness of mine that I felt I had to strengthen. The people in the masses, though, do better than the teachers. They come out. They're willing to fight anyhow.

You know, I had to go away for twenty years from Charleston. I couldn't get a job here, nowhere in South Carolina. Not only that, but the black teachers here, my sorority, Alpha Kappa Alpha, gave me a testimonial. Alpha Kappa Alpha is an organization of black women college graduates. Do you know that at that party my [sorority sisters] would not stand beside me and have their picture made with me? If they had, they would have lost their jobs.

I can't say that I kept from being frightened about this whole episode. For three solid months after I took a new job at Highlander Folk School, I couldn't sleep. Night after night I stayed up listening to the tape of the workshop that we had conducted during the day. One morning, it must have been a September morning, I felt a kind of a free feeling in my mind, and I said, "Now I must have been right." I was able to fall asleep and to sleep after that. I decided that I had worried about the thing enough.

Cynthia Stokes Brown, ed., *Septima Clark and the Civil Rights Movement: Ready from Within*, Trenton, NJ: Africa World Press, 1990.

SUPREME COURT OF THE UNITED STATES, *BROWN V. BOARD OF EDUCATION OF TOPEKA, KANSAS*, 1954

The United States Supreme Court's decision in the Brown v. Board of Education *case was unusual for the Court in two ways. First, it directly overturned a previous Court decision: the 1896* Plessy v. Ferguson *decision in which the Court had decided that segregation on the basis of race was legal.* Brown *was also a unanimous decision; indeed, Chief Justice Earl Warren worked hard to achieve the compromises necessary for a unanimous decision because he believed that the full Court should be behind such a dramatic order. It is hard for people living more than a half-century after the* Brown *decision to understand how controversial the order was when the Court handed it down in spite of many previous court decisions declaring racial segregation to be unconstitutional in specific educational contexts. On the other hand, it is essential that we see* Brown *as just one step on a very long road. Years of local organizing and legal action had gone into building the judicial base and the community support that made* Brown *possible. Many more years of legal action, civil rights activity, and local organizing across the country would be necessary to implement* Brown. *Still, the case is a marker of great significance in the history of education, and worth reading with special attention.*

Mr. Chief Justice Warren delivered the opinion of the Court.

These cases come to us from the States of Kansas, South Carolina, Virginia, and Delaware. They are premised on different facts and different local conditions, but a common legal question justifies their consideration together in this consolidated opinion.

In each of the cases, minors of the Negro race, through their legal representatives, seek the aid of the courts in obtaining admission to the public schools of their community on a nonsegregated basis. In each instance, they had been denied admission to schools attended by white children under laws requiring or permitting segregation according to race. This segregation was alleged to deprive the plaintiffs of the equal protection of the laws under the Fourteenth Amendment. In each of the cases other than the Delaware case, a three-judge federal district court denied relief to the plaintiffs on the so-called "separate but equal" doctrine announced by this Court in *Plessy v Ferguson*, 163 U.S. 537. Under that doctrine, equality of treatment is accorded when the races are provided substantially equal facilities, even though these facilities be separate. In the Delaware case, the Supreme Court of Delaware adhered to that doctrine, but ordered that the plaintiffs be admitted to the white schools because of their superiority to the Negro schools.

The plaintiffs contend that segregated public schools are not "equal" and cannot be made "equal," and that hence they are deprived of the equal protection of the laws. Because of the obvious importance of the question presented, the Court took jurisdiction. Argument was heard in the 1952 Term, and reargument was heard this Term on certain questions propounded by the Court.

Reargument was largely devoted to the circumstances surrounding the adoption of the Fourteenth Amendment in 1868. It covered exhaustively consideration of the Amendment in Congress, ratification by the states, then existing practices in racial segregation, and the views of proponents and opponents of the Amendment. This discussion and our own investigation convince us that, although these sources cast some light, it is not enough to resolve the problem with which we are faced. At best, they are inconclusive. The most avid proponents of the post-War Amendments undoubtedly intended them to remove all legal distinctions among "all persons born or naturalized in the United States." Their opponents, just as certainly, were antagonistic to both the letter and the spirit of the Amendments and wished them to have the most limited effect. What others in Congress and the state legislatures had in mind cannot be determined with any degree of certainty . . .

In the first cases in this Court construing the Fourteenth Amendment, decided shortly after its adoption, the Court interpreted it as proscribing all state-imposed discriminations against the Negro race. The doctrine of "separate but equal" did not make its appearance in this Court until 1896 in the case of *Plessy v. Ferguson, supra*, involving not education but transportation. American courts have since labored with the doctrine for over half a century. In this Court, there have been six cases involving the "separate but equal" doctrine in the field of public education. In *Gumming v. County Board of Education*, 175 U.S. 528, and *Gong Lum v Rice*, 275 U.S. 78, the validity of the doctrine itself was not challenged. In more recent cases, all on the graduate school level, inequality was found in that specific benefits enjoyed by white students were denied to Negro students of the same educational qualifications. *Missouri ex rel. Gaines v. Canada*, 305 U.S. 337; *Sipuel v. Oklahoma*, 332 U.S. 631; *Sweatt v. Painter*, 339 U.S. 629; *McLaurin v. Oklahoma State Regents*, 339 U.S. 637. In none of these cases was it necessary to reexamine the doctrine to grant relief to the Negro plaintiff. And in *Sweatt v. Painter, supra*, the Court expressly reserved decision on the question whether *Plessy v. Ferguson* should be held inapplicable to public education.

In the instant case, that question is directly presented. Here, unlike *Sweatt v Painter*, there are findings below that the Negro and white schools involved have been equalized, or are being equalized, with respect to buildings, curricula, qualifications and salaries of teachers, and other "tangible" factors. Our decision, therefore, cannot turn on merely a comparison of these tangible factors in the Negro and white schools involved in each of the cases. We must look instead to the effect of segregation itself on public education.

In approaching this problem, we cannot turn the clock back to 1868 when the Amendment was adopted, or even to 1896 when *Plessy v. Ferguson* was written. We must consider public education in the light of its full development and its present place in American life throughout the Nation. Only in this way can it be determined if segregation in public schools deprives these plaintiffs of the equal protection of the laws.

Today, education is perhaps the most important function of state and local governments. Compulsory school attendance laws and the great expenditures for education both demonstrate our recognition of the importance of education to our democratic society. It is required in the performance of our most basic public responsibilities, even service in the armed forces. It is the very foundation of good citizenship. Today it is a principal instrument in awakening the child to cultural values, in preparing him for later professional training, and in helping him to adjust normally to his environment. In these days, it is doubtful that any child may reasonably be expected to succeed in life if he is denied the opportunity of an education. Such an opportunity, where the state has undertaken to provide it, is a right which must be made available to all on equal terms.

We come then to the question presented: Does segregation of children in public schools solely on the basis of race, even though the physical facilities and other "tangible" factors may be equal, deprive the children of the minority group of equal educational opportunities? We believe that it does.

In *Sweatt v. Painter, supra,* in finding that a segregated law school for Negroes could not provide them equal educational opportunities, this Court relied in large part on "those qualities which are incapable of objective measurement but which make for greatness in a law school." In *McLaurin v. Oklahoma State Regents, supra,* the Court, in requiring that a Negro admitted to a white graduate school be treated like all other students, again resorted to intangible considerations: ". . . his ability to study, to engage in discussions and exchange views with other students, and, in general, to learn his profession." Such considerations apply with added force to children in grade and high schools. To separate them from others of similar age and qualifications solely because of their race generates a feeling of inferiority as to their status in the community that may affect their hearts and minds in a way unlikely ever to be undone. The effect of this separation on their educational opportunities was well-stated by a finding in the Kansas case by a court which nevertheless felt compelled to rule against the Negro plaintiffs:

> Segregation of white and colored children in public schools has a detrimental effect upon the colored children. The impact is greater when it has the sanction of the law; for the policy of separating the races is usually interpreted as denoting the inferiority of the negro group. A sense of inferiority affects the motivation of a child to learn. Segregation with the sanction of law, therefore, has a tendency to [retard] the educational and mental development of negro children and to deprive them of some of the benefits they would receive in a racial[ly] integrated school system.

Whatever may have been the extent of psychological knowledge at the time of *Plessy v Ferguson*, this finding is amply supported by modern authority. Any language in *Plessy v. Ferguson* contrary to this finding is rejected.

We conclude that in the field of public education, the doctrine of "separate but equal" has no place. Separate educational facilities are inherently unequal. Therefore, we hold that the plaintiffs and others similarly situated for whom the actions have been brought are, by reason of the segregation complained of, deprived of the equal protection of the laws guaranteed by the Fourteenth Amendments. This disposition makes unnecessary any discussion whether such segregation also violates the Due Process Clause of the Fourteenth Amendment.

It is so ordered.

Supreme Court of the United States, *Brown et al. v. Board of Education of Topeka et al.*, No. 1, Supreme Court of the United States 347 U.S. 483; 1954.

KENNETH B. CLARK, "HOW CHILDREN LEARN ABOUT RACE," 1950

The Supreme Court's reasoning in the Brown *case was based on many considerations, but one of the most important was Kenneth Clark's research on the impact of segregation on the self-image and learning potential of African American children. Clark had presented his findings at a White House Conference in 1950. While he faced significant challenges later in the century, Clark's study showing the harmful impact of "separate but equal" schooling influenced the Court, and much of American society, to conclude that legally enforced separation was inherently unequal. Clark published his findings in 1955, but they had already made their most significant impact through the Supreme Court's 1954 decision.*

Are children born with racial feelings? Or do they have to learn, first, what color they are and, second, what color is "best"?

Less than fifty years ago, some social theorists maintained that racial and religious prejudices are inborn—that they are inherent and instinctive. These theorists believed that children do not have to learn to dislike people who differ from them in physical characteristics; it was considered natural to dislike those different from oneself and to like those similar to oneself.

However, research over the past thirty years has refuted these earlier theories. Social scientists are now convinced that children learn social, racial, and religious prejudices in the course of observing, and being influenced by, the existence of patterns in the culture in which they live. Students of the problem are now facing these questions:

1. How and when do children learn to identify themselves with some people and to differentiate themselves from others?
2. How and when do children acquire racial attitudes and begin to express these attitudes in their behavior?
3. What conditions in the environment foster the development of these racial attitudes and behavior?

4. What can be done to prevent the development and expression of destructive racial prejudices in children?

Until quite recently, there were differences in opinion concerning the age at which children develop and express racial prejudices. Some observers (in the tradition of those who believed that prejudices are inborn) said that even infants express racial preferences and that therefore such preferences play little or no role in the life of the child until the early teens. They pointed out that children of different races have been observed playing together and sometimes developing close friendships; this fact, they thought, showed that young children are unaware of racial or religious differences.

Within the past two decades, social scientists have made a series of studies of this problem. They indicate, on the one hand, that there is no evidence that racial prejudices are inborn; and, on the other hand, that it is equally false to assume that the child remains unaffected by racial considerations until his teens or preteens.

Racial attitudes appear early in the life of children and affect the ideas and behavior of children in the first grades of school. Such attitudes—which appear to be almost inevitable in children in our society—develop gradually.

According to one recent study, white kindergarten children in New York City show a clear preference for whites and a clear rejection of Negroes. Other studies show that Negro children in the kindergarten and early elementary grades of a New England town, in New York City, in Philadelphia, and in two urban communities in Arkansas know the difference between Negroes and whites; realize they are Negro or white; and are aware of the social meaning and evaluation of racial differences.

The development of racial awareness and racial preferences in Negro children has been studied by the author and his wife. To determine the extent of consciousness of skin of color in these children between three and seven years old, we showed the children four dolls all from the same mold and dressed alike; the only difference in the dolls was that two were brown and two were white. We asked the children to choose among the dolls in answer to certain requests:

1. "Give me the white doll."
2. "Give me the colored doll."
3. "Give me the Negro doll."

These children reacted with strong awareness of skin color. Among three-year-old Negro children in both northern and southern communities, more that 75 percent showed that they were conscious of the difference between "white" and "colored." Among older children, an increasingly greater number made the correct choices.

These findings clearly support the conclusion that racial awareness is present in Negro children as young as three years old. Furthermore, this knowledge develops in stability and clarity from year to year, and by the age of seven, it is a part of the knowledge of all Negro children. Other investigators have shown that the same is true of white children.

Some children whose skin color is indistinguishable from that of white people, but who are nonetheless classified as Negroes by the society, have difficulty in making a correct racial identification of themselves at an age when other children do so. Soon, however—by the age of five or six—the majority of these children also begin to accept the social definition of themselves, even though this differs from their observance of their own skin color.

There is now no doubt that children learn the prevailing social ideas about racial differences early in their lives. Not only are they aware of race in terms of physical characteristics such as skin color, but also they are generally able to identify themselves in terms of race . . .

In addition to Negro children's awareness of differences in skin color, the author and his wife studied the ability of these children to identify themselves in racial terms . . . We asked the children to point out the doll "which is most like you." Approximately two-thirds of all the children answered correctly. Correct answers were more frequent among the older ones. (Only 37 percent of the three-year-olds but 87 percent of the seven-year-olds responded accurately.) Negro children of light skin color had more difficulty in choosing the brown doll than Negro children of medium-brown or dark-brown skin color. This was true for older as well as younger children.

Many personal and emotional factors probably affected the ability of these Negro children to select the brown doll. In an effort to determine their racial preferences, we asked the children the following four questions:

1. "Give me the doll that you like to play with" or "the doll you like best."
2. "Give me the doll that is the nice doll."
3. "Give me the doll that looks bad."
4. "Give me the doll that is a nice color."

The majority of these Negro children at each age indicated an unmistakable preference for the white doll and a rejection of the brown doll.

Studies of the development of racial awareness, racial identification, and racial preference in both Negro and white children thus present a consistent pattern. Learning about races and racial differences, learning one's own racial identity, learning which race is to be preferred and which rejected—all these are assimilated by the child as part of the total pattern of ideas he acquires about himself and the society in which he lives. These acquired patterns of social and racial ideas are interrelated both in development and in function. The child's first awareness of racial differences is found to be associated with some rudimentary evaluation of these differences. Furthermore, as the average child learns to evaluate these differences according to the standards of the society, he is at the same time required to identify himself with one or another group. This identification necessarily involves a knowledge of the status assigned to the group with which he identifies himself, in relation to the status of other groups. The child therefore cannot learn what racial group he belongs to without being involved in a larger pattern of emotions, conflict, and desires which are part of his growing knowledge of what society thinks about his race.

Many independent studies enable us to begin to understand how children learn about race, how they identify themselves and others in terms of racial, religious, or nationality differences, and what meaning these differences have for the growing child. Racial and religious identification involves the ability of the child to identify himself with others of similar characteristics and to distinguish himself from those who appear to be dissimilar.

The fact that young Negro children would prefer to be white reflects their knowledge that society prefers white people. White children are generally found to prefer their white skin—an indication that they, too, know that society like whites better. It is clear, therefore, that the self-acceptance or self-rejection found so early in a child's developing complex of racial ideas reflects the awareness and acceptance of the prevailing racial attitudes in his community.

Some children as young as three years of age begin to express racial and religious attitudes similar to those held by adults in their society. The racial and religious attitudes of sixth graders are more definite than the attitudes of preschool children, and hardly distinguishable from the attitudes of high school students. Thereafter, there is an increase in the intensity and complexity of these attitudes, until they become similar (at least, as far as words go) to the prevailing attitudes held by the average adult American.

Kenneth B. Clark, "How Children Learn about Race," *Prejudice and Your Child*, Boston, MA: Beacon Press, 1963.

SCHOOL DESEGREGATION IN THE SOUTH: LITTLE ROCK, 1957

Daisy Bates, *The Long Shadow of Little Rock, Reflections on 1957*

Daisy Bates, editor of a newspaper in the African American community in Little Rock, Arkansas, and president of the Arkansas chapter of the NAACP in 1957, was a major actor in the desegregation of Little Rock High School. She tells of the experience that as an adult she shared with the students in her book, The Long Shadow of Little Rock *(1962). Clearly she and her coworkers never expected the massive resistance to the federal court orders that occurred in Little Rock and elsewhere. Yet when it appeared, they faced it with courage. Bates's account provides a moving personal glimpse of the desegregation struggle.*

It was Labor Day, September 2, 1957. The nine pupils who had been selected by the school authorities to enter Central High School—Carlotta Walls, Jefferson Thomas, Elizabeth Eckford, Thelma Mothershed, Melba Pattillo, Ernest Green, Terrance Roberts, Gloria Ray, and Minnijean Brown—were enjoying the last day of their summer vacation . . . About mid-afternoon, young Jefferson Thomas was on his way home from the pool and stopped at my house for a brief visit. While Jeff was raiding the refrigerator, a news flash came over the radio that the Governor would address the citizens of Arkansas that night.

"I wonder what he's going to talk about," said Jeff. The youngster then turned to me and asked, "Is there anything they can do—now that they lost in court? Is there any way they can stop us from entering Central tomorrow morning?"

"I don't think so," I said.

About seven o'clock that night, a local newspaper reporter rang my doorbell. "Mrs. Bates, do you know that national guardsmen are surrounding Central High?"

L. C. [Bates] and I stared at him incredulously for a moment. A friend who was visiting us volunteered to guard the house while we drove out to Central. L. C. gave him the shotgun. We jumped into our car and drove to Central High . . . Men in full battle dress-helmets, boots, and bayonets were piling out of the trucks and lining up in front of the school.

As we watched, L. C. switched on the car radio. A newscaster was saying, "National guardsmen are surrounding Central High School. No one is certain what this means. Governor Faubus will speak later this evening . . ."

I don't recall all the details of what Governor Faubus said that night. But his words electrified Little Rock. By morning, they shocked the United States. By noon the next day, his message horrified the world.

Faubus's alleged reason for calling out the troops was that he had received information that caravans of automobiles filled with white supremacists were heading toward Little Rock from all over the state. He therefore declared Central High School off limits to Negroes. For some inexplicable reason, he added that Horace Mann, a Negro high school, would be off limits to whites.

Then, from the chair of the highest office of the State of Arkansas, Governor Orval Eugene Faubus delivered the infamous words, "blood will run in the streets," if Negro pupils should attempt to enter Central High School.

In a half dozen ill-chosen words, Faubus made his contribution to the mass hysteria that was to grip the city of Little Rock for several months.

The citizens of Little Rock gathered on September 3 to gaze upon the incredible spectacle of an empty school building surrounded by two-hundred fifty National Guard troops. At about eight fifteen in the morning, Central students starting passing through the line of national guardsmen—all but the nine Negro students.

I had been in touch with their parents throughout the day. They were confused, and they were frightened. As the parents voiced their fears, they kept repeating Governor Faubus's words that "blood would run in the streets of Little Rock" should their teenage children try to attend Central—the school to which they had been assigned by the school board?

On the afternoon of the same day, September 3, when the school was scheduled to open, Superintendent [Virgil] Blossom called a meeting of leading Negro citizens and parents of the nine children . . . [and] instructed the parents not to accompany their children the next morning when they were scheduled to enter Central. "If violence breaks out," the Superintendent told them, "it will be easier to protect the children if the adults aren't there."

During the conference, Superintendent Blossom had given us little assurance that the children would be adequately protected. As we left the building, I was aware of how deeply worried the parents were, although they did not voice their fears.

About ten o'clock that night, I was alone in the downstairs recreation room.

I sat huddled in my chair, dazed, trying to think, yet not knowing what to do. I don't recall how much time went by . . . before some neighbors entered. One of them was the Reverend J. C. Crenshaw, President of the Little Rock branch of the NAACP.

"Maybe," I said, "maybe we could round up a few ministers to go with the children tomorrow. Maybe then the mob wouldn't attack them. Maybe with the ministers by their side—"

I called a white minister, Reverend Dunbar Ogden, Jr., President of the Interracial Ministerial Alliance. I did not know Mr. Ogden. I explained the situation, then asked if he thought he could get some ministers to go with the children to school the next morning.

Tensely, I waited for his return call. When it came, he sounded apologetic. The white ministers he had talked to had questioned whether it was the thing to do. Some of the Negro ministers had pointed out that the Superintendent of Schools had asked that no Negro adults go with the children, and that in view of this, they felt they shouldn't go. Then he added gently, "I'll keep trying—and, God willing, I'll be there."

Next I called the city police. I explained to the officer in charge that we were concerned about the safety of the children and that we were trying to get ministers to accompany them to school the next morning. I said that the children would assemble at eight thirty at Twelfth and Park Avenue. I asked whether a police car could be stationed there to protect the children until the ministers arrived.

The police officer promised to have a squad car there at eight o'clock. "But you realize," he warned, "that our men cannot go any closer than that to the school. The school is off limits to the city police while it's 'occupied' by the Arkansas National Guardsmen."

By now it was two thirty in the morning. Still, the parents had to be called about the change in plan. At three o'clock I completed my last call, explaining to the parents where the children were to assemble and the plan about the ministers. Suddenly I remembered Elizabeth Eckford. Her family had no telephone. Should I go to the Union Station and search for her father? Someone had once told me that he had a night job there. Tired in mind and body, I decided to handle the matter early in the morning. I stumbled into bed.

A few hours later, at about eight fifteen in the morning, L. C. and I started driving to Twelfth Street and Park Avenue. On the way I checked out in my mind the possibilities that awaited us . . .

The bulletin over the car radio interrupted. The voice announced: "A Negro girl is being mobbed at Central High . . ."

"Oh my God!" I cried. "It must be Elizabeth! I forgot to notify her where to meet us!"

L. C. jumped out of the car and rushed to find her. I drove on to Twelfth Street. There were the ministers—two white—Mr. Ogden and Reverend Will Campbell, of the National Council of Churches, Nashville, Tennessee—and two colored—the Reverend Z. A. Driver, of the African Methodist Episcopal Church, and the Reverend Harry Bass, of the Methodist Church. With them also was Mr. Ogden's twenty-one-year-old son, David. The children were already there. And, yes, the police had come as promised. All of the children were there—all except Elizabeth.

Elizabeth, whose dignity and control in the face of jeering mobsters had been filmed by television cameras and recorded in pictures flashed to newspapers over the world, had overnight become a national heroine . . . The first day that her parents agreed she might come out of seclusion, she came to my house, where the reporters awaited her. Elizabeth was very quiet, speaking only when spoken to. I took her to my bedroom to talk before I let the reporters see her. I asked her how she felt now. Suddenly all her pent-up emotion flared.

"Why am I here?" she said, turning blazing eyes on me. "Why are you so interested in my welfare now? You didn't care enough to notify me of the change of plans—"

Little by little, Elizabeth came out of her shell. Up to now she had never talked about what happened to her at Central. Once when we were alone in the downstairs recreation room of my house, I asked her simply, "Elizabeth, do you think you can talk about it now?"

She remained quiet for a long time. Then she began to speak.

"You remember the day before we were to go in, we met Superintendent Blossom at the school board office. He told us what the mob might say and do, but he never told us we wouldn't have any protection. He told our parents not to come because he wouldn't be able to protect the children if they did.

"That night I was so excited I couldn't sleep. The next morning I was about the first one up. While I was pressing my black-and-white dress—I had made it to wear on the first day of school—my little brother turned on the TV set. They started telling about a large crowd gathered at the school. The man on TV said he wondered if we were going to show up that morning.

"Before I left home, Mother called us into the living room. She said we should have a word of prayer. Then I caught the bus and got off a block from the school. I saw a large crowd of people standing across the street from the soldiers guarding Central. As I walked on, the crowd suddenly got quiet. Superintendent Blossom had told us to enter by the front door. I looked at all the people and thought, 'Maybe I will be safer if I walk down the block to the front entrance behind the guards.'

"At the corner, I tried to pass through the long line of guards around the school so as to enter the grounds behind them. One of the guards pointed across the street. So I pointed in the same direction and asked whether he meant for me to cross the street and walk down. He nodded 'yes.' So, I walked across the street, conscious of the crowd that stood there, but they moved away from me.

"For a moment all I could hear was the shuffling of their feet. Then someone shouted, 'Here she comes, get ready!' I moved away from the crowd on the sidewalk and into the street. If the mob came at me I could then cross back over so the guards could protect me.

"The crowd moved in closer and then began to follow me, calling me names. I still wasn't afraid. Just a little bit nervous. Then my knees started to shake all of a sudden and I wondered whether I could make it to the center entrance a block away. It was the longest block I ever walked in my whole life.

"Even so, I still wasn't too scared, because all the time I kept thinking that the guards would protect me.

"When I got in front of the school, I went up to a guard again. But this time he just looked straight ahead and didn't move to let me pass him. I didn't know what to do. Then I looked and saw the path leading to the front entrance was a little further ahead. So I walked until I was right in front of the path to the front door.

"I stood looking at the school—it looked so big! Just then the guards let some white students through.

"The crowd was quiet. I guess they were waiting to see what was going to happen. When I was able to steady my knees, I walked up to the guard who had let the white students in. He, too, didn't move. When I tried to squeeze past him, he raised his bayonet and then the other guards moved in and they raised their bayonets.

"They glared at me with a mean look and I was very frightened and didn't know what to do. I turned around and the crowd came toward me.

"They moved closer and closer. Somebody started yelling, 'Lynch her! Lynch her!' I tried to see a friendly face somewhere in the mob—someone who maybe would help. I looked into the face of an old woman and it seemed a kind face, but when I looked at her again, she spat on me.

"They came closer, shouting, 'No nigger bitch is going to get in our school. Get out of here!'

Figure 10.2 Little Rock. Courtesy of the Library of Congress, LC-DIG-ppmsca-03140.

"I turned back to the guards but their faces told me I wouldn't get any help from them. Then I looked down the block and saw a bench at the bus stop. I thought, 'If I can only get there, I will be safe.' I don't know why the bench seemed a safe place to me, but I started walking toward it. I tried to close my mind to what they were shouting, and kept saying to myself, 'If I can only make it to the bench, I will be safe.'

"When I finally got there, I don't think I could have gone another step. I sat down and the mob crowded up and began shouting all over again. Someone hollered, 'Drag her over to this tree! Let's take care of that nigger.' Just then a white man sat down beside me, put his arm around me and patted my shoulder. He raised my chin and said, 'Don't let them see you cry.'

"Then, a white lady—she was very nice—she came over to me on the bench. She spoke to me but I don't remember what she said. She put me on the bus and sat next to me. She asked my name and tried to talk to me, but I don't think I answered. I can't remember much about the bus ride, but the next thing I remember I was standing in front of the School for the Blind, where Mother works."

Daisy Bates, *The Long Shadow of Little Rock*, Fayetteville, AR: University of Arkansas Press, 1962. Reprinted by permission of the University of Arkansas Press.

NAACP BOSTON BRANCH, STATEMENT TO THE BOSTON SCHOOL COMMITTEE, JUNE 11, 1963

Ruth Batson was the Chairman of the Education Committee of the NAACP, Boston Branch, in 1963. A well-known community and civil rights leader, Batson emerged as part of a group that steadily challenged the inequality and the poor education offered to the children of Boston's small African American community. She preserved her statement as part of a history of the desegregation effort in Boston that she assembled.

Madame Chairman, Members of the Boston School Committee:

The National Association for the Advancement of Colored People is an organization dedicated to the elimination of discrimination and prejudice from all phases of American life. Our goal is First-Class Citizenship, and we will settle for nothing less. All immigrants to the American shores have suffered from discrimination, but in most cases, as soon as they lost their identifying accents, they were able to blend into the American culture and enjoy the fruits of our democratic system. The Negro, brought here in chains, bears visible identification of his race, and we have spent our lives tearing down wall after wall of resistance raised in our path, because of our color.

One of the most frustrating and devastating obstacles confronting us is the lack of educational opportunity. Education constitutes our strongest hope for pulling ourselves out of the inferior status to which society has assigned us. For a boy of eight or nine years, who is receiving an inferior education today, will feel the effects at age thirty-five, forty-five, and until he dies, as he struggles, as a father, to rear and educate his children. His lack of educational opportunity will make it impossible for him to motivate his children properly, and thus, this burden is inherited by each succeeding generation. Since you, our School Committee, are the caretakers of our educational school system, a job which each of you sought voluntarily, we are here tonight to express our dissatisfaction, to air our complaints, and to make certain demands in connection with our schools.

I know that the word *demand* is a word that is disliked by many public officials, but I am afraid that it is too late for pleading, begging, requesting, or even reasoning. The NAACP's concern with the plight of Negro pupils in the Boston schools is of long duration. Please allow me a few minutes to review. Several years ago, because of many complaints of a varying nature from parents, I received permission from the then superintendent, Dr. Haley, to visit and interview certain principals. I interviewed six principals of predominantly Negro schools. Three of these principals refused to acknowledge the existence of any problems. They tossed off the complaints parents had made and, in general, inferred that the NAACP was making a "mountain out of a molehill." One principal acknowledged that it could be true that his graduates, 99 percent Negro, might have difficulty in high school when competing with students from all over Boston, because, he stated, "Negroes do not make their kids learn." He said further that we should be like Jewish parents, who see that their children learn. Another principal told me that she just didn't think that Negroes could learn at the same rate as white children. She had just left a school in Roslindale which was an all-white school, and felt that she could come to this conclusion. Another principal, very pleasant and affable, said that he saw no differences in children, and that he was sure that his attitude was reflected in his staff. Time has proven that this rather nonchalant attitude did not produce the results desired by the complaining parents.

We are here because the claim from the community is too anxious to be ignored, the dissatisfaction and complaints too genuine and deep-seated to be passed over lightly, and the injustices present in our school system hurt our pride, rob us of our dignity, and produce results which are injuries not only to our future, but to that of our city, our commonwealth, and our nation.

Paul Parks, a member of the Education Committee of the NAACP, has produced certain facts that call for serious attention. Mr. Parks' research brings out that there are 13 schools in Boston with predominantly Negro populations. The youngest of these buildings was built in 1937. The rest were built in 1932, 1912, 1910, 1909, 1922, 1906, 1900, 1870, and 1868. According to the Sargent Report of May 1962, at least four of these buildings have been recommended to be abandoned because of health and safety reasons. Eight have been recommended to be renovated in order to meet present educational requirements.

We then make this charge ... There is segregation in fact in our Boston Public School System. To be sure, the May 17, 1954 Supreme Court decision dealt with deliberate segregation, but there can be no misinterpretation of the language used in that decision which stated that the "separation of children solely on the basis of race generates a feeling of inferiority that may affect their hearts and minds in a way unlikely ever to be undone." The steady migration of Negroes to Boston has intensified this problem. The 1960 census showed a total Negro population of 112,000. 63,000 of that total live in Boston, and 57,000 live in the Roxbury-Dorchester section of Boston. Our schools' population as of last Spring was 93,000, and of that, approximately 14,000 are Negroes.

The NAACP's position on northern school segregation is clear ... We must work to reduce and eliminate school segregation wherever it exists. In the discussions of segregation in fact in our public schools, we do not accept residential segregation as an excuse for countenancing this situation. We feel that it is the responsibility of school officials to take an affirmative and positive stand on the side of the best possible education for all children. This "best possible education" is not possible where segregation exists. Inadequate educational standards, unequal facilities, and discriminatory educational practices exist wherever there is school segregation.

Therefore, we state that it is imperative that the Boston School Committee take immediate steps to eliminate and reduce segregation from our school system. We recognize that some of the methods advised pose problems when related to younger children; therefore, we recommend that the immediate concentration be centered on our Jr. High Schools. There should be a review of the Open Enrollment plan which would allow transfers without the present limitations. This plan should be accompanied by rezoning designed deliberately to integrate our schools. Site selections and additions to existing school buildings must be planned to achieve integration. Segregation in fact is a problem existing in all urban communities today. This problem must be acknowledged and faced up to by all citizens and public officials ...

The unjust conditions created by segregation should also come under our scrutiny tonight. There are many conditions that must be corrected as we move forward to give to Negro students what rightfully belongs to them.

We are indebted to the many known and unknown dedicated principals and teachers who have seen their duty clearly and have performed in the true spirit of their profession. We acknowledge and honor their presence in our system. However, too many others approach the Negro schools with their minds poisoned by stereotyped, preconceived notions of Negro people. They believe that Negroes are lazy, stupid, and inferior. This attitude does not go unnoticed by the youngest Negro child ... for at an early age, our youngest become skilled in their ability to recognize prejudice. This recognition is always accompanied by resentment, hostility, and a feeling of humiliation. This is an unhealthy situation which cannot create an atmosphere in which the teacher is at his or her best, or where the child can perform at his highest level. We realize that teachers in these schools do teach under difficult conditions, and these conditions should be remedied in order to encourage teachers not only to remain in these districts, but to improve the quality of their teaching. Training programs should be expanded to establish a liaison between the school administration and colleges from which we get our teachers so that they can start their teaching careers able to distinguish myth from reality. Such a program should create an understanding of the child in congested Negro school districts, which would be [an] invaluable aid to well-meaning teachers who want to do a good job wherever they are assigned.

We also urge that permanent teachers be assigned to grades 1–3 and that the size of these classes be reduced to 25. I know that it is not necessary to stress the importance of a good beginning. Our teachers should have at their disposal sufficient supplies . . . books and other materials.

We should use books and other visual aids that include illustrations of people of all races. To use material depicting only white people is unrealistic in today's world. Please do not minimize the importance of this statement. It is important that the Negro child see recognition of himself as a person of worth, and it is important that the white child see people of other races in a positive setting. This material is available and is being used in other school systems.

The statement often made by school officials to refute charges of discrimination—that we have a uniform curriculum—concerns thoughtful people. We know that needs vary from district to district. We know that many of our predominantly Negro schools are located in the older, underprivileged sections of Boston. We acknowledge that many of our children come from deprived homes. Many of our parents, handicapped by lack of training or formal education, are consumed with the day-to-day struggle of just trying to make ends meet. For many reasons that go hand-in-hand with deprivation, inadequate and dilapidated over-crowded housing, discrimination, bitterness, and frustration, our schools must consider the plight of the pupil in these congested Negro areas. As a good teacher gears her program to the individual child, the school administration must gear its curriculum to the individual districts. We must have concentrated developmental reading programs in these schools in grades 1–8. In each school, the programs for the gifted and the slow learners should be expanded and taught by qualified, specially trained teachers. The needs of the average child in this setting must not be overlooked. The curriculum must be enriched to enable this child to compete in a society where the removal of the barriers of segregation will force them to compete with those who have not been handicapped as they have been.

Because ghetto living produces children with problems, we cannot emphasize too strongly the importance of the school adjustment counselors and the need for more such programs.

The vocational program should be expanded to include grade 7, and Negro children should be counseled by people who believe that America is the land of opportunity for all. To steer Negro students into certain trades or into certain training programs because the counselor believes other programs out of their reach is unfair, and this happens often in our schools. We are disturbed by the small number of our youngsters who take advantage of the cooperative programs. This, we feel, is the result of poor guidance programs, and the fact that many are discouraged from attending schools outside of their assigned school districts. This discouraging of students in the Industrial Arts courses prohibits them from gaining an entry into union and apprenticeship programs. We should see that all students, Negro and white, have the opportunity during specially observed weeks and in assemblies, to hear and see people of all races who have achieved in many fields. The value of this type of learning experience cannot be over-emphasized and should be planned. This is something that can be accomplished without affecting our school budget, and the dividends are great.

We feel that there should be no discrimination in the hiring or assigning of teachers. We take note of the fact there is no Negro school principal in our system and ask you to examine the reasons for this.

We recommend that you accept in toto the section of the Sargent Report that refers to Roxbury and North Dorchester. This portion of the survey, we feel, will achieve maximum integration in this section of Boston.

We also urge that you review the system of intelligence testing in our schools. The Boston school system mainly uses a group test to determine the intelligence and capability of a child to learn. When we realize that many of the Negro children coming to Boston are from rural communities, we feel that a group test is unfair and does not give a true picture of ability. As a result of this kind of testing, many Negro children are declared slow learners and unteachable.

We are aware of the problems confronting this school administration. We, like any citizens, are vitally concerned with good sound educational policies. Our demands tonight have centered around de facto segregation and its evil effects because we know that this issue has not been faced by Boston school officials. This issue must be dealt with, if we are to move along with the plans and blueprints that proclaim a New Boston . . . we will rise to the occasion to see that our children are no longer shortchanged in the education they receive.

> Ruth Batson, Chairman, Education Committee NAACP, Boston Branch
> Elizabeth Price, Barbara Erna Ballantyne, Melvin King, Paul Parks

Ruth Batson, "NAACP Statement to the Boston School Committee," 1963, in Clayborne Carson, David J. Garrow, Gerald Gill, Vincent Harding, and Darlene Clark Hine, eds., *The Eyes on the Prize Civil Rights Reader*, New York: Penguin Books, 1991, pp. 596–601.

School Desegregation in the North: Boston, 1965

Jonathan Kozol, *Death at an Early Age*, 1967

Jonathan Kozol, who has become well known to education audiences for his many later books focusing on the lives of poor children, most recently Fire in the Ashes: Twenty-Five Years Among the Poorest Children in America *(2013), was a young college graduate just hired by the Boston public schools when he began his career at the predominantly African American Gibson School in Roxbury in 1965. He paints a vivid picture of the Boston schools before desegregation. It is interesting to compare his experience with teaching in Boston in 1965 to Herb Kohl's experience in New York (see Chapter 9) at about the same time.*

Perhaps a reader would like to know what it is like to go into a new classroom in the same way that I did and to see before you suddenly, and in terms you cannot avoid recognizing, the dreadful consequences of a year's wastage of real lives.

You walk into a narrow and old wood-smelling classroom and you see before you thirty-five curious, cautious, and untrusting children, aged eight to thirteen, of whom about two-thirds are Negro. Three of the children are designated to you as special students. Thirty percent of the class is reading at the Second-Grade level in a year and in a month in which they should be reading at the height of Fourth-Grade performance or at the beginning of the Fifth. Seven children out of the class are up to par. Ten substitutes or teacher changes. Or twelve changes. Or eight. Or eleven. Nobody seems to know how many teachers they have had. Seven of their lifetime records are missing: symptomatic and emblematic at once of the chaos that has been with them all year long. Many more lives than just seven have already been wasted, but the seven missing records become an embittering symbol of the lives behind them which, equally, have been lost or mislaid. (You have to spend the first three nights staying up until dawn trying to reconstruct these records out of notes and scraps.) On the first math test you give, the class average comes out to 36. The children tell you with embarrassment that it has been like that since fall.

You check around the classroom. Of forty desks, five have tops with no hinges. You lift a desktop to fetch a paper, and you find that the top has fallen off. There are three windows. One cannot be opened. A sign on it written in the messy scribble of a hurried teacher or some custodial person warns you: DO NOT UNLOCK THIS WINDOW IT IS BROKEN. The general look of the room is as a bleak-light photograph of a mental hospital. Above the one poor blackboard, gray rather than really black, and hard to write on, hangs from one tack, lopsided, a motto attributed to Benjamin Franklin: *Well begun is half done.* Everything, or almost everything like that, seems a mockery of itself.

Into this grim scenario, drawing on your own pleasures and memories, you do what you can do to bring some kind of life. You bring in some cheerful and colorful paintings by Joan Miro and Paul Klee. While the paintings by Miro do not arouse much interest, the ones by Klee become an instantaneous success. One picture in particular, a watercolor titled "Bird Garden," catches the fascination of the entire class. You slip it out of the book and tack it up on the wall beside the doorway, and it creates a traffic jam every time the children have to file in or file out. You discuss with your students some of the reasons why Klee may have painted the way he did, and you talk about the things that can be accomplished in a painting which could not be accomplished in a photograph. None of this seems to be above the children's heads. Despite this, you are advised flatly by the Art Teacher that your naiveté has gotten the best of you and that the children cannot possibly appreciate this. Klee is too difficult. Children will not enjoy it. You are unable to escape the idea that the Art Teacher means herself instead.

For poetry, in place of the recommended memory gems, going back again into your own college days, you make up your mind to introduce a poem of William Butler Yeats. It is about a lake isle called Innisfree, about birds that have the funny name of "linnets" and about a "bee-loud glade." The children do not all go crazy about it, but a number of them seem to like it as much as you do, and you tell them how once, three years before, you were living in England and you helped a man in the country to make his home from wattles and clay. The children become intrigued. They pay good attention, and many of them grow more curious about the poem than they appeared at first. Here again, however, you are advised by older teachers that you are making a mistake: Yeats is too difficult for children. They can't enjoy it, won't appreciate it, wouldn't like it. You are aiming way above their heads . . . Another idea comes to mind and you decide to try out an easy and well-known and not very complicated poem of Robert Frost. The poem is called "Stopping by the Woods on a Snowy Evening." This time, your supervisor happens to drop in from the School Department. He looks over the mimeograph, agrees with you that it's a nice poem, then points out to you—tolerantly, but strictly—that you have made another mistake. "Stopping by Woods" is scheduled for Sixth Grade. It is not "a Fourth-Grade poem," and it is not to be read or looked at during the Fourth Grade. Bewildered as you are by what appears to be kind of idiocy, you still feel reproved and criticized and muted and set back, and you feel that you have been caught in the commission of a serious mistake.

On a series of other occasions, the situation is repeated. The children are offered something new and something lively. They respond to it energetically, and they are attentive and their attention does not waver. For the first time in a long while, perhaps, there is actually some real excitement and some growing and some thinking going on within that one small room. In each case, however, you are advised sooner or later that you are making a mistake. Your mistake, in fact, is to have impinged upon the standardized condescension on which the entire administration of the school is based. To hand Paul Klee's pictures to the children of this classroom, and particularly in a twenty-dollar volume, constitutes a threat to this school system. It is not different from sending a little girl from the Negro ghetto into an art class near Harvard Yard. Transcending the field of familiarity of the administration, you are endangering its authority and casting a blow at its self-confidence. The way the threat is handled is by a continual and standardized underrating of the children: They can't do it, couldn't do it, wouldn't like it, don't deserve it . . . In such a manner, many children are tragically and unjustifiably held back from a great many of the good things that they might come to like or admire and are pinned down instead to books the teacher knows and to easy tastes that she can handle. This includes, above all, of course, the kind of material that is contained in the Course of Study.

Try to imagine, for a child, how great the gap between the outside world and the world conveyed within this kind of school must seem: A little girl, maybe Negro, comes in from a street that is lined with car-carcasses. Old purple Hudsons and one-wheel missing Cadillacs represent her horizon and mark the edges of her dreams. In the kitchen of her house, roaches creep and large rats crawl. On the way to school, a wino totters. Some teenage white boys slow down their car to insult her, and speed on. At school, she stands frozen for fifteen minutes in a yard of cracked cement that overlooks a hillside on which trash has been unloaded and at the bottom of which the New York, New Haven, and Hartford railroad rumbles past. In the basement, she sits upon broken or splintery seats in filthy toilets and she is yelled at in the halls. Upstairs, when something has been stolen, she is told that she is the one who stole it and is called a liar and forced abjectly to apologize before a teacher who has not the slightest idea in the world of who the culprit truly was. The same teacher, behind the child's back, ponders audibly with imagined compassion: "What can you do with this kind of material? How can you begin to teach this kind of child?"

Of all of the poems of Langston Hughes that I read to my Fourth Graders, the one that the children liked most was a poem that has the title "Ballad of the Landlord." The poem is printed along with some other material in the back part of this book. This poem may not satisfy the taste of every critic, and I am not making any claims to immortality for a poem just because I happen to like it a great deal. But the reason this poem did have so much value and meaning for me and, I believe, for many of my students, is that it not only seems moving in an obvious and immediate human way but that it *finds* its emotion in something ordinary. It is a poem which really does allow both heroism and pathos to poor people, sees strength and awkwardness, and attributes to a poor person standing on the stoop of his slum house every bit as much significance as William Wordsworth saw in daffodils, waterfalls, and clouds. At the request of the children, later on I mimeographed that poem and, although nobody in the classroom was asked to do this, several of the children took it home and memorized it on their own. I did not assign it for memory, because I do not think that memorizing a poem has any kind of special value. Some of the children just came in and asked if they could recite it. Before long, almost every child in the room had asked to have a turn.

All of the poems that you read to Negro children obviously are not going to be by or about Negro people. Nor would anyone expect that all poems which are read to a class of poor children ought to be grim or gloomy or heartbreaking or sad. But when, among the works of many different authors, you do have the will to read children a poem by a man so highly renowned as Langston Hughes, then I think it is important not to try to pick a poem that is innocuous, being like any other poet's kind of poem, but I think you ought to choose a poem that is genuinely representative and then try to make it real to the children in front of you in the way that I tried. I also think it ought to be taken seriously by a teacher when a group of young children come in to him one morning and announce they have liked something so much that they have memorized it voluntarily. It surprised me and impressed me when that happened. It was all I needed to know to confirm for me the value of reading that poem and the value of reading many other poems to children which will build upon, and not attempt to break down, the most important observations and very deepest foundations of their lives.

On a day a week later, about fifteen minutes before lunchtime, I was standing in front of the class, and they were listening to a record I had brought in. The record was a collection of French children's songs. We had been spending the month reading and talking about Paris and about France. As lunchtime drew near, I decided to let the children listen to the music while they were having their meal. While the record was playing, a little signal on the wall began to buzz. I left the room and hurried to the Principal's office. A white man whom I had never seen before was sitting by the Principal's desk. This man, bristling and clearly hostile to me, as was the Principal, instantly attacked me for having read to my class and distributed at their wish the poem I have talked about that was entitled "Ballad of the Landlord." It turned out that he was the father of one of the white boys in the class. He was also a police officer. The mimeograph of the poem, in my handwriting, was waved before my eyes. The Principal demanded to know what right I had to allow such a poem—not in the official Course of Study—to be read and memorized by the children in my class. I said I had not asked anyone to memorize it, but that I would defend the poem and its use against her or anyone on the basis that it was a good poem. The Principal became incensed with my answer and blurted out that she did not consider it a work of art. I remember that I knew right away I was not going to give in to her. I replied, in my own anger, that I had spent a good many years studying poetry and that I was not going to accept her judgment about a poem that meant that much to me and to my pupils. Although I did not say it in these words, it was really a way of telling her that I thought myself a better judge of poetry than she. I hope that I am.

The parent attacked me, as well, for having forced his son to read a book about the United Nations. I had brought a book to class, one out of sixty or more volumes, that told about the U.N. and its Human Rights Commission. The man, I believe, had mistaken "human rights" for "civil rights" and he was consequently in a patriotic rage. The Principal, in fairness, made the point that she did not think there was anything really wrong with the United Nations, although in the report that she later filed on the matter, she denied this for some reason and said, instead, "I then spoke and said that I felt there was no need for this material in the classroom." The Principal's report goes on to say that, after she dismissed me to my own room, she assured the parent that "there was not another teacher in the district who would have used this poem or any material like it. I assured him that his children would be very safe from such incidents."

As the Principal had instructed, I returned to my class, where the children had remained quiet and had not opened up their lunch because I had not told them to, and they were patiently waiting for me to come back. We had our lunch and listened to more music and did the rest of our lessons, and at quarter to two, just before school ended, the Principal called me back again. She told me I was fired. This was about eight days before the end of school. I asked her whether this was due to the talk we had had earlier, but she said it was not. I asked her if it was due to an evaluation, a written report, which I had sent in on the compensatory program about a week before. This was a report that I had written, as all teachers had, in answer to a request from the School Department and in which I had said that the program seemed to me to be very poor. I was told, at the time I passed it in, that the Principal had been quite angry. But again she said it was not that. I asked her finally if my dismissal was at her request, and she said, No, it came from higher up, and she didn't know anything about it except that I should close up my records and leave school and not come back. She said that I should not say goodbye to the children in my class. I asked her if she really meant this, and she repeated it to me as an order.

I returned to my class, taught for ten more minutes, then gave assignments for the following morning as if I would be there and saw the children file off. After all but one were gone, that one, a little girl, helped me to pile up the books and posters and pictures with which I had tried to fill the room. It took an hour to get everything out, and when it was all in my car, it filled up the back seat and the space behind it and the floor, as well as the floor and half the seat in front. Outside my car, on the sidewalk, I said goodbye to this one child and told her that I would not be back again. I told her I had had a disagreement with the Principal and I asked her to say goodbye to the other children. I regretted very much now that I had not disobeyed the Principal's last order and I wished that I could have had one final chance to speak to all my pupils. The little girl, in any case, took what I had said with great solemnity and promised that she would relay my message to the other children. Then I left the school.

The next morning, an official who had charge of my case at the School Department contradicted the Principal by telling me that I was being fired at her wish. The woman to whom I spoke said the reason was the use of the poem by Langston Hughes, which was punishable because it was not in the Course of Study. She also said something to me at the time that had never been said to me before, and something that represented a much harder line on curriculum innovation than I had ever seen in print. No literature, she said, which is not in the Course of Study can *ever* be read by a Boston teacher without permission from someone higher up. When I asked her about this in more detail, she said further that no poem, anyway, by any Negro author can be considered permissible if it involves suffering. I thought this a very strong statement and I asked her several times again if that was really what she meant. She insisted that it was.

I asked if there would be many good poems left to read by such a standard. Wouldn't it rule out almost all great Negro literature? Her answer evaded the issue. No poetry that described suffering was felt to be suitable. The only Negro poetry that could be read in the Boston schools, she indicated, must fit a certain kind of standard or canon. The kind of poem she meant, she said by example, might be a poem that "accentuates the positive," or "describes nature" or "tells of something hopeful." Nothing was wanted of suffering, nothing that could be painful, nothing that might involve its reader in a moment of self-questioning or worry. If this is an extremely conservative or eccentric viewpoint, I think that it is nonetheless something which has to be taken seriously. For an opinion put forward in the privacy of her office by a School Department official who has the kind of authority that the woman had must be taken to represent a certain segment of educational opinion within the Boston school system, and, in some ways, it seems more representative even than the carefully written and carefully prepared essays of such a lady as the Deputy Superintendent. For in those various writings, Miss Sullivan unquestionably has had one ear tuned to the way they were going to come across in print and sound in public, whereas, in the office of a central bureaucratic person such as the lady with whom I now was talking, you receive an absolutely innocent and unedited experience in what a school system really feels and believes.

The same official went on a few minutes later to tell me that, in addition to having made the mistake of reading the wrong poem, I also had made an error by bringing in books to school from the Cambridge Public Library. When I told her that there were no books for reading in our classroom, except for the sets of antiquated readers, and that the need of the children was for individual reading which they would be able to begin without delay, she told me that that was all very well, but still this was the Boston school system, and that meant that you must not use a book that the Cambridge Library supplied. She also advised me, in answer to my question, that any complaint from a parent means automatic dismissal of a teacher anyway, and that this, in itself, was therefore sufficient grounds for my release. When I repeated this later to some Negro parents, they were embittered and startled. For they told me of many instances in which they had complained that a teacher whipped their child black and blue or called him a nigger openly, and yet the teacher had not been released. It seemed obvious to them, as it seems to me, and would to anyone, that a complaint from a white police officer carries more weight in the Boston school system than the complaint of the mother of a Negro child.

I asked this official finally whether I had been considered a good teacher and what rating I had been given. She answered that she was not allowed to tell me. An instant later, whimsically reversing herself, she opened her files and told me that my rating was good. The last thing she said was that deviation from a prescribed curriculum was a serious offense and that I would never be permitted to teach in Boston again. The words she used were these: "You're out. You cannot teach in the Boston schools again. If you want to teach, why don't you try a private school someday?" I left her office, but before I left the building, I stopped at a table and I took out a pad of paper and wrote down what she had said.

The firing of a "provisional teacher" from a large public school system is not generally much of an event. As Mr. Ohrenberger was to say later, it happens commonly. When the firing is attributed to something as socially relevant and dramatically specific as a single poem by a well-known Negro poet, however, it is not apt to go unnoticed; and, in this case, I was not ready to let it go unnoticed. I telephoned one of the civil rights leaders of Roxbury and told him what had happened. He urged me to call Phyllis Ryan, press spokesman for the Boston chapter of CORE. Mrs. Ryan decided to set up a press conference for the same day. That afternoon, sitting at the side of the Negro minister who had begun and carried on a lonely vigil for so many days outside the Boston School Committee, I described what had just happened.

The reaction of the reporters seemed, for the most part, as astonished as my own, and the direct consequence of this was that Miss Sullivan and Mr. Ohrenberger were obliged in a hurry, and without checking carefully, to back up the assertions of their own subordinates. The consequences of this, in turn, was that both of them allowed themselves to repeat and to magnify misstatements. Mr. Ohrenberger came out with a statement that I had been "repeatedly warned" about deviation from the Course of Study. Miss Sullivan's statement on my dismissal was much the same as Mr. Ohrenberger's, adding, however, a general admonition about the dangers of reading to Negro children poems written in bad grammar. Although Langston Hughes "has written much beautiful poetry," she said, "we cannot give directives to the teachers to use literature written in native dialects." It was at this time that she also made the statement to which I have alluded earlier: "We are trying to break the speech patterns of these children, trying to get them to speak properly. This poem does not present correct grammatical expression and would just entrench the speech patterns we want to break." I felt it was a grim statement.

The reactions of a large number of private individuals were recounted in the press during the following weeks, and some of them gave me a better feeling about the city in which I grew up than I had ever had before. One school employee who asked, for his safety, to remain anonymous, gave a statement to the press in which he reported that the atmosphere at school on the civil rights subject was like the atmosphere of a Gestapo. I believe that the person in question was a teacher in my school, but the fact that he had felt it necessary to keep his name anonymous, and his position unspecified, made his statement even more revelatory than if his name and position had appeared.

Another thing that reassured me was the reaction of the parents of the children in my class and in the school. I did not have any means of contacting them directly, but dozens of CORE members went out into the neighborhood, knocked at doors, and told parents very simply that a teacher had been fired for reading their children a good poem written by a Negro. A meeting was called by the chairman of the parent group, a woman of great poise and courage, and the parents asked me if I would come to that meeting and describe for them what had gone on. I arrived at it late and I was reluctant to go inside, but when I did go in, I found one of the most impressive parent groups that I had ever seen gathered in one hall. Instead of ten or eleven or twelve or fifteen or even twenty or thirty, which was the number of parents that usually could be rallied for a meeting on any ordinary occasion during the year, there were in the church building close to two hundred people, and I discovered that several of my pupils were in the audience as well as over half the parents of the children in my class.

I do not want to describe all the things that were said that night, what statements of strong loyalty came forward from those mothers and fathers, or how they developed, step by step, the plan of protest which they would put into effect on the following morning and which was to be the subject of intensive press attention for a good many days to come. Looking back on it, I am sure that it was one of the most important and most valuable and most straightforward moments in my life. A white woman who was present, and who has observed race relations in Roxbury for a long while, said to me after the meeting: "I hope that you understand what happened tonight between you and those parents. Very few white people in all of their lives are ever going to be given that kind of tribute. You can do anything in your life—and I don't know what plans you have. But you will never have a better reason to feel proud."

I believed that what she said was true. It is hard to imagine that any other event in my life can matter more.

Jonathan Kozol, *Death at an Early Age*, Boston, MA: Houghton Mifflin, 1967.

LOOKING BACK AT AN ERA: RUCKER C. JOHNSON, *THE DREAM REVISITED—IN SEARCH OF INTEGRATION: BEYOND BLACK AND WHITE*, 2014

Writing sixty years after the U.S. Supreme Court's Brown v. Board *decision, Rucker Johnson, a professor of public policy at the University of California, Berkeley, looks back at these years and describes some of the successes and many of the failures of the movement for true school integration and equal educational opportunity for all Americans. Like other twenty-first-century observers, Johnson notes that while schools became less and less racially segregated in the years between 1954 and about 1980, the process of desegregation seemed to stop in the 1980s, and across the country schools are at least as segregated as they were in the late 1970s. Equally important, Johnson notes that even in integrated schools, true integration requires more—changes in attitudes, in an openness to "other people," and truly equal facilities in things like Advanced Placement and other elite courses and programs. While celebrating the promise of* Brown, *Johnson also notes the important steps needed before that promise is a reality.*

As we commemorate the 50th anniversary of one of the singular high points of the Civil Rights Movement—the March on Washington—it is important to recall that its educational goal was the desegregation of all school districts. Despite the March and the resulting policy changes, today as a nation, we sit in a backslidden condition. America's schools are more segregated now than they were in the early 1970s.

Often, the words desegregation and integration are used interchangeably, as if they are one and the same. Conflating the two is erroneous, and lacks an understanding of the process MLK envisioned—"to change behavior, not only laws." Desegregation alone was not enough. Along the highway of justice, desegregation was to be an immediate point of origination—the final destination: equal opportunity for all. Integration, however, was to be the map guiding the hearts and minds to a paradigm shift that would take us beyond legalistic compliance with desegregation into the spirit of the democratic dream of integration and inclusion. Brown was intended not only to promote equitable access to school quality, but also to alter the attitudes and socialization of all children—beginning at the youngest ages. Beyond the removal of the legal and social prohibitions of segregation, beyond law enforcement agencies and the courts, desegregation was a necessary but not sufficient condition that represented the partial down-payment, the lay away plan, toward the final goals of equal educational opportunity and inclusion.

Outmoded and unjust laws are not the only barriers to change. While the rollout of civil rights laws washed away segregated public facilities, it could not wash away the greatest barriers to true equality: fear, prejudice, and irrationality. Efforts to achieve either desegregation or integration singularly have proven elusive because the two are inseparable. King anticipated this when he said, "Desegregation is enforceable . . . integration is not," because it requires changes in attitudes. The response—white and middle class flight, segregated classes within desegregated schools, lower expectations for students of color, disparate disciplinary measures, and racist attitudes—certainly short-circuited the efforts to move beyond desegregation to integrated communities. Too often policy makers have settled for superficial fixes to the complexities of integration. As a result, we are fifty years down the path, but in many respects, virtually no closer to the destination.

Because of the persistent patterns of segregation, many view segregation as inevitable. Spoiler Alert: not so . . . and history is our witness that policy choices play a key role. Urban cities are hyper-segregated because of the legacy of historic patterns of racial discrimination in mortgage lending, the geography of public housing units, racially-motivated city planning and zoning policy, highway construction, and gentrified development strategies that price poor families out of their existing neighborhoods, to name a few. Such unfairness creates greater inequities and exacerbates existing poverty. It is unconscionable that in 1968, when MLK died, the black child poverty rate was 35%, and it is the same rate today. Poverty, like segregation, is man-made, and thus can be unmade by man.

Focusing again on desegregation . . . at first glance, the initial effort toward school desegregation may appear to have been about merely placing people as pawns, mixing up the social Rubik's Cube, or constructing a color compound for success. Placing brown bodies next to white bodies does not osmotically improve the life trajectory of Blacks, nor does it infuse Blacks' wealth holdings or resources with that of whites. Though the cultural mosaic of diversity is a positive outcome of integration, for the proponents of Brown, diversity per se was not the steam propelling the train down the "long road to freedom." More than anything, for many in the black community, the goal was to galvanize and redistribute school resources to ensure a quality education in every district, for every child, from every neighborhood, of any race, ethnicity, and class. Brown insisted that America acknowledge and make reparations for the existing inequities that left one People a step behind in education, and therefore earnings, and therefore health, wealth, and so forth . . .

The black–white achievement gap narrowed substantially in the 1970s and 80s and has been stagnant since then. We can learn from our previous success. Desegregation and improved access to quality (reductions in class size, increases in school spending) were key contributors to closing the gaps back then. For blacks a generation ago, school desegregation significantly increased both educational and occupational attainments, college quality and adult earnings, reduced the probability of incarceration, and improved adult health status; desegregation had no effects on whites across each of these outcomes. The mechanisms through which school desegregation led to beneficial adult attainment outcomes for blacks include improvement in access to school resources reflected in reductions in class size and increases in per-pupil spending. Also at that time, the federal government began to invest in early childhood education. Case in point: those very investments set me, and people like me, on a path to experience and achieve things beyond what my parents attained. These approaches work and will work again, if we invest in them.

Unfortunately, some of the gains of the '70s and '80s eroded as both whites and middle-class blacks left the cities, and urban school systems became in some ways as socioeconomically and racially segregated as they were at the time of the Brown decision. The combination of racial segregation and concentrated poverty can be toxic without addressing school and non-school educational needs of our most disadvantaged children. Such toxicity is further exacerbated in the heat of any economic crisis when we seem more drawn to the loss of financial capital than the need for human and health capital investments. We ought not leave such jaded footprints on children's early-life experiences.

Today, segregation may not be as conspicuous as 30–40 years ago. Contemporary segregation takes on more nuanced forms, but the consequences are no less pernicious. We have desegregated schools, yet segregated classrooms. The quality of curricular content between districts differs substantially (e.g., access to early education programs, gifted and talented programs, AP offerings, tracking beginning at young ages). There are larger between-district differences than within-district, and inter-district metro-wide desegregation plans have been ruled unconstitutional, limiting that policy lever's efficacy. A new legal environment, beginning in the early 1990s, diminished desegregation standards and resulted in the release of hundreds of districts from their court-mandated desegregation orders, which led to a re-segregation of schools. Since then, more than one-half of school districts that were ever under court order have now been released.

Furthermore, contemporary segregation and effects on racial inequality have taken an even more negative turn with regard to criminal justice policy, and the early antecedents of them are witnessed in elevated minority school suspension rates. Profound changes in sentencing policy since the 1980s were fueled, in part, by the politics of fear—perceptions of neighborhood safety were colored by race. To underscore how much this has changed things, we would have to release 4 out of 5 people from behind bars in order to return to the rates of incarceration of the 1970s. In today's schools, these fears are evident in the assumptions and judgments that teachers make about black boys, in particular, and underscore that ultimately without parent advocacy and agency, institutions will foster and sustain disparate outcomes. Regardless of our dogged intentions, true integration has escaped our grasp, and American apartheid haunts us over and again. The more we slam the hammer of justice on the head of segregation, the more it evades us and rears its nefarious head in a different place and a different guise.

These negative outcomes are recorded in history, but there are some promising models of successful modern-day interventions that provide a blueprint for us to follow. The Harlem Children's Zone is noteworthy for its comprehensive, full-scale initiatives that seek to improve children's educational opportunities with wrap-around services from birth to college and beyond, by providing family support and programs in pre-school academics, media and technology, fitness and nutrition, as well as college and career preparation. Another meritorious enterprise is the mixed-housing income intervention of Montgomery County, Maryland, which demonstrates that achievement among poor black children increases with integration, attendance in middle-class schools, and increased compensatory education funding for disadvantaged children. These policies have promise to break the vicious cycle of poor school performance leading to poverty, and poverty leading to poor school performance, and constitute reform models for other cities to follow.

Consider that, within the next 10 years, the majority of children in our country will be minorities. The era of integration that existed during the Civil Rights Movement is not the same as the world we now inherit: the black–white dichotomy is an old paradigm. We have shifted from communities that are black and white to ones that are multi-ethnic in a globally competitive, 21st-century knowledge economy. The global community requires multi-cultural competencies. No matter where our children live and work in the future, their neighborhood will be part of a multi-cultural and global community; our failure will be in not adequately preparing them for that new reality.

Newsletter, Furman Center, School of Law, New York University, January 2014.

11

Rights, Opportunities, and Limits in American Education, 1965–1980

- Introduction

- Supreme Court of the United States, *Engel v. Vitale*, 1962

- The Elementary and Secondary Education Act and the Great Society, 1965

- Supreme Court of the United States, *Tinker et al. v. Des Moines Independent Community School District*, 1969

- Title IX, the Education Amendments of 1972

- Supreme Court of the United States, *Lau et al. v. Nichols et al.*, 1974

- Public Law 94-142, Education for All Handicapped Children Act, 1975

- Dillon Platero, The Rough Rock Demonstration School, Navajo Nation, 1970

- Supreme Court of the United States, *San Antonio Independent School District v. Rodriguez*, Argued October 12, 1972, Decided March 21, 1973

Introduction

The initial focus of the civil rights movement in education was on school integration and quality education for African American children. In time, however, the movement affected wider and wider spheres of activity. By the mid-1960s, and for the decade that followed, few Americans were unaffected by the civil rights movement, and fewer still lacked opinions about these developments. Civil rights leaders properly remind members of other groups that many of the rights won during the 1960s and 1970s were won first through the civil rights movement and only later expanded to include a wider circle of citizens.

One group of Americans who had begun asserting their rights in the 1950s became the center of a still unresolved national debate in the early 1960s. The nation has long debated the proper relationship between religion and public education, and in 1962 the United States Supreme Court ruled in *Engel v. Vitale* that the New York state policy requiring students to recite a state written prayer at the beginning of the school day was unconstitutional. The following year, the Court expanded its ruling in *Abington v. Schempp*, stating that all required prayers as well as the devotional reading of the Bible in school were unconstitutional. While the Court carefully protected objective teaching about religion from its ban, the charge that the Court was "banning God from the schools" led to a battle about who controls the content of public culture, and about the proper relationship of personal piety and values to the educational process.

The federal government's role in school reform expanded dramatically as part of Lyndon Johnson's War on Poverty. The War on Poverty was itself a direct outgrowth of the civil rights movement. If not for the pressure of civil rights activities all across the country, it is doubtful that either the president or Congress would have initiated the Great Society programs, including dramatically expanded federal aid to education. Johnson's speeches as he proposed and, three months later, signed the Elementary and Secondary Education Act of 1965 reveal the change of thinking that occurred as a result of civil rights activism as it became linked to the reform of public education.

As the 1960s wore on, the war in Vietnam came to overshadow the times. Schools were not exempt from the firestorm that swept the land. While the most significant antiwar demonstrations took place on college campuses, high schools—and even elementary schools—were not immune. The case of *Tinker v. Des Moines Independent Community District* is particularly noted in legal history for its significance in expanding the rights of high school students. The specific issue involved three young people who wore black armbands to their schools in Des Moines, Iowa to protest the war. Reading the case, one gains a sense of the changing educational scene in the late 1960s, as well as of the divided judicial—and national—views on how society should respond to these changes.

Following the black freedom struggle of the 1950s and 1960s, many other groups also began to demand their rights. While women of all races, Latinos, Asians, and American Indians had certainly fought for their rights throughout American history, they had been relatively quiet during the post-World War II era. The civil rights movement sparked them to life again. Earlier documents in this book revealed the expanded roles women filled as they entered the teaching profession in large numbers early in the nineteenth century. Many women teachers in the turn-of-the-twentieth-century progressive era became militant advocates for their right to have input in the schools where they taught as well as just compensation for their efforts. Nineteenth-century American Indians fought wars and resisted the efforts of European American soldiers and missionaries to school them in the ways of an alien culture. Immigrant groups had long sought to maintain their first language while in schools. During the 1960s and 1970s, these and other previously marginalized groups in American society initiated a dramatic resurgence of militancy and successful advocacy. While none of the groups won total victories, and American schools and the larger society remained discriminatory in many ways, some very significant changes were won during these years. The documents included here describe some of the changes of these dramatic years, including:

- Title IX of the Elementary and Secondary Education Act, added in 1972, which expanded opportunities for women and girls in schools by requiring any educational institution that received federal money—by 1972, virtually all schools in the country—to provide equal resources and opportunities for women, not only in sports but also in curricular options and in individual choices, including the decision by pregnant and parenting teens whether or not to stay in schools where a pregnant student had previously been excluded.
- In the *Lau v. Nichols Supreme Court* and other state and federal actions, students who came to school not speaking English were guaranteed services that they had often previously been denied.

- Public Law 94-142, which provided equality of opportunity for students with disabilities. While never enforced to the satisfaction of its advocates, PL 94-142 and similar state legislation ended the virtual exclusion of students with handicapping conditions from American schools.
- The community control movement developed among many groups in many different parts of the country. The example provided here—in which Chicago's Mexican American community successfully demanded a far greater level of autonomy in running their schools—is just one of many possible examples. While the New York City public schools were virtually paralyzed by the issue during the 1968–1969 school year, they were not alone: community control struggles were taking place in many places.
- One of the most dramatic examples of expanded civil rights and community control occurred within the American Indian community. The federally funded but Navajo-controlled Rough Rock Demonstration School remains a model of self-directed education.

Many more worthy examples exist, but these provide a flavor of the times.

Figure 11.1 Herb Block, perhaps the most popular cartoonist of the day, caught some of the tensions that the U.S. Supreme Court's 1962 and 1963 decisions about prayer and Bible reading in school caused. A 1963 Herblock Cartoon, © The Herb Block Foundation.

Not everything that happened in education in the 1960s and '70s expanded educational opportunity, however. In one key area, opportunity did not necessarily expand at all. In 1973, in a sharply divided opinion, the U.S. Supreme Court ruled in *San Antonio School Independent School District v. Rodriguez* that school funding did not need to be equalized across rich and poor districts. Since most schools across the country are supported by local property taxes, and as a result the schools in the best-off communities have many times the budgets of the schools in the worst-off communities, many people consider this a gross inequality. While agreeing in principle, the Court decided that there was no basic constitutional right involved and that while states were free to equalize school spending, they did not need to do so, resulting in many poor children attending poorly funded communities for the next several decades.

Supreme Court of the United States, *Engel v. Vitale*, 1962

Few decisions in the history of the Supreme Court have created such long-lasting animosity as Engel v. Vitale *in 1962 and the Court's subsequent 1963 decision in* Abington School Board v. Schempp. *The* Engel *case only banned a state-written prayer, but* Abington *expanded the field to include all official prayers and the devotional reading of the Bible in public schools. While* Abington *was, therefore, significantly broader, the fact that* Engel *came first made it the target of debate. Many believed that these rulings represented the exclusion not only of faith, but also of what they had long seen as the properly dominant Protestant-European-Christian faith from the education of their children. All of the debates about cultural domination versus cultural inclusion came to a head here. At the same time, for others, the issue was much simpler—they wanted the right to affirm their own faith and piety at the beginning of the school day. The overlap of so many issues and fundamental debates in these cases—shown clearly in the majority and minority opinions that follow—meant that resolution would never be easy or final.*

Majority Opinion: Mr. Justice Black delivered the opinion of the Court.

The respondent Board of Education of Union Free School District No. Nine, New Hyde Park, New York, acting in its official capacity under state law, directed the School District's principal to cause the following prayer to be said aloud by each class in the presence of a teacher at the beginning of each school day:

"Almighty God, we acknowledge our dependence upon Thee, and we beg Thy blessings upon us, our parents, our teachers, and our Country."

This daily procedure was adopted on the recommendation of the State Board of Regents, a governmental agency created by the State Constitution to which the New York Legislature has granted broad supervisory, executive, and legislative powers over the State's public school system. These state officials composed the prayer which they recommended and published as a part of their "Statement on Moral and Spiritual Training in the Schools," saying: "We believe that this Statement will be subscribed to by all men and women of good will, and we call upon all of them to aid in giving life to our program."

Shortly after the practice of reciting the Regents' prayer was adopted by the School District, the parents of ten pupils brought this action in a New York State Court, insisting that use of this official prayer in the public schools was contrary to the beliefs, religions, or religious practices of both themselves and their children. Among other things, these parents challenged the constitutionality of both the state law authorizing the School District to direct the use of prayer in Public Schools and the District's regulation ordering the recitation of this particular prayer on the ground that these actions of official governmental agencies violate that part of the First Amendment of the Federal Constitution which commands that "Congress shall make no law respecting an establishment of religion"—a command which was "made applicable to the State of New York by the Fourteenth Amendment of the said Constitution." The New York Court of Appeals, over the dissents of Judges Dye and Fuld, sustained an order of the lower state courts which had upheld the power of New York to use the Regents' prayer as a part of the daily procedures of its public schools so long as the schools did not compel any pupil to join in the prayer over his or his parents' objection. We granted *certiorari* to review this important decision involving rights protected by the First and Fourteenth Amendments.

We think that by using its public school system to encourage recitation of the Regents' prayer, the State of New York has adopted a practice wholly inconsistent with the Establishment Clause. There can, of course, be no doubt that New York's program of daily classroom invocation of God's blessings as prescribed in the Regents' prayer is a religious activity. It is a solemn avowal of divine faith and supplication for the blessings of the Almighty. The nature of such a prayer has always been religious, none of the respondents has denied this, and the trial court expressly so found:

The religious nature of prayer was recognized by Jefferson and has been concurred in by theological writers, the United States Supreme Court, and State courts and administrative officials, including New York's Commissioner of Education. A committee of the New York Legislature has agreed.

The Board of Regents as amicus curiae, the respondents, and intervenors all concede the religious nature of prayer, but seek to distinguish this prayer because it is based on our spiritual heritage.

The petitioners contend among other things that the state laws requiring or permitting use of the Regents' prayer must be struck down as a violation of the Establishment Clause because that prayer was composed by governmental officials as a part of a governmental program to further religious beliefs. For this reason, petitioners argue, the State's use of the Regents' prayer in its public school system breaches the constitutional wall of separation between Church and State. We agree with that contention since we think that the constitutional prohibition against laws respecting an establishment of religion must at least mean that in this country it is no part of the business of government to compose official prayers for any group of the American people to recite as a part of a religious program carried on by government . . .

It is true that New York's establishment of its Regents' prayer as an officially approved religious doctrine of that State does not amount to a total establishment of one particular religious sect to the exclusion of all others—that, indeed, the governmental endorsement of that prayer seems relatively insignificant when compared to the governmental encroachments upon religion which were commonplace two hundred years ago. To those who may subscribe to the view that because the Regents' official prayer is so brief and general there can be no danger to religious freedom in its governmental establishment, however, it may be appropriate to say in the words of James Madison, the author of the First Amendment:

"It is proper to take alarm to the first experiment in our liberties . . . Who does not see that the same authority which can establish Christianity, in exclusion of all other Religions, may establish with the same ease any particular sect of Christians, in exclusion of all other Sects? That the same authority which can force a citizen to contribute three pence only of his property for the support of any one establishment, may force him to conform to any other establishment in all cases whatsoever?"

The judgment of the Court of Appeals of New York is reversed and the cause remanded for further proceedings not consistent with this opinion.

Dissent: Mr. Justice Stewart, dissenting.

A local school board in New York has provided that those pupils who wish to do so may join in a brief prayer at the beginning of each school day, acknowledging their dependence upon God and asking His blessing upon them and upon their parents, their teachers, and their country. The Court today decides that in permitting this brief nondenominational prayer the school board has violated the Constitution of the United States. I think this decision is wrong.

The Court does not hold, nor could it, that New York has interfered with the free exercise of anybody's religion. For the state courts have made clear that those who object to reciting the prayer must be entirely free of any compulsion to do so, including any "embarrassments and pressures." Cf. *West Virginia State Board of Education v. Barnette, 319 U.S. 624*. But the Court says that in permitting school children to say this simple prayer, the New York authorities have established "an official religion."

With all respect, I think the Court has misapplied a great constitutional principle. I cannot see how an "official religion" is established by letting those who want to say a prayer say it. On the contrary, I think that to deny the wish of these school children to join in reciting this prayer is to deny them the opportunity of sharing in the spiritual heritage of our Nation . . .

At the opening of each day's Session of the Court we stand, while one of our officials invokes the protection of God. Since the days of John Marshall, our Crier has said, "God save the United States and this Honorable Court." Both the Senate and the House of Representatives open their daily Sessions with prayer. Each of our Presidents, from George Washington to John F. Kennedy, has, upon assuming his Office, asked the protection and help of God . . .

In 1954, Congress added a phrase to the Pledge of Allegiance to the Flag so that it now contains the words "one Nation *under God*, indivisible, with liberty and justice for all." In 1952, Congress enacted legislation calling upon the President each year to proclaim a National Day of Prayer. Since 1865, the words "In God We Trust" have been impressed on our coins.

Countless similar examples could be listed, but there is no need to belabor the obvious. It was all summed up by this Court just ten years ago in a single sentence: "We are a religious people whose institutions presuppose a Supreme Being" *Zorach v. Clauson, 343 U.S. 306, 313*.

I do not believe that this Court, or the Congress, or the President has by the actions and practices I have mentioned established an "official religion" in violation of the Constitution. And I do not believe the State of New York has done so in this case. What each has done has been to recognize and to follow the deeply entrenched and highly cherished spiritual traditions of our Nation—traditions which come down to us from those who almost two hundred years ago avowed their "firm Reliance on the Protection of divine Providence" when they proclaimed the freedom and independence of this brave new world.

I dissent.

Supreme Court of the United States, *Engel v. Vitalel*, 1962, 370 U.S. 421; 82S. Ct. 1261; 1962.

The Elementary and Secondary Education Act and the Great Society, 1965

The civil rights movement had a significant impact on federal legislation in the 1960s. Soon after his inauguration in 1961, John F. Kennedy began to lobby for a federal role in improving the nation's schools. However, it was Kennedy's successor, Lyndon B. Johnson, who called for a national "War on Poverty," and who coined the phrase "The Great Society" for his wide-reaching social program. As he sought to end poverty and transform American society, Johnson also believed that education was the key to improved economic opportunity. As the president never tired of saying, "Poverty has many roots, but the taproot is ignorance." Improved school-ing, Johnson believed, was thus the key to the whole Great Society effort.

Since the time of the New Deal, federal aid to education had generally floundered over two key concerns. Many southern Democrats who chaired key congressional committees feared that fed-eral aid would lead to a federal requirement that schools stop segregating students by race. And while many northern Catholic representatives in Congress would not vote for funds that did not aid students in Catholic parochial schools, many Protestants in Congress would not vote for any bill that provided such aid. The Civil Rights Act of 1964 ended the first concern since it banned federal aid to any racially segregated institution. Johnson then formulated the "child benefit theory" in which federal funds followed the child rather than the school, thus allowing limited aid to students in parochial schools in a way that satisfied most Catholics and Protestants.

The Kennedy–Johnson commitment to ending poverty and improving schools did not spring from nothing. The civil rights movement exerted a strong influence on presidential policies and decisions during the 1960s. Moreover, Lyndon Johnson had begun his career as a schoolteacher in rural Texas. He brought a personal passion to the debate, as is evidenced in the two speeches that follow. By the mid-1960s, Johnson was advocating a significant national effort to improve the educational experience of every citizen in a way no president before—or since—has done. Johnson's initial Special Message to Congress, "Toward Full Educational Opportunity," was submitted on January 12, 1965. He signed the Act, which included all of the major provisions he had requested, on April 11 of the same year—just three months later, with a speed rarely seen in federal legislation.

Lyndon B. Johnson, Towards Full Educational Opportunity, January 12, 1965

To the Congress of the United States:

In 1787, the Continental Congress declared in the Northwest Ordinance: "schools and the means of education shall forever be encouraged."

America is strong and prosperous and free because for one hundred and seventy eight years, we have honored that commitment.

In the United States today:

- One quarter of all Americans are in the nation's classroom.
- High school attendance has grown 18-fold since the turn of the century—6 times as fast as the population.
- College enrollment has advanced 80-fold. Americans today support a fourth of the world's institutions of higher learning and a third of its professors and college students.

In the life of the individual, education is always an unfinished task.

And in the life of this nation, the advancement of education is a continuing challenge.

There is a darker side to education in America;

- One student in every three now in the fifth grade will drop out before finishing high school—if the present rate continues.
- Almost a million young people will continue to quit school each year—if our schools fail to stimulate their desire to learn.
- Over one hundred thousand of our brightest high school graduates each year will not go to college—and many others will leave college—if the opportunity for higher education is not expanded.

The cost of this neglect runs high—both for the youth and the nation.

- Unemployment of young people with an eighth grade education or less is four times the national average.
- Jobs filled by high school graduates rose by 40 percent in the last ten years. Jobs for those with less schooling decreased by nearly 10 percent.

We can measure the cost in even starker terms. We now spend about $450 a year per child in our public schools. But we spend $1,800 a year to keep a delinquent youth in a detention home, $2,500 a year for a family on relief, $3,500 a year for a criminal in state prison.

The growing numbers of young people reaching school age demand that we move swiftly even to stand still.

- Attendance in elementary and secondary schools will increase by 4 million in the next five years; 400,000 new classrooms will be needed to meet this growth. But almost 1/2 million of the nation's existing classrooms are already more than 30 years old.
- The post-World War II boom in babies has now reached college age. And by 1970, our colleges must be prepared to add 50 percent more enrollment to their presently over-crowded facilities.

In the past, Congress has supported an increasing commitment to education in America. Last year, I signed historic measures passed by the Eighty-eighth Congress to provide:

- facilities badly needed by universities, colleges, and community colleges;
- major new resources for vocational training;
- more loans and fellowships for students enrolled in higher education;
- enlarged and improved training for physicians, dentists, and nurses.

I propose that the Eighty-ninth Congress join me in extending the commitment still further. I propose that we declare a national goal of *Full Educational Opportunity*. Every child must be encouraged to get as much education as he has the ability to take.

We want this not only for his sake—but for the nation's sake.

Nothing matters more to the future of our country: not our military preparedness— for armed might is worthless if we lack the brain power to build a world of peace; not our productive economy—for we cannot sustain growth without trained manpower; not our democratic system of government—for freedom is fragile if citizens are ignorant.

We must demand that our schools increase not only the quantity but the quality of America's education. For we recognize that nuclear-age problems cannot be solved with horse-and-buggy learning. The *three R's* of our school system must be supported by the three *T's—teachers* who are superior, *techniques* of instruction that are modern, and *thinking* about education which places it first in all our plans and hopes.

Specifically, four major tasks confront us:

- to bring better education to millions of disadvantaged youth who need it most;
- to put the best educational equipment and ideas and innovations within reach of all students;
- to advance the technology of teaching and the training of teachers;
- to provide incentives for those who wish to learn at every stage along the road to learning.

Our program must match the magnitude of these tasks. The budget on education which I request for fiscal year 1966 will contain a total of $4.1 billion. This includes $1.1 billion to finance programs established by the Eighty-eighth Congress. I will submit a request for $1.5 billion in new obligational authority to finance the programs described in this message. This expenditure is a small price to pay for developing our nation's most price- less resource.

In all that we do, we mean to strengthen our state and community education systems. Federal assistance does not mean federal control—as past programs have proven. The late Senator Robert Taft declared: "Education is primarily a state function—but in the field of education, as in the fields of health, relief, and medical care, the Federal Government has a secondary obligation to see that there is a basic floor under those essential services for all adults and children in the United States."

In this spirit, I urge that we now push ahead with the number one business of the American people—the education of our youth in preschools, elementary and secondary schools, and in the colleges and universities.

Lyndon B. Johnson, Remarks in Johnson City, Texas, Upon Signing the Elementary and Secondary Education Bill, April 11, 1965

For too long, political acrimony held up our progress. For too long, children suffered while jarring interests caused stalemate in the efforts to improve our schools. Since 1946, Congress tried repeatedly, and failed repeatedly, to enact measures for elementary and sec- ondary education.

Now, within the past 3 weeks, the House of Representatives, by a vote of 263 to 153, and the Senate, by a vote of 73 to 18, have passed the most sweeping educational bill ever to come before Congress. It represents a major new commitment of the Federal Government to quality and equality in the schooling that we offer our young people. I predict that all of those of both parties of Congress who supported the enactment of this legislation will be remembered in history as men and women who began a new day of greatness in American society.

By passing this bill, we bridge the gap between helplessness and hope for more than 5 million educationally deprived children.

We put into the hands of our youth more than 30 million new books, and into many of our schools their first libraries.

We reduce the terrible time lag in bringing new teaching techniques into the nation's classrooms.

We strengthen state and local agencies which bear the burden and the challenge of better education.

And we rekindle the revolution—the revolution of the spirit against the tyranny of ignorance.

As a son of a tenant farmer, I know that education is the only valid passport from poverty.

As a former teacher—and, I hope, a future one—I have great expectations of what this law will mean for all of our young people.

Figure 11.2 President Lyndon B. Johnson invited one of his own former teachers, Kate Deadrich Loney, to sit beside him when he signed the Elementary and Secondary Education Act in April, 1965. Courtesy of the Lyndon B. Johnson Library and Museum, public domain.

As President of the United States, I believe deeply no law I have signed or will ever sign means more to the future of America.

To each and every one who contributed to this day, the nation is indebted.

Lyndon B. Johnson, "Special Message to the Congress Toward Full Educational Opportunity, January 12, 1965," and "Remarks in Johnson City, Texas, Upon Signing the Elementary and Secondary Education Bill, April 11, 1965," *Public Papers of the Presidents, Lyndon B. Johnson*, 1965, Book I, Washington, DC, 1966, pp. 25–27 and 413–414.

SUPREME COURT OF THE UNITED STATES, *TINKER ET AL. V. DES MOINES INDEPENDENT COMMUNITY SCHOOL DISTRICT*, 1969

While the U.S. Supreme Court had dealt with a number of cases, dating back to the 1940s, having to do with the free speech rights of teachers and professional staff in schools, few cases had been heard in the courts regarding students' rights. It is not surprising that the student protests of the late 1960s created new legal questions. In this case, three students, with the support of their parents, wore black armbands to school to protest the war in Vietnam in 1965. They did this in spite of the fact that the school district, fearing such a protest, had declared armbands against school rules, warning that any student who wore one would be asked to remove it and, if he or she refused to do so, they would be suspended. The three students refused to remove their armbands and the school district suspended them. The federal District Court ruled in favor of the school district. In the opinion provided here, the Supreme Court sided with the students, seven to two. The divided opinions of the justices provide a window into their thinking on several issues, including the rights of students to speak their minds in school.

Mr. Justice Fortas delivered the opinion of the Court.

Petitioner John R Tinker, fifteen years old, and petitioner Christopher Eckhardt, sixteen years old, attended high schools in Des Moines, Iowa. Petitioner Mary Beth Tinker, John's sister, was a thirteen-year-old student in junior high school.

In December 1965, a group of adults and students in Des Moines held a meeting at the Eckhardt home. The group determined to publicize their objections to the hostilities in Vietnam and their support for a truce by wearing black armbands during the holiday season and by fasting on December 16 and New Year's Eve. Petitioners and their parents had previously engaged in similar activities, and they decided to participate in the program.

The principals of the Des Moines schools became aware of the plan to wear armbands. On December 14, 1965, they met and adopted a policy that any student wearing an armband to school would be asked to remove it, and if he refused he would be suspended until he returned without the armband. Petitioners were aware of the regulation that the school authorities adopted.

On December 16, Mary Beth and Christopher wore black armbands to their schools. John Tinker wore his armband the next day. They were all sent home and suspended from school until they would come back without their armbands. They did not return to school until after the planned period for wearing armbands had expired—that is, until after New Year's Day . . .

First Amendment rights, applied in light of the special characteristics of the school environment, are available to teachers and students. It can hardly be argued that either students or teachers shed their constitutional rights to freedom of speech or expression at the schoolhouse gate. This has been the unmistakable holding of this court for almost fifty years. In *Meyer v. Nebraska*, 262 U.S. 390 (1923), and *Bartels v. Iowa*, 262 U.S. 404 (1923), this Court, in opinions by Mr. Justice McReynolds, held that the Due Process Clause of the Fourteenth Amendment prevents States from forbidding the teaching of a foreign language to young students. Statutes to this effect, the Court held, unconstitutionally interfere with the liberty of teacher, student, and parent. See also *Pierce v. Society of Sisters*, 268 U.S. 510 [*507] (1925); *West Virginia v. Barnette*, 319 U.S. 624 (1943); *McCollum v. Board of Education*, 333 U.S. 203 (1948); *Wieman v. Updegraff*, 344 U.S. 183, 195 (1952) (concurring opinion); *Sweezy v. New Hampshire*, 354 U.S. 234 (1957); *Shelton v. Tucker*, 364 U.S. 479, 487 (1960); *Engel v. Vitale*, 370 U.S. 421 (1962); *Keyishian v. Board of Regents*, 385 U.S. 589, 603 (1967); *Epperson v. Arkansas, ante,* p. 97 (1968).

In *West Virginia v. Barnette, supra,* this Court held that under the First Amendment, the student in public school may not be compelled to salute the flag. Speaking through Mr. Justice Jackson, the Court said:

"The Fourteenth Amendment, as now applied to the States, protects the citizen against the State itself and all of its creatures—Boards of Education not excepted. These have, of course, important, delicate, and highly discretionary functions, but none that they may not perform within the limits of the Bill of Rights. That they are educating the young for citizenship is reason for scrupulous protection of Constitutional freedoms of the individual, if we are not to strangle the free mind at its source and teach youth to discount important principles of our government as mere platitudes." 319 U.S. at 637.

On the other hand, the Court has repeatedly emphasized the need for affirming the comprehensive authority of the States and of school officials, consistent with fundamental constitutional safeguards, to prescribe and control conduct in the schools. See *Epperson v. Arkansas, supra,* at 104; *Meyer v. Nebraska, supra,* at 402. Our problem lies in the area where students in the exercise of the First Amendment rights collide with the rules of the school authorities.

The problem posed by the present case does not relate to regulation of the length of skirts or the type of clothing, to hair style, or deportment. Cf. *Ferrell v. Dallas Independent School District*, 392 R 2d 697 (1968); *Pugsley v. Sellmeyer*, 158 Ark. 247, 250 S. W. 538 (1923). It does not concern aggressive, disruptive action or even group demonstrations. Our problem involves direct, primary First Amendment rights akin to "pure speech."

The school officials banned and sought to punish petitioners for a silent, passive expression of opinion, unaccompanied by any disorder or disturbance on the part of petitioners. There is here no evidence whatever of petitioners' interference, actual or nascent, with the schools' work or of collision with the rights of other students to be secure and to be let alone. Accordingly, this case does not concern speech or action that intrudes upon the work of the schools or the rights of other students.

Only a few of the 18,000 students in the school system wore the black armbands. Only five students were suspended for wearing them. There is no indication that the work of the schools or any class was disrupted. Outside the classrooms, a few students made hostile remarks to the children wearing armbands, but there were no threats or acts of violence on school premises. The District Court concluded that the action of the school authorities was reasonable because it was based upon their fear of a disturbance from the wearing of the armbands. But, in our system, undifferentiated fear or apprehension of disturbance is not enough to overcome the right to freedom of expression. Any departure from absolute regimentation may cause trouble. Any variation from the majority's opinion may inspire fear. Any word spoken, in class, in the lunchroom, or on the campus, that deviates from the views of another person may start an argument or cause a disturbance. But our Constitution says we must take this risk, *Terminiello v. Chicago*, 337 U.S. 1 (1949); and our history says that it is this sort of hazardous freedom this kind of openness-that is the basis of our national strength and of the independence and vigor of Americans who grow up and live in this relatively permissive, often disputatious, society.

In order for the State in the person of school officials to justify prohibition of a particular expression of opinion, it must be able to show that its action was caused by something more than a mere desire to avoid the discomfort and unpleasantness that always accompany an unpopular viewpoint. Certainly where there is no finding and no showing that engaging in the forbidden conduct would "materially and substantially interfere with the requirements of appropriate discipline in the operation of the school," the prohibition cannot be sustained. *Burnside v. Byars, supra*, at 749 . . .

It is also relevant that the school authorities did not purport to prohibit the wearing of all symbols of political or controversial significance. The record shows that students in some of the schools wore buttons relating to national political campaigns, and some even wore the Iron Cross, traditionally a symbol of Nazism. The order prohibiting the wearing of armbands did not extend to these. Instead, a particular symbol—black armbands worn to exhibit opposition to this Nation's involvement in Vietnam—was singled out for prohibition. Clearly, the prohibition of expression of one particular opinion, at least without evidence that it is necessary to avoid material and substantial interference with schoolwork or discipline, is not constitutionally permissible.

In our system, state-operated schools may not be enclaves of totalitarianism. School officials do not possess absolute authority over their students. Students in school as well as out of school are "persons" under our Constitution. They are possessed of fundamental rights which the State must respect, just as they themselves must respect their obligations to the State. In our system, students may not be regarded as closed-circuit recipients of only that which the State chooses to communicate. They may not be confined to the expression of those sentiments that are officially approved. In the absence of a specific showing of constitutionally valid reasons to regulate their speech, students are entitled to freedom of expression of their views. As Judge Gewin, speaking for the Fifth Circuit, said, school officials cannot suppress "expressions of feelings with which they do not wish to contend." *Burnside v. Byars, supra*, at 749 . . .

This principle has been repeated by this Court on numerous occasions during the intervening years. In *Keyishian v. Board of Regents*, 385 U.S. 589, 603, Mr. Justice Brennan, speaking for the Court, said:

"The vigilant protection of constitutional freedom is nowhere more vital than in the community of American schools. *Shelton v. Tucker* [364 U.S. 479], at 487. The classroom is peculiarly the 'marketplace of ideas.' The Nation's future depends upon leaders trained through wide exposure to that robust exchange of ideas which discovers truth 'out of a multitude of tongues, [rather] than through any kind of authoritative selection.'"

The principle of these cases is not confined to the supervised and ordained discussion which takes place in the classroom. The principal use to which the schools are dedicated is to accommodate students during prescribed hours for the purpose of certain types of activities. Among those activities is personal intercommunication among the students. This is not only an inevitable part of the process of attending school; it is also an important part of the educational process. A student's rights, therefore, do not embrace merely the classroom hours. When he is in the cafeteria, or on the playing field, or on the campus during the authorized hours, he may express his opinions, even on controversial subjects like the conflict in Vietnam, if he does so without "materially and substantially interfer[ing] with the requirements of appropriate discipline in the operation of the school" and without colliding with the rights of others. *Burnside v. Byars, supra*, at 749. But conduct by the student, in class or out of it, which for any reason—whether it stems from time, place, or type of behavior—materially disrupts Classwork or involves substantial disorder or invasion of the rights of others is, of course, not immunized by the constitutional guarantee of freedom of speech. Cf. *Blackwell v. Issaquena County Board of Education*, 363 R 2d 749 (C.A. 5th Cir. 1966) . . .

Under our Constitution, free speech is not a right that is given only to be so circumscribed that it exists in principle but not in fact. Freedom of expression would not truly exist if the right could be exercised only in an area that a benevolent government has provided as a safe haven for crackpots. The Constitution says that Congress (and the States) may not abridge the right to free speech. This provision means what it says. We properly read it to permit reasonable regulation of speech-connected activities in carefully restricted circumstances. But we do not confine the permissible exercise of First Amendment rights to a telephone booth or the four corners of a pamphlet, or to supervised and ordained discussion in a school classroom.

If a regulation were adopted by school officials forbidding discussion of the Vietnam conflict, or the expression by any student of opposition to it anywhere on school property except as part of a prescribed classroom exercise, it would be obvious that the regulation would violate the constitutional rights of students, at least if it could not be justified by a showing that the students' activities would materially and substantially disrupt the work and discipline of the school. Cf. *Hammond v. South Carolina State College*, 272 F. Supp. 947 (D.C.S.C. 1967) (orderly protest meeting on state college campus); *Dickey v. Alabama State Board of Education*, 273 ft Supp. 613 (D.C.M.D. Ala. 1967) (expulsion of student editor of college newspaper). In the circumstances of the present case, the prohibition of the silent, passive "witness of the armbands," as one of the children called it, is no less offensive to the Constitution's guarantees.

As we have discussed, the record does not demonstrate any facts which might reasonably have led school authorities to forecast substantial disruption of or material interference with school activities, and no disturbances or disorders on the school premises in fact occurred. These petitioners merely went about their ordained rounds in school. Their deviation consisted only in wearing on their sleeve a band of black cloth, not more than two inches wide.

They wore it to exhibit their disapproval of the Vietnam hostilities and their advocacy of a truce, to make their views known, and, by their example, to influence others to adopt them. They neither interrupted school activities nor sought to intrude in the school affairs or the lives of others. They caused discussion outside of the classrooms, but no interference with work and no disorder. In the circumstances, our Constitution does not permit officials of the State to deny their form of expression.

We express no opinion as to the form of relief which should be granted, this being a matter for the lower courts to determine. We reverse and remand for further proceedings consistent with this opinion.

Dissent: Mr. Justice Black, dissenting.

The Court's holding in this case ushers in what I deem to be an entirely new era in which the power to control pupils by the elected "officials of state-supported public schools" in the United States is in ultimate effect transferred to the Supreme Court. The Court brought this particular case here on a petition for certiorari urging that the First and Fourteenth Amendments protect the right of school pupils to express their political views all the way "from kindergarten through high school." Here the constitutional right to "political expression" asserted was a right to wear black armbands during school hours and at classes in order to demonstrate to the other students that the petitioners were mourning because of the death of United States soldiers in Vietnam and to protest that war, which they were against. Ordered to refrain from wearing the armbands in school by the elected school officials and the teachers vested with state authority to do so, apparently only seven out of the school system's eighteen-thousand pupils deliberately refused to obey the order. One defying pupil was Paul Tinker, 8 years old, who was in the second grade; another, Hope Tinker, was 11 years old and in the fifth grade; a third member of the Tinker family was 13, in the eighth grade; and a fourth member of the same family was John Tinker, 15 years old, an 11th-grade high school pupil. Their father, a Methodist minister without a church, is paid a salary by the American Friends Service Committee. Another student who defied the school order and insisted on wearing an armband in school was Christopher Eckhardt, an 11th-grade pupil and a petitioner in this case. His mother is an official in the Women's International League for Peace and Freedom.

As I read the Court's opinion, it relies upon the following grounds for holding unconstitutional the judgment of the Des Moines school officials and the two courts below. First, the Court concludes that the wearing of armbands is "symbolic speech" which is "akin to 'pure speech'" and therefore protected by the First and Fourteenth Amendments. Secondly, the Court decides that the public schools are an appropriate place to exercise "symbolic speech" as long as normal school functions are not "unreasonably" disrupted. Finally, the Court arrogates to itself, rather than to the State's elected officials charged with running the schools, the decision as to which school disciplinary regulations are "reasonable."

Assuming that the Court is correct in holding that the conduct of wearing armbands for the purpose of conveying political ideas is protected by the First Amendment, cf., e.g., *Giboney v. Empire Storage and Ice Co.*, 336 U.S. 490 (1949), the crucial remaining questions are whether students and teachers may use the schools at their whim as a platform for the exercise of free speech—"symbolic" or "pure"—and whether the courts will allocate to themselves the function of deciding how the pupils' school day will be spent. While I have always believed that under the First and Fourteenth Amendments neither the State nor the Federal Government has any authority to regulate or censor the content of speech, I have never believed that any person has a right to give speeches or engage in demonstrations where he pleases and when he pleases. This Court has already rejected such a notion. In *Cox v. Louisiana*, 379 U.S. 536, 554 (1965), for example, the Court clearly stated that the rights of free speech and assembly "do not mean that everyone with opinions or beliefs to express may address a group at any public place and at any time."

While the record does not show that any of these armband students shouted, used profane language, or were violent in any manner, detailed testimony by some of them shows their armbands caused comments, warnings by other students, the poking of fun at them, and a warning by an older football player that other, nonprotesting students had better let them alone. There is also evidence that a teacher of mathematics had his lesson period practically "wrecked" chiefly by disputes with Mary Beth Tinker, who wore her armband for her "demonstration." Even a casual reading of the record shows that this armband did divert students' minds from their regular lessons, and that talk, comments, etc., made John Tinker "self-conscious" in attending school with his armband. While the absence of obscene remarks or boisterous and loud disorder perhaps justifies the Court's statement that the few armband students did not actually "disrupt" the Classwork, I think the record overwhelmingly shows that the armbands did exactly what the elected school officials and principals foresaw they would, that is, took the students' minds off their Classwork and diverted them to thoughts about the highly emotional subject of the Vietnam war. And I repeat that if the time has come when pupils of state-supported schools, kindergartens, grammar schools, or high schools, can defy and flout orders of school officials to keep their minds on their own schoolwork, it is the beginning of a new revolutionary era of permissiveness in this country fostered by the judiciary. The next logical step, it appears to me, would be to hold unconstitutional laws that bar pupils under twenty-one or eighteen from voting, or from being elected members of the boards of education . . .

In my view, teachers in state-controlled public schools are hired to teach there. Although Mr. Justice McReynolds may have intimated to the contrary in *Meyer v. Nebraska*, *supra*, certainly a teacher is not paid to go into school and teach subjects the State does not hire him to teach as a part of its selected curriculum. Nor are public school students sent to the schools at public expense to broadcast political or any other views to educate and inform the public. The original idea of schools, which I do not believe is yet abandoned as worthless or out of date, was that children had not yet reached the point of experience and wisdom which enabled them to teach all of their elders. It may be that the Nation has outworn the old-fashioned slogan that "children are to be seen not heard," but one may, I hope, be permitted to harbor the thought that taxpayers send children to school on the premise that at their age they need to learn, not teach . . . And, as I have pointed out before, the record amply shows that public protest in the school classes against the Vietnam War "distracted from that singleness of purpose which the State [here Iowa] desired to exist in its public educational institutions." Here the Court should accord Iowa educational institutions the same right to determine for themselves to what extent free expression should be allowed in its schools as it accorded Mississippi with reference to freedom of assembly. But even if the record were silent as to protests against the Vietnam War distracting students from their assigned class work, members of this Court, like all other citizens, know, without being told, that the disputes over the wisdom of the Vietnam War have disrupted and divided this country as few other issues ever have. Of course students, like other people, cannot concentrate on lesser issues when black armbands are being ostentatiously displayed in their presence to call attention to the wounded and dead of the war, some of the wounded and the dead being their friends and neighbors. It was, of course, to distract the attention of other students that some students insisted up to the very point of their own suspension from school that they were determined to sit in school with their symbolic armbands.

Change has been said to be truly the law of life, but sometimes the old and the tried and true are worth holding. The schools of this Nation have undoubtedly contributed to giving us tranquility and to making us a more law-abiding people. Uncontrolled and uncontrollable liberty is an enemy to domestic peace. We cannot close our eyes to the fact that some of the country's greatest problems are crimes committed by the youth, too many of school age. School discipline, like parental discipline, is an integral and important part of training our children to be good citizens—to be better citizens. Here a very small number of students have crisply and summarily refused to obey a school order designed to give pupils who want to learn the opportunity to do so. One does not need to be a prophet or the son of a prophet to know that after the Court's holding today, some students in Iowa schools and indeed in all schools will be ready, able, and willing to defy their teachers on practically all orders. This is the more unfortunate for the schools since groups of students all over the land are already running loose, conducting break-ins, sit-ins, lie-ins, and smash-ins. Many of these student groups, as is all too familiar to all who read the newspapers and watch the television news programs, have already engaged in rioting, property seizures, and destruction. They have picketed schools to force students not to cross their picket lines and have too often violently attacked earnest but frightened students who wanted an education that the pickets did not want them to get. Students engaged in such activities are apparently confident that they know far more about how to operate public school systems than do their parents, teachers, and elected school officials. It is no answer to say that the particular students here have not reached such high points in their demands to attend classes in order to exercise their political pressures. Turned loose with lawsuits for damages and injunctions against their teachers as they are here, it is nothing but wishful thinking to imagine that young, immature students will not soon believe it is their right to control the schools rather than the right of the States that collect the taxes to hire the teachers for the benefit of the pupils. This case, therefore, wholly without constitutional reasons in my judgment, subjects all the public schools in the country to the whims and caprices of their loudest-mouthed, but maybe not their brightest, students. I, for one, am not fully persuaded that school pupils are wise enough, even with this Court's expert help from Washington, to run the 23,390 public school systems in our 50 states. I wish, therefore, wholly to disclaim any purpose on my part to hold that the Federal Constitution compels the teachers, parents, and elected school officials to surrender control of the American public school system to public school students. I dissent.

Supreme Court of the United States, *Tinker et al. v. Des Moines Independent Community School District*, No. 21, Supreme Court of the United States 393 U.S. 503; 1969.

TITLE IX, THE EDUCATION AMENDMENTS OF 1972

Sometimes, a very short statement makes a very large difference. This is certainly true in Title IX, an education amendment passed by Congress and signed by President Richard Nixon in 1972. Congress spent more than two years of debate leading up to the passage of Title IX. The then U.S. Department of Health, Education, and Welfare, which was charged with implementing the Act, spent another three years developing the interpretative regulations before they were published in 1975. It is likely that some of those who voted for the Act expected little from it. In fact, most of the detailed language of the legislation lists all of the types of cases to which it would not apply, including admission to private colleges, military academies, and student housing facilities. Nevertheless, because of patient and determined advocacy over the years after its passage, Title IX brought more and more changes to every aspect of American education, from more nearly equal sports facilities, to new initiatives to encourage women to participate in nontraditional programs, to the rights of pregnant girls to remain in school, to very different portraits of women in textbooks.

No person in the United States shall, on the basis of sex, be excluded from participation, be denied the benefits of, or be subjected to discrimination under any education program or activity receiving federal financial assistance.

For purposes of this title, an educational institution means any public or private preschool, elementary, or secondary school, or any institution of vocational, professional, or higher education, except that in the case of an educational institution composed of more than one school, college, or department which are administratively separate units, such term means each such school, college, or department.

Laws of the 92nd Congress, P.L. 92–318, "Title IX, Women's Education Equity Act, 1972," June 23, 1972.

SUPREME COURT OF THE UNITED STATES, *LAU ET AL. V. NICHOLS ET AL.*, 1974

Many different groups of Americans began to demand their rights in the 1960s and 1970s, and the energy and passion of the civil rights movement as well as the specific protections of the Civil Rights Act of 1964 meant that these demands carried more and more weight. Among the important changes wrought in education in these years was the development of programs in bilingual education. As the majority opinion in the following case indicates, prior to this time many students who came to school with little or no English-language proficiency were simply told to learn English somewhere else and then come to school. In 1968 the U.S. Congress passed the Bilingual Education Act that made funds available to those school districts that wanted to develop programs for students who did not speak English, but offering bilingual education remained a voluntary local decision. That situation changed in 1974 when a suit by Chinese American citizens of San Francisco came before the U.S. Supreme Court. In the Court's opinion, the Civil Rights Act was very clear: discrimination, whatever the original intent, was discrimination. And asking a student to sit in a classroom when the language of instruction simply made no sense was clearly discrimination. Neither the plaintiffs nor the

Court demanded a specific form of instruction for limited-English-proficiency students. And the debates have continued in subsequent decades between those who favor two-way bilingual education—retaining the speaker's native language while helping him/her learn English—those who favor a transitional form of bilingual education in which instruction in many subjects is carried on in their student's language of origin while they also learn English, and those who favor intensive immersion in the English language followed by an all-English curriculum. But the basic principle that every student has a basic civil right to be taught in a language that makes sense was established by the Court in this 1974 ruling.

SUMMARY: Non-English speaking students of Chinese ancestry brought a class suit in the United States District Court for the Northern District of California against officials of the San Francisco Unified School District, seeking relief against alleged unequal educational opportunities resulting from the officials' failure to establish a program to rectify the students' language problem. The District Court denied relief, and the United States Court of Appeals for the Ninth Circuit affirmed, holding that there was no violation of the equal protection clause of the Fourteenth Amendment nor of 601 of the Civil Rights Act of 1964 (42 USCS 2000d) (483 F2d 791). On certiorari, the United States Supreme Court reversed and remanded . . .

MR. JUSTICE DOUGLAS delivered the opinion of the Court.

The District Court found that there are 2,856 students of Chinese ancestry in the school system who do not speak English. Of those who have that language deficiency, about 1,000 are given supplemental courses in the English language. About 1,800, however, do not receive that instruction.

A report adopted by the Human Rights Commission of San Francisco and submitted to the Court by respondents after oral argument shows that, as of April 1973, there were 3,457 Chinese students in the school system who spoke little or no English. The document further showed 2,136 students enrolled in Chinese special instruction classes, but at least 429 of the enrollees were not Chinese but were included for ethnic balance. Thus, as of April 1973, no more than 1,707 of the 3,457 Chinese students needing special English instruction were receiving it.

This class suit brought by non-English-speaking Chinese students against officials responsible for the operation of the San Francisco Unified School District seeks relief against the unequal educational opportunities, which are alleged to violate, *inter alia*, the Fourteenth Amendment. No specific remedy is urged upon us. Teaching English to the students of Chinese ancestry who do not speak the language is one choice. Giving instructions to this group in Chinese is another. There may be others. Petitioners ask only that the Board of Education be directed to apply its expertise to the problem and rectify the situation . . .

This is a public school system of California and [HN1] § 71 of the California Education Code states that "English shall be the basic language of instruction in all schools." That section permits a school district to determine "when and under what circumstances instruction may be given bilingually." That section also states as "the policy of the state" to insure "the mastery of English by all pupils in the schools." And bilingual instruction is authorized "to the extent that it does not interfere with the systematic, sequential, and regular instruction of all pupils in the English language."

Moreover, [HN2] § 8573 of the Education Code provides that no pupil shall receive a diploma of graduation from grade 12 who has not met the standards of proficiency in "English," as well as other prescribed subjects. Moreover, by § 12101 of the Education Code (Supp. 1973) children between the ages of six and 16 years are (with exceptions not material here) "subject to compulsory full-time education."

Under these state-imposed standards there is no equality of treatment merely by providing students with the same facilities, textbooks, teachers, and curriculum; for students who do not understand English are effectively foreclosed from any meaningful education.

Basic English skills are at the very core of what these public schools teach. Imposition of a requirement that, before a child can effectively participate in the educational program, he must already have acquired those basic skills is to make a mockery of public education. We know that those who do not understand English are certain to find their classroom experiences wholly incomprehensible and in no way meaningful.

We do not reach the Equal Protection Clause argument which has been advanced but rely solely on § 601 of the Civil Rights Act of 1964, 42 U. S. C. § 2000d, to reverse the Court of Appeals.

That section bans discrimination based "on the ground of race, color, or national origin," in "any program or activity receiving Federal financial assistance." The school district involved in this litigation receives large amounts of federal financial assistance. [HN4] The Department of Health, Education, and Welfare (HEW), which has authority to promulgate regulations prohibiting discrimination in federally assisted school systems in 1968 issued one guideline that "school systems are responsible for assuring that students of a particular race, color, or national origin are not denied the opportunity to obtain the education generally obtained by other students in the system." 33 Fed. Reg. 4956. In 1970 HEW made the guidelines more specific, requiring school districts that were federally funded "to rectify the language deficiency in order to open" the instruction to students who had "linguistic deficiencies," 35 Fed. Reg. 11595...

Discrimination is barred which has that *effect* even though no purposeful design is present: a recipient "may not ... utilize criteria or methods of administration which have the effect of subjecting individuals to discrimination" or have "the effect of defeating or substantially impairing accomplishment of the objectives of the program as respect individuals of a particular race, color, or national origin." *Id.*, § 80.3 (b)(2).

It seems obvious that the Chinese-speaking minority receive fewer benefits than the English-speaking majority from respondents' school system which denies them a meaningful opportunity to participate in the educational program—all earmarks of the discrimination banned by the regulations ...

Senator Humphrey, during the floor debates on the Civil Rights Act of 1964, said: "Simple justice requires that public funds, to which all taxpayers of all races contribute, not be spent in any fashion which encourages, entrenches, subsidizes, or results in racial discrimination." 4 110 Cong. Rec. 6543 (Sen. Humphrey, quoting from President Kennedy's message to Congress, June 19, 1963).

We accordingly reverse the judgment of the Court of Appeals and remand the case for the fashioning of appropriate relief.

Reversed and remanded.

Supreme Court of the United States, *Lau et al. v. Nichols et al.*, No. 72–6520, 414 U.S. 563; 94 S. Ct. 786; 39L. Ed. 2d 1; 1974.

PUBLIC LAW 94-142, EDUCATION FOR ALL HANDICAPPED CHILDREN ACT, 1975

Perhaps the last group petitioning Congress to recognize their civil rights in the 1960s and 1970s were students with disabilities and their parents. While schools have still not met the goal of offering fully equal treatment to all students regardless of disability, Public Law 94-142 made an extraordinary difference. Prior to the law (and its predecessors in a few states), many special needs students were simply excluded from school or separated into special classes, often in the symbolic basements of the schools, which were properly described as warehouses. Because of the costs associated with implementing the law, Public Law 94-142 has aroused continual debate in many school districts across the country. Nevertheless, few advocate returning to the days of segregation and exclusion of students with special needs.

Be it enacted by the Senate and House of Representatives of the United States of America in Congress assembled, That this Act may be cited as the "Education for All Handicapped Children Act of 1975."

Statement of Findings and Purpose

Section 3 (a) Section 601 of the Act (20 U.S.C. 1401) is amended by inserting "(a)" immediately before "This title" and by adding at the end thereof the following new subsections:

(b) The Congress finds that

(1) there are more than eight million handicapped children in the United States today;
(2) the special educational needs of such children are not being fully met;
(3) more than half of the handicapped children in the United States do not receive appropriate educational services which would enable them to have full equality of opportunity;
(4) one million of the handicapped children in the United States are excluded entirely from the public school system and will not go through the educational process with their peers;
(5) there are many handicapped children throughout the United States participating in regular school programs whose handicaps prevent them from having a successful educational experience because their handicaps are undetected;
(6) because of the lack of adequate services within the public school system, families are often forced to find services outside the public school system, often at great distance from their residence and at their own expense;
(7) developments in the training of teachers and in diagnostic and instructional procedures and methods have advanced to the point that, given appropriate funding, State and local educational agencies can and will provide effective special education and related services to meet the needs of handicapped children;
(8) State and local educational agencies have a responsibility to provide education for all handicapped children, but present financial resources are inadequate to meet the special educational needs of handicapped children; and
(9) it is in the national interest that the Federal Government assist State and local efforts to provide programs to meet the educational needs of handicapped children in order to assure equal protection of the law.

(c) It is the purpose of this Act to assure that all handicapped children have available to them, within the time periods specified in section 612(2) (B), a free appropriate public education which emphasizes special education and related services designed to meet their unique needs, to assure that the rights of handicapped children and their parents or guardians are protected, to assist States and localities to provide for the education of all handicapped children, and to assess and assure the effectiveness of efforts to educate handicapped children.

(d) The heading for section 601 of the Act (20 U.S.C. 1401) is amended to read as follows: "Short title; statement of findings and purpose."

Laws of the 94th Congress, P.L. 94-142, "Education of All Handicapped Children Act of 1975," November 29, 1975, p. 774. [Renamed and expanded with the "Americans with Disabilities Act of 1990."]

DILLON PLATERO, THE ROUGH ROCK DEMONSTRATION SCHOOL, NAVAJO NATION, 1970

In March of 1970, a unique academic convention of scholars, Native American students, and tribal representatives met at Princeton University. The convocation heard a range of presentations on Indian matters. Indian Voices: The First Convocation of American Indian Scholars *is a record of the papers presenters gave at panels and discussions held at the Convocation. Dillon Platero, Director of the Rough Rock Demonstration School in Chinle, Arizona, reported on the school, then four years old. The Rough Rock Demonstration School represents a different type of community control, and a very significant shift in the culture of Indian schooling that had begun in the 1960s. With federal funding but local Navajo energy and control, the school could not have been further from the Indian Boarding school or even the federal reservation school model (see Chapter 7).*

In 1965, like-minded persons from the Navajo tribe, governmental agencies, and institutions of higher learning came together and were able to propose, and get funded, an experimental school. A demonstration school if you will, which would show to the many skeptics that Navajo people could run their own educational affairs, *now* . . . The school was not then successful and its supporters agonized over this apparent failure, as the decision to terminate the project was seriously considered. However, everyone understood what had happened. The principle underlying the experiment was felt still to be sound. Only the manner of attempted implementation needed improvement.

And so we tried again, this time with a more experienced administrator and in a locale where only the demonstration school would be functioning. A new facility was turned over to the Navajo people, only the broadest restrictions were imposed as to its use. A private, nonprofit corporation was formed as the legal entity which could accept funds from government agencies, as well as from private sources for the operation of the Rough Rock Demonstration School. This was accomplished in the spring of 1966 and in July 1 of that year, the experiment began anew.

From the very beginning, cooperation and even more importantly, freedom, have characterized our relationships with other involved agencies. Rough Rock now truly became responsible for its own school. With the election of a five-member board of education in June, 1966, the governing body was ready to begin functioning by the time the school came into being.

The Navajo people of Rough Rock wanted to accomplish two things: (1) the development of educational experiences comparable to those offered in the federal and state schools, in order to equip Indian children with knowledge of English, and the subject areas usually taught in any elementary school in the state of Arizona; (2) the development of educational experiences in Navajo-oriented subjects in order to enrich our children's academic work and enhance their total educational program.

When Rough Rock first began operation, the community had been used to having their school serve children from the ages of six through the highest grade taught. Not even a kindergarten program existed, to say nothing of a nursery school. In 1966–67, for the first time, a Head Start unit was established, affiliated with the Demonstration School. These children were among the most enthusiastic in the entire community. Our gravest problem is how to keep the class to a reasonable size. The office of Navajo Economic Opportunity set up a unit to provide for 20 children; in its first year, average daily attendance in that was 20.9. In 1967–68 it was 19.7; in 1968–69, it was 22.8. In response to increasing pressure from local parents to extend the entrance age downward, Rough Rock began a nursery school, accommodating two-, three-, and four-year-olds. The kindergarten program bridges the gap between this group and the regular school-age children . . . In this fashion, the child's self-image and feeling of worthy personhood is not shattered so mercilessly as often happens, when the difference between what is actual life and what is taught in school strikes the child at the age of six. School at Rough Rock is an extension of the child's normal world, in which he is competent to communicate and react in fashions sanctioned by his community and culture. Recently, the community has also begun a child care center for infants. It's so new that no general statement can be made about it.

Rough Rock is a bilingual school. We believe this term embraces the concept of fluency in two media of communication: in our case, in Navajo and in English. This is a little different from the usual "bilingual" programs at other schools, that merely treat the language other than English as a necessary evil. All students receive instruction in the Navajo language one period a day. The school was thus firmly committed to the concept of equality of value of the two most commonly used languages in the community. At the same time, thought was seriously being given to actually providing instruction in Navajo to certain children for certain periods of time. In 1968–69, our "Follow Through" students, at the early primary grade level, began receiving all their teaching in Navajo, with exception of a daily English lesson. Today we have six classes being taught in the Navajo language, in addition to our kindergarten and nursery school. As the children gain confidence in their ability to handle the intricacies of school learning, Navajo gives way as the basic medium of instruction, and English replaces it by the end of the third-grade age level.

The Rough Rock community, through their elected school board, hold to the philosophy that we teach the Navajo language for the reason that proficiency in it is a tool needed by our children and a skill worthy of formal educational efforts. Just as there is a wide range of fluency in the speaking of English, so in Navajo some handle the language better than others. All too often in the past, the Navajo child has been removed from his home environment at an early age and thrown into a completely alien cultural milieu and language. Great efforts were made to inhibit the speaking of such Navajo as he already knew, which not only stunted the quality of his native tongue, but actually made him ashamed of himself and of his language, as something inferior to English. The result was often a person who was fluent in neither language—one who was handicapped linguistically. Once the parents of Rough Rock actually had control of their school, the Navajo language ceased to be considered as a patois to be eliminated, or suppressed, and instead took its rightful place as the co-language of the school, a place it continues to hold with dignity.

Navajo culture is taught daily at Rough Rock. But we recognize that there is no clear-cut dichotomy, with Navajo culture occupying one compartment and non-Indian culture another. Recognizing and accepting the inevitability of our children's biculturalness, the school board emphasizes the values found in each and helps our students understand that neither is "right" nor "wrong" as such.

The school board also realizes that our children's familiarity with Navajo culture needs to be systematically expanded, and the non-Indian culture taught as well. The early primary grade levels find what is probably the best teaching done in this area, inasmuch as these children all have Navajo-speaking teachers whose knowledge of Navajo culture is better than any non-Navajo's could possibly be. Speakers from the community who have special knowledge of various aspects of Navajo culture spend an entire day at the school, lecturing to the older students on their specialty, once a week. These presentations are followed with vocabulary study, composition, and consideration of the specific topic during the following five days, in the social studies classes and homerooms.

Such extensive and systematic teaching of Navajo language and culture calls for both texts and teaching aids. In this respect, the school's Navajo Curriculum Center has proved to be invaluable. Rough Rock has found that there are teachers of Navajo language and culture . . . and others, who merely think they can teach. Too often a person not professionally trained to teach has attempted to provide instruction only to find himself running out of pedagogic steam within a few weeks. This is one explanation for our school's attempt to hire as many Navajo teachers as possible: They have both the knowledge of Navajo language and culture and the professional acumen to organize and present their subject. During the past three and a half years, the Navajo Curriculum Center has published such texts as Black Mountain Boy for intermediate grades, several beginning readers, and a book of Navajo biographies for older students. Emphasis at the present time is being placed on getting more works in the Navajo language. The center has also completed materials explaining the school, and the principles upon which it is founded, and such ancillary teaching aids as film strips, puppets, and dramatic presentations.

We need leadership, of course. And in cooperation with the Navajo Community College, the Chinle Public School District, and Arizona State University, we have had four teacher aides in full-time training for the past year. These are people who spent several years as practical aides in our classrooms and showed such potential for the teaching profession that the opportunity was given them to upgrade their skills and prepare for entrance into the profession. We have also been able to provide rotating employment opportunities for parents in the community whose lack of special, non-Indian skills makes it impractical to engage them on a full-time basis. The U.S. Office of Education has provided funds for this purpose.

Since the school began in 1966, Rough Rock has had dormitory parent aides. They have functioned as less experienced instructional aides and have the same benefits as our classroom parent aides. It is recognized that a most sensitive point with parents is the way their children are treated in the dormitories. At Rough Rock, our community parents have nearly all had the opportunity to actually work in the dorms and find out for themselves what is involved in group living with large numbers of children. The dormitory program itself may slowly go out of business, but right now, the Navajo communities don't have facilities such as would normally be found in cities.

Community development is an integral part of the demonstration project. All too often, people equate the activities of the project solely with that of operating an elementary school. Our entire community development building, built of adobe with local labor, is a service to our total population, as well as to our school and our students. For example, the postal facilities serve the entire community with mail service that was not available before the demonstration project began. The personnel office serves the entire community as well as the school. The community recreation office, office of community development director, office of special services, all serve the entire community. The funds expended for these largely non-school-related functions cannot justifiably be considered legitimate expenses in the education of children. The old bureaucratic accountancy method of figuring cost per pupil for education cannot be utilized at Rough Rock.

The uses of existing leadership and the consistent training of new leadership is the keynote for the success of Rough Rock. It is to be emphasized that the Rough Rock Community School Board controls policy and has the decision-making power. I could stand here and be fired right now, and may not know it, but the school board has that power. They hire and fire teachers. They make the policies of the school. Recently, they made the decision to make Rough Rock into a high school, so that we are working on this now.

Of particular interest in this discussion are the basic principles used:

1. The work to be accomplished must be recognized by Indian people as being needed. Only after a realization of need for change by Indian people, can such change be effective.
2. Indian people must be afforded recognition as competent human beings whose decisions (and rationale for them) merit the respect of all. An end to paternalism is demanded—though not to the services, which were brought and paid for hundreds of years ago. Here is a fine distinction that too often is completely overlooked by persons who would turn Indians into copies of non-Indian peoples. For example, on the Navajo reservation, the federal government is responsible for providing educational opportunities for our children. This is no largess that has been handed down to us. It is part of the spoils of war which was written into the Treaty of 1868 between the United States government and the Navajo Nation.
3. Indian people must be involved with the efforts their community is making to improve their lot. Such involvement can take many forms, such as participation on a Parents Advisory Committee, service on the school board, work as a dormitory aide, work as a classroom parent aide, helping supervise an off-reservation field trip, or addressing a convocation of scholars, as have several of our local leaders. Following these basic principles, Rough Rock has been an example . . .

Indian people need to be doers, rather than objects to which things are done. They need to be masters of their own destinies, a dream that has been constant with American people ever since this nation was founded—a dream that Indian people, whose nationhood predates America itself, are now fulfilling for themselves, thus returning to their ancient and original rights as the first and only true Americans.

Dillon Platero, remarks recorded in *Indian Voices: The First Convocation of American Indian Scholars*, San Francisco, CA: The Indian Historian Press, 1970.

Supreme Court of the United States, *San Antonio Independent School District v. Rodriguez*, Argued October 12, 1972, Decided March 21, 1973

After the 1954 Brown v. Board *Supreme Court decision mandating an end to racial segregation in schools, many began to talk about educational equity. How, they asked, could the nation use its public schools to provide equal educational opportunity to those long denied it—people of color, poor people, and many others described in this chapter? Especially, they asked, how could the nation move toward equality when the financing of public elementary and secondary schools was so extremely unequal? Rich districts could spend many times what poor districts could spend on education, even neighboring districts in the same state. In Texas, as in many states, each school district supplemented its basic state aid through a tax on property within its jurisdiction. Given the value of property, and therefore the tax base in more prosperous districts, these districts had many times the budgets of less prosperous ones. People challenged these arrangements in many places and eventually the issue made it to the Supreme Court. In a 5–4 decision, the Court ruled that the U.S. Constitution did not guarantee equality in educational opportunity even if it did ban discrimination against a particular group. Justice Powell spoke for the majority, Justice Marshall for the minority.*

MR. JUSTICE POWELL delivered the opinion of the Court.

This suit attacking the Texas system of financing public education was initiated by Mexican-American parents whose children attend the elementary and secondary schools in the Edgewood Independent School District, an urban school district in San Antonio, Texas. They brought a class action on behalf of schoolchildren throughout the State who are members of minority groups or who are poor and reside in school districts having a low property tax base. Named as defendants were the State Board of Education, the Commissioner of Education, the State Attorney General, and the Bexar County (San Antonio) Board of Trustees. The complaint was filed in the summer of 1968 and a three-judge court was impaneled in January 1969. In December 1971 the panel rendered its judgment . . . holding the Texas school finance system unconstitutional under the Equal Protection Clause of the Fourteenth Amendment. The State appealed, and we noted probable jurisdiction to consider the far-reaching constitutional questions presented. (1972). For the reasons stated in this opinion, we reverse the decision of the District Court . . .

The wealth discrimination discovered by the District Court in this case, and by several other courts that have recently struck down school-financing laws in other States, is quite unlike any of the forms of wealth discrimination heretofore reviewed by this Court . . . However described, it is clear that appellees' suit asks this Court to extend its most exacting scrutiny to review a system that allegedly discriminates against a large, diverse, and amorphous class, unified only by the common factor of residence in districts that happen to have less taxable wealth than other districts. The system of alleged discrimination and the class it defines have none of the traditional indicia of suspectness: the class is not saddled with such disabilities, or subjected to such a history of purposeful unequal treatment, or relegated to such a position of political powerlessness as to command extraordinary protection from the majoritarian political process.

We thus conclude that the Texas system does not operate to the peculiar disadvantage of any suspect class . . .

Nothing this Court holds today in any way detracts from our historic dedication to public education. We are in complete agreement with the conclusion of the three-judge panel below that "the grave significance of education both to the individual and to our society" cannot be doubted. But the importance of a service performed by the State does not determine whether it must be regarded as fundamental for purposes of examination under the Equal Protection Clause . . .

Education, of course, is not among the rights afforded explicit protection under our Federal Constitution. Nor do we find any basis for saying it is implicitly so protected. As we have said, the undisputed importance of education will not alone cause this Court to depart from the usual standard for reviewing a State's social and economic legislation. It is appellees' contention, however, that education is distinguishable from other services and benefits provided by the State because it bears a peculiarly close relationship to other rights and liberties accorded protection under the Constitution. Specifically, they insist that education is itself a fundamental personal right because it is essential to the effective exercise of First Amendment freedoms and to intelligent utilization of the right to vote. In asserting a nexus between speech and education, appellees urge that the right to speak is meaningless unless the speaker is capable of articulating his thoughts intelligently and persuasively. The "marketplace of ideas" is an empty forum for those lacking basic communicative tools. Likewise, they argue that the corollary right to receive information becomes little more than a hollow privilege when the recipient has not been taught to read, assimilate, and utilize available knowledge . . .

We need not dispute any of these propositions. The Court has long afforded zealous protection against unjustifiable governmental interference with the individual's rights to speak and to vote. Yet we have never presumed to possess either the ability or the authority to guarantee to the citizenry the most effective speech or the most informed electoral choice. That these may be desirable goals of a system of freedom of expression and of a representative form of government is not to be doubted. These are indeed goals to be pursued by a people whose thoughts and beliefs are freed from governmental interference. But they are not values to be implemented by judicial intrusion into otherwise legitimate state activities . . .

We have carefully considered each of the arguments supportive of the District Court's finding that education is a fundamental right or liberty and have found those arguments unpersuasive . . .

The consideration and initiation of fundamental reforms with respect to state taxation and education are matters reserved for the legislative processes of the various States, and we do no violence to the values of federalism and separation of powers by staying our hand. We hardly need add that this Court's action today is not to be viewed as placing its judicial imprimatur on the status quo. The need is apparent for reform in tax systems which may well have relied too long and too heavily on the local property tax. And certainly innovative thinking as to public education, its methods, and its funding is necessary to assure both a higher level of quality and greater uniformity of opportunity. These matters merit the continued attention of the scholars who already have contributed much by their challenges. But the ultimate solutions must come from the lawmakers and from the democratic pressures of those who elect them.

MR. JUSTICE MARSHALL, with whom MR. JUSTICE DOUGLAS concurs, dissenting.

The Court today decides, in effect, that a State may constitutionally vary the quality of education which it offers its children in accordance with the amount of taxable wealth located in the school districts within which they reside. The majority's decision represents an abrupt departure from the mainstream of recent state and federal court decisions concerning the unconstitutionality of state educational financing schemes dependent upon taxable local wealth. More unfortunately, though, the majority's holding can only be seen as a retreat from our historic commitment to equality of educational opportunity and as unsupportable acquiescence in a system which deprives children in their earliest years of the chance to reach their full potential as citizens. The Court does this despite the absence of any substantial justification for a scheme which arbitrarily channels educational resources in accordance with the fortuity of the amount of taxable wealth within each district.

In my judgment, the right of every American to an equal start in life, so far as the provision of a state service as important as education is concerned, is far too vital to permit state discrimination on grounds as tenuous as those presented by this record. Nor can I accept the notion that it is sufficient to remit these appellees to the vagaries of the political process which, contrary to the majority's suggestion, has proved singularly unsuited to the task of providing a remedy for this discrimination. I, for one, am unsatisfied with the hope of an ultimate "political" solution sometime in the indefinite future while, in the meantime, countless children unjustifiably receive inferior educations that "may affect their hearts and minds in a way unlikely ever to be undone." *Brown v. Board of Education* (1954). I must therefore respectfully dissent.

The Court acknowledges that "substantial interdistrict disparities in school expenditures" exist in Texas . . . When the Texas financing scheme is taken as a whole, I do not think it can be doubted that it produces a discriminatory impact on substantial numbers of the school-age children of the State of Texas . . .

Under Texas law, the only mechanism provided the local school district for raising new, unencumbered revenues is the power to tax property located within its boundaries. At the same time, the Texas financing scheme effectively restricts the use of monies raised by local property taxation to the support of public education within the boundaries of the district in which they are raised, since any such taxes must be approved by a majority of the property-taxpaying voters of the district.

The significance of the local property tax element of the Texas financing scheme is apparent from the fact that it provides the funds to meet some 40% of the cost of public education for Texas as a whole. Yet the amount of revenue that any particular Texas district can raise is dependent on two factors—its tax rate and its amount of taxable property. The first factor is determined by the property-taxpaying voters of the district. But, regardless of the enthusiasm of the local voters for public education, the second factor—the taxable property wealth of the district—necessarily restricts the district's ability to raise funds to support public education. Thus, even though the voters of two Texas districts may be willing to make the same tax effort, the results for the districts will be substantially different if one is property rich while the other is property poor. The necessary effect of the Texas local property tax is, in short, to favor property-rich districts and to disfavor property-poor ones . . .

The seriously disparate consequences of the Texas local property tax, when that tax is considered alone, are amply illustrated by data presented to the District Court by appellees. These data included a detailed study of a sample of 110 Texas school districts for the 1967–1968 school year conducted by Professor Joel S. Berke of Syracuse University's Educational Finance Policy Institute. Among other things, this study revealed that the 10 richest districts examined, each of which had more than $100,000 in taxable property per pupil, raised through local effort an average of $610 per pupil, whereas the four poorest districts studied, each of which had less than $10,000 in taxable property per pupil, were able to raise only an average of $63 per pupil. And, as the Court effectively recognizes . . . this correlation between the amount of taxable property per pupil and the amount of local revenues per pupil holds true for the 96 districts in between the richest and poorest districts . . .

The Court seeks solace for its action today in the possibility of legislative reform. The Court's suggestions of legislative redress and experimentation will doubtless be of great comfort to the schoolchildren of Texas' disadvantaged districts, but considering the vested interests of wealthy school districts in the preservation of the status quo, they are worth little more. The possibility of legislative action is, in all events, no answer to this Court's duty under the Constitution to eliminate unjustified state discrimination. In this case we have been presented with an instance of such discrimination, in a particularly invidious form, against an individual interest of large constitutional and practical importance. To support the demonstrated discrimination in the provision of educational opportunity the State has offered a justification which, on analysis, takes on at best an ephemeral character. Thus, I believe that the wide disparities in taxable district property wealth inherent in the local property tax element of the Texas financing scheme render that scheme violative of the Equal Protection Clause.

Supreme Court of the United States, *San Antonio School District v. Rodriguez*, 411 U.S. 1 (1973) 411
U.S. 1, No. 71–1332. Decided March 21, 1973.

Reform Efforts of the 1980s and 1990s and the New Century, 1980–2005

- Introduction

- National Commission on Excellence
  in Education, *A Nation at Risk:
  The Imperative for Educational
  Reform*, 1983

- Ann Bastian et al., *Choosing Equality:
  The Case for Democratic
  Schooling*, 1985

- David C. Berliner and Bruce J. Biddle,
  The Manufactured Crisis, 1995

- Sonia Nieto, *Affirming Diversity:
  The Sociopolitical Context of
  Multicultural Education*, 1992

- Arthur M. Schlesinger, Jr., *The
  Disuniting of America*, 1991

- Seymour Papert, *The Children's
  Machine*, 1993

- Neil Postman, *Technopoly*, 1993

- United States Department of Education,
  Executive Summary of the No
  Child Left Behind Act, 2002

- Different Schools of Thought Regarding
  the No Child Left Behind Act
  (NCLB), 2003–2004

Introduction

With the election of Ronald Reagan as president in 1980, the Great Society era was clearly over. Reagan had pledged to abolish the federal Department of Education. More substantially, the Reagan revolution involved cutting all of the nonmilitary functions of the federal government so that they would revert to the states, or—for most of the social programs that had expanded in the previous two decades, including education—simply shrink or disappear. Reagan engineered the massive transfer of funds from the poor and middle class to the rich, which became his lasting legacy, by cutting many of the services that had opened doors of opportunity for poor and working-class Americans during the previous era. Given such a philosophy of governance, it was a surprise to many observers when Reagan's Secretary of Education, Terrell Bell, created the National Commission on Excellence in Education. The Commission's 1983 report, *A Nation at Risk: The Imperative for Educational Reform*, brought significantly more national attention to school reform than any act of the Carter-era Department of Education; indeed, it called more attention to school reform than virtually any federal action in education since Richard Nixon had signed Public Law 94-142 in the early 1970s. To say the report "burst on the scene" is not an overstatement. The report's authors framed their plea for school reform as a matter of national crisis. While careful to avoid offending the sensibilities of their federal patrons by calling for federal funds (a logical assumption given their martial rhetoric), they launched a series of further reform reports and studies, and fueled a significant range of state spending, state and local reform efforts, and a national debate about "school reform" that has lasted into the new century. Ironically, while the authors of the report did not end the continued cuts in federal spending for education, they probably did save the federal Department itself.

While President Reagan was reportedly appalled by the report and the limits it placed on his ability to maneuver for further cuts in education, the most vocal critics of the report were on the left. While glad for the attention to school issues, progressive educators feared that the rhetoric of *A Nation at Risk* would focus on punishing students, punishing teachers, and sometimes punishing parents (all themes that would appear again and again in the next decades), but would avoid responsibility to remediate the problems. One of the most cogent arguments for a more humane and generous stance on the issue of school reform came from Ann Bastian and her colleagues in the Report of the New World Foundation, *Choosing Equality: The Case for Democratic Schooling*. A selection from the book included here summarizes the arguments of some of those who sought a much broader definition of school reform. At the same time, others critiqued the core ideas behind many of the calls for reform. David C. Berliner and his colleagues have argued in *The Manufactured Crisis* that all the talk about school reform has masked the successes of the schools and is, in fact, part of an effort to undermine public schooling altogether.

One of the issues that dominated the educational debates of the late twentieth century is multiculturalism. How can schools attract and reflect increasing diversity in their student bodies? How can schools celebrate the contributions to American culture that many different ethnic groups have made? How can schools counter discrimination by race, class, or gender that has so long been a part of the American story? These and other questions have caused the flowering of multicultural curricula, which attempt to educate students about the many contributions people of diverse heritage have made to our nation and culture. At the same time, this multicultural approach has provoked heated debate; a surprising range of people defend a single cultural norm or national story and see any other approach as dangerously divisive.

Sonia Nieto's *Affirming Diversity: The Sociopolitical Context of Multicultural Education* makes the case for multicultural education clearly. On the other side of the debate, noted historian Arthur M. Schlesinger, Jr. argues in *The Disuniting of America* that multiculturalism is both a distortion of history and a political project with dangerous consequences for the nation's future. In the comparison of Nieto and Schlesinger the debate about multicultural education can be seen in stark contrast.

Another issue that came to the fore in the last decades of the twentieth century was the use of computers in schools and schooling. While the issue had been raised much earlier (see Chapter 6), the role of technology generally and computers specifically expanded greatly in the world of education in the 1990s. Seymour Papert emerged as perhaps the greatest defender of the role of computers in education, while Neil Postman became a major critic. Their two articles frame the debates of the era.

Finally, a major movement to institute national educational standards began to build on the call for change in *A Nation at Risk* and led to many developments during the presidency of George H. W. Bush and Bill Clinton. With the election of the second President Bush, the standards movement was embedded in federal law in the No Child Left Behind Act, signed in January 2002. No issue dominated education in the first decade of the twenty-first century as much as the discussions and debates about the federal No Child Left Behind legislation.

NCLB—as it came to be called—changed the daily life and preoccupations of teachers, principals, and school leaders across the United States. With its demand for annual testing of all students in the third to eighth grade and the use of the test results to measure whether individual schools and districts were making "adequate yearly progress," or AYP, the law highlighted testing—and too often test preparation—as never before. And AYP was not to be measured on the average progress of all students but by carefully disaggregated data collection. Students in eight categories or subgroups—white, black, Hispanic, American Indian, Asian or Pacific Islander, students eligible for free or reduced lunches, those with limited English proficiency, and those in special education—were measured separately and all had to be making progress for a school to meet its goals. Schools that failed to make AYP could suffer serious consequences. No wonder the Act received so much attention and was the subject of so much controversy.

The law that emerged from the Congress was 670 pages long and it is doubtful that anyone knew every provision of the legislation when it was passed and signed. The overarching goals, however, were clear. NCLB's sponsors wanted to use federal legislation to close the achievement gap between traditionally high-performing students, often those of white and middle-class backgrounds, and those who often did less well in school, students of color, poor students, students who came to school with limited knowledge of the English language, and students in special education programs. And in order to do this they created an accountability system that would reward schools that were succeeding and either prod or punish those that were seen as failing their students.

NCLB dominated educational discussions in the decade after it was signed. The U.S. Department of Education web page (posted during the years of the Bush administration) describes the Act in the most positive terms; as it was envisioned by its supporters. The chart that follows tracks the views of four very different critics of NCLB; critics with quite different perspectives. All of these differing views continue to be reflected in the educational debates of the twenty-first century.

NATIONAL COMMISSION ON EXCELLENCE IN EDUCATION, *A NATION AT RISK: THE IMPERATIVE FOR EDUCATIONAL REFORM*, 1983

It is hard to imagine the surprise and the energy surrounding A Nation at Risk when the report first appeared in 1983. Few federal reports have stirred as much debate. In part, the debate was so intense because a number of other reports appeared within the following year. A number of individual scholars, including Ernest Boyer, Theodore Sizer, Mortimer J. Adler, Robert Wood, Sarah Lawrence Lightfoot, Seymour Sarason, and John Goodlad, wrote their own telling reports at about the same time. Education was in the news. Debates about education were in the air. And the Nation at Risk *report, along with its many successors, continues to influence school policy to the present.*

Our Nation is at risk. Our once unchallenged preeminence in commerce, industry, science, and technological innovation is being overtaken by competitors throughout the world. This report is concerned with only one of the many causes and dimensions of the problem, but it is the one that undergirds American prosperity, security, and civility. We report to the American people that while we can take justiciable pride in what our schools and colleges have historically accomplished and contributed to the United States and the well-being of its people, the educational foundations of our society are presently being eroded by a rising tide of mediocrity that threatens our very future as a Nation and a people. What was unimaginable a generation ago has begun to occur—others are matching and surpassing our educational attainments.

If an unfriendly foreign power had attempted to impose on America the mediocre educational performance that exists today, we might well have viewed it as an act of war. As it stands, we have allowed this to happen to ourselves. We have even squandered the gains in student achievement made in the wake of the Sputnik challenge. Moreover, we have dismantled essential support systems which helped make those gains possible. We have, in effect, been committing an act of unthinking, unilateral educational disarmament.

Our society and its educational institutions seem to have lost sight of the basic purposes of schooling, and of the high expectations and disciplined effort needed to attain them. This report, the result of 18 months of study, seeks to generate reform of our educational system in fundamental ways and to renew the Nation's commitment to schools and colleges of high quality throughout the length and breadth of our land. That we have compromised this commitment is, upon reflection, hardly surprising, given the multitude of often conflicting demands we have placed on our Nation's schools and colleges. They are routinely called on to provide solutions to personal, social, and political problems that the home and other institutions either will not or cannot resolve. We must understand that these demands on our schools and colleges often exact an educational cost as well as a financial one.

On the occasion of the Commission's first meeting, President Reagan noted the central purpose of education in American life when he said, "Certainly there are few areas of American life as important to our society, to our people, and to our families as our schools and colleges." This report, therefore, is as much an open letter to the American people as it is a report to the Secretary of Education. We are confident that the American people, properly informed, will do what is right for their children and for the generations to come.

The Risk

History is not kind to idlers. The time is long past when America's destiny was assured simply by an abundance of natural resources and inexhaustible human enthusiasm, and by our relative isolation from the malignant problems of older civilizations. The world is indeed one global village. We live among determined, well-educated, and strongly motivated competitors. We compete with them for international standing and markets, not only with products but also with the ideas of our laboratories and neighborhood workshops. America's position in the world may once have been reasonably secure with only a few exceptionally well-trained men and women. It is no longer.

The risk is not only that the Japanese make automobiles more efficiently than Americans and have government subsidies for development and export. It is not just that the South Koreans recently built the world's most efficient steel mill, or that American machine tools, once the pride of the world, are being displaced by German products. It is also that these developments signify a redistribution of trained capability throughout the globe. Knowledge, learning, information, and skilled intelligence are the new raw materials of international commerce and are today spreading throughout the world as vigorously as miracle drugs, synthetic fertilizers, and blue jeans did earlier. If only to keep and improve on the slim competitive edge we still retain in world markets, we must dedicate ourselves to the reform of our educational system for the benefit of all—old and young alike, affluent and poor, majority, and minority. Learning is the indispensable investment required for success in the "information age" we are entering.

Our concern, however, goes well beyond matters such as industry and commerce. It also includes the intellectual, moral, and spiritual strengths of our people which knit together the very fabric of our society. The people of the United States need to know that individuals in our society who do not possess the levels of skill, literacy, and training essential to this new era will be effectively disenfranchised, not simply from the material rewards that accompany competent performance, but also from the chance to participate fully in our national life. A high level of shared education is essential to a free, democratic society and to the fostering of a common culture, especially in a country that prides itself on pluralism and individual freedom.

For our country to function, citizens must be able to reach some common understandings on complex issues, often on short notice and on the basis of conflicting or incomplete evidence. Education helps form these common understandings, a point Thomas Jefferson made long ago in his justly famous dictum:

> I know no safe depository of the ultimate powers of the society but the people themselves; and if we think them not enlightened enough to exercise their control with a wholesome discretion, the remedy is not to take from but to inform their discretion.

Part of what is at risk is the promise first made on this continent: All, regardless of race or class or economic status, are entitled to a fair chance and to the tools for developing their individual powers of mind and spirit to the utmost. This promise means that all children by virtue of their own efforts, competently guided, can hope to attain the mature and informed judgment needed to secure gainful employment and to manage their own lives, thereby serving not only their own interests but also the progress of society itself.

Indicators of the Risk

The educational dimensions of the risk before us have been amply documented in testimony received by the Commission. For example:

- International comparisons of student achievement, completed a decade ago, reveal that on 19 academic tests, American students were never first or second, and, in comparison with other industrialized nations, were last seven times.

- Some 23 million American adults are functionally illiterate by the simplest tests of everyday reading, writing, and comprehension.
- About 13 percent of all 17-year-olds in the United States can be considered functionally illiterate. Functional illiteracy among minority youth may run as high as 40 percent.
- Average achievement of high school students on most standardized tests is now lower than 26 years ago, when Sputnik was launched.
- Over half the population of gifted students do not match their tested ability with comparable achievement in school.
- The College Board's Scholastic Aptitude Test (SAT) demonstrates a virtually unbroken decline from 1963 to 1980. Average verbal scores fell over 50 points and average mathematics scores dropped nearly 40 points.
- College Board achievement tests also reveal consistent declines in recent years in such subjects as physics and English.
- Both the number and proportion of students demonstrating superior achievement on the SATs (i.e., those with scores of 650 or higher) have also dramatically declined.
- Many 17-year-olds do not possess the "higher-order" intellectual skills we should expect of them. Nearly 40 percent cannot draw inferences from written material; only one-fifth can write a persuasive essay; and only one-third can solve a mathematics problem requiring several steps.
- There was a steady decline in science achievement scores of U.S. 17-year-olds as measured by national assessments of science in 1969, 1973, and 1977.
- Between 1975 and 1980, remedial mathematics courses in public 4-year colleges increased by 72 percent and constitute one-quarter of all mathematics courses taught in those institutions.
- Average tested achievement of students graduating from college is also lower. Business and military leaders complain that they are required to spend millions of dollars on costly remedial education and training programs in such basic skills as reading, writing, spelling, and computation. The Department of the Navy, for example, reported to the Commission that one-quarter of its recent recruits cannot read at the ninth-grade level, the minimum needed to simply understand written safety instructions. Without remedial work they cannot even begin, much less complete, the sophisticated training essential in much of the modern military.

These deficiencies come at a time when the demand for highly skilled workers in fields is accelerating rapidly. For example:

- Computers and computer-controlled equipment are penetrating every aspect of our lives—homes, factories, and offices.
- One estimate indicates that by the turn of the century, millions of jobs will involve laser technology and robotics.
- Technology is radically transforming a host of other occupations. They include health care, medical science, energy production, food processing, construction, and the building, repair, and maintenance of sophisticated scientific, educational, military, and industrial equipment . . .

Our final word, perhaps better characterized as a plea, is that all segments of our population give attention to the implementation of our recommendations. Our present plight did not appear overnight, and the responsibility for our current situation is wide spread. Reform of our educational system will take time and unwavering commitment. It will require equally widespread, energetic, and dedicated action. For example, we call upon the National Academy of Sciences, National Academy of Engineering, Institute of Medicine, Science Service, National Science Foundation, Social Science Research Council, American Council of Learned Societies, National Endowment for the Humanities, National Endowment for the Arts, and other scholarly, scientific, and learned societies for their help in this effort. Help should come from students themselves; from parents, teachers, and school boards; from colleges and universities; from local, State, and Federal officials; from teachers' and administrators' organizations; from industrial and labor councils; and from other groups with interest in and responsibility for educational reform.

It is their America, and the America of all of us, that is at risk; it is to each of us that this imperative is addressed. It is by our willingness to take up the challenge, and our resolve to see it through, that America's place in the world will be either secured or forfeited. Americans have succeeded before, and so we shall again.

National Commission on Excellence in Education, *A Nation at Risk: The Imperative for Educational Reform*, Washington, DC: U.S. Government Printing Office, 1983, pp. 5–23.

Ann Bastian, Norm Fruchter, Marilyn Gittell, Colin Greer, and Kenneth Haskins, *Choosing Equality: The Case for Democratic Schooling*, 1985

Many people praised A Nation at Risk, *and many were critical.* Choosing Equality *represents a thoughtful critique of* A Nation at Risk *asking fundamentally different questions about the nature of the risk to education and the social values that schools should reflect. It also poses a series of important questions about the relationship of education to the larger social good.*

When the question is asked, "What should we do about the public schools?" it almost always means, "What should public schools do?" For the past two years, this has been the fundamental issue in the intense national debate over school reform. Beyond the focus on teacher morale or academic standards, we are probing the purposes of schooling, sorting out which needs schools should meet and what expectations they should fulfill.

For the general public, the debate expresses a rising fear about declining school performance and, perhaps more basically, fear about the future for youth in our society. This concern seems a natural product of recurring economic and social insecurity. The country is in the midst of profound structural shifts in technology, in job and income distribution, in family life and in government commitments. These shifts intensify existing inequities and threaten familiar patterns of individual mobility and community cohesion. Yet the debate also expresses hope. People turn to the schools as a social tool, one of few institutions which are public and local, for adapting to new demands and for protecting the coming generation.

Underlying the impulses to fear and hope is an unspoken tension between priorities for school change. We see this as a tension between two divergent goals for public education: a desire for schools to serve the competitive demands of a stratified society, and a desire for schools to play a socially integrative and democratic role, serving the right of all children to develop to their fullest potential. Some people do not see these as incompatible functions; others deny that they require different kinds of schooling. Yet, choices are being made, and in the current wave of school reform, democratic values of education have not been the central concern.

When we look beyond the universal call for excellence, we find new standards for achievement, but not new strategies for ensuring that all children will have the appropriate means to meet them. We find a new emphasis on accountability, but not institutional reforms which open the schools to those they serve. We find new tests for performance, but not analysis which measures the total school experience—including the patterns of inequality, rigidity, and exclusion which remain fundamental barriers to learning for millions of American schoolchildren.

This essay attempts to explore the tension between elitist and democratic goals in education in the present debate. Clearly, we feel that the democratic concepts of schooling should govern the direction of change and, in particular, that the massive school failure experienced in low-income communities should be of primary concern. We believe that equality in education is the inalienable right of all Americans. We believe that schools belong to citizens, not as clients but as owners of a public institution. And we believe that equality and participation in the educational process are essential conditions of educational excellence.

Yet we are also aware that our beliefs require a much firmer vision of what constitutes quality schooling and what is necessary to make quality a [more] universal commitment than has emerged in the debate thus far. This essay has, therefore, a threefold purpose: to understand where the current thrust for school change is leading, to examine alternative frameworks and approaches for restructuring our schools, and to consider what constituencies can be set in motion so that reform enlarges the democratic promise of education.

We are presenting an image of the opportunities for change, not a blueprint or formula which can ensure progressive outcomes in school reform. The agenda for democratic schooling will itself be incomplete until a more active and cohesive citizens' movement develops in education. What we propose are ways of viewing the options which would help break through the polarities of equity and excellence and move beyond the limits of past reform or present reaction. We try to connect what happens in the classroom to organizational and institutional contexts. We discuss the multiple levels of structural change necessary to achieve fundamental change. We explore the political processes which set priorities for education, and thus decide what we expect or tolerate in school performance . . .

In surveying these multiple dimensions of school reform, we have developed the following basic arguments.

The Mission of Schooling

The opening rounds of the school debate have been dominated by a neoconservative consensus which, by design or by default, identifies excellence with an elitist concept of meritocracy. The thrust has been to reinforce competitive structures of achievement, modeled on and serving the economic marketplace. This perspective misconstrues the crisis in education, which in our view is twofold: There is a catastrophic failure to provide decent schools and adequate skills to low-income students; there is also a chronic failure to provide reasoning and citizenship skills among all students. Moreover, school failure in the bottom tiers and narrow achievement throughout the system, cited to justify meritocratic practices, are in fact the result of such practices.

In establishing a framework for progressive alternatives, it is necessary to project a concept of education in which quality and equality are mutually inclusive standards. We must answer the questions: How do we measure equality? What defines democratic education?

Three Myths of School Performance

In further challenging the meritocratic framework, we examine three popular beliefs which underlie the neoconservative side of the school debate. These myths serve to narrow the vision of reform and to lower the expectations placed on education, particularly its role in meeting social needs and promoting capacities for citizenship.

Myth One is that today's school failures represent a recent development, in contrast with a "golden age" of public schooling which once served well both the elite and mass of students. But in our view, the gulf between elite and mass goals and methods of education has been a constant feature of our education system; today's failures express the tradition of a historically stratified system.

Myth Two is that the equity reforms attempted in the '60s and '70s have proven either diverting or damaging to the quest for excellence. In fact, the reforms enacted were not fully egalitarian, were actively subverted in their implementation, and have remained marginal to the education system. The reform era achieved a shift from exclusive meritocracy to inclusive meritocracy, but it did not transform the schools. Our choices are not limited to embracing either deficient reform or an elitist backlash; we can also choose to pursue more fundamental change.

Myth Three is that national economic growth and individual mobility are contingent on establishing more rigorous standards of education competition. Yet current economic trends contradict the notion that education will fuel economic recovery and broadly distribute economic rewards. The employment functions of schooling do not constitute a sufficient mechanism or rationale for structuring educational goals . . .

School Constituencies: Directions for Change

To secure progressive changes in instruction, it is essential to go beyond the classroom focus and to challenge the arrangements of institutional power which subvert responsive education. School systems are typically constructed to deny parents, teachers, and communities a positive role in guiding school practice. These frontline constituencies are vital both as resources for school improvement and as activists for democratic priorities in the reform process. But it is often the case, particularly in the most deprived school systems, that parents are regularly excluded from participating in school affairs and even blamed for student failure. Teachers are frequently viewed as custodians and technicians, denied control over their working conditions and their professional development by the lack of supportive resources, by bureaucratic professionalism, by autocratic management. And schools, especially the worst schools, remain isolated from and often antagonistic toward the communities they serve.

The educational value of schools which empower their constituents and function as community institutions can be clearly demonstrated. Pursuing this goal on a broad scale, however, quickly raises the problem of making such reforms tangible, not token. We look at four topical issues which are proving important in defining our concept of the school as an open institution: voucher or optional enrollment systems, the Effective Schools Movement, community-based campaigns, and youth service programs.

Today's Agenda

Taken as a whole, this essay rejects the notion of a one best reform or a one best school system. This essay is an effort to clarify the choices before us and the steps that promote or deter democratic purposes in education. Reviewing the major issues of the current debate, we look not only to specific proposals, but to the context in which they are offered: Are they seen as panaceas or as leverage points for restructuring? Do they substitute for fundamental changes or move toward them? Do they preempt the empowerment of school constituents or enlarge their capacities to shape policy in practice?

The school debate of the 1980s is far from over. While we question many of the initiatives launched in the name of excellence, the current excellence movement has at least focused public attention on the conditions of schooling. A broader vision of alternatives is being forged, in defense of past gains and in support of new models. This essay seeks to further enlarge our sense of opportunity and possibility by looking beyond the alarm over the school crisis, by moving toward a democratic conception of the public school mission, and by posing the priorities for change that democratic education demands.

Ann Bastian, Norm Frachter, Marilyn Gittell, Colin Greer, and Kenneth Haskins, *Choosing Equality: The Case for Democratic Schooling*, Philadelphia, PA: Temple University Press, 1985.

DAVID C. BERLINER AND BRUCE J. BIDDLE, *THE MANUFACTURED CRISIS*, 1995

While Ann Bastian and her colleagues tried to redirect the discussion of school reform to focus on a more inclusive democratic ideal, some educators began to ask different questions. Was so much reform necessary? Was so much really wrong with the schools? David Berliner and Bruce Biddle offered a new perspective in their book, charging that the crisis in the schools is manufactured—developed not to improve schools, but to dismantle them.

This book was written in outrage.

Throughout much of recent history our federal government seemed to be willing to promote the interests of public education. Advocates who favored public schools appeared regularly in both the White House and Congress; various programs to support the needs of our schools passed into law over the years; and although we knew that those schools continued to face many problems, our political leaders seemed to be aware of those problems and to be willing to respect the results of research on education in their pronouncements. Thus, like many other Americans, we came to believe that in their discussions of education, our federal leaders were, within limits, well-intentioned and honest people.

Events in the last decade have certainly challenged these beliefs. In 1983, the Reagan White House began to make sweeping claims attacking the conduct and achievements of America's public schools—claims that were contradicted by evidence we knew about. We thought at first this might have been a mistake, but these and related hostile and untrue claims were soon to be repeated by many leaders of the Reagan and Bush administrations. The claims were also embraced in many documents issued by industrialists and business leaders and were endlessly repeated and embroidered on by the press. And, as time passed, even leading members of the education community—including a number of people whom we knew personally—began to state these lies as facts.

Slowly, then, we began to suspect that something was not quite right, that organized malevolence might actually be underway . . . The more we poked into our story, the more nasty lies about education we unearthed; the more we learned about how government officials and their allies were ignoring, suppressing, and distorting evidence; and the more we discovered how Americans were being misled about schools and their accomplishments. This, then, has been the source of our outrage. We also began to wonder why this was happening—why were some people in Washington so anxious to scapegoat educators, what were they really up to, what problems were they trying to hide, what actions did they want to promote or prevent?

We also learned that the answers to these questions are not simple. Some of those who have accepted hostile myths about education have been genuinely worried about our schools, some have misunderstood evidence, some have been duped, and some have had other understandable reasons for their actions. But many of the myths seem also to have been told by powerful people who—despite their protestations—were pursuing a political agenda designed to weaken the nation's public schools, redistribute support for those schools so that privileged students are favored over needy students, or even abolish those schools altogether. To this end, they have been prepared to tell lies, suppress evidence, scapegoat educators, and sow endless confusion. We consider this conduct particularly despicable.

This book, then, is designed to set the record straight about these events; to examine the evidence and correct the hostile myths that have been told about our schools; to explore why they were told and what the myth-tellers were up to; to examine the real problems of education that have too often been masked; and to explore what might be done about those problems . . .

Manufacturing a Crisis in Education

Seldom in the course of policymaking in the U.S. have so many firm convictions held by so many been based on so little convincing proof.

—Clark Kerr

President Emeritus of the University of California (1991)

Given the serious problems of Japanese education, why have so many Americans come to believe that *American* education is so deficient and that we should look to the Japanese to find out how to run our schools? The answer is that for more than a dozen years, this groundless and damaging message has been proclaimed by major leaders of our government and industry and has been repeated endlessly by a compliant press. Good-hearted Americans have come to believe that the public schools of their nation are in a crisis state because they have so often been given this false message by supposedly credible sources.

To illustrate, in 1983, amid much fanfare, the White House released an incendiary document highly critical of American education. Entitled *A Nation at Risk*, this work was prepared by a prestigious committee under the direction of then Secretary of Education Terrell Bell and was endorsed in a speech by President Ronald Reagan. It made many claims about the "failures" of American education, how those "failures" were confirmed by "evidence," and how this would inevitably damage the nation. (Unfortunately, none of the supposedly supportive "evidence" actually appeared in *A Nation at Risk*, nor did this work provide citations to tell Americans where that "evidence" might be found.)

But leaders in this disinformation campaign were not content merely to attack American schools. *A Nation at Risk* charged that American students never excelled in international comparisons of student achievement and that this failure reflected systematic weaknesses in our school programs and lack of talent and motivation among American educators. Thus, it came as little surprise when the White House soon sent a team of Americans to Japan to discover and report on why Japanese education was so "successful." Following this visit, the then Assistant Secretary of Education, Chester Finn, a leader of the team, said of the Japanese:

> They've demonstrated that you can have a coherent curriculum, high standards, good discipline, parental support, a professional teaching force and a well-run school. They have shown that the average student can learn a whole lot more.

This enthusiasm was echoed by others on the team. According to team member Herbert Walberg, an educational researcher, features of the Japanese system could be adopted in America and would help to solve the many "problems" of American education. Walberg suggested, "I think it's portable. Gumption and willpower, that's the key." This was far from the end of White House criticisms of American education. Indeed, the next decade witnessed a veritable explosion of documents and pronouncements from government leaders—two American presidents, Ronald Reagan and George Bush, secretaries of education, assistant secretaries, and chiefs and staff members in federal agencies—telling Americans about the many "problems" of their public schools. As in *A Nation at Risk*, most of these claims were said to reflect "evidence," although the "evidence" in question either was not presented or appeared in the form of simplistic, misleading generalizations.

During the same years, many leaders in industry claimed in documents and public statements that American education was in deep trouble, that as a result our country was falling behind foreign competitors, and that these various charges were all confronted by "evidence" (which somehow was rarely presented or appeared in simple, misleading formats). And these many charges, documents, and pronouncements from leaders of government and industry, often seconded by prominent members of the educational community, were dutifully reported and endlessly elaborated upon by an unquestioning press.

So it is small wonder that many Americans have come to believe that education in our country is now in a deplorable state. Indeed, how could they have concluded anything else, given such an energetic and widely reported campaign of criticism, from such prestigious sources, attacking America's public schools? To the best of our knowledge, no campaign of this sort had ever before appeared in American history. Never before had an American government been so critical of the public schools, and never had so many false claims been made about education in the name of "evidence." We shall refer to this campaign of criticism as the Manufactured Crisis.

The Manufactured Crisis was not an accidental event. Rather, it appeared within a specific historical context and was led by identifiable critics whose political goals could be furthered by scapegoating educators. It was also supported from its inception by an assortment of questionable techniques—including misleading methods for analyzing data, distorting reports of findings, and suppressing contradictory evidence. Moreover, it was tied to misguided schemes for "reforming" education—schemes that would, if adopted, seriously damage American schools.

Unfortunately, the Manufactured Crisis has had a good deal of influence—thus, too many well-meaning, bright, and knowledgeable Americans have come to believe some of its major myths, and this has generated serious mischief. Damaging programs for educational reform have been adopted, a great deal of money has been wasted, effective school programs have been harmed, and morale has declined among educators.

But myths need not remain unchallenged; in fact, they have become shaky when they are exposed to the light of reason and evidence. When one actually looks at the evidence, one discovers that most of the claims of the Manufactured Crisis are, indeed, myths, half-truths, and sometimes outright lies. Thus, as our first major task, we undertake, through reason and displays of relevant evidence, to dispel some of the mischief of the Manufactured Crisis—to place the crisis in context, to counter its myths, to explain why its associated agenda will not work, to set the record straight.

But accomplishing only this first task would leave many questions unanswered. One of the worst effects of the Manufactured Crisis has been to divert attention away from the *real* problems faced by American education—problems that are serious and that are escalating in today's world. To illustrate, although many Americans do not realize it, family incomes and financial support for schools are *much* more poorly distributed in our country than in other industrialized nations. This means that in the United States, very privileged students attend some of the world's best private and public schools, but it also means that large numbers of students who are truly disadvantaged attend public schools whose support is far below that permitted in other Western democracies. Thus, opportunities are *not* equal in America's schools. As a result, the achievements of students in schools that cater to the rich and the poor in our country are also far from equal.

In addition, America's school system has expanded enormously since World War II and now serves the needs of a huge range of students. This increased diversity has created many opportunities—but also many dilemmas—and debates now rage over how to distribute resources and design curricula to meet the needs of students from diverse backgrounds, with many different skills and interests. Problems such as these *must* be addressed if Americans are to design a school system that truly provides high standards and equal opportunities for all students.

Our second major task, then, is to direct attention away from the fictions of the Manufactured Crisis and toward the real problems of American schools.

David C. Berliner and Bruce J. Biddle, *The Manufactured Crisis: Myths, Fraud, and the Attack on America's Public Schools*, New York: Perseus Books Publishers, 1995.

SONIA NIETO, *AFFIRMING DIVERSITY: THE SOCIOPOLITICAL CONTEXT OF MULTICULTURAL EDUCATION*, 1992

James Banks is often called the father of multicultural education. Certainly he has been a towering figure in the field for many years. A number of other scholars have also developed their own views on multicultural education. As with any topic in education, there are almost as many definitions of multicultural education as there are writers discussing the subject. Sonia Nieto from the University of Massachusetts at Amherst provides a clear definition of multicultural education and a compelling case for its value.

Multicultural education cannot be understood in a vacuum, but rather must be seen in its personal, social, historical, and political context. Assuming that multicultural education is "the answer" to school failure is simplistic at best, for it overlooks important social and educational issues that affect daily the lives of students. Educational failure is too complex and knotty an issue to be "fixed" by any single program or approach. However, if broadly conceptualized and implemented, multicultural education can have a substantive and positive impact on the educational experience of most students. That is the thesis of this book.

I have come to this understanding as a result of many experiences, including my childhood and my life as a student, teacher, researcher, and parent. As a young child growing up in Brooklyn, New York, during the 1940s, I was able to experience firsthand the influence that poverty, discrimination, and the perception of one's culture and language as inferior can have. Speaking only Spanish when I entered the first grade, I was immediately confronted with the arduous task of learning a second language while my already quite developed native language was all but ignored. Some 40 years later, I still recall the frustration of groping for words I did not know to express thoughts I could very capably say in Spanish. Equally vivid are memories of some teachers' expectations that because of our language and cultural differences, my classmates and I would not do well in school. This explains my fourth-grade teacher's response when mine was the only hand to go up when she asked if anybody in the class wanted to go to college. "Well, that's O.K.," she said, "because we always need people to clean toilets."

I also recall teachers' perceptions that there was something wrong with speaking a language other than English. "Is there anybody in this class who started school without speaking English?" my tenth-grade homeroom teacher asked loudly, filling out one of the endless forms that teachers are handed by the central office. By this time, my family had moved to what was at the time a working-class and primarily European-American neighborhood. My classmates looked in hushed silence as I, the only Puerto Rican in the class, raised my hand timidly. "Are you in a special English class?" he asked in front of the entire class. "Yes," I

Figure 12.1 Sonia Nieto has been one of the major advocates for multicultural education even as others, like Arthur M. Schlesinger, Jr., attacked the movement. Photo courtesy Sonia Nieto.

said, "I'm in Honors English." Although there is nothing wrong with being in a special class for English as a second language (ESL), I felt fortunate that I was able to respond in this way. I had learned to feel somewhat ashamed of speaking Spanish and wanted to make it very clear that I was intelligent in spite of it. Many students in similar circumstances who are in bilingual and ESL classes feel guilty and inferior to their peers.

Those first experiences with society's responses to cultural differences did not, of course, convince me that something was wrong with the *responses*. Rather, I assumed, as many of my peers did, that there was something wrong with us. We learned to feel ashamed of who we were, how we spoke, what we ate, and everything else that was "different" about us. "Please," I would beg my mother, "make us hamburgers and hot dogs for dinner." Luckily, she never paid attention and kept right on cooking rice, beans, platanos, and all those other good foods that we grew up with. She and my father also continued speaking Spanish to us, in spite of our teachers' pleas to speak to us only in English. And so, alongside the messages at school and in the streets that being Puerto Rican was not something to be proud of, we learned to keep on being who we were. As the case studies point out, these conflicting messages are still being given to many young people.

Immigration is not a phenomenon of the past. In fact, the experience of immigration is still fresh in the minds of a great many people in our country. It is an experience that begins anew every day that planes land, ships reach our shores, and people make their way on foot to our borders. Many of the students in our schools, even if they themselves are not immigrants, have parents or grandparents who were. The United States is thus not only a nation of immigrants as seen in some idealized and romanticized past; it is also a living nation of immigrants even today.

The pain and alienation of the immigrant experience, however, have rarely been confronted in our schools. This experience includes the forced immigration of enslaved Africans, and the colonization of American Indians and Mexicans from within. Because schools have traditionally perceived their role to be that of an assimilating agent, the isolation and rejection that come hand-in-hand with immigration and colonization have simply been left at the schoolhouse door. Curriculum and pedagogy, rather than using the lived experiences of students as a foundation, have been based on what can be described as an alien and imposed reality. The rich experiences of millions of our students, their parents, grandparents, and neighbors have been kept strangely quiet. Although we almost all have an immigrant past, very few of us know or even acknowledge it.

What the research reported in this book suggests to me is that we need to make this history visible by making it part of the curriculum, instruction, and educational experience in general. Whether through the words of Manuel, who claims that he cannot be an American because it would mean forsaking his Cape Verdean background, or those of Vanessa, who knows nothing about her European-American past and even feels uncomfortable discussing it, it has become clear that the immigrant experience is an important point of departure for beginning our journey into multicultural education. This journey needs to begin with teachers, who themselves are frequently unaware of or uncomfortable with their own ethnicity. By going through a process of reeducation about their own backgrounds, their families' pain, and their rich legacy of stories, teachers can lay the groundwork for students to reclaim their own histories and voices.

As an adult, I have come to the conclusion that no child should have to go through the painful dilemma of choosing between family and school and of what inevitably becomes a choice between belonging and succeeding. The costs for going through such an experience are high indeed, from becoming a "cultural schizophrenic" to developing doubts about one's self-worth and dignity. This is nowhere more poignantly described than Richard Rodriguez's painful recollection of growing up as a "scholarship boy," an academically promising student who is doomed to lose his family, culture, and language in the process. His conclusion is that one's public and private worlds cannot be reconciled:

My awkward childhood does not prove the necessity of bilingual education. My story discloses instead an essential myth of childhood—inevitable pain. If I rehearse here the changes in my private life after my Americanization, it is finally to emphasize the public gain. The loss implies the gain.

Because of his wrenching loss of language and culture, Rodriguez decides that bilingual-multicultural education and affirmative action are all policies that cannot work because they in effect delay the inevitable loss. My conclusion is quite the opposite: *The loss implies the pain.* Just as the title of an important book on the issue asserts (*Minority Education: From Shame to Struggle*), our society must move beyond causing and exploiting students' shame to using their cultural and linguistic differences to struggle for an education that is more in tune with society's rhetoric of equal and high-quality education for all students. That is the fundamental lesson I have relearned while doing the research for this book.

Some Assumptions

It is necessary to clarify a number of assumptions embedded in the text. The first concerns who is included in multicultural education. My perspective is that multicultural education is for everyone regardless of ethnicity, race, language, social class, religion, gender, or sexual preference. My framework for multicultural education is thus a very broad and inclusive one. Nevertheless, although I refer in the text to many kinds of differences, I am particularly concerned with race, ethnicity, and language. These are the major issues that provide a lens through which I view multicultural education. This perspective is probably based on a number of reasons, not the least of which is my own experience. Another reason concerns the very history of multicultural education. A direct outgrowth of the civil rights movement, multicultural and bilingual education was developed as a response to inequality in education based on racism, ethnocentrism, and language discrimination. Although I believe it is imperative to include other differences, for me it is necessary to approach an understanding of multicultural education with a firm grounding in these three areas.

This brings up another dilemma related to inclusion. It is easier for some educators to embrace a very inclusive and comprehensive framework of multicultural education because they have a hard time facing racism. They may prefer to deal with issues of class, exceptionality, or religious diversity because, for them, these factors may be easier to confront. Racism is an excruciatingly difficult issue for most of us. Given our history of exclusion and discrimination, this is not surprising. Nevertheless, I believe it is only through a thorough investigation of discrimination based on race and other differences related to it that we can understand the genesis as well as the rationale for multicultural education. I will also refer to gender, social class, and exceptionality because these areas provide other important lenses with which to view inequality in education. However, because no one book can possibly give all of these issues the central importance they deserve, I have chosen to focus on race, ethnicity, and language.

Another assumption that guides this book is that teachers should not be singled out as the villains in the failure of so many students. Although some teachers do indeed bear the responsibility for having low expectations, being racist and elitist in their interactions with students and parents, and providing educational environments that discourage many students from learning, most do not do so consciously. Most teachers are sincerely concerned about their students and want very much to provide the best education they can. Nevertheless, they are often at the mercy of decisions made by others far removed from the classroom. In addition, they have little to do with developing the policies and practices in operation in their schools and frequently do not even question them.

Teachers are also the products of educational systems that have a history of racism, exclusion, and debilitating pedagogy. As such, they put into practice what they themselves have been subjected to and thus perpetuate structures that may be harmful to many of their students. Furthermore, the disempowerment felt by so many teachers is a palpable force in many schools. Finally, schools cannot be separated from communities or from our society in general. Oppressive forces that limit opportunities in the schools are a reflection of such forces in the society at large. Thus, the purpose of this book is not to point a finger, but to provide a forum for reflection and discussion so that teachers take responsibility for their actions, challenge the actions of schools and society that affect their students' education, and help effect positive change.

Overview

Multicultural education cannot be understood in a vacuum. Yet it is often presented as somehow divorced from the policies and practices of schools and from the society in which we live. The result is a fairyland kind of multicultural education disassociated from the lives of teachers, students, and their communities. The premise of this book is quite different: No educational philosophy or program is worthwhile unless it focuses on two primary concerns:

- Raising the achievement of all students and thus providing them with an equal and equitable education
- Giving students the opportunity to become critical and productive members of a democratic society

To the extent that it remains education to help students get along, or to help them feel better about themselves, or to "sensitize" them to one another, without tackling the central but far more difficult issues of stratification, empowerment, and inequity, multicultural education becomes another approach that simply scratches the surface of educational failure. Although we may all want our students to get along and to be sensitive to and respect one another, this by itself will make little difference when it comes to the options they have as a result of their schooling. Because the choices they make are inexorably affected by social and political forces in schools and society, it is necessary to consider them in our understanding of multicultural education.

Equal education in this context goes beyond providing the same resources and opportunities for all students, although this alone would be a crucial step in affording a better education for a wide variety of students. By remaining at this level, however, it completely misses the point that education is a two-way process. That is, education must involve the interaction of students with teachers and schools, not simply the action of teachers and schools on students. Equal education thus also means that the skills, talents, and experiences that all students bring to their education need to be considered valid starting points for further schooling. *Equity* is a more comprehensive term because it includes equal educational opportunities while at the same time demanding fairness and the real possibility of *equality of outcomes* for a broader range of students. Throughout this book, multicultural education will be considered as fundamental to educational equity.

Sonja Nieto, *Affirming Diversity*, Boston, MA: Addison Wesley Longman, 1992.

ARTHUR M. SCHLESINGER, JR., *THE DISUNITING OF AMERICA*, 1991

While many educators rallied to the cause of multicultural education, others were critical, some highly so. Few issues have cut so deeply to the core questions of the nature and purpose of schooling and the fundamental nature of the American story. The historian Arthur M. Schlesinger, advisor to President John F. Kennedy and well-known liberal icon, surprised many with the vehemence of his attack on multicultural education. For Schlesinger, multiculturalism can quickly lead to division and separation; he wanted none of it.

The attack on the common American identity is the culmination of the cult of ethnicity. That attack was mounted in the first instance by European Americans of non-British origin ("unmeltable ethnics") against the British foundations of American culture; then, latterly and massively, by Americans of non-European origin against the European foundations of that culture. As Theodore Roosevelt's foreboding suggests, the European immigration itself palpitated with internal hostilities, everyone at everybody else's throats—hardly the "monocultural" crowd portrayed by ethnocentric separatists. After all, the two great "world" wars of the 20th century began as fights among European states. Making a single society out of this diversity of antagonistic European peoples is a hard enough job. The new salience of non-European, nonwhite stocks compounds the challenge. And the non-Europeans, or at least their self-appointed spokesmen, bring with them a resentment, in some cases a hatred, of Europe and the West provoked by generations of Western colonialism, racism, condescension, contempt, and cruel exploitation.

Will not this rising flow of non-European immigrants create a "minority majority" that will make Europeans obsolete by the 21st century? This is the fear of some white Americans and the hope (and sometimes the threat) of some nonwhites.

Immigrants were responsible for a third of population growth during the 1980s. More arrived than in any decade since the second of the century. And the composition of the newcomers changed dramatically. In 1910, nearly 90 percent of immigrants came from Europe. In the 1980s, more than 80 percent came from Asia and Latin America. Still, foreign-born residents constitute only about 7 percent of the population today, as against nearly 15 percent when the first Roosevelt and Wilson were worrying about hyphenated Americans. Stephan Thernstrom doubts that the minority majority will ever arrive. The black share in the population has grown rather slowly—9.9 percent in 1920, 10 percent in 1950, 11.1 percent in 1970, 12.1 percent in 1990. Neither Asian Americans nor Hispanic Americans go in for especially large families; and family size in any case tends to decline as income and intermarriage increase. "If today's immigrants assimilate to American ways as readily as their predecessors at the turn of the century—as seems to be happening," Thernstrom concludes, "there won't be a minority majority issue anyway."

America has so long seen itself as the asylum for the oppressed and persecuted—and has done itself and the world so much good thereby—that any curtailment of immigration offends something in the American soul. No one wants to be a Know-Nothing. Yet uncontrolled immigration is an impossibility; so the criteria of control are questions the American democracy must confront. We have shifted the basis of [immigration policy] administration three times this century—from national origins in 1924, to family reunification in 1965, to needed skills in 1990. The future of immigration policy depends on the capacity of the assimilation process to continue to do what it has done so well in the past: to lead newcomers to an acceptance of the language, the institutions, and the political ideals that hold the nation together.

Is Europe really the root of all evil? The crimes of Europe against lesser breeds without the law (not to mention even worse crimes—Hitlerism and Stalinism—against other Europeans) are famous. But these crimes do not alter other facts of history: that Europe was the birthplace of the United States of America, that European ideas and culture formed the republic, that the United States is an extension of European civilization, and that nearly 80 percent of Americans are of European descent.

When Irving Howe, hardly a notorious conservative, dared write, "The Bible, Homer, Plato, Sophocles, Shakespeare are central to our culture," an outraged reader ("having graduated this past year from Amherst") wrote, "Where on Howe's list is the Quran, the Gita, Confucius, and other central cultural artifacts of the peoples of our nation?" No one can doubt the importance of these works, nor the influence they have had on other societies. But on American society? It may be too bad that dead white European males have played so large a role in shaping our culture. But that's the way it is. One cannot erase history.

These humdrum historical facts, and not some dastardly imperialist conspiracy, explain the Eurocentric slant in American schools. Would anyone seriously argue that teachers should conceal the European origins of American civilization? Or that schools should educate the 20 percent and ignore the 80 percent? Of course the 20 percent and their contributions should be integrated into the curriculum, too, which is the point of cultural pluralism.

But self-styled "multiculturalists" are very often ethnocentric separatists who see little in the Western heritage beyond Western crimes. The Western tradition, in this view, is inherently racist, sexist, "classist," hegemony; irredeemably repressive, irredeemably oppressive. The spread of Western culture is due not to any innate quality but simply to the spread of Western power. Thus the popularity of European classical music around the world—and, one supposes, of American jazz and rock, too—is evidence not of wide appeal but of "the pattern of imperialism, in which the conquered culture adopts that of the conqueror."

Such animus toward Europe lay behind the well-known crusade against the Western Civilization course at Stanford ("Hey-hey, ho-ho, Western Culture's got to go!"). According to the National Endowment for the Humanities, students can graduate from 78 percent of American colleges and universities without taking a course in the history of Western civilization. A number of institutions—among them Dartmouth, Wisconsin, Mount Holyoke—require courses in third-world or ethnic studies, but not in Western civilization. The mood is one of divesting Americans of the sinful European inheritance and seeking redemptive infusions from non-Western cultures.

One of the oddities of the situation is that the assault on the Western tradition is conducted very largely with analytical weapons forged in the West. What are the names invoked by the coalition of latter-day Marxists, deconstructionists, poststructuralists, radical feminists, Afrocentrists? Marx, Nietzsche, Gramsci, Derrida, Foucault, Lacan, Sartre, de Beauvoir, Habermas, the Frankfurt "critical theory" school—Europeans all. The "unmasking," "demythologizing," "decanonizing," "dehegomizing" blitz against Western culture depends on methods of critical analysis unique to the West—which surely testifies to the internally redemptive potentialities of the Western tradition.

Even Afrocentrists seem to accept subliminally the very Eurocentric standards they think they are rejecting. "Black intellectuals condemn Western civilization," Professor Pearce Williams says, "yet ardently wish to prove it was founded by their ancestors." And, like Frantz Fanon and Leopold Senghor, whose books figure prominently on their reading lists, Afrocentric ideologues are intellectual children of the West they repudiate. Fanon, the eloquent spokesman of the African wretched of the earth, had French as his native tongue and based his analyses on Freud, Marx, and Sartre. Senghor, the prophet of Negritude, wrote in French, established the Senegalese educational system on the French model and, when he left the presidency of Senegal, retired to France.

Western hegemony, it would seem, can be the source of protest as well as of power. Indeed, the invasion of American schools by the Afrocentric curriculum, not to mention the conquest of university departments of English and comparative literature by deconstructionists, poststructuralists, etc., are developments that by themselves refute the extreme theory of "cultural hegemony." Of course, Gramsci had a point.

Ruling values do dominate and permeate any society; but they do not have the rigid and monolithic grip on American democracy that academic leftists claim . . .

It is time to adjourn the chat about hegemony. If hegemony were as real as the cultural radicals pretend, Afrocentrism would never have got anywhere, and the heirs of William Lyons Phelps would still be running the Modern Language Association.

Is the Western tradition a bar to progress and a curse on humanity? Would it really do America and the world good to get rid of the European legacy?

No doubt Europe has done terrible things, not least to itself. But what culture has not? History, said Edward Gibbon, is little more than the register of the crimes, follies, and misfortunes of mankind. The sins of the West are no worse than the sins of Asia or of the Middle East or of Africa.

There remains, however, a crucial difference between the Western tradition and the others. The crimes of the West have produced their own antidotes. They have provoked great movements to end slavery, to raise the status of women, to abolish torture, to combat racism, to defend freedom of inquiry and expression, to advance personal liberty and human rights.

Whatever the particular crimes of Europe, that continent is also the source—the *unique* source—of those liberating ideas of individual liberty, political democracy, the rule of law, human rights, and cultural freedom that constitute our most precious legacy and to which most of the world today aspires. These are *European* ideas, not Asian, nor African, nor Middle Eastern ideas, except by adoption.

The freedoms of inquiry and of artistic creation, for example, are Western values. Consider the differing reactions to the case of Salman Rushdie: what the West saw as an intolerable attack on individual freedom, the Middle East saw as a proper punishment for an evildoer who had violated the mores of his group. Individualism itself is looked on with abhorrence and dread by collectivist cultures in which loyalty to the group overrides personal goals— cultures that, social scientists say, comprise about 70 percent of the world's population.

There is surely no reason for Western civilization to have guilt trips laid on it by champions of cultures based on despotism, superstition, tribalism, and fanaticism. In this regard, the Afrocentrists are especially absurd. The West needs no lectures on the superior virtue of those "sun people" who sustained slavery until Western imperialism abolished it (and, it is reported, sustain it to this day in Mauritania and the Sudan), who still keep women in subjection and cut off their clitorises, who carry out racial persecutions not only against Indians and other Asians but against fellow Africans from the wrong tribes, who show themselves either incapable of operating a democracy or ideologically hostile to the democratic idea, and who, in their tyrannies and massacres, their Idi Amins and Boukassas, have stamped with utmost brutality on human rights.

Certainly the European overlords did little enough to prepare Africa for self-government. But democracy would find it hard in any case to put down roots in a tribalist and patrimonial culture that, long before the West invaded Africa, had sacralized the personal authority of chieftains and ordained the submission of the rest. What the West would call corruption is regarded through much of Africa as no more than the prerogative of power. Competitive political parties, an independent judiciary, a free press, the rule of law are alien to African traditions.

It was the French, not the Algerians, who freed Algerian women from the veil (much to the irritation of Frantz Fanon, who regarded deveiling as symbolic rape); as in India it was the British, not the Indians, who ended (or did their best to end) the horrible custom of *suttee-widows* burning themselves alive on their husbands' funeral pyres. And it was the West, not the non-Western cultures, that launched the crusade to abolish slavery—and in doing so encountered mighty resistance, especially in the Islamic world (where Moslems, with fine impartiality, enslaved whites as well as blacks). Those many brave and humane Africans who are struggling these days for decent societies are animated by Western, not by African, ideals. White guilt can be pushed too far.

The Western commitment to human rights has unquestionably been intermittent and imperfect. Yet the ideal remains—and movement toward it has been real, if sporadic. Today it is the *Western* democratic tradition that attracts and empowers people of all continents, creeds, and colors. When the Chinese students cried and died for democracy in Tiananmen Square, they brought with them not representations of Confucius or Buddha, but a model of the Statue of Liberty.

The great American asylum, as Crevecoeur called it, open, as Washington said, to the oppressed and persecuted of all nations, has been from the start an experiment in a multiethnic society. This is a bolder experiment than we sometimes remember. History is littered with the wreck of states that tried to combine diverse ethnic or linguistic or religious groups within a single sovereignty. Today's headlines tell of imminent crisis or impending dissolution in one or another multiethnic polity—the Soviet Union, India, Yugoslavia, Czechoslovakia, Ireland, Belgium, Canada, Lebanon, Cyprus, Israel, Ceylon, Spain, Nigeria, Kenya, Angola, Trinidad, Guyana . . . The list is almost endless. The luck so far of the American experiment has been due in large part to the vision of the melting pot. "No other nation," Margaret Thatcher has said, "has so successfully combined people of different races and nations within a single culture."

But even in the United States, ethnic ideologues have not been without effect. They have set themselves against the old American ideal of assimilation. They call on the republic to think in terms not of individual but of group identity and to move the polity from individual rights to group rights. They have made a certain progress in transforming the United States into a more segregated society. They have done their best to turn a college generation against

Europe and the Western tradition. They have imposed ethnocentric, Afrocentric, and bilingual curricula on public schools, well designed to hold minority children out of American society. They have told young people from minority groups that the Western democratic tradition is not for them. They have encouraged minorities to see themselves as victims and to live by alibis rather than to claim the opportunities opened for them by the potent combination of black protest and white guilt. They have filled the air with recrimination and rancor and have remarkably advanced the fragmentation of American life.

Yet I believe the campaign against the idea of common ideals and a single society will fail. Gunnar Myrdal was surely right: For all the damage it has done, the upsurge of ethnicity is a superficial enthusiasm stirred by romantic ideologues and unscrupulous hucksters whose claim to speak for their minorities is thoughtlessly accepted by the media. I doubt that the ethnic vogue expresses a reversal of direction from assimilation to apartheid among the minorities themselves. Indeed, the more the ideologues press the case for ethnic separatism, the less they appeal to the mass of their own groups. They have thus far done better in intimidating the white majority than in converting their own constituencies.

"No nation in history," writes Lawrence Fuchs, the political scientist and immigration expert in his fine book *The American Kaleidoscope*, "had proved as successful as the United States in managing ethnic diversity. No nation before had ever made diversity itself a source of national identity and unity." The second sentence explains the success described in the first, and the mechanism for translating diversity into unity has been the American Creed, the civic culture—the very assimilating, unifying culture that is today challenged, and not seldom rejected, by the ideologues of ethnicity.

A historian's guess is that the resources of the Creed have not been exhausted. Americanization has not lost its charms. Many sons and daughters of ethnic neighborhoods still want to shed their ethnicity and move to the suburbs as fast as they can where they will be received with far more tolerance than they would have been seventy years ago. The desire for achievement and success in American society remains a potent force for assimilation. Ethnic subcultures, Stephen Steinberg, author of *The Ethnic Myth*, points out, fade away "because circumstances forced them to make choices that undermined the basis for cultural survival."

Others may enjoy their ethnic neighborhoods but see no conflict between foreign descent and American loyalty. Unlike the multiculturalists, they celebrate not only what is distinctive in their own backgrounds but what they hold in common with the rest of the population ...

Our democratic principles contemplate an open society founded on tolerance of individuals with differences and on mutual respect. In practice, America has been more open to some than to others. But it is more open to all today than it was yesterday and is likely to be even more open tomorrow than today. The steady movement of American life has been from exclusion to inclusion.

Historically and culturally, this republic has an Anglo-Saxon base; but from the start the base has been modified, enriched, and reconstituted by transfusions from other continents and civilizations. The movement from exclusion to inclusion causes a constant revision in the texture of our culture. The ethnic transfusions affect all aspects of American life—our politics, our literature, our music, our painting, our movies, our cuisine, our customs, our dreams ...

The American identity will never be fixed and final; it will always be in the making. Changes in the population have always brought changes in the national ethos and will continue to do so; but not, one must hope, at the expense of national integration. The question America confronts as a pluralistic society is how to vindicate cherished cultures and traditions without breaking the bonds of cohesion—common ideals, common political institutions, common language, common culture, common fate—that hold the republic together.

Our task is to combine due appreciation of the splendid diversity of the nation with due emphasis on the great unifying Western ideas of individual freedom, political democracy, and human rights. These are the ideas that define the American nationality—and that today empower people of all continents, races, and creeds.

"What then is the American, this new man? . . . Here individuals of all nations are melted into a new race of men." Still a good answer—still the best hope.

Arthur M. Schlesinger, Jr., *The Disuniting of America: Reflections on a Multicultural Society*, New York: W. W. Norton & Company, 1991/1992.

Seymour Papert, *The Children's Machine*, 1993

Seymour Papert (1928–2016) was a mathematician and computer scientist who taught for most of his career at the Massachusetts Institute of Technology. In the course of his career, he turned most of his attention to the development of artificial intelligence and especially the ways in which computers could be used to enhance education. His 1993 book, The Children's Machine: Rethinking School in the Age of the Computer, *was perhaps his strongest defense of the role computers could play in the lives of children and their education.*

Across the world children have entered a passionate and enduring love affair with the computer. What they do with computers is as varied as their activities. The greatest amount of time is devoted to playing games, with the result that names like Nintendo have become household words. They use computers to write, to draw, to communicate, to obtain information. Some use computers as a means to establish social ties, while others use them to isolate themselves. In many cases their zeal has such force that it brings the word *addiction* to the minds of concerned parents.

The love affair involves more than the desire to do things with computers. It also has an element of possessiveness and, most importantly, of assertion of intellectual identity. Large numbers of children see the computer as "theirs"—as something that belongs to them, to their generation. Many have observed that they are more comfortable with the machines than their parents and teachers are. They learn to use them more easily and naturally. For the moment some of us old fogeys may somehow have acquired the special knowledge that makes one a master of the computer, but children know that it is just a matter of time before they inherit the machines. They are the computer generation . . .

Imagine a party of time travelers from an earlier century, among them one group of surgeons and another of school-teachers, each group eager to see how much things have changed in their profession a hundred or more years into the future. Imagine the bewilderment of the surgeons finding themselves in the operating room of a modern hospital.

Although they would know that an operation of some sort was being performed, and might even be able to guess at the target organ, they would in almost all cases be unable to figure out what the surgeon was trying to accomplish or what was the purpose of the many strange devices he and the surgical staff were employing. The rituals of antisepsis and anesthesia, the beeping electronics, and even the bright lights, all so familiar to television audiences, would be utterly unfamiliar to them.

The time-traveling teachers would respond very differently to a modern elementary school classroom. They might be puzzled by a few strange objects. They might notice that some standard techniques had changed—and would likely disagree among themselves about whether the changes they saw were for the better or the worse—but they would fully see the point of most of what was being attempted and could quite easily take over the class. I use this parable to provide a rough-and-ready measure of the unevenness of progress across the broad front of historical change. In the wake of the startling growth of science and technology in our recent past, some areas of human activity have undergone megachange. Telecommunications, entertainment, and transportation, as well as medicine, are among them. School is a notable example of an area that has not. One cannot say that there has been no change at all in the way we dish out education to our students. Of course there has; the parable gives me a way of pointing out what most of us know about our system of schooling: Yes, it has changed, but not in ways that have substantially altered its nature. The parable sets up the question: Why, through a period when so much human activity has been revolutionized, have we not seen comparable change in the way we help our children learn? . . .

The time-traveling teachers of my parable who saw nothing in the modern classroom they did not recognize would have found many surprises had they simply gone home with one or two of the students. For there they would have found that with an industriousness and eagerness that School can seldom generate, many of the students had become intensely involved in learning the rules and strategies of what appeared at first glance to be a process much more demanding than any homework assignment. The students would define the subject as video games and what they were doing as play.

While the technology itself might first catch the eye of our visitors, they would in time, being teachers, be struck by the level of intellectual effort that the children were putting into this activity and the level of learning that was taking place, a level that seemed far beyond that which had taken place just a few hours earlier in school. The most open and honest of our time-traveling teachers might well observe that never before had they seen so much being learned in such a confined space and in so short a time.

School would have parents—who honestly don't know how to interpret their children's obvious love affair with video games—believe that children love them and dislike homework because the first is easy and the second hard. In reality, the reverse is more often true. Any adult who thinks these games are easy need only sit down and try to master one. Most are hard, with complex information—as well as techniques—to be mastered, the information often much more difficult and time consuming to master than the technique.

If that argument did not convince parents that the games are not serious, surely a second argument would: Video games are toys—electronic toys, no doubt, but toys—and of course children like toys better than homework. By definition, play is entertaining, homework is not. What some parents may not realize, however, is that video games, being the first example of computer technology applied to toy making, have nonetheless been the entry way for children into the world of computers. These toys, by empowering children to test out ideas about working within prefixed rules and structures in a way few other toys are capable of doing, have proved capable of teaching students about the possibilities and drawbacks of a newly presented system in ways many adults should envy.

Video games teach children what computers are beginning to teach adults—that some forms of learning are fast-paced, immensely compelling, and rewarding. The fact that they are enormously demanding of one's time and require new ways of thinking remains a small price to pay (and is perhaps even an advantage) to be vaulted into the future. Not surprisingly, by comparison School strikes many young people as slow, boring, and frankly out of touch . . .

Seymour Papert, *The Children's Machine: Rethinking School in the Age of the Computer*, New York: Basic Books, 1993, selections from pp. vii–x, 1–16.

Neil Postman, *Technopoly*, 1993

Neil Postman (1931–2003) spent his career as a professor of Communications at New York University, as a critic of schools that were boring and did not allow students to reach their full potential, and as an iconoclast who asked hard questions of all educational practices. In 1993, as computers were becoming more common, especially in classrooms, he published Technoploy: The Surrender of Culture to Technology, *challenging the growth of computer use in schools and society—and Papert's work specifically—as he asked hard questions not only about computer use in school but the way it was changing thinking.*

[N]ew technologies compete with old ones—for time, for attention, for money, for prestige, but mostly for dominance of their world-view . . . In the United States, we can see such collisions everywhere—in politics, in religion, in commerce—but we see them most clearly in the schools . . .

In introducing the personal computer to the classroom, we shall be breaking a four-hundred-year-old truce between the gregariousness and openness fostered by orality and the introspection and isolation fostered by the printed word . . . Over four centuries, teachers, while emphasizing print, have allowed orality its place in the classroom, and have therefore achieved a kind of pedagogical peace between these two forms of learning, so that what is valuable in each can be maximized. Now comes the computer, carrying anew the banner of private learning and individual problem-solving. Will the widespread use of computers in the classroom defeat once and for all the claims of communal speech? Will the computer raise egocentrism to the status of a virtue?

Technological change is neither additive nor subtractive. It is ecological. I mean "ecological" in the same sense as the word is used by environmental scientists. One significant change generates total change. If you remove the caterpillars from a given habitat, you are not left with the same environment minus caterpillars: you have a new environment, and you have reconstituted the conditions of survival; the same is true if you add caterpillars to an environment that has had none. This is how the ecology of media works as well. A new technology does not add or subtract something. It changes everything. In the year 1500, fifty years after the printing press was invented, we did not have old Europe plus the printing press. We had a different Europe. After television, the United States was not America plus television; television gave a new coloration to every political campaign, to every home, to every school, to every church, to every industry. And that is why the competition among media is so fierce. Surrounding every technology are institutions whose organization—not to mention their reason for being—reflects the world-view promoted by the technology. Therefore, when an old technology is assaulted by a new one, institutions are threatened. When institutions are threatened, a culture finds itself in crisis. This is serious business, which is why we learn nothing when educators ask, Will students learn mathematics better by computers than by textbooks? Or when businessmen ask, Through which medium can we sell more products? Or when preachers ask, Can we reach more people through television than through radio? Or when politicians ask, How effective are messages sent through different media? Such questions have an immediate practical value to those who ask them, but they are diversionary. They direct our attention away from the serious social, intellectual, and institutional crisis that new media foster.

What we need to consider about the computer has nothing to do with its efficiency as a teaching tool. We need to know in what ways it is altering our conception of learning, and how in conjunction with television, it undermines the old idea of school. Who cares how many boxes of cereal can be sold via television? We need to know if television changes our conception of reality, the relationship of the rich to the poor, the idea of happiness itself. A preacher who confines himself to considering how a medium can increase his audience will miss the significant question: In what sense do new media alter what is meant by religion, by church, even by God? And if the politician cannot think beyond the next election, then *we* must wonder about what new media do to the idea of political organization and to the conception of citizenship.

To help us do this, we have what Harold Innis [author of *The Bias of Communication* who described "knowledge monopolies" to describe the power accumulated by those with control over any new technology], in his way, tried to. New technologies alter the structure of our interests: the things we think *about*. They alter the character of our symbols: the things we think *with*. And they alter the nature of community: the arena in which thoughts develop. For something has happened in America that is strange and dangerous, and there is only a dull and even stupid awareness of what it is—in part because it has no name. I call it Technopoly.

Neil Postman, *Technopoly: The Surrender of Culture to Technology*, New York: Vintage Books, 1993.

UNITED STATES DEPARTMENT OF EDUCATION, EXECUTIVE SUMMARY OF THE NO CHILD LEFT BEHIND ACT, 2002

After two decades of non-stop discussion of education reform, in January 2002, just before the first anniversary of his inauguration as president, George W. Bush signed the No Child Left Behind Act that had been passed by Congress the month before. Both George Bush and Al Gore had run on a promise to reform public education in the November 2000 election and as early as his first week in office, Bush had announced that a significant change in the direction of federal support for education would be part of his agenda. As a Republican president, Bush was not the only supporter of the legislation that emerged. In Congress two of the most liberal Democrats, Senator Edward M. Kennedy and Representative George Brown, led the fight for No Child Left Behind. Not even the events of September 2001 diverted the administration and Congress from the agenda. The summary of the law posted on the Department of Education website during the Bush years provides a useful overview of the major provisions of the legislation as well as the thinking behind those within the administration who sponsored it and were responsible for its implementation for its first seven years of existence.

These reforms express my deep belief in our public schools and their mission to build the mind and character of every child, from every background, in every part of America.

President George W. Bush, January 2001

Three days after taking office in January 2001 as the 43rd President of the United States, George W. Bush announced *No Child Left Behind*, his framework for bipartisan education reform that he described as "the cornerstone of my Administration." President Bush emphasized his deep belief in our public schools, but an even greater concern that "too many of our neediest children are being left behind," despite the nearly $200 billion in Federal spending since the passage of the Elementary and Secondary Education Act of 1965 (ESEA).

Figure 12.2 President George W. Bush was reading to schoolchildren in Sarasota, Florida on September 11, 2001 as part of his campaign to build support for the No Child Left Behind legislation when he was informed that planes had hit the World Trade Center in New York. Photo by Eric Draper, courtesy of the George W. Bush Presidential Library.

The President called for bipartisan solutions based on accountability, choice, and flexibility in Federal education programs.

Less than a year later, despite the unprecedented challenges of engineering an economic recovery while leading the Nation in the war on terrorism following the events of September 11, President Bush secured passage of the landmark *No Child Left Behind Act of 2001* (NCLB Act). The new law reflects a remarkable consensus-first articulated in the President's *No Child Left Behind* framework—on how to improve the performance of America's elementary and secondary schools while at the same time ensuring that no child is trapped in a failing school.

The NCLB Act, which reauthorizes the ESEA, incorporates the principles and strategies proposed by President Bush. These include increased accountability for States, school districts, and schools; greater choice for parents and students, particularly those attending low-performing schools; more flexibility for States and local educational agencies (LEAs) in the use of Federal education dollars; and a stronger emphasis on reading, especially for our youngest children.

Increased Accountability

The NCLB Act will strengthen Title I accountability by requiring States to implement statewide accountability systems covering all public schools and students. These systems must be based on challenging State standards in reading and mathematics, annual testing for all students in grades 3–8, and annual statewide progress objectives ensuring that all groups of students reach proficiency within 12 years. Assessment results and State progress objectives must be broken out by poverty, race, ethnicity, disability, and limited English proficiency to ensure that no group is left behind. School districts and schools that fail to make adequate yearly progress (AYP) toward statewide proficiency goals will, over time, be subject to improvement, corrective action, and restructuring measures aimed at getting them back on course to meet State standards. Schools that meet or exceed AYP objectives or close achievement gaps will be eligible for State Academic Achievement Awards.

More Choices for Parents and Students

The NCLB Act significantly increases the choices available to the parents of students attending Title I schools that fail to meet State standards, including immediate relief—beginning with the 2002–03 school year—for students in schools that were previously identified for improvement or corrective action under the 1994 ESEA reauthorization.

LEAs must give students attending schools identified for improvement, corrective action, or restructuring the opportunity to attend a better public school, which may include a public charter school, within the school district. The district must provide transportation to the new school, and must use at least 5 percent of its Title I funds for this purpose, if needed.

For students attending persistently failing schools (those that have failed to meet State standards for at least 3 of the 4 preceding years), LEAs must permit low-income students to use Title I funds to obtain supplemental educational services from the public- or private-sector provider selected by the students and their parents. Providers must meet State standards and offer services tailored to help participating students meet challenging State academic standards.

To help ensure that LEAs offer meaningful choices, the new law requires school districts to spend up to 20 percent of their Title I allocations to provide school choice and supplemental educational services to eligible students.

In addition to helping ensure that no child loses the opportunity for a quality education because he or she is trapped in a failing school, the choice and supplemental service requirements provide a substantial incentive for low-performing schools to improve. Schools that want to avoid losing students—along with the portion of their annual budgets typically associated with those students—will have to improve or, if they fail to make AYP for 5 years, run the risk of reconstitution under a restructuring plan.

Greater Flexibility for States, School Districts, and Schools

One important goal of *No Child Left Behind* was to breathe new life into the "flexibility for accountability" bargain with States first struck by President George H.W. Bush during his historic 1989 education summit with the Nation's Governors at Charlottesville, Virginia. Prior flexibility efforts have focused on the waiver of program requirements; the NCLB Act moves beyond this limited approach to give States and school districts unprecedented flexibility in the use of Federal education funds in exchange for strong accountability for results.

New flexibility provisions in the NCLB Act include authority for States and LEAs to transfer up to 50 percent of the funding they receive under 4 major State grant programs to any one of the programs, or to Title I. The covered programs include Teacher Quality State Grants, Educational Technology, Innovative Programs, and Safe and Drug-Free Schools.

The new law also includes a competitive State Flexibility Demonstration Program that permits up to 7 States to consolidate the State share of nearly all Federal State grant programs—including Title I, Part A Grants to Local Educational Agencies—while providing additional flexibility in their use of Title V Innovation funds. Participating States must enter into 5-year performance agreements with the Secretary covering the use of the consolidated funds, which may be used for any educational purpose authorized under the ESEA. As part of their plans, States also must enter into up to 10 local performance agreements with LEAs, which will enjoy the same level of flexibility granted under the separate Local Flexibility Demonstration Program.

The new competitive Local Flexibility Demonstration Program would allow up to 80 LEAs, in addition to the 70 LEAs under the State Flexibility Demonstration Program, to consolidate funds received under Teacher Quality State Grants, Educational Technology State Grants, Innovative Programs, and Safe and Drug-Free Schools programs. Participating LEAs would enter into performance agreements with the Secretary of Education, and would be able to use the consolidated funds for any ESEA-authorized purpose.

Putting Reading First

No Child Left Behind stated President Bush's unequivocal commitment to ensuring that every child can read by the end of third grade. To accomplish this goal, the new Reading First initiative would significantly increase the Federal investment in scientifically based reading instruction programs in the early grades. One major benefit of this approach would be reduced identification of children for special education services due to a lack of appropriate reading instruction in their early years.

The NCLB Act fully implements the President's Reading First initiative. The new Reading First State Grant program will make 6-year grants to States, which will make competitive subgrants to local communities. Local recipients will administer screening and diagnostic assessments to determine which students in grades K-3 are at risk of reading failure, and provide professional development for K-3 teachers in the essential components of reading instruction.

The new Early Reading First program will make competitive 6-year awards to LEAs to support early language, literacy, and pre-reading development of preschool-age children, particularly those from low-income families. Recipients will use instructional strategies and professional development drawn from scientifically based reading research to help young children to attain the fundamental knowledge and skills they will need for optimal reading development in kindergarten and beyond . . .

www.ed.gov/nclb/overview/intro/execsumm.html. Released February 10, 2004, recovered December 30, 2008.

DIFFERENT SCHOOLS OF THOUGHT REGARDING THE NO CHILD LEFT BEHIND ACT (NCLB), 2003–2004

NCLB generated extraordinary controversy in the years after the law was adopted. Some believed the law did too little, that the accountability standards were too low, and that there are too many loopholes. Others saw it as an inappropriate federal intrusion into local matters. Many liberals found several aspects of the legislation to be objectionable, especially the closing of schools that failed to meet AYP—an ever-expanding demand—and the testing that NCLB demands of schools.

Debates about NCLB were never simple, and not likely to be resolved anytime soon. While NCLB was supposed to be up for reauthorization in 2008, Congress after Congress could not agree on a replacement. Only in 2015, with the passage of the bipartisan Every Student Succeeds Act, were some aspects of NCLB modified while others were retained.

Supporters and opponents of the legislation cannot easily be divided into two camps. Educational liberals disagreed with each other about many aspects of NCLB. Alfie Kohn saw the law as, from the start, a calculated attack on all aspects of public education as we have known it in the United States, and opposed virtually every aspect of the legislation. Kohn saw little hope in rescuing any aspect of NCLB and urged educators to do everything possible to ensure the repeal of the Act. Linda Darling-Hammond described NCLB as basically a set of good intentions gone awry. Whereas both authors were highly critical of the ways in which the testing aspects of NCLB could narrow the curriculum and, in their views, force teachers to "teach to the test," Darling-Hammond believed there was significant opportunity to reform the law and, if such reforms were linked to adequate funding, NCLB could make a positive contribution to American education.

Among authors traditionally viewed as educational conservatives, Frederick M. Hess and Chester E. Finn, Jr. were upbeat in their description of NCLB. However, they viewed the law as only a small first step in implementing a much larger accountability movement in the future. Terry M. Moe, more conservative than Hess and Finn, had grave doubts about NCLB.

Moe, a champion of charter schools and educational vouchers, doubted that any government intervention could by itself undercut the deeply established traditions in contemporary school structures. For him, only a much higher level of decentralization linked to more powerful parental choice will bring about effective changes.

Alfie Kohn, "NCLB and the Effort to Privatize Public Education," chapter five in Deborah Meier and George Wood, eds., *Many Children Left Behind: How the No Child Left Behind Act is Damaging Our Children and Our Schools*, Boston, MA: Beacon Press, 2004, pp. 79–81.

Linda Darling-Hammond, "From 'Separate but Equal' to 'No Child Left Behind': The Collision of New Standards and Old Inequities," chapter one in Deborah Meier and George Wood, eds., *Many Children Left Behind: How the No Child Left Behind Act is Damaging Our Children and Our Schools*, Boston, MA: Beacon Press, 2004, pp. 3–4, 6, 9–13, 15–16, 18–21.

Frederick M. Hess and Chester E. Finn, Jr., "Introduction," *Leaving No Child Behind? Options for Kids in Failing Schools*, New York: Palgrave Macmillan, 2004, pp. 1–6.

Terry M. Moe, "Politics, Control, and the Future of School Accountability," chapter four in Paul E. Peterson and Martin R. West, eds., *No Child Left Behind? The Politics and Practice of School Accountability*, Washington, DC: Brookings Institution Press, 2003, pp. 80–86, 91, 99–102.

Table 12.1 Different schools of thought regarding the No Child Left Behind Act (NCLB), 2003–2004

Alfie Kohn, "NCLB and the Effort to Privatize Public Education," 2004	Linda Darling-Hammond, "The Collision of New Standards and Old Inequalities," 2004	Frederick M. Hess and Chester E. Finn, "Leaving No Child Behind?", 2004	Terry M. Moe, "Politics, Control, and the Future of School Accountability," 2003
NCLB usurps the power of local communities to choose their own policies and programs. It represents a power grab on the part of the federal government that is unprecedented in the history of U.S. education. It compromises the quality of teaching by forcing teachers to worry more about raising test scores than about promoting meaningful learning. It punishes those who most need help and sets back efforts to close the gap between rich and poor, and between black and white . . . But to fully assess the impact of this law, we need to understand it in context. Some of NCLB's most energetic supporters are people and organizations opposed to the whole idea of public schooling—and, indeed, to public institutions in general. Their idea of "reform" turns out to entail some sort of privatization.	The broad goal of NCLB is to raise the achievement levels of all students, especially underperforming groups, and to close the achievement gap that parallels race and class distinctions . . . While these are troubling aspects of the law's implementation, one could also argue, quite legitimately, that many of the schools identified as "needing improvement" (a designation that changes to "failing" if not corrected after three years) indeed are dismal places where little learning occurs, or are complacent schools . . . However, its complex regulations for showing "Adequate Yearly Progress" toward test score targets aimed at "100% proficiency" within ten years have created a bizarre situation in which most of the nation's public schools will be deemed failing within the next few years.	For the first time, the federal government required that academic performance lead to concrete consequences for schools—and that children in inadequate schools have the opportunity to seek assistance or move elsewhere . . . Nobody should be surprised that such ambitious and untested provisions in a sweeping federal law would run into all manner of diverse local realities, some of which mesh nicely with them but others of which tend to frustrate them; or that it will take fine-tuning and revision to get them working right. There are many moving parts here, and much that can go wrong. The legislation rests upon a tangled set of expectations regarding the behavior of families, schools, districts, private providers, and states. How these elements actually mesh is crucial to the fate of this effort.	The authorities are up against a control problem of formidable proportions. They do not know how to produce student achievement nor do they necessarily know student achievement when they see it . . . The movement for school accountability is essentially a movement for more effective top-down control of schools . . . When all is said and done, then the top-down approach to accountability—taken alone—is destined to be a disappointment. The good news, however, is that this is not the only approach to accountability available to us, and it need not be adopted all by itself. Schools can also be held accountable from below through well-designed systems of school choice. And there is much good reason to think that the combination of the two approaches might be much more effective.

Curriculum, Technology, and New Tensions, 2005–2018

- Introduction
- Common Core State Standards Initiative, FAQ, 2018
- Joseph P. McDonald, James W. Fraser, and Susan B. Neuman, *Where Are the Common Core State Standards Headed? Oblivion, Probably*, 2016
- Arthur Levine, "Digital Students, Industrial-Era Universities," 2010
- Benjamin Harold, "Technology in Education: An Overview," *Education Week*, February 5, 2016
- Emma Gonzalez, Address at Gun Control Rally, 2018
- President Donald Trump, Governor Jay Inslee (D-Washington), and Governor Greg Abbott (R-Texas) on Guns in Schools, 2018

- Secretary of Education Betsy DeVos, Remarks to Turning Point USA High School Leadership Summit, July 25, 2018
- AFT Resolution, "Defeating the DeVos Agenda," 2018
- Josh Eidelson and Sarah Jaffe, "Defending Public Education: An Interview with Karen Lewis of the Chicago Teachers Union," *Dissent*, Summer 2013
- Frederick M. Hess, "The Facts Behind the Teacher Strikes," *Forbes*, April 30, 2018
- Randi Weingarten, "Hope in Darkness," 2018
- Johann N. Neem, "Schools Have a Nobler Purpose Than Just Career Prep," 2018

Introduction

In the first decades of the twenty-first century, a number of contentious issues dominated the discussion in education. The long-simmering debate about educational standards—an issue from *A Nation at Risk* in the 1980s to No Child Left Behind in 2002—morphed into a quest for a common core for the curriculum across the country. The result, the Common Core State Standards, was officially released on June 2, 2010, at Peachtree Ridge High School in Suwanee, GA. The location was chosen to symbolize distance from Washington, DC. So were the first presenters of the standards: two sitting governors (a Republican and a Democrat) and two chief state school officers—all from different regions of the country. As former North Carolina Governor James B. Hunt told it, the CCSS originated in a commitment among a significant number of governors and state school heads to the following goals:

(1) to promote educational equity in the face of a well-documented achievement gap by race and income; (2) to promote American competitiveness in a globalizing economy; and (3) to preserve state control of American education while advancing a more integrated and less fragmented American curriculum (by ensuring that the various states built and adopted the standards, not the federal government). As the two documents that follow show, some of the high hopes for CCSS have not materialized, but others have.

Technology, its use and its pluses and minuses, has also continued to dominate educational discussions and especially education budgets. A relatively new issue—school shootings—also burst on the scene in the new century. While the shooting at Columbine High School in Colorado in 1999 in which twelve students and a teacher were killed and that at an elementary school in Newtown, Connecticut in 2012 in which twenty students and six teachers were killed horrified the nation, the reality is that a school shooting happens every few days in the United States. But the violence at a high school in Parkland, Florida in February 2018 in which seventeen were killed changed the conversation; most of all because of the activism of the students who demanded change in every forum which they could reach and the nation seemed, for a time, to listen in a new way. Again, action was not as easy and the debates about which action was best—from banning assault rifles to arming teachers—continued.

Other issues continued, though in new forms. The effort to divert state and federal funds from district-based public schools to charter schools picked up steam with the appointment of charter advocate Betsy DeVos as U.S. Secretary of Education in 2017, but also generated new opposition from public school advocates, especially those in teacher unions. And unions also became increasingly active as teachers in a number of states went on strike in the 2017–2018 school year demanding better salaries and more funding for their work.

Finally, the unresolved issue of the ultimate purpose of schooling—preparation for college and work, or building a more vibrant and inclusive democracy, or something else—is discussed in the final document of the chapter by Johann Neem.

Common Core State Standards Initiative, Frequently Asked Questions, 2018

Released in 2010, the Common Core State Standards (CCSS) were a decade in the making and have been another decade in a checkered path to implementation. An organization dedicated to the success of the CCSS offers a website with answers—from their perspective—to many of the frequently asked questions about the standards.

The following provides answers to some of the frequently asked questions about the Common Core State Standards, from how they were developed to what they mean for states and local communities.

Overview

What Are Educational Standards?

Educational standards are the learning goals for what students should know and be able to do at each grade level. Educational standards help teachers ensure their students have the skills and knowledge they need to be successful, while also helping parents understand what is expected of their children.

What Is the Common Core?

State education chiefs and governors in 48 states came together to develop the Common Core, a set of clear college- and career-ready standards for kindergarten through 12th grade in English language arts/literacy and mathematics. Today, 43 states have voluntarily adopted and are working to implement the standards, which are designed to ensure that students graduating from high school are prepared to take credit bearing introductory courses in two- or four-year college programs or enter the workforce.

Who Led the Development of the Common Core State Standards?

The nation's governors and education commissioners, through their representative organizations, the National Governors Association Center for Best Practices (NGA) and the Council of Chief State School Officers (CCSSO), led the development of the Common Core State Standards and continue to lead the initiative. Teachers, parents, school administrators, and experts from across the country, together with state leaders, provided input into the development of the standards.

The actual implementation of the Common Core, including how the standards are taught, the curriculum developed, and the materials used to support teachers as they help students reach the standards, is led entirely at the state and local levels.

Were Teachers Involved in the Creation of the Standards?

Yes, teachers have been a critical voice in the development of the standards. The Common Core drafting process relied on teachers and standards experts from across the country. The National Education Association (NEA), American Federation of Teachers (AFT), National Council of Teachers of Mathematics (NCTM), and National Council of Teachers of English (NCTE), among other organizations, were instrumental in bringing together teachers to provide specific, constructive feedback on the standards.

Why Are the Common Core State Standards Important?

High standards that are consistent across states provide teachers, parents, and students with a set of clear expectations to ensure that all students have the skills and knowledge necessary to succeed in college, career, and life upon graduation from high school, regardless of where they live. These standards are aligned to the expectations of colleges, workforce training programs, and employers. The standards promote equity by ensuring all students are well prepared to collaborate and compete with their peers in the United States and abroad. Unlike previous state standards, which varied widely from state to state, the Common Core enables collaboration among states on a range of tools and policies, including the:

- Development of textbooks, digital media, and other teaching materials
- Development and implementation of common comprehensive assessment systems that replace existing state testing systems in order to measure student performance annually and provide teachers with specific feedback to help ensure students are on the path to success
- Development of tools and other supports to help educators and schools ensure all students are able to learn the new standards.

Who Was Involved in the Development of the Common Core State Standards?

States across the country collaborated with teachers, researchers, and leading experts to design and develop the Common Core State Standards. Each state independently made the decision to adopt the Common Core. Local teachers, principals, and superintendents lead the implementation of the Common Core in their states. The federal government was not involved in the development of the standards.

What Guidance Do the Common Core State Standards Provide to Teachers?

The Common Core State Standards are a clear set of shared goals and expectations for the knowledge and skills students need in English language arts and mathematics at each grade level so they can be prepared to succeed in college, career, and life. The standards establish what students need to learn, but they do not dictate how teachers should teach. Teachers will devise their own lesson plans and curriculum, and tailor their instruction to the individual needs of the students in their classrooms.

How Do the Common Core State Standards Compare to Previous State Education Standards?

The Common Core was developed by building on the best state standards in the United States; examining the expectations of other high-performing countries around the world; and carefully studying the research and literature available on what students need to know and be able to do to be successful in college, career, and life. No state was asked to lower their expectations for students in adopting the Common Core. The evidence-based standards were developed in consultation with teachers and parents from across the country, so they are also realistic and practical for the classroom.

How Much Will It Cost States to Implement the Common Core State Standards?

Costs for implementing the standards will vary from state to state and territory. While states already spend significant amounts of money on professional development, curriculum materials, and assessments, there will be some additional costs associated with the Common Core, such as training teachers to teach the standards, developing and purchasing new materials, and other aspects of implementation. However, there are also opportunities for states to save considerable resources by using technology, open-source materials, and taking advantage of cross-state opportunities that come from sharing consistent standards . . .

What Role Did International Benchmarking Play in the Development of the Standards?

International benchmarking refers to analyzing high-performing education systems and identifying ways to improve our own system based on those findings. One of the ways to analyze education systems is to compare international assessments, particularly the Programme for International Student Assessment (PISA) and Trends in International Mathematics and Science Study (TIMSS). Prior to the development of the Common Core State Standards, research revealed striking similarities among the standards in top-performing nations, along with stark differences between those world-class expectations and the standards adopted by most U.S. states. As a result, standards from top-performing countries were consulted during the development of the Common Core State Standards. The college- and career-ready standards appendix lists the evidence consulted.

What Grade Levels Are Included in the Common Core State Standards?

The English language arts and math standards are for grades K-12. Research from the early childhood and higher education communities also informed the development of the standards.

What Does This Work Mean for Students with Disabilities and English Language Learners?

The Common Core State Standards give states the opportunity to share experiences and best practices, which can lead to an improved ability to serve young people with disabilities and English language learners. Additionally, the standards include information on application for these groups of students.

Why Are the Common Core State Standards Only for English Language Arts and Math?

English language arts and math were the subjects chosen for the Common Core State Standards because they are areas upon which students build skill sets that are used in other subjects. Students must learn to read, write, speak, listen, and use language effectively in a variety of content areas, so the standards specify the literacy skills and understandings required for college and career readiness in multiple disciplines.

It is important to note that the literacy standards in history/social studies, science, and technical subjects for grades 6–12 are meant to supplement content standards in those areas, not replace them. States determine how to incorporate these standards into their standards for those subjects or adopt them as content area literacy standards . . .

Implementation and Future Work

What Do the Common Core State Standards Mean for Students?

Today's students are preparing to enter a world in which colleges and businesses are demanding more than ever before. To ensure all students are prepared for success after graduation, the Common Core establishes a set of clear, consistent guidelines for what students should know and be able to do at each grade level in math and English language arts.

How Do the Common Core State Standards Impact Teachers?

The standards impact teachers by:

- Providing them with consistent goals and benchmarks to ensure students are progressing on a path for success in college, career, and life
- Providing them with consistent expectations for students who move into their districts and classrooms from other states
- Providing them the opportunity to collaborate with teachers across the country as they develop curricula, materials, and assessments linked to high-quality standards
- Helping colleges and professional development programs better prepare teachers

What Supports Are Being Provided to Teachers to Help Them Ensure Students Are Prepared to Reach the New Goals Established by the Common Core?

Decisions on how to implement the standards, including the right supports to put in place, are made at the state and local levels. As such, states and localities are taking different approaches to implementing the standards and providing their teachers with the supports they need to help students successfully reach the standards. To learn how states are supporting teachers and implementing their new standards, visit the "Standards in Your State" section for a map linking to the state-specific implementation page.

Do the Standards Tell Teachers What to Teach?

Teachers know best about what works in the classroom. That is why these standards establish what students need to learn, but do not dictate how teachers should teach. Instead, schools and teachers decide how best to help students reach the standards.

Who Will Manage the Common Core State Standards in the Future?

The Common Core State Standards are and will remain a state-led effort, and adoption of the standards and any potential revisions will continue to be a voluntary state decision. The National Governors Association Center for Best Practices and the Council of Chief State School Officers will continue to serve as the two leading organizations with ownership of the Common Core and will make decisions about the timing and substance of future revisions to the standards in consultation with the states.

Federal funds have never and will never be used to support the development or governance of the Common Core or any future revisions of the standards. Any future revisions will be made based on research and evidence. Governance of the standards will be independent of governance of related assessments.

Will Common Assessments Be Developed?

Two state-led consortia, Partnership for Assessment of Readiness for College and Careers (PARCC) and the Smarter Balanced Assessment Consortium (Smarter Balanced), are currently working to develop assessments that aim to provide meaningful feedback to ensure that students are progressing toward attaining the necessary skills to succeed in college, career, and life. These assessments are expected to be available in the 2014–2015 school year. Most states have chosen to participate in one of the two consortia. For more information, visit the website of your state's assessment consortium.

Two additional consortia, working through the National Center and State Collaborative Partnership and the Dynamic Learning Maps Alternative Assessment System Consortium, are developing a new generation of assessments for students with the most significant cognitive disabilities.

Will CCSSO and the NGA Center Be Creating Common Instructional Materials and Curricula?

No. The standards are not curricula and do not mandate the use of any particular curriculum. Teachers are able to develop their own lesson plans and choose materials, as they have always done. States that have adopted the standards may choose to work together to develop instructional materials and curricula. As states work individually to implement their new standards, publishers of instructional materials and experienced educators will develop new resources around these shared standards.

Are There Data Collection Requirements Associated with the Common Core State Standards?

No. Implementing the Common Core State Standards does not require data collection. Standards define expectations for what students should know and be able to do by the end of each grade. The means of assessing students and the data that result from those assessments are up to the discretion of each state and are separate and unique from the Common Core.

Content and Quality of the Standards

Do the Common Core State Standards Incorporate Both Content and Skills?

Yes. In English language arts, the standards require certain critical content for all students, including:

- Classic myths and stories from around the world
- America's founding documents
- Foundational American literature
- Shakespeare

The remaining crucial decisions about what content should be taught are made at the state and local levels. In addition to content coverage, the Common Core State Standards require that students systematically acquire knowledge in literature and other disciplines through reading, writing, speaking, and listening.

In mathematics, the standards lay a solid foundation in:

- Whole numbers
- Addition
- Subtraction
- Multiplication
- Division
- Fractions
- Decimals.

Taken together, these elements support a student's ability to learn and apply more demanding math concepts and procedures. The middle school and high school standards call on students to practice applying mathematical ways of thinking to real-world issues and challenges.

Across the English language arts and mathematics standards, skills critical to each content area are emphasized. In particular, problem-solving, collaboration, communication, and critical-thinking skills are interwoven into the standards . . .

JOSEPH P. MCDONALD, JAMES W. FRASER, AND SUSAN B. NEUMAN, *WHERE ARE THE COMMON CORE STATE STANDARDS HEADED? OBLIVION, PROBABLY*, 2016

In September 2016, New York University held a forum on education at which McDonald, Fraser, and Neuman presented a paper on the state of the Common Core State Standards, a selection of which follows. In writing the paper about the state of the common core the authors came to two seemingly opposite conclusions. If one looks at the CCSS goal of a common curriculum core across the many different United States, the common core is a failure in spite of the best hopes of its advocates including the FAQ authors. Different states have clearly gone their own way and there is no guarantee that a fourth-grade class in New York, Oklahoma, or Idaho will study the same general area or that a student moving from one state to another will pick up where they left off. On the other hand, as these authors note, at a less public level—at the level of what teachers are thinking and the way curriculum is developing—CCSS are a great success. More and more of the now different state standards point in the same general direction and reflect similar concerns; and probably will for the coming decades. The CCSS effort, the authors conclude, is truly a failure and a success.

The Common Core State Standards (CCSS) initiative has aimed to create and install a set of student learning standards and assessments across the United States. The purpose is to redress shortcomings of state-based systems with respect to student achievement and equity. Originally supported by nearly all states, the initiative today is in trouble nearly everywhere, though with variation across states. This paper looks at the trouble in New York, where the velocity and turbulence in CCSS implementation resulted in substantial public push-back, but where CCSS resilience is also evident. The New York Common Core story affords a good opportunity, we think, to examine a phenomenon not uncommon in U.S. policymaking, whereby innovation under political pressure moves underground. *Oblivion* as we use the word here need not involve abandonment. It can mean, instead, a state of being *still* present but also overlooked . . .

Common Core Today

The online policy journal, *Education Next*, began tracking support for and opposition to the Common Core State Standards in 2012. In that pinnacle year of support, 63 percent of the general public expressed support, and only 7 percent outright opposition. Teachers participating in the poll then were even more supportive (at 72 percent)—though, ominously, showed more outright opposition too (16 percent); and Democrats and Republicans then were virtually indistinguishable in their views. However, the next two years of *EdNext* polling found declining support, as well as inclining political divergence. And the latest *EdNext* poll (2015) puts public support for CCSS at only 49 percent, with 35 percent voicing outright opposition; and it puts teacher support at only 40 percent (with 50 percent opposed). Moreover, in this latest poll, Republicans and Democrats diverge dramatically in their views—with Republicans 50 percent in opposition, compared to Democrats at 25 percent.

The latest (2015) PDK/Gallup Poll of attitudes on public schooling reports even higher CCSS opposition among public school parents (54 percent opposed overall)—though with significant racial differences. White parents were more likely than Black or Hispanic ones to express opposition. This is a finding that seems to track the history mentioned above of association between equity on the one hand, and standards and testing on the other; and it may also track the difference between suburban parent satisfaction with schooling and urban parent dissatisfaction. Usefully, the 2015 PDK/Gallup poll also asked parents how much they feel they know about CCSS, and how they learned what they know. Some 30 percent of parents reported knowing a great deal, and another 42 percent a fair amount. Their reported sources of knowledge especially include teachers or other educational professionals, and school communication (for example, a newsletter). Together these sources account for 46 percent of the variance in reported sources. Clearly, many parents rely on educators when it comes to judging educational policy. Thus rising opposition to CCSS among teachers has had a multiplying impact.

What else may underlie the fast-rising opposition to and politicization of the Common Core State Standards? One factor, we think, is that the new reformers could do no better than the 1990s reformers in pulling off the trick of creating nonfederal national standards—even with a cross-generational team alert to past mistakes. In this case, the heavy-handed support of the Obama administration did not help. But even if the CCSS effort had never benefited from Race to the Top, the recovery funding of new assessment consortia, and NCLB waivers, it would likely have become on its own a Republican target in the 2016 election cycle, given the intensity of general political polarization. And funding by the Bill and Melinda Gates Foundation would hardly have escaped critical notice. Indeed, all the devices that the CCSS initiative used to portray itself as just a conversation among states seem in retrospect to have produced a very thin disguise.

That said, the changes suggested by the polling above seem to us to have much more to do with exhaustion with standardized testing among parents, students, and teachers, than they do with the Common Core Standards themselves, and in particular with concern about participation in the national testing consortia. This seems borne out by the still relatively stable set of state *standards* adopters, versus the dwindling set of state *testing consortia* adopters. As of July 2016, 38 states were still officially committed to the CCSS (albeit with some related legislation pending in some), whereas the current count on states still committed to the assessment consortia is down to 20 from the original 45, with only 15 states using the assessments K-12. PARCC is particularly hard hit, with only six states and the District of Columbia still involved. Meanwhile, with respect to the standards, the experience of the states that have formally withdrawn suggest that withdrawal may not be as dramatic as it sounds. Mike Cohen of Achieve, an old standards enthusiast, has suggested that the new Indiana standards look a lot like the Indiana Common Core Standards. And this is the case in South Carolina, too. Even in Oklahoma, where the legislature forbade the state school board from taking the CCSS into account in constructing new standards, what the board approved this year seems to us hardly the primitive throwback that some press reports have suggested. And one of the most recent states to withdraw—Louisiana—after adopting a very Common Core-like new set of standards, went on to create a very EngageNY-like set of free, online curriculum materials to help teachers meet the standards.

Even the current dust-up in New York policymaking seems clearly more about testing than about the Common Core, again despite press reports. It derives from the enormous success of the opt-out movement in both the spring 2015 and spring 2016 testing seasons, and blowback from the teachers' unions on Governor Andrew Cuomo's call for ratcheting up the role of student test data in teacher evaluations from 20 percent to 50 percent. In September 2015, Cuomo dealt with the growing opposition in classical political fashion by convening a task force that he charged with making recommendations "to overhaul the Common Core system—to do a total reboot." But reporting back three months later, the task force made very few suggestions for revision, and explicitly called for maintaining the CCSS "instructional shifts"—for example, the emphasis in English language arts classes on text discussions, and on balancing informational and literary texts, and in mathematics on narrowing and deepening the curriculum, and on building mathematical fluency. In fact, the task force aligns with the governor's and his staff's repeated criticism not of the standards themselves, but of their hasty and "mismanaged" rollout by the State Education Department under the leadership of former Chancellor Merryl Tisch, and former Commissioner (later U.S. Secretary of Education) John King . . .

Common Core Overall: More Dead or Alive?

From the perspective of those who hoped that the Common Core standards might herald a transformation in American education—from fragmentation to consistency in aspiration, expectation, and achievement—the vital signs are fading. As one of us recently put it at a public panel on the Common Core State Standards at New York University, the whole point of the CCSS initiative was, after all, to form the *common core* of accountability across all states, and use them in a common pursuit of educational equity and of an American schooling system more attuned than the current one to the demands of the 21st-century economy. From this perspective, the fact that multiple states are in the process of doing what Oklahoma has done—repudiating the standards—or of doing what Indiana, Florida,

Ohio, New Jersey, Louisiana, and other states have done (and now New York, too)—lowering the profile of the standards—seems a bad sign. Moreover, the politicization of the CCSS, the fact that the Republican National Committee has passed a resolution condemning them, and that more than half of the states originally committed to the testing consortia have now ditched them (including New York), seem mortal signs. And the goal of standards explicitly held in common across the United States, guiding a student's learning (and the measurement of it) whether the student lives in California or Oklahoma, or has recently moved to New York from New Hampshire, or goes to a district, charter, or online school—seems imperiled. Of course, in hindsight, one can ask whether such a goal was ever really achievable *by means of the CCSS initiative*. This brings us back to this word in the title of our paper, *oblivion*.

It is possible that the theory of action underlying the CCSS, and the long stretch of American educational policymaking we identified above, may have exhausted itself, and may seem suddenly to many Americans a bad fit for circumstances they perceive in their own families and schools. By *theory of action*, we mean the logic model underlying the policymaking. This logic model presumes a set of joints (or connections), beginning with an articulation of what students at different levels of schooling should know and be able to do, and ending with what *A Nation at Risk* called equity and excellence. In between, there are joints between standards and teaching materials, between teaching materials and teaching, between teaching and learning, between learning and testing, and between test data and re-learning as needed. For a long time, this pattern of joints has seemed to many—who perhaps should have known better—as a straight-forward action path rather than a useful heuristic to guide capacity-building. When policymaking grows *really* ambitious, David Cohen and Susan Moffit warn, it can outstrip the capacity of practitioners to implement it, and, we would add, the capacity of parents to comprehend and support it. At such moments, a theory of action can burst a joint, even several joints.

On the other hand, astute champions of long-term goals like educational equity and economic relevance in schooling know how to construct new theories of action to replace spent ones. Chris Argyris and Donald Schon have a name for this. They call it double-loop learning—or learning that causes one to re-think original premises. Double-loop learning begins in a confrontation with obstacles, and ends in imaginative re-routings—sometimes under the cover of oblivion.

This may perhaps be the way forward for CCSS energy, and it is the answer we give to the question that begins this paper's title. Where are the Common Core Standards headed? To a state of being that calls less attention to itself politically, but continues to function as a heuristic for educators, policymakers, and curriculum developers *nationally*.

We end the paper with three brief, illustrative examples of imaginative re-routing—under the cover of oblivion, under pressure from political push-back, in response to the realization that the Common Core State Standards Initiative in a number of places (especially New York) pushed too hard and too fast. What these re-routings have in common is what one of us has called *connections*—or deliberate efforts to build on, rather than avoid, the shards of broken policy effort; to emphasize continuity over discontinuity.

New York University, Steinhardt School of Culture, Education, and Human Development, Education Solutions Initiative, September 2016.

ARTHUR LEVINE, "DIGITAL STUDENTS, INDUSTRIAL-ERA UNIVERSITIES," 2010

While he wrote primarily about the development of technology in American colleges and universities, Arthur Levine—president of the Woodrow Wilson National Fellowship Foundation—could just as well have been writing about K-12 schooling. Technology is in the process of transforming the very structure of schools—the ways students learn and the way schools are organized—and the future is yet to be known but, as Levine says here, it will most certainly be different from the present.

The American university, like the nation's other major social institutions—government, banks, the media, health care—was created for an industrial society. Buffeted by dramatic changes in demography, the economy, technology, and globalization, all these institutions function less well than they once did. In today's international information economy, they appear to be broken and must be refitted for a world transformed.

At the university, the clash between old and new is manifest in profound differences between institutions of higher education and the students they enroll. Today's traditional students, aged 18 to 25, are digital natives. They grew up in a world of computers, Internet, cell phone, MP3 players, and social networking.

They differ from their colleges on matters as fundamental as how they conceive of and utilize physical plant and time. For the most part, universities operate in fixed locales, campuses, and on fixed calendars, semesters and quarters with classes typically set for 50 minutes, three times per week. In contrast, digital natives live in an anytime/anyplace world, operating 24 hours a day, seven days a week, unbounded by physical location.

There is also a mismatch between institutions of higher education and digital natives on the goals and dynamics of education. Universities focus on teaching, the *process* of education, exposing students to instruction for specific periods of time; digital natives are more concerned with the *outcomes* of education—learning and the mastery of content, achieved in the manner of games.

Higher education and digital natives also favor different methods of instruction. Universities have historically emphasized passive means of instruction—lectures and books—while digital natives tend to be more active learners, preferring interactive, hands-on methods of learning such as case studies, field study and simulations. The institution gives preference to the most traditional medium, print, while the students favor new media—the Internet and its associated applications.

This is mirrored in a split between professors and students, who approach knowledge in very different ways. Faculty might be described as hunters who search for and generate knowledge to answer questions. Digital natives by contrast are gatherers, who wade through a sea of data available to them online to find the answers to their questions. Faculty are rooted in the disciplines and depth of knowledge, while students think in increasingly interdisciplinary or a-disciplinary ways, with a focus on breadth . . . Today's digital natives are oriented more toward group learning and social networking, characterized by collaboration and sharing of content. This approach is causing an ethical challenge for universities, which under certain circumstances view collaboration as cheating and content sharing as plagiarism.

These are substantial gaps, complicated by the disparities in the way colleges and digital learners see their roles in education. Higher education is provider-driven in belief and practice. That is, the university, through its faculty, determines the curriculum, the content, the instructional methods, the study materials, and the class schedule. Digital natives tend to be consumer-driven, preferring to choose, if not the curriculum and content they wish to study, then the instructional method by which they learn best, the materials they use to learn, and the schedule by which they choose to study . . .

What must change, however, is the means by which we educate the digital natives who are and will be sitting in our classrooms—employing calendars, locations, pedagogies, and learning materials consistent with ways our students learn most effectively. It means that the curriculum must meet our students where they are, not where we hope they might be or where we are. All education is essentially remedial, teaching students what they do not know. This, for example, is a generation that is stronger in gathering than hunting skills. So let the curriculum begin with breadth and move to depth.

It doesn't make sense anymore to tie education to a common process; a uniform amount of seat time exposed to teaching and a fixed clock is outdated. We all learn at different rates. Each of us even learns different subject matters at different rates. As a consequence, higher education must in the years ahead move away from its emphasis on teaching to learning, from its focus on common processes to common outcomes. With this shift will come the possibility of offering students a variety of ways to achieve those outcomes rooted in the ways they learn best, an approach Alverno College in Milwaukee embraced four decades ago.

This needed transformation of the American university is merely the task of taking a healthy institution and maintaining its vitality. In an information economy, there is no more important social institution than the university in its capacity to fuel our economy, our society and our minds. To accomplish these ends, the university must be rooted simultaneously in our past and our present, with its vision directed toward the future.

Arthur Levine, "Digital Students, Industrial-Era Universities," *Inside Higher Education*, June 24, 2010.

BENJAMIN HAROLD, "TECHNOLOGY IN EDUCATION: AN OVERVIEW," *EDUCATION WEEK*, FEBRUARY 5, 2016

In its February 5, 2016 issue, Education Week, *the recognized "newspaper of record" for K-12 schooling, published a detailed overview of the place of technology in schools in the second decade of the new century. After the dreams of Papert and the warnings of Postman (see Chapter 12), the article represents as good a summary as there is as to what is actually happening with technology in the nation's K-12 schools.*

Technology is everywhere in education: Public schools in the United States now provide at least one computer for every five students. They spend more than $3 billion per year on digital content. Led by the federal government, the country is in the midst of a massive effort to make affordable high-speed Internet and free online teaching resources available to even the most rural and remote schools. And in 2015–16, for the first time, more state standardized tests for the elementary and middle grades will be administered via technology than by paper and pencil.

To keep up with what's changing (and what isn't), observers must know where to look.

There's the booming ed-tech industry, with corporate titans and small startups alike vying for a slice of an $8 billion-plus yearly market for hardware and software. Much attention is also paid to the "early adopters"—those districts, schools, and teachers who are making the most ingenious and effective uses of the new tools at their disposal.

But a significant body of research has also made clear that most teachers have been slow to transform the ways they teach, despite the influx of new technology into their classrooms. There remains limited evidence to show that technology and online learning are improving learning outcomes for most students. And academics and parents alike have expressed concerns about digital distractions, ways in which unequal access to and use of technology might widen achievement gaps, and more.

State and federal lawmakers, meanwhile, have wrestled in recent years with the reality that new technologies also present new challenges. The rise of "big data," for example, has led to new concerns about how schools can keep sensitive student information private and secure.

What follows is an overview of the big trends, opportunities, and concerns associated with classroom technology . . .

What Is Personalized Learning?

Many in the ed-tech field see new technologies as powerful tools to help schools meet the needs of ever-more-diverse student populations. The idea is that digital devices, software, and learning platforms offer a once-unimaginable array of options for tailoring education to each individual student's academic strengths and weaknesses, interests and motivations, personal preferences, and optimal pace of learning.

In recent years, a group of organizations including the Bill & Melinda Gates Foundation, the Michael and Susan Dell Foundation, and EDUCAUSE have crafted a definition of "personalized learning" that rests on four pillars:

- Each student should have a "learner profile" that documents his or her strengths, weaknesses, preferences, and goals;
- Each student should pursue an individualized learning path that encourages him or her to set and manage personal academic goals;
- Students should follow a "competency-based progression" that focuses on their ability to demonstrate mastery of a topic, rather than seat time; and,
- Students' learning environments should be flexible and structured in ways that support their individual goals.

How does technology support that vision?

In many schools, students are given district-owned computing devices or allowed to bring their own devices from home. The idea is that this allows for "24-7" learning at the time and location of the student's choosing.

Learning management systems, student information systems, and other software are also used to distribute assignments, manage schedules and communications, and track student progress.

And educational software and applications have grown more "adaptive," relying on technology and algorithms to determine not only what a student knows, but what his or her learning process is, and even his or her emotional state.

For all the technological progress, though, implementation remains a major challenge. Schools and educators across the country continue to wrestle with the changing role of teachers, how to balance flexible and "personalized" models with the state and federal accountability requirements they still must meet, and the deeper cultural challenge of changing educators' long-standing habits and routines.

Despite the massive investments that many school systems are making, the evidence that digital personalized learning can improve student outcomes or narrow achievement gaps at scale remains scattered, at best.

What Is 1-to-1 Computing?

Increasingly, schools are moving to provide students with their own laptop computer, net-book, or digital tablet. Schools purchased more than 23 million devices for classroom use in 2013 and 2014 alone. In recent years, iPads and then Chromebooks (inexpensive Web-based laptops) have emerged as the devices of choice for many schools.

The two biggest factors spurring the rise in 1-to-1 student computing have been new mandates that state standardized tests be delivered online and the widespread adoption of the Common Core State Standards.

Generally, the hope is that putting devices in the hands of students will help with some or all of the following goals:

- Allowing teachers and software to deliver more personalized content and lessons to students, while allowing students to learn at their own pace and ability level;
- Helping students to become technologically skilled and literate and thus better prepared for modern workplaces;
- Empowering students to do more complex and creative work by allowing them to use digital and online applications and tools;
- Improving the administration and management of schools and classrooms by making it easier to gather information on what students know and have done;
- Improving communications among students, teachers, and parents.

Despite the potential benefits, however, many districts have run into trouble when attempting to implement 1-to-1 computing initiatives. Paying for the devices can be a challenge, especially as the strategy of issuing long-term bonds for short-term technology purchases has come into question. Many districts have also run into problems with infrastructure (not enough bandwidth to support all students accessing the Internet at the same time) and deployment (poor planning in distributing and managing thousands of devices.)

The most significant problem for schools trying to go 1-to-1, though, has been a lack of educational vision. Without a clear picture of how teaching and learning is expected to change, experts say, going 1-to-1 often amounts to a "spray and pray" approach of distributing many devices and hoping for the best.

Some critics of educational technology also point to a recent study by the Organization for Economic Cooperation and Development, which found that countries where 15-year old students use computers most in the classroom scored the worst on international reading and math tests.

What Is Blended Learning?

In its simplest terms, blended learning combines traditional, teacher-to-student lessons with technology-based instruction.

Many schools and districts use a "rotation" model, which is often viewed as an effective means of providing students with more personalized instruction and smaller group experiences. In some cases, saving money (through larger overall class sizes, for example) is also a goal. The basic premise involves students rotating between online and in-person stations for different parts of the day. There are many versions of this approach, however: Do students stay in the classroom or go to a computer lab?

Does online instruction cover core content, or is it primarily for remediation? Are all students doing the same thing online, or do different students have different software and learning experiences?

One big trend for schools involves trying to make sure that what happens online is connected with what happens during face-to-face interactions with teachers. That could involve giving teachers a say in selecting the software that students use, for example, or making a concerted effort to ensure online programs provide teachers with data that is useful in making timely instructional decisions.

Another trend involves boosting students' access to the Internet outside of school. Robust blended learning programs involve "anytime, anywhere" access to learning content for students—a major challenge in many communities.

Perhaps the biggest hurdle confronting educators interested in blended learning, though, is the lack of a solid research base. As of now, there is still no definitive evidence that blended learning works (or doesn't). While some studies have found encouraging results with specific programs or under certain circumstances, the question of whether blended learning positively impacts student learning still has a mostly unsatisfactory answer: "It depends."

What Is the Status of Tech Infrastructure and the E-Rate?

The promise of technology in the classroom is almost entirely dependent on reliable infrastructure. But in many parts of the country, schools still struggle to get affordable access to high-speed Internet and/or robust wireless connectivity.

A typical school district network involves multiple components. In 2014, the Federal Communications Commission established connectivity targets for some of the pieces:

- A connection to the broader Internet provided by an outside service provider to the district office (or another central district hub).

  Target: 100 megabits per second per 1,000 students in the short-term, and 1 Gigabit per second per 1,000 students in the long-term.

- A "Wide Area Network" that provides network connections between the district's central hub and all of its campuses, office buildings, and other facilities.

Target: Connections capable of delivering 10 Gigabits per second per 1,000 students.

- "Local Area Networks" that provide connections within a school, including the equipment necessary to provide Wi-Fi service inside classrooms.

  Target: The FCC recommended a survey to determine a suitable measure. Many school-technology advocates call for internal connections that support 1-to-1 computing.

To support schools (and libraries) in building and paying for these networks, the FCC in 1996 established a program known as the E-rate. Fees on consumers' phone bills fund the program, which has paid out more than $30 billion since its inception.

In 2014, the commission overhauled the E-rate, raising the program's annual spending cap from $2.4 billion to $3.9 billion and prioritizing support for broadband service and wireless networks. The changes were already being felt as of Fall 2015; after steadily declining for years, the number of schools and libraries applying for E-rate funds for wireless network equipment skyrocketed, with nearly all of the applicants expected to receive a portion of the $1.6 billion in overall wireless-related requests.

As part of the E-rate overhaul, the FCC also approved a series of regulatory changes aimed at leveling the playing field for rural and remote schools, which often face two big struggles: accessing the fiber-optic cables that experts say are essential to meeting the FCC's long-term goals, and finding affordable rates.

Infrastructure in some contexts can also be taken to include learning devices, digital content, and the policies and guidelines that govern how they are expected to be used in schools (such as "responsible use policies" and "digital citizenship" programs aimed to ensure that students and staff are using technology appropriately and in support of learning goals).

Another big—and often overlooked—aspect of infrastructure is what's known as interoperability. Essentially, the term refers to common standards and protocols for formatting and handling data so that information can be shared between software programs. A number of frameworks outline data interoperability standards for different purposes. Many hope to see the field settle on common standards in the coming years.

How Is Online Testing Evolving?

The biggest development on this front has been states' adoption of online exams aligned with the Common Core State Standards. During the 2014–15 school year, 10 states (plus the District of Columbia) used exams from the Partnership for Assessment of Readiness for College and Careers (PARCC), and 18 states used exams from the Smarter Balanced Assessment Consortium, all of which were delivered primarily online. Many of the other states also used online assessments.

The 2015–16 school year will be the first in which more state-required summative assessments in U.S. middle and elementary schools will be delivered via technology rather than paper and pencil, according to a recent analysis by EdTech Strategies, an educational technology consulting firm.

Beyond meeting legislative mandates, perceived benefits include cost savings, ease of administration and analysis, and the potential to employ complex performance tasks.

But some states—including Florida, Minnesota, Montana, and Wisconsin—have experienced big problems with online tests, ranging from cyber attacks to log-in problems to technical errors. And there is growing evidence that students who take the paper-and-pencil version of some important tests perform better than peers who take the same exams online, at least in the short term.

Nevertheless, it appears likely that online testing will continue to grow—and not just for state summative assessments. The U.S. Department of Education, for example, is among those pushing for a greater use of technologically enhanced formative assessments that can be used to diagnose students' abilities in close to real time. In the department's 2016 National Education Technology Plan, for example, it calls for states and districts to "design, develop, and implement learning dashboards, response systems, and communication pathways that give students, educators, families, and other stakeholders timely and actionable feedback about student learning to improve achievement and instructional practices."

How Are Digital Materials Used in Classrooms?

Digital instructional content is the largest slice of the (non-hardware) K-12 educational technology market, with annual sales of more than $3 billion. That includes digital lessons in math, English/language arts, and science, as well as "specialty" subjects such as business and fine arts. The market is still dominated by giant publishers such as Houghton Mifflin Harcourt and Pearson, who have been scrambling to transition from their print-centric legacy products to more digital offerings.

But newcomers with one-off products or specific areas of expertise have made inroads, and some apps and online services have also gained huge traction inside of schools.

As a result, many schools use a mix of digital resources, touting potential benefits such as greater ability to personalize, higher engagement among students, enhanced ability to keep content updated and current, and greater interactivity and adaptivity (or responsiveness to individual learners).

Still, though, the transition to digital instructional materials is happening slowly, for reasons that range from the financial (for districts that haven't been able to purchase devices for all students, for example) to the technical (districts that lack the infrastructure to support every student being online together). Print still accounts for about 70 percent of pre-K-12 instructional materials sales in the United States.

What Are Open Educational Resources?

Rather than buying digital instructional content, some states and districts prefer using "open" digital education resources that are licensed in such a way that they can be freely used, revised, and shared. The trend appears likely to accelerate: The U.S. Department of Education, for example, is now formally encouraging districts to move away from textbooks and towards greater adoption of OER.

New York and Utah have led the way in developing open educational resources and encouraging their use by schools. The K-12 OER Collaborative, which includes 12 states and several nonprofit organizations, is working to develop OER materials as well.

Proponents argue that OER offer greater bang for the buck, while also giving students better access to a wider array of digital materials and teachers more flexibility to customize instructional content for individual classrooms and students. Some also believe OER use encourages collaboration among teachers. Concerns from industry and others generally focus on the quality of open materials, as well as the challenges that educators face in sifting through voluminous one-off resources to find the right material for every lesson.

How Are Virtual Education and Distance Learning Doing?

One technology trend that has come under increasing scrutiny involves full-time online schools, particularly cyber charters. About 200,000 students are enrolled in about 200 publicly funded, independently managed online charter schools across 26 states.

But such schools were found to have an "overwhelming negative impact" on student learning in a comprehensive set of studies released in 2015 by a group of research organizations, including Stanford University's Center for Research on Education Outcomes at Stanford University.

That research did not cover the more than two dozen full-time online schools that are state-run, however, nor did it cover the dozens more that are run by individual school districts. Thousands upon thousands of students who are enrolled in traditional brick-and-mortar schools also take individual courses online. Five states—Alabama, Arkansas, Florida, Michigan, and Virginia—now require students to have some online learning to graduate. Other states, such as Utah, have passed laws encouraging such options for students.

For many students, especially those in rural and remote areas, online and distance learning can offer access to courses, subjects, and teachers they might otherwise never be able to find. Such opportunities can also benefit advanced and highly motivated students and those with unusual schedules and travel requirements, and be a useful tool to keep schools running during snow days.

But so far, achieving positive academic outcomes at scale via online learning has proven difficult, and many observers have expressed concerns about the lack of accountability in the sector, especially as relates to for-profit managers of online options.

Benjamin Herold (2016, February 5), "Issues A–Z: Technology in Education: An Overview," *Education Week*, Retrieved December 29, 2017 from www.edweek.org/ew/issues/technology-in-education.

EMMA GONZALEZ, ADDRESS AT GUN CONTROL RALLY, 2018

On February 14, 2018 a former student at the school entered Marjory Stoneman Douglas High School in Parkland, Florida armed with automatic rifles and killed seventeen people—students and teachers. It was far from the first time that such a shooting had taken place. Large-scale school shootings had shocked the nation in Columbine, Colorado in 1999 and Sandy Hook Elementary School in Newtown, Connecticut in 2012. But school shootings happen in the United States every few days, often killing one, two, or three students. But at Parkland, the student reaction was different. Rather than simply grieving for the terrible loss, many of the students determined that they would do something; that indeed they would make sure that they were heard and that their experience would be the last time such a terrible tragedy took place. Three days after the shooting at her school, Emma Gonzalez, a senior at the Parkland school, addressed a gun control rally on Saturday in Fort Lauderdale. Students around the country took up the challenge with marches, boycotts, and other actions.

Figure 13.1 The Marjorie Stoneman Douglas High School in Parkland, Florida was the scene of a shooting in February 2018, one of too many school shootings in recent years. Stoneman Douglas students rallied in ways that had not been seen before and began a nationwide drive for gun control and an end to the terrible violence.

Every single person up here today, all these people should be home grieving. But instead we are up here standing together because if all our government and President can do is send thoughts and prayers, then it's time for victims to be the change that we need to see. Since the time of the Founding Fathers and since they added the Second Amendment to the Constitution, our guns have developed at a rate that leaves me dizzy. The guns have changed but our laws have not.

We certainly do not understand why it should be harder to make plans with friends on weekends than to buy an automatic or semi-automatic weapon. In Florida, to buy a gun you do not need a permit, you do not need a gun license, and once you buy it you do not need to register it. You do not need a permit to carry a concealed rifle or shotgun. You can buy as many guns as you want at one time.

I read something very powerful to me today. It was from the point of view of a teacher. And I quote: When adults tell me I have the right to own a gun, all I can hear is my right to own a gun outweighs your student's right to live. All I hear is mine, mine, mine, mine . . .

We are going to be the kids you read about in textbooks. Not because we're going to be another statistic about mass shooting in America, but because, just as David said, we are going to be the last mass shooting. Just like *Tinker v. Des Moines*, we are going to change the law. That's going to be Marjory Stoneman Douglas in that textbook and it's going to be due to the tireless effort of the school board, the faculty members, the family members and most of all the students. The students who are dead, the students still in the hospital, the student now suffering PTSD, the students who had panic attacks during the vigil because the helicopters would not leave us alone, hovering over the school for 24 hours a day.

There is one tweet I would like to call attention to. So many signs that the Florida shooter was mentally disturbed, even expelled for bad and erratic behavior. Neighbors and classmates knew he was a big problem. Must always report such instances to authorities again and again. We did, time and time again. Since he was in middle school, it was no surprise to anyone who knew him to hear that he was the shooter. Those talking about how we should have not ostracized him, you didn't know this kid. OK, we did. We know that they are claiming mental health issues, and I am not a psychologist, but we need to pay attention to the fact that this was not just a mental health issue. He would not have harmed that many students with a knife.

And how about we stop blaming the victims for something that was the student's fault, the fault of the people who let him buy the guns in the first place, those at the gun shows, the people who encouraged him to buy accessories for his guns to make them fully automatic, the people who didn't take them away from him when they knew he expressed homicidal tendencies, and I am not talking about the FBI. I'm talking about the people he lived with. I'm talking about the neighbors who saw him outside holding guns.

If the President wants to come up to me and tell me to my face that it was a terrible tragedy and how it should never have happened and maintain telling us how nothing is going to be done about it, I'm going to happily ask him how much money he received from the National Rifle Association.

You want to know something? It doesn't matter, because I already know. Thirty million dollars. And divided by the number of gunshot victims in the United States in the one and one-half months in 2018 alone, that comes out to being $5,800. Is that how much these people are worth to you, Trump? If you don't do anything to prevent this from continuing to occur, that number of gunshot victims will go up and the number that they are worth will go down. And we will be worthless to you.

To every politician who is taking donations from the NRA, shame on you.

[Crowd chants, shame on you.]

If your money was as threatened as us, would your first thought be, how is this going to reflect on my campaign? Which should I choose? Or would you choose us, and if you answered us, will you act like it for once? You know what would be a good way to act like it? I have an example of how to not act like it. In February of 2017, one year ago, President Trump repealed an Obama-era regulation that would have made it easier to block the sale of firearms to people with certain mental illnesses.

From the interactions that I had with the shooter before the shooting and from the information that I currently know about him, I don't really know if he was mentally ill. I wrote this before I heard what Delaney said. Delaney said he was diagnosed. I don't need a psychologist and I don't need to be a psychologist to know that repealing that regulation was a really dumb idea.

Republican Senator Chuck Grassley of Iowa was the sole sponsor on this bill that stops the FBI from performing background checks on people adjudicated to be mentally ill and now he's stating for the record, "Well, it's a shame the FBI isn't doing background checks on these mentally ill people." Well, duh. You took that opportunity away last year.

The people in the government who were voted into power are lying to us. And us kids seem to be the only ones who notice and our parents to call BS. Companies trying to make caricatures of the teenagers these days, saying that all we are self-involved and trend-obsessed and they hush us into submission when our message doesn't reach the ears of the nation, we are prepared to call BS. Politicians who sit in their gilded House and Senate seats funded by the

NRA telling us nothing could have been done to prevent this, we call BS. They say tougher guns laws do not decrease gun violence. We call BS. They say a good guy with a gun stops a bad guy with a gun. We call BS. They say guns are just tools like knives and are as dangerous as cars. We call BS. They say no laws could have prevented the hundreds of senseless tragedies that have occurred. We call BS. That us kids don't know what we're talking about, that we're too young to understand how the government works. We call BS.

If you agree, register to vote. Contact your local congress people. Give them a piece of your mind.

[Crowd chants, throw them out.]

PRESIDENT DONALD TRUMP, GOVERNOR JAY INSLEE (D-WASHINGTON), AND GOVERNOR GREG ABBOTT (R-TEXAS) ON GUNS IN SCHOOLS, 2018

Less than two weeks after the shooting and the impassioned speech by Emma Gonzalez asking political leaders to make guns harder to get and to ban the most lethal military weapons, President Trump, in a meeting with state governors, provided his own response—arm teachers. By most polls the majority of teachers rejected the solution, though some teachers and some governors embraced it. At the February 26, 2018 meeting at which the president made the proposal, Governor Jay Inslee of Washington rejected the idea while favoring strict gun control but Governor Greg Abbott of Texas agreed with the president and described implementation in his home state. What follows is from the official White House transcript of the event.

State Dining Room—10:53 A.M. EST

THE PRESIDENT: Thank you, everybody. Thank you very much. And I want to thank our Vice President for that really lovely introduction. That was very nice, Mike, and I appreciate it.

This is a time of great opportunity for our country. We've created nearly 3 million jobs since the election—a number that nobody would have thought possible. You go back and take a look at what they were saying just prior to the election. Nobody thought it was even possible.

And we've done many other things, as you know. And I won't go over them because I want to be hearing from you today, but many other things that, frankly, nobody thought possible . . .

Today, I want to hear your ideas on a number of critical issues. But, most importantly, we want to discuss the public safety in schools and public safety, generally. But school safety. We can't have this go on.

I'm grateful that Governor Rick Scott is here, and we thank him for his leadership in the aftermath of the terrible tragedy in Parkland, Florida. Horrible. Our nation is heartbroken. We continue to mourn the loss of so many precious, innocent young lives. These are incredible people. I visited a lot of them.

But we will turn our grief into action. We have to have action. We don't have any action. It happens, a week goes by, "let's keep talking." Another week goes by, we keep talking. Two months go by—all of the sudden, everybody is off to the next subject. Then, when it happens again, everybody is angry and "let's start talking again." We got to stop.

By the way, bump stocks—we're writing that out. I'm writing that out myself. I don't care if Congress does it or not. I'm writing it out myself, okay? (Applause.) You put it into the machine gun category—which is what it is—it becomes, essentially, a machine gun, and nobody is going to be able to—it's going to very hard to get them. So we're writing out bump stocks.

But we have to take steps to harden our schools so that they are less vulnerable to attack. This includes allowing well-trained and certified school personnel to carry concealed firearms. At some point, you need volume. I don't know that a school is going to be able to hire a hundred security guards that are armed. Plus, you know, I got to watch some deputy sheriffs performing this week. And they weren't exactly Medal of Honor winners. All right?

The way they performed was, frankly, disgusting. They were listening to what was going on. The one in particular, he was then—he was early. And then you had three others that probably a similar deal a little bit later, but a similar kind of a thing.

You know, I really believe—you don't know until you test it—but I really believe I'd run in there, even if I didn't had a weapon. And I think most of the people in this room would have done that, too, because I know most of you. But the way they performed was really a disgrace.

Second, we must confront the issue of mental health. And here is the best example of mental health. This kid—they had 39 red flags. They should have known. They did know. They didn't do anything about it. That was really a bad time, I have to tell you. Nobody bigger for law enforcement than I am. But between the people that didn't go into that school and protect those lives, and the fact that this should have been solved long before it happened—pretty sad.

So we have to confront the issue, and we have to discuss mental health, and we have to do something about it. You know, in the old days, we had mental institutions. We had a lot of them, and you could nab somebody like this. Because, you know, they did—they knew he was—something was off. You had to know that. People were calling all over the place.

But you used to be able to bring him into a mental institution, and hopefully he gets help or whatever—but he's off the streets. You can't arrest him, I guess, because he hasn't done anything, but you know he's like a boiler ready to explode, right? So he just—you have to do something. But you can't put him in jail, I guess, because he hasn't done anything.

But, in the old days, you would put him into a mental institution. And we had them in New York, and our government started closing them because of cost. And we're going to have to start talking about mental institutions, because a lot of the folks in this room closed their mental institutions also.

So we have no halfway. We have nothing between a prison and leaving him at his house, which we can't do anymore. So I think you folks have to start thinking about that.

Third, we have to improve our early warning response system so that when friends, family, and neighbors do warn the authorities about a violent or dangerous individual, action is taken quickly and decisively. Look, you had the one mother—you remember, in Connecticut, how horrible that was. She was begging—begging—to take her son in and help him—do something, anything, he's so dangerous. And nobody really listened to her. And he ended up killing her, and then the rest. You know what happened. It was a horror. But she was begging to do something about her own son.

Recently, you had a grandmother that got to see the notes of her grandchild, and she reported him. And they nabbed him. He was ready to go in for a school—looked like. She reported him. And there, the law enforcement did a very good job.

Fourth, we must pursue commonsense measures that protect the constitutional rights of law-abiding Americans while keeping guns out of the hands of those who pose a threat to themselves and to others.

And fifth, we must strive to create a culture in our country that cherishes life and condemns violence and embraces dignity.

Now, with all of that, over the weekend—I cannot believe the press didn't find this out, I can't believe it. I think they're getting a little bit—I could never use the word "lazy"; you don't want to say that. We don't want to give them any more enthusiasm than they already have. But I can't believe they didn't figure this one—because I had lunch with Wayne LaPierre, Chris Cox, and David Lehman of the NRA. And I want to tell you, they want to do something. And I said, "Fellas, we got to do something. It's too long now. We got to do something."

And we're going to do very strong background checks—very strong. We got to do background checks. If we see a sicko, I don't want him having a gun. And, you know, I know there was a time when anybody could have—I mean, even if they were sick, they were fighting. And I said, "Fellas, we can't do it anymore." And there's no bigger fan of the Second Amendment than me, and there's no bigger fan of the NRA. And these guys are great patriots. They're great people. And they want to do something. They're going to do something. And they're going to do it, I think, quickly. I think they want to see it.

But we don't want to have sick people having the right to have a gun. Plus, when we see somebody is sick like this guy, when the police went to see him, they didn't do a good job. But they have restrictions on what they can do. We got to give them immediate access to taking those guns away so that they don't just leave and he's sitting there with seven different weapons. (Applause.) Got to give immediate access.

Don't worry, you're not going to get any—you won't—don't worry about the NRA. They're on our side. You guys—half of you are so afraid of the NRA. There's nothing to be afraid of. And you know what? If they're not with you, we have to fight them every once and a while. That's okay. They're doing what they think is right. I will tell you, they are doing what they think is right.

But sometimes we're going to have to be very tough and we're going to have to fight them. But we need strong background checks. For a long period of time, people resisted that. But now people, I think, are really into it.

And John Cornyn—great guy—senator, Mitch McConnell, Paul Ryan, and Kevin McCarthy hopefully are going to work on some legislation. I hope you guys—they started already. In fact, John has legislation in. We're going to strengthen it, we're going to make it more pertinent to what we're discussing, but he's already started the process. We've already started it. And the other thing—we need hardened sites. We have to have hardened sites.

So just in concluding, we have tremendous things happening. The country is doing well, and then we have a setback like this that's so heart-wrenching. It's so heart-wrenching. And we have to—we have to clean it up. We have to straighten it out . . .

And I'm here as long as you need me. Let's get it all out. We want to help the governors, we want to help our states, and we want to make our schools safe . . .

GOVERNOR INSLEE: Thanks, Mr. President. Two comments. One from the state of Washington. Thank you.

We have a program called the Extreme Risk Protection Orders System that has been supremely effective in allowing family members that realize there's a risk, to have them separated from their firearm. It involves a judicial decision. It involves a hearing. And it has saved lives, and I'm sure, in the state of Washington.

And I would commend it to you for national attention, because it makes sure that when you have an uncle that might be—you have concern about depression—it allows law enforcement to separate your uncle, and depressed uncle, from his firearm. If you have somebody in your family that might have some violent tendencies, after a hearing and a potential ex parte order, you get an order to actually allow law enforcement to remove them. It's been in operation for a year. It's been extremely successful. I would commend it to you.

Second issue. Now I know that you have suggested arming our teachers. And I just—

THE PRESIDENT: No. No, no. Not your teachers.

GOVERNOR INSLEE: Not your teachers.

THE PRESIDENT: Arming a small portion that are very gun adept, that truly know how to handle it. Because I do feel, Governor, it's very important that gun-free zones—you have a gun-free zone, it's like an invitation for these very sick people to go there.

I do think that there has to be some form of major retaliation if they're able to enter a school. And if that happens, you're not going have any problems anymore, because they're never going to the school. You're never going to have a problem.

So it would just be a very small group of people that are very gun adept. Anyway, go ahead, Governor.

GOVERNOR INSLEE: If I may respond to that. Let me just suggest, whatever percentage it is—I heard at one time you might have suggested 20 percent—whatever percentage it is, speaking as a grandfather, speaking as the Governor of the state of Washington, I have listened to the people who would be affected by that. I have listened to the biology teachers, and they don't want to do that, at any percentage. I've listened to the first-grade teachers that don't want to be pistol-packing first-grade teachers. I've listened to law enforcement who have said they don't want to have to train teachers as law enforcement agents, which takes about six months.

Now, I just think this is a circumstance where we need to listen, that educators should educate, and they should not be foisted upon this responsibility of packing heat in first grade classes.

Now, I understand you have suggested this. And we suggest things, and sometimes then we listen to people about it, and maybe they don't look so good a little later. So I just suggest we need a little less tweeting here and a little more listening. And let's just take that off the table and move forward.

THE PRESIDENT: All right. Thank you very much. You know, we have a number of states right now that do that. And I think, with that in mind, I'll call on Greg Abbott, the great governor of Texas. Greg.

GOVERNOR ABBOTT: Sure. Texas authorized schools to adopt policies to implement a school marshal program where individuals would be trained to have a weapon and to be able to use that weapon. And we now have well over a hundred school districts in the state of Texas where teachers or other people who work in the school do carry a weapon, and are trained to be able to respond to an attack that occurs.

Now, it's not always a schoolteacher. It could be a coach, it could be an administrator, it could be anybody who works in that school. But it's a well-thought-out program with a lot of training in advance. And, candidly, some school districts, they promote it. Because they will have signs out front—a warning sign: "Be aware, there are armed personnel on campus"—warning anybody coming on there that they—if they attempt to cause any harm, they're going to be in trouble.

THE PRESIDENT: Well, I think that's great. And so, essentially, what you're saying is that when a sick individual comes into that school, they can expect major trouble. Right? Major trouble. The bullets are going to be going toward him, also. And I think that's great. And you know what's going to happen? Nobody is going into that school, Greg. That's a big difference.

Secretary of Education Betsy DeVos, Remarks to Turning Point USA High School Leadership Summit, July 25, 2018

In the summer of 2018, U.S. Secretary of Education, Betsy DeVos, spoke to a gathering of high school students. While her speech made headlines for her question, "how many of you have been bored in one or more of your classes?" the heart of the speech was her ringing endorsement of charter and parochial schools and other forms of school choice. Some were delighted; some appalled; and few uninterested.

Thank you, Kyle Kashuv, for that introduction. I was so pleased to meet and visit with you some months ago. The adage of good things coming from bad situations was proven once again. I hope you know just how impressed we are by your courage and your determination to stay engaged.

Many of you know Kyle, and you know what he and his classmates went through in Parkland, Florida. No student, no parent, no teacher should ever have to worry about their safety at school.

We've suffered too many heartbreaking reminders that our nation must come together to address the underlying issues that create a culture of violence.

Enough is enough. America demands action. I don't say this to score political points. School safety is not a partisan issue. It is about protecting students' lives. Your lives.

President Trump took swift action. He also asked me to chair the Federal Commission on School Safety. We are seeking input from students, parents, teachers, school safety personnel, administrators, law enforcement officials, mental health professionals, school counselors . . . anyone and everyone who is focused on identifying and elevating solutions. That's right, solutions. Plural. Our aim is not to impose a one-size-fits-all solution for everyone, everywhere. The primary responsibility for the physical security of schools—and their students—naturally rests with states and local communities. It's not up to the Commission. It's not up to me. Actually, it's not up to anyone in Washington.

And that's not just for school safety. There is no one-size-fits-all solution for any issue in public life. For eight long years, many in Washington seemed to think that because they had power here, they should make decisions on behalf of people there, and everywhere.

And that is why Donald Trump is president.

President Trump was elected to return power and control to people and their communities. There's nowhere that's needed more than in education.

My work in education over thirty years has revolved around time invested on the "outside." Outside the Department of Education. Outside "the system." Outside Washington.

I think that's a good thing, don't you?

Way too many in the education world believe they need more involvement, more intrusion, more mandates, more money, more government.

But what do we believe? We believe in more freedom!

We are committed to expanding education freedom for all families across America. You've probably heard me described as "pro-school choice." Well, I am, but choice in education is not defined by picking this building or that school, using this voucher or that scholarship. And it's not public versus private. Parochial versus charter. Homeschool versus virtual.

It shouldn't be "versus" anything, because choice in education is bigger than that.

Choice is really about freedom! Freedom to learn, and to learn differently. Freedom to explore. Freedom to fail, to learn from falling and to get back up and try again. It's freedom to find the best way for you to learn and grow . . . to find the engaging combination that unleashes your curiosity and unlocks your individual potential.

You and your families already exercise freedom when you make choices about next steps for education after high school. I suspect many of you are going through this process right now.

You compare options, and make an informed decision.

If you choose to go to Georgetown, are you somehow against the Wolverines or the Fighting Irish? Well, you're not—except when they're on the basketball court.

If you decide to go to George Washington University, are you somehow against public universities? Of course not!

No one criticizes those choices. No one thinks choice in higher education is wrong. So why is it wrong in elementary school, middle school, or high school?

Truth is: there is nothing wrong with that! There is nothing wrong with wanting to pursue the education that's right for you!

Let me ask you this: how many of you have been bored in one or more of your classes?

I was too!

How many of you wish you could study a subject but your school doesn't offer it?

How many of you feel like you need more or less time than your classmates in some subjects?

And how many of you are told that there's nothing you can do about it?

That's not right! You deserve better. Parents deserve better. Our country deserves better. And we must do better!

It's time to reorient our approach to education. We need a paradigm shift. A rethink.

"Rethink" means we question everything to ensure nothing limits you from pursuing your passion, and achieving your potential.

You—and all students—deserve learning environments that are agile, relevant, exciting. You should be able to pursue customized, self-paced, and challenging life-long learning journeys.

I recently visited a SkillsUSA conference where students competed with each other in a wide range of activities they had learned about: developing computer games, building homes, welding, baking, graphic design—to name just a few. They were all clearly excited about what they were doing!

And last week, I met a 70-year-old man who was in his fourth career. His first was a helicopter pilot in Vietnam. He went on to work in the defense contracting industry, followed by another career in banking. He found retirement to be quite boring, so he learned the necessary skills to drive big rigs across the country. And he said his fourth career is his best one yet!

So be open to possibilities that aren't pre-planned. I suspect some—or maybe many—of you feel like your life thus far has been ordered for you. Class to class, grade to grade, graduation to graduation. But you will find that nothing—not your families, your careers, your faith journeys—is as predictable as it seems.

So what you learn is about much more than just acquiring "skills" or diplomas. You are your most important resource. Your education is about you. It's about your aspirations and abilities. Your passions and pursuits. Your ingenuity and what you do with it is what gives life to your education.

There's one thing for sure: you'll enter an economy that's the strongest it's been in years! After the historic Tax Cut and Jobs Act, confidence is at a new high and unemployment—in nearly every sector—is at a new low. Nearly 3 million jobs have been created since President Trump took office, and Americans are more hopeful about their futures!

Today, you are at a "turning point." You have more opportunities at your fingertips than any other generation in the history of the world. You are making choices today that will lay the foundation for your future.

But, keep in mind, when it comes to your education, it's not only about making a good salary or getting that big promotion.

Getting a great education is also about becoming a great citizen. It's learning about ideas—and not just the ones you agree with! It's way more than putting a face or a phrase on a tee shirt. It's discerning what's behind that phrase and knowing what the person pictured stood for and accomplished.

So, let's conclude by returning to the idea that made this country great: freedom! You're blessed to live in the most free and most prosperous country in the history of human civilization.

Most free and most prosperous. That's no accident. You cannot have one without the other.

So study freedom. Learn it. And—importantly—protect it. Because freedom is fragile.

And freedom is not a fad. Freedom is for everyone, everywhere. It's not just an American "thing." Freedom is a human thing.

Each of us has been created with unique talents. We each need the freedom to develop them through learning—and then the freedom to choose what to do with them.

Because as it's been said: freedom is not about doing what we want, it's about having the right to do what we ought.

Thank you and God bless America's future, all of you!

Downloaded from the U.S. Department of Education website, www.ed.gov, July 26, 2019.

AFT Resolution, "Defeating the DeVos Agenda," 2018

In the above remarks, Secretary DeVos advocated greater and greater support for what is called school choice; allowing students to move from district-based public schools to charter schools or to different kinds of schooling altogether. The American Federation of Teachers, one of the nation's two main teacher unions, would have none of it and passed a resolution at its 2018 conference urging the defeat of what it labeled the DeVos agenda.

WHEREAS, Betsy DeVos was not qualified to be U.S. secretary of education when she was confirmed; and

WHEREAS, over the course of the 18 months that she has had the job, she has continued to display her lack of qualification by demonstrating through her actions that her goal is to hurt, not help, public education; and

WHEREAS, even though early in her term she accepted an invitation to visit a quality public school in Van Wert, Ohio, and saw the impact those teachers have on their students and community, she has demonstrated no further interest in visiting, listening to or learning about public schools and their students, educators or communities, preferring instead to visit only private schools and charter schools that fit her "choice" agenda; and

WHEREAS, while DeVos often speaks of "choice," she never lifts up public schools as quality choices, showing that this rhetoric of choice cloaks her true education agenda, which is to defund and destabilize public education in America, from early childhood through college; and

WHEREAS, from her confirmation hearing, where she identified the threat of grizzly bears as a reason to bring guns to schools and was unable to answer basic questions about federal education law; to her testimony on the federal budget; to her most recent sparring with a state teacher of the year over DeVos' prioritization of private schools over public ones, she has consistently demonstrated she does not have the prerequisite knowledge of the programs that she is supposed to be overseeing; and

WHEREAS, DeVos is not respected by the general public, given that polls have found DeVos' "very unfavorable" rating is higher than any other Cabinet member included in the polls; and

WHEREAS, the DeVos agenda of privatization and disinvestment—which is the result of an intentional, decades-long campaign to protect the economic and political power of the few against the rights of the many—has taken the form of division and expresses itself as racism, sexism, classism, xenophobia and homophobia; and

WHEREAS, with the support of the Trump administration, DeVos proposed nearly $9 billion in unprecedented cuts in education programs, including eliminating class-size reduction, after-school and professional development programs; and

WHEREAS, even the Republican-led Congress has rejected the DeVos proposal for a federal voucher program and has so far rejected her proposal to slash the federal investment in public education; and

WHEREAS, DeVos eliminated the requirements that states be required to explain to the Department of Education how they have worked with stakeholders to develop their plans to implement provisions of the Every Student Succeeds Act, indicating support for top-down education reform without regard for participation from the field; and

WHEREAS, under DeVos' leadership, the Department of Education has favored wealthy former for-profit college executives over students and has failed to execute the department's mission to promote student access to continued and postsecondary learning, by removing regulations designed to protect borrowers, allowing student loan servicers like Navient and Nelnet to engage in deceptive practices and defraud borrowers, leading them deeper and deeper into debt; and

WHEREAS, in conjunction with the one-year anniversary of DeVos' tenure as education secretary, the AFT and stakeholders with an interest in promoting the success of public education collected 80,000 comments from teachers, students and parents encouraging her to do her job to strengthen and support the great work happening in public schools across the country; and

WHEREAS, the overwhelming majority of those comments indicate that DeVos is failing to listen to those who educate in, learn in and send their children to public schools—the schools that 90 percent of America's children attend:

RESOLVED, that the American Federation of Teachers and our members call for Betsy DeVos to do her job as secretary of education by prioritizing and championing public schools and public school students, parents and educators; and

RESOLVED, that the AFT will continue to educate and mobilize everyone in our communities who shares our values and our support for public education, and will work to defeat the DeVos agenda because of the danger her policies and agenda pose to public education and our students; and

RESOLVED, that the AFT will urge federal and state lawmakers to reject the DeVos efforts to defund and destabilize public education and to instead invest in public education, including early childhood education and higher education.

JOSH EIDELSON AND SARAH JAFFE, "DEFENDING PUBLIC EDUCATION: AN INTERVIEW WITH KAREN LEWIS OF THE CHICAGO TEACHERS UNION," *DISSENT*, SUMMER 2013

In September 2012 the Chicago Teachers Union went on strike after negotiations with city officials failed to win them the contract they wanted. While teacher strikes had been common in the 1960s and 1970s, the number of strikes by teachers has declined significantly in recent decades;

a process that would reverse itself dramatically in 2018 under new leaders like Lewis. As this interview with the president of Chicago union by authors for Dissent Magazine shows, by 2012 there were relatively new issues of concern to teachers, not just the traditional issues of salary and hours of work but teacher evaluations, school closings, and a changing attitude toward public school teachers by many. Karen Lewis and her colleagues in the union were ready to point to a new direction in teacher unions and in defining education reform for the twenty-first century. How significant the new direction will be is yet to be seen, but there are signs of resistance to the reform agenda of the last two decades in many places.

In 2010, a slate led by Karen Lewis ousted the incumbent leadership of the Chicago Teachers Union, promising deeper community engagement and a more aggressive defense of teachers and public education. In 2012, with Lewis as president, CTU mounted the city's first teachers' strike in a quarter-century, and the most dramatic recent challenge to the bipartisan education reform consensus. For the inaugural episode of Dissent magazine's podcast series, labor journalists Josh Eidelson and Sarah Jaffe sat down with Lewis to discuss teaching and gender discrimination, professionalism and solidarity, unions and the Democratic Party . . . —Eds.

DISSENT: How does the current fight over school closures in Chicago fit into the larger aims of the union?

KAREN LEWIS: The school closures are one symptom of a really bad school policy that we as Chicagoans have been struggling with for over ten years. The leaders of No Child Left Behind came around and said, "Oh, if the school's bad, we're going to close it down because, you know, it's *bad*." As if the building makes something bad. And what's happened is, as schools close, they destabilize other schools that are close by. So there's this domino effect they never took into consideration.

Children don't do better when schools close. They lose anywhere from three to six months on their learning or at least on their testing.

I kept saying, "Why are they continuing to close schools, open up charter schools that don't do any better, and not even taking the kids that were in the schools that were closed?"

But that was never good enough for the "reformers," so they started stepping it up. Instead of closing just one or two schools, they would close seven, eight, nine, ten. And they weren't keeping up with the children. So when schools would close, if kids didn't go to the school they were sent to, there was no way to find out where those kids went.

Not all of them went to private school, not all of them went to charters, and not all of them left town. So where were these kids going?

What inevitably happened was the increasing disruption of neighborhoods. Where I live, which is a kind of a gentrifying neighborhood, if I wanted to send my child to a traditional K–8 school, there would be none for my child to go to. And there didn't seem to be a "master plan" about why they were closing these schools. It wasn't like these were the worst performing schools. So it just seemed arbitrary and capricious.

D: How is the problem of violent crime in Chicago connected to problems with the schools?

KL: Chicago has a very different gang structure than most other cities. We've got a lot of Capulets and Montagues. There's no hierarchy. In Chicago, this block may be fighting against the next block. And they're not just defending drug territory. They're defending respect. Because our children have so little of it, if somebody disrespects them, it escalates outrageously.

Part of the problem is that we don't have counseling programs for children early enough. And we have almost gotten rid of play in preschool and kindergarten because we are so busy trying to get them to pass tests that we don't focus on the things that actually build their social and emotional learning along with their academics. Some of the conflict resolution that you should learn in play has disappeared.

In Chicago, we have issues of safety and a murder rate that is out of control. Think about Hadiya Pendleton, the young woman who was murdered after she'd performed at Obama's inauguration. She actually went to the school where I taught before I left the classroom, and I knew one of the kids that was involved in her killing. In Chicago, this stuff touches everybody.

"Why are they continuing to close schools, open up charter schools that don't do any better, and not even taking the kids that were in the schools that were closed?"

When a school closes, our children have to walk from a neighborhood they know, where they know where the safe streets are, to one they don't know. It takes a while to do this process right. But the authorities want to rush it through, and this won't even save the money they claim it will.

D: I'm also interested in the role that gender plays in the fight over education. I know that Gloria Steinem wrote to you, saying that teacher-bashing was anti-feminist.

KL: Well, some 87 percent of K–12 teachers are women. There was a time when teachers were revered in the community, and now they're often demonized. Teachers have been an easy target, primarily because we're not used to fighting. We're not used to a lot of confrontation. We're used to saying, "Whatever you want me to do I'll do it because we all care about what's best for kids."

So, when people told us, "Go get masters degrees, because that will make you better," teachers rushed out and got masters degrees. Then it was: "Get endorsements in ESL [English as a second language], or special ed, or whatever," and we rushed out and did that. Then it was, "Become National Board-certified."

But it is never enough when the goal is really to destroy public education. That narrative that "teachers don't care about children" makes no sense. So I get up every morning to deal with children I don't like or I don't care about? It's just not the kind of thing you do.

We have to turn this discussion around and make sure people understand that we are now living in bizarro-world. We're supposed to think that the elite, who are very wealthy and very well educated and don't send their children to public schools, care more about black and brown children they don't know?

Part of the issue about gender is something that we don't ever bring up because it makes people very uncomfortable. There's still this paternalistic attitude of, "I'd like to protect women" combined with, on the other hand, "Let's cut them off at the knees. Let's put women out of work"—women who may be caring for their own children and families.

And it's also a kind of mythical thinking, as if children don't have their own parents who love them, that they don't live in communities with few appropriate places for the parents to work. So my question has always been, "If you love black and brown children so much, why do you hate their parents?"

D: I want to ask you about teachers and professionalism. To counter the attacks on teachers' benefits and bargaining rights, we hear some union leaders emphasizing the training that goes into being a teacher and the idea that they belong to unions of professional workers.

At the same time, you have some teacher unionists who specifically reject professionalism as an organizing principle and call themselves education workers. They argue that talking about professionalism obscures class dynamics and divides teachers from the person who watches the kids during lunch and the person who cooks the kids' food. What do you make of that?

KL: I think people need to find where they feel most comfortable. It's not an either/or.

My experience has been that the people who serve the food, the people who work as paraprofessionals, those are the people who actually have experience with children in those neighborhoods, because most work in the neighborhoods in which they live. And they are also the ones who can tell you exactly what's going on in a building. If you want to know something about a child, well, ask one of the lunchroom workers. They will tell you exactly what's going on in that child's family.

Still, professionalism is important on one level because the billionaires boys' club is saying, "We don't need professionals. We could just train somebody for five weeks and throw them in there and let them do it," like in the army.

But, in Chicago, there is a coming-together of the different unions. We're working right now with other unions that represent the janitors, the security workers, and the lunchroom workers, because school closings affect all of us. We have to defend professionalism, but we can't defend it as the only thing we're doing . . .

D: You've talked and written about recognizing who your enemies are. Just because people are Democrats does not mean that they are not enemies. Does there need to be a break in the relationship between the teachers unions and Democrats?

KL: You know, this is the part that's the most difficult for me, because I hate politics, actually. For a long time I've felt we live in a one-party system. We just have two branches of it.

The key is to use the political system to hold our elected officials accountable through mass movements. I would like to see a whole new party that speaks for working people. But the way our system is set up, it's very difficult to have good conversations about third parties.

Let me give you an example of why that doesn't work well. In Illinois, in 2010, before we got elected, the teachers unions in Illinois decided *not* to give to the Democratic Party. So that's how we ended up with Senate Bill 7 [which includes restrictions on teachers' right to strike and revisions of tenure procedures]. We got punished for not giving them money. The reason we hadn't given them money was because the year before they came up with a really horrible pension bill.

In 2012, we had that same conversation. A lot of members asked, "Why are we giving the Democrats money?" Because when we didn't, we got smooshed. You cannot put all your eggs in a legislative basket. The problem with business unionists is that they rely on having good relationships with legislators. But if you don't have a mass movement behind you to move legislators, they don't take you seriously.

Then our members say, "Well, why aren't we suing [the Board of Education]?" OK, we have sued. But people watch too much TV. They don't understand that lawsuits aren't over in an hour or at the end of the show, when everybody walks away because they've been vindicated. Because the other side will keep fighting you.

So we started a case in 2010 after the school board illegally laid off our members, and we're still fighting that case! It's still in federal court three years later!

If you only go the legislative route and the legal route, you're playing by somebody else's rules. As [civil rights lawyer and Harvard law professor] Lani Guinier says, whoever makes the rules has an advantage. The legislative piece and the legal piece are out of our hands. But what we can control is our membership and having them active, having them involved, and having them push their legislators—but also having them take to the streets. And having the authorities understand that we will shut down your city. You will not be able to function without dealing with us fairly.

That's the way it is right now in Chicago. In the past, when school-closing hearings would happen, ten or twelve people would show up. We're now getting thousands of people to come to those hearings. And what they are saying with one voice is, "Keep your hands off my school."

Another question Lani Guinier asks is, "What are the stories the winners tell the losers to keep them playing the game?" A lot of people don't think about that. When you're playing on somebody else's turf, you don't have control. So the key is to change the rules of the game.

Dissent, Summer 2013, reprinted with permission of the University of Pennsylvania Press.

Frederick M. Hess, "The Facts Behind the Teacher Strikes," *Forbes*, April 30, 2018

Frederick M. (Rick) Hess is an education researcher at the American Enterprise Institute in Washington, DC, a relatively conservative "think tank." In this article, Hess discusses the wave of teacher strikes that began in West Virginia early in 2018 and spread to many parts of the nation. While sympathetic to the strikes and strikers, Hess makes much less far-reaching recommendations than the article that follows from the president of the American Federation of Teachers.

This spring has been marked by a remarkable phenomenon: the first statewide teacher strikes in recent memory. The strikes have been greeted with glowing press coverage and a remarkable degree of public support. After starting in West Virginia, things spread to Kentucky, Oklahoma, and most recently to Arizona and Colorado. Given all the claims and confusion surrounding these developments, it's worth taking a moment to explain what's going on, why both teachers and taxpayers have valid complaints, and how understanding all this can help point the way forward.

First off, the teachers have a legitimate concern. Teacher pay is mediocre for college-educated professionals, and has fallen over time. Teacher pay declined by two percent in real terms (after adjusting for inflation) between 1992 and 2014. According to data tracked by the

National Education Association (NEA), in 2016–2017, the most recent year for which data are available, average teacher pay nationally was $59,660. In the states where teachers have walked out, average pay is generally substantially lower than that. For instance, Kentucky's teachers rank 29th nationally at $52,338; Arizona's teachers 44th at $47,403; West Virginia's 49th, at $45,555; and Oklahoma's 50th, at $45,292.

Second, the notion that stingy taxpayers are to blame for stagnant teacher pay is hard to credit—despite frenzied media coverage suggesting just that. Now, it's wholly true that Arizona has modestly cut school spending over the past decade and that Oklahoma's per-pupil spending is flat over that same span, but the notion that taxpayers are defunding schools is just wrong. Indeed, in the two-plus decades between 1992 and 2014, even as teacher salaries declined across the land by two percent, inflation-adjusted per-pupil spending actually grew by 27 percent. In Kentucky and West Virginia, over that same period, teacher pay fell by three percent even as real per-pupil spending increased by more than 35 percent. In Oklahoma, over that same stretch, a 26-percent increase in real per-pupil spending translated only into a four-percent salary boost for teachers. As Grant Addison and I have noted in the case of West Virginia, "If teacher salaries had simply increased at the same rate as per-pupil spending, teacher salaries would have increased more than $17,000 since 1992—to an average of more than $63,000 today."

Third, teachers have raced to defend two of the big culprits responsible for their stagnant pay: costly employee benefits packages and added ranks of non-instructional staff. Even as teachers are frustrated by their take-home pay, their total compensation is a lot higher than many realize. That's because teacher retirement and health-care benefits are far more generous than those of the taxpayers who pay for them. As former Obama-administration official Chad Aldeman has observed, "While the average civilian employee receives $1.78 for retirement benefits per hour of work, public school teachers receive $6.22 per hour in retirement compensation." Between 2003 and 2014, even as teacher salaries declined, per-teacher average benefits spending increased from $14,000 to $21,000—much of which goes to paying down pension debt rather than benefits for current teachers. In the case of Kentucky, where teachers have been fighting pension reform, Aldeman has calculated that if the state wasn't forced to spend vast sums paying down pension debt, teacher salaries would be $11,400 higher today. There's a big disconnect; taxpayers see dollars flowing out of their wallets, but current teachers don't see those funds showing up in their paychecks.

Meanwhile, as organizations add employees, it becomes harder to pay them all well. Yet, in West Virginia, while student enrollment fell by 12 percent between 1992 and 2014, the number of non-teaching staff actually grew by ten percent. The story is similar in other strike states: In Kentucky, over that same stretch, enrollment grew by seven percent while the non-teaching workforce grew at nearly six times that rate—by a remarkable 41 percent. And Oklahoma saw a 17-percent growth in enrollment accompanied by a 36-percent increase in non-teaching staff. Nationally, while student enrollment grew 20 percent over that period, non-teaching staff grew by 47 percent. While some of these hires can represent a good investment, many represent little more than administrative bloat—and their sheer numbers soak up dollars that could otherwise fund teacher pay.

While it's not unreasonable to argue that we should have increased school spending in recent years more than we have, it's a mistake to blame stagnant teacher pay on a lack of taxpayer support. If teachers want sustainable pay increases and more than stopgap Band-Aids, school spending needs to be tackled in a way that addresses the concerns of teachers, taxpayers, and students. The contours of such a deal aren't that hard to see, though they're far tougher to enact. In any event, I'll try sketch them in my next column.

Randi Weingarten, "Hope in Darkness," 2018

Randi Weingarten is president of the American Federation of teachers and one of the nation's most vocal defenders of teachers and public education in general. Her July 13, 2018 speech to the AFT Annual Convention represents a clarion call to support striking teachers but also to do much more in support of American public education.

I. Introduction

Teachers weren't walking out on our students. We were walking out for our students—creating a human shield for the public schools they deserve; caring, fighting and showing up; creating hope in darkness. And we need that in these most surreal of times.

II. Two moments.

There has been no shortage of lows—or highs—these last couple of months. In one moment you can be saying, "What the heck?!" And the next, "Heck yeah!" (That's the sanitized version—because my swear jar is getting pretty full this year.)

My "What the heck" moment was Feb. 26. I was at the Supreme Court, listening to the oral arguments in *Janus v. ASFCME*. Bruce Rauner, the anti-union Illinois governor who brought the case, was there, as was Betsy DeVos, who snuck in. The oral arguments made it crystal clear what the right-wing supporters of this case want. And the right-wing justices made it equally clear they are willing accomplices.

In one exchange between Justice Kennedy and David Frederick, the lawyer for AFSCME, Kennedy asked if unions would have less political influence if AFSCME lost the case. Frederick responded that, if the *Janus* supporters prevailed, he believed unions would have less political influence. To which Kennedy replied, "Isn't that the end of this case?" Then, Justice Alito lectured Frederick about the First Amendment, asserting that collective bargaining in the public sector violates freedom of speech.

Our lawyer again pushed back, but the one-two punch had been thrown. The justices were attacking the two surest pathways working people have to a better life: the bargaining table and the ballot box. And these right-wing judges were trying to take both away, in one fell swoop.

Well, we know their decision now, and Justice Kagan's dissent nailed it: Her five conservative colleagues were "weaponizing the First Amendment," perverting it from its intended purpose of securing the political freedom necessary for democracy—just as Justice Kennedy did in *Citizens United*, equating unlimited corporate political donations with protected speech. Why would those justices, as Kagan put it, "overthrow a decision entrenched in this Nation's law and its economic life for over 40 years"? Because the court's right-wing 5–4 majority wants to destroy unions and, with them, the aspirations and dreams of working folks.

Figure 13.2 Randi Weingarten, president of the American Federation of Teachers, one of the nation's two large professional unions of public school teachers, has been an outspoken defender of teacher rights including the right to strike and influence education policy nationally and locally.

And then, just two weeks later: March 6, Charleston, W.Va; the start of the recent school walkouts.

I arrived at Fred's high school to find teachers, parents, students and others picketing, many for the first time ever. And at the state Capitol in Charleston, educators were in the streets, in a sea of red and blue T-shirts and signs. "This is what democracy looks like."

Democracy looked like students and school aides, teachers and bus drivers, children and parents, standing in solidarity. Democracy sounded like defiant chants of "55 strong" and "55 united" from voices representing each of the 55 school districts in West Virginia. It sounded like students lobbying their representatives, using the skills their teachers taught them to make the case for why educators deserve better. And democracy even tasted like something: pizza.

Seven hundred pizzas to be exact, courtesy of California educators who understood that, while unity can feed the soul, you still need something in your stomach. So Lita Blanc, the former president of the United Educators of San Francisco, started a GoFundMe campaign to feed her brothers and sisters 2,500 miles away (#union). Oh, and she made sure they ordered the pizzas from Husson's, a local family business.

Nine days later, still strong, still united, but nervous, the West Virginia House of Delegates had agreed to honor the deal the governor made with our unions, but nobody knew what the Republican-controlled Senate would do. And some state senators were playing hard-ball, threatening that West Virginians would face painful cuts if lawmakers conceded to educators' demands. But the public support was strong and growing—support from clergy and coal miners and our students. And the human shield worked; the Senate agreed. The moratorium on health insurance costs would hold, and teachers would be getting a 5 percent raise. And so would state employees. That was one heck of a "Heck yeah!" moment.

Throughout the capitol, you heard: "West Virginia first! Oklahoma next!" Educators saw that, together, we could accomplish what would be impossible alone. And that spirit of solidarity spread from red state to blue state to territory: from West Virginia to Arizona, Colorado to California, Pennsylvania to Puerto Rico.

Like so much of the recent activism, the teacher walkouts are stoking a movement for social justice, for workers' rights, for women's rights, for civil rights and children's rights, for decent healthcare and well-funded public schools, for safety—on the streets and in our schools. People acting together and accomplishing together what individuals can't do on their own, and doing it in places that no one predicted.

And that makes us a huge target. Right-wing groups and their wealthy allies want us gone, because unions are often the only organized force challenging their enormous power in politics and the economy. It's part of their trifecta strategy: suppress the vote, privatize public education and eliminate unions—the three ways working folks have any agency, any real power in America.

They know that working people gain strength in numbers. And they know working people do better when they join together in unions. So the right wing is doing everything they can to stop us, so people will have to fend for themselves.

That is why, in the days since the *Janus* decision, right-wing billionaires have spent millions of dollars, literally millions, on opt-out campaigns and lawsuits. The Mackinac Center, for example, funded by the Koch brothers and Betsy DeVos, is spamming every educator in nearly a dozen states on their school email accounts.

And speaking of Secretary DeVos, I think it's safe to say the whole country now knows what we knew the day her nomination was announced: that Betsy DeVos is the worst secretary of education ever.

Look at how the Freedom Foundation tries to pick off union members in Washington state: "Give yourself a raise . . ." *Give me a break.* You know who's paying for this? The American Legislative Exchange Council and the Walton Foundation, among others—the same groups that fight for huge tax cuts for the rich that end up decimating education funding, so students get scraps and many school employees can barely scrape by; the same groups that go after our pensions and wages and due process and on and on and on. Spare me the hypocrisy.

But you know what? Where our opponents have waged their bare-knuckle opt-out campaigns, the stories of drops have been few and far between. We have seen just the opposite: members recommitting and new members joining. Over and over members are sticking with their union.

The day the *Janus* decision came down, 2,400 faculty at Oregon State University joined our AFT and American Association of University Professors joint local. That same day, our nurses at the University of Cincinnati Medical Center won a contract that boosts salaries and will help prevent dangerous fatigue for nurses. And in the first three hours after the Professional Staff Congress announced the *Janus* decision, the union received 238 completed online membership applications. And they just kept coming.

Today, one of our locals is not here because it's on strike. Nurses at the University of Vermont Medical Center are on a two-day strike for fair wages and safe conditions. We'll show our support in a solidarity action at the end of this session.

Working people see that, through their union, they can accomplish together what would be impossible on their own. That's why the AFT is growing. And today, your union has 1,755,000 members, the highest number ever.

Caring, fighting, showing up.

III. More WVA, less scotus

How many of you were with us for the AFT TEACH conference, way back in 2015? If you were, I introduced you to this formula—for so-called value-added measurement. Some officials claimed it's the formula for teacher quality. Except, it isn't. It's really about trying to strip teachers' professional latitude from the equation. It's about reducing students to a test score and teachers to an algorithm, to create a pretext to starve and privatize public schools.

The good news is that, because of our work, the last administration and Congress replaced No Child Left Behind with a new federal education law, the Every Student Succeeds Act. And ESSA prohibits the secretary of education from mandating the use of student test scores in teacher evaluation. That has now helped our affiliates do the same in Houston; in New Mexico; in Ohio, where we're waiting for Gov. Kasich's signature; and we're "this close" in New York.

So they have their formula, but we have one too. It's a little more accessible and a lot more aspirational: $(ME+CI)I = A BETTER LIFE$. That is, member engagement + community involvement around issues that matter is the pathway to a better life . . .

IX. Conclusion: hope in darkness

A decade ago, you gave me the honor of leading this union I love. And what a decade it's been. It gave us President Obama, and President Trump. Waiting for Superman, and true superheroes. Testing obsession, and mass mobilization. Supreme Court decisions like *Janus*, and ones like the case recognizing the right to marry for people like myself who never in our lifetimes thought we could or would.

We are in a battle for the soul of our nation. It's terrifying, but we have confronted dreadful times before: slavery and the Civil War, two world wars, the Great Depression, Jim Crow and lynchings, Native Americans forced onto reservations, Japanese-Americans confined to internment camps.

But I come down on the side of hope. Because of you, we bring hope in the darkness.

America can and does change. Yes, power concedes nothing without a demand, as Frederick Douglass taught us, and we have been fighting powerful forces for centuries— millennia, in the case of Moses, who was the first labor organizer, fighting for the emancipation out of Egypt. Mother Jones fought another West Virginia battle, that time for coal miners, and the freedom riders fought Jim Crow. The arc of the universe does bend toward justice—but not on its own. It bends because people like you and me put our hands on it and bend it.

So now it's our turn. This is on us. This is our moment. This is our movement.

There are very few times in life you can look back and say that because of our movement, our actions, our human shield, we have turned back cruelty and created decency. That we have exercised all our muscles to bend that arc. That we have turned back darkness into hope.

Johann N. Neem, "Schools Have a Nobler Purpose Than Just Career Prep," 2018

In a commentary piece for the weekly newspaper of K-12 education professionals, EdWeek, Johann Neem reminded educators and parents that they "need regular reminders of the broader purposes of public schools." And in the brief article that followed he spelled out a little more about just what those broader purposes could be. By the 1990s and the early twenty-first century, most commentators assumed that the mantra of "college and career ready" answered the question of what schools were meant to accomplish. Yet as Neem and other historians know, the answer to that question has changed greatly over time, from the early nineteenth century when Thomas Jefferson and Horace Mann insisted that schools were primarily to prepare citizens for a democracy, to the civil war and civil rights eras when schools were often seen as the key to freedom, especially for those who had been unfree in the United States, to the focus on the best possible development for the individual child in the progressive era. As an immigrant (from India as a child), a product of California's public schools, and a parent of two children in Washington State, and as a scholar who had written extensively about the possibilities of public education, especially in his Democracy's Schools: The Rise of Public Education in America *(Baltimore, MD: Johns Hopkins University Press, 2017), Neem calls educators and parents to a new vision of the democratic potentialities of schools.*

We Americans are busy. We work, shop, cook, take care of the kids, and have little time left over. At a time of growing inequality, for many it feels like a struggle just to stay in place. Naturally, we are concerned about our children's future. We wonder whether schools are preparing them for a changing economy.

I'm a parent. I want to do all that I can to help my children, although I'm not always sure what that might be.

That's why we parents need regular reminders of the broader purposes of public schools. Instead of providing us those reasons, education reformers of the 21st century appeal to our fears and our pocketbooks. We are told again and again that our children will not get jobs unless they excel—and that our schools are failing. Children need to be prepared for "college and career," but not, it seems, to be citizens or flourishing human beings.

This is a problem that has been growing for years. The Common Core State Standards' authors considered the civic and humanistic benefits of education as a "natural outgrowth" of high standards, not a purpose for them. As one Dayton, Ohio, Chamber of Commerce member put it in 2014, students are educated "so that they can be an attractive product for business to consume and hire." Or, as former U.S. Secretary of Education Arne Duncan stated in 2012 that then-President Barack Obama "knows education is about jobs."

There is nothing wrong with schools preparing Americans for work and encouraging social mobility. Parents reasonably expect schools to offer their children economic opportunities, and all Americans benefit from a vibrant economy. But these goals are not enough. Today, we need reformers who appeal to the better angels of our nature. We need the kind of reformers who promote the ideals that the founders of our schools did over a century ago, most notably Horace Mann.

Mann—the first Massachusetts Board of Education Secretary in the 1830s—called us to be better selves. He used his bully pulpit to celebrate the true purpose of public education. He argued that a child's right to public education "begins with the first breath he draws." Children need more than food and shelter; they have minds, hearts, and souls."

Mann reasserted what the founders had said: In a republic, every citizen must be educated with the knowledge to make good decisions and to have empathy. "As each citizen is to participate in the power of governing others," he wrote, "it is an essential preliminary that he should be imbued with a feeling for the wants, and a sense of the rights, of those whom he is to govern; because the power of governing others, if guided by no higher motive than our own gratification, is the distinctive attribute of oppression."

Indeed, Mann hoped that public schools would foster economic opportunity, but not place economic success above other goods. To Mann, public schools should encourage public-mindedness, not just personal ambition.

Other antebellum education reformers agreed. John Pierce, the new state of Michigan's first superintendent of public schools, celebrated public schools where "all classes are blended together; the rich mingle with the poor . . . and mutual attachments are formed." James Henry Jr., then superintendent of schools in Herkimer County, N.Y., believed that public schools would prepare every American to "discharge his duties as an individual, as a member of society, and as a citizen of a free State."

We have struggled to meet these aspirations in a society segregated by class and race. Yet, antebellum reformers' civic ideals continued to inspire advocates of public education.

In the 1990s, supporters of national standards in the George H.W. Bush administration offered three reasons to improve achievement: "to promote educational equality, to preserve democracy and enhance the civic culture, and to improve economic competitiveness."

But that pursuit of "economic competitiveness" seems to crowd out the others today. This a real lowering of our expectations.

That's why we need a new generation of reformers to inspire us Americans again with the public purposes of public education. They will not come from the top down in the form of corporate reform; they must emerge from the grass roots. In many communities across the country, this is already happening.

When we vote or attend PTA and school board meetings, we can remind our leaders and—perhaps more importantly—each other, that we value more than getting ahead. Ideally, public schools bring together a diverse community and promote equality and empathy. They will not do so, however, unless we remember what, deep down, we already know to be true. Public schools shape hearts and minds and sustain our democracy.

Education Week, Commentary, July 25, 2018.

Bibliography
For Further Reading

Basic Background Information for Studying the History of American Education

There are many excellent books providing an overview of the history of American education, including:

Reese, William J., *America's Public Schools: From Common School to "No Child Left Behind"*, Baltimore, MD: Johns Hopkins University Press, 2011.

Urban, Wayne, Wagoner, Jennings, Jr., and Gaither, Milton, *American Education: A History*, 6th edition, New York: Routledge, 2019.

Chapter 1: The School in Colonial America, 1620–1770

Bailyn, Bernard, *Education in the Forming of American Society*, Chapel Hill, NC: University of North Carolina Press, 1960.

Berlin, Ira, *Many Thousands Gone: The First Two Centuries of Slavery in North America*, Cambridge, MA: Harvard University Press, 1998.

Calam, John, *Parsons and Pedagogues: The Society for the Propagation of the Gospel Adventure in American Education*, New York: Columbia University Press, 1971.

Richter, Daniel K., *Facing East from Indian Country: A Native History of Early America*, Cambridge, MA: Harvard University Press, 2001.

Szasz, Margaret Connell, *Indian Education in the American Colonies, 1607–1783*, Albuquerque, NM: University of New Mexico Press, 1988.

Wood, Gordon S., *The Americanization of Benjamin Franklin*, New York: Penguin Books, 2004.

Chapter 2: The American Revolution and Schools for the New Republic, 1770–1820

Bailyn, Bernard, *The Ideological Origins of the American Revolution*, Cambridge, MA: Harvard University Press, 1967.

Kaestle, Carl F., *Pillars of the Republic: Common Schools and American Society, 1780–1860*, New York: Hill and Wang, 1983.

Kendall, Joshua, *The Forgotten Founding Father: Noah Webster's Obsession and the Creation of an American Culture*, New York: G. P. Putnam's Sons, 2010.

Nash, Gary B., *The Unknown American Revolution: The Unruly Birth of Democracy and the Struggle to Create America*, New York: Viking, 2005.

Neem, Johann N., *Democracy's Schools: The Rise of Public Education in America*, Baltimore, MD: Johns Hopkins University Press, 2017.

Wood, Gordon S., *The Radicalism of the American Revolution*, New York: Vintage, 1993.

Chapter 3: The Common School Movement, 1820–1860

Glenn, Charles Leslie, Jr., *The Myth of the Common School*, Amherst, MA: The University of Massachusetts Press, 1988.

Kaestle, Carl F., *The Evolution of an Urban School System: New York City, 1750–1850*, Cambridge, MA: Harvard University Press, 1973.

—. *Pillars of the Republic: Common Schools and American Society, 1780–1860*, New York: Hill and Wang, 1983.

—. and Vinovskis, Marias, *Education and Social Change in Nineteenth-Century Massachusetts*, New York: Cambridge University Press, 1980.

Katz, Michael, *The Irony of Early School Reform*, Cambridge, MA: Harvard University Press, 1968.

Lannie, Vincent P., *Public Money and Parochial Education: Bishop Hughes, Governor Seward, and the New York School Controversy*, Cleveland, OH: Case Western Reserve University Press, 1968.

Messerli, Jonathan, *Horace Mann: A Biography*, New York: Alfred A. Knopf, 1972.

Nash, Margaret A., *Women's Education in the United States, 1780–1840*, New York: Palgrave Macmillan, 2005.

Reese, William J., *Testing Wars in the Public Schools: A Forgotten History*, Cambridge, MA: Harvard University Press, 2013.

Schultz, Stanley K., *The Culture Factory: Boston Public Schools, 1789–1860*, New York: Oxford University Press, 1973.

Sklar, Kathryn Kish, *Catharine Beecher: A Study in American Domesticity*, New Haven, CT: Yale University Press, 1973.

Solomon, Barbara Miller, *In the Company of Educated Women: A History of Women and Higher Education in America*, New Haven, CT: Yale University Press, 1985.

Chapter 4: Schooling Moves West, 1835–1860

Berkhofer, Robert F., Jr., *Salvation and the Savage: An Analysis of Protestant Missions and American Indian Response, 1787–1862*, Lexington, KY: University of Kentucky Press, 1965.

Brown, Dee, *Bury My Heart at Wounded Knee: An Indian History of the American West*, New York: Henry Holt, 1970.

Fraser, James W., *Pedagogue for God's Kingdom: Lyman Beecher and the Second Great Awakening*, Lanham, MD: University Press of America, 1985.

Kaufman, Polly Welts, *Women Teachers on the Frontier*, New Haven, CT: Yale University Press, 1984.

See also Sklar and Solomon, Chapter 3.

Chapter 5: Slavery, Reconstruction, and the Schools of the South, 1820–1937

Anderson, James D., *The Education of Blacks in the South, 1860–1935*, Chapel Hill, NC: University of North Carolina Press, 1988.

Blight, David W., *Frederick Douglass: Prophet of Freedom*, New York: Simon & Schuster, 2018.

Boylan, Anne M., *Sunday School: The Formation of an American Institution, 1790–1880*, New Haven, CT: Yale University Press, 1988.

Butchart, Ronald E., *Northern Schools, Southern Blacks, and Reconstruction: Freedmen's Education, 1862–1875*, Westport, CT: Greenwood Press, 1980.

—. *Schooling the Freed People: Teaching, Learning, and the Struggle for Black Freedom, 1861–1876*, Charlotte, NC: University of North Carolina Press, 2010.

DuBois, W. E. B., *Black Reconstruction: An Essay Towards a History of the Part Which Black Folk Played in the Attempt to Reconstruct Democracy in America, 1860–1880*, New York: Russell and Russell, 1935.

Franklin, John Hope, and Moss, Alfred A., Jr., *From Slavery to Freedom: A History of African Americans*, 7th edition, New York: Alfred A. Knopf, 1994.

Genovese, Eugene D., *Roll, Jordan, Roll: The World the Slaves Made*, New York: Vintage Books, 1972.

Jones, Jacqueline, *Soldiers of Light and Love: Northern Teachers and Georgia Blacks, 1865–1873*, Chapel Hill, NC: University of North Carolina Press, 1980.

Malczewski, Joan, *Building a New Educational State: Foundations, Schools, and the American South*, Chicago, IL: University of Chicago Press, 2016.

McAfee, Ward M., *Religion, Race, and Reconstruction: The Public School in the Politics of the 1870s*, Albany, NY, NY: State University of New York Press, 1998.

Webber, Thomas L., *Deep Like the Rivers: Education in the Slave Quarter Community, 1831–1865*, New York: W. W. Norton, 1978.

Chapter 6: The Emergence of the High School, 1821–1959

Angus, David L., and Mirel, Jeffrey E., *The Failed Promise of the American High School, 1890–1995*, New York: Teachers College Press, 1999.

Herbst, Jurgen, *The Once and Future School: Three Hundred and Fifty Years of American Secondary Education*, New York: Routledge, 1996.

Kliebard, Herbert M., *The Struggle for the American Curriculum*, 2nd edition, New York: Routledge, 1995.

Kridel, Craig, and Bullough, Robert V., Jr., *Stories of the Eight-Year Study: Reexamining Secondary Education in America*. Albany, NY, NY: State University of New York Press, 2007.

Labaree, David F., *The Making of an American High School: The Credentials Market and the Central High School of Philadelphia, 1838–1939*, New Haven, CT: Yale University Press, 1988.

Reese, William J., *The Origins of the American High School*, New Haven, CT: Yale University Press, 1995.

Chapter 7: Growth and Diversity in Schools and Students, 1880–1960

Adams, David Wallace, *Education for Extinction: American Indians and the Boarding School Experience, 1875–1928*, Lawrence, KS: University Press of Kansas, 1995.

Allen, Paula Gunn, *The Sacred Hoop: Recovering the Feminine in American Indian Traditions*, Boston, MA: Beacon Press, 1992.

Antin, Mary, *The Promised Land*, Boston, MA: Houghton Mifflin, 1911.

Burns, J. A., *The Catholic School System in the United States: Its Principles, Origin, and Establishment*, New York, 1908.

Dog, Mary Crow, with Erdoes, Richard, *Lakota Woman*, New York: Harper, 1990.

Franklin, Barry M., *From "Backwardness" to "At-Risk": Childhood Learning Difficulties and the Contradictions of School Reform*, Albany, NY, NY: State University of New York Press, 1994.

Gonzalez, Gilbert, *Chicano Education in the Era of Segregation*, Philadelphia, PA: Balch Institute Press, 1990.

Lazerson, Marvin, *Origins of the Urban School: Public Education in Massachusetts, 1870–1915*, Cambridge, MA: Harvard University Press, 1971.

Low, Victor, *The Unimpressible Race: A Century of Educational Struggle by the Chinese in San Francisco*, San Francisco, CA: East/West Publishing, 1982.

Prucha, Francis Paul, *The Great Father: The United States Government and the American Indians*, 2 vols, Lincoln, NE: University of Nebraska Press, 1984.

—. ed., *Documents of United States Indian Policy*, 2nd edition expanded, Lincoln, NE: University of Nebraska Press, 1990.

Ravitch, Diane, *The Great School Wars: New York City, 1805–1973*, New York: Basic Books, 1974.

Rury, John L., *Education and Women's Work: Female Schooling and the Division of Labor in Urban America, 1870–1930*, Albany, NY: State University of New York Press, 1991.

Sanders, James W., *The Education of an Urban Minority: Catholics in Chicago, 1833–1965*, New York: Oxford University Press, 1977.

—. *Irish vs. Yankee: A Social History of the Boston Public Schools*, New York: Oxford University Press, 2018.

San Miguel, Guadalupe, Jr., *"Let All of Them Take Heed": Mexican Americans and the Campaign for Educational Equality in Texas, 1910–1981*, Austin, TX: University of Texas Press, 1987.

Takaki, Ronald, *Strangers from a Different Shore: A History of Asian Americans*, New York: Penguin Books, 1989.

Walsh, Catherine, *Pedagogy and the Struggle for Voice: Issues of Language, Power, and Schooling for Puerto Ricans*, New York: Bergin and Garvey, 1991.

Chapter 8: The Progressive Era, 1890–1950

Blount, Jackie M., *Destined to Rule the Schools: Women and the Superintendency, 1873–1995*, Albany, NY: State University of New York Press, 1998.

Bowers, C. A., *The Progressive Educator and the Depression: The Radical Years*, New York: Random House, 1969.

Counts, George S., *Dare the School Build a New Social Order?* Edited and with an introduction by Wayne Urban, Carbondale, IL: Southern Illinois University Press, 1978.

Cremin, Lawrence A., *The Transformation of the School: Progressivism in American Education, 1876–1957*, New York: Random House, 1961.

Cuban, Larry, *How Teachers Taught: Constancy and Change in American Classrooms, 1890–1990*, 2nd edition, New York: Teachers College Press, 1993.

Dewey, John, *The School and Society*, Chicago, IL: University of Chicago Press, 1900.

—. *The Child and the Curriculum*, Chicago, IL: The University of Chicago Press, 1902.

—. *Democracy and Education*, New York: Macmillan, 1916.

Graham, Patricia Albjerg, *Progressive Education: From Arcady to Academe*, New York: Teachers College Press, 1967.

Katz, Michael B., *Class, Bureaucracy, and Education: The Illusion of Educational Change in America*, New York: Praeger, 1975.

Lemann, Nicholas, *The Big Test: The Secret History of American Meritocracy*, New York: Farrar, Straus and Giroux, 2000.

Murphy, Marjorie, *Blackboard Unions: The AFT and the NEA, 1900–1980*, Ithaca, NY: Cornell University Press, 1990.

Reese, William J., *Power and the Promise of School Reform: Grass-Roots Movement During the Progressive Era*, Boston, MA: Routledge & Kegan Paul, 1986.

Steffes, Tracy L., *School, Society, and State: A New Education to Govern Modern America, 1890–1940*, Chicago, IL: University of Chicago Press, 2012.

Tyack, David, *The One Best System: A History of American Urban Education*, Cambridge, MA: Harvard University Press, 1974.

Tyack, David and Hansot, Elisabeth, *Managers of Virtue: Public School Leadership in America, 1820–1980*, New York: Basic Books, 1982.

Tyack, David, Lowe, Robert, and Hansot, Elisabeth, *Public Schools in Hard Times: The Great Depression and Recent Years*, Cambridge, MA: Harvard University Press, 1984.

Urban, Wayne J., *Why Teachers Organized*, Detroit, MI: Wayne State University Press, 1982.

Westbrook, Robert, *John Dewey and American Democracy*, Ithaca, NY: Cornell University Press, 1991.

Wrigley, Julia, *Class Politics and Public Schools: Chicago, 1900–1950*, New Brunswick, NJ: Rutgers University Press, 1982.

Chapter 9: Schools in the Cold War Era, 1950–1970

Blount, Jackie M., *Fit to Teach: Same Sex Desire, Gender, and School Work in the Twentieth Century*, Albany, NY: State University of New York Press, 2006.

Cremin, Lawrence A., *The Transformation of the School: Progressivism in American Education, 1876–1957*, New York: Alfred A. Knopf, 1961.

Fitzgerald, Frances, *America Revised: History Schoolbooks in the Twentieth Century*, New York: Vintage Books, 1979.

Kliebard, Herbert M., *The Struggle for the American Curriculum, 1893–1958*, Boston, MA: Routledge & Kegan Paul, 1986.

Mirel, Jeffrey, *The Rise and Fall of an Urban School System: Detroit, 1907–1981*, 2nd edition, Ann Arbor, MI: University of Michigan Press, 1999.

Ravitch, Diane, *The Troubled Crusade: American Education, 1945–1980*, New York: Basic Books, 1983.

Spring, Joel, *The Sorting Machine: National Educational Policy Since 1945*, New York: McKay, 1976.

Trace, Arthur S., *What Ivan Knows That Johnny Doesn't*, New York: Random House, 1961.

See also Cuban, Chapter 8.

Chapter 10: Civil Rights, Integration, and School Reform, 1954–1980

Carson, Clayborne, Garrow, David J., Gill, Gerald, Harding, Vincent, and Hine, Darlene Clark, *The Eyes on the Prize Reader: Documents, Speeches, and Firsthand Accounts from the Black Freedom Struggle, 1954–1990*, New York: Penguin Books, 1991.

Coleman, James S., et al., *Trends in School Segregation, 1968–1973*, Washington, DC: Urban Institute, 1975.

Coleman, James, Campbell, Ernest Q., Hobson, Carol J., McPortland, James, Mood, Alexander M., Weinfeld, Fredrick D., and York, Robert L., *Equality of Educational Opportunity*, Washington, DC: U.S. Government Printing Office, 1966.

Cronin, Joseph M., *The Control of Urban Schools: Perspectives on the Power of Educational Reformers*, New York: Free Press, 1973.

Kluger, Richard, *Simple Justice*, New York: Alfred A. Knopf, 1976.

Kozol, Jonathan, *Death at an Early Age: The Destruction of the Hearts and Minds of Negro Children in the Boston Public Schools*, Boston, MA: Houghton Mifflin, 1967.

Myrdal, Gunnar, *An American Dilemma: The Negro Problem and Modern Democracy*, New York: Harper & Row, 1944.

Orfield, Gary, *The Reconstruction of Southern Education: The Schools and the 1964 Civil Rights Act*, New York: Wiley Interscience, 1969.

Pattterson, James T., *Brown v. Board of Education: A Civil Rights Milestone and Its Troubled Legacy*, New York: Oxford University Press, 2001.

Perrillo, Jonna, *Uncivil Rights: Teachers, Unions, and Race in the Battle for School Equality*, Chicago, IL: University of Chicago Press, 2012.

Chapter 11: Rights, Opportunities, and Limits in American Education, 1965–1980

Berke, Joel S., and Kirst, Michael W., *Federal Aid to Education: Who Benefits? Who Governs?*, Lexington, MA: D. C. Heath, 1972.

Fellman, David, *The Supreme Court and Education*, 3rd edition, New York: Teachers College Press, 1976.

Graham, Hugh Davis, *Uncertain Triumph: Federal Educational Policy in the Kennedy and Johnson Years*, Chapel Hill, NC: University of North Carolina Press, 1984.

Hanson, Katherine, Vivian Guilfoy, and Sarita Pillai, *More Than Title IX: How Equity in Education Has Shaped the Nation*, Lanham, MD: Rowman & Littlefield, 2009.

Jordan, Barbara C., and Rostow, Elspeth D., *The Great Society: A Twenty Year Critique*, Austin, TX: Lyndon Baines Johnson Library, 1986.

Porter, Rosalie Pedalino, *Forked Tongue: The Politics of Bilingual Education*, New York: Basic Books, 1990.

Chapter 12: Reform Efforts of the 1980s and 1990s and the New Century, 1980–2005

Apple, Michael, *Official Knowledge: Democratic Education in a Conservative Age*, New York: Routledge, 1993.

—. *Cultural Politics and Education*, New York: Teachers College Press, 1996.

Asante, Molefi Kete, *Afrocentricity*, Trenton, NJ: Africa World Press, 1988.

Bell, Terrell, *The Thirteenth Man: A Reagan Cabinet Memoir*, New York: The Free Press, 1988.

Berliner, David C., and Biddle, Bruce J., *The Manufactured Crisis: Myths, Fraud, and the Attack on America's Schools*, Reading, MA: Addison-Wesley, 1995.

Chubb, J., and Moe, T., *Politics, Markets, and America's Schools*, Washington, DC: Brookings Institution, 1990.

Cornbleth, Catherine, and Waugh, Detter, *The Great Speckled Bird: Multicultural Politics and Education Policy Making*, New York: St. Martin's Press, 1995.

Cuban, Larry, *Teachers and Machines: Classroom Use of Technology Since 1920*, New York: Teachers College Press, 1986.

—. *Hugging the Middle: How Teachers Teach in an Era of Testing and Accountability*, New York: Teachers College Press, 2009.

—. *Oversold and Underused: Computers in the Classroom*, Cambridge, MA: Harvard University Press, 2009.

Darling-Hammond, Linda, *The Flat World and Education: How America's Commitment to Equity Will Determine Our Future*, New York: Teachers College Press, 2010.

Foster, Michele, *Black Teachers on Teaching*, New York: The New Press, 1997.

Fraser, James W., *Between Church and State: Religion and Public Education in a Multicultural America*, 2nd edition, Baltimore, MD: Johns Hopkins University Press, 2016.

Hess, Frederick M., and Finn, Chester E., Jr., *Leaving No Child Behind? Options for Kids in Failing Schools*, New York: Palgrave, 2004.

Kozol, Jonathan, *Savage Inequalities: Children in America's Schools*, New York: Crown, 1991.

McLaren, Peter, *Revolutionary Multiculturalism: Pedagogies of Dissent for the New Millennium*, Boulder, CO: Westview Press, 1997.

Meier, Deborah, *The Power of Their Ideas*, Boston, MA: Beacon Press, 1995.

Meier, Deborah, and Wood, George, eds., *Many Children Left Behind: How the No Child Left Behind Act Is Damaging Our Children and Our Schools*, Boston, MA: Beacon Press, 2004.

Nieto, Sonia, *Affirming Diversity: The Sociopolitical Context of Multicultural Education*, New York: Addison-Wesley Longman, 1992.

Sarason, Seymour B., *Revisiting "The Culture of the School and the Problem of Change"*, New York: Teachers College Press, 1996.

Tyack, David, and Larry Cuban, *Tinkering Toward Utopia: A Century of Public School Reform*, Cambridge, MA: Harvard University Press, 1995.

Zimmerman, Jonathan, *Whose America? Culture Wars in the Public Schools*, Cambridge, MA: Harvard University Press, 2002.

Chapter 13: Curriculum, Technology, and New Tensions, 2005–2018

Berner, Ashley, *Pluralism in American Public Education: No One Way to Go to School*, New York: Palgrave Macmillan, 2017.

Duncan, Arne, *How Schools Work: An Inside Account of Failure and Success From One of the Nation's Longest-Serving Secretaries of Education*, New York: Simon & Schuster, 2018.

Hess, Frederick M., and McShane, Michael Q., *Common Core Meets Education Reform: What It All Means for Politics, Policy, and the Future of Schooling*, New York: Teachers College Press, 2013.

Ivery, Curtis, and Bassett, Joshua, eds., *Reclaiming Integration and the Language of Race in the "Post Racial" Era*, New York: Rowman and Littlefield, 2015.

Kumashiro, Kevin K., *The Seduction of Common Sense: How the Right Has Framed the Debate on America's Schools*, New York: Teachers College Press, 2008.

Lewis-McCoy, and L'Heureux, R., *Race, Resources, and Suburban Schools*, Palo Alto, CA: Stanford University Press, 2014.

Nunez, Isabel, Michie, Gregory, and Konkol, Pamela, *Worth Striking For: Why Education Policy Is Every Teacher's Concern*, New York: Teachers College Press, 2015.

Orfield, Gary, and Frankenbury, Erica, *Educational Delusions? Why Choice Can Deepen Inequality and How to Make Schools Fair*, Berkeley, CA: University of California Press, 2013.

Ravitch, Diane, *Reign of Error: The Hoax of the Privatization Movement and the Danger to America's Public Schools*, New York: Alfred A. Knopf, 2013.

About the Author

James W. Fraser is Professor of History and Education and Chair of the Department of Applied Statistics, Social Science, and Humanities at the Steinhardt School of Culture, Education, and Human Development at New York University. He was the Senior Vice President for Programs at the Woodrow Wilson National Fellowship Foundation in Princeton, New Jersey from 2008 to 2012 and the founding dean of Northeastern University's School of Education, serving from 1999 to 2004.

His teaching includes survey courses in American history and courses in the History of American Education, Introduction to Education and Global Culture Wars, and Religion and Education, and many workshops for high school history teachers. He was a lecturer in the Program in Religion and Secondary Education at the Harvard University Divinity School from 1997 to 2004. He has also taught at Lesley University, University of Massachusetts at Boston, Boston University, and Public School 76 Manhattan. Fraser is an historian of education. His colleagues in the History of Education Society elected him as the society's president for 2013–2014.

Author or editor of twelve books, Fraser wrote *By the People: A History of the United States* (second edition, Pearson, 2019), a textbook specifically focused on AP U.S. History. Fraser's latest book, co-authored with Lauren Lefty, is *Teaching Teachers: Changing Paths and Enduring Debates* (Johns Hopkins University Press, 2019). A revised second edition of his *Between Church and State: Religion and Public Education in a Multicultural America* was published by Johns Hopkins University Press in 2016. His current research interests include the place of religion in K-12 schools around the globe, the recent—and fast-changing—history of the ways in which teachers are taught in the United States and globally, and the ongoing discussions about the teaching of U.S. History in middle and high schools in the United States.

Fraser lives in New York City with his wife Katherine Hanson and their dog Pebble.

Index

Abbott, Greg 362
Abington School Board v. Schempp (1963) 275, 278
Adams, John 9; *Diary* entries (1756) 3, 9–10; Massachusetts constitution 18
Addison, Grant 371
adequate yearly progress (AYP) 306, 332, 333
Adler, Mortimer J. 224, 306
adolescence 108, 116–18; *see also* high schools
African Americans 61; civil rights 240, 245–50, 275; education 37, 76, 77–8, 93–7, 101–3, 245–8, 275; high schools 106; impact of segregation on children 253–6; literacy 76; teachers 77, 88; *see also* DuBois, W. E. B.; Forten, Charlotte; Garvey, Marcus; NAACP; slavery; Washington, Booker T.
Aldeman, Chad 371
American Creed 326
American Federation of Teachers (AFT): Common Core State Standards 339; Randi Weingarten's speech (2018) 372–6; Resolution: "Defeating the DeVos Agenda" (2018) 365–6
American Indians *see* Native Americans
American Revolution (1765–1783) 17–20
The American Spelling Book (1783) 30–2, *31*, 82
Anderson, James D.: *The Education of Blacks in the South, 1860–1935* 76–7
Andrus, Ethel P. 167
Angus, David L. 107
Antin, Mary 141; *The Promised Land* (1912) 141, 145–9
Argyris, Chris 347
Arkansas: *Epperson v. Arkansas* (1968) 286; Little Rock Central High School (1957) 241, 256–60, *260*
Articles of Confederation (1787) 19
Asian Americans 240; California (1919–1920) 155–63, 240, 242; school segregation 240, 242
AYP *see* adequate yearly progress

Baldwin, Roger 212
Baltimore: Third Plenary Council (1884) 142–5
Banks, James 317
Barnard, Henry 35
Bartels v. Iowa (1923) 286
Bastian, Ann *et al.*: *Choosing Equality: The Case for Democratic Schooling* (1985) 305, 310–13
Bates, Daisy 241, 256; *The Long Shadow of Little Rock, Reflections on 1957* 256–60, *260*
Batson, Ruth 241, 260; Statement to the Boston School Committee (June 11, 1963) 260–4
Beecher, Catherine E. 35, 43, 60, 61, 69, *71*; *An Essay on the Education of Female Teachers for the United States* (1835) 36, 43–5

Beecher, Lyman 65; *The Memory of Our Fathers* 63, 65–6; *A Plea for the West* 60–1
Bell, Terrell 304, 315
Berkeley, Sir William 2, 6, 7
Berliner, David C. and Bruce J. Biddle: *The Manufactured Crisis* (1995) 305, 313–17
Bestor, Arthur: *Educational Wastelands* 217
Biddle, Bruce J. *see* Berliner, David C.
Bigelow, Cora: "World Democracy and School Democracy" (1918) 189–90, 191
Bilingual Education Act (1968) 292–3
bilingualism 164, 166, 170, 297, 318, 319–20
Bill & Melinda Gates Foundation 350
Binet-Simon Intelligence Scale 167, 199–200, 203–4
Blanc, Lita 373
blended learning 352
Block, Herb: cartoon *277*
Blossom, Virgil 257, 258–9
Board of National Popular Education 61, 69; Correspondence (1849–1850) 68–70, 71
Boston: Abiel Smith School 37, 38; African American schools 37, 38, 241–2; colonial America 2; elementary teachers' organization 189; English Classical High School (1821) 104; Latin School 2, 3, 8, 104; *Morgan v. Hennigan* (1972) 242; Museum of African America History *59*; progressive movement 177; Public Schools (1901–1906) 177–81; school desegregation 38, 53–9, 241–2, 260–71; "Steamer Glass" *142*
Bourne, Randolph S. 191
Boyer, Ernest 306
Brock, G. E. 180
Brooks, Stratton D. 180, 181
Brown, George 331
Brown, John 79
Brown v. Board of Education of Topeka, Kansas (1954) 38, 240, 241, 250–3, 272, 300
Bryan, William Jennings 106, 135; "Who Shall Control?" (1925) 135–6
Burnside v. Byars 287
Bush, George H. W. 305, 315, 333, 377
Bush, George W. 305–6, 330–2, *331*
Butler, Nicholas Murray 176

California: Asian Americans 155–63, 240, 242; Gonzalo and Felicitas Mendez School, Santa Ana 242; *Mendez v. Westminster* (1946) 242–5; Mexican Americans 163–9, 240, 242–5; school segregation 155, 165–6, 242
Cardinal Principles of Secondary Education (NEA, 1981) 109, 126; I. The Need for

Reorganization 126–8; II. The Goal of Education in a Democracy 128; III. The Main Objectives of Education 128–9; IV. The Role of Secondary Education 129–30; VII. Education as a Process of Growth 130; X. Division of Education into Elementary and Secondary 130–1; XV. The Specializing and Unifying Functions of Secondary Education 131–3; XVI. The Comprehensive High School as The Standard Secondary School 133; XX. Conclusion 133–4

Carnegie Corporation of New York 109, 136

Carolina: state standards 346

Carroll, John 142

Carter, Jimmy 304

Catholicism 35, 36; and the common school fund 36, 49–53; education 140–1, 142–5; Third Plenary Council of Baltimore (1884) 142–3

CCSS see Common Core State Standards

charter schools 338; AFT resolution: "Defeating the DeVos Agenda" (2018) 365–6; Betsy DeVos' remarks 362–5; online charter schools 355

Chicago: High School 104, 105; Mexican Americans 277; school councils 185–7

Chicago Teachers Federation 181

Chicago Teachers Union 366–7

child benefit 281

child-centred education 176, 191, 205, 214

Chinese Americans 155; see also Asian Americans; Lau et al. v. Nichols et al. (1974)

Chinese Exclusion Act (1882) 155

Cincinnati: High School 104

civil rights (1954–1980) 240–2, 275–8; bilingual education 292–4; equal opportunities for women 276, 292; freedom of speech 276, 285–91; The Great Society 276, 281–5, 304; integration 271–2, 273, 274; prayer in school 275, 277, 278–81; Septima Clark 240–1, 245–50, 246; students with disabilities 295–6, 341, 343; see also school desegregation; school segregation

Civil Rights Act (1964) 281, 292

Civilization Fund Act (1819) 33

Clark, Kenneth B.: "How Children Learn About Race" (1950) 253–6

Clark, Septima 240–1, 245, 246; Ready From Within (ca. 1950) 245–50

Clinton, Bill 305

co-education 105

Cohen, David 347

Cohen, Mike 346

Cold War era (1950–1970) 214–15; How Children Fail (1964) 235–9; National Defense Education Act (1958) 215, 219, 220–1; science education 215–19; Scott Foresman Readers (1955) 221–4; Thirty-Six Children (1967) 227–35

college entrance requirements 107

Colonial America (1620–1770) 1–3; Benjamin Franklin, Autobiography 8–9; education 6–8; John Adams' Diary 3, 9–10; Native Americans 24; The New England Primer 10, 11–16; religious education 3–6; slaves 4–6

Columbine High School, Colorado (1999) 338, 355

Commager, Henry Steele 61, 63

Committee of Ten (1893) 106, 107, 108, 109–16, 112, 126

Common Core 339

Common Core State Standards (CCSS, 2010) 337–8, 376; 1-1 computing 351; frequently asked questions (2018) 338–44; online testing 353–4; Where Are the Common Core State Standards Headed? Oblivion, Probably (2016) 344–7

common school fund 36, 49–53

Common School Journal: Debate Over Plan to Abolish the Board of Education (1840) 36, 45–9

common school movement (1820–1860) 34–8; moral education 40; religious education 35, 36, 41–2; school integration 37–8; women teachers 35–6

community control of education 36

computers 327–30, 351–2

Conant, James Bryant 109, 136; The American High School Today (1959) 109, 136–9

Cornyn, John 360–1

Council of Chief State School Officers 339, 342

Counts, George S. 177, 205, 214; Dare the School Build a New Social Order? (1932) 205–10; see also The Social Frontier

Cox v. Louisiana (1965) 290

Cram, Jacob 73–5

Cremin, Lawrence A. 175, 214

Crèvecoeur, J. Hector St John 325

Cuomo, Andrew 346

curriculum 237; Boston (1963) 263, 268–9; child-centered curriculum 176, 191, 205, 214, 215, 217; Common Core State Standards (CCSS) 337–8, 343; high schools 106, 107–9, 110–15, 117, 126, 130, 132, 133; history 319, 323; Native Americans 152, 153; Progressive Era 176, 189, 191, 197; Puerto Rican schools 169, 171–3; science education 215–19; and technology 346, 349

Darling-Hammond, Linda: "The Collision of New Standards and Old Inequalities" (2004) 334, 336

DeLima, Agnes 191

democracy 189–90, 191

Desegregation of the Boston Public Schools (1846–1855) 53–4; Act in Amendment of An Act Concerning Public Schools (1855) 58–9; Argument of Charles Sumner, Esq. 56–7; Report to the Primary School Committee 53–4; Report of the Primary School Committee in Response 54–5; Sarah C. Roberts v. The City of Boston (1849) 37, 38, 55–8

DeVos, Betsy 338, 372, 374; AFT resolution: "Defeating the DeVos Agenda" (2018) 365–6; Remarks to Turning Point USA High School Leadership Summit (July 25, 2018) 362–5

Dewey, John 190; "A Policy of Industrial Education" (1914) 119–21; "Can education share in social reconstruction?" 211–13; "Education vs. Trade-Training–Dr. Dewey's Reply" (1915) 106,

108, 124–5; "learning by doing" 226; progressive education 175, 177, 185, 215; *The School and Society* (1899) 191–8, 224; *The Social Frontier* 210; on teacher organization 183

Dickey v. Alabama State Board of Education (1967) 288

digital materials in classrooms 354

digital natives 348–9

disabilities, students with 277, 295–6, 304, 341, 343

Dissent (magazine, 2013): "Defending Public Education: An Interview with Karen Lewis" (2013) 366–70

distance learning 355

diversity in schools and students (1880–1960) 140–2, 305; *see also* African Americans; Asian Americans; Catholicism; Japanese Americans; Jewish Americans; Mexican Americans; Native Americans; Puerto Ricans

Donovan, Jim 179

double-loop learning 347

Douglass, Frederick 76, 78–9, 375; *Narrative of the Life of Frederick Douglass: An American Slave* (1845) 78–83

DuBois, W. E. B. 78, 97, *98*, 101; *Black Reconstruction in America* (1935) 76; *The Souls of Black Folk* (1903) 97–101

Duncan, Arne 376

Durr, Virginia 247

Dwight, Dr. Timothy 65

E-rate program 353

Eckford, Elizabeth 258–60

Eckhardt, Christopher *see Tinker et al. v. Des Moines Independent Community School District* (1969)

Edison, Thomas 106; Film Will Replace Teacher, Books (1923) 134–5

EdTech Strategies 353

Education for All Handicapped Children Act (1975) 295–6

Education Next (journal) 345

Education Week: Harold, Benjamin 349–55

educational standards 338–9; *see also* Common Core State Standards

EDUCAUSE 350

EdWeek *see* Neem, Johann N.

Eidelson, John and Sarah Jaffe: "Defending Public Education: An Interview with Karen Lewis" (2013) 366–70

Eisenhower, Dwight D. 215–16, 241

Elementary and Secondary Education Act (ESEA, 1965) 276, 281, 283–5, 331, 332

Elementary Public Instruction in Europe (1837) 66–8

elementary schools 106; science in 218–19; *see also* Common School Movement (1820–1860)

Eliot, Charles W. 107, 108, 110, 126

Elliott, Harrison 210

Ellis, A. 180

elocution 63–4

Engel v. Vitale (1962) 275, 278–81, 286

English language learners 147–8, 158, 170, 171, 172–4, 317–18, 341

Epperson v. Arkansas (1968) 286

equality and equity 252, 321

ESEA *see* Elementary and Secondary Education Act

Every Student Succeeds Act (2015) 334

evolution, teaching of 106, 135–6

fairness in schooling *see* civil rights; school desegregation; school reform (1980s–1990s)

Fanon, Frantz 324

Faubus, Orval 241, 257

Federal Commission on School Safety 363

Federal Communications Commission (FCC) 352–3

Finn, Chester E., Jr.: on Japanese education 315; "Leaving No Child Behind?" (2004) 334, **336**

Fitzgerald, John F. 179, 180

Flesch, Rudolf: *Why Johnny Can't Read* 217

Florida *see* Marjory Stoneman Douglas High School, Parkland, Florida

Forten, Charlotte 88; *The Journal of Charlotte Forten* (1862) 77, 88–93

Fourteenth Amendment (1868) 251, 253, 279, 286

Franklin, Benjamin: *Autobiography* (1714–1718) 3, 8–9

Fraser, James W. *see* McDonald, Joseph P. *et al.*

Frederick, David 372

freedom of speech 286; *see also Tinker et al. v. Des Moines Independent Community School District* (1969)

Freedom Schools 241

Freedom Train 247

Fruchter, Norm *see* Bastian, Ann *et al.*

Fuchs, Lawrence 326

Galton, Francis 199

Gardner, John W. 136

Garrison, William Lloyd 37, 79, 84

Gartland, Arthur 242

Garvey, Marcus 78, 101; *Lessons from the School of African Philosophy: The New Way to Education* (1937) 101–3

Gates, Sir Thomas 3–4

Gibbon, Edward 324

Gittell, Marilyn *see* Bastian, Ann *et al.*

Glass, Bentley 218

Gonzalez, Emma: address at gun control rally (2018) 355–8, *356*

Goodlad, John 306

Gore, Al 330–1

Grassley, Chuck 357

Great Society 276, 281–5, 304

Greer, Colin *see* Bastian, Ann *et al.*

Griffith, Beatrice: *American Me* (1948) 163–9

Guinier, Lani 370

Gulick, Sidney L.: *The American-Japanese Problem* 162–3

gun control (2018) 355–8

guns in schools (2018) 338, 355–62

Haley, Margaret 181; *Why Teachers Should Organize* (1904) 181–5
Hall, G. Stanley 108, 116; *Adolescence* (1904) 108, 116–18
Hammond v. South Carolina State College (1967) 288
Hanus, Paul 178
Harlem Children's Zone 273–4
Harold, Benjamin: "Technology in Education: An Overview" (2016) 349–55
Harris, William T. 109–10
Haskins, Kenneth *see* Bastian, Ann *et al.*
Hawaii: Japanese Americans 161, 162–3
health: education 129; Native Americans 149, 150–1
Henry, James, Jr. 377
Henry, Patrick 64; Speech before the Virginia Convention (1765) 63, 64–5
Herbst, Jurgen 107
Hess, Frederick M. 334; "Leaving No Child Behind?" (2004) 334, **336**; "The Facts Behind the Teacher Strikes" (2018) 370–2
Hicks, Louise Day 242
High School, Palmyra, Wisconsin *105*
high schools: (1821–1959) 104–39; *Adolescence* (1904) 108, 116–18; *The American High School Today* (1959) 136–9; *Cardinal Principles of Secondary Education* (1981) 109, 126–34; coeducation 105; comprehensive high schools 136, 137; curriculum 106, 107–9, 110–15, 117, 126, 130, 132, 133; diplomas 106–7; entrance requirements 116; graduates 107; industrial training 119–21, 153; Palmyra, Wisconsin *105*; Report of the Committee of Ten (1893) 106, 107, 108, 109–16, **112**; teacher training 115; teaching of evolution 106, 135–6; Thomas Edison Predicts Film Will Replace Teacher, Books (1923) 134–5; vocational education 108, 109, 121–5; *see also Tinker et al. v. Des Moines Independent Community School District* (1969); Turning Point USA High School Leadership Summit (July 25, 2018)
Highlander Folk School, Tennessee 245–8, 249, 250
Holmes, Henry W. 179
Holt, John 215; *How Children Fail* (1964) 235–9
Holton, Gerald 218
Hoover, Herbert 212
Horton, Myles 246, 247
Houston, Charles 240
Howe, Irving 323
Hughes, John 36, 141
Hunt, James B. 337–8
Hutcheson, Anne 2

Indian Voices: The First Convocation of American Indian Scholars (1970) 296
Indiana: Board of National Popular Education correspondence 70; state standards 346
industrial education 119–21, 153
Inslee, Jay: guns in schools 361–2
integration 271–2, 273, 274
intelligence tests 176, 199–205; Binet tests 167, 199–200, 203–4; and culture 166–7;

group testing 204–5; mental age 200–1, **202**; significance of mental tests 200
intelligent quotient (IQ) 201–2; as basis for prediction 202, 203; effects of environment on 203–4
international benchmarking 341

Jaffe, Sarah *see* Eidelson, John
Janus v. ASFCME (2018) 372, 374
Japan, education in 315
Japanese Americans 155; in California 155–63; education 161–2; home influence 162–3
Japanese Association of America 141, 155–9, 161, 163
Japanese language schools 159, 161–2, 163
Jefferson, Thomas 17–18, 19, *19*, 279; A Bill for the More General Diffusion of Knowledge (1779) 17, 20–1; Notes on the State of Virginia (1783) 17, 21–3
Jewish Americans 145–9
Johnson, Lyndon B. 281, *284*; Remarks upon signing the Elementary and Secondary Education Bill (April 11, 1965) 283–5; Towards Full Educational Opportunity (Jan. 12, 1965) 281–3; War on Poverty 276, 281
Johnson, Rucker C. 242, 271; *The Dream Revisited—In Search of Integration: Beyond Black and White* (2014) 271–4

K-12 OER Collaborative 354
Kagan, Justice 372
Kansas *see Brown v. Board of Education of Topeka, Kansas*
Kashuv, Kyle 362
Katz, Michael 36
Kaufman, Polly Welts 71
Kennedy, Edward M. 331
Kennedy, John F. 281, 322
Kennedy, Justice 372
Kenney, W. S. 180
Kenny, T. J. 180
Kerr, Clark 314
Keyishian v. Board of Regents (1967) 286–7
Kilpatrick, William H. 210
Kilpatrick, William K. 191
kindergartens: chldren's awareness of race 254; Mexican–Americans 166; Rough Rock Demonstration School 297
King, John 346
King, Martin Luther 271, 272
King, Mel 242
Kingsley, Clarence D. 126
Kliebard, Herbert M. 107
Kohl, Herbert 215, 227; *Thirty-Six Children* (1967) 227–35
Kohn, Alfie: "NCLB and the Effort to Privatize Public Education" (2004) **336**
Korean Americans 155
Kozol, Jonathan 264; *Death at an Early Age* (1967) 241–2, 264–71
Krug, Edward A. 107

Labaree, David F. 107
language 205, 276; Bilingual Education Act (1968) 292; bilingualism 164, 166, 170, 297, 318, 319–20; Common Core State Standards 339, 341; English language learners 147–8, 158, 170, 171, 172–4, 317–18, 341; freedom of speech 286; Greek and Latin 22, 26, 110; Japanese language schools 159, 161–2, 163; *Lau et al. v. Nichols et al.* (1974) 276, 292–4; modern languages 29, 110, 113, 138–9, 220–1; *see also McGuffey's Sixth Eclectic Reader*; school segregation; Webster, Noah
Latinos *see* Mexican Americans
Lau et al. v. Nichols et al. (1974) 276, 292–4
Lawrence-Lightfoot, Sarah 306
Lemon Grove v. Alvarez (1931) 242
Levine, Arthur: "Digital Students, Industrial-Era Universities" (2010) 348–9
Lewis, Karen *see Dissent* (magazine, 2013)
Lewis, Samuel 35
Lincoln, Abraham 79, 224
literacy 2–3; African Americans 76; Midwestern schools 61–6; in slavery 76–7, 79–83; *see also McGuffey's Sixth Eclectic Reader*; Webster, Noah
Little Rock High School (Arkansas, 1957) 241, 256–60, *260*
Loney, Kate Deadrich *284*
Louisiana: *Cox v. Louisiana* (1965) 290; state standards 346
Lynn, Albert: *Quackery in the Public Schools* 217

McCarthy, Kevin 360
McCarty, Revered Thaddeus 9
McConnell, Mitch 360
McCormaek, Paul J. 165
McDonald, Joseph P. *et al.*: *Where Are the Common Core State Standards Headed? Oblivion, Probably* (2016) 344–7
McGuffey's Sixth Eclectic Reader (1836) 61–3, *62*, 87; Elocution and Reading 63–4; Introduction (to 1879 Edition) 63; *The Memory of Our Fathers* 65–6; Patrick Henry's Speech before the Virginia Convention 63, 64–5
Mackinac Center 374
McLaurin v. Oklahoma State Regents (1950) 251, 252
Madison, James 279–80
Mann, Horace *37*; and abolitionism 37; and the common school movement 34, 36, 45, 192, 376, 377; *Tenth Annual Report to the Massachusetts Board of Education* (1846) 38–9; *Twelfth Annual Report to the Massachusetts Board of Education* (1848) 34, 35, 38, 39–42; *see also Common School Journal*
Marcus, David 165
Marjory Stoneman Douglas High School, Parkland, Florida 338, 355, *356*, 362; Emma Gonzalez, address at gun control rally (2018) 355–8
Marshall, Thurgood 240
Mason, Priscilla 23

Massachusetts: Anti-Slavery Society 79; and the Common School Movement 36, 38–42; constitution 18; debate to abolish the Board of Education 45–9; education legislation 2–3, 18; integration of public schools 38; John Adams' *Diary* 9–10; Old Deluder Satan Law (1647) 3, 7–8; racial segregation 37; *see also* Boston
mathematics: Committee of Ten (1893) 110; Common Core State Standards (2010) 339, 341
Mathews, Nathan 179
Maude, Daniel 2
Mendez v. Westminster (Federal District Court, 1946) 165–6, 242–5
mental age 200–1; as basis for school grading 201, **202**
Meriam, Lewis: *The Problem of Indian Administration* (1928) 141, 149–55, *150*
Mexican Americans 141; Beatrice Griffith, *American Me* (1948) 163–9; Chicago 277; *Mendez v. Westminster* (1946) 242–5; school segregation 240, 242
Meyer v. Nebraska (1923) 286, 290
Michael and Susan Dell Foundation 350
Michigan: Letters from Mill Point, Michigan (1842–1854) 71–3
Midwestern schools (1835–1860) 60–1; literacy 61–6; speech to a missionary 73–5; women teachers 68–73
Millis, Professor 158–9, 163
Minnesota: Board of National Popular Education correspondence 69–70
Mirel, Jeffrey E. 107
missionaries 33, 73; Jacob Cram 73–5; and Japanese Americans 158–9; report from Mr. Taylor to the society in North Carolina (1719) 5–6; speech of Red Jacket (ca. 1805) 73–5
Moe, Terry M.: "Politics, Control, and the Future of School Accountability" (2003) 334, **335**, 336
Moffit, Susan 347
Montgomery County, Maryland 274
moral education 40–1
Morgan v. Hennigan (1972) 242
motion pictures 134–5
multiculturalism 305; *Affirming Diversity* (1992) 305, 317–21; *The Disuniting of America* (1991) 322–7
Myrdal, Gunnar 326

NAACP (National Association for the Advancement of Colored People): Legal Defense Fund 240, 241; Statement to the Boston School Committee (June 11, 1963) 241, 260–4; *see also* Bates, Daisy; Clark, Septima
A Nation at Risk: The Imperative for Educational Reform (1983) 304–5, 306–10, 315, 347
National Commission on Excellence in Education 304; *A Nation at Risk: The Imperative for Educational Reform* (1983) 304–5, 306–10, 315
National Council of Teachers of English (NCTE) 339
National Council of Teachers of Mathematics (NCTM) 339

National Defense Education Act (NDEA, 1958) 215, 219, 220–1
national educatioinal standards 305–6
National Education Association (NEA) 371; Common Core State Standards 339; high school entrance requirements (1890) 116; Report of the Committee of Ten (1893) 107, 108, 109–16, **112**, 126; teacher organization (1904) 181–5; *see also Cardinal Principles of Secondary Education*
National Education Technology Plan (2016) 354
National Endowment for the Humanities 323
National Governors Association (NGA) 339
National Rifle Association (NRA) 357, 360
National Science Foundation 215, 217, 218, 221
Native Americans 24, 61, 141; Civilization Fund Act (1819) 19, 33; conversion to Christianity 2, 3–4; education 2, 4, 19, *150*; Indian Voices: The First Convocation of American Indian Scholars (1970) 296; Navajo Rough Rock Demonstration School 277, 296–300; *The Problem of Indian Administration* (1928) 141, 149–55, *150*; speech of Red Jacket, Seneca Chief (ca. 1805) 73–5
NCLB *see* No Child Left Behind Act
NCTE (National Council of Teachers of English) 339
NCTM (National Council of Teachers of Mathematics) 339
NDEA *see* National Defense Education Act
NEA *see* National Education Association
Neem, Johann N. 338, 376; "Schools Have a Nobler Purpose Than Just Career Prep" (2018) 376–7
Nell, William C. 37
Neuman, Susan B. *see* McDonald, Joseph P. *et al.*
New England Freedmen's Aid Society 77; Correspondence (1865–1874) 85–6, 88; *Freedmen's Reader 87*; Official Records (1862–1872) 83–4
The New England Primer (1768) 10, *11–16*
New Republic (1770–1820) 17–20; Civilization Fund Act 33; diffusion of knowledge 20–1; education in Virginia 21–3; education of youth 25–30; female education 23–4; Noah Webster, *The American Spelling Book* 30–2, *31*, 82; The Northwest Ordinance 32
The New Republic (1914–1915) 108, 121, 124
New York City: *Equal Pay for Equal Work* (1910) 187–9; Petition of the Catholics of New York for a Portion of the Common School Fund (1840) 36, 49–53; Public School Society 36, 49–53; Teaching Children of Puerto Rican Background (1954) 169–74
New York Dramatic Mirror 134
New York State: Common Core State Standards (CCSS) 344–5
NGA (National Governors Association) 339
Nieto, Sonia *318*; *Affirming Diverstiy: The Sociopolitical Context of Multicultural Education* 305, 317–21
Nixon, Richard 292, 304
No Child Left Behind Act (NCLB, 2002) 306; different schools of thought (2003–2004) 334–6,

336; U.S. Department of Education Executive Summary 330–4
Nordhoff, Charles 77
North Carolina: baptism of slaves (1719) 5–6; education 84; school desegregation 241
Northwest Ordinace (1787) 19, 32
NRA *see* National Rifle Association

Obama, Barack 345, 357, 368, 376
Ogden, Reverend Dunbar, Jr. 257–8
Ohio: Cleveland Central High School 104; public schools 61, 66
Oklahoma: *McLaurin v. Oklahoma State Regents* (1950) 251, 252; state standards 346
online charter schools 355
open educational resources (OER) 354–5
Organization for Economic Cooperation and Development 351–2
Overstreet, H.A. 167

Papert, Seymour 305, 327; *The Children's Machine* (1993) 327–9
Parker, Francis W. 191
Parks, Paul 261–2
Parks, Rosa 246–8
Partnership for Assessment of Readiness for College and Careers (PARCC) 342–3, 346, 353
Pearl Harbor 216
personalized learning 350–1
Petition of the Catholics of New York for a Portion of the Common School Fund (1840) 36, 49–53
Philadelphia high schools 104
Pierce, Edward L. 77
Pierce, John 377
PISA (Programme for International Student Assessment) 341
Platero, Dillon: The Rough Rock Demonstration School, Navajo Nation (1970) 296–300
Pledge of Allegiance to the Flag 280
Plessy v. Ferguson (1896) 38, 250, 251, 252, 253
Pormort, Philemon 2
Postman, Neil 305, 329; *Technopoly* (1993) 329–30
poverty: and segregation 272, 273, 274; War on Poverty 276, 281, 284
prayer in school 275, *277*, 278–81
Programme for International Student Assessment (PISA) 341
Progressive Era (1890–1950) 175–7, 214, 215; Boston Public Schools 177–81; equal pay for equal work 187–9; intelligence tests 199–205; a new social order 205–10; the school and society 191–8; school councils 185–7; social reconstruction 210–13; teacher organization 181–5; world democracy and school democracy 189–91
Protestantism 8, 33, 35, 36, 61
Prussian schools (1837) 67–8
psychology 108
Public Law 94-142, Education for All Handicapped Children Act (1975) 277, 295–6, 304

Puerto Ricans 142; Teaching Children of Puerto Rican Background (1954) 169–74; *see also* Nieto, Sonia

Puritans 2

purpose of schooling 338, 376–7

Putnam, James 9, 10

Quincy, Josiah 179

racism 37; *see also* Clark, Kenneth B.; school segregation

Rauner, Bruce 372

reading 63–4

Reading First 333–4

Reagan, Ronald 304, 305, 307, 314, 315

Red Jacket (Sagoyewatha), Seneca Chief: speech to a missionary (c. 1805) 73–5

Reese, William J. 104, 107

religion and education: colonial era 2–4; Common School Movement 35, 36, 41–2; conversion of slaves 2, 4–6; prayer in school 275, *277*, 278–81; Protestantism 8, 26, 33, 35, 61; *see also* Catholicism; Jewish Americans

Rickover, Hyman G. 215, *225*; *Education and Freedom* 215; *Education for All Children: What We Can Learn from England* (1962) 224–7

Rodriguez, Richard 319–20

Roosevelt, Theodore 155, 157, 163–4, 175, 322

Roper, Mary Augusta: Letters from Mill Point, Michigan (1842–1854) 71–3

Rough Rock Demonstration School(1970) 277, 296–300

Rugg, Harold 210

Rush, Benjamin 18, 23; Thoughts Upon Female Education (1787) 18, 23–5

Rushdie, Salman 324

Rutherford, F. James 215–16; Sputnik and Science Education, Reflections on (1957) 216–19

Ryan, Paul 360

San Antonio Independent School District v. Rodriguez (1972–1973) 278, 300–3

San Francisco: "Gentlemen's Agreement" 155, 156, 157

San Francisco Association 158

Sanchez, George I. 166

Sandy Hook Elementary School, Newtown, Connecticut (2012) 338, 355

Sarah C. Roberts v. The City of Boston (1849) 37, 38, 55–8

Sarason, Seymour 306

Schlesinger, Arthur M., Jr.: *The Disuniting of America* (1991) 305, 322–7

Schon, Donald 347

school choice: Betsy DeVos' remarks 362–5

school councils 185–7

school desegregation: *Brown v. Board of Education* (1954) 38, 240, 241, 250–3, 272, 300; *The Dream Revisited* (2014) 271–4; in the north 37–8, 53–9, 241–2, 260–71; in the south 241, 256–60, *260*

school funding: federal funding 108; taxes 36; *see also San Antonio Independent School District v. Rodriguez* (1972–1973)

school integration *see* school desegregation

school reform (1980s–1990s) 304–10; computers 327–30, 351–2; equality 305, 310–13, 321; a manufactured crisis 313–17; multiculturalism 305, 317–21, 322–7; *A Nation at Risk* (1983) 304–5, 306–10, 315, 347

school segregation 240, 242; *de jure* v. *de facto* segregation 241, 272, 273; impact on African American children 253–6; "separate but equal" 57, 240, 251, 253; in the south 155, 165–6, 240–1, 242, 245–50, 256–60

school shootings *see* guns in schools

schools of the South (1820–1937) 76–8; Charlotte Forten 88–93; Frederick Douglass 78–83; *Freedmen's Reader* 87; The Future of the American Negro 93–7; Lessons from the School of African Philosophy 101–3; New England Freedmen's Aid Society 83–4, 85–6, 88; The Souls of Black Folk 97–101

science education 110, 215–19

Scopes, John T. 106, 135–6

Scott Foresman Readers (1955) 221–4

Scott, Rick 358

Seaborg, Glenn 218

secondary schools *see* high schools

Senghor, Leopold 324

Shaw, Lemuel 37–8

Sizer, Theodore 306

Slade, William 69

slavery: conversion to Christianity 2, 4–6; education 2, 37; Frederick Douglass 79–83, 375; literacy 76–7, 79–83; reconstruction 76–8; *see also* schools of the South

Smarter Balanced Assessment Consortium 342–3, 353

Smith, Frederick James 134

Smith-Hughes Act (1917) 108, 119

Smith, Timothy L. 35

Snedden, David 106, 108, 124–5, 126; "Vocational Education" (1915) 121–4

The Social Frontier (journal, 1934) 210–13

social reconstruction 211–13

South Carolina: civil rights 245–50; education 84, 88; Statute on Conversion of Slaves to Christianity (1711) 4–5

southern schools *see* schools of the South

speech, freedom of 286; *see also Tinker et al. v. Des Moines Independent Community School District* (1969)

Sputnik 214–16, *219*

Sputnik and Science Education, Reflections on (1957) 216–19

Stamp Act 64–5

Stanford University: Center for Research on Education Outcomes 355

Steinberg, Stephen 326

Stephens, William D. 159–61, 162

Storrow, James Jackson 176, 177; *Son of New England* (1932) 177–81

Stowe, Calvin E. 35, 61, 66; Report on Elementary Public Instruction in Europe (1837) 66–8

Stowe, Harriet Beecher 77

Strachan, Grace, C.: *Equal Pay for Equal Work* (1910) 187–9

students' rights *see Tinker et al. v. Des Moines Independent Community School District* (1969)

Summer, Charles, Esq.: Argument Against the Constitutionality of Separate Colored Schools 56–7

Supreme Court of the U.S. *see Brown v. Board of Education of Topeka, Kansas* (1954); *Engel v. Vitale* (1962); *Lau et al. v. Nichols et al.* (1974); *Plessy v. Ferguson* (1896); *San Antonio Independent School District v. Rodriquez* (1972–1973); *Tinker et al. v. Des Moines Independent Community School District* (1969)

Sweatt v. Painter (1950) 251, 252

Taylor, Mr. (missionary) 5–6

Teacher Corps 61

teacher strikes 338, 366–7, 370–2

teacher unions 181–5, 214

teachers: normal courses 106; pay 187–9, 370–1; in the South 85–6, 88–93; training 115; women 35–6, 43–5, 61, 68–73, 77, 187–9, 276

technology 305, 338, 349–50; 1-1 computing 351–2; blended learning 352; computers 327–30, 351–2; digital materials in classrooms 354; digital natives 348–9; distance learning 355; Film Will Replace Teacher, Books (1923) 187–9; infrastructure and the E-rate 352–3; online testing 353–4; open educational resources (OER) 354–5; personalized learning 350–1; virtual education 355

Terman, Lewis M. 199; *National Intelligence Tests* (1919) 199–205

Terminiello v. Chicago (1949) 287

testing of students 306; adequate yearly progress (AYP) 306, 332, 333; online testing 353–4; *see also* intelligence tests

textbooks 221; *The American Spelling Book* (1783) 30–2, *31*, 82; *McGuffey's Sixth Eclectic Reader* (1836) 61–3, *62*, 87; *The New England Primer* (1768) 10, *11–16*; science textbooks 215, 218; *Scott Foresman Readers* (1955) 221–4

Thatcher, Margaret 325

Thernstrom, Stephan 322

Thorndike, Edward L. 199

Tinker et al. v. Des Moines Independent Community School District (1969) 276, 285–91

Tisch, Merryl 346

Title IX, the Education Amendments of 1972 276, 292

Treat, P. J. 156–7

Trends in International Mathematics and Science Study (TIMSS) 341

Trump, Donald *et al.*: guns in schools (2018) 358–62, 363; and National Rifle Association 357, 360

Turning Point USA High School Leadership Summit (July 25, 2018): remarks by Betsy DeVos 362–5

United States Congress: Civilization Fund Act (1819) 33; The Northwest Ordinance (1787) 19, 32

Universal Negro Improvement Association (UNIA) 78, 101

U.S. Department of Commerce 106–7

U.S. Department of Education 304–5; National Education Technology Plan (2016) 354; No Child Left Behind Act (NCLB, 2002) 330–4

U.S. Department of the Interior: Meriam report (1928) 141, 149–55

U.S. Federal Trade Commission 134

Vietnam War 276; *see also Tinker et al. v. Des Moines Independent Community School District* (1969)

Virginia: A Bill for the More General Diffusion of Knowledge (1779) 17, 20–1; education 7, 21–3, 84; Notes on the State of Virginia (1783) 17, 21–3; Patrick Henry's Speech (1765) 63, 64–5; *Statutes at Large* on the education of Indian children held hostage (1656) 4; University of Virginia (1819) 20

Virginia Council [London] (1636) 2, 3–4

Virginia's Cure, or An Advisive Narrative (1662) 6–7

vocational education 108, 109, 119–25

Walberg, Herbert 315

War on Poverty 276, 281

Washburne, Carleton 191

Washington, Booker T. 77–8, *96*, 97, 98–101; *The Future of the American Negro* (1899) 93–7

Washington, George 325

Webster, Noah 18, 25–6, 63; *The American Spelling Book* (1783) 30–2, *31*, 82; On the Education of Youth in America, Boston (1790) 18, 25–30; *Grammatical Institute of the English Language* 18

Weingarten, Randi *373*; "Hope in Darkness" (2018) 372–6

West Virginia State Board of Education v. Barnette (1943) 280, 286

Williams, Pearce 324

Wilson, Woodrow 108, 141, 175, 322

women: education 23–5, 43; equal opportunities 276, 292; equal pay 187–9; teachers 35–6, 43–5, 61, 68–73, 77, 187–9, 276

Wood, Robert 306

Woods, Elizabeth 167

Young, Ella Flagg 185, *186*; *Isolation in the School* (1901) 185–7

Zacharias, Gerald 218

Zorach v. Clauson (1952) 280

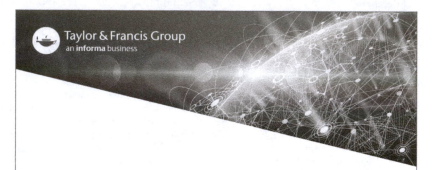